The
Encyclopaedia of
FORMS
AND
PRECEDENTS

Fifth Edition

2001 Reissue

The Rt. Hon. Lord Millett, P.C.

A Lord of Appeal in Ordinary

Editor–in–Chief

Volume 40(1)

Trusts and Settlements

Butterworths

A Member of the LexisNexis Group

Members of the LexisNexis Group worldwide

United Kingdom	Butterworths Tolley, a Division of Reed Elsevier (UK) Ltd, Halsbury House, 35 Chancery Lane, LONDON, WC2A 1EL, and 4 Hill Street, EDINBURGH EH2 3JZ
Argentina	Abeledo Perrot, Jurisprudencia Argentina and Depalma, BUENOS AIRES
Australia	Butterworths, a Division of Reed International Books Australia Pty Ltd, CHATSWOOD, New South Wales
Austria	ARD Betriebsdienst and Verlag Orac, VIENNA
Canada	Butterworths Canada Ltd, MARKHAM, Ontario
Chile	Publitecsa and Conosur Ltda, SANTIAGO DE CHILE
Czech Republic	Orac sro, PRAGUE
France	Editions du Juris-Classeur SA, PARIS
Hong Kong	Butterworths Asia (Hong Kong), HONG KONG
Hungary	Hvg Orac, BUDAPEST
India	Butterworths India, NEW DELHI
Ireland	Butterworths (Ireland) Ltd, DUBLIN
Italy	Giuffré, MILAN
Malaysia	Malayan Law Journal Sdn Bhd, KUALA LUMPUR
New Zealand	Butterworths of New Zealand, WELLINGTON
Poland	Wydawnictwa Prawnicze PWN, WARSAW
Singapore	Butterworths Asia, SINGAPORE
South Africa	Butterworths Publishers (Pty) Ltd, DURBAN
Switzerland	Stämpfli Verlag AG, BERNE
USA	LexisNexis, DAYTON, Ohio

A CIP Catalogue record for this book is available from the British Library.

First Edition: Published between 1902 and 1909

Second Edition: Published in 1925 and 1926

Third Edition: Published between 1939 and 1950

Fourth Edition: Published between 1964 and 1983

Fifth Edition: Published from 1985 with selective reissues between 1993 and 2001

ISBN *for complete set of volumes:*   0 406 02360 3
ISBN for this volume: 0 406 94139 4

ISBN 0-406-94139-4

9 780406 941398

Set in 10 on 11 pt Bembo and printed in Great Britain by Butler & Tanner Ltd, Frome and London

Visit Butterworths LexisNexis *direct* **at www.butterworths.com**

Editor–in–Chief

THE RT. HON. LORD MILLETT, P.C.

A Lord of Appeal in Ordinary

Consulting Editors

For Land Registry matters:

RICHARD FEARNLEY, B.A., Solicitor

District Land Registrar,
Her Majesty's Land Registry

For Direct Taxation matters:

JOHN JEFFREY-COOK, F.T.I.I., F.C.A., F.C.I.S.

For Value Added Tax and Stamp Duty matters:

IAN HYDE, B.A., Partner

Pinsent Curtis Biddle

Publishing Manager

JAN JASTRZEBSKI, B.A., Solicitor

Managing Editor

ROBERT I. WALKER, B.A., Solicitor

Principal Editor on this Volume

BRENDA RAMSDEN, B.A., LL.B., Solicitor

Commissioning and Development Editor

LISA ZOLTOWSKA, B.A.

Editors

JENNIFER BARTHORPE, M.A., Solicitor
ADELENE CHINNICK, B.Sc., Solicitor
JEM CONNOR, B.A. (Oxon)
CLAIRE HEELEY, LL.B.
JEAN HURLEY, B.A.
CATHERINE JACKSON, M.A. (Cantab)
SHARON RODNEY, LL.B., Solicitor
DOMINIC SAVAGE, LL.M., Solicitor

Production Editor

SOPHIE PELLS, B.A.

Indexer

ALEXANDRA CORRIN, LL.B., of Gray's Inn, Barrister

Contributors

TRUSTS AND SETTLEMENTS

HELEN GALLEY, LL.B., Barrister
Ground Floor, 24 Old Buildings, Lincoln's Inn, London

PHILIP H. PETTIT, M.A., Barrister
Emeritus Professor of Equity
The Universities of Bristol and Buckingham

NICHOLAS RADCLIFFE, Solicitor

CHRIS WHITEHOUSE, B.A., B.C.L., Barrister
8, Gray's Inn Square, London

Volume 40(1)
2001 Reissue

For current information on the titles published in the Encyclopaedia, subscribers should refer to the *List of Titles*, in the Information Binder of the Service, which will always represent the most recent position of titles.

This volume will be kept up to date by material in the Fifth Edition Service which is issued quarterly and which should be filed in the appropriate Fifth Edition Service Binders.

Summary of Titles

(For full details of the contents of the volume see the Table of Contents to the title and the index to the volume)

reference no

TRUSTS AND SETTLEMENTS . . . . [1]

The title TRUSTS AND SETTLEMENTS is concerned with the law relating to the creation of trusts and settlements, their administration, their variation and their taxation. The revised title is published in two volumes. This volume deals with establishment and administration generally, whilst volume 40(2) is concerned with areas of a more specialised nature.

Full account is taken of the major legislative changes that have occurred in this area: the Trusts of Land and Appointment of Trustees Act 1996 (which is considered in detail in volume 40(2)), the Trustee Delegation Act 1999 (which is considered in a new Part 7 in this volume) and the Trustee Act 2000. The Trustee Act 2000 has meant that the administrative provisions have been rethought throughout. In the event, the contributors have concluded that the Act is unlikely to result in a significant shortening of the standard express trust deed.

The text and precedent sections have been reviewed, expanded and redrafted to ensure that the title reflects the changes introduced by these Acts, and the title has been thoroughly updated to incorporate other legislative and case law developments. In view of the fact that many more dispositions involve registered land, full account has been taken of the Land Registration Act 1997 and the Land Registration Rules 1997–1999. All transfers of land have been redrafted to reflect changes to the Land Registry prescribed forms.

The first volume includes:

- A substantial commentary setting out the current law and practice on trusts and settlements and explaining the taxation factors that practitioners should take into account in setting up or modifying trusts and settlements.

- The standard provisions of the Society of Trust and Estate Practitioners which are intended to deal with routine administration matters commonly included in both will trusts and inter vivos settlements.

- A collection of complete precedents (together with full explanatory footnotes) including both flexible and fixed interest trusts.

- A selection of administrative powers and typical beneficial trusts.

- Delegation of their functions by trustees.

- Ancillary documentation such as letters of wishes and trustee resolutions, as well as precedents relating to the exercise by trustees of their dispositive powers.

The second volume is to be published in December 2001 and will contain an in-depth treatment of trusts of land (including a section by section analysis of the Trusts of Land and Appointment of Trustees Act 1996), as well as retaining coverage of strict settlements. The volume also considers a number of other areas of interest to the practitioner such as change of trustees, protective trusts, disabled trusts, maintenance trusts, purpose trusts and trusts for minors and older children. An outline of the contents of the second volume appears at the end of the volume 40(1) Table of Contents.

TABLE OF STATUTES

References are to the numbers in square brackets which appear
on the right-hand side of the pages of text

TABLE OF
STATUTORY INSTRUMENTS

References are to the numbers in square brackets which appear
on the right-hand side of the pages of text

TABLE OF CASES

*References are to the numbers in square brackets which appear
on the right-hand side of the pages of text*

A

D

G

J

M

R

S

TRUSTS AND SETTLEMENTS

References are to the numbers in square brackets which appear
on the right hand side of the pages of text

reference no

PART 1:   GENERAL COMMENTARY

Commentary

D: CONSTITUENTS OF A TRUST OR SETTLEMENT

1:   WHO CAN BENEFIT?

2:   WHAT CAN BE SETTLED?

3:   WHO CAN BE TRUSTEE?

(3) ADVISING THE SETTLOR AND CONSIDERATIONS FOR THE DRAFTSMAN

A: SETTLOR'S MOTIVES AND OBJECTIVES

B: PROPERTY TO BE SETTLED

C: DETERMINING THE BENEFICIAL INTERESTS

D: EXCLUSION OF SETTLOR AND SPOUSE

E: CHOICE OF TRUSTEES

(5) ACCEPTANCE BY TRUSTEES AND DEVOLUTION OF TRUST PROPERTY

A: THE TRUST ESTATE

1: EXTENT OF ESTATE TAKEN BY TRUSTEES IN LAND

2: CHARACTER IN WHICH PROPERTY IS TAKEN

3: POSSESSION AND INCIDENTS

B: ACCEPTANCE OF THE TRUST

(For a detailed discussion of disclaimer of trusts see vol 40(2) (2001 Reissue) TRUSTS AND SETTLEMENTS Part 10 [5201].)

C: RELEASE OF TRUSTEES ON DETERMINATION OF TRUST

D: DEVOLUTION ON DEATH OF A TRUSTEE

(6) LAND SETTLED ON A TRUST OF LAND

(For a detailed commentary on the provisions of the Trusts of Land and Appointment of Trustees Act 1996 Parts I and III see further vol 40(2) (2001 Reissue) TRUSTS AND SETTLEMENTS Part 8 [3001]. As to the appointment and retirement of trustees under Part II of the Act see vol 40(2) Part 10 [5201].)

(7) PERSONALTY SETTLEMENTS

A: FORM

B: NATURE OF PROPERTY

C: BENEFICIAL INTERESTS

1:   LIFE AND LIMITED INTERESTS

2:   PROTECTED LIFE INTERESTS

(For a detailed consideration of protected life interests, together with a specimen protective trust, see vol 40(2) (2001 Reissue) TRUSTS AND SETTLEMENTS) Part 12 [6901].)

3:   BENEFICIARIES UNDER A DISCRETIONARY TRUST

(8)   RIGHTS AND POSITION OF BENEFICIARIES

A: RIGHTS AS BETWEEN LIFE TENANT AND REMAINDERMAN

B: PROTECTION OF TRUSTEES

1: TRUSTEES IN GENERAL

2: TRUSTEES UNDER THE SETTLED LAND ACT 1925

C: INDEMNITY OF TRUSTEES

D: TRUSTEE AS FIDUCIARY

(10) REMUNERATION OF TRUSTEES

A: INTRODUCTION

B: WHERE REMUNERATION MAY BE ALLOWED

(11) ADMINISTRATIVE PROVISIONS AND POWERS

A: INTRODUCTION

B: PROVISIONS RELATING TO TRUSTS OF LAND

(For a detailed commentary on the provisions of the Trusts of Land and Appointment of Trustees Act 1996 Parts I and III see further vol 40(2) (2001 Reissue) TRUSTS AND SETTLEMENTS Part 8 [3001]. As to Part II of the Act see vol 40(2) Part 10 [5201].)

C: GENERAL STATUTORY POWERS OF TRUSTEES

1: SOURCES AND AVAILABILITY

2: POWERS OF MAINTENANCE

3: POWERS OF ADVANCEMENT

4: POWERS OF INVESTMENT

(12) VARIATION OF TRUSTS

A: GENERAL

B: VARIATION OF BENEFICIAL INTERESTS

C: CAPITAL GAINS TAX

D: INCOME TAX

1: LIABILITY OF TRUSTEES

PART 2:   TAKING   INSTRUCTIONS   FOR   A   NEW SETTLEMENT AND STANDARD CONDITIONS

Forms and Precedents

A: TAKING INSTRUCTIONS

1:    INTRODUCTION

2:    FORMS

B: STANDARD PROVISIONS OF THE SOCIETY OF TRUST AND ESTATE
    PRACTITIONERS

1:    INTRODUCTION

2:    STANDARD PROVISIONS FORMS

PART 3:   COMPLETE TRUST DEEDS

(For other complete trust precedents see vol 40(2) (2001 Reissue) TRUSTS AND SETTLEMENTS, including: discretionary trust of land (see vol 40(2) Part 8 [3501]), employee trusts (see vol 40(2) Part 14 [8101]), offshore trusts (see vol 40(2) Part 15 [8701]), disabled trusts (see vol 40(2) Part 16 [9301]), personal injury compensation trusts (see vol 40(2) Part 17 [9451]) and pension policy trusts (see vol 40(2) Part 18 [9601]).)

Forms and Precedents

PART 4:   DECLARATIONS OF TRUST, AND ASSIGNMENTS AND TRANSFERS TO TRUSTEES

Forms and Precedents

A: DECLARATIONS OF TRUST

1: INTRODUCTION

2:   GENERAL FORMS

3:   SPECIFIC CASES

PART 5:   GENERAL CLAUSES FOR USE IN SETTLEMENTS

Forms and Precedents

A: PARTIES

1:     INTRODUCTION

2:     FORMS

B: RECITALS

1:     INTRODUCTION

2:    FORMS

C: TESTATUM

D: COMMON BENEFICIAL TRUSTS

1:    INTRODUCTION

2:    TRUSTS OF INCOME

F: PROVISION FOR FUTURE MARRIAGE AND FOR REVOCATION

G: INVESTMENT CLAUSES AND APPLICATION OF CAPITAL MONEY

1:   INTRODUCTION

2:   MISCELLANEOUS POWERS PERMITTING THE ACQUISITION OF STOCKS AND SHARES

I: CLAUSES CONCERNING ADMINISTRATIVE POWERS OF TRUSTEES

J: DIRECTIONS AS TO LAND AND OTHER PROPERTY HELD OR PURCHASED

K: INDEMNITY, EXONERATION, CHARGING AND AUDIT

(For releases and indemnities of trustees see vol 40(2) (2001 Reissue) TRUSTS AND SETTLEMENTS *Part 20 [9821].)*

L: APPOINTMENT AND REMOVAL OF TRUSTEES

(As to the appointment and retirement of trustees under the Trusts of Land and Appointment of Trustees Act 1996 Part II and as to the change of trustees generally, see vol 40(2) (2001 Reissue) TRUSTS AND SETTLEMENTS *Part 10 [5201].)*

M: MISCELLANEOUS PROVISIONS

PART 6:   DOCUMENTS SUBSIDIARY TO, MODIFYING AND EXTINGUISHING TRUSTS

Forms and Precedents

A: LETTERS OF WISHES

B: TRUSTEE RESOLUTIONS ETC

C: CONSENTS AND AUTHORITIES ETC GIVEN TO TRUSTEES

D: CONVEYANCES AND DECLARATIONS ETC IN FAVOUR OF BENEFICIARIES ABSOLUTELY ENTITLED

E: DEEDS EXERCISING DISPOSITIVE POWERS—ADVANCEMENT, PAY OR APPLY, APPOINTMENT

H: MISCELLANEOUS   DOCUMENTS   MODIFYING   AND   ENDING
EXISTING TRUSTS

1:   MODIFICATIONS TO AN EXISTING TRUST

2:   ENDING THE TRUST

PART 7:   TRUSTEE DELEGATION

Forms and Precedents

A: INTRODUCTION

B: POWERS PROVIDING FOR COLLECTIVE DELEGATION

C: POWERS PROVIDING FOR INDIVIDUAL DELEGATION

FURTHER COMMENTARY AND FORMS AND PRECEDENTS UNDER THE FOLLOWING HEADINGS APPEAR IN VOL 40(2).

Pt 8   Trusts of Land: Trusts of Land and Appointment of Trustees Act 1996 Parts I and III

Pt 9   Settlements of Land under the Settled Land Act 1925

Pt 10   Change of Trustees

Pt 11   Trusts for Minors and for Older Children

Pt 12   Protective Trusts and Asset Protection

Pt 13   Purpose Trusts

Pt 14   Employee Trusts

Pt 15   Offshore Trusts

Pt 16   Disabled Trusts

Pt 17   Personal Injury Compensation Trusts

Pt 18   Pension Policy Trusts

Pt 19   Applications by the Trustees and Others to the Court

Pt 20   Releases and Indemnities

PART 1: GENERAL COMMENTARY

Commentary

(1) NATURE OF TRUSTS AND SETTLEMENTS

A: INTRODUCTION

1   Scope of title
This title is concerned with the law relating to the creation of trusts and settlements, their administration, their variation and their taxation. It is divided into two volumes: this volume deals with establishment and administration generally, whilst volume 40(2) is concerned with topics of a more specialised nature such as trusts and settlements of land, change of trustees, trusts for minors and older children, protective trusts (and asset protection generally), non-charitable purpose trusts, employee trusts, offshore trusts, and court applications by trustees. Trusts created by testamentary disposition and charitable trusts are dealt with in detail elsewhere[1].

1   As to trusts created by testamentary disposition see vol 42(1) (1998 Reissue) WILLS AND
        ADMINISTRATION Paragraph 118 [271] et seq; for coverage of charitable trusts see vol 6(2)
        (2001 Reissue) CHARITIES AND CHARITABLE GIVING.

[1]

2   Meaning of trust
A trust[1] may be defined as an obligation under which a person to whom property is transferred is bound in equity to deal with the beneficial interest in such property in a particular manner in favour of a specified person or persons (including a corporation), or class of persons. In general, a trust cannot be set up for a 'purpose' or 'object' unless the purpose or object is charitable[2].

Three characters are concerned in a trust, namely, the creator of the trust, the trustee, and the beneficiary or *cestui que trust*; but the creator of the trust, or settlor, may be the trustee or one of several trustees, and he may also be the trustee and one of the beneficiaries. Under no circumstances, however, can a sole trustee be the sole beneficiary, for, directly he becomes so, the beneficial interest is merged and extinguished in the legal ownership[3].

[2]

1   For the meanings of trust and trustee in the Trustee Act 1925 (48 Halsbury's Statutes (4th Edn) TRUSTS
        AND SETTLEMENTS) see the Trustee Act 1925 s 68(1).
2   *Morice v Bishop of Durham* (1804) 9 Ves 399 at 405; on appeal (1805) 10 Ves 522; *Re Wood, Barton v
        Chilcott* [1949] Ch 498 at 501, [1949] 1 All ER 1100 at 1101; *Re Astor's Settlement Trusts, Astor v
        Scholfield* [1952] Ch 534, [1952] 1 All ER 1067; *Leahy v A-G for New South Wales* [1959] AC 457 at
        478, 479, [1959] 2 All ER 300 at 307, PC; *Re Recher's Will Trusts, National Westminster Bank Ltd v
        National Anti-Vivisection Society Ltd* [1972] Ch 526, [1971] 3 All ER 401. But see Paragraph 47 [112]
        post and vol 40(2) (2001 Reissue) TRUSTS AND SETTLEMENTS Part 13 [1701] et seq.
3   *Re Cook, Beck v Grant* [1948] Ch 212, [1948] 1 All ER 231.

[3]

3   Distinction between charitable trusts and private trusts

Trusts may be divided into charitable (or public) trusts and private trusts.

Charitable trusts comprise trusts created for:

3.1   the relief of poverty;

3.2   the advancement of education;

3.3   the advancement of religion; and

3.4   other purposes beneficial to the community not falling under any of the preceding heads[1].

Certain other trusts are charitable if they fall within the provisions of the Recreational Charities Act 1958. Charitable trusts differ from private trusts in certain respects[2].

All non-charitable trusts are called private trusts. They may arise either:

3.5   by express declaration, in which case they are called express or declared trusts;

3.6   by statute (for example, where land is held in undivided shares[3], or on intestacy under the Administration of Estates Act 1925)[4]; or

3.7   by implication of equity, in which case they are called implied or constructive trusts.

Resulting trusts, which form a sub-division of implied trusts, arise where the beneficial interest results or springs back to the creator of the trust who has failed to dispose of his entire beneficial interest[5]. Express private trusts are created by settlements, wills[6], or by declaration of trust.

[4]

---

1   *Income Tax Special Purposes Comrs v Pemsel* [1891] AC 531 at 583, HL. See also vol 6(2) (2001 Reissue) CHARITIES AND CHARITABLE GIVING Paragraph 3 [5] et seq.

2   Charitable trusts differ from private trusts in the following particulars:

    (a)   they are not limited in duration by the rule against perpetuities: see vol 6(2) (2001 Reissue) CHARITIES AND CHARITABLE GIVING Paragraph 15 [61];

    (b)   they are not void for uncertainty if there is a general intention in favour of charity, as distinguished from a mere wish to benefit a particular charity; in the former case the court will administer the trust cy-près: see further vol 6(2) (2001 Reissue) CHARITIES AND CHARITABLE GIVING Paragraph 16 [63];

    (c)   the trustees of a charitable trust act by majority, whereas private trustees (unless authorised to the contrary) must be unanimous: see further 48 Halsbury's Laws (4th Edn 2000 Reissue) para 851; and

    (d)   the restriction on the number of trustees of settlements and dispositions creating trusts of land imposed by the Trustee Act 1925 s 34 as amended by the Trusts of Land and Appointment of Trustees Act 1996 s 25(1), Sch 3 para 3(9) (48 Halsbury's Statutes (4th Edn) TRUSTS AND SETTLEMENTS) (see further Paragraph 109 [269] post) does not apply in the case of land vested in trustees for charitable, ecclesiastical, or public purposes, or where the net proceeds of sale of the land are held for like purposes: Trustee Act 1925 s 34(3)(a), (b).

3   See the Law of Property Act 1925 s 34 as amended by the Trusts of Land and Appointment of Trustees Act 1996 ss 5, 25(2), Sch 2 para 3, Sch 4 (37 Halsbury's Statutes (4th Edn) REAL PROPERTY); the Settled Land Act 1925 s 36 as amended by the Trusts of Land and Appointment of Trustees Act 1996 s 25(1), Sch 3 para 2(11) (48 Halsbury's Statutes (4th Edn) TRUSTS AND SETTLEMENTS).

4   See the Administration of Estates Act 1925 s 33 as amended by the Trusts of Land and Appointment of Trustees Act 1996 s 5, Sch 2 para 5 and by the Trustee Act 2000 Sch 2 Pt II para 27 (17 Halsbury's Statutes (4th Edn) EXECUTORS AND ADMINISTRATORS); and see generally vol 42(2) (1998 Reissue) WILLS AND ADMINISTRATION Paragraph 513 [3051] et seq.

5   The terms 'implied', 'resulting' and 'constructive' trust overlap and are not used consistently in the same sense.

6   As to the creation of express private trusts by will see generally vol 42(1) (1998 Reissue) WILLS AND ADMINISTRATION Paragraph 75 [184] and Form 214 [1309] et seq.

[5]

4   Meaning of settlement

Parliament has from time to time defined the word 'settlement' for the purposes of particular statutes[1], but there is no generally accepted definition. It may, however, be defined as any disposition of property, of whatever nature, by any instrument or number of instruments, so that trusts are constituted for the purpose of regulating the enjoyment of the settled property successively among the persons or classes of persons nominated by the settlor[2]. The term 'compound settlement' is used to describe a settlement that subsists by virtue of several different instruments, often a series of successive dispositions such as, for example, a deed of settlement, a disentailing deed and a deed of resettlement[3].

The settlements considered in this title are voluntary settlements[4] made inter vivos and marriage settlements[5].

[6]

1   For some definitions of 'settlement' see, eg, the Settled Land Act 1925 s 1 as amended by the Married Women (Restraint upon Anticipation) Act 1949 s 1(4), Sch 2, by the Law of Property (Amendment) Act 1926 s 7, Schedule and by the Trusts of Land and Appointment of Trustees Act 1996 s 25(1), Sch 3 para 2(2) (48 Halsbury's Statutes (4th Edn) TRUSTS AND SETTLEMENTS); the Income and Corporation Taxes Act 1988 s 660G as inserted by the Finance Act 1995 s 74, Sch 17 para 1 (42–44 Halsbury's Statutes (4th Edn) TAXATION). The definition of 'settlement' adopted in the Income and Corporation Taxes Act 1988 s 660G includes a 'transfer of assets' and goes far beyond the meaning of a settlement as understood by Chancery lawyers and as considered in this title. The Inland Revenue contends that a series of settlements with a common settlor, trustees and beneficiaries, although created on separate days and separately documented, constitutes a single settlement for inheritance tax purposes. It also takes the view that additions to an existing settlement (whether by the settlor or another) create a new settlement: *Tax Bulletin*, February 1997.
2   See generally 42 Halsbury's Laws (4th Edn Reissue) para 601. The term 'settlement' has two different senses in law; it can mean either the documents which express the dispositions that are the settlement, or the state of affairs which the documents bring about: see, eg, *Re Ogle's Settled Estates* [1927] 1 Ch 229 at 233, per Romer J. Proprietary estoppel has been held to give rise to a settlement under the Settled Land Act 1925: see *Dodsworth v Dodsworth* (1973) 228 Estates Gazette 1115, CA; *Griffiths v Williams* (1977) 248 Estates Gazette 947, CA; but note that it has not been possible to create a new settlement under the Settled Land Act 1925 since the coming into force of the Trusts of Land and Appointment of Trustees Act 1996 (37 Halsbury's Statutes (4th Edn) REAL PROPERTY) on 1 January 1997.
3   See *Re Earl of Carnarvon's Chesterfield Settled Estates, Re Earl of Carnarvon's Highclere Settled Estates* [1927] 1 Ch 138 at 143. The term 'compound settlement' is used in, but is not defined by, the Settled Land Act 1925. As to compound settlements and resettlement see vol 40(2) (2001 Reissue) TRUSTS AND SETTLEMENTS Part 9 [4101]. It has not been possible to create a new settlement under the Settled Land Act 1925 since the coming into force of the Trusts of Land and Appointment of Trustees Act 1996.
4   A voluntary settlement is a settlement not supported by consideration.
5   A marriage settlement is, in practice, the only form of settlement made for valuable consideration. As to settlements by will generally see vol 42(1) (1998 Reissue) WILLS AND ADMINISTRATION Paragraph 118 [271] et seq. Many of the clauses in that title are, however, equally appropriate to settlements inter vivos, and many of the clauses in this title are applicable to settlements by will.

[7]–[10]

B: TYPES OF TRUST AND SETTLEMENT

5   Life interest trust

In the classic life interest trust the life tenant is entitled to income produced by the trust fund or to the use of trust assets. He has no entitlement to capital which is held for the beneficiaries entitled in remainder on the termination of the life interest. In recent years this relatively inflexible structure has been loosened so that it is now common for the modern life interest settlement to confer express powers on the trustees to advance capital to the life tenant, as well as giving them power to revoke the life interest in whole or in part and either in their absolute discretion or on the occurrence of certain events[1]. The term 'an interest in possession' settlement derives from the capital transfer tax legislation (now found in the Inheritance Tax Act 1984)[2]. Although not defined in that Act, the term has been judicially construed as embracing not only life interest trusts, but any trusts under which a beneficiary has an immediate right to income as it arises. For instance, a beneficiary under an accumulation and maintenance settlement who has just turned 18 years and become entitled to income from the fund (or from his share of the fund) under the Trustee Act 1925 Section 31 is entitled to an interest in possession. More recently the term has been adopted by the draftsman of the Trusts of Land and Appointment of Trustees Act 1996[3].

1   As to life and limited interests generally see Paragraph 121 [301] et seq post. For a life interest settlement see Form 5 [1107] post.

2   See the Inheritance Tax Act 1984 s 49 as amended by the Finance Act 1986 s 101(1), (3), Sch 19 Pt I para 14 and by the Finance (No 2) Act 1987 s 96(1), (4) (42–44 Halsbury's Statutes (4th Edn) TAXATION). For a detailed discussion of the meaning of the term, including an analysis of the leading House of Lords authority, *Pearson v IRC* [1981] AC 753, [1980] 2 All ER 479, see Paragraph 286 [723] post.

3   See especially the Trusts of Land and Appointment of Trustees Act 1996 ss 9, 11, 12, 13, 22(3) as amended by the Trustee Act 2000 Sch 2 Pt II para 46 (37 Halsbury's Statutes (4th Edn) REAL PROPERTY).

[11]

6   Discretionary trusts

Wide discretionary trusts flourished in the 1960s, being developed in large measure to avoid the imposition of estate duty. The Finance Act 1975, which introduced capital transfer tax, included a draconian method of taxing such settlements, which led to their declining use throughout the late 1970s and early 1980s. Many such trusts were converted into accumulation and maintenance form and, in their place, flexible life interest trusts were created. With a relaxation of the capital transfer tax regime from 1984 onwards there has been something of a revival in their use, although the preference remains for flexible accumulation and maintenance or life interest trusts[1].

1   As to discretionary trusts generally see Paragraph 124 [307] et seq post. For the inheritance tax treatment of discretionary trusts see Paragraph 316 [821] et seq post. The inheritance tax legislation distinguishes between trusts with and without an interest in possession. For a full discretionary settlement see Form 4 [1081] post and for a discretionary express trust of land see vol 40(2) (2001 Reissue) TRUSTS AND SETTLEMENTS Part 8 [3501].

The following extract taken from Pettit, *Equity and the Law of Trusts* (8th Edn, 1997) p 68 aptly describes the nature of discretionary trusts:

'Trustees are often given discretions of varying kinds, eg as to how the trust funds should be invested, but the phrase discretionary trust means a trust under which the trustees are given a discretion to pay or apply income or capital, or both, to or for the benefit of all, or any one or more exclusively of the others, of a specified class or group of persons, no beneficiary being able to claim as of right that all or any part of the income or capital is to be paid to him or applied for his benefit.

The trustees may thus have power to decide both who shall benefit and what the benefits shall be. A potential beneficiary cannot be said to be the owner of an equitable interest unless and until the trustees exercise their discretion in his favour.'

[12]

7   Settlements on children and issue ('accumulation and maintenance trusts')

It is common practice for settlors to make settlements for their children and grandchildren, both born and unborn, with a view not only to benefiting them but also of avoiding or reducing liability to income tax, inheritance tax and capital gains tax[1]. In settlements under which a minor[2] has an interest, express powers of maintenance, accumulation and advancement may be included; but, even if there are no express powers, there are, subject to certain limitations, statutory powers for the same purposes[3].

Under the 1925 property legislation a conveyance of a legal estate in land to a minor operated as an agreement for valuable consideration to execute a settlement in his favour and in the meantime to hold the land in trust for him. The relevant provisions[4] were repealed by the Trusts of Land and Appointment of Trustees Act 1996[5], and that Act now provides as follows[6]:

7.1   where a person purports to convey a legal estate to a minor (or minors) the conveyance operates as a declaration that the land is held in trust for the minor (or minors);

7.2   where a person purports to convey a legal estate to a minor (or minors) and another person (or persons) of full age, the conveyance operates to vest the land in the other person (or persons) in trust for the minor (or minors) and the other person (or persons).

Driven by tax considerations, the classic settlement for such beneficiaries is the accumulation and maintenance trust[7].

[13]

---

1   For a detailed treatment of accumulation and maintenance trusts with precedents see vol 40(2) (2001 Reissue) TRUSTS AND SETTLEMENTS Part 11 [6501]. As to the taxation of trusts and settlements generally see Paragraph 282 [711] et seq post.

2   The age of majority is 18 years: see the Family Law Reform Act 1969 s 1 (6 Halsbury's Statutes (4th Edn) CHILDREN).

3   As to the statutory powers of maintenance, accumulation and advancement see Paragraph 235 [558] et seq post.

4   Ie the Settled Land Act 1925 s 27 (repealed) and the Law of Property Act 1925 s 19 (repealed).

5   Trusts of Land and Appointment of Trustees Act 1996 s 25(2), Sch 4 (37 Halsbury's Statutes (4th Edn) REAL PROPERTY).

6   Trusts of Land and Appointment of Trustees Act 1996 s 2, Sch 1 para 1. There are corresponding provisions where, by reason of intestacy or in any other circumstances, a legal estate in land would vest in a person who is a minor if he were a person of full age: Trusts of Land and Appointment of Trustees Act 1996 Sch 1 para 2.
      Where the land is registered, the position is governed by the Land Registration Act 1925 s 111(1) as amended by the Trusts of Land and Appointment of Trustees Act 1996 s 25(1), Sch 3 para 5(11) (37 Halsbury's Statutes (4th Edn) REAL PROPERTY).

7   For long and short forms of accumulation and maintenance settlement and for a 25-year accumulation and maintenance settlement see vol 40(2) (2001 Reissue) TRUSTS AND SETTLEMENTS Part 11 [6501].

[14]

8   Protective settlements[1]

Protective settlements may be made by a settlor for his own benefit and protection or for that of a third party. Sometimes referred to as 'spendthrift trusts' they are useful in protecting assets both against spendthrift beneficiaries and against outside claimants. Such settlements normally contain provisions designed to enable the principal beneficiary to enjoy the beneficial interest intended for him without allowing him any power of alienation[2]. Such a settlement, if made by a third party, will be valid against a beneficiary's creditors or trustee in bankruptcy[3], but not if made by the settlor for his own benefit[4].

[15]

1   For a detailed treatment of protective settlements with precedents see vol 40(2) (2001 Reissue) TRUSTS AND SETTLEMENTS Part 12 [6901]. See also Paragraph 123 [305] post.
2   See the Trustee Act 1925 s 33 as amended by the Family Law Reform Act 1987 s 33(1), Sch 2 para 2 (48 Halsbury's Statutes (4th Edn) TRUSTS AND SETTLEMENTS).
3   *Re Ashby, ex p Wreford* [1892] 1 QB 872; *Re Throckmorton, ex p Eyston* (1877) 7 Ch D 145, CA.
4   *Re Burroughs-Fowler, Burroughs-Fowler's Trustee v Burroughs-Fowler* [1916] 2 Ch 251. See *Re Trusts of the Scientific Investment Pension Plan* [1999] Ch 53, [1998] 3 All ER 154, per Rattee J at 59, 158.

[16]

9   Marriage settlements

A marriage settlement is a settlement made in consideration of marriage either before the marriage or after it, but in the latter case only if made in pursuance of an ante-nuptial agreement to settle. The form of a marriage settlement has to a large extent become stereotyped[1]: such settlements are now rarely created.

1   As to marriage settlements generally see Paragraph 128 [318] et seq post. For a specimen marriage settlement see Form 7 [1136] post.

[17]

10   Post-nuptial settlements

A post-nuptial settlement is merely a species of voluntary settlement[1] unless it is made in pursuance of an agreement made prior to the marriage[2], in which case it will be deemed to have been made in consideration of the marriage[3], or unless it is the result of a bargain made after the marriage[4] or it is made for valuable consideration given by some other person[5].

[18]

1   *Goodright d Humphreys v Moses* (1775) 2 Wm Bl 1019; *Evelyn v Templar* (1787) 2 Bro CC 148; *Doe d Barnes v Rowe* (1838) 6 Scott 525; *Currie v Nind* (1836) 1 My & Cr 17; *Shurmur v Sedgwick, Crossfield v Shurmur* (1883) 24 Ch D 597; *Re Gillespie, ex p Knapman, The Trustee v Gillespie* (1913) 20 Mans 311. See also *Pownall v Anderson* (1856) 2 Jur NS 857 where articles entered into after marriage were held inoperative.
2   As to contracts for settlements generally see 42 Halsbury's Laws (4th Edn Reissue) para 627 et seq.
3   As to marriage as consideration for a settlement see 42 Halsbury's Laws (4th Edn Reissue) para 660 et seq.
4   *Hewison v Negus* (1853) 16 Beav 594; *Teasdale v Braithwaite* (1876) 4 Ch D 85 (affd (1877) 5 Ch D 630, CA); *Schreiber v Dinkel* (1884) 54 LJ Ch 241. See also *Stephens v Green, Green v Knight* [1895] 2 Ch 148, CA. In this situation the consideration does not extend to the children of the marriage, who are volunteers and, apart from statute, cannot enforce the settlement, unless they are parties to it (*Green v Paterson* (1886) 32 Ch D 95, CA; *Joyce v Hutton* (1860) 11 I Ch R 123 (on appeal (1861) 12 I Ch R 71, CA); cf *Gandy v Gandy* (1885) 30 Ch D 57, CA), or there is an executed trust in their favour (*Joyce v Hutton* above; *Green v Paterson* above). Now, however, they may be able to sue under the Contracts (Rights of Third Parties) Act 1999, though as volunteers they will not be able to obtain specific performance.
5   *Bayspoole v Collins* (1871) 6 Ch App 228; cf *Re Dickinson, ex p Hall* (1810) 1 Ves & B 112; *Ford v Stuart* (1852) 15 Beav 493; *Townend v Toker* (1866) 1 Ch App 446.

[19]

11   Other types of trust

Many other types of trust are mutants of the above described trusts, frequently variants of the discretionary trust[1]. The complex trusts marketed by insurance companies make use of a combination of revocable life interest with wide discretionary powers vested in the trustees.

1   See, eg, disabled trusts (vol 40(2) (2001 Reissue) TRUSTS AND SETTLEMENTS Part 16 [9301]), employee trusts (vol 40(2) (2001 Reissue) TRUSTS AND SETTLEMENTS Part 14 [8101]) and pension trusts (vol 40(2) (2001 Reissue) TRUSTS AND SETTLEMENTS Part 18 [9601]).

[20]

12   Why are trusts created?

Trusts are widely employed in what may loosely be termed 'family situations'; in commercial and business transactions; and as a vehicle for charitable or for non-charitable purposes. For example:

12.1	to provide for property to be held for successive generations of a family (in the case of land it was traditionally via the strict settlement)[1];
12.2	to hold property on behalf of minors[2];
12.3	to protect property against spendthrift beneficiaries[3];
12.4	to provide secretly for dependants[4];
12.5	to make provision for a couple on their marriage whilst ensuring that the property so provided is 'tied up' in the event of that marriage failing;
12.6	to obtain fiscal advantages[5];
12.7	to establish a fund which is available to benefit family members according to future need as and when that need arises[6];
12.8	as an investment vehicle (typically via unit trusts);
12.9	to provide pensions for employees and dependants[7];
12.10	to provide an incentive to the workforce: eg via employee trusts of various kinds[8];
12.11	to make provision for abstract purposes which are of benefit to individuals but are not charitable ('the purpose trust')[9];
12.12	to enable charitable objects to be carried out[10]; and
12.13	as part of commercial arrangements: eg to protect commercial lenders and customers[11].

Fundamentally, trust law is the same whatever the type of trust, but the trend over the last decade has been to introduce specific legislation to deal with problems that have arisen in particular types of case and to provide additional regulation in what are perceived to be areas of key public interest: for example, the Pensions Act 1995 was introduced in the wake of the Maxwell pension fiasco; the regulation of charities has been carried further by the Charities Act 1993; and unit trusts come within the regulatory framework of the financial services industry. It may be that we are seeing the development of a law for specific types of trust out of the core body of trust law.

[21]

---

1   Of course the trustees will usually have powers to sell the property, but the 'fund' will be protected. On excluding the power to sell land consider the effects of the Trusts of Land and Appointment of Trustees Act 1996 ss 6, 8 as amended by the Trustee Act 2000 Sch 2 Pt II para 45 (37 Halsbury's Statutes (4th Edn) REAL PROPERTY): see Paragraph 224 [538] post and for commentary on those provisions see vol 40(2) (2001 Reissue) TRUSTS AND SETTLEMENTS Part 8 [3001].

2   Land cannot be owned directly by minors: see the Law of Property Act 1925 s 1(6) (37 Halsbury's Statutes (4th Edn) REAL PROPERTY) and note the Trusts of Land and Appointment of Trustees Act 1996 s 2, Sch 1 paras 1, 2 where land is purported to be conveyed to a minor. Note also that co-ownership of land takes effect via the mechanism of a trust: see the Law of Property Act 1925 ss 34, 36 as amended by the Trusts of Land and Appointment of Trustees Act 1996 s 5, Sch 2 paras 3, 4, Sch 4.

Where the land is registered, the position is governed by the Land Registration Act 1925 s 111(1) as amended by the Trusts of Land and Appointment of Trustees Act 1996 s 25(1), Sch 3 para 5(11) (37 Halsbury's Statutes (4th Edn) REAL PROPERTY).

3   As to protective trusts see Paragraphs 8 [15] ante, 123 [305] post and vol 40(2) (2001 Reissue) TRUSTS AND SETTLEMENTS Part 12 [6901].

4   On so-called secret and half-secret trusts see Paragraph 26 [68] post.

5   For a typical example consider the accumulation and maintenance trust: see Paragraphs 7 [13] ante, 127 [316] post and vol 40(2) (2001 Reissue) TRUSTS AND SETTLEMENTS Part 11 [6501].

6   For a typical discretionary trust see Form 4 [1081] post; for a discretionary trust of land see vol 40(2) (2001 Reissue) TRUSTS AND SETTLEMENTS Part 8 [3501].

7   On pension trusts see 'Some Trust Principles in the Pensions Context' by Sir Robert Walker in Oakley (ed) *Trends in Contemporary Trust Law* (1996) p 123.

8   As to employee trusts see Paragraph 333 [880] post and vol 40(2) (2001 Reissue) TRUSTS AND
     SETTLEMENTS Part 14 [8101].
9   As to purpose trusts see Paragraph 47 [112] post and vol 40(2) (2001 Reissue) TRUSTS AND
     SETTLEMENTS Part 13 [7501].
10   For a detailed consideration of charities see vol 6(2) (2001 Reissue) CHARITIES AND CHARITABLE
     GIVING.
11   Consider for instance the arrangements set up in *Re Kayford* [1975] 1 All ER 604, [1975] 1 WLR 279;
     Barclays Bank v Quistclose Investments Ltd [1970] AC 567, [1968] 3 All ER 651, HL; *R v Common
     Professional Examination Board, ex p Mealing-McCleod* (2000) Times, 2 May, CA.

[22]

C: MAIN LEGISLATION RELATING TO TRUSTS AND SETTLEMENTS

13   Main legislation

The principal statute in force relating to trusts remains the Trustee Act 1925[1]. The powers conferred by this Act on trustees are in addition to the powers conferred by the instrument, if any, creating the trust[2], but those powers, unless otherwise stated, apply if and so far only as a contrary intention is not expressed in the instrument, if any, creating the trust[3], and have effect subject to the terms of that instrument[4].

Other statutes of importance relating to trusts are the Variation of Trusts Act 1958, by which the court is given wide powers to vary the terms of trusts[5], the Trustee Delegation Act 1999[6] and, most importantly, the Trustee Act 2000[7]. The Administration of Estates Act 1925[8] also affects to some extent the law relating to trusts.

The Charities Act 1993 is the main Act governing the administration of charitable trusts and the appointment of charity trustees[9].

The Recognition of Trusts Act 1987 ratifies the Convention, adopted in draft form by the 1984 Hague Conference on Private International Law, on the law applicable to trusts and on their recognition.

The principal statutes now in force relating to settlements are the Settled Land Act 1925[10] and, in relation to a settlement of land by way of a trust of land, the Law of Property Act 1925 and the Trusts of Land and Appointment of Trustees Act 1996[11].

[23]

1   The Trustee Act 1925 (48 Halsbury's Statutes (4th Edn) TRUSTS AND SETTLEMENTS) came into
     force on 1 January 1926 and applies, except where otherwise expressly provided, to trusts including, so
     far as the Act applies to them, executorships and administratorships constituted or created either before
     or after the commencement of the Act: Trustee Act 1925 s 69(1). Except where otherwise expressly
     provided, the Act extends to England and Wales only: Trustee Act 1925 s 71(3). The Act binds the
     Crown: Trustee Act 1925 s 71(4).
2   'Trust' does not include the duties incident to an estate conveyed by way of mortgage, but with this
     exception the expressions 'trust' and 'trustee' extend to implied and constructive trusts, and to cases
     where the trustee has a beneficial interest in the trust property, and to the duties incident to the office
     of a personal representative, and 'trustee' where the context admits, includes a personal representative
     and 'new trustee' includes an additional trustee: Trustee Act 1925 s 68(1).
3   For cases where a contrary intention was shown see *Re Turner's Will Trusts, District Bank Ltd v Turner*
     [1937] Ch 15, [1936] 2 All ER 1435, CA; *Re Rider's Will Trusts, Nelson v Rider* [1958] 3 All ER 135,
     [1958] 1 WLR 974; *IRC v Bernstein* [1961] Ch 399, [1961] 1 All ER 320, CA. For cases where no
     contrary intention was held to have been shown see *Re Warren, Public Trustee v Fletcher* [1939] Ch 684,
     [1939] 2 All ER 599; *Re Rees, Lloyds Bank Ltd v Rees* [1954] Ch 202, [1954] 1 All ER 7.
4   Trustee Act 1925 s 69(2).
5   As to the variation of trusts generally see further Paragraph 267 [661] et seq post.
6   As to delegation of trustee functions by power of attorney see further Paragraph 227 [543] post.
7   The main matters dealt with by this Act relate to the imposition of a statutory duty of care (see
     Paragraph 183 [453] post); the powers of trustees in respect of investments and the acquisition of land
     (see Paragraph 184 [454] post); the appointment of agents, nominees and custodians (see Paragraph 246
     [611] et seq post); and remuneration (see Paragraph 212 [511] et seq post).

8   As to the administration of estates see generally vol 42(2) (1998 Reissue) WILLS AND
         ADMINISTRATION Paragraph 495 [3001] et seq.
9   As to charitable trusts and the appointment of charity trustees see generally vol 6(2) (2001 Reissue)
         CHARITIES AND CHARITABLE GIVING Paragraph 42 [226] et seq.
10   As to settlements under the Settled Land Act 1925 (48 Halsbury's Statutes (4th Edn) TRUSTS AND
         SETTLEMENTS) see further vol 40(2) (2001 Reissue) TRUSTS AND SETTLEMENTS Part 9 [4101]. It
         has not been possible to create a new settlement under the Settled Land Act 1925 since the coming into
         force of the Trusts of Land and Appointment of Trustees Act 1996 (37 Halsbury's Statutes (4th Edn)
         REAL PROPERTY) on 1 January 1997: Trusts of Land and Appointment of Trustees Act 1996 s 2.
11   As to trusts of land see further Paragraph 107 [266] et seq post.

[24]–[40]

(2) CREATION OF TRUSTS AND SETTLEMENTS

A: PERSONS WHO CAN CREATE

14   General

As a general rule every person who is able to acquire and dispose of property is able to
create a trust. Exceptions to this rule exist in the case of minors, of persons mentally
disordered and bankrupts[1].

1   As to the exceptions to this rule see further Paragraphs 15 [42]–17 [46] post.

[41]

15   Minors

A minor[1] cannot make a binding settlement, or enter into a binding contract to make a
settlement. Such a settlement is not, however, void ab initio but voidable[2], and is binding
if confirmed on attaining full age[3], or acted upon[4]. Ratification upon coming of age is
not necessary, though desirable; it is enough if the settlor or covenantor does not, within
a reasonable time of attaining majority, repudiate the act done while a minor[5]. The
reasonable time begins to run from the date when the minor attains full age, not from
the date when the property falls into possession[6]. In many cases the benefit of the
settlement is enough to preclude the likelihood of the minor objecting to it on attaining
his majority; and the interest of the repudiating party in property brought into settlement
by another may become liable to be impounded to make up the loss of persons affected
by the repudiation[7].

[42]

1   A minor is a person under the age of 18 years: see the Family Law Reform Act 1969 s 1 (6 Halsbury's
         Statutes (4th Edn) CHILDREN). Before 1 January 1970 the age of majority was 21 years.
2   *Zouch d Abbot and Hallet v Parsons* (1765) 3 Burr 1794 at 1801; *Allen v Allen* (1842) 4 I Eq R 472;
         Burnaby v Equitable Reversionary Interest Society (1885) 28 Ch D 416 at 419, 420.
3   *Re Hodson, Williams v Knight* [1894] 2 Ch 421.
4   Eg if a wife mortgages her interest on attaining her majority: see *Greenhill v North British and Mercantile
         Insurance Co* [1893] 3 Ch 474.
5   *Edwards v Carter* [1893] AC 360, HL; *Viditz v O'Hagan* [1900] 2 Ch 87, CA.
6   *Carnell v Harrison* [1916] 1 Ch 328, CA.
7   *Carter v Silber, Carter v Hasluck* [1891] 3 Ch 553 (revsd on other grounds [1892] 2 Ch 278, CA; affd
         sub nom *Edwards v Carter* [1893] AC 360, HL); *Hamilton v Hamilton* [1892] 1 Ch 396.

[43]

16   Persons mentally disordered

Where a patient[1] is incapable by reason of mental disorder of managing and administering his property and affairs, and a receiver has been appointed, any disposition, including a settlement executed by him, would appear to be void under the Mental Health Act 1983[2]. Where a receiver has not been appointed, the question in each case is whether the person concerned is capable of understanding what he does by executing the deed in question when its general purport has been fully explained to him. For the making of a valid will, a high degree of understanding is required, including an understanding of the claims of all potential beneficiaries and the extent of the property to be disposed of. The same degree of understanding may be required in the case of an inter vivos gift or settlement, though it varies with the circumstances of the transaction, and a much lower degree of understanding would suffice if the subject matter and value of the gift or settlement are trivial in relation to the donor's or settlor's other assets[3]. In the case of a marriage settlement, if the settlor is a party to the marriage, and the marriage is subsequently annulled on the grounds of mental disorder[4], there will be a resulting trust of the settled property for the settlor[5].

In relation to a contract to settle property, a party who seeks to avoid the contract on the ground of mental incapacity must first show that at the time of entering into the contract he was suffering from such a degree of mental disability that he was incapable of understanding the nature of the contract[6]. If this can be shown, the contract is not void, but voidable at his option, provided that the incapacity was known or ought to have been known by the other contracting party[7]. The onus of proof lies on the person seeking to avoid the contract[8].

Under the Mental Health Act 1983, the judge[9] has wide powers over the property of a patient for the purpose of the maintenance or benefit of the patient and members of his family, and for making provision for other persons or purposes for whom or which the patient might be expected to provide if he were not mentally disordered. The judge also has express power to order a settlement of the patient's property for these purposes[10]. The power of the judge, however, to make or give an order, direction or authority for the execution of a will for a patient is not exercisable at any time when the patient is a minor[11].

A donee of an enduring power of attorney has power to provide for and meet the 'needs' of any person if the donor might have been expected to do so[12]. In *Re Cameron*[13] the attorneys were held to have acted within the scope of this power in establishing a trust for the education of the donor's grandson: it was further held that this provision for the grandson adeemed *pro tanto* the share of the donor's son (the father of the grandson) of the residue of his mother's estate.

[44]

1   A person in relation to whom a judge under the Mental Health Act 1983 Part VII (ss 93–113) (28 Halsbury's Statutes (4th Edn) MENTAL HEALTH) is satisfied is incapable, by reason of mental disorder, of managing and administering his property and affairs is in that part referred to as a patient: Mental Health Act 1983 s 94(2).

2   For the power to appoint a receiver see Mental Health Act 1983 s 99.

3   *Re Beaney* [1978] 2 All ER 595, [1978] 1 WLR 770. As to the capacity to execute a will see vol 42(1) (1998 Reissue) WILLS AND ADMINISTRATION Paragraphs 13 [42] et seq and 285 [2001] et seq. Reforms are envisaged in 'Making Decisions' a report from the Lord Chancellor's Department which sets out the Government's proposals for making decisions on behalf of mentally incapacitated adults (CM 4465: October 1999). It is intended that there will be a new (statutory) test of capacity.

4   See the Matrimonial Causes Act 1973 s 12(d) as amended by the Mental Health Act 1983 s 148, Sch 4 para 34 (27 Halsbury's Statutes (4th Edn) MATRIMONIAL LAW).

5   See *Re Garnett, Richardson v Greenep* (1905) 74 LJ Ch 570; *Re Wombwell's Settlement, Clerke v Menzies* [1922] 2 Ch 298.

6   *Boughton v Knight* (1873) LR 3 P & D 64 at 72.

7   *Molton v Camroux* (1848) 2 Exch 487 (affd (1849) 4 Exch 17); *Imperial Loan Co Ltd v Stone* [1892] 1 QB
     599, CA; *York Glass Co Ltd v Jubb* (1925) 134 LT 36, CA; *Hart v O'Connor* [1985] AC 1000, [1985]
     2 All ER 880, PC.
8   See note 7 above.
9   The functions expressed to be conferred on the judge under the Mental Health Act 1983 Pt VII
     (ss 93–113) are exercisable by the Lord Chancellor or by any judge of the Supreme Court nominated
     by him for this purpose; also by the Master of the Court of Protection, by the Public Trustee or by
     any nominated officer: see the Mental Health Act 1983 s 94(1), (1A) as amended and inserted by the
     Public Trustee and Administration of Funds Act 1986 s 2(1), (2).
10   See the Mental Health Act 1983 ss 95, 96(1). In exercising this jurisdiction the judge is guided by what
     it is thought likely the patient would himself do if he were not under disability, but on the assumption
     that the circumstances in other respects are what they are in fact: *Re DML* [1965] Ch 1133, [1965] 2 All
     ER 129; *Re L(WJG)* [1966] Ch 135, sub nom *Re WJGL* [1965] 3 All ER 865; *Re TB* [1967] Ch 247,
     [1966] 3 All ER 509; *Re S (gifts by mental patient)* [1997] 2 FCR 320, [1997] 1 FLR 96. See also
     Re CMG [1970] Ch 574, [1970] 2 All ER 740n; *Re CWHT* [1978] Ch 67, [1978] 1 All ER 210. As
     to applications for settlements see the Court of Protection Rules 1994, SI 1994/3046 r 20.
11   Mental Health Act 1983 s 96(4)(a).
12   Enduring Powers of Attorney Act 1985 s 3(4) (1 Halsbury's Statutes (4th Edn) AGENCY).
13   *Re Cameron* [1999] Ch 386, [1999] 2 All ER 924. The attorney does not, however, have authority to
     enter into estate planning arrangements on behalf of the donor: these require the approval of the Court
     of Protection.

[45]

17   Bankruptcy

On a person having a bankruptcy order made against him, all property which belongs to
or is vested in him at the commencement of the bankruptcy with certain exceptions
only[1], vests in his trustee immediately on his appointment taking effect or, in the case of
the official receiver, on his becoming trustee[2]. It follows that a bankrupt cannot make
any settlement of the property so vesting. He is, however, entitled to any surplus
remaining after payment in full of his creditors, with interest, and the expenses of the
bankruptcy proceedings[3]; and this he can settle[4]. Since the repeal of the Bankruptcy Act
1914 and its replacement, with modifications, by the Insolvency Act 1986, property
acquired by or devolving on the bankrupt between the commencement of the
bankruptcy and his discharge does not automatically vest in the trustee. The trustee may,
however, by notice in writing claim for the bankrupt's estate any property acquired by
or devolving on him since the commencement of the bankruptcy[5].

[46]

1   See the Insolvency Act 1986 s 283 (4 Halsbury's Statutes (4th Edn) BANKRUPTCY AND
     INSOLVENCY).
2   Insolvency Act 1986 s 306(1).
3   Insolvency Act 1986 s 330(5).
4   *Bird v Philpott* [1900] 1 Ch 822.
5   Insolvency Act 1986 s 307(1). As to after-acquired property generally see further 3(2) Halsbury's Laws
     (4th Edn Reissue) para 433 et seq.

[47]

18   Settlement by trustees of a settlement ('settled advances')

Trustees of a settlement may properly settle funds they advance, whether under an
express power of advancement contained in the settlement[1] or under the statutory power
of advancement where that applies[2]. If the trustees are satisfied that the proposed
settlement is for the benefit of the object of the power, it is no objection to the exercise
of the statutory power of advancement that other persons may incidentally benefit as the
result of its exercise; nor is it bad merely because money is to be tied up in a proposed
settlement[3].

Although no settlement made by way of advancement upon an object of the power by trustees must conflict with the maxim *delegatus non potest delegare*, the law is not that trustees cannot delegate, but that they cannot delegate unless they have power to do so; and, if the power is so read as to allow the trustees to raise money for the purpose of having it settled on the trusts of a new settlement, then they have authority to let the money pass out of the old settlement into the new trusts[4].

The exercise of a power of advancement, however, which takes the form of a settlement, is a special power akin to a special power of appointment, and as such, must be exercised within the period permitted by the rule against perpetuities, and its exercise must, for the purposes of that rule, be written into the instrument creating the power[5].

[48]

1   *Roper-Curzon v Roper-Curzon* (1871) LR 11 Eq 452; *Re Halsted's Will Trusts, Halsted v Halsted* [1937] 2 All ER 570; *Re Ropner's Settlements Trusts, Ropner v Ropner* [1956] 3 All ER 332n, [1956] 1 WLR 902; *Re Wills' Will Trusts, Wills v Wills* [1959] Ch 1, [1958] 2 All ER 472. As to advancement see further Paragraph 238 [573] et seq post and for advancement by way of resettlement see Form 290 [2020] post. For a discussion of settled advances see Parker & Mellows Modern Law of Trusts (7th Edn, 1998) pp 623–629. For trustee resolutions exercising the power of advancement see Forms 256 [1852] and 257 [1854] post.

2   *Re Ropner's Settlements Trusts, Ropner v Ropner* [1956] 3 All ER 332n, [1956] 1 WLR 902; *Pilkington v IRC* [1964] AC 612, [1962] 3 All ER 622, HL.

3   *Pilkington v IRC* [1964] AC 612, [1962] 3 All ER 622, HL at 636, 628. A beneficiary may derive a benefit from knowing that funds are tied up for his wife and children: see *Re Halsted's Will Trusts, Re Halsted v Halsted* [1937] 2 All ER 570.

4   See, eg, Form 157(2) clause 0.2 [1614] post which is a 'power in the wider form' permitting capital to be resettled on trusts with overriding powers of appointment. See also *Pilkington v IRC* [1964] AC 612, [1962] 3 All ER 622, HL. In *Re Wills' Will Trusts, Wills v Wills* [1959] Ch 1, Upjohn J commented that 'a settlement created in exercise of the power of advancement cannot in general delegate any powers or discretions, at any rate in relation to beneficial interests, to any trustees or other persons, and in so far as the settlement purports to do so, it is *pro tanto* invalid'. This has led to concerns that:
     (a)   an advance into a discretionary trust would be ineffective;
     (b)   if an advance on protective trusts was made, the discretionary trust arising on the forfeiture of the principal beneficiary's life interest would be ineffective; and
     (c)   if an advance was made onto life interest trusts, a discretionary power to advance capital to the life tenant would be ineffective.
     The dictum is based upon the maxim *delegatus non potest delegare*, but it is by no means certain that it accurately represents the law. In *Pilkington v IRC* [1964] AC 612, [1962] 3 All ER 622, HL at 639 and 630, there is a statement of Lord Radcliffe apparently to the contrary. In any event, it has been accepted that the 'new' trustees may themselves have powers of advancement: *Re Hunter's Will Trusts, Gilks v Harris* [1963] Ch 372, [1962] 3 All ER 1050. See further *Lewin on Trusts* (17th Edn, 2000) para 32.18, and, for a contrary view, see Underhill and Hayton *Law of Trusts and Trustees* (15th Edn, 1995) p 704.

5   *Pilkington v IRC* [1964] AC 612, [1962] 3 All ER 622, HL. As to the rule against perpetuities, the 'wait and see' provisions and the power to specify a perpetuity period see Paragraph 77 [183] et seq post. For the capital gains tax consequences of resettlement see Paragraph 342 [919] post.

[49]–[55]

B: MODE OF CREATION AND DURATION

1: MODE OF CREATION

19   Settlements of land before 1 January 1997

Prior to the coming into force of the Trusts of Land and Appointment of Trustees Act 1996 on 1 January 1997 there were two methods of settling land: by what was known as a 'strict settlement' under the Settled Land Act 1925, or by means of a trust for sale. If the former method was employed the land was vested in the tenant for life, or statutory owner, by a vesting instrument, the trusts being declared by a separate instrument[1]. All powers over the land, such as sale and leasing, were then exercisable by the tenant for life or statutory owner. If a trust for sale was employed the land was vested in trustees who held it on trust for sale, and the trusts of the net proceeds of sale and of the net rents and profits until sale were again normally declared by a separate instrument[2]. All the powers were then exercisable by the trustees[3]. Money might also be settled upon trust to purchase land to be held upon trusts appropriate to a settlement of realty.

In the case of registered land, the relevant vesting deed or assurance would have needed to be (as now) in the prescribed form of transfer and the transfer would need to have been lodged for registration in order to achieve the vesting of the legal estate in the appropriate person[4].

[56]

---

1   As to settlements of land under the Settled Land Act 1925 (48 Halsbury's Statutes (4th Edn) TRUSTS AND SETTLEMENTS) see vol 40(2) (2001 Reissue) TRUSTS AND SETTLEMENTS Part 9 [4101].
2   As to land settled by way of trust for sale before 1 January 1997 see Paragraph 107 [266] post. As to the current position see Paragraph 108 [267] post.
3   As to the powers of trustees of land see Paragraph 221 [532] et seq post.
4   Land Registration Act 1925 ss 20(1), 23(1), 69(1) (37 Halsbury's Statutes (4th Edn) REAL PROPERTY).

[57]

20   Settlements of land after 31 December 1996

The Trusts of Land and Appointment of Trustees Act 1996, which was brought into force on 1 January 1997, has taken an important step towards ending the dual system of settlements of land. Section 2(1) of the Act provides that no new settlement under the Settled Land Act 1925 can be created, or will be deemed to arise, after the commencement of the 1996 Act[1]. Any existing settlement, however, continues to be governed by the Settled Land Act 1925, and there are no provisions enabling it to be converted into a trust of land under the Trusts of Land and Appointment of Trustees Act 1996. It will, therefore, be many years before the provisions of the Settled Land Act 1925 become obsolete, although they will be of continually diminishing relevance. It is not possible to bring additional land into an existing settlement by way of further settlement[2], and if at any time there ceases to be any relevant property[3] subject to the settlement, the settlement ceases permanently to be a settlement for the purposes of the Settled Land Act 1925[4].

Every settlement of land is now a 'trust of land' which is defined as meaning any trust of property which consists of or includes land[5]. 'Trust' is itself defined as referring to any description of trust[6], expressly including a trust for sale and a bare trust[7]. Accordingly, every settlement of land is created by vesting the land in trustees to be held upon the declared trusts, which is normally, though not essentially, declared by a separate instrument.

[58]

1   However, a new settlement resulting from any alteration of an interest under a Settled Land Act 1925 settlement (eg a resettlement), or occurring as a result of a person becoming entitled under an existing Settled Land Act settlement (eg on the exercise of a power of appointment), will continue to be governed by the Settled Land Act 1925 unless there is a contrary provision in the relevant instrument: Trusts of Land and Appointment of Trustees Act 1996 s 2(2), (3) (37 Halsbury's Statutes (4th Edn) REAL PROPERTY).

2   It is possible to bring further land into the settlement by purchase under the provisions of the Settled Land Act 1925 s 10 (48 Halsbury's Statutes (4th Edn) TRUSTS AND SETTLEMENTS) (in which case a subsidiary vesting deed is necessary, in the prescribed form if registered).

3   'Relevant property' means land and personal chattels to which the Settled Land Act 1925 s 67(1) (heirlooms) applies: Trusts of Land and Appointment of Trustees Act 1996 s 2(4).

4   Trusts of Land and Appointment of Trustees Act 1996 s 2(4).

5   Trusts of Land and Appointment of Trustees Act 1996 s 1(1)(a). Land in a pre-1997 Act settlement within the Settled Land Act 1925, or to which the Universities and College Estates Act 1925 applies, is excluded: Trusts of Land and Appointment of Trustees Act 1996 s 1(3).

6   Whether express, implied, resulting or constructive.

7   Trusts of Land and Appointment of Trustees Act 1996 s 1(2)(a). A trust created, or arising, before the commencement of the 1996 Act is included: Trusts of Land and Appointment of Trustees Act 1996 s 1(2)(b).

[59]

21   Settlements of pure personalty

A trust of pure personalty is properly constituted by the transfer of the trust property to trustees who are directed to hold it on trust for the persons or purposes intended to benefit; or by the settlor declaring that from that time onwards he holds the property on the specified trusts[1].

1   As to settlements of personalty see further Paragraph 112 [275] et seq post. As to what property is capable of being held in trust see Paragraph 113 [276] post.

[60]

2: CONSTITUTION OF TRUSTS

22   Constitution generally

A voluntary settlement is fully constituted when the instrument declaring the trusts has been executed[1] and everything has been done by the settlor which is necessary, according to the nature of the property comprised in the settlement, to transfer the property to the trustees[2]. Alternatively he may declare himself to be a trustee of the gifted property for the donee[3]. In principle there is no distinction between the case where the donor declares himself to be the sole trustee for a donee and the case where he declares himself to be one of the trustees for that donee[4]. If a voluntary settlement is not completely constituted, the settlement and the covenants contained in it will be unenforceable.

In the case of a settlement made for valuable consideration, such as marriage, the court will treat an incompletely constituted settlement as a contract to transfer the property which the settlor covenanted to transfer and will enforce it[5]. Where a proposed marriage does not take place, or is later annulled, there is a total failure of the consideration for an ante-nuptial settlement, which generally causes a resulting trust of the settled property to the settlor[6]. Hitherto the only persons who have been able to enforce any covenants contained in incompletely constituted marriage settlements have been the parties to the marriage and the issue of the marriage being the persons falling within the marriage consideration[7] but this rule has been modified by the Contracts (Rights of Third Parties) Act 1999, though not so as to enable a volunteer to obtain specific performance.

Where a sum of money or property passing by delivery is being settled, only a trust instrument is necessary, but in other cases deeds or instruments of transfer or assignment are required[8].

[61]

1   If the settlor intends to retain the property himself, but to declare himself to be a trustee of it for a donee, no instrument in writing is necessary, unless the trust property consists of land or the declaration constitutes a disposition of an equitable interest: see the Law of Property Act 1925 s 53(1) (37 Halsbury's Statutes (4th Edn) REAL PROPERTY); see also *Grey v IRC* [1960] AC 1, [1959] 3 All ER 603, HL. As to the distinction between incomplete gifts and declarations of trust see vol 17(2) (2000 Reissue) GIFTS Paragraph 27 [628]. In the case of so-called 'pilot' settlements (ie where the deed recites that a small cash sum is initially settled and that further property will be added in the future) it is important to ensure that the cash sum is paid to the trustees: otherwise the trust will not be constituted and this may have disastrous results (especially for inheritance tax).

2   *Milroy v Lord* (1862) 4 De GF & J 264. The test is whether any act remains to be done by the settlor, and not by the beneficiaries or trustees: see *Re Rose, Midland Bank Executor and Trustee Co Ltd v Rose* [1949] Ch 78, [1948] 2 All ER 971; *Re Rose, Rose v IRC* [1952] Ch 499, [1952] 1 All ER 1217, CA; see also *Jaffa v Taylor Gallery Ltd* (1990) Times 21 March. Once a settlement is completely constituted, it is immaterial whether it is voluntary or not; it will be enforced against the settlor, whether he afterwards obtains possession of the settled property or not: see *Vandervell v IRC* [1967] 2 AC 291, [1967] 1 All ER 1, HL. As to irrevocability of perfect gifts generally see vol 17(2) (2000 Reissue) GIFTS Paragraph 5 [508].

3   *Milroy v Lord* (1862) 4 De GF & J 264.

4   *T Choithram International SA v Pagarani* [2001] 2 All ER 492, [2001] 1 LRC 694, PC.

5   *Pullan v Koe* [1913] 1 Ch 9.

6   See *Re Garnett, Richardson v Greenep* (1905) 74 LJ Ch 570; *Re Wombwell's Settlement, Clerke v Menzies* [1922] 2 Ch 298; *Re Ames' Settlement, Dinwiddy v Ames* [1946] Ch 217, [1946] 1 All ER 689; *Re Rodwell, Midgley v Rumbold* [1970] Ch 726, [1969] 3 All ER 1363.

7   As to persons within the marriage consideration see further 42 Halsbury's Laws (4th Edn Reissue) para 661.

8   *De Mestre v West* [1891] AC 264, PC.

[62]

3: EVIDENCE OF AN EXPRESS TRUST

23   Evidence of trust in land or disposition of equitable interest

Apart from statute, a trust inter vivos can be created by word of mouth. An oral declaration and a deed may, however, form one single transaction for stamp duty purposes[1]. The Law of Property Act 1925 Section 53 provides that:

23.1   no interest in land can be created or disposed of except by writing signed by the person creating or conveying it, or by his agent who is lawfully authorised in writing, or by will, or by operation of law[2];

23.2   a declaration of trust respecting any land or any interest in it must be manifested and proved by some writing signed by some person who is able to declare such trust or by his will[3]; and

23.3   a disposition of an equitable interest or trust subsisting at the time of the disposition, must be in writing signed by the person disposing of it, or by his agent who is lawfully authorised in writing, or by will[4].

[63]

A declaration of trust, therefore, needs merely to be evidenced by writing; it does not have to be created by writing. The written evidence should contain all the terms of the trust (namely, parties, property and the way in which the property should be dealt with)[5]. The provision set out in Paragraph 23.2 above does not sanction signature by an agent.

On the other hand, the disposition of an equitable interest or trust must be in writing[6], although signature by an agent lawfully authorised in writing is sufficient. The word 'disposition' has been widely construed and accordingly oral directions given by the settlor may be treated as dispositions[7]. It is, however, important to notice for this purpose that Paragraph 23.3 above has no application in cases where the disposition intended to be made is not merely of the equitable interest but also of the legal interest in the property[8]. In other words, in dealing with the disposition of an equitable interest, Paragraph 23.3 above only applies when the disposer is not also the controller of the legal interest.

All interests in land created by parol and not put into writing and signed by the persons creating them, or by their agents lawfully authorised in writing, have the force and effect of interests at will only[9]. However, this does not invalidate dispositions by will, or the right to acquire an interest in land by virtue of taking possession, or affect the operation of the law relating to part performance[10].

[64]

1   *Cohen and Moore v IRC* [1933] 2 KB 126. As to stamp duty generally see Information Binder: Stamp Duties [1].
2   Law of Property Act 1925 s 53(1)(a) (37 Halsbury's Statutes (4th Edn) REAL PROPERTY).
3   Law of Property Act 1925 s 53(1)(b).
4   Law of Property Act 1925 s 53(1)(c). The creation or operation of resulting, implied or constructive trusts are not affected by s 53: Law of Property Act 1925 s 53(2). Such trusts are clearly exempt from Law of Property Act 1925 s 53(1)(b): see *Hodgson v Marks* [1971] Ch 892, [1971] 2 All ER 684, CA. In relation to s 53(1)(c) it was held in *Neville v Wilson* [1997] Ch 144, [1996] 3 All ER 171, CA, that where there is an oral agreement for value for the sale and purchase of an equitable interest in personalty, the vendor becomes a constructive trustee for the purchaser and s 53(2) applies to dispense with the requirement of writing.
5   See *Forster v Hale* (1798) 3 Ves 696; affd (1800) 5 Ves 308.
6   For the meaning of 'writing' see *Re Danish Bacon Co Ltd Staff Pension Fund, Christensen v Arnett* [1971] 1 All ER 486 at 491–493, [1971] 1 WLR 248 at 254, 255 per Megarry J.
7   *Grey v IRC* [1960] AC 1, [1959] 3 All ER 603, HL. See also *Re Tyler's Fund Trusts, Graves v King* [1967] 3 All ER 389, [1967] 1 WLR 1269; *Crowden v Aldridge* [1993] 3 All ER 603, [1993] 1 WLR 433.
8   *Vandervell v IRC* [1967] 2 AC 291, [1967] 1 All ER 1, HL.
9   Law of Property Act 1925 s 54(1).
10   Law of Property Act 1925 s 55. By the Law of Property Act 1925 s 54(2) nothing in the preceding provisions of the Law of Property Act 1925 Pt II (ss 40–54(1)) is to affect the creation by parol of leases taking effect in possession for a term not exceeding three years (whether or not the lessee has power to extend the term) at the best rent which can be reasonably obtained without taking a fine. Law of Property Act 1925 s 40 has now been repealed and replaced by the Law of Property (Miscellaneous Provisions) Act 1989 (37 Halsbury's Statutes (4th Edn) REAL PROPERTY) under which an agreement to settle land can only be made in writing and only by incorporating all the terms which the parties have expressly agreed in one document (which may include a reference to another document), or, where contracts are exchanged, in each; the document(s) must be signed by or on behalf of each party to the contract: Law of Property (Miscellaneous Provisions) Act 1989 s 2(1)–(3). As a consequence of the Law of Property (Miscellaneous Provisions) Act 1989 the law relating to part performance can now only be relevant in relation to contracts entered into before the Law of Property (Miscellaneous Provisions) Act 1989 s 2 came into force on 27 September 1989: see the Law of Property (Miscellaneous Provisions) Act 1989 s 5(3), (4).

[65]

24   Rectification on account of error

Where, by mistake, an instrument creating a trust of property does not express the intention of the disposer, it may be cancelled or rectified according to the true intention of the disposer[1].

1   *Thompson v Whitmore* (1860) 1 John & H 268 at 273, per Wood V-C; *Lister v Hodgson* (1867) LR 4 Eq 30; *Weir v Van Tromp* (1900) 16 TLR 531; *Van der Linde v Van der Linde* [1947] Ch 306; *Re Butlin's Settlement Trusts, Butlin v Butlin* [1976] Ch 251, [1976] 2 All ER 483; *Gibbon v Mitchell* [1990] 3 All ER 338; (1990) 1 WLR 1304. But see *Tankel v Tankel* [1999] 1 FLR 676 (rectification refused where it could not be said that the settlement in question differed, by reason of some mistake, from that which the settlor intended to execute. It was not enough for the judge to consider that the proposed rectification would improve the settlement, or that if the settlor's attention had been drawn to the point he would have approved it).

[66]

25   Evidence of a trust of personalty

Personal chattels, money, or any other form of personal property, are not within the statutory provisions requiring a declaration of trust to be in writing[1]. A valid trust of such property inter vivos can be created by word of mouth[2], and writing is not necessary to prove it[3].

1   Ie the Law of Property Act 1925 s 53(1)(b) (37 Halsbury's Statutes (4th Edn) REAL PROPERTY). See further Paragraph 23 [63] ante.
2   *Kilpin v Kilpin* (1834) 1 My & K 520; *Jones v Lock* (1865) 1 Ch App 25.
3   See *Cohen and Moore v IRC* [1933] 2 KB 126; and see further Paragraph 23 [63] ante.

[67]

26   Testamentary trusts (including secret and half-secret trusts)

A trust of either real or personal property, which is not intended to take effect until after the death of the creator, must be created by a document properly attested as a will or codicil[1]. For instance, if a testator appoints by duly executed will a trustee to whom he gives property expressed to be upon trust, but does not by the will declare the trusts, a declaration of trust subsequently made by a document not executed as a will is invalid, and the trustee becomes trustee for the persons interested as residuary legatees or on an intestacy[2]. Similarly, if a testator gives property by will to a person absolutely, and makes no reference to any trust on the face of the will, but privately communicates to that person that he is to hold the property bequeathed to him on certain trusts, prima facie those trusts are invalid unless declared by a duly executed testamentary instrument[3]. To this rule, however, there is an exception arising where the testator has been induced to make a will in a particular form by a promise on the part of the devisee or legatee to deal with the property or some part of it in a specified manner. In such a case equity compels performance of the promise, treating it as a trust binding the conscience of the devisee or legatee, the trust operating outside the will. Because it is presumed that, had it not been for such promise, the testator would not have made the gift[4], where there are two trustees, communication to and acceptance of the trust by one of them is, in certain circumstances, enough[5].

This exception does not operate, however, where the communication to the alleged trustee is accompanied by a statement on the part of the testator that it is not to create a trust[6]. Nor does it apply in a case where the gift is made to trustees on the face of the will, but the trusts are not disclosed and communication of the trusts is only made to the trustees after the execution of the will[7], for a testator cannot reserve to himself a power of making further unwitnessed dispositions by merely naming a trustee and leaving the purposes of the trust to be supplied afterwards[8]. Likewise, where the amount of the gift is increased, but the increase is not communicated to the trustee, the additional gift will fail[9].

Although the principle has generally only been applied in gifts by will, it may operate also where the gift is by settlement inter vivos[10].

[68]

1   As to the formalities for the execution of wills and codicils see in particular the Wills Act 1837 s 9 as substituted by the Administration of Justice Act 1982 s 17 (50 Halsbury's Statutes (4th Edn) WILLS) and see vol 42(1) (1998 Reissue) WILLS AND ADMINISTRATION Paragraph 182 [423].

2   See eg *Johnson v Ball* (1851) 5 De G & Sm 85. Where the trust is referred to but not defined in the will it is enforceable if, but only if: (a) it is described in the will as having been defined and communicated to the trustees prior to, or contemporaneously with, the execution of the will and (b) it is also proved that it was so defined and communicated to some, even though not to all, of the trustees: *Re Keen, Evershed v Griffiths* [1937] Ch 236, [1937] 1 All ER 452, CA; *Re Bateman's Will Trusts, Brierley v Perry* [1970] 3 All ER 817, [1970] 1 WLR 1463. See further vol 42(1) (1998 Reissue) WILLS AND ADMINISTRATION Paragraph 10 [28].

3   *Re Boyes, Boyes v Carritt* (1884) 26 Ch D 531.

4   *Re Boyes, Boyes v Carritt* (1884) 26 Ch D 531 at 535; *Re Gardner, Huey v Cunnington* [1920] 2 Ch 523, CA; *Re Williams, Williams v Parochial Church Council of the Parish of All Souls, Hastings* [1933] Ch 244; *Blackwell v Blackwell* [1929] AC 318 at 334, 335, HL per Lord Sumner; *Ottaway v Norman* [1972] Ch 698, [1971] 3 All ER 1325; *Re Snowden* [1979] Ch 528, [1979] 2 All ER 172. See also *Re Young, Young v Young* [1951] Ch 344, [1950] 2 All ER 1245.

5   If the gift by will is made to persons as tenants in common, then the communication of the trust must be made to all such persons in the testator's lifetime; otherwise only the persons to whom it is communicated are bound: *Re Stead, Witham v Andrew* [1900] 1 Ch 237. If, however, the gift is made to persons as joint tenants a distinction is drawn between two cases: (a) if one of the joint tenants accepts the trust before execution of the will, all joint tenants are bound; (b) if acceptance is after the execution of the will, only the joint tenants who accept are bound: *Moss v Cooper* (1861) 1 John & H 352; *Re Stead, Witham v Andrew* above.

6   *Re Falkiner, Mead v Smith* [1924] 1 Ch 88, distinguishing *Re Spencer's Will* (1887) 57 LT 519, CA and itself distinguished in *Re Williams, Williams v Parochial Church Council of the Parish of All Souls, Hastings* [1933] Ch 244 but applied in *Re Stirling, Union Bank of Scotland Ltd v Stirling* [1954] 2 All ER 113, [1954] 1 WLR 763.

7   *Re Keen, Evershed v Griffiths* [1937] Ch 236, [1937] 1 All ER 452, CA; *Re Bateman's Will Trusts, Brierley v Perry* [1970] 3 All ER 817, [1970] 1 WLR 1463. The Australian courts have refused to apply this rule: *Legerwood v Perpetual Trustee Co Ltd* (1997) 41 NSWLR 532. Moreover the English courts have refused to apply the rule to the analogous case of nomination under a life insurance policy: *Gold v Hill* [1999] 1 FLR 54.

8   *Blackwell v Blackwell* [1929] AC 318 at 339 per Viscount Sumner.

9   *Re Cooper, Le Neve-Foster v National Provincial Bank Ltd* [1939] Ch 811, [1939] 3 All ER 586, CA.

10   *Re Gardner, Huey v Cunningham* [1923] 2 Ch 230 at 233; *Ottaway v Norman* [1972] Ch 698, [1971] 3 All ER 1325; *Nichols v IRC* [1973] 3 All ER 632, [1974] 1 WLR 296 (affd on different grounds [1975] 2 All ER 120, [1975] 1 WLR 534, CA). There is much to be said, however, for the contrary view expressed by Pennycuick J in *Re Tyler's Fund Trusts, Graves v King* [1967] 3 All ER 389 at 392.

[69]

27   Voluntary trusts

Valuable consideration is not necessary to render a trust inter vivos enforceable. If the trust is in the first instance completely constituted, it will be enforced in favour of volunteers[1]. The law is that anybody of full age and sound mind who has executed a voluntary deed by which he has knowingly denuded himself of his own property is bound by his own act[2], unless that act was induced by undue influence, fraud or mistake[3]. The case where the disposition of the property is not complete must be distinguished, and trusts of this nature have not hitherto been able to be enforced by mere volunteers. Therefore, a covenant in a marriage settlement for the settlement of after-acquired property could not be enforced by persons, such as the wife's next of kin, who are outside the marriage consideration[4]. The law has now been modified by the Contracts (Rights of Third Parties) Act 1999, but not so as to enable a volunteer to obtain specific performance.

[70]

1   *Ellison v Ellison* (1802) 6 Ves 656; *Kekewich v Manning* (1851) 1 De GM & G 176.
2   *Henry v Armstrong* (1881) 18 Ch D 668.
3   As to undue influence see Paragraph 93 [224] post.
4   *Re D'Angibau, Andrews v Andrews* (1880) 15 Ch D 228, CA; *Re Pryce, Nevill v Pryce* [1917] 1 Ch 234; *Re Kay's Settlement, Broadbent v Macnab* [1939] Ch 329, [1939] 1 All ER 245; *Re Cook's Settlement Trusts, Royal Exchange Assurance v Cook* [1965] Ch 902, [1964] 3 All ER 898. As to agreements and covenants to settle property see further Paragraph 34 [91] et seq post.

[71]

4: NECESSITY FOR CERTAINTY

28   Matters in respect of which certainty is required

It has been laid down[1] that 'three certainties' are required for the creation of a trust:

28.1   the words used must be so couched that taken as a whole they are deemed to be imperative;

28.2   the subject matter of the trust must be certain; and

28.3   the persons or objects intended to be benefited must also be certain.

1   *Knight v Knight* (1840) 3 Beav 148.

[72]

29   Certainty of words

Equity looks to the intent rather than the form. No particular form of words is required for the creation of a trust. The use of the word 'trust' is not essential, although, of course, highly desirable. It is therefore possible that words expressing desire, belief, recommendation or hope (known as precatory words) may create a trust. It is entirely a question of construction of the instrument whether the settlor intended to create a trust[1]. A similar question of construction will arise when it has to be determined whether a trust or a mere power of appointment was intended by the settlor, for what appears to be a power may be treated, as a matter of construction, as a trust, in which case it is often referred to as a trust power or a power in the nature of a trust[2].

The same principles apply where it is alleged that a person has declared himself a trustee of property which he owns for the intended beneficiary[3].

[73]

1   For cases where a trust was held to be created see eg *Comiskey v Bowring-Hanbury* [1905] AC 84, HL; *Re Johnson, Public Trustee v Calvert* [1939] 2 All ER 458; *Re Steele's Will Trusts, National Provincial Bank Ltd v Steele* [1948] Ch 603, [1948] 2 All ER 193; *Re Endacott, Corpe v Endacott* [1960] Ch 232, [1959] 3 All ER 562, CA. For cases where a trust was held not to have been created see eg *Lambe v Eames* (1871) 6 Ch App 597; *Mussoorie Bank Ltd v Raynor* (1882) 7 App Cas 321, PC; *Re Adams and Kensington Vestry* (1884) 27 Ch D 394, CA; *Re Hamilton, Trench v Hamilton* [1895] 2 Ch 370, CA; *Re Williams, Williams v Williams* [1897] 2 Ch 12, CA. See also *Re Challoner Club Ltd (in liquidation)* (1997) Times 4 November (terms of intended trust not certain: no trust created).

The above cases arose under wills, but the same question may arise in a commercial context: see *Re Kayford Ltd* [1975] 1 All ER 604, [1975] 1 WLR 279; *Re Chelsea Cloisters Ltd* (1980) 41 P & CR 98, CA; *Re Multi Guarantee Co Ltd* [1987] BCLC 257, CA; *Re Eastern Capital Futures Ltd* [1989] BCLC 371; *Re English and American Insurance Co Ltd* [1994] 1 BCLC 649; *Re Lewis's of Leicester Ltd* [1995] 1 BCLC 428; *Re B (child: property transfer)* [1999] 3 FCR 266, [1999] 2 FLR 418, CA (held an order under the Guardianship of Minors Act 1971 transferring property from the father to the mother 'for the benefit of the child' did not create a trust in favour of the child).

2   *Burrough v Philcox* (1840) 5 My & Cr 72. Cf *Re Perowne, Perowne v Moss* [1951] Ch 785, [1951] 2 All ER 201. See also *McPhail v Doulton* [1971] AC 424, [1970] 2 All ER 228, HL; *Re Baden's Deed Trusts (No 2)* [1973] Ch 9, [1972] 2 All ER 1304, CA; *Blausten v IRC* [1972] Ch 256, [1972] 1 All ER 41, CA.

3   See *Paul v Constance* [1977] 1 All ER 195, [1997] 1 WLR 527, CA, applied in *Rowe v Prance* [1999] 2 FLR 787.

[74]

30   Certainty of subject matter

The expression 'certainty of subject matter' can mean either that the trust property should be certain or that the beneficial interest of the *cestui que trust* must be certain.

If the trust property cannot be identified, the purported trust is void ab initio[1]. If, however, there is both certainty of words and certainty of the trust property but the beneficial interests are uncertain, then the property should be held on a resulting trust for the settlor[2]. In such a case, a trust will clearly have been intended and its failure on grounds of uncertainty of the beneficial interests will not enable the trustees to take beneficially[3].

1   *Palmer v Simmonds* (1854) 2 Drew 221; *Sprange v Barnard* (1789) 2 Bro CC 585; *Re London Wine Co (Shippers) Ltd* (1975) 126 NLJ 977, distinguished in the much criticised case of *Hunter v Moss* [1994] 3 All ER 215, [1994] 1 WLR 452 where the Court of Appeal agreed with the decision at first instance that the requirement of certainty does not apply in the same way to trusts of intangible assets such as, in that case, 50 out of 950 indistinguishable shares. It is submitted that intangible assets are not in a different position from tangible. Nor is the analogy drawn by the court with a demonstrative legacy of shares valid, for a trust of such shares will become completely constituted only when the particular shares have been vested in the trustee. This decision was necessarily followed by Neuberger J in *Re Harvard Securities Ltd (in liquidation)* [1998] BCC 567. See also *Re Goldcorp Exchange Ltd (in receivership)* [1995] 1 AC 74, [1994] 2 All ER 806, PC; *Re Stapylton Fletcher Ltd (in administrative receivership)* [1995] 1 All ER 192, [1994] 1 WLR 1181; and *Re Harvard Securities Ltd (in liquidation), Holland v Newbury* (1998) BCC 567.

     As a general proposition 'all property real or personal, legal or equitable, at home or abroad and whether in possession or action, remainder or reversion, and whether vested or contingent, may be made the subject of a trust': Underhill and Hayton *Law of Trusts and Trustees* (15th Edn, 1995) p 159. As to the validity of trusts of future property see the materials in Maudsley and Burn's *Trusts and Trustees—Cases and Materials* (5th Edn, 1996) pp 134–140.

2   *Boyce v Boyce* (1849) 16 Sim 476; cf *Re Golay, Morris v Bridgewater* [1965] 2 All ER 660, [1965] 1 WLR 969.

3   *Briggs v Penny* (1851) 3 Mac & G 546 at 557 per Lord Truro LC.

[75]

31   Certainty of objects

Except in the case of charitable trusts[1] it is necessary for the objects of the trust to be certain. For the purpose of deciding whether the range of beneficiaries is ascertainable a distinction must be drawn between a power of appointment in their favour, on the one hand, and a trust, on the other. If a mere power of appointment is given it is established that the test of certainty is whether or not it can be postulated of any given person whether or not he is an object of the power[2]. If, however, a trust, rather than a power of appointment, is created, the test was formerly thought to be that the whole range of objects eligible for selection should be ascertained or capable of ascertainment[3]. This test has now, however, been overruled, with regard to trust powers and discretionary trusts, by the House of Lords[4] which has held that the test for a power is the appropriate one to apply, subject to the qualification, it would appear, that a 'wider and more comprehensive range of inquiry is called for in the case of trust powers than in the case of powers'[5]. Furthermore, even where the meaning of the words is clear, the definition of beneficiaries may be so hopelessly wide as not to form 'anything like a class', so that the trust is administratively unworkable[6]. It is not yet established, however, whether this test applies merely to trust powers and discretionary trusts, which, it is submitted, is the better view, or whether it applies to all trusts.

Subject to the above, the objects of the trusts should be sufficiently ascertainable[7].

[76]

1   As to charitable trusts generally see vol 6(2) (2001 Reissue) CHARITIES AND CHARITABLE GIVING.
2   *Whishaw v Stephens* [1970] AC 508, [1968] 3 All ER 785, HL; applying *Re Gestetner Settlement, Barnett v Blumka* [1953] Ch 672, [1953] 1 All ER 1150.
3   *IRC v Broadway Cottages Trust* [1955] Ch 20, [1954] 3 All ER 120, CA.
4   *McPhail v Doulton* [1971] AC 424, [1970] 2 All ER 228, HL. See also *Re Baden's Deed Trusts (No 2)* [1973] Ch 9, [1972] 2 All ER 1304, CA; *Blausten v IRC* [1972] Ch 256, [1972] 1 All ER 41, CA.
5   *McPhail v Doulton* [1971] AC 424, [1970] 2 All ER 228 at 457, 247 per Lord Wilberforce. A power conferred on trustees of a settlement to add to the class of beneficiaries, being a power exercisable in favour of anyone with certain exceptions, was held valid in *Re Manisty's Settlement, Manisty v Manisty* [1974] Ch 17, [1973] 2 All ER 1203, applying *Whishaw v Stephens* [1970] AC 508, [1968] 3 All ER 785, *Re Gestetner Settlement, Barnett v Blumka* above, *McPhail v Doulton* above and *Re Baden's Deed Trusts (No 2)* [1973] Ch 9, [1972] 2 All ER 1304, CA. See Form 4 clause 6 [1087] post.
6   *McPhail v Doulton* [1971] AC 424, [1970] 2 All ER 228 at 457, 247 per Lord Wilberforce; *Re Manisty's Settlement, Manisty v Manisty* [1974] Ch 17, [1973] 2 All ER 1203; *Re Hay's Settlement Trusts* [1981] 3 All ER 786, [1982] 1 WLR 202; *R v District Auditor No 3 Audit District of West Yorkshire Metropolitan County Council, ex p West Yorkshire Metropolitan County Council* [1986] RVR 24, DC.
7   See eg *Re Astor's Settlement Trusts, Astor v Scholfield* [1952] Ch 534, [1952] 1 All ER 1067; *Re Endacott, Corpe v Endacott* [1960] Ch 232, [1959] 3 All ER 562, CA. The so-called 'complete list' test is thought still to apply to fixed (as opposed to discretionary trusts).

[77]

5: TERMINATION OF TRUSTS

32   Duration of trust

Apart from the restrictions imposed on the duration of trusts by the rules directed against remoteness of vesting and against the creation of trusts of perpetual or indefinite duration otherwise than for charitable purposes, and by the statutory restrictions upon accumulations of income[1], an express trust after it has become operative may be terminated by the subsequent failure or satisfaction of the purposes of the trust, or by the cessation of particular circumstances for which the trust was created to provide. It may be terminated by the action of the beneficiaries if they are all ascertained and sui juris[2], and by the trustees in the exercise of dispositive powers.

1   As to the rule against remoteness of vesting etc and the statutory restrictions upon accumulations of income see further Paragraph 77 [183] post.
2   As to the termination of trusts generally see further 48 Halsbury's Laws (4th Edn 2000 Reissue) para 644 et seq. Substantial tax charges may arise on the termination of a trust.

[78]

33   Revocation and setting aside

Where an express trust is completely constituted, it is generally binding and irrevocable whether it was or was not constituted or declared for valuable consideration, unless a power of revocation is expressly reserved[1]. In order to effect a valid revocation, such a power must be exercised in the manner specifically directed[2].

A disposition of property in trust may in certain circumstances be set aside under the provisions relating to the avoidance of transactions at an undervalue[3], or under the statutory provisions relating to dispositions in fraud of creditors[4], or on the ground that the disposition was induced by fraud, duress or undue influence[5]. In the case of matrimonial proceedings, the court has power to adjust interests in settlements[6]; to set aside a disposition intended to defeat a claim for financial relief in such proceedings[7]; and even to set aside a settlement made in compliance with a property adjustment order in matrimonial proceedings where this would amount to a transaction at an undervalue in an insolvency[8].

[79]

1   *Ellison v Ellison* (1802) 6 Ves 656. See further 48 Halsbury's Laws (4th Edn 2000 Reissue) para 567. In practice, a power of revocation is rarely found today.

2   *Lane v Debenham* (1853) 11 Hare 188 at 192. A power to revoke the trusts of a settlement with the consent of a judge of the Chancery Division is invalid, since a private individual cannot impose upon a judge the jurisdiction or duty to adjudicate on a matter: *Re Hooker's Settlement, Heron v Public Trustee* [1955] Ch 55, [1954] 3 All ER 321; and see *Re H's Settlement, H v S* [1939] WN 318.

3   See the Insolvency Act 1986 ss 339, 341, 342 as amended by the Criminal Justice Act 1988 s 170(2), Sch 16 from a day to be appointed and by the Insolvency (No 2) Act 1994 s 2 (4 Halsbury's Statutes (4th Edn) BANKRUPTCY AND INSOLVENCY) and see further Paragraph 90 [216] post.

4   See the Insolvency Act 1986 ss 423–425 and see further Paragraph 90 [216] post.

5   As to the setting aside of a disposition on the ground that it was induced by undue influence see Paragraph 93 [224] post.

6   See currently the Matrimonial Causes Act 1973 s 24 (27 Halsbury's Statutes (4th Edn) MATRIMONIAL LAW). See also the Matrimonial Causes Act 1973 s 21(2) as substituted by the Family Law Act 1996 s 15, Sch 2 para 2 from a day to be appointed.

7   See the Matrimonial Causes Act 1973 s 37 as amended by the Family Law Act 1996 s 66(1), Sch 8 para 21 from a day to be appointed.

8   See the Matrimonial Causes Act 1973 s 39 as amended by the Insolvency Act 1985 s 235(1), Sch 8 para 23 and by the Insolvency Act 1986 s 439(2), Sch 14.

[80]–[90]

C: AGREEMENTS AND COVENANTS TO SETTLE PROPERTY

34   Agreements for settlements and marriage articles

Most agreements for settlements were formerly made in contemplation of marriage, but they are now frequently made on other occasions. The agreement for a settlement may be in the form of a covenant to settle and such covenant may itself be contained in a settlement; for example, a covenant to settle after-acquired property. The term 'marriage articles' is employed to mean an agreement in consideration of a marriage to settle property on terms subsequently to be embodied in a formal document[1].

If there is valuable consideration for the articles, it is available for the support of a settlement made subsequently, although it will then be a past consideration. Such agreements to settle are not very often needed; but sometimes they are necessary because the consideration, for instance marriage, is to be effected too soon as to permit the possibility of preparing a proper settlement before its occurrence. Cases may occur, moreover, in which it is expedient to postpone the settlement until the parties have time for deliberation and for resorting to proper professional assistance.

A settlement pursuant to articles of land on a trust of land is a conveyance to trustees of land to be held on the trusts declared either in the conveyance itself or more commonly, and better, in a separate document. In the cases in which time precludes the preparation of a proper settlement the articles should be short, defining precisely, even if generally, the property to be settled and the interests to be created in it, and leaving the draftsman of the settlement the utmost liberty in framing the language by which the settlement is to give effect to the articles.

1   For a specimen marriage settlement see Form 7 [1136] post. For an assignment pursuant to a marriage
     agreement see Form 34 [1284] post.

[91]

35   Covenants to settle

Covenants to settle property are frequently inserted in settlements for such purposes as the provision of income during a period which is likely to elapse before some settled expectant interest will fall into possession; for the payment to the trustees at a specified future time of a capital fund intended to become subject to trusts declared by the deed which contains the covenant; or for bringing into settlement property to which during the intended marriage either party may become entitled. These covenants differ from articles for settlement not merely in being part of a settlement, but also in being designed to secure the payment of money or the transfer of property, and not to express, except by reference, the terms of settlement[1].

1   Covenants to settle have hitherto not been enforceable by volunteers who are not parties to the
     covenant: *Re Cook's Settlement Trusts, Royal Exchange Assurance v Cook* [1965] Ch 902, [1964] 3 All ER
     898, but see now the Contracts (Rights of Third Parties) Act 1999. The Act does not appear to affect
     the rule that equity will not assist a volunteer so specific performance will not be available.

[92]

36   Requirements for agreement to settle land

An agreement to settle an interest in land[1] can only be made in writing and only by incorporating all the terms which the parties have expressly agreed in one document or, where contracts are exchanged, in each[2]. The terms may be incorporated in a document either by being set out in it or by reference to some other document[3]. The document incorporating the terms or, where contracts are exchanged, one of the documents incorporating them (but not necessarily the same one) must be signed by or on behalf of each party to the agreement[4]. Non-compliance with these provisions makes the agreement a complete nullity. A contract to convey a legal estate in land for the purposes of a settlement is registrable as an estate contract under the Land Charges Act 1972[5].

[93]

1   An 'interest in land' means any estate, interest or charge in or over land: Law of Property (Miscellaneous
     Provisions) Act 1989 s 2(6) as amended by the Trusts of Land and Appointment of Trustees Act 1996
     s 25(2), Sch 4 (37 Halsbury's Statutes (4th Edn) REAL PROPERTY).
2   Law of Property (Miscellaneous Provisions) Act 1989 s 2(1).
3   Law of Property (Miscellaneous Provisions) Act 1989 s 2(2).
4   Law of Property (Miscellaneous Provisions) Act 1989 s 2(3). See *Firstpost Homes Ltd v Johnson* [1995]
     4 All ER 355, [1995] 1 WLR 1567, CA.
5   See the Settled Land Act 1925 s 11 (48 Halsbury's Statutes (4th Edn) TRUSTS AND SETTLEMENTS)
     and the Land Charges Act 1972 s 2(4), Class C(iv) (37 Halsbury's Statutes (4th Edn) REAL PROPERTY).
     As to land charges generally see vol 25(1) (1999 Reissue) LAND CHARGES Paragraph 2 [4] et seq. An
     estate contract may be protected in the case of registered land by the entry of a notice, caution or
     restriction: see the Land Registration Act 1925 ss 49, 54, 58 amended inter alia by the Trusts of Land
     and Appointment of Trustees Act 1996 s 25(1), Sch 3 para 5(5) (37 Halsbury's Statutes (4th Edn) REAL
     PROPERTY). See further vol 25(1) (1999 Reissue) LAND REGISTRATION Paragraph 174 [2461] et seq.

[94]

37   Covenants to settle property not specified

A covenant is sometimes inserted in marriage settlements to settle property other than that which is the specific subject of the settlement. Such covenants may be so framed as to sweep in all property, both present and future, even though not specifically referred to[1], of one or both of the contracting parties, but as a rule they are confined to property to be acquired in the future by the wife during the marriage[2]. Such a covenant is not a 'usual covenant' and ought not to be inserted without express instructions[3]. As it is executory it has hitherto been enforceable only in favour of parties within the marriage consideration[4], but see now the Contracts (Rights of Third Parties) Act 1999[5].

1   *Caldwell v Fellowes* (1870) LR 9 Eq 410 at 417 per James VC.
2   A covenant to settle all the covenantor's after-acquired property is not too vague or general to be enforced: *Re Turcan* (1888) 40 Ch D 5, CA; *Re Reis, ex p Clough* [1904] 2 KB 769, CA; affd on other grounds sub nom *Clough v Samuel* [1905] AC 442, HL; see also *Syrett v Egerton* [1957] 3 All ER 331 at 334, [1957] 1 WLR 1130 at 1134, DC.
3   *Re Maddy's Estate, Maddy v Maddy* [1901] 2 Ch 820.
4   As to persons within the marriage consideration see 42 Halsbury's Laws (4th Edn Reissue) para 661 et seq.
5   See Paragraph 35 note 1 [92] ante.

[95]

38   Construction of covenants to settle after-acquired property

Covenants to settle are contracts which must be performed in strict accordance with their terms[1]. Therefore general words are rejected, and a covenant to settle property derived from a particular source does not attach to property coming from another source or under another title[2]. If land is purchased out of the proceeds of personal property bound by a covenant of this kind, the land is charged with the money thus improperly invested[3].

1   *Re Van Straubenzee, Boustead v Cooper* [1901] 2 Ch 779 (where it was held that there is no ground for applying the rule in *Howe v Earl of Dartmouth, Howe v Countess of Aylesbury* (1802) 7 Ves 137 (see Paragraph 146 [356] post) to property settled by such a covenant); and see *Hope v Hope* (1855) 1 Jur NS 770; *Brooke v Hicks* (1864) 10 LT 404. The propositions in the text may require reconsideration in the light of *Investors Compensation Scheme Ltd v West Bromwich Building Society* [1998] 1 All ER 98, [1998] WLR 896, HL. See 13 Halsbury's Laws (4th Edn Reissue) para 163 et seq.
2   *Williams v Williams* (1782) 1 Bro CC 152. See further 42 Halsbury's Laws (4th Edn Reissue) para 645.
3   *Lewis v Madocks* (1810) 17 Ves 48.

[96]

39   Property incapable of assignment

The proper construction of a covenant to settle after-acquired property is that the property is to be conveyed for such estate and interest as is actually taken in it by the covenantor. Therefore, property which is incapable of assignment[1], or in which the covenantor acquires an interest which cannot be effectively assigned, or a protected life interest[2], or a mere *spes successionis*, or a contingent claim for damages which could not arise until after the husband's death[3], is not caught by the covenant.

1   *Re Pearse's Settlement, Pearse v Pearse* [1909] 1 Ch 304 (land in Jersey and Jersey law made transfer to trustees inoperative).
2   *Brooks v Keith* (1861) 1 Drew & Sm 462; *Re Allnutt, Pott v Brassey* (1882) 22 Ch D 275; *Re Currey, Gibson v Way* (1886) 32 Ch D 361; *Re Crawshay, Walker v Crawshay* [1891] 3 Ch 176; *Re Smith, Franklin v Smith* [1928] Ch 10; but see *Re Haynes' Will Trusts, Pitt v Haynes* [1949] Ch 5, [1948] 2 All ER 423, where the acquisition of the protected life interest preceded the covenant.
3   *Re Simpson, Simpson v Simpson* [1904] 1 Ch 1, CA; see also *Re Mudge* [1914] 1 Ch 115, CA.

[97]

40   Effect of covenant to settle after-acquired property on interests existing at date of covenant

Interests existing at the date of the covenant are not caught by a covenant to settle property to which the covenantor is to become entitled during marriage[1]. Such interests will, however, be caught by a covenant which on its true construction extends to present interests. Whether a covenant extends to property to which the covenantor is entitled at the date of the covenant depends in every case upon the language of the particular instrument[2], but such property is not subsequently brought within its operation by reason of an increase in value[3], or by a change of investment[4] or character, as, for instance, by the sale for a lump sum of an annuity which was not caught by the covenant[5].

[98]

1   *Prebble v Boghurst* (1818) 1 Swan 309 at 321; and see *Re Bland's Settlement, Bland v Perkin* [1905] 1 Ch 4; *Re Peel's Settlement, Millard v Peel* [1964] 3 All ER 567, [1964] 1 WLR 1232. See further 42 Halsbury's Laws (4th Edn Reissue) para 648.
2   See *Re Peel's Settlement, Millard v Peel* [1964] 3 All ER 567, [1964] 1 WLR 1232.
3   *Re Browne's Will* (1869) LR 7 Eq 231; cf *Re Garnett, Robinson v Gandy* (1886) 33 Ch D 300, CA.
4   *Mackenzie v Allardes* [1905] AC 285 at 293, HL per Lord Macnaghten.
5   *Churchill v Denny* (1875) LR 20 Eq 534; *Re Biscoe, Biscoe v Biscoe* (1914) 111 LT 902.

[99]

41   Reversionary interests of covenantor

A covenant to settle property to which the covenantor may or will at any time during the marriage become entitled does not extend to a reversionary interest which is already vested in interest at the date of the covenant, whether it falls into possession during[1] or after[2] the marriage; but a covenant which binds a wife to settle her present and future property extends to reversionary interests to which she is entitled at the date of the covenant or acquires during marriage, and a covenant which binds her to settle all her future acquired property extends to reversionary interests to which she becomes entitled during marriage, notwithstanding in either case that the reversion does not fall in during the marriage[3]. Even if there are technical difficulties in the way of getting a conveyance, such property is bound in the hands of everyone, including the personal representatives of the covenantor[4].

[100]

1   *Re Bland's Settlement, Bland v Perkin* [1905] 1 Ch 4; followed in *Re Yardley's Settlement, Milward v Yardley* (1908) 124 LT Jo 315; see also *Re Peel's Settlement, Millard v Peel* [1964] 3 All ER 567, [1964] 1 WLR 1232.
2   *Re Pedder's Settlement Trusts* (1870) LR 10 Eq 585; *Re Clinton's Trusts, Holloway's Fund, Re Clinton's Trust, Weare's Fund* (1871) LR 13 Eq 295; see also *Cannon v Hartley* [1949] Ch 213, [1949] 1 All ER 50.
3   *Grafftey v Humpage* (1839) 3 Jur 622.
4   *Lloyd v Prichard* [1908] 1 Ch 265.

[101]

42   Contingent and defeasible interests of covenantor

A covenant which binds a wife to settle all her present and future property extends to contingent or defeasible interests, whether in possession or remainder[1] and whether the contingency happens or the interest becomes indefeasible during or after the marriage[2]; but a covenant to settle future property only does not extend to a contingent or defeasible interest existing at the date of the covenant merely because it vests in interest or becomes indefeasible during the marriage[3], although it will extend to any such interest which falls into possession during the marriage[4].

[102]

1   *Agar v George* (1876) 2 Ch D 706; *Cornmell v Keith* (1876) 3 Ch D 767; *Re Jackson's Will* (1879)
     13 Ch D 189; *Re Ware, Cumberlege v Cumberlege-Ware* (1890) 45 Ch D 269; *Re Hewett, Hewett v Hallett*
     [1894] 1 Ch 362 at 365; *Lloyd v Prichard* [1908] 1 Ch 265. *Atcherley v Du Moulin* (1855) 2 K & J 186
     and *Dering v Kynaston* (1868) LR 6 Eq 210, where it was held that contingent interests are not within
     such a covenant, must be treated as overruled: *Agar v George* above.
2   *Brooks v Keith* (1861) 1 Drew & Sm 462; *Agar v George* (1876) 2 Ch D 706; *Lloyd v Prichard* [1908]
     1 Ch 265.
3   *Re Michell's Trusts* (1878) 9 Ch D 5, CA; cf *Re Cazenove, Perkin v Bland* (1919) 122 LT 181.
4   *Archer v Kelly* (1860) 1 Drew & Sm 300; *Brooks v Keith* (1861) 1 Drew & Sm 462; *Re Worsley's Trusts*
     (1867) 16 LT 826; *Re Williams' Settlement, Williams v Williams* [1911] 1 Ch 441; *Re Crook's Settlement,*
     Re Glasier's Settlement, Crook v Preston [1923] 2 Ch 339; and see also *Re Peel's Settlement, Millard v Peel*
     [1964] 3 All ER 567, [1964] 1 WLR 1232.

[103]

43   Interests under appointments and in default of appointment

An interest in default of appointment is a vested interest subject to defeasance and is
capable of being bound by a covenant to settle present or future acquired property[1]; but
property acquired under an exercise of a power is derived under a new title, even when
there is a gift over to the covenantor in default of appointment, and such property is not
caught by a covenant which does not extend to future property[2]. Property over which
the covenantor possesses a general power of appointment will not be caught unless the
power is so exercised as to bring the property within the covenant[3].

1   *Re Jackson's Will* (1879) 13 Ch D 189.
2   *Sweetapple v Horlock* (1879) 11 Ch D 745; *Re De la Bere's Marriage Settlement Trusts, De La Bere v Public*
     Trustee [1941] Ch 443, [1941] 2 All ER 533. See also *Muir (or Williams) v Muir* [1943] AC 468, HL;
     Re Dowie's Will Trusts, Re Marriage Settlement of 24th September 1936, Barlas v Pennefather [1949] Ch 547,
     [1949] 1 All ER 968; *Re Maltby Marriage Settlement, Aylen v Gaud* [1953] 2 All ER 220, [1953] 1 WLR
     765.
3   *Ewart v Ewart* (1853) 1 Eq Rep 536; *Townshend v Harrowby* (1858) 27 LJ Ch 553; *Bower v Smith* (1871)
     LR 11 Eq 279.

[104]

44   Property and interests commonly excepted from a covenant

It is usual to exclude from the operation of a covenant:
44.1   property of less than a specified value acquired from a single source;
44.2   gifts by the husband to the wife inter vivos;
44.3   property purchased by the wife with savings from her income;
44.4   life and other limited interests;
44.5   jewels and personal chattels;
44.6   property which, if bound, would be liable to forfeiture; and
44.7   property as to which the donor has expressed an intention that it should be
            exempt from the covenant or any similar provision.
    Other kinds of property may also be excepted. It is desirable that any property which
it is intended to exclude should be expressly mentioned[1].

1   Consumable goods are not included in a general covenant: *Willoughby v Middleton* (1862) 2 John & H
     344 at 355; and see also *Re Cunliffe-Owen, Mountain v IRC* [1953] Ch 545, [1953] 2 All ER 196, CA.

[105]

45   Limitation as to amount, time and source

If it is intended to except from the operation of the covenant after-acquired property not exceeding a specified amount, it is usual to provide expressly that this exception is to apply to property acquired at any one time from any one source. Even if the words 'from any one source' are not inserted they are implied, and any particular fund to which the covenantor becomes entitled does not fall within the covenant unless by itself it amounts to the specified sum[1]. In estimating whether the specified amount is reached, the beneficial receipt of the covenantor and not the amount of the gift must be considered[2].

1   *Re Hooper's Trust* (1865) 11 Jur NS 479; *Hood v Franklin* (1873) LR 16 Eq 496; *Re Hughes' Settlement, Hughes v Schooling, Re Smith, Hughes v Schooling* [1924] 2 Ch 356. As to such limitations see further 42 Halsbury's Laws (4th Edn Reissue) para 654.
2   *Re Pares, Re Scott Chad, Scott Chad v Pares* [1901] 1 Ch 708. As to estimates of the value of property for the purposes of the covenant see further 42 Halsbury's Laws (4th Edn Reissue) para 655.

[106]–[110]

D: CONSTITUENTS OF A TRUST OR SETTLEMENT

1: WHO CAN BENEFIT?

46   Persons who may be beneficiaries

Any person capable of holding property may be a beneficiary under a trust, but persons incapable of holding property at law cannot be entitled to it under a trust. Minors, however, can be beneficiaries under a trust even though they cannot hold the legal estate in trust land.

[111]

47   Valid but unenforceable trusts and *Denley* trusts

It is not essential in all cases to the validity of a trust, that there should be some living person by whom it can be enforced[1]. For example, a trust may be created for charitable purposes. Furthermore, in certain limited instances trusts have been held valid even though they are not charitable and there is no person by whom they can be enforced. These trusts are commonly called trusts of imperfect obligation. Thus trusts for the building or maintenance of monuments and tombs have been held valid[2], as have trusts for the maintenance of particular animals[3], so long as such trusts are limited in duration to the period allowed by the rule against perpetuities[4]. If the trustee elects not to carry out such a trust, he cannot keep the property for himself beneficially but must deal with it as a resulting trust. It seems, however, that in general equity will refuse to recognise a trust, other than a charitable trust, unless it is for the benefit of ascertained or ascertainable beneficiaries[5]. Accordingly, it would appear that the decisions by which trusts for the building or maintenance of monuments or tombs, or trusts relating to specific animals, have been held valid, are to be regarded as anomalous and exceptional and their scope is not to be extended[6].

The principle that a trust cannot be created for a 'purpose' or 'object' unless the purpose or object is charitable[7] does not apply to a trust which, although apparently expressed as a purpose, is directly or indirectly for the benefit of an individual or individuals[8]. The need for enforceability of the trust is met by the existence of factual beneficiaries; ie persons who, though not actually *cestuis que trust*, are interested in the disposal of the property[9].

[112]

1   In *Morice v Bishop of Durham* (1804) 9 Ves 399 at 405 Sir William Grant MR stated that 'there must be someone in whose favour the court can decree performance'. For a consideration of recent developments in this area see 'The New Trust: Obligations without Rights?' by Paul Matthews in Oakley (ed) *Trends in Contemporary Trust Law* (1996) p 1.

2   *Trimmer v Danby* (1856) 25 LJ Ch 424; *Pirbright v Salwey* [1896] WN 86; *Re Hooper, Parker v Ward* [1932] 1 Ch 38. As to purpose trusts see further vol 40(2) (2001 Reissue) TRUSTS AND SETTLEMENTS Part 13 [7501].

3   *Pettingall v Pettingall* (1842) 11 LJ Ch 176; *Mitford v Reynolds* (1848) 16 Sim 105; *Re Dean, Cooper-Dean v Stevens* (1889) 41 Ch D 552. Some trusts in favour of animals 'useful to man', such as dogs and horses, have been held to be charitable, and, as such, enforceable: see *Re Wedgwood, Allen v Wedgwood* [1915] 1 Ch 113, CA; *Re Grove-Grady, Plowden v Lawrence* [1929] 1 Ch 557, CA; on appeal sub nom *A-G v Plowden* [1931] WN 89, HL; *Re Thompson, Public Trustee v Lloyd* [1934] Ch 342.

4   As to the rule against perpetuities see further Paragraph 77 [183] post; and see *Re Vaughan, Vaughan v Thomas* (1886) 33 Ch D 187 and cf *Re Dean, Cooper-Dean v Stevens* (1889) 41 Ch D 552.
        A trust to repair a tomb 'for the longest period allowed by law, ie until the period of 21 years from the death of the last survivor of all persons who shall be living at my death' is void for uncertainty: *Re Moore, Prior v Moore* [1901] 1 Ch 936 (distinguished in *Muir v IRC* [1966] 3 All ER 38, [1966] 1 WLR 1269, CA); but see *Re Villar, Public Trustee v Villar* [1929] 1 Ch 243, CA; *Re Leverhulme, Cooper v Leverhulme (No 2)* [1943] 2 All ER 274; *Re Hooper, Parker v Ward* [1932] 1 Ch 38; *Re Vaux, Nicholson v Vaux* [1939] Ch 465, [1938] 4 All ER 297, CA.

5   As to the requirement of certainty of objects see Paragraph 31 [76] ante.

6   See eg *Re Astor's Settlement Trusts, Astor v Scholfield* [1952] Ch 534, [1952] 1 All ER 1067; and *Re Endacott, Corpe v Endacott* [1960] Ch 232, [1959] 3 All ER 562, CA in which Harman LJ commented '… there have been decisions at times which are not satisfactorily classified, but are perhaps merely occasions when Homer has nodded, at any rate these cases stand by themselves and ought not to be increased in number, nor indeed followed, except when the one is exactly like another'.

7   As to this principle see further Paragraph 2 [2] ante.

8   It is the difference between 'on trust for the upkeep of a garden' and 'on trust for the upkeep of a garden for the benefit of X', which can be construed as 'for the benefit of X with the hope that it will be spent on the upkeep of a garden'.

9   *Re Denley's Trust Deed, Holman v HH Martyn & Co Ltd* [1969] 1 Ch 373, [1968] 3 All ER 65. See also *Re Grant's Will Trusts* [1979] 3 All ER 359, [1980] 1 WLR 360; and see *Barclays Bank Ltd v Quistclose Investments Ltd* [1970] AC 567, [1968] 3 All ER 651, HL. Problems in this area may be overcome by the formation of a company.

[113]

48   Trusts for the benefit of unincorporated associations

An unincorporated association does not have a legal personality and cannot therefore be a beneficiary under a trust. If a trust is purported to be created for a non-charitable unincorporated association it must be determined first how the trust is to be construed, and then decided what results flow from that construction. It appears that four interpretations of such a trust are possible[1].

48.1   It may be construed as a trust for the individual members of the association at the date it takes effect for their own benefit as joint tenants or tenants in common, so that they could at once, if they pleased, agree to divide it amongst themselves, each putting his share into his own pocket. The association on this construction is used in effect as a convenient label or definition of the class which is intended to take. This construction may even be adapted to a trust for the general purposes of the association, although it may clearly not be contemplated that the individual members will divide it among themselves[2], provided that there is nothing in the constitution of the association to prohibit it[3].

[114]

48.2   It may be construed as a trust not only for present members, but also for future members forever or for an indefinite period. On this construction, unless the duration was limited to the perpetuity period, it would, prior to the Perpetuities and Accumulations Act 1964, have failed for perpetuity. Since that Act it is submitted that it will not fail for perpetuity, but will operate in favour of those members ascertained within the perpetuity period[4].

48.3   It may be construed as a trust for the trustees or other proper officers of the association, who are to hold the beneficial interest on trust to carry into effect the purposes of the association. On this construction the trust will fail as an invalid purpose trust[5].

48.4   It may be construed as a trust for the existing members of the association beneficially, but on the basis that the subject matter of the trust is to be held as an accretion to the funds of association and falls to be dealt with in accordance with the rules of the association by which the members are contractually bound inter se. On this construction the trust will be valid. Though beneficially entitled, an individual member cannot claim to be paid out his share. His share will accrue to the other members on his death or resignation, even though members include persons who became members after the trust took effect[6]. This construction may apply where there is a trust for an association for a specific purpose, that purpose being within the powers of the association and being one of which the members were beneficiaries[7].

[115]

1   *Re Recher's Will Trusts, National Westminster Bank Ltd v National Anti-Vivisection Society Ltd* [1972] Ch 526, [1971] 3 All ER 401; following *Leahy v A-G of New South Wales* [1959] AC 457, [1959] 2 All ER 300, PC and *Neville Estates Ltd v Madden* [1962] Ch 832, [1961] 3 All ER 769. Cf. *Artistic Upholstery Ltd v Art Forma (Furniture) Ltd* [1999] 4 All ER 277, [2000] FSR 311. As to unincorporated members' clubs see vol 7 (1994 Reissue) CLUBS Paragraph 4 [3013].
2   *Bowman v Secular Society Ltd* [1917] AC 406, HL; *Re Ogden, Brydon v Samuel* [1933] Ch 678.
3   *Re Clarke, Clarke v Clarke* [1901] 2 Ch 110.
4   See the Perpetuities and Accumulations Act 1964 ss 3(1), (4), 4(4) (33 Halsbury's Statutes (4th Edn) PERPETUITIES). The effect of the Act was not considered by Vinelott J in *Re Grant's Will Trusts, Harris v Anderson* [1979] 3 All ER 359, [1980] 1 WLR 360 nor by Brightman J in *Re Recher's Will Trusts, National Westminster Bank Ltd v National Anti-Vivisection Society Ltd* [1972] Ch 526, [1971] 3 All ER 401 who restated the old rule that if construed as a gift to all members, present and future, beneficially it would be void for perpetuity.
5   As to invalid purpose trusts see Paragraph 47 [112] ante. See also Paragraph 2 [2] ante.
6   *Re Recher's Will Trusts, National Westminster Bank Ltd v National Anti-Vivisection Society Ltd* [1972] Ch 526, [1971] 3 All ER 401.
7   *Re Lipinski's Will Trusts, Gosschalk v Levy* [1976] Ch 235, [1977] 1 All ER 33; *Re Grant's Will Trusts* [1979] 3 All ER 359, [1980] 1 WLR 360.

[116]

2: WHAT CAN BE SETTLED?

49   Property which may be made subject of trust

Property of all kinds, real or personal, legal or equitable, may be made the subject of a trust, unless:

49.1   the policy of the law or any statutory enactment prohibits the settlor from parting with the beneficial interest in it; or

49.2   being real estate, the tenure under which it is held is inconsistent with the trust sought to be created[1].

There can, accordingly, be a trust of a chattel or of a chose in action, or of a right or obligation under an ordinary legal contract, just as much as a trust of land or money[2]. It even seems that there is no objection to a party to a contract involving skill and confidence or containing non-assignment provisions becoming trustee of the benefit of being the contracting party as well as of the benefit of the rights conferred[3].

1   *Earl Nelson v Lord Bridport* (1846) 8 Beav 547; *Allen v Bewsey* (1877) 7 Ch D 453, CA. Where leasehold
     property is settled, the trustee is under a duty to obtain for the benefit of the trust a renewal of the lease
     if he can and the court will not permit him to retain for himself the benefit of any such renewal: *Keech
     v Sandford* (1726) 2 Eq Cas Abr 741; *Re Knowles' Will Trusts, Nelson v Knowles* [1948] 1 All ER 866,
     CA. Legal rights may be settled: see for a consideration in the context of capital gains tax *Kirby v Thorn
     EMI* [1986] 1 WLR 851; revsd [1988] 2 All ER 947, [1988] 1 WLR 445, CA.

2   See *Lord Strathcona Steamship Co Ltd v Dominion Coal Co Ltd* [1926] AC 108, 124, [1925] All ER Rep
     87, 95, per Lord Shaw, cited by Lightman J in *Don King Productions Inc v Warren* [1998] 2 All ER 608,
     affd [1999] 2 All ER 218, CA. In *Abrahams v Trustee in Bankruptcy of Abrahams* [1999] 31 LS Gaz R 38,
     it was held that where a person paid money to a lottery syndicate she gained the right to have any
     winnings received duly administered in accordance with whatever rules of the syndicate then applied.
     That right was property which was capable of being held on a resulting trust. In *Swift v Dairywise Farms
     Ltd* [2000] 1 All ER 320, [2000] 1 WLR 1177 it was held that a milk quota which must be attached
     to a holding of appropriate land, known as a euroholding, could be the subject of a trust. If T held a
     quota on trust for B, then where B had no euroholding he could not, therefore, require T to transfer
     the quota to him. He could, however, require T to realise the quota and transfer the proceeds to him.

3   *Don King Productions Inc v Warren* [1998] 2 All ER 608, per Lightman J at 634, affd [2000] Ch 291,
     [1999] 2 All ER 218, CA; but a provision in the contract prohibiting a party from declaring himself a
     trustee would be effective.

[117]

3: WHO CAN BE TRUSTEE?

50   Persons who can be a trustee

Any person who can hold property is capable of being a trustee of it, although he may
be displaced by the court if unfit: for example, if he is a person mentally disordered, a
person permanently resident abroad, a bankrupt, or a person who has been detected in
dishonest practices, or even if he be a very quarrelsome person who cannot carry on the
trust in harmony with his co-trustees[1]. There is no bar to a beneficiary being a trustee
nor indeed to the settlor being a trustee, although there may be tax disadvantages in the
latter case[2].

1   See generally the Trustee Act 1925 ss 36, 41 as amended by the Criminal Law Act 1967 s 10, Sch 3,
     by the Mental Health Act 1959 s 149(1), Sch 7, by the Mental Health Act 1983 s 148, Sch 4 para 4 and
     by the Trusts of Land and Appointment of Trustees Act 1996 s 25(1), Sch 3 para 3(11) (48 Halsbury's
     Statutes (4th Edn) TRUSTS AND SETTLEMENTS); *Letterstedt v Broers* (1884) 9 App Cas 371 at 386, PC.
         The court has jurisdiction in an administration action at any time to remove a trustee if it
     considers such removal necessary for the protection of the trust estate or the welfare of the *cestui que
     trust*: *Re Wrightson, Wrightson v Cooke* [1908] 1 Ch 789.
         As to the appointment of a judicial trustee see 48 Halsbury's Laws (4th Edn 2000 Reissue)
     para 654 et seq and as to the classes of bodies which are constituted trust corporations see 48 Halsbury's
     Laws (4th Edn 2000 Reissue) para 693 et seq.

2   If a settlor is to be one of the trustees, it is normal to insert a provision in the settlement that he cannot
     be paid for so acting (see Form 4 clauses 10.3 [1089] post), as well as including a general clause
     prohibiting the conferring of any benefit on him (see Form 4 clause 14 [1091] post). For the power of
     beneficiaries to dismiss and appoint trustees see the Trusts of Land and Appointment of Trustees Act
     1996 Pt II (ss 19–21) (37 Halsbury's Statutes (4th Edn) REAL PROPERTY) which is considered in detail
     in vol 40(2) (2001 Reissue) TRUSTS AND SETTLEMENTS Part 10 [5201].

[118]

51   Minors

A minor cannot be appointed a trustee and any attempted appointment is void but without prejudice to the power to appoint a new trustee to fill the vacancy[1].

1   Law of Property Act 1925 s 20 (37 Halsbury's Statutes (4th Edn) REAL PROPERTY). A minor may, however, be a trustee under a resulting, implied or constructive trust: see *Re Vinogradoff, Allen v Jackson* [1935] WN 68. As to the effect of conveying land to a minor alone or jointly with others see the Trusts of Land and Appointment of Trustees Act 1996 s 2, Sch 1 para 1 (37 Halsbury's Statutes (4th Edn) REAL PROPERTY). In relation to registered land see the Land Registration Act 1925 s 111 as amended by the Mental Health Act 1959 s 149(1), Sch 7 Pt I, by the Mental Health Act 1983 s 148, Sch 4 para 6 and by the Trusts of Land and Appointment of Trustees Act 1996 s 25(1), Sch 3 para 5(11) (37 Halsbury's Statutes (4th Edn) REAL PROPERTY).

[119]

52   The Crown

The Crown, it seems, can be a trustee[1], at any rate if it deliberately chooses to act as such[2], but in practice should never be appointed a trustee if only by reason of the doubts and difficulties in enforcing the trust[3].

1   *Penn v Lord Baltimore* (1750) 1 Ves Sen 444 at 453 per Hardwicke LC; *Burgess v Wheate, A-G v Wheate* (1759) 1 Eden 177. As to an officer of state, see *Town Investments Ltd v Department of the Environment* [1978] AC 359, [1977] 1 All ER 813, HL.
2   *Civilian War Claimants Association v R* [1932] AC 14 at 27, HL per Lord Atkin. Note, however, that circumstances which may at first sight appear to constitute the Crown as a trustee may well be explicable by reference to the governmental powers and obligations of the Crown and may not set up a true trust at all: *Tito v Waddell (No 2)* [1977] Ch 106, [1977] 3 All ER 129.
3   See *Dyson v A-G* [1911] 1 KB 410, CA; *Esquimalt and Nanaimo Rly Co v Wilson* [1920] AC 358, PC.

[120]

53   Trustee need not be named

It is not necessary in a trust created by will, or based on valuable consideration, to name a trustee at all, for a court of equity never allows a trust to fail for want of a trustee, but will either appoint trustees, or, alternatively, will itself administer the trust in an action for its administration[1]. However, in the case of a voluntary trust purported to be created inter vivos, there can be no valid trust if the document relied on as constituting the trust is a purported conveyance or transfer to trustees who are not named or otherwise identified, or who are already dead, or have otherwise ceased to exist or are not capable grantees. Such a document would be a nullity and completely ineffective to constitute a trust.

1   See *Moggridge v Thackwell* (1803) 7 Ves 36, HL.

[121]–[130]

(3) ADVISING THE SETTLOR AND CONSIDERATIONS FOR THE DRAFTSMAN

A: SETTLOR'S MOTIVES AND OBJECTIVES

54   Preliminary considerations

Before commencing his work it is essential for the draftsman to be clear in his mind what he is seeking to achieve. One difficulty is that the settlor may have motives and objectives that are conflicting; for example, retention of the beneficial interest may be incompatible with the tax savings he seeks to make. The motives and objectives of the settlor may, apart from a wish to confer benefits on members of his family, or others, and to avoid tax, include the following:

54.1   He may wish to shield himself and his assets from future changes in legislation and to keep the trust property secure from creditors[1].

54.2   He may wish to transfer the management of and responsibility for assets to trustees who may in his view have the necessary expertise and be better qualified to conserve and develop them than he is himself.

54.3   His aim may be to achieve confidentiality. Although it may be known where the legal title is to be found, the equitable interest can be dealt with confidentially without any means being available to disclose what has been done[2].

[131]

---

1   But note the Insolvency Act 1986 ss 339–342 (as amended by the Criminal Justice Act 1988 s 170(2), Sch 16 from a day to be appointed and by the Insolvency (No 2) Act 1994 s 2), 423–425 (4 Halsbury's Statutes (4th Edn) BANKRUPTCY AND INSOLVENCY) which may defeat such an attempt: see further Paragraph 90 [216] et seq post. As to the possibility of shielding property from a spouse on divorce see currently the Matrimonial Causes Act 1973 s 24 (27 Halsbury's Statutes (4th Edn) MATRIMONIAL LAW). See also Matrimonial Causes Act 1973 s 21(2) as substituted by the Family Law Act 1996 s 15, Sch 2 para 2 from a day to be appointed.

2   But note the rights of beneficiaries to information regarding the trust and the obligation on a settlor to disclose the existence of a trust: see *Re Murphy's Settlements, Murphy v Murphy* [1998] 3 All ER 1, [1999] 1 WLR 282 and *Lewin on Trusts* (17th Edn, 2000) para 23.03.

[132]

---

55   In general

The matters for consideration in constituting settlements vary with the occasions on which, and the circumstances in which, the settlements are to be made. Marriage has traditionally been an occasion for the making of a settlement; and, in relation to existing settlements under the Settled Land Act 1925[1], the arrival at majority of the tenant in tail or person entitled to an entailed interest in remainder may also provide the occasion for a resettlement. Other occasions for the making of settlements are many and various: settlements may be made on the attainment of the age of majority of the child or children, grandchild or grandchildren or other relatives of the settlor; on the birth of a child or grandchild of the settlor; on the retirement from business of the settlor whether that business be the property of a company or not; for the protection of particular persons whom it may be considered should be protected from their own financial misfortunes or incompetence, or who need protection because they are incapable of managing their own affairs by reason of youth, old age, or mental incapacity; or for the benefit of a domestic employee or other persons.

[133]

A principal object in the case of many settlements, whatever the occasion, is the mitigation of the burden of taxation in so far as it falls, or will fall, on the settlor or his estate, and the form of a settlement may be governed as much by the incidence of the burdens of income tax, capital gains tax and inheritance tax in so far as they affect both the settlor and the beneficiaries, as by other factors[2]. In most cases in which settlors are possessed of substantial properties, the occasions on which it was once common to effect settlements (for example on the coming of age of a child or on marriage) are merely selected as being the most opportune moments at which to effect a disposition of property, the primary object of which is to pass on the benefit of the properties to the persons whom they wish to benefit, freed from the burdens of tax which the properties might have to bear if they remained in the possession of the settlors.

Upon the receipt of instructions to make a settlement on any occasion other than marriage, the adviser has to satisfy himself that the settlor understands the facts and circumstances upon and in which the settlement will operate, and the operation it will have in the events which will or may happen, and that he wishes to do what he asks the adviser to help him in doing, and is not acting under the undue influence of another person[3]. In so satisfying himself, an adviser should consider whether the settlement is one which it is right and proper for the settlor to make in all the circumstances, and if not, he should so advise the settlor, although the settlor is not bound to act on this advice[4]. This duty does not extend so far as to require a solicitor to refuse to act for a settlor who, being fully aware of all the implications, continues to wish to make a settlement which the solicitor thinks he ought not to make[5]. Where the solicitor is to follow a client's instructions when these are contrary to his advice, it is generally prudent to ensure that the position as to the giving of advice and the receipt of contrary instructions is adequately recorded in writing.

[134]

1   As to settlements of land after 31 December 1996 see Paragraph 19 [56] ante. In view of the disadvantages of settlements under the Settled Land Act 1925 (48 Halsbury's Statutes (4th Edn) TRUSTS AND SETTLEMENTS) in attracting inheritance tax on the death of the tenant for life, it may be desirable to bring an existing settlement to an end by an arrangement under which the tenant in tail will enter into a disentailing assurance and then partition the settled property with the existing tenant for life. For a deed of disentail and partition between tenant for life and tenant in tail see Form 304 [2113] post. As to settlements under the Settled Land Act 1925 generally see vol 40(2) (2001 Reissue) TRUSTS AND SETTLEMENTS Part 9 [4101].

2   As to the various tax liabilities see generally Paragraph 282 [711] et seq post.

3   As to undue influence and its effect on settlements see Paragraph 93 [224] post.

4   See *Powell v Powell* [1900] 1 Ch 243 at 247; *Wright v Carter* [1903] 1 Ch 27 at 57, CA; *Inche Noriah v Shaik Allie Bin Omar* [1929] AC 127, PC. Cf *Re Coomber, Coomber v Coomber* [1911] 1 Ch 723, CA.

5   See *Wingrove v Wingrove* (1885) 11 PD 81; *Baudains v Richardson* [1906] AC 169 at 184, 185, PC; *Craig v Lamoureux* [1920] AC 349 at 357, PC.

[135]

56   Negotiation of marriage settlements

The practice of negotiations for settlements on marriage will vary with the circumstances and, as a rule, the parties to the marriage themselves come to an understanding as to what should be settled before they instruct their advisers. The first step would normally be that the adviser of one party will call on the other party's adviser. They will consider what property is to be settled by each side and the terms of the settlement. Subsequently, each adviser submits to the other proposals for settlement of the property to be contributed by, or on behalf of, his client. The proposals are considered by the recipients and suggestions for variation, if any, are accepted or refused. When such variations or opinion, if any, are determined, the proposals are approved by both advisers, and then left with the adviser of the intended wife to prepare the necessary documents. If only one party is settling property (which is probably the more usual today), the negotiations, if any, leading to the constitution of the settlement, will probably differ little from the discussions leading to the constitution of settlements made on other occasions.

Marriage settlements have certain unique features. The forms of beneficial interests and administrative provisions contained in marriage settlements are increasingly likely to resemble those of settlements made on other occasions (the primary object of which may be the mitigation of the burden of tax)[1] though, with respect to the negotiation of settlements, the circumstances under which marriage settlements are negotiated will remain substantially the same.

1   As to considerations which are peculiar to marriage settlements see Paragraph 57 [137] post.

[136]

57   Considerations peculiar to marriage settlements

Additional points requiring consideration in the case of marriage settlements include the following:

57.1   The property to be settled on either side.

57.2   The beneficial trusts. If separate properties are brought in whether they are to be settled separately; if so, consideration of the trusts of the husband's fund and the trusts of the wife's fund[1].

57.3   Whether after-acquired property is to be settled; if so, whether any such property can be specifically referred to, and what should be excepted[2].

57.4   Whether power to withdraw property from the settlement is desired and to what extent:

57.4.1   on death and remarriage of one spouse; and

57.4.2   on any other event[3].

57.5   Costs of preparing the settlement.

In the absence of any agreement to the contrary, the wife's adviser normally prepares the settlement and the husband pays that adviser's costs, as well as those of his own adviser[4]. This applies not only to the settlement itself but also to articles entered into before marriage, to settlements executed after marriage pursuant to the articles, and to conveyances by a settlor to the trustees of the settlement[5].

[137]

1   As to beneficial interests in relation to Settled Land Act settlements see vol 40(2) (2001 Reissue) TRUSTS AND SETTLEMENTS Part 9 [4101]. As to beneficial interests in relation to personalty settlements see Paragraph 121 [301] post.
2   As to after-acquired property see Paragraph 42 [102] et seq ante.
3   As to the power to withdraw funds from a marriage settlement see Paragraph 141 [342] et seq post.
4   *Helps v Clayton* (1864) 17 CBNS 553; *Re Lawrance, Bowker v Austin* [1894] 1 Ch 556.
5   As to the costs of preparing the settlement generally see further 42 Halsbury's Laws (4th Edn Reissue) para 624.

[138]

B: PROPERTY TO BE SETTLED

58   The property to be settled

In advising the settlor on the property to be settled the adviser will have regard not only to the nature and value of that property, but also the nature and value of the property left remaining to the settlor and the income likely to be produced from it, so as to enable the adviser to determine whether or not the settlor is left with sufficient means to provide for himself. An important consideration in advising on the nature of the property settled, where there is any choice in the matter, may be the likely incidence of capital gains tax payable in respect of the transfers or disposals necessary as the result of the constitution of the settlement[1]. It may be that the settlor is able to dispose of some property attracting exemption for capital gains tax purposes.

When, as is frequently the case, the settlor desires to settle shares in a company controlled by him so as to relinquish that control, the adviser should consider whether the interests of the settlor are adequately protected. Consideration might be given, prior to the execution of the settlement, to the settlor's entering into a service contract with the company. Any special rights attached to the shares settled should also be reviewed and any desired amendments made, prior to settlement[2].

In connection with the property to be settled the adviser should ascertain whether the property transferred to the trustees is to be kept in its existing form or is to be converted and, if converted, whether the trustees are to have power to postpone the conversion. This will always be the case where land in England and Wales is settled, whether upon trust for sale or upon a trust of land[3], but is not necessarily the case with other property. If the property consists of or includes property situated outside the United Kingdom there may be special formalities required to effect its transfer. If stocks and shares are to be transferred, it must be ascertained whether there are any restrictions on transfer in the articles of the company[4]. It should also be borne in mind that, depending on the nature of the property, notices may be required to be given to trustees, insurance companies or other persons of the transfer of the property[5].

[139]

1   As to capital gains tax generally see Paragraph 338 [896] et seq post and note that 'hold-over' relief is only available in limited circumstances (for instance, on the creation of a discretionary trust). The creation of a settlement is a 'disposal' for the purpose of this tax even if the settlor (or his spouse) retains a life interest in the property or is the trustee. Particular care should be exercised if the settlor is proposing to settle an interest in his principal residence.
2   As to inheritance tax generally see Paragraph 283 [712] et seq post. Taking out a service contract before disposing of the shares may assist in rebutting any suggestion that by continuing to receive benefits from the company in the form of salary the settlor has reserved a benefit, but the terms of that contract should be 'reasonable'. With the advent of 100% business property relief great care should be exercised to ensure that the transfer into trust will attract (and continue to attract) maximum relief. Note the problems of a clawback if the assets are sold by the trustees within seven years of creation of the settlement: Inheritance Tax Act 1984 s 113A as amended (42–44 Halsbury's Statutes (4th Edn) TAXATION).
3   As to land settled on trust for sale before 1 January 1997 see Paragraph 107 [266] post. As to land settled on trust of land see Paragraph 108 [267] post.
4   As to the transfer of shares generally see vol 10 COMPANIES (2001 Reissue) Paragraph 181 [958] et seq. Other important examples of the need to be wary of restrictions upon the ability to transfer the property are land subject to a mortgage (where the mortgagee's consent will normally need to be sought) and leasehold land (where the consent of the landlord to an assignment is likely to be needed).
5   As to the requisite procedure when a policy of insurance is made the subject of a settlement see Paragraph 117 [282] post.

[140]

C: DETERMINING THE BENEFICIAL INTERESTS

59   Persons whom it is desired to benefit

The settlor will usually decide which persons he wishes to benefit before he considers any further questions. He should be reminded of the tax consequences if he fails to dispose of his whole interest in the property[1]. In exceptional cases, he may desire that the property should ultimately return to him. In other cases, however, a resulting trust could have serious disadvantages, particularly if the purpose of the settlement is to mitigate tax. The settlor should therefore be asked to consider what further objects he wishes to benefit if the objects of his immediate benefit fail to attain vested interests. It may be, particularly in the case of discretionary trusts extending over a substantial number of years, that, unless the settlement is carefully drawn, persons to whom the settlor has no intention of giving benefit will ultimately come to acquire a substantial part of the trust property. Discretionary settlements should, therefore, provide for trusts in default of appointment in favour of those persons (for example, the issue of the settlor living on a particular date) whom the settlor desires immediately to benefit and should always be supplemented by a letter of wishes[2].

Where a beneficiary or potential beneficiary is referred to by reference to his or her relationship to the settlor or any other person, it should be ascertained whether illegitimate, legitimated and adopted persons are intended to benefit[3].

[141]

1   As to the tax implications of settlements generally see further Paragraph 283 [712] et seq post.
2   For a letter of wishes see Forms 252 [1841] post.
3   See the Family Law Reform Act 1987 s 1 (6 Halsbury's Statutes (4th Edn) CHILDREN) and Form 4 clause 1.2 [1083] post.

[142]

60   Beneficial trusts

The beneficial trusts will be governed by the settlor's intentions with regard to the persons whom he wishes to benefit. Particular regard should be had to the possibilities of saving tax on the death of the individual beneficiaries and to any savings of tax that may be effected during their lives, although the opportunities may be circumscribed by the choice of beneficiaries[1]. The settlor should be asked what primary interests he wishes to create in the income and capital of the trust fund, and whether these are to be protective trusts, life interests (whether revocable or not), contingent interests or discretionary trusts. The settlor should be asked about and advised on the precise form of trusts if the primary trusts created by the settlement fail. The settlor should also be asked whether or not he wishes to include a power or direction to accumulate income, what powers of appointment he wishes to include and by whom he wishes such powers to be exercisable, and whether he wishes to include a power to vary the settlement by allowing the trustees to add to the number of beneficiaries[2].

1   As to the tax implications of settlements generally see Paragraph 283 [712] et seq post.
2   Exceptionally a protector may be thought appropriate; especially in the case of non-UK settlements.

[143]

61   Period of settlement

The period of the settlement will be determined in some cases by the class of beneficiaries. In many of the Forms contained in this title, the settlement provides for the vesting of the property in certain specified persons on their attaining a certain age, and the attainment of this age, or the remainders over in default, will determine the duration of the settlement. In the case of discretionary trusts in favour of a wide class of persons a longer period may be selected[1].

1   All interests should, however, vest within the perpetuity period: see further Paragraph 77 [183] et seq post.

[144]

D: EXCLUSION OF SETTLOR AND SPOUSE

62   Exclusion of benefit

It is common in settlements in which substantial assets are involved (with potentially heavy liabilities for tax) to provide specifically that the settlor and any spouse shall in no way benefit from the exercise of any power, discretion or duty under the settlement[1]. The reason for the insertion of this provision is to avoid so far as possible liability to tax falling on the settlor in respect of the income or capital of the trust. This applies with regard to income tax[2], capital gains tax[3], and in practice inheritance tax[4] for although the reservation of benefit rules in relation to trusts do not in theory apply to benefits reserved to the settlor's spouse, it is best, for safety's sake, to exclude the spouse to guard against the risk of an indirect benefit. It is desirable both as a reminder to the trustees, and as a means by which any argument that the settlor might in fact derive some benefit under the settlement can be forestalled. In this connection trustees should be reminded that when they are given extensive powers of borrowing and lending, no money should be lent to or borrowed from the settlor[5]. Particular care is needed where private family companies are involved[6]. It is sometimes expedient to insert a specific reminder in the settlement to this effect since the test for liability in such cases is not the benefit derived by the settlor but the making of the loan (or its repayment) itself. Apart from this it may be to the advantage of those beneficially interested under the settlement if wide powers of borrowing and lending are inserted[7].

[145]

1   For the exclusion of the settlor and his spouse from benefit see Form 250 [1813] post. Note that 'spouse' does not include a widow or widower of the settlor: enabling such a person to benefit does not usually have adverse tax consequences. For the construction of 'settlor exclusion' clauses, see *IRC v Botnar* [1999] STC 711, CA and *Fuller v Evans* [2000] 1 All ER 636.

2   See the Income and Corporation Taxes Act 1988 s 660A as inserted by the Finance Act 1995 s 74, Sch 17 para 1 (42–44 Halsbury's Statutes (4th Edn) TAXATION).

3   See the Taxation of Chargeable Gains Act 1992 s 77 as substituted by the Finance Act 1995 s 74, Sch 17 para 27 (42–44 Halsbury's Statutes (4th Edn) TAXATION).

4   As to the inheritance tax consequences generally see Paragraph 289 [749] et seq post.

5   If such money is borrowed or lent there is a risk that on payment or repayment to the settlor such a sum will be treated as his income for tax purposes: see the Income and Corporation Taxes Act 1988 s 677 as amended.

6   See *IRC v Bates* [1965] 3 All ER 64, [1965] 1 WLR 1133, CA.

7   For a power to borrow see Form 168 [1641] post; the borrowing is for the general purposes of the settlement and the assets purchased will usually form part of the capital of the trust fund. As to lending see Form 156 [1599] et seq post.

[146]

E: CHOICE OF TRUSTEES

63   The trustees

Although it is increasingly common to appoint a corporate trustee and many settlements contain provision for the appointment of such a body, the settlor may, in particular if the trustees will become obliged to exercise powers requiring an intimate knowledge of family affairs[1], prefer to appoint as trustees individuals who are likely to be in a position to know more about those affairs. If the settlor fears dispute between members of his family, or if none or few of those members are capable of acting as a trustee, he may prefer to appoint a solicitor or other independent person[2]. It should be remembered that a corporate trustee imposes charges for its services and, if it is proposed to appoint such a body, confirmation as to its rates of charges and of the terms and conditions upon which it will act should be obtained[3]. There are now statutory provisions under which a trust corporation or a professional trustee may be entitled to reasonable remuneration out of the trust funds[4].

The adviser must, therefore, ascertain from the settlor:

63.1   whether he has any particular wishes concerning the identity of the trustees;

63.2   whether any particular person is to be debarred from appointment as trustee;

63.3   whether a corporate trustee is to be appointed;

63.4   whether professional trustees, who are also directors of companies by virtue of their office as trustees, are to be allowed to retain their remuneration as directors; and

63.5   whether other trustees may charge for their services[5].

The adviser should ascertain who is to have power to appoint new trustees[6]. Consideration should also be given as to whether the settlement should contain a provision that the Trusts of Land and Appointment of Trustees Act 1996 Sections 19 and 20 (appointment of new trustees at instance of beneficiaries) is not to apply[7].

The settlor or his spouse may be a trustee without tax disadvantage provided that there is no possibility of their receiving remuneration or any other benefit by virtue of their position[8].

[147]

---

1   Eg powers of appointment or to hold directorships in family companies.

2   An ideal combination will often be one trustee who is a family member (with the requisite 'knowledge') and one who is a professional (and who will, hopefully, get things done). It should be noted that there are limitations on the possible number of trustees holding land: see Paragraph 109 [269] post.

3   In relation to ascertaining the likely rates of charge of a corporate trustee, such a trustee is likely to be in place for a considerable period of time, so that some assurance as to the rates which will apply in the future is desirable (eg rates will not be reviewed more frequently than annually and will not increase above the rate of increase in the retail prices index).

4   See Trustee Act 2000 ss 28, 29 (48 Halsbury's Statutes (4th Edn) TRUSTS AND SETTLEMENTS) and Paragraph 213 [513] et seq post.

5   See Trustee Act 2000 ss 28, 29 and Paragraph 213 [523] et seq post.

6   As to the appointment of new trustees see vol 40(2) (2001 Reissue) TRUSTS AND SETTLEMENTS Part 10 [5201].

7   Trusts of Land and Appointment of Trustees Act 1996 s 21(5) (37 Halsbury's Statutes (4th Edn) REAL PROPERTY). In the case of a settlement created before 1 January 1997 the sections may be excluded by a deed executed by the settlor or, if more than one, by those of the settlors who are alive and of full capacity: Trusts of Land and Appointment of Trustees Act 1996 s 21(6)–(8).

8   As to the exclusion of benefit to the settlor and his spouse see Paragraph 62 [145] ante.

[148]–[155]

F: EXTENT OF TRUSTEES' POWERS AND FURTHER ADMINISTRATIVE PROVISIONS

64   Dispositive powers

Trustees may be, and commonly are, given wide powers either as powers of appointment or under a discretionary trust, and may even be given wide powers to vary the trust. The powers, having been given to the trustees, cannot be controlled by the settlor, but there is nothing improper in the settlor providing the trustees, when he creates the trust, with a memorandum of his wishes. The provision of a letter of wishes is strongly recommended: it will not in any way be binding on the trustees, but they may find it useful guidance in the administration of the trust both during the lifetime of the settlor and after his death[1].

1   For specimen letters of wishes see Form 252 [1841] et seq post. On the question of whether the beneficiary is entitled to see a letter of wishes, there is some authority that this is a matter which depends upon the intention of the settlor: see Form 252 note 1 [1844] post and the Australian case *Hartigan Nominees Pty Ltd v Rydge* (1992) 29 NSWLR 405 and the Jersey case of *Re Rabaiotti Settlements* (2000) WTLR 953, Royal Crt (Jer).

[156]

65   Other matters to be considered

The settlor should be advised of the statutory powers and provisions relating to trustees and any additional powers and provisions which may be desirable. The choice of any additional powers and provisions will depend on the nature of the property settled, the numbers of the beneficiaries, their circumstances, the situation of the property and like matters. Consideration should be given whether to insert a provision for the remuneration of professional trustees or to rely on the statutory provisions[1]; likewise in relation to a power of investment[2]; and whether to insert provisions excluding the settlor from benefit[3]. Where houses are held on a trust of land in the case of family settlements, a statement of the intentions of the settlor or settlors, and of the purposes for which the land is held, may be included in the settlement so as to confirm or qualify the right of beneficiaries to occupy trust land[4]. Some of the more commonly included additional powers and provisions are discussed below.

[157]

Other questions which may be put to the settlor include:

65.1   whether the settlor wishes to vary the statutory powers of maintenance and advancement or to include any other special powers of advancement[5];

65.2   whether any particular item of expenditure is to be treated as between the beneficiaries as capital or income[6];

65.3   whether the trustees are to be given any wider protection against their breaches of trust than that provided by law[7], or can act if they are personally interested in a transaction;

65.4   whether the trustees are to be given power to appropriate any particular item of property to any one beneficiary[8];

65.5   whether the settlor wishes to include power to insure his own life or that of any one of the beneficiaries[9];

65.6   whether extended powers of borrowing or lending are to be included[10];

65.7   whether any more extensive powers than those provided by law are to be included to employ agents and servants, to appoint nominees[11], to audit the trust accounts[12] and value trust property[13], to raise money on mortgage[14], or to manage land[15];

65.8   whether any consents are required to the exercise of any of the powers contained in the settlements; and

65.9   whether any of the powers or directions can be surrendered by the person entitled to exercise them and if so by what means[16].

Special provisions may be needed when it is intended to settle large holdings of land; where a business or shares in a family company are being settled; or where it is contemplated that the trust property or part of it may be situated or transferred abroad or the administration of the trust transferred abroad[17].

[158]

1   As to the remuneration of professional trustees see Trustee Act 2000 s 28 et seq (48 Halsbury's Statutes (4th Edn) TRUSTS AND SETTLEMENTS) and see Paragraph 213 [513] et seq post and, for a remuneration of trustees clause, see Form 233 [1769] post. Express provision should always be made: the statutory rules merely provide a safety net in *some* cases.

2   As to the statutory powers of investment see Trustee Act 2000 s 3 et seq and Paragraph 241 [591] et seq post.

3   As to the exclusion of the settlor from benefit see Paragraph 62 [145] ante and for a clause excluding the settlor from benefit see Form 250 [1813] post.

4   As to the right of beneficiaries to occupy trust land see Paragraph 73 [169] post, Form 4 schedule paragraph 22 [1100] and Form 210 [1727] post.

5   As to the statutory powers of maintenance and advancement, see Paragraph 235 [568] et seq post and for clauses varying these statutory powers see Forms 150 [1586]–153 [1594] post.

6   For clauses permitting trustees to charge expenditure to capital or income, see Form 173 [1649] et seq post.

7   As to the protection of trustees generally, see Paragraph 193 [473] et seq post.

8   For powers to appropriate and fix values, see Forms 165 [1629], 166 [1631] post.

9   As to the statutory power to insure, see Paragraph 259 [641] post and for a clause giving trustees the power to insure the lives of the settlor and any of the beneficiaries see Form 109 [1504] and Form 191 [1684] post

10   As to extending the powers of borrowing and lending, see Paragraph 62 [145] ante.

11   As to the power to employ agents and to delegate powers, see Paragraph 246 [611] et seq post and see Form 195 [1690] and Form 316 [2194] et seq post. It is thought that the statutory powers in the Trustee Act 2000 s 11 et seq will commonly be adequate.

12   As to the power to audit trust accounts, see Paragraph 266 [655] post and see Forms 230 [1763], 231 [1764] post.

13   As to the power to value trust property, see Paragraph 262 [647] post and see Form 165 [1629] post.

14   As to the tenant for life's power to raise money by mortgage, see vol 27 MORTGAGES (1999 Reissue) Paragraph 75 [75] et seq and for powers to borrow and to effect all kinds of dealings in land see Forms 168 [1641], 169 [1642] post.

15   For additional powers to manage farms and woodlands and to carry on a business, see Forms 178 [1659], 179 [1660] et seq post.

16   For a power to delegate see eg Form 195 [1690] post.

17   For a power to remove the forum of a trust from the United Kingdom, see Form 197 [1694] post.

[159]

66   Power of investment

The wider powers of investment conferred on trustees by the Trustee Act 2000[1] will commonly be adequate. They may however be restricted or extended[2].

[160]

1   Trustee Act 2000 ss 3–10 (48 Halsbury's Statutes (4th Edn) TRUSTS AND SETTLEMENTS). See Paragraph 241 [591] et seq post.

2   Eg by giving power to acquire land outside the United Kingdom; to dispense with the need for diversification where, for instance, the settlor wishes the trust funds to continue to be invested in a family company. For an express power, see Form 4 schedule paragraphs 1–4 [1092] post.

[161]

67   Where company shares are held in trust

Where the trust investments include stocks or shares in companies, the inclusion of a power enabling trustees to retain director's or other fees, and to vote as they think fit notwithstanding the trust shareholding may be appropriate[1].

1   For a power to hold directorships and retain remuneration see Form 183 [1670] post and for a power to retain commissions and brokerages see Form 228 [1761] post.

[162]

68   Exoneration of trustees for loss to the trust fund

Clauses commonly inserted in settlements relieve trustees from liability except in the case of wilful default and individual fraud or dishonesty on the part of the trustee who is sought to be made liable[1]. Arguably this gives the trustees, and especially professional trustees, an undue amount of protection as they should be liable for their own negligence. Express instructions should be given by the settlor, to whom the consequences should be clearly spelt out before such clauses are included.

It may be desirable to distinguish between:

68.1   lay or non-professional trustees;

68.2   professional trustees such as banks and trust corporations; and

68.3   professional people such as solicitors and accountants who are not professional trustees but professionals acting as trustees.

[163]

1   As to the liability of trustees generally see further Paragraph 185 [456] et seq post and for the exoneration of trustees from liability for the acts of agents see Form 221 [1749] post. Compare the Society of Trust and Estate Practitioners' Standard Provisions paragraph 12 at Form 3 [1071] post and see *Armitage v Nurse* [1998] Ch 241, [1997] 2 All ER 705 at 713, CA, *Bogg v Raper*, [1998] CLY 4592, (1998) Times 22 April, CA; *Wight v Olswang*, (1998) Times, 17 September, reversed on a question of construction (1999) Times, 18 May, CA; *Walker v Stones* [2000] 4 All ER 412, [2001] 2 WLR 623, CA. Note that at the time of writing the case of *Walker v Stones* is before the House of Lords, whose judgment is expected shortly. See also Trust Law Committee Consultation Paper 'Trustee Exemption Clauses' (June 1999).

[164]

69   Power to insure

The power to insure is considered subsequently[1].

1   Trustee Act 1925 s 19(1) as amended by the Trusts of Land and Appointment of Trustees Act 1996 s 25(1), (2), Sch 3 para 3(4), Sch 4 (48 Halsbury's Statutes (4th Edn) TRUSTS AND SETTLEMENTS). See further Paragraph 259 [641] post.

[165]

70   Power to carry on business

A power to enable trustees to carry on a business (including a farming business) alone or in partnership, or to incorporate a company for this purpose, and to make such arrangements as they think fit upon the reconstruction of a company in which the trust holds stocks, shares or securities should be included in a settlement in appropriate cases[1]. Trustees will be personally liable for business debts although they should be given a right of indemnity against the trust fund. It may be appropriate in such cases to incorporate the business, or to form a limited liability partnership, so that advantage can be taken of limited liability[2].

1   For powers to carry on business see Forms 179 [1660]–182 [1669] post.
2   For the position of trustees see 'Rights of Creditors Against Trustees and Trust Funds', Report of the Trust Law Committee (June 1999). For power to form a limited liability partnership, see Form 182 [1669] post.

[166]

71   Power to export a trust

Power to export a trust by appointing non-resident trustees, and to transfer the trust property out of the jurisdiction, may be desirable[1]. Where a power to appoint non-resident trustees is included, the provision of the Trustee Act 1925[2] for the replacement of a trustee who remains out of the United Kingdom for more than 12 months should be excluded.

1   For a power to remove the forum of a trust from the United Kingdom see Form 197 [1694] post.
2   See the Trustee Act 1925 s 36(1) (48 Halsbury's Statutes (4th Edn) TRUSTS AND SETTLEMENTS).

[167]

72   Power to insure life of settlor

A clause may be inserted in a settlement empowering the trustees to take out policies of insurance on the life of the settlor to provide for the payment of inheritance tax (or any substituted tax) on the death of the settlor within the period of seven years of creating the settlement (or other substituted period)[1].

1   For a power for trustees to insure the lives of the settlor and any of the beneficiaries see Form 109 [1504] and Form 191 [1684] post. As to the inheritance tax implications of settlements generally see Paragraph 283 [712] et seq post.

[168]

73   Power for trustees to permit beneficiaries to reside in trust property and use chattels

Under the Trusts of Land and Appointment of Trustees Act 1996[1] a beneficiary who is beneficially entitled to an interest in possession in land subject to a trust of land may be entitled to occupy the land. The right does not, however, extend to a beneficiary under a discretionary trust, but the trust instrument may provide that the trustees can permit a discretionary beneficiary to occupy, use or enjoy personally any movable or immovable property comprised in the trust fund upon such terms and conditions as the trustees think fit. The inclusion of such a provision may be desirable even though the trustees appear to have statutory power to allow such a beneficiary into occupation[2]. All trustees have power to acquire land under the power conferred by the Trustee Act 2000 for occupation by a beneficiary[3].

If a settlor does not wish any beneficiary to enjoy a right of occupation it is important that this should be clearly indicated in the trust instrument. The 1996 Act does not appear to contemplate the exclusion of Section 12, but a recital that it is not the wish of the settlor that any beneficiary should enjoy such a right and stating that any beneficial occupation should always be a matter exclusively within the discretion of the trustees is possible[4].

1   Trusts of Land and Appointment of Trustees Act 1996 ss 12, 13 (37 Halsbury's Statutes (4th Edn) REAL
     PROPERTY): see Paragraph 228 [545] post. For a detailed consideration of these sections see further
     vol 40(2) (2001 Reissue) TRUSTS AND SETTLEMENTS Part 8 [3001].
2   Trusts of Land and Appointment of Trustees Act 1996 s 6(1).
3   Trustee Act 2000 s 8 (48 Halsbury's Statutes (4th Edn) TRUSTS AND SETTLEMENTS).
4   For a recital as to the purposes of the settlement having regard to Trusts of Land and Appointment of
     Trustees Act 1996 s 12(1) see vol 40(2) (2001 Reissue) TRUSTS AND SETTLEMENTS Part 8 [3001].

[169]

74   Appropriation

A settlement may provide for the appropriation of trust property by the trustees in
satisfaction of the share of particular beneficiaries. Such a power may be particularly
useful when the assets consist of property that is not readily reducible to cash; for
example, chattels or shares in a family company[1]. The statutory powers of appropriation
applicable to the estates of deceased persons[2] may be applied for the purpose, and it is
usual to exclude the necessity of obtaining consents[3]. However, those powers do not
apply automatically to trustees holding funds under a settlement.

Trustees of land have power to partition the land where beneficiaries of full age are
absolutely entitled in undivided shares and to provide for the payment of equality
money[4]. The trustees, after obtaining the consent of the beneficiaries[5], give effect to any
such partition by conveying the partitioned land in severalty, either absolutely or in trust,
in accordance with the rights of the beneficiaries[6]. The power of partition may be
excluded by the disposition creating the trust[7], or the disposition may require a consent
which, in that case, must be obtained[8].

[170]

1   For powers to appropriate and fix values see Forms 165 [1629], 166 [1631] post. See also Form 167
     [1632] post enabling trustees to make transfers between separate funds.
2   See the Administration of Estates Act 1925 s 41 as amended by the Mental Health Act 1959 s 149(1),
     Sch 7 Pt I, by the Mental Health Act 1983 s 148, Sch 4 para 7, by the County Courts Act 1984 s 148(1),
     Sch 2 para 13 and by the Trusts of Land and Appointment of Trustees Act 1996 s 25(1), Sch 3 para 6(3)
     (17 Halsbury's Statutes (4th Edn) EXECUTORS AND ADMINISTRATORS).
3   As to the consents required see vol 42(2) (1998 Reissue) WILLS AND ADMINISTRATION Paragraph
     627 [3336]. The draftsman should also consider problems that may arise if property has been
     appropriated into separate funds within the settlement and it is desired to switch those properties. In an
     accumulation and maintenance trust, for instance, it is common (when there is more than one
     beneficiary) for separate funds to arise in due course. See Form 167 [1632] post.
4   Trusts of Land and Appointment of Trustees Act 1996 s 7(1) (37 Halsbury's Statutes (4th Edn) REAL
     PROPERTY): see Paragraph 223 [536] post and for a detailed consideration of the section see further
     vol 40(2) (2001 Reissue) TRUSTS AND SETTLEMENTS Part 8 [3001]. This section applies to personal
     representatives: Trusts of Land and Appointment of Trustees Act 1996 s 18(1).
5   Trusts of Land and Appointment of Trustees Act 1996 s 7(3). If a beneficiary refuses his consent an
     application could be made to the court under the Trusts of Land and Appointment of Trustees Act
     1996 s 14.
6   Trusts of Land and Appointment of Trustees Act 1996 s 7(2). The Trusts of Land and Appointment of
     Trustees Act 1996 s 7(4) deals with the situation where a share in the land is affected by an incumbrance;
     and if a share in the land is absolutely vested in a minor, the trustees, under the Trusts of Land and
     Appointment of Trustees Act 1996 s 7(5), may act on his behalf and retain land or other property
     representing his share in trust for him.
7   Trusts of Land and Appointment of Trustees Act 1996 s 8(1).
8   Trusts of Land and Appointment of Trustees Act 1996 s 8(2). If consent is refused an application to
     dispense with it may be made to the court under the Trusts of Land and Appointment of Trustees Act
     1996 s 14.

[171]

75   Power for trustees to enlarge their administrative powers

A power may be included in a settlement allowing trustees to add to their administrative powers such powers as would otherwise have required the sanction of the court[1]. Such a power could be included in settlements in which property of substantial value is likely to be involved, but with the cautionary remark that, although it would appear to allow for the trustees to include almost any other administrative provision (which, when exercised, can itself have an effect on the interests of the persons beneficially entitled under the trusts) it would probably be construed as restricted to providing for the inclusion of those powers which the court would consider to be for the benefit of the beneficiaries. It would probably not allow for the inclusion of the power to export the trust[2].

The tax status of a settlement is not affected by administrative powers, however wide[3]. It is not always easy, however, to distinguish between an administrative and a dispositive power, and the exercise of the latter may have tax consequences. It may be possible to avoid the risks by the insertion of a clause prohibiting the exercise of any specified power (ie those which might cause difficulty) in such a way as to prevent an interest in possession from continuing[4].

[172]

1   Ie under the Trustee Act 1925 s 57 (48 Halsbury's Statutes (4th Edn) TRUSTS AND SETTLEMENTS). Note that under the Trusts of Land and Appointment of Trustees Act 1996 s 6 (37 Halsbury's Statutes (4th Edn) REAL PROPERTY) trustees of land, for the purpose of exercising their functions as trustees, have in relation to the land subject to the trust all the powers of an absolute owner. For a power of trustees to confer additional powers on themselves or nominees see Form 194 [1688] post.

2   As to the power to export a trust see Paragraph 71 [167] ante; and as to offshore trusts generally see vol 40(2) (2001 Reissue) TRUSTS AND SETTLEMENTS Part 15 [8701]. See also *Re Weston's Settlements, Weston v Weston* [1969] 1 Ch 223, [1968] 3 All ER 338, CA; *Richards v Mackay* (1987) 11 Tru LI 23; *Re Beatty's Will Trusts (No 2)* (1991) 11 Tru LI 77.

3   See *Pearson v IRC* [1981] AC 753, [1980] 2 All ER 479, HL.

4   Or, in the case of an accumulation and maintenance trust, to prevent the Inheritance Tax Act 1984 s 71(1) (42–44 Halsbury's Statutes (4th Edn) TAXATION) from continuing to apply. As to the tax implications of accumulation and maintenance trusts see vol 40(2) (2001 Reissue) TRUSTS AND SETTLEMENTS Part 11 [6301]. See the Society of Trust and Estate Practitioners' Standard Provisions paragraph 14 at Form 3 [1072] post.

[173]–[180]

(4) VALIDITY AND SETTING ASIDE OF TRUSTS AND SETTLEMENTS

A: ILLEGALITY

76   Unlawful trusts

A trust created for an unlawful purpose is invalid and void. Unlawful trusts include the following:

76.1   trusts infringing the rule against remoteness of vesting[1] or the rule against the creation of a trust of perpetual or indefinite duration otherwise than for charitable purposes[2];

76.2   trusts for accumulation beyond the period allowed by the statutes in that respect[3];

76.3   trusts restricting the power of alienation[4];

76.4   trusts in fraud of creditors[5];

76.5   trusts tending to restraint of marriage[6];

76.6   trusts designed or tending to induce a future separation of husband and
            wife[7]; and

76.7   trusts tending to prevent the carrying out of parental duties[8].

[181]

1   As to the rule against remoteness of vesting see Paragraph 77 [183] et seq post.
2   As to trusts for charitable purposes generally see vol 6(2) (2001 Reissue) CHARITIES AND
        CHARITABLE GIVING.
3   As to restrictions on the accumulation of income see Paragraph 83 [194] et seq post.
4   As to trusts restricting the power of alienation see further 48 Halsbury's Laws (4th Edn 2000 Reissue)
        para 637.
5   As to trusts set up to defraud creditors see Paragraph 91 [219] post.
6   A general restraint is prima facie void in relation to personalty, and probably in relation to realty, unless
        the intention is not to promote celibacy, but, for instance, to make provision until marriage takes place:
        Jones v Jones (1876) 1 QBD 279 (realty); *Re Hewett, Eldridge v Iles* [1918] 1 Ch 458; *Re Fentem, Cockerton
        v Fentem* [1950] 2 All ER 1073 (personalty). Partial restraints, whether with regard to realty or
        personalty, are prima facie valid: as to the differing effect according to the nature of the property see
        Leong v Lim Beng Chye [1955] AC 648 at 662, [1955] 2 All ER 903 at 908, PC per Lord Radcliffe. See
        further 50 Halsbury's Laws (4th Edn Reissue) para 371 et seq.
7   It is trusts made in contemplation of the future separation of a husband and wife then living together
        which are void, for their existence might tend to bring about a separation which would not otherwise
        take place: *Re Thompson, Lloyds Bank Ltd v George* [1939] 1 All ER 681; *Re Caborne, Hodge and Nabarro
        v Smith* [1943] Ch 224, [1943] 2 All ER 7; *Re Johnson's Will Trusts, National Provincial Bank Ltd v Jeffrey*
        [1967] Ch 387, [1967] 1 All ER 553. Where a husband and wife have already decided upon an
        immediate separation, trusts created in a deed of separation are valid: *Wilson v Wilson* (1848) 1 HL Cas
        538; *Vansittart v Vansittart* (1858) 2 De G & J 249.
8   *Re Sandbrook, Noel v Sandbrook* [1912] 2 Ch 471; *Re Borwick, Borwick v Borwick* [1933] Ch 657; *Re Piper,
        Dodd v Piper* [1946] 2 All ER 503; *Blathwayt v Baron Cawley* [1976] AC 397, [1975] 3 All ER 625, HL.

[182]

B: PERPETUITIES AND ACCUMULATIONS

77   The rule against perpetuities

In drafting a settlement care must be taken not to violate the rule against perpetuities.
That rule, shortly stated, was, and in some cases still is, that a future interest must vest, if
it vests at all, within a period consisting of a life or lives in being and 21 years afterwards,
plus an extended period if there is a child en ventre sa mere[1]. It is not sufficient that it
may vest within that period; it *must* necessarily so vest, otherwise it is void. In the case of
instruments taking effect after 15 July 1964, the Perpetuities and Accumulations Act
1964 has introduced a 'wait and see' provision by which a disposition is not void for
remoteness until such time (if any) as it becomes established that the interest disposed of
or created cannot vest within the perpetuity period[2]. Similarly, a general power of
appointment[3] is not subject to the rule as to its exercise until it becomes established that
it will not become exercisable within the period[4] and a disposition consisting of or
conferring any power, option or other right is only treated as void for remoteness if, and
so far as, the right is not fully exercised within the period[5].

In the case of instruments taking effect after 15 July 1964, where the instrument so
provides, the perpetuity period applicable to the disposition made by the instrument,
instead of being of any other duration, may be of a duration equal to such number of
years, not exceeding 80 years, as may be specified in the instrument[6].

This power to specify an alternative period does not apply, however, where a
disposition is made in exercise of a special power of appointment[7], although, where a
period is specified in the instrument creating such a power, the period does apply in
relation to any disposition under the power as it applies in relation to the power itself[8].

The use of a 'royal lives' clause to achieve a lengthy perpetuity period[9] is still permissible, but the power conferred by statute to fix a period of up to 80 years should make such clauses, with their attendant uncertainty, unnecessary.

Where, in the case of instruments coming into effect after 15 July 1964, the duration of the perpetuity period is not determined by reference to a fixed period of years, for the purpose of the 'wait and see' provision it must be determined by reference to the lives of certain specified persons in being and ascertainable at the commencement of the perpetuity period[10]. If there are no such lives, or if they are so numerous as to render it impracticable to ascertain the date of death of the survivor, the period is 21 years[11].

[183]

1   As to the perpetuity rule generally see 35 Halsbury's Laws (4th Edn Reissue) para 1008 et seq. The courts have not yet had to consider the effect of scientific advances in relation to artificial insemination and in vitro fertilisation. It is now possible to freeze, preserve and thaw semen, ova and embryos for many years: see 35 Halsbury's Laws (4th Edn Reissue) para 1026.

2   See the Perpetuities and Accumulations Act 1964 ss 3(1), 15(5) (33 Halsbury's Statutes (4th Edn) PERPETUITIES).

3   For the purposes of the rule against perpetuities, a power of appointment is to be treated as a special power unless:
       (a)   in the instrument creating the power it is expressed to be exercisable by one person only; and
       (b)   it could, at all times during its currency when that person is of full age and capacity, be exercised by him so as immediately to transfer to himself the whole of the interest governed by the power without the consent of any other person or compliance with any other condition, not being a formal condition relating only to the mode of exercise of the power;
       provided that, for the purpose of determining whether a disposition made under a power of appointment exercisable by will only is void for remoteness, the power is to be treated as a general power where it would have fallen to be so treated if exercisable by deed: Perpetuities and Accumulations Act 1964 s 7.

4   See Perpetuities and Accumulations Act 1964 ss 3(2), 15(5).

5   See Perpetuities and Accumulations Act 1964 ss 3(3), 15(5). As to the meaning of disposition see Perpetuities and Accumulations Act 1964 s 15(2).

6   Perpetuities and Accumulations Act 1964 ss 1(1), 15(5). It should be noted that the fixed period of years in question must be specified in the instrument; it is not sufficient if it is merely implied by, say, a gift to the survivors of a class living 80 years after the date of the settlement. In that case, if there is uncertainty as to whether the gift might not become vested until too remote a time, its validity will be determined by reference to the 'wait and see' rule.

[184]

7   As to the meaning of a special power of appointment see note 3 above.

8   Perpetuities and Accumulations Act 1964 ss 1(2), 15(5). As to the possible effect of a variation of trusts order by the court see Form 91 note 3 [1465] post.

9   See eg Re Villar, Public Trustee v Villar [1929] 1 Ch 243, CA, where a period consisting of the lives of all the lineal descendants of Queen Victoria living at the testator's death was held valid; see also Re Leverhulme, Cooper v Leverhulme (No 2) [1943] 2 All ER 274.

10   See the Perpetuities and Accumulations Act 1964 s 3(4). The specified persons are as follows:
       (a)   the person by whom the disposition was made;
       (b)   a person to whom or in whose favour the disposition was made, ie:
               (i)   in the case of a disposition to a class of persons, any member or potential member of the class;
               (ii)   in the case of an individual disposition to a person taking only on certain conditions being satisfied, any person as to whom some of the conditions are satisfied and the remainder may in time be satisfied;
               (iii) in the case of a special power of appointment exercisable in favour of members of a class, any member or potential member of the class;
               (iv)   in the case of a special power of appointment exercisable in favour of one person only, that person or, where the object of the power is ascertainable only on certain conditions being satisfied, any person as to whom some of the conditions are satisfied and the remainder may in time be satisfied;
               (v)   in the case of any power, option or other right, the person on whom the right is conferred;
       (c)   a person having a child or grandchild within (i) to (iv) of paragraph (b) above, or any of whose children or grandchildren, if subsequently born, would by virtue of his or her descent fall within those sub-paragraphs; and

(d)   any person on the failure or determination of whose prior interest the disposition is limited to take effect: Perpetuities and Accumulations Act 1964 s 3(5).

See also *Re Thomas Meadows & Co Ltd and Subsidiary Companies (1960) Staff Pension Scheme Rules, Fetherston v Thomas Meadows & Co Ltd* [1971] Ch 278, [1971] 1 All ER 239 (as to the application of this section to a staff pension scheme).

11   See the Perpetuities and Accumulations Act 1964 s 3(4).

[185]

78   Presumption as to capacity to have children

At common law, for the purposes of the rule against perpetuities, a person was never deemed to be incapable of procreating or bearing a child[1]. Now, however, where in any proceedings there arises on the rule against perpetuities a question which turns on the ability of a person to have a child at some future time, it is presumed that a man can have a child at the age of 14 years or over, but not under that age, and that a woman can have a child at the age of 12 years or over, but not under that age or over the age of 55 years; but in the case of a living person evidence may be given to show that he or she will or will not be able to have a child at the time in question[2].

Where any such question is decided by treating a person as unable to have a child at a particular time, and he or she does so, the court may make such order as it thinks fit for placing the persons interested in the property comprised in the disposition, so far as may be just, in the position which they would have held if the question had not been so decided[3].

[186]

1   See *Re Gaite's Will Trusts, Banks v Gaite* [1949] 1 All ER 459. Cf *Re Atkins' Will Trusts, National Westminster Bank Ltd v Atkins* [1974] 2 All ER 1, [1974] 1 WLR 761; and see, in the context of capital gains tax, *Figg v Clarke* [1997] STC 247.
2   Perpetuities and Accumulations Act 1964 s 2(1) (33 Halsbury's Statutes (4th Edn) PERPETUITIES).
3   Perpetuities and Accumulations Act 1964 s 2(2). References to having a child in the Perpetuities and Accumulations Act 1964 s 2 (except the provision as to the giving of evidence to show that a living person will or will not be able to have a child at the time in question) include references to the possibility of having a child by adoption, legitimation or other means: see the Perpetuities and Accumulations Act 1964 s 2(4).

[187]

79   Reduction of age and exclusion of class members to avoid remoteness

Where a disposition is limited by reference to the attainment by any person or persons of a specified age exceeding 21 years, and it is apparent at the time the disposition is made or becomes apparent at a subsequent time:

79.1   that the disposition would otherwise be void for remoteness, but

79.2   that it would not be void if the specified age had been 21 years,

the disposition is treated for all purposes as if, instead of being limited by reference to the age in fact specified, it had been limited by reference to the age nearest to that age[1] which would, if specified instead, have prevented the disposition from being void[2].

Where it is apparent at the time the disposition is made or becomes apparent at a subsequent time[3] that the inclusion of any persons, being potential members of a class or unborn persons who at birth would become members or potential members of the class, would cause the disposition to be treated as void for remoteness, they are deemed for all purposes of the disposition to be excluded from the class, unless their exclusion would exhaust the class[4].

[188]

1   Therefore, where the specified age is 25 years, and no more than a reduction to 23 years is necessary
     in order to save the disposition from being void as infringing the rule against perpetuities, 23 years (and
     not, as would have been the case under the Law of Property Act 1925 s 163 (repealed), 21 years) will
     be substituted for the specified age.
2   Perpetuities and Accumulations Act 1964 s 4(1) (33 Halsbury's Statutes (4th Edn) PERPETUITIES). If
     different ages exceeding 21 years are specified, each may be reduced accordingly: see Perpetuities and
     Accumulations Act 1964 s 4(2).
3   The validity of anything previously done in relation to the interest disposed of by way of advancement,
     application of intermediate income or otherwise is not affected: Perpetuities and Accumulations Act
     1964 s 4(5).
4   Perpetuities and Accumulations Act 1964 s 4(4). Similarly, if the interest of a class member still fails to
     comply with the perpetuity rule after the age at which it is to vest has been reduced to 21 years he is
     excluded from the class: see Perpetuities and Accumulations Act 1964 s 4(3).

[189]

80   Validity of interests subsequent to void interests—acceleration

At common law, where a limitation was void for remoteness, any subsequent limitation
depending on it was also void[1]. In the case of instruments coming into effect after 15 July
1964, a disposition is not to be treated as void for remoteness by reason only that the
interest disposed of is ulterior to and dependent upon an interest under a disposition
which is so void, and the vesting of an interest is not prevented from being accelerated
on the failure of a prior interest by reason only that the failure arises because of
remoteness[2].

1   See eg *Re Buckton's Settlement Trusts, Public Trustee v Midland Bank Executor and Trustee Co Ltd* [1964]
     Ch 497, [1964] 2 All ER 487. Cf *Re Robinson's Will Trusts, Public Trustee v Gotto* [1963] 1 All ER 777,
     [1963] 1 WLR 628.
2   Perpetuities and Accumulations Act 1964 ss 6, 15(5) (33 Halsbury's Statutes (4th Edn) PERPETUITIES).
     'Disposition' includes the conferring of a power of appointment and any other disposition of an interest
     in or right over property: Perpetuities and Accumulations Act 1964 s 15(2).

[190]

81   Application of rule to administrative powers

The rule against perpetuities does not operate to invalidate a power conferred on trustees
or other persons to sell, lease, exchange or otherwise dispose of any property for full
consideration, or to do any other act in the administration (as opposed to distribution)
of any property, and does not prevent the payment to trustees or other persons of
reasonable remuneration for their services[1].

1   Perpetuities and Accumulations Act 1964 s 8(1) (33 Halsbury's Statutes (4th Edn) PERPETUITIES).
     This applies whether the power is conferred by an instrument taking effect before 16 July 1964 or after
     15 July 1964: see Perpetuities and Accumulations Act 1964 s 8(2). It is open to question whether
     Perpetuities and Accumulations Act 1964 s 8 applies to a power to mortgage, for such a power would
     not amount to one to dispose of property for full consideration. It may be advisable, therefore, expressly
     to limit the exercise of the power by specifying a period (up to 80 years) for its exercise (see the
     Perpetuities and Accumulations Act 1964 s 1(1)), or by limiting the exercise to a time within the
     perpetuity period. If no express perpetuity period is specified, the validity of any exercise of the power,
     so far as remoteness is concerned, will be determined in accordance with the Perpetuities and
     Accumulations Act 1964 s 3(3)–(5).

[191]

82 Charitable and purpose trusts

Trusts for charitable purposes, once they have taken effect, have never been subject to the rule against perpetuities[1]; although prior to 1964 a gift to a charity was void if it could possibly take effect initially outside the period, unless it was a gift over following another charitable gift. Now, in the case of instruments coming into effect after 15 July 1964, the 'wait and see' principle applies[2].

Nothing in the Perpetuities and Accumulations Act 1964 affects the operation of the rule of law rendering void for remoteness certain dispositions under which property is limited to be applied for purposes other than the benefit of any person or class of persons in cases where the property may be so applied after the end of the perpetuity period[3].

[192]

1   As to charitable trusts and the rule against perpetuities generally see vol 6(2) (2001 Reissue) CHARITIES AND CHARITABLE GIVING Paragraph 15 [61].
2   See the Perpetuities and Accumulations Act 1964 s 3(1) (33 Halsbury's Statutes (4th Edn) PERPETUITIES). See further Paragraph 77 [183] ante.
3   Perpetuities and Accumulations Act 1964 s 15(4). Examples of such dispositions are gifts for building tombs or monuments that are not part of the fabric of the church.

[193]

83 Restrictions on accumulations of income

The period permitted for the accumulation of the income of property is restricted by statute[1], and a settlor[2] who desires the income of settled property to be accumulated is restricted to choosing one, and only one[3], of the following periods:

83.1   the life of the grantor or settlor[4];
83.2   a term of 21 years from the death of the grantor, settlor or testator[5];
83.3   the minority[6] or respective minorities of any person or persons living or en ventre sa mère at the death of the grantor, settlor or testator[7];
83.4   the minority or respective minorities of any person or persons who, under the limitations of the settlement would, for the time being, if of full age, be entitled to the income directed to be accumulated[8];
83.5   a term of 21 years from the date of the making of the disposition[9]; or
83.6   the duration of the minority or respective minorities of any person or persons in being at the date of the disposition[10].

The restriction applies to a power to accumulate income whether or not there is a duty to exercise that power, and it applies whether or not the power to accumulate extends to income produced by the investment of income previously accumulated[11].

An accumulation of income for the purchase of land may be directed for no longer period than the duration of the minority or respective minorities of any person or persons who, under the limitations of the instrument directing the accumulation, would for the time being, if of full age, be entitled to the income so directed to be accumulated[12], but that restriction does not apply to accumulations to be held as capital money for the purposes of the Settled Land Act 1925, whether or not the accumulations are primarily liable to be laid out in the purchase of land[13].

The appropriate accumulation period is a question of construction that must be determined according to the language of the instrument and the facts of the particular case[14].

[194]

1   See the Law of Property Act 1925 s 164 (37 Halsbury's Statutes (4th Edn) REAL PROPERTY). See also the amendment to Law of Property Act 1925 s 164 in the Perpetuities and Accumulations Act 1964 s 13 (33 Halsbury's Statutes (4th Edn) PERPETUITIES).

2   The restriction applies only to a settlor who is a natural person, not a corporate settlor: *Re Dodwell & Co Ltd's Trust, Baker v Timmins* [1979] Ch 301, [1978] 3 All ER 738. The Law of Property Act 1925 s 164 uses the word 'person', and it replaces the Accumulations Act 1800 which was formed in terms of natural persons only. Since the Law of Property Act 1925 is a consolidating Act, the law remained unaltered. See also *Dinari Ltd v Hancock Prospecting Pty Ltd* [1972] 2 NSWLR 385.

3   The question of which one has been chosen is one of construction: see note 14 below. See also *Re Earl Berkeley, Inglis v Countess Berkeley* [1968] Ch 744, [1968] 3 All ER 364, CA (the mere retention by trustees of income from residuary estate by way of security for annuitants is not accumulation; accumulation involves the addition of income to capital against the interests of those entitled to the capital); cf *Re Rochford's Settlement Trusts, Rochford v Rochford* [1965] Ch 111, [1964] 2 All ER 177 (an accumulation of income of an income share, for purpose of making good or paying estate duty on death of beneficiary, is void).

4   Law of Property Act 1925 s 164(1)(a).

5   Law of Property Act 1925 s 164(1)(b).

6   The period of minority was reduced from 21 years to 18 years as from 1 January 1970 by the Family Law Reform Act 1969 s 1(1), (2) (6 Halsbury's Statutes (4th Edn) CHILDREN). The reduction does not affect any direction for accumulation made before 1 January 1970: see Family Law Reform Act 1969 s 1(4), Sch 3 para 7.

7   Law of Property Act 1925 s 164(1)(c).

8   Law of Property Act 1925 s 164(1)(d).

9   Perpetuities and Accumulations Act 1964 s 13(1)(a).

10   Perpetuities and Accumulations Act 1964 s 13(1)(b).

11   Perpetuities and Accumulations Act 1964 s 13(2).

12   This is the period permitted by the Law of Property Act 1925 s 164(1)(d): see the Law of Property Act 1925 s 166(1). As to the duration of the minority see note 6 above.

13   Law of Property Act 1925 s 166(2). It should be noted that by virtue of the Trusts of Land and Appointment of Trustees Act 1996, no new settlement under the Settled Land Act 1925 (48 Halsbury's Statutes (4th Edn) TRUSTS AND SETTLEMENTS) can come into being since the coming into force of the 1996 Act on 1 January 1997.

14   See *Re Watt's Will Trusts, Watt v Watt* [1936] 2 All ER 1555; *Re Ransome, Moberly v Ransome* [1957] Ch 348, [1957] 1 All ER 690; *Re Bourne's Settlement Trusts, Bourne v Mackay* [1946] 1 All ER 411, CA. In *Jagger v Jagger* (1883) 25 Ch D 729 and in *Re Bourne's Settlement Trusts, Bourne v Mackay* above, it was held that, no other period being applicable, the appropriate period was the life of the settlor; but now the Perpetuities and Accumulations Act 1964 s 13 has introduced a new period of 21 years from the date of the settlement.

[195]

84   Accumulations of surplus income during minority

If a beneficiary under a trust is a minor, subject to any contrary direction in the settlement, the trustees have power to maintain him out of income and must accumulate any surplus[1].

Where surplus income has been accumulated during a minority, whether under this statutory power or under the general law, the period for which such accumulations are made is not to be taken into account in determining the periods for which accumulations are permitted to be made under the statutory power, and accordingly an express trust for accumulation for any other permitted period is not to be deemed to have been invalidated by reason of accumulations also having been made during such minority[2].

1   See the Trustee Act 1925 s 31 as amended by the Family Law Reform Act 1969 s 1(3), Sch 1 Pt 1 (48 Halsbury's Statutes (4th Edn) TRUSTS AND SETTLEMENTS). See further Paragraph 235 [568] post.

2   Law of Property Act 1925 s 165 (37 Halsbury's Statutes (4th Edn) REAL PROPERTY). See also *Re Maber, Ward v Maber* [1928] Ch 88.

[196]

85   Power to terminate accumulations

Where there is an absolutely vested gift in favour of a beneficiary, but subject to a trust that the income is to be accumulated until he attains an age exceeding his minority, he may, on attaining his majority, put an end to the accumulations[1]. Once the property belongs to him absolutely his free enjoyment of it cannot be fettered. This does not apply where there is the possibility of another beneficiary coming into existence, and the court would formerly never assume that a woman was past the age of childbearing; but now the presumption, introduced by the Perpetuities and Accumulations Act 1964, that no woman over the age of 55 can have a child applies to the right of beneficiaries to put an end to accumulations[2].

1   *Saunders v Vautier* (1841) Cr & Ph 240; *Wharton v Masterman* [1895] AC 186, HL.
2   Perpetuities and Accumulations Act 1964 s 14 (33 Halsbury's Statutes (4th Edn) PERPETUITIES). As to the presumption as to capacity to have children generally see Paragraph 78 [186] ante.

[197]

86   Exceptions to the restrictions on accumulation of income

The restrictions on accumulation do not extend to any provision:
86.1   for the payment of the debts[1] of any grantor, settlor, testator or any other person[2];
86.2   for raising portions for:
    86.2.1   any child, children or remoter issue of the grantor, settlor or testator[3]; or
    86.2.2   any child, children or remoter issue of a person taking any interest under any settlement or other disposition directing the accumulations or to whom any interest is thereby limited[4]; or
86.3   respecting the accumulation of the produce of timber or wood[5];
and accordingly such provisions may be made as if no statutory restrictions on accumulation of income had been imposed[6]. The restrictions on accumulation do not extend either to transactions that cannot fairly be described as settlements or dispositions[7].

[198]

1   To be within the exception the debt must be in existence as a legal liability, even though contingent, when the instrument providing for accumulation took effect: *Re Rochford's Settlement Trusts, Rochford v Rochford* [1965] Ch 111, [1964] 2 All ER 177 (accumulation to pay future estate duty).
2   Law of Property Act 1925 s 164(2)(i) (37 Halsbury's Statutes (4th Edn) REAL PROPERTY).
3   Law of Property Act 1925 s 164(2)(ii)(a).
4   Law of Property Act 1925 s 164(2)(ii)(b).
5   Law of Property Act 1925 s 164(2)(iii).
6   Law of Property Act 1925 s 164(2).
7   If a settlement directs or authorises the trustees to expend the income of the settled property in paying the premiums of a policy of assurance, such a direction or power will not offend the rules relating to excessive accumulation despite the fact that the trustees might pay the premiums outside the periods authorised by law for the accumulation of income and despite any direction in the settlement that the policy money is to be treated as capital: see *Bassil v Lister* (1851) 9 Hare 177 at 184 (cited in *Re AEG Unit Trust (Managers) Ltd's Deed, Midland Bank Executor and Trustee Co Ltd v AEG Unit Trust (Managers) Ltd* [1957] Ch 415 at 421, [1957] 2 All ER 506 at 509). See further 35 Halsbury's Laws (4th Edn Reissue) para 1144.

[199]

87   Effect of void direction to accumulate

If a direction to accumulate is void as exceeding the statutory period, the income of the property directed to be accumulated, in so far as the direction is void[1], is receivable by the person or persons who would have been entitled to it if no accumulations had been directed[2]. Therefore, if a beneficiary would have been entitled to the income in specie had no accumulations been directed, he will be entitled to any in respect of which the direction is invalid; but if there is no such beneficiary, there is a resulting trust to the settlor[3].

[200]

1   Ie the period specified is curtailed to the length of the appropriate statutory period, and the direction is void as to the excess: see eg *Re Watt's Will Trusts, Watt v Watt* [1936] 2 All ER 1555. See further 35 Halsbury's Laws (4th Edn Reissue) para 1124.
2   See the Law of Property Act 1925 s 164(1) (37 Halsbury's Statutes (4th Edn) REAL PROPERTY).
3   *Re O'Hagan, O'Hagan v Lloyds Bank Ltd* [1932] WN 188. As to the application of surplus accumulations see 35 Halsbury's Laws (4th Edn Reissue) para 1146 et seq.

[201]

88   Application to charities

The restriction on accumulation applies in the case of charities, and a charitable institution, to which a fund is given subject to a trust for accumulation, has the same right as an individual to stop the accumulations and call for immediate payment[1].

1   As to accumulations in relation to charitable trusts see further 5(2) Halsbury's Laws (4th Edn Reissue) para 136.

[202]

89   Reform

The Law Commission produced a final report on 'The Rules against Perpetuities and Excessive Accumulations' in March 1998 (see Law Com 251). It proposes a standard perpetuity period of 125 years and that trustees should be able (if the trust instrument so provides) to accumulate income throughout this period. A draft Bill is attached but it does not seem likely that these proposals will be legislated in the near future.

[203]–[215]

C: RIGHTS OF TRUSTEE OF A BANKRUPT SETTLOR'S ESTATE, CREDITORS AND OTHERS

90   Avoidance by trustee of the bankrupt's estate of transactions at an undervalue

Where an individual is adjudged bankrupt and he has at a relevant time[1] entered into a transaction with any person[2] at an undervalue:

90.1   the trustee of the bankrupt's estate may apply to the court for an order[3]; and
90.2   the court must make such an order as it thinks fit for restoring the position to what it would have been if that individual had not entered into that transaction[4].

[216]

An individual enters into a transaction with a person at an undervalue if:

90.3   he makes a gift to that person or he otherwise enters into a transaction with
            that person on terms that provide for him to receive no consideration[5];

90.4   he enters into a transaction with that person in consideration of marriage[6];
            or

90.5   he enters into a transaction with that person for a consideration the value
            of which, in money or money's worth, is significantly less than the value,
            in money or money's worth, of the consideration provided by the
            individual[7].

The time at which an individual enters into a transaction at an undervalue is a
relevant time if the transaction is entered into at a time in the period of five years ending
with the day of the presentation of the bankruptcy petition on which that individual is
adjudged bankrupt[8]. Where an individual enters into a transaction at an undervalue
within that five year period, not being a time less than two years before the end of that
period, that time is not a relevant time unless the individual:

90.6   is insolvent at that time[9]; or

90.7   becomes insolvent in consequence of the transaction[10].

An individual is insolvent if:

90.8   he is unable to pay his debts as they fall due[11]; or

90.9   the value of his assets is less than the amount of his liabilities, taking into
            account his contingent and prospective liabilities[12].

[217]

---

1   'Relevant time' is defined in the Insolvency Act 1986 s 341(1) (4 Halsbury's Statutes (4th Edn)
     BANKRUPTCY AND INSOLVENCY).

2   The expression 'any person' in the corresponding provision dealing with companies (see the Insolvency
     Act 1986 s 238) has been held to have its literal and natural meaning of any person wherever resident.
     The safeguards are that the court's power to make an order is discretionary and, in the case of persons
     who are abroad, the leave of the court must be obtained for service abroad: *Re Paramount Airways Ltd*
     [1993] Ch 223, [1992] 3 All ER 1, CA.

3   Ie an order under the Insolvency Act 1986 s 339: see the Insolvency Act 1986 s 339(1). For particular
     orders that may be made see the Insolvency Act 1986 s 342 as amended by the Insolvency (No 2) Act
     1994 s 2.

4   Insolvency Act 1986 s 339(2).

5   Insolvency Act 1986 s 339(3)(a).

6   Insolvency Act 1986 s 339(3)(b).

7   Insolvency Act 1986 s 339(3)(c). See *Re Kumar (a bankrupt), ex p Lewis v Kumar* [1993] 2 All ER 700,
     [1993] 1 WLR 224; *Clarkson v Clarkson (a bankrupt)* [1994] BCC 921, CA; *Agricultural Mortgage Corpn
     plc v Woodward* [1995] 1 BCLC 1, CA; *Barclays Bank plc v Eustice* [1995] 4 All ER 511, [1995] 1 WLR
     1238, CA; *National Bank of Kuwait v Menzies* [1994] 2 BCLC 306, CA.

8   Insolvency Act 1986 s 341(1)(a).

9   Insolvency Act 1986 s 341(2)(a).

10   Insolvency Act 1986 s 341(2)(b). However, these requirements are presumed to be satisfied, unless the
     contrary is shown, in relation to any transaction at an undervalue which is entered into by an individual
     with a person who is an associate of his (otherwise than by reason only of being his employee):
     Insolvency Act 1986 s 341(2). As to the meaning of 'associate' see the Insolvency Act 1986 s 435. In
     appropriate circumstances a settlor may make a statutory declaration of solvency: see vol 17(2)
     (2000 Reissue) GIFTS Form 1 [1251].

11   Insolvency Act 1986 s 341(3)(a).

12   Insolvency Act 1986 s 341(3)(b).

[218]

91   Transactions defrauding creditors

Where:

91.1   a person has entered into a transaction with any other person at an undervalue[1]; and

91.2   the court is satisfied that the transaction was entered into for the purpose[2] of putting assets beyond the reach of a person[3] who is making, or may at some time make, a claim against the relevant person or of otherwise prejudicing the interests of such a person in relation to the claim which he is making or may make[4],

the court may make such order as it thinks fit for restoring the position to what it would have been if the transaction had not been entered into and for protecting the interests of persons who are victims of the transaction[5].

[219]

For the purposes of these provisions, a person enters into a transaction with another at an undervalue if:

91.3   he makes a gift to that other person or he otherwise enters into a transaction with that other person on terms that provide for him to receive no consideration[6];

91.4   he enters into a transaction with that other person in consideration of marriage[7]; or

91.5   he enters into a transaction with that other person for a consideration the value of which, in money or money's worth, is significantly less than the value, in money or money's worth, of the consideration provided by himself[8].

An application for an order under the above provisions can only be made by specified persons, namely:

91.6   in a case where the person entering into the transaction at an undervalue has been adjudged bankrupt, the official receiver, the trustee of the bankrupt's estate or, with the leave of the court, a victim of the transaction[9];

91.7   in a case where a victim of the transaction is bound by a voluntary arrangement approved under the Insolvency Act 1986 Part VIII[10], the supervisor of the voluntary arrangement or any person who (whether or not so bound) is such a victim[11]; or

91.8   in any other case, a victim of the transaction[12].

[220]

---

1   As to when a person enters into a transaction at an undervalue see the Insolvency Act 1986 s 423(1) (4 Halsbury's Statutes (4th Edn) BANKRUPTCY AND INSOLVENCY) and see further Paragraph 90 [216] ante.

2   The purpose must be at least a 'substantial' purpose. It does not matter that there may be other motives for the transaction: *Chohan v Saggar* [1992] BCC 306, order varied [1994] 1 BCLC 706, CA. In this case the judge at first instance construed the Insolvency Act 1986 s 423(3) as requiring the purpose to be a dominant purpose. This point was not discussed on appeal. In *Royscott Spa Leasing Ltd v Lovett* [1995] BCC 502, CA, without deciding the point, it was assumed that it would suffice if the relevant purpose which had to be established was a substantial purpose, rather than the stricter test of dominant purpose. In *Re Pinewood Joinery* [1994] 2 BCLC 412 the judge in arguendo doubted the proposition that a dominant purpose must be established, but reached no final view on the matter. If legal advice is sought to devise a structure to prejudice the interests of creditors and there is strong prima facie evidence that the structured transaction does prejudice creditors, then communications between lawyer and client are not privileged, thereby making it easier to establish requisite intent: *Barclays Bank plc v Eustice* [1995] 4 All ER 511 [1995] 1 WLR 1238, CA.

3   The section does not require the applicant to establish that the purpose of the transaction was to put assets beyond the applicant's reach: *Jyske Bank (Gibraltar) Ltd v Spjeldnaes* [1999] 2 BCLC 101.

4   Insolvency Act 1986 s 423(3).

5   Insolvency Act 1986 s 423(2). For particular orders that may be made see the Insolvency Act 1986
    s 425.
6   Insolvency Act 1986 s 423(1)(a).
7   Insolvency Act 1986 s 423(1)(b).
8   Insolvency Act 1986 s 423(1)(c). In *Agricultural Mortgage Corpn plc v Woodward* [1995] 1 BCLC 1, CA
    a husband granted his wife a tenancy of mortgaged property whilst he was in serious arrears with his
    mortgage. At first instance it was held that the transaction was entered into by the husband for the
    purpose of prejudicing his creditors. This was not challenged on appeal. What was challenged was the
    finding at first instance that the transaction was not at an undervalue within the Insolvency Act 1986
    s 423(1)(c) as W was paying a market rent for the property. The trial judge refused to take into account
    the detriment to H consisting of the diminution in value of his freehold interest now that he had a
    sitting tenant and could not give vacant possession of the land. The Court of Appeal reversed this,
    saying that the transaction had to be viewed as a whole and that it was clear that the benefits conferred
    on W were far greater than the consideration provided by her, as by making her a secure tenant H had
    placed her in a 'ransom' position vis-a-vis a creditor, who would in effect have had to pay her to vacate
    the premises in order that he could realise his security.
9   See the Insolvency Act 1986 s 424(1)(a). A victim of the transaction is a person who is, or is capable of
    being, prejudiced by it: Insolvency Act 1986 s 423(5).
10 Ie a proposal made by the debtor to his creditors for a composition in satisfaction of his debts or a
    scheme of arrangement of his affairs: see the Insolvency Act 1986 ss 252–263.
11 Insolvency Act 1986 s 424(1)(b).
12 Insolvency Act 1986 s 424(1)(c). Whoever makes the application, it is to be treated as made on behalf
    of every victim of the transaction: Insolvency Act 1986 s 424(2).

[221]

92   Asset protection trusts[1]

The earlier discussion of transactions at undervalue and transactions defrauding
creditors[2], is relevant when a settlor has established an 'asset protection trust'. Primarily
developed in the United States, these trusts (commonly set up in tax haven jurisdictions
such as the Turks and Caicos or Cook Islands) are designed to hold assets beyond the
reach of the settlor's creditors, his divorced spouse or other family members (typically in
the situation where he resides in a forced heirship jurisdiction). For a UK resident (and
his professional advisers) the creation of asset protection vehicles is beset with problems.
If a substantial purpose behind setting up the trust was to put assets out of the reach of
creditors, the Insolvency Act 1986 Section 423 may be invoked by such creditors. The
case of *Midland Bank plc v Wyatt*[3] provides a recent illustration, with the court holding
that the purported declaration of trust should be set aside under that section[4]. Apart from
civil redress, Section 357 of the Act provides for criminal penalties and a professional
adviser who is involved in an asset protection scheme designed to defraud third parties
may become engaged in either a criminal conspiracy or in aiding and abetting a Section
357 crime[5].

The position of trustees when faced with a claim to set aside a transaction at
undervalue under Section 423 was considered by the Court in *Alsop Wilkinson v Neary*[6].
Lightman J made it plain that the old idea that trustees of settlements have a duty to
defend actions challenging the validity of their settlement and are entitled to costs
irrespective of the outcome of the action does not accord with modern authority. He
considered that if the matter was in reality a dispute between rival claimants to the
beneficial interest in the property subject to the trust, then the trustees' duty was to
remain neutral and to offer to submit to the court's direction, thereby leaving the rival
parties to dispute ownership of the property.

[222]

1   As to protective trusts and asset protection generally see vol 40(2) (2001 Reissue) TRUSTS AND
    SETTLEMENTS Part 12 [6901].
2   See Paragraphs 90 [216], 91 [219] ante.
3   *Midland Bank plc v Wyatt* [1997] 1 BCLC 242.

4   As an alternative ground for the decision, the court also held the trust void as a sham: see further *Private Client Business*, 1994, p 410 and Paragraph 94 [226] post.

5   See further 'Asset Protection Trusts—Promise or Threat?' by Richard Citron and Michael Steiner in *Private Client Business*, 1994, p 96; and note the remarks of the Court of Appeal in *Barclays Bank plc v Eustice* [1995] 4 All ER 511, [1995] 1 WLR 1238, CA.

6   *Alsop Wilkinson v Neary* [1995] 1 All ER 431, [1996] 1 WLR 1220.

[223]

D: UNDUE INFLUENCE

93   Avoidance by reason of undue influence

Settlements, whether made for the benefit of the settlor himself, or of third parties, are liable to be set aside in equity if their execution was obtained as the result of undue influence[1]. In *Barclays Bank plc v O'Brien* the House of Lords classified situations of undue influence as follows[2]:

93.1   **'Class 1'** (actual undue influence). In these cases, it is necessary for the claimant to prove affirmatively that the wrongdoer exerted undue influence on the complainant to enter into the particular transaction which is impugned[3].

93.2   **'Class 2'** (presumed undue influence). In these cases, the complainant only has to show, in the first instance, that there was a relationship of trust and confidence between the complainant and the wrongdoer of such a nature that it is fair to presume that the wrongdoer abused that relationship in procuring the complainant to enter into the impugned transaction. In Class 2 cases, therefore, there is no need to produce evidence that actual undue influence was exerted in relation to the particular transaction impugned: once a confidential relationship has been proved, the burden then shifts to the wrongdoer to prove that the complainant entered into the impugned transaction freely; for example, by showing that the complainant had independent advice. Such a confidential relationship can be established in two ways:

93.2.1   **'Class 2A'**. Certain relationships (for example solicitor and client, medical adviser and patient) as a matter of law raise the presumption that undue influence has been exercised[4].

93.2.2   **'Class 2B'**. Even if there is no relationship falling within Class 2A, if the complainant proves the de facto existence of a relationship under which the complainant generally reposed trust and confidence in the wrongdoer, the existence of such a relationship raises the presumption of undue influence. In a Class 2B case therefore, in the absence of evidence disproving undue influence, the complainant will succeed in setting aside the impugned transaction merely by proof that the complainant reposed trust and confidence in the wrongdoer without having to prove that the wrongdoer exerted actual undue influence or otherwise abused such trust and confidence in relation to the particular transaction impugned[5].

In the case of transactions falling within Class 2 (but not Class 1), there is a further requirement to be satisfied before the transaction is set aside; namely that it constituted 'a disadvantage sufficiently serious to require evidence to rebut the presumption that in the circumstances of the relationship between the parties it was procured by the exercise of undue influence'[6].

[224]

1   As to undue influence generally see 18 Halsbury's Laws (4th Edn) para 330 et seq.
2   See *Barclays Bank plc v O'Brien* [1994] 1 AC 180 at 189, [1993] 4 All ER 417 at 423, HL per Lord Browne-Wilkinson. The cases were reviewed and the law set out in some detail by Stuart-Smith J, giving the judgment of the court, in *Royal Bank of Scotland v Etridge (No 2)* [1998] 4 All ER 705, CA. See also *Bank of Cyprus (London) Ltd v Markou* [1999] 2 All ER 707; *Barclays Bank plc v Caplan* [1998] 1 FLR 532.
3   See *CIBC Mortgages plc v Pitt* [1994] 1 AC 200, [1993] 4 All ER 433, HL categorising undue influence of this type as a species of fraud so that if successful the claimant may have the transaction set aside as of right whether or not it was to his manifest disadvantage.
4   Other relationships include parent and child, trustee and beneficiary, spiritual adviser and disciple etc It is important that independent legal advice is taken in the common situation where a child on attaining majority is 'encouraged' by his father and legal adviser to resettle property which has vested in him absolutely.
5   The relationship of husband and wife does not fall within Class 2A. However, such an emotional relationship may fall within Class 2B (as may cohabitation).
6   *National Westminster Bank plc v Morgan* [1985] AC 686 at 704, [1985] 1 All ER 821 at 827, HL.

[225]

E: SHAM TRUSTS

94   General

Although a trust may appear to be created with trustees owning property and owing fiduciary duties to the beneficiaries, it may transpire that the reality is that the settlor has retained a full beneficial entitlement to the property with the trustees being no more than cyphers in carrying out his wishes[1].

In *Rahman v Chase Bank*, Mrs Rahman persuaded the Jersey court that the trust apparently set up by her husband ('KAR') was a sham. The headnote of the case records that:

> 'the trustee was empowered to pay or apply the capital or income to or for the benefit of KAR and was directed to have regard exclusively to his interests in determining whether or not to exercise such power. Many of the administrative powers contained in the settlement required his prior consent for their exercise in his lifetime. KAR referred to the fund as "my assets" and to the trustee as his "trust manager". The trustee made no independent investment decisions and invariably complied with KAR's instructions. Moreover, KAR obtained moneys and made distributions from the fund of which the trustee was only later informed and often gave direct instructions to banks holding trust property concerning its investment'.

[226]

When will a trust be set aside on these grounds? Consider the following:

94.1   *Midland Bank plc v Wyatt.* A man made a declaration of trust in favour of his wife and children and put the relevant instrument away in his safe. Subsequently, he incurred various liabilities to the bank which obtained a charging order over the property. The bank had throughout been in ignorance of the declaration of trust which only came to light after the charging order had been obtained. The court held that he had no intention of benefiting his wife and children and that the declaration was a pretence or sham[2].

94.2   *Red Cross 'trusts'.* A trust in wide discretionary form is set up with a single named beneficiary (eg the Red Cross), but with the trustees having wide powers to add the settlor and his family. There is evidence that the Red Cross is not intended to benefit. Often such trusts are purchased 'off the peg' in a similar way to ready made companies[3].

94.3   *Terms in the trust deed denying the 'irreducible trust core'.* If it is clear from a clause in the trust deed that the beneficiaries are to have no rights as against the trustees, it may result either in the clause being struck out or in the court concluding that no trust can have been intended so that the settlor never disposed of any equitable interest in the property. The question of the 'irreducible trust core' has recently been considered by the Court of Appeal in the context of whether a clause purporting to relieve the trustees against liability for acts of negligence (or indeed of gross negligence) was valid and enforceable. Millett LJ commented as follows:

> 'I accept ... that there is an irreducible core of obligations owed by the trustees to the beneficiaries and enforceable by them which is fundamental to the concept of a trust. If the beneficiaries have no rights enforceable against the trustees there are no trusts. But I do not accept the further submission that these core obligations include the duties of skill and care, prudence and diligence. The duty of the trustees to perform the trusts honestly and in good faith for the benefit of the beneficiaries is the minimum necessary to give substance to the trusts, but in my opinion it is sufficient. ... a trustee who relied on the presence of a trustee exemption clause to justify what he proposed to do would thereby lose its protection: he would be acting recklessly in the proper sense of the term'[4]

94.4   *The settlor leaves a detailed letter of wishes which the trustees slavishly follow*[5]. In this case an argument can be mounted that the trust deed by itself does not record the full terms of the trust which can only be ascertained by incorporating the letter of wishes. Similar arguments can be raised if the settlor's consent is required to the exercise of powers (eg of distribution and investment) and in reality it is the settlor who initiates whilst the trustees provide the consent[6].

[227]

1   See in particular *Midland Bank plc v Wyatt* [1995] 3 FCR 11; *Rahman v Chase Bank (CI) Trust Co Ltd* [1991] JLR 103, Royal Ct (Jer). Judgment in the *Rahman* case is reproduced in Butterworths *Offshore Cases and Materials* (1996) vol 1 at p 433. The classic definition of a sham in English law is found in the judgment of Diplock LJ in *Snook v London and West Riding Investments Ltd* [1967] 2 QB 786 at 802, [1967] 1 All ER 518 at 528, CA where he commented: '... if it has any meaning in law, it means acts done or documents executed by the parties to the "sham" which are intended by them to give to third parties or to the court the appearance of creating between the parties legal rights and obligations different from the actual legal rights and obligations (if any) which the parties intend to create.' See also *Turner v Turner* [1984] Ch 100, [1983] 2 All ER 745 in which the purported exercise of a power of appointment by trustees was set aside because they never applied their minds to the exercise of the discretion entrusted to them: they did unthinkingly what the settlor asked.

2   The transaction was also set aside under the Insolvency Act 1986 s 423 (4 Halsbury's Statutes (4th Edn) BANKRUPTCY AND INSOLVENCY): see Paragraph 91 [219] ante. The judge concluded that the declaration had in effect been put away in case it should ever be needed: in the event of a rainy day!

3   See the Isle of Man litigation in *Steele v Paz Ltd (in liquidation)* (10 October 1995, unreported) extracts from which appear in Butterworths *Offshore Cases and Materials* (1996) vol 1 at p 338.

4   *Armitage v Nurse* [1997] 2 All ER 705 at 713, CA. The clause in that case offered no protection against fraud or recklessness: 'No Trustee shall be liable for any loss or damage which may happen to [the Trust] or any part thereof or the income thereof at any time or from any cause whatsoever unless such loss or damage shall be caused by his own actual fraud'. A clause seeking to protect a trustee against fraud would have offended the irreducible trust core. Millett LJ further commented that whilst the difference between fraud and negligence was one of kind, the difference between negligence and gross negligence was merely one of degree. See further 'The Irreducible Core Content of Trusteeship' by Professor David Hayton in Oakley *Trends in Contemporary Trust Law* (1996) p 47. In this connection consider the extent to which the restrictions were placed on a beneficiary's right to information that would infringe the 'fundamental trust core'.

5   For examples of such letters see Form 252 [1841] et seq post.

6   In appropriate circumstances the trust may be used as a disguised will: eg if the settlor retains a life interest with the remainder being held for such persons as the settlor may in writing declare.

[228]–[235]

(5) ACCEPTANCE BY TRUSTEES AND DEVOLUTION OF TRUST PROPERTY

A: THE TRUST ESTATE

1: EXTENT OF ESTATE TAKEN BY TRUSTEES IN LAND

95   Legal estates

The only legal estates capable of existing in land after 1925 and therefore capable of being transferred to and held by trustees are an estate in fee simple absolute in possession and a term of years absolute[1]. In the case of a trust of land the legal estate is vested in the trustees of land, and in the case of a settlement under the terms of the Settled Land Act 1925 the legal estate is vested either in the tenant for life or statutory owners[2].

1   Law of Property Act 1925 s 1(1) (37 Halsbury's Statutes (4th Edn) REAL PROPERTY).
2   As to land settled on a trust of land see Paragraph 107 [266] et seq post and as to settlements under the Settled Land Act 1925 (48 Halsbury's Statutes (4th Edn) TRUSTS AND SETTLEMENTS) see vol 40(2) (2001 Reissue) TRUSTS AND SETTLEMENTS Part 9 [4101]. It has not been possible to create a new settlement under the Settled Land Act 1925 since the coming into force of the Trusts of Land and Appointment of Trustees Act 1996 on 1 January 1997: Trusts of Land and Appointment of Trustees Act 1996 s 2 (37 Halsbury's Statutes (4th Edn) REAL PROPERTY).

[236]

96   Equitable interests

An equitable interest in land may be transferred to trustees and where the owner of an absolute equitable interest in land vests it in trustees, they have a right to call for the legal estate from the bare trustees[1].

1   *Angier v Stannard* (1834) 3 My & K 566; *Poole v Pass* (1839) 1 Beav 600.

[237]

2: CHARACTER IN WHICH PROPERTY IS TAKEN

97   Presumption that no beneficial interest taken

Where property is given to a person on trust, there is a presumption that the property is given to him entirely as a trustee and not to any extent beneficially[1]. However, if the trust does not exhaust the whole beneficial interest in the property, this presumption can be rebutted by an indication in the trust instrument that he was intended to take the residue for his own benefit[2]. A gift by will to a person on trust to carry out certain purposes creates a resulting trust of so much as is not required for the fulfilment of those purposes[3]. A gift to a person for a trust or purpose which he is left at liberty either to perform or not at his option, is a beneficial gift to him[4]. The trust or purpose in that case is rather the motive for the gift than the specified object for which it is given[5].

[238]

1   *Burgess v Wheate, AG v Wheate* (1759) 1 Eden 177. This applies *a fortiori* to a trustee taking by
     representation: see *Re Booth, Hattersley v Cowgill* (1917) 86 LJ Ch 270.
2   *Croome v Croome* (1888) 59 LT 582, CA; affd (1889) 61 LT 814, HL; *AG v Jeffreys* [1908] AC 411, HL;
     cf *Re Foord, Foord v Conder* [1922] 2 Ch 519. Extrinsic evidence is not admissible to show that a trustee
     is intended to take the surplus beneficially: *Re Rees, Williams v Hopkins* [1950] Ch 204, CA.
3   *Re West, George v Grose* [1900] 1 Ch 84.
4   *Thorp v Owen* (1843) 2 Hare 607; *Barrs v Fewkes* (1864) 2 Hem & M 60.
5   *Andrews v Partington* (1790) 2 Cox Eq Cas 223 at 224 per Lord Thurlow LC; *Brown v Casamajor* (1799)
     4 Ves 498; *Hammond v Neame* (1818) 1 Swan 35 at 38; *Benson v Whittam, Hemming v Whittam* (1831)
     5 Sim 22; *Thorp v Owen* (1843) 2 Hare 607.

[239]

3: POSSESSION AND INCIDENTS

98   Possession of trust estate

As against strangers, a trustee and his beneficiaries are regarded in equity as one person,
so that possession of the trust property, whether real or personal, by the beneficiaries is,
in general, possession by the trustee[1]. Similarly, while the relation between trustee and
beneficiary subsists, the possession of the trust property by the trustee is the possession of
the beneficiaries[2]. If property is given to the trustee to sell, it remains in him for that
purpose until something is done to put an end to the character in which he stands[3]. The
trustee is bound to protect the interest of the beneficiaries and the length of time during
which he has omitted to discharge his trust is no bar to his power or duty to perform it[4].
Where a trustee has as such taken possession of trust property, he cannot hold it adversely
to the beneficiaries after his estate as trustee has determined[5]; his continuance in
possession is deemed that of the beneficiaries.

[240]

1   *Earl of Pomfret v Lord Windsor* (1752) 2 Ves Sen 472.
2   *Lord Grenville v Blyth* (1809) 16 Ves 224.
3   Trustees of a trust of land, which includes a trust for sale, have powers to postpone the sale indefinitely,
     despite any provision to the contrary made by the disposition on trust for sale: Trusts of Land and
     Appointment of Trustees Act 1996 ss 1(2)(a), 4(1) (37 Halsbury's Statutes (4th Edn) REAL
     PROPERTY).
4   *Chalmer v Bradley* (1819) 1 Jac & W 51. As to the effect of the running of time upon an action by a
     beneficiary under a trust see the Limitation Act 1980 s 21 (24 Halsbury's Statutes (4th Edn)
     LIMITATION OF ACTIONS).
5   See the Limitation Act 1980 s 21(1)(b), (2).

[241]

99   Trustees' liability for outgoings

The possession by a trustee of the legal estate or legal ownership of trust property invests
him with the legal burdens and privileges incident to that estate or ownership[1]. If the
estate is leasehold, he is liable to pay rent and perform the covenants under which it
is held[2].

1   *Burgess v Wheate, A-G v Wheate* (1759) 1 Eden 177.
2   *Walters v Northern Coal Mining Co* (1855) 5 De GM & G 629.

[242]

100   Trustees' liability for taxes

Trustees are liable to make returns and are assessable and chargeable to income tax and capital gains tax. The statutory income of trustees is calculated in the same way as for an individual by applying the rules of the Income and Corporation Taxes Act 1988 Schedules A to F. Although they may deduct expenses permitted by the appropriate schedule, they cannot deduct the expense of managing the trust itself, nor may they claim any personal reliefs since for this purpose, trustees are not 'individuals'[1]. The trustees are normally liable for income tax at the lower rate of 20%[2] only, irrespective of the amount of the trust income, although with discretionary and accumulation trusts liability is to pay tax at the rate applicable to trusts on income of the trust other than that applied in defraying administrative expenses (which remains taxed at the lower rate)[3].

Trustees may also be liable for inheritance tax and are under a duty to render accounts in relation to that tax[4].

1   For a full account of the income tax position of trustees see Paragraph 347 [956] et seq post; for capital gains tax see Paragraph 338 [896] et seq post.
2   See the Income and Corporation Taxes Act 1988 s 1A as inserted by the Finance Act 1996 s 73(1), (3) and as amended (42–44 Halsbury's Statutes (4th Edn) TAXATION).
3   See the Income and Corporation Taxes Act 1988 ss 686, 687 as amended; see also Paragraph 348 [959] post.
4   See generally the Inheritance Tax Act 1984 ss 199–214, 216, 217 (42–44 Halsbury's Statutes (4th Edn) TAXATION); see further Paragraph 283 [712] et seq post.

[243]–[250]

B: ACCEPTANCE OF THE TRUST

101   Mode of acceptance

Acceptance of office may be either express, for example, by execution of the deed by which the appointment is made or by verbal assent[1], or inferred from the conduct of the person nominated[2], or perhaps by lapse of time. To avoid doubt, every person who is to be appointed trustee by deed should be made a party to and execute such deed.

1   *Doe d Chidgey v Harris* (1847) 16 M & W 517.
2   *Conyngham v Conyngham* (1750) 1 Ves Sen 522.

[251]

102   Acceptance or disclaimer of whole

A trustee must accept the trust as a whole. He is not permitted to accept the office as regards part of the trust property and at the same time refuse it in respect of some other part. A partial disclaimer has no effect and any purported acceptance of part is treated as acceptance of the whole[1].

(For a detailed discussion of disclaimer of trusts see vol 40(2) (2001 Reissue) TRUSTS AND SETTLEMENTS Part 10 [5201].)

1   *Re Lord and Fullerton's Contract* [1896] 1 Ch 228, CA. A personal representative who is not a trustee of a settlement of land may (inter alia) before representation has been granted, renounce his office in respect of the settled land without renouncing it as regards other property: Administration of Estates Act 1925 s 23(1) (17 Halsbury's Statutes (4th Edn) EXECUTORS AND ADMINISTRATORS).

[252]

C: RELEASE OF TRUSTEES ON DETERMINATION OF TRUST

103   General

Where a trustee pays income or transfers capital in strict accordance with the terms of a clearly defined trust, he may on the termination of the trust require an acknowledgement that the accounts are settled[1]. It is usual on the distribution of the trust fund for the beneficiaries to execute a release. Although a trustee may strictly not be entitled to such[2], in practice it is not objected to and affords protection to the trustee. In cases where the trustee is requested to deal with property in a manner differing from the strict tenor of the trust, he can demand a formal release by deed.

---

1   *Chadwick v Heatley* (1845) 2 Coll 137. If an acknowledgement is refused, he can insist on the account being taken by the court: *Re Wright's Trusts* (1857) 3 K & J 419.
2   *King v Mullins* (1852) 1 Drew 308 at 311. In many cases the receipt of the beneficiary is a sufficient discharge: *Re Robert's Trusts* (1869) 38 LJ Ch 708 at 709.

[253]

104   Discharge of trustees under the Settled Land Act 1925

Where the estate owner of land settled under the Settled Land Act 1925 holds the land free from all equitable interests and powers under the trust instrument, the trustees must at the cost of the trust estate execute a deed declaring that they are discharged from the trust as regards that land[1]. If they refuse, or if the discharge cannot be executed without undue delay or expense, the court may make an order[2]. In the absence of a statement in the deed or order of discharge to the contrary, a purchaser may assume that the land has ceased to be settled land and is not subject to a trust of land[3].

Until there is a deed of discharge, the legal estate in land which has become the subject of a vesting deed can only be disposed of in pursuance of the statutory powers or any extended powers in the settlement, and a conveyance to a purchaser is only to take effect if any capital money is paid to or by the direction of the trustees (being at least two persons or a trust corporation) or into court[4]; but this restriction does not affect the right of a person of full age who has become absolutely entitled (whether beneficially or as trustee of land, or as personal representative or otherwise) to the settled land, free from all limitations, powers and charges taking effect under the trust instrument, to require the land to be conveyed to him[5].

[254]

---

1   Settled Land Act 1925 s 17(1) (48 Halsbury's Statutes (4th Edn) TRUSTS AND SETTLEMENTS). See, however, the Settled Land Act 1925 s 17(1) proviso as amended by the Trusts of Land and Appointment of Trustees Act 1996 s 25(1), Sch 3 para 2(6)(a) where the trustees have notice of a derivative settlement or trust of land or equitable charge.
      Where a trustee under the Settled Land Act 1925 is discharged without fresh appointment, otherwise than on the termination of the settlement, a deed must be executed supplemental to the last or only principal vesting instrument containing a declaration that the persons named in it are the future trustees for the purpose of the Act and a memorandum must be indorsed on or annexed to the last or only principal vesting instrument in accordance with the Trustee Act 1925 (48 Halsbury's Statutes (4th Edn) TRUSTS AND SETTLEMENTS): see the Settled Land Act 1925 s 35(1). The persons required to execute the deed are specified in the Settled Land Act 1925 s 35(2) and the effect of the declaration on purchasers is contained in the Settled Land Act 1925 s 35(3).
2   Settled Land Act 1925 s 17(2) as amended by the Trusts of Land and Appointment of Trustees Act 1996 s 25(1), Sch 3 para 2(6)(b).

3   Settled Land Act 1925 s 17(3) as amended by the Trusts of Land and Appointment of Trustees Act 1996
     s 25(1), Sch 3 para 2(6)(c). In simple cases, a discharge of trustees is often included in a deed by which
     the settlement is brought to an end and not made the subject of a separate document. An informal
     discharge may be effected under the Settled Land Act 1925 s 110(5) as amended by the Trusts of Land
     and Appointment of Trustees Act 1996 s 25(1), Sch 3 para 2(12). In the case of registered land see the
     Land Registration Act 1925 s 87(4) (37 Halsbury's Statutes (4th Edn) REAL PROPERTY) and the Land
     Registration Rules 1925, SR & O 1925/1093 r 106.
4   Settled Land Act 1925 ss 17(3), 18(1).
5   Settled Land Act 1925 s 18(2)(b) as amended by the Trusts of Land and Appointment of Trustees Act
     1996 s 25(1), Sch 3 para 2(7); Land Registration Act 1925 s 87(6).

[255]

D: DEVOLUTION ON DEATH OF A TRUSTEE

105   Devolution to survivor of trustees

Trustees are joint tenants of the trust estate and on the death of one trustee the estate
vests in the survivor or survivors[1]. Therefore, the remaining trustee or trustees can carry
on with the running of the trust and there is no need to replace the deceased trustee
except where this is necessary to comply with the terms of the trust[2] or a statutory
provision[3], or is desirable in the interests of good administration. The trust property vests
automatically in the surviving trustee or trustees but proper steps should be taken to bring
up to date any document of title or register reflecting ownership of the trust property[4].

[256]

1   Trustee Act 1925 s 18(1) (48 Halsbury's Statutes (4th Edn) TRUSTS AND SETTLEMENTS).
2   Certain powers may be expressed as being exercisable provided that there are at least two or more
     trustees.
3   The statutory provision by which a receipt in writing of a trustee for money or other personal property
     is in general a sufficient discharge to the person paying or delivering the same does not, except where
     the trustee is a trust corporation, enable a sole trustee to give a valid receipt for the proceeds of sale or
     other capital money arising under a trust of land or capital money arising under the Settled Land Act
     1925 (48 Halsbury's Statutes (4th Edn) TRUSTS AND SETTLEMENTS): see the Trustee Act 1925 s 14
     as amended by the Law of Property (Amendment) Act 1926 s 7, 8(2), Schedule, the Trusts of Land and
     Appointment of Trustees Act 1996 s 25(1), Sch 3 para 3(3) and the Trustee Act 2000 Sch 2 para 19;
     see also the Law of Property Act 1925 s 27(2) as substituted by the Law of Property (Amendment) Act
     1926 s 7, Schedule and amended by the Trusts of Land and Appointment of Trustees Act 1996 s 25(1),
     Sch 3 para 4(8)(b) (37 Halsbury's Statutes (4th Edn) REAL PROPERTY); and see the Settled Land Act
     1925 s 94.
4   Eg if the trustees hold land on a trust of land with an unregistered title, a copy of the death certificate
     should be placed with the title documents; in the case of registered title, the death certificate and land
     certificate should be forwarded to the appropriate district land registry with a request to delete the
     deceased trustee's name from the proprietorship register. Similarly, where the trust holds shares and
     similar investments, application should be made to amend the appropriate register and for the issue of
     a new share certificate showing the present trustees.

[257]

106   Devolution on death of sole trustee

On the death of a sole or last surviving trustee, the trust property and all trust powers vest
in his personal representatives[1]. The personal representatives may exercise all the powers
of the former trustee although they are not obliged to do so[2]. Consequently, they may
decline to accept the position and duties of a trustee if they so wish[3]. Otherwise, the
personal representatives can act until such time as new trustees are appointed[4].

[258]

1   Trustee Act 1925 s 18(2) (48 Halsbury's Statutes (4th Edn) TRUSTS AND SETTLEMENTS). 'Personal
     representative' does not include an executor who has renounced or who has not proved: Trustee Act
     1925 s 18(4).
2   Trustee Act 1925 s 18(2).
3   *Re Benett, Ward v Benett* [1906] 1 Ch 216 at 225, CA.
4   The powers given to the personal representatives by the Trustee Act 1925 s 18(2) take effect subject to
     the restrictions imposed in regard to receipts by a sole trustee, not being a trust corporation: Trustee
     Act 1925 s 18(3). It is not certain whether the Trustee Act 1925 s 18(2) enables the personal
     representatives of a sole surviving trustee, if two or more persons, to give a receipt for capital money
     received on the exercise of a trust of land. They can only (in the words of the Trustee Act 1925 s 18(2))
     exercise any power which was capable of being exercised by the sole or last surviving trustee; but since
     there are in fact two persons to receive the money, the statutory requirement appears to be satisfied.
         In the case of trustees of a settlement under the Settled Land Act 1925 (48 Halsbury's Statutes
     (4th Edn) TRUSTS AND SETTLEMENTS) the above problem does not arise, since the Settled Land Act
     1925 s 95 makes valid the receipt of: (1) the trustees (being two or more, as required by Settled Land
     Act 1925 s 94); (2) a sole trustee where a trust corporation; or (3) the personal representatives of the
     last surviving or continuing trustee. The personal representatives (if two or more) can therefore give
     receipts for money or securities payable or transferable under the Settled Land Act 1925.

                                                                                          [259]–[265]

(6) LAND SETTLED ON A TRUST OF LAND

*(For a detailed commentary on the provisions of the Trusts of Land and Appointment of Trustees
Act 1996 Parts I and III see further vol 40(2) (2001 Reissue) TRUSTS AND SETTLEMENTS Part 8
[3001]. As to the appointment and retirement of trustees under Part II of the Act see vol 40(2)
Part 10 [5201].)*

107   Land settled by way of trust for sale before 1 January 1997

As has previously been noted[1] there were two methods of settling land available before
the coming into force of the Trusts of Land and Appointment of Trustees Act 1996 on
1 January 1997; namely the strict settlement under the Settled Land Act 1925[2], and the
settlement by means of a trust for sale. Where the latter method was employed, which
for many years had been the more popular alternative, the legal estate in the land was
held by the trustees and the beneficial interests were in the net proceeds of sale. While
the beneficial interests might be the same as those under a strict settlement, the most
common function of the trust for sale was as a device for holding land where the interests
were concurrent: as where the land was purchased by a husband and wife to hold as
beneficial joint tenants or tenants in common.

If a legal estate in land was settled inter vivos on trust for sale, the usual practice was
for the legal estate to be conveyed to the trustees on trust to sell and to hold the net
proceeds of sale, and the net rents and profits of the land until sale, on the trusts declared
by a deed of even date.

There was no statutory provision requiring the transaction to be carried out by means
of two deeds, and a purchaser was not concerned with the trusts affecting the proceeds
of sale even if those trusts were declared by the same instrument by which the trust for
sale was created. It was, however, clearly convenient to carry out the transaction by two
separate deeds, so that on a sale the conveyance could be handed over to the purchaser
and the settlement retained by the trustees[3].

A trust for sale also arose by statute in a number of cases[4].

1   See Paragraph 19 [56] ante.
2   As to settlements under the Settled Land Act 1925 see vol 40(2) (2001 Reissue) TRUSTS AND SETTLEMENTS Part 9 [4101].
3   As to the use of two instruments see further vol 40(2) (2001 Reissue) TRUSTS AND SETTLEMENTS Part 8 [3001].
4   See eg the Law of Property Act 1925 ss 31(1), 32(1), 34(2), (3), 36(1) now amended or repealed (37 Halsbury's Statutes (4th Edn) REAL PROPERTY); Administration of Estates Act 1925 s 33 now amended (17 Halsbury's Statutes (4th Edn) EXECUTORS AND ADMINISTRATORS).

[266]

108   Trusts of land

The trust for sale was not abolished by the Trusts of Land and Appointment of Trustees Act 1996[1], but it is now subsumed within a 'trust of land' as defined in that Act. This phrase means any trust of property which consists of or includes land[2], and the reference to a trust is to any description of trust (whether express, implied, resulting or constructive), including a trust for sale and a bare trust[3]. The Act applies to trusts whenever created or arising[4]. Land held on charitable, ecclesiastical or public trusts is included, even if it was, or was deemed to be, settled land within the Settled Land Act 1925 before 1 January 1997[5].

Trusts of land can be regarded as a development of trusts for sale and are used for the same purposes. A trust of land should be carried out by means of two deeds, as was the usual practice before 1 January 1997 in relation to a trust for sale[6], but it remains the case that it is not essential, and even if two deeds are not used a purchaser is not concerned with the trusts of the land or the proceeds of sale[7].

The abolition of the doctrine of conversion in relation to the trust for sale has the effect that whether or not an express trust for sale is created, which is still possible, the beneficiaries have an interest in land and not merely in the proceeds of sale[8]. In every case the trustees now have a power to postpone sale of the land, notwithstanding any provision to the contrary that may be made by the disposition[9], whenever the trust was created[10]. The difference made by the imposition of a trust for sale is that, as was the case before 1 January 1997[11], it imposes a duty to sell, and the power to postpone which the trustees now always have can only be exercised by unanimity.

Since the Trusts of Land and Appointment of Trustees Act 1996 came into force there are no situations where a trust for sale is imposed by statute, and most of the statutory provisions which before 1 January 1997 imposed a trust for sale have been amended so as to transmute the trust for sale into a trust of the land without a duty to sell[12].

[267]

1   The statutory definition of a trust for sale in the Law of Property Act 1925 s 205(1)(xxix) (37 Halsbury's Statutes (4th Edn) REAL PROPERTY) has, however, been amended. As originally enacted it read: 'Trust for sale, in relation to land, means an immediate binding trust for sale, whether or not exercisable at the request or with the consent of any person, and with or without a power at discretion to postpone the sale'. By the Trusts of Land and Appointment of Trustees Act 1996 s 25(2), Sch 4 (37 Halsbury's Statutes (4th Edn) REAL PROPERTY), the word 'binding' and the words 'and with' onwards have been repealed. For a discussion of the sections of this Act see vol 40(2) (2001 Reissue) TRUSTS AND SETTLEMENTS Part 8 [3001].
2   Trusts of Land and Appointment of Trustees Act 1996 s 1(1)(a). 'Land' has the same meaning as in the Law of Property Act 1925: Trusts of Land and Appointment of Trustees Act 1996 s 23(2). See further the Law of Property Act 1925 s 205(1)(ix) as amended by the Trusts of Land and Appointment of Trustees Act 1996 s 25(2), Sch 4.
3   Trusts of Land and Appointment of Trustees Act 1996 s 1(2)(a). The Act does not apply to existing settlements under the Settled Land Act 1925, nor to land to which the Universities and College Estates Act 1925 applies: Trusts of Land and Appointment of Trustees Act 1996 s 1(3).
4   Trusts of Land and Appointment of Trustees Act 1996 s 1(2)(b).
5   Trusts of Land and Appointment of Trustees Act 1996 s 2(5).

6   Although the Land Registration Act 1925 (37 Halsbury's Statutes (4th Edn) REAL PROPERTY) does not require use of a separate trust deed as such, it is clear from the Land Registration Act 1925 s 74, which provides that neither the Registrar nor any person dealing with a registered estate shall be affected with notice of any trust and that reference to trusts shall, so far as possible, be excluded from the register, that a separate trust deed is appropriate in the case of registered land: see further Paragraph 111 [272] post. A further reason to prefer two deeds is that a transfer to trustees containing trust provisions would be retained by the Land Registry and would therefore not be available for reference.

7   The theoretical basis for overreaching is more confused than ever. The Law of Property Act 1925 s 2(1)(ii) as amended by the Trusts of Land and Appointment of Trustees Act 1996 Sch 3 para 4(2) provides for overreaching in the case of trusts of land either under the provisions of the Law of Property Act 1925 s 2(2) (which is limited to ad hoc trusts of land) or 'independently of that sub-section' provided, in both cases, that capital money is paid in accordance with the Law of Property Act 1925 s 27 as amended by the Trusts of Land and Appointment of Trustees Act 1996 Sch 3 para 4(8) (ie to two trustees or a trust corporation). The Law of Property Act 1925 s 27 does not make it clear that the protection in the Law of Property Act 1925 s 27(1) is dependent on the Law of Property Act 1925 s 27(2) procedure being followed, although that is how the section has been interpreted.

     Prior to 1 January 1997, overreaching outside the Law of Property Act 1925 s 2(2) was explicable in the case of trusts for sale on the basis of the doctrine of conversion: *City of London Building Society v Flegg* [1988] AC 54, [1987] 3 All ER 435, HL. With the abolition of that doctrine in the Trusts of Land and Appointment of Trustees Act 1996 s 3, a new basis has to be found for overreaching in the case of trusts for land which presumably lies in the powers of sale enjoyed by the trustees: Trusts of Land and Appointment of Trustees Act 1996 s 6(1) as amended by the Trustee Act 2000 Sch 2 para 45(1). See generally Whitehouse and Hassall: *Trusts of Land, Trustee Delegation and the Trustee Act 2000* (2nd Edn, 2001) paras 1.18–26 and 6.63–64; and see the comments of Charles Harpum in 'Overreaching, Trustees' Powers and the Reform of the 1925 Legislation' (1990) 49 CLJ 300. See also *Birmingham Midshires Mortgage Services Ltd v Sabherwal* (2000) 80 P & CR 256, CA, [2000] Conv 267 (M Dixon), [2001] Conv 221 (G Ferris and G Battersby).

     Provisions for the protection of purchasers are contained in the Trusts of Land and Appointment of Trustees Act 1996 s 16.

8   Trusts of Land and Appointment of Trustees Act 1996 s 3(1). The Section excludes a trust created by will if the testator died before 1 January 1997: Trusts of Land and Appointment of Trustees Act 1996 s 3(2).

9   Trusts of Land and Appointment of Trustees Act 1996 s 4(1).

10   Trusts of Land and Appointment of Trustees Act 1996 s 4(2).

11   See *Re Mayo, Mayo v Mayo* [1943] Ch 302, [1943] 2 All ER 440.

12   Trusts of Land and Appointment of Trustees Act 1996 s 5, Sch 2.

[268]

109   Number of trustees

It is not necessary to have more than one trustee of a conveyance on trust of land, but in practice at least two trustees (or a trust corporation) should be appointed, because it will be impossible to carry out a transaction in which capital money arises unless there are at least two trustees or the trustee is a trust corporation[1]. The number of the trustees must not exceed four[2]. If more than four persons are named as trustees the first four named (who are able and willing to act) will alone be the trustees[3].

1   See the Law of Property Act 1925 s 27(2) as substituted by the Law of Property (Amendment) Act 1926 s 7, Schedule and amended by the Trusts of Land and Appointment of Trustees Act 1996 s 25(1), Sch 3 para 4(8)(b) (37 Halsbury's Statutes (4th Edn) REAL PROPERTY). This provision does not affect the right of a sole personal representative as such to give valid receipts for, or direct the application of, proceeds of sale or other capital money. As to the meaning of 'trust corporation' see the Law of Property Act 1925 s 205(1)(xxviii) as extended by the Law of Property (Amendment) Act 1926 s 3.

     Even when a transfer of registered land is to a sole trustee, the transferee is still under an obligation to apply for the usual trustee restriction preventing dispositions by a sole trustee (other than a trust corporation) where capital money arises: see the Land Registration Rules 1925, SR & O 1925/1093 rr 213, 236, (both substituted by SI 1996/2975) Sch 2 Form 62 (as substituted by SI 1989/801 and amended by SI 1996/2975).

2   Trustee Act 1925 s 34(2) as amended by the Trusts of Land and Appointment of Trustees Act 1996 s 25(1), Sch 3 para 3(9) (48 Halsbury's Statutes (4th Edn) TRUSTS AND SETTLEMENTS).

3   Trustee Act 1925 s 34(2)(a). This restriction does not apply in the case of land vested in trustees for charitable, ecclesiastical, or public purposes, or where the net proceeds of sale are held for like purposes: Trustee Act 1925 s 34(3).

[269]

110   New trustees after constitution of trust of land

After the trust of land has been constituted, appointments of new trustees[1] of land on the one hand and of new trustees of any trust of the proceeds of sale on the other hand must, subject to any order of the court, be effected by separate instruments, but in such manner as to secure that the same persons become trustees of land and trustees of the settlement of the proceeds of sale[2].

Where new trustees of land are appointed, a memorandum of the persons who are for the time being the trustees of the land must be indorsed on or annexed to the conveyance by which the land was vested in trustees of land and that conveyance must be produced to the persons who are for the time being the trustees of the land by the person in possession of it in order for that to be done when the trustees require its production[3]. As regards registered land, memoranda cannot be endorsed on transfers which are retained in the Land Registry; instead, the correct procedure is to ensure that the new trustees are registered as proprietors of the land in place of the old trustees or, in the case of settled land where the tenant for life is the registered proprietor, application should be made by the previous trustees, the new trustees, the continuing trustees and the tenant for life in Form 77 for the restriction in Form 9 to be modified so as to substitute the new trustees for the old trustees[4].

[270]

---

1   'New trustee' includes an additional trustee: Trustee Act 1925 s 68(17) (48 Halsbury's Statutes (4th Edn) TRUSTS AND SETTLEMENTS).

2   Law of Property Act 1925 s 24 as substituted by the Trusts of Land and Appointment of Trustees Act 1996 s 25(1), Sch 3 para 4(7) (37 Halsbury's Statutes (4th Edn) REAL PROPERTY); Trustee Act 1925 s 35(1) as substituted by the Trusts of Land and Appointment of Trustees Act 1996 s 25(1), Sch 3 para 3(10)(a).

3   Trustee Act 1925 s 35(3) as substituted by the Trusts of Land and Appointment of Trustees Act 1996 s 25(1), Sch 3 para 3(10)(b). There is no statutory provision requiring a memorandum to be indorsed on or annexed to the conveyance on the discharge of a trustee under the Trustee Act 1925 s 39(1) as amended by the Trusts of Land and Appointment of Trustees Act 1996 s 25(1), Sch 3 para 3(13), but the same course should be followed in that case.

4   See the Land Registration Rules 1925, SR & O 1925/1093 r 236B (substituted by SI 1996/2975), Sch 2, Form 77 (amended by SI 1996/2975, SI 1997/3037 and SI 1999/128).

[271]

111   Trust of land of registered land

The Land Registration Act 1925 gives effect to the general scheme of the Law of Property Act 1925 and the Trusts of Land and Appointment of Trustees Act 1996 with regard to trusts of land when they affect registered land. Where registered land is subject to a trust of land, the land must be registered in the names of the trustees or in the name of a nominee appointed under the Trustee Act 2000 Section 16[1]. There must also be entered on the register such restrictions as may be prescribed, or may be expedient, for the protection of the rights of the persons beneficially interested in the land[2]. The beneficial interests under the trust are accordingly kept behind the curtain of the registered legal estate[3] so that they can be overridden on a sale by the trustees. It is expressly provided by the Land Registration Act 1925[4] that, subject to its provisions as to settled land, neither the Registrar nor any person dealing with a registered estate is to be affected with notice of an express, implied or constructive trust and that references to trusts are, as far as possible, to be excluded from the register.

If registered land is to be settled inter vivos on trust, this should be effected by two instruments; namely a trust instrument executed off the register[5] setting out the terms of the trust and an instrument of transfer following the registered form[6] transferring the registered estate to the trustees to hold on the trusts contained in the trust instrument[7].

On registering the transfer, the Registrar will enter a restriction on the register to the effect that no disposition by one proprietor of the land, being the survivor of joint proprietors and not being a trust corporation, under which capital money arises is to be registered except under an order of the Registrar or of the court[8]. This restriction accords with the statutory provisions relating to the payment of capital money[9]. In view of the wide statutory powers conferred on trustees of land, it is not the usual practice to enter any further general restriction on the register. Nevertheless, if some express limitation on their powers is contained in the trust instrument, as, for example, where there is a provision that the land is not to be sold without the consent of one of the beneficiaries, it will be the duty of the trustees to apply for a further restriction as appropriate[10]. If there is a change in the trustees, the necessary alteration will have to be made to the names of the proprietors entered on the register[11].

[272]

1   Land Registration Act 1925 s 94(1) as substituted by the Trusts of Land and Appointment of Trustees Act 1996 s 25(1), Sch 3 para 5(8)(a) and amended by the Trustee Act 2000 Sch 2 para 26 (37 Halsbury's Statutes (4th Edn) REAL PROPERTY). As to transitional provisions see the Land Registration Act 1925 ss 78, 94(3) as amended by the Trusts of Land and Appointment of Trustees Act 1996 s 25(1), Sch 3 para 5(6), (8); the Land Registration Rules 1925, SR & O 1925/1093 r 134 as amended by SI 1996/2975. The statutory restrictions as to the number of trustees apply: see the Land Registration Act 1925 s 95 as amended by the Trusts of Land and Appointment of Trustees Act 1996 s 25, Sch 3 para 5(9) and Paragraph 109 [269] ante.
2   Land Registration Act 1925 s 94(4) as inserted by the Trusts of Land and Appointment of Trustees Act 1996 s 25(1), Sch 3 para 5(8)(c).
3   The beneficial interests take effect as minor interests: see the Land Registration Act 1925 ss 3(xv), 101 as amended by the Trusts of Land and Appointment of Trustees Act 1996 s 25(1), Sch 3 para 5(2). See further vol 25(1) (1999 Reissue) LAND REGISTRATION Paragraph 11 [1601] et seq.
4   Land Registration Act 1925 s 74.
5   See the Land Registration Act 1925 ss 74, 101.
6   See vol 25(1) (1999 Reissue) LAND REGISTRATION Paragraph 98 [2064] et seq.
7   On registration, the transfer will be retained in the Land Registry: SR & O 1925/1093 r 90.
8   Land Registration Act 1925 s 58(3); SR & O 1925/1093 rr 213, 236, (both substituted by SI 1996/2975) Sch 2 Form 62 (as substituted by SI 1989/801 and amended by SI 1996/2975). For the usual form of restriction see vol 40(2) (2001 Reissue) TRUSTS AND SETTLEMENTS Part 8 [3501]. The Registrar is only obliged to enter the restriction where there is a transfer to joint proprietors. In other cases, such as a transfer to a sole trustee, or a declaration of trust by registered proprietors without an accompanying transfer, it is the duty of the trustee(s) to apply for the restriction.
9   Law of Property Act 1925 s 27(2) as substituted by the Law of Property (Amendment) Act 1926 s 7, Schedule and amended by the Trusts of Land and Appointment of Trustees Act 1996 s 25(1), Sch 3 para 4(8)(b) (37 Halsbury's Statutes (4th Edn) REAL PROPERTY).
10 See SR & O 1925/1093 rr 59A, 106A, 236, Sch 2 Form 11A as inserted by SI 1996/2975.
11 See further the Land Registration Act 1925 s 47; and the Trustee Act 1925 s 40 as amended by the Trusts of Land and Appointment of Trustees Act 1996 s 25(1), Sch 3 para 3(14) (48 Halsbury's Statutes (4th Edn) TRUSTS AND SETTLEMENTS).

[273]–[274]

(7) PERSONALTY SETTLEMENTS

A: FORM

112   Form of personalty settlements made otherwise than on marriage

The form of settlements of personalty made otherwise than on marriage will vary with the objects whom the settlor desires to benefit and to a certain extent the property available for settlement. The primary purpose of many settlements is the mitigation of the burden of tax which would otherwise fall on the settlor or his estate[1], and attention is usually paid also to the potential liability of individual beneficiaries or their estates in deciding on the form of settlement.

1   As to taxation generally see further Paragraph 282 [711] et seq post.

[275]

B: NATURE OF PROPERTY

113   Stocks and shares

Stocks and shares are possibly the most frequent subject of personalty settlements. A voluntary settlement of the stocks and shares of public and private companies requires the transfer of them to the trustees in accordance with the regulations of the company concerned, or, if the company is registered abroad, in accordance with the law of the country where that company is registered[1]. In the case of government stocks and funds the transfer is effected by entry in the books of the Bank of England[2]. Bearer securities are transferred by delivery[3]. The transfer of local government stock is regulated by special provisions[4]. In each case the settlement normally recites that the transfer has been, or is intended to be, made, as the case may be[5].

[276]

1   As to the transfer of shares generally see vol 10 COMPANIES (2001 Reissue) Paragraph 181 [958] et seq. The settlor must have done everything which was in his power to do: see *Re Rose, Midland Bank Executor and Trustee Co Ltd v Rose* [1949] Ch 78, [1948] 2 All ER 971 (transfer complete but registration of transfer required). A settlement may itself operate as an effective disposition of the equitable interest of the settlor where the legal title is outstanding at the date of the settlement: see *Re Wale, Wale v Harris* [1956] 3 All ER 280, [1956] 1 WLR 1346.
2   See the Government Stock Regulations 1965, SI 1965/1420 regs 4–11 as amended by SI 1981/1004, SI 1985/1146, SI 1990/2253, SI 1997/1709 and SI 2000/1681.
3   Bearer securities must, in general, be held by a custodian: see Paragraph 249 [617] post.
4   As to the transfer of local government stock see vol 26 (2000 Reissue) LOCAL GOVERNMENT AND RATING Paragraph 62 [135] et seq.
5   An erroneous recital that investments have been transferred does not invalidate the settlement if, on its true construction, it operates as an equitable assignment of the settlor's interest in them: see *Re Wale, Wale v Harris* [1956] 3 All ER 280, [1956] 1 WLR 1346.

[277]

114   Debts

A debt is normally settled by assignment to the trustees of the settlement. Such an assignment, coupled with notice in writing of it to the debtor, vests in the trustees the legal right to the debt and the remedies for it, with power to give a good discharge[1]. Money secured by a mortgage is settled by transferring the mortgage[2] to the trustees by one deed, without disclosing that the mortgage debt is trust money, and declaring the trusts by another. This avoids the inconvenience that would otherwise arise on the sale or redemption of the mortgaged property, of having to produce and acknowledge the right to production of the deed containing the trusts, and for similar reasons, a portion charged on land is settled by assigning it to the trustees of the settlement by a separate deed.

1   See the Law of Property Act 1925 s 136(1) (37 Halsbury's Statutes (4th Edn) REAL PROPERTY).
2   For transfers of a mortgage and registered charge by way of gift see vol 17(2) (2000 Reissue) GIFTS Form 47 [1667], Form 48 [1670].

[278]

115   Reversionary interests

A reversionary interest is settled by assignment to the trustees of the settlement, who should perfect their title, as in the case of other choses in action, by giving notice in writing of the assignment to the trustees of the instrument under which the reversionary interest is derived[1]. The principle on which the court acts in discouraging dealings by expectant heirs with their reversionary interests has no application to the case of a settlement by an expectant heir[2].

1   For forms of assignment of reversionary interests see Form 310 [2142] post and see vol 7 (1994 Reissue) CHOSES IN ACTION Form 84 [767] et seq.
2   *Shafto v Adams* (1864) 4 Giff 492. As to bargains with expectant heirs see 18 Halsbury's Laws (4th Edn) para 345 et seq. The treatment of reversionary interests as 'excluded property' has encouraged their settlement as part of an inheritance tax mitigation exercise.

[279]

116   Share of personalty under or in default of appointment

A fund or share of a fund of personalty to which the settlor is entitled, either under or in default of appointment, in the estate of a testator or intestate, is settled by assigning to the trustees the settlor's interest[1]. This should be described with precision, since settlements of an interest in a fund derived, under a will, by survivorship, or otherwise, do not include a share in the fund coming to the settlor as next of kin of another beneficiary under the will, and shares taken under appointments do not pass under settlements which deal with shares in the same property taken in default of appointment[2].

[280]

1   For forms of assignments of interests in trust funds see vol 7 (1994 Reissue) CHOSES IN ACTION Form 81 [755] et seq.
2   *Re Newbolt's Trust* (1856) 4 WR 735; cf *Re Walpole's Marriage Settlement, Thomson v Walpole* [1903] 1 Ch 928; *Re Dowie's Will Trusts, Re Marriage Settlement of September 24 1936, Barlas v Pennefather* [1949] Ch 547, [1949] 1 All ER 968. In the case of a settlement for valuable consideration, a purported assignment of an interest in a fund to which the settlor has no title will catch any interest in the fund subsequently acquired by him: *Re Harper's Settlement, Williams v Harper* [1919] 1 Ch 270.

[281]

117   Policies of insurance

Policies of insurance, generally on the life of the settlor, are frequently made the subject of settlements[1]. The settlement may either declare the trusts of money to arise from a policy, which is taken out by the trustees in their own names[2], or more usually the settlor will take out the policy in his own name and assign it to the trustees to be held upon the trusts declared by the settlement. The trustees should give notice in writing of such assignment to the insurance company[3]. An assignment of a policy generally carries with it any bonuses or profits which may accrue[4], although the settlor may be entitled to exercise any option that is given him by the rules of the insurance company to apply the bonuses or profits in reduction of premiums or receive them in cash[5]. Where bonuses or profits are excluded from the settlement, the trustees who receive them are not allowed to retain them, as against the personal representatives of the settlor, to make good a misappropriation of trust funds by him[6].

[282]

A marriage settlement usually, and a voluntary settlement occasionally, contains covenants with the trustees by the person whose life is insured to pay the premiums, to effect a substituted policy if necessary, to observe and perform the other stipulations contained in the policy, not to avoid the policy, and not to prejudice the trustees' rights to the policy money. If the covenant is merely to keep up the policy, there is no right of action against the covenantor's estate on the forfeiture of the policy by reason of a breach of the stipulations contained in it[7]. In the case of those settlements where there is no such covenant, it is desirable on the payment of each premium for the settlor to address a short memorandum to the trustees indicating that the payment of the premium does not create any lien in his favour.

Failure to effect a substituted policy in pursuance of a covenant requiring it will render the covenantor liable in damages to the trustees, even though the reason for the failure is that his life has in fact become uninsurable[8]. If a settlor in breach of covenant allows a policy to become void, neither he nor his assigns can claim any interest in other property comprised in the settlement until the loss has been made good[9]. Failure to pay premiums gives the trustees a right to substantial damages[10], and, should the covenantor become bankrupt, his contingent future liability to pay premiums is a debt which may be proved in his bankruptcy[11]. It is always desirable for the trustees to be given the power to surrender the policy for a fully paid up one of a smaller amount.

Payment of the premiums may be further secured by trusts or powers directing or authorising the trustees to apply the income and even the capital of settled property in making such payment or to borrow money and use it for the purpose. Insurance companies often give undertakings to let some premium or premiums remain outstanding at interest on the security of the policies. In framing the trusts, the expectant character of the interest settled must be borne in mind, and the trusts of such policies as do, or may, give a right to any payment to the insured in the lifetime of the settlor should provide for the application of the income which may in his lifetime accrue from that money and its investments, as well as its yearly produce after his death. If the trustees may become entitled to options concerning the form in which they may receive benefit of bonuses, directions or powers should be given to them with reference to that choice.

[283]

Where a policy is subject to a charge or debt and is afterwards settled or assigned, care should be taken to make provision for how the charge is to be borne. Where the charge is not created by the settlor the grantee may be liable to discharge or contribute to the charge[12], but if the charge is a debt due by the settlor his estate may be required to bear it[13].

A trustee of the policy who pays the premium to prevent lapse is ordinarily entitled to a lien for repayment by reason of the right of trustees to indemnity out of their trust property[14]; but where the trustee of a term of years who is not trustee of the policy pays the premiums to prevent lapse, he has no lien[15]. A wife, however, who pays the premiums on her husband's life policies to prevent them lapsing has no lien on them for repayment[16]. Power to restore a policy does not authorise a new policy to replace one that has lapsed[17].

Covenants to substitute a new policy for one which had become void formerly required the new policy to be for the sum which would have been payable under that which had become void if the life had then determined. The modern variety in policies suggests that it is more practical for covenants to describe in more general terms the benefits to be secured, and also that it may be expedient to authorise the trustees to accept a new policy differing from the old one if, in the opinion of the trustees, it will not be less advantageous to the beneficiaries under the settlement generally[18].

[284]

1   For a life insurance settlement see Form 6 [1120] post. A covenant by an intending husband to effect a policy with an insurance company is not satisfied by effecting a less beneficial policy with a friendly society: *Courtenay v Courtenay* (1846) 3 Jo & Lat 519. For clauses for use in a life insurance settlement see Form 101 [1488] et seq post. For the voluntary assignment of a life insurance policy see Form 33 [1284] post.

2   *Tidswell v Ankerstein* (1792) Peake 151; *Collett v Morrison* (1851) 9 Hare 162. As relief is not available for policies issued after 13 March 1984: Income and Corporation Taxes Act 1988 s 266 as amended (42-44 Halsbury's Statutes (4th Edn) TAXATION).

3   See the Policies of Assurance Act 1867 s 3 (22 Halsbury's Statutes (4th Edn) INSURANCE). For a notice of assignment of a life policy see Form 298 [2084] post. A policy of insurance of his life subsequently effected by the settlor may be caught by a covenant by him to settle after-acquired property: *Re Turcan* (1888) 40 Ch D 5, CA.

4   Bonuses do not pass if the policies are only securities for a specified sum which is settled: *Domville v Lamb* (1853) 1 WR 246.

5   *Hughes v Searle* [1885] WN 79. The application of bonuses in reduction of premiums will reduce entitlement to tax relief on premiums: see *Watkins (Inspector of Taxes) v Jones* (1928) 14 TC 94; and see 23 Halsbury's Laws (4th Edn Reissue) para 976 et seq.

6   *Hallett v Hallett* (1879) 13 Ch D 232. The position is different where the claim is made under the trusts of the settlement: *Re Weston, Davies v Tagart* [1900] 2 Ch 164.

7   *Dormay v Borrodaile* (1874) 10 Beav 335. For a covenant see Form 102 [1489] post.

8   *Re Arthur, Arthur v Wynne* (1880) 14 Ch D 603.

9   *Re Jewell's Settlement, Watts v Public Trustee* [1919] 2 Ch 161.

10   *Schlesinger and Joseph v Mostyn* [1932] 1 KB 349.

11   See the Insolvency Act 1986 s 382 as amended by the Criminal Justice Act 1988 s 170(2), Sch 16 as from a day to be appointed (4 Halsbury's Statutes (4th Edn) BANKRUPTCY AND INSOLVENCY).

12   *Ker v Ker* (1869) IR 4 Eq 15, CA.

13   *Re Darby's Estate, Rendall v Darby* [1907] 2 Ch 465; *Re Best, Parker v Best* [1924] 1 Ch 42; and cf *Re Jones, Farrington v Forrester* [1893] 2 Ch 461; *Re Mainwaring, Mainwaring v Verden* [1937] Ch 96, [1936] 3 All ER 540, CA.

14   *Re Leslie, Leslie v French* (1883) 23 Ch D 552 (where the cases where lien may arise were considered by Pearson J) and cf *Re Foster, Hudson v Foster (No 2)* [1938] 3 All ER 610; *Schlesinger and Joseph v Mostyn* [1932] 1 KB 349.

15   *Re Earl of Winchilsea's Policy Trusts* (1888) 39 Ch D 168.

16   *Re Jones' Settlement, Stunt v Jones* [1915] 1 Ch 373.

17   *Re Jewell's Settlement, Watts v Public Trustee* [1919] 2 Ch 161.

18   For the taxation consequences involved in the settlement of a life insurance policy see Form 6 note 1 [1135] post.

[285]

118   Chattels

Chattels are sometimes made the subject of a settlement[1], which may provide that the beneficiaries should have the enjoyment of the settled chattels, and that the trustees should not interfere with the custody or management of them, or that the trustees should not be responsible for the custody, preservation, or insurance of the chattels against fire, or other damage or loss. It is expedient to provide for the substitution of new articles of equal value for those originally settled[2].

A settlement of chattels on marriage does not require registration as a bill of sale[3]. The transfer of chattels is usually effected by delivery.

[286]

1   As to settlements of chattels to devolve with land see vol 40(2) (2001 Reissue) TRUSTS AND SETTLEMENTS Part 9 [4101]. For a deed transferring chattels to trustees see Form 35 [1285] post.
2   For a case where new furniture was substituted see *Lane v Grylls* (1862) 6 LT 533.
3   See the Bills of Sale Act 1878 s 4 (5 Halsbury's Statutes (4th Edn) BILLS OF SALE). As to registration under this Act see vol 17(2) (2000 Reissue) GIFTS Paragraph 38 [675].

[287]

119   Other subjects of personalty settlements

Copyrights, patents, or a share in a partnership may be the subject of a settlement[1].

1   The mode of assignment of these types of property is discussed elsewhere in this work: see eg vol 21(1) (1997 Reissue) INTELLECTUAL PROPERTY Paragraph 82 [125] et seq, see vol 21(2) (1999 Reissue) INTELLECTUAL PROPERTY Paragraph 403 [3180], and see vol 30 (1996 Reissue) PARTNERSHIP Paragraph 73 [90] et seq. For a consideration of the position when the purported assignment is of future property see the discussion in *Williams v IRC* [1965] NZLR 395.

[288]

120   Trusts including both land and personalty

A trust including both land and personalty comes within the definition of a trust of land[1]. If all the land were to be sold by the trustees it would cease to be a trust of land. By contrast, if trustees of a fund made up entirely of pure personalty were to acquire land, they would become trustees of a trust of land.

1   Trusts of Land and Appointment of Trustees Act 1996 s 1(1)(a) (37 Halsbury's Statutes (4th Edn) REAL PROPERTY) and see Paragraph 108 [267] ante.

[289]–[300]

C: BENEFICIAL INTERESTS

1: LIFE AND LIMITED INTERESTS

121   Creation of life interests

In a marriage settlement of personalty the first life interest in the settled property is usually taken by whichever party to the marriage brings property into the settlement. If both parties bring property into the settlement, each, as a rule, takes the first life interest in the property settled by him or her; and, after the death of either spouse, the survivor[1] is generally given a life interest in the entire fund. Careful thought should be given to the incidence of inheritance tax and capital gains tax before creating life interests in voluntary settlements: often trustees are given power to determine the life interest in so far as it affects the whole or any part of the settled property prior to death[2]. Settlements on children, grandchildren and other objects of the settlor's bounty may take the form of a discretionary trust or a trust of income and capital accompanied by an overriding power of appointment, but for tax reasons an accumulation and maintenance settlement is usually preferred if it is appropriate in the circumstances[3].

[301]

1   A marriage settlement, in so far as it is not varied by the court, remains unaffected by the dissolution of the marriage: *Fitzgerald v Chapman* (1875) 1 Ch D 563. The interest of the survivor is sometimes made to determine on remarriage. A trust to pay the income of the husband's fund, after his death, to the wife during her life or until she marries again, is not determined, after the marriage has been dissolved, by her remarriage during the lifetime of the first husband: *Re Monro's Settlement, Monro v Hill* [1933] Ch 82. For inheritance tax purposes the spouse exemption may apply on the termination of the first life interest: see the Inheritance Tax Act 1984 s 18 (42–44 Halsbury's Statutes (4th Edn) TAXATION).

2   As to taxation generally see Paragraph 282 [711] et seq post. For a revocable life interest settlement see Form 5 [1107] post.

3   As to such trusts generally see Paragraph 127 [316] post; and vol 40(2) (2001 Reissue) TRUSTS AND SETTLEMENTS Part 11 [6301]. For specimen accumulation and maintenance settlements see vol 40(2) (2001 Reissue) TRUSTS AND SETTLEMENTS Part 11 [6501].

[302]

122   Acceleration of subsequent interests

The doctrine of acceleration usually arises in relation to gifts by will, but it may also apply to settlements[1]. Where there is a gift to a person for life, and a vested gift in remainder expressed to take effect on the death of the first taker, the gift in remainder is construed as a gift taking effect on the death of the first taker or on any earlier failure or determination of his interest; the result is that if the gift to the first taker fails in his lifetime or is disclaimed or surrendered, then the person entitled in remainder will take immediately on the failure or determination of the prior interest, and will not be kept waiting until the death of the first taker[2]. The principle applies to personalty as well as to realty[3], and applies if the remainder is vested, but subject to defeasance[4], but not if it is contingent[5].

[303]

1   See *Re Flower's Settlement Trusts, Flower v IRC* [1957] 1 All ER 462 at 465, [1957] 1 WLR 401 at 405, CA per Jenkins LJ; *Re Young's Settlement Trusts, Royal Exchange Assurance v Taylor-Young* [1959] 2 All ER 74 at 78, [1959] 1 WLR 457 at 462. See also *Re Dawson's Settlement, Lloyds Bank Ltd v Dawson* [1966] 3 All ER 68, [1966] 1 WLR 1456.

2   *Re Flower's Settlement Trusts, Flower v IRC* [1957] 1 All ER 462, [1957] 1 WLR 401 at 465, 405, CA per Jenkins LJ.

3   *Re Flower's Settlement Trusts, Flower v IRC* [1957] 1 All ER 462, [1957] 1 WLR 401 at 465, 405, CA per Jenkins LJ; *Re Hodge, Midland Bank Executor and Trustee Co Ltd v Morrison* [1943] Ch 300 at 301, [1943] 2 All ER 304 at 305 per Simonds J.

4   *Re Conyngham, Conyngham v Conyngham* [1921] 1 Ch 491, CA; *Re Taylor, Lloyds Bank Ltd v Jones* [1957] 3 All ER 56, [1957] 1 WLR 1043.

5   *Re Townsend's Estate, Townsend v Townsend* (1886) 34 Ch D 357. See *Re Bellville's Settlement, Westminster Bank Ltd v Bellville* [1964] Ch 163, [1963] 3 All ER 270. There is, however, no distinction drawn between vested and contingent interests where the person contingently entitled is in being and his interest is contingent on some personal qualification and in no way relates to the words of futurity or the determination of the prior interest: see *Re Dawson's Settlement, Lloyds Bank Ltd v Dawson* [1966] 3 All ER 68, [1966] 1 WLR 1456 (principle applied to accelerate the interest of beneficiary in being contingently upon the beneficiary attaining 21 or marrying). See also *Re Scott, Widdows v Friends of the Clergy Corpn* [1975] 2 All ER 1033 at 1041, [1975] 1 WLR 1260 at 1267 per Walton J: '... never has the doctrine of acceleration been used, nor, in my judgment, can it ever be used, to carry an interest to somebody to whom the testatrix never intended it to go, if something else happened, and that something else is still capable of happening.'

[304]

2: PROTECTED LIFE INTERESTS

(For a detailed consideration of protected life interests, together with a specimen protective trust, see vol 40(2) (2001 Reissue) TRUSTS AND SETTLEMENTS) Part 12 [6901].)

123   Protected life interests[1]

Protective trusts are primarily designed to guard against the possibility that the life tenant may be a spendthrift. They operate by a combination of a life interest determinable on specified events, including bankruptcy, followed by discretionary trusts. The statutory protective trusts[2] provide that where any income is held on protective trusts[3] for the benefit of any person ('the principal beneficiary') for his life or any lesser period, then during that period the income is to be held on trust for him unless and until he does anything or any event happens as a result of which if the income were payable to him he would be deprived of the right to receive it. This covers both voluntary alienation and involuntary inalienation on bankruptcy. If a determining event occurs discretionary trusts arise under which the trustees hold the income for such of the following persons as they in their absolute discretion select, namely:

123.1   the principal beneficiary, his or her wife or husband, and children or more remote issue; or

123.2   if there is no wife or husband or issue, the principal beneficiary and the persons who would be entitled to the trust property or the income if he were dead.

The statutory protective trusts take effect subject to any modifications in the trust instrument, but neither they, nor any express protective trusts, can operate so as to defeat the bankruptcy laws. Thus if a settlor settles property on protective trusts for himself for his life, on the one hand if he becomes bankrupt his life interest will vest indefeasibly in the trustee in bankruptcy[4], and, on the other hand if one of the other determining events is the first to happen, the life interest will automatically come to an end and if the life tenant subsequently becomes bankrupt the bankrupt will have no interest in the property which can pass to the trustee in bankruptcy[5].

[305]

1   For a detailed treatment of protective trusts see vol 40(2) (2001 Reissue) TRUSTS AND SETTLEMENTS Part 12 [6901].

2   See the Trustee Act 1925 s 33 as amended by the Family Law Reform Act 1987 s 33(1), Sch 2 para 2 (48 Halsbury's Statutes (4th Edn) TRUSTS AND SETTLEMENTS).

3   It is not necessary in order to invoke the section to use the words 'on protective trusts', provided the reference is sufficiently clear: see *Re Wittke, Reynolds and Gorst v King Edward's Hospital Fund for London and Custodian of Enemy Property* [1944] Ch 166, [1944] 1 All ER 383; *Re Platt, Westminster Bank v Platt* [1950] CLY 4386.

4   *Re Burroughs-Fowler, Trustee of the Property of Burroughs-Fowler (a bankrupt) v Burroughs-Fowler* [1916] 2 Ch 251.

5   *Re Richardson's Will Trusts, Public Trustee v Llewellyn-Evans' Trustee* [1958] Ch 504, [1958] 1 All ER 538.

[306]

3: BENEFICIARIES UNDER A DISCRETIONARY TRUST

124   Nature of discretionary trusts

Under a discretionary trust trustees are given a discretion to pay or apply income or capital, or both, to or for the benefit of all, or any one or more exclusively of the others, of a specified class or group of persons, no beneficiary being able to claim as of right that all or any part of the income or capital is to be paid to him or applied for his benefit. The trustees may therefore have power to decide both who shall benefit and what the benefits shall be. A potential beneficiary cannot be said to be the owner of an equitable interest in the trust property unless and until the trustees exercise their discretion in his favour.

A discretionary trust may be exhaustive, that is where the trustees are bound to distribute the whole income, but have a discretion as to how the distribution is to be made between the objects. Alternatively, a discretionary trust may be non-exhaustive, in which case the trustees have a discretion not only as to how the distribution is to be made, but also as to whether and to what extent it is to be made at all. It is thought that the term 'non-exhaustive discretionary trust' in fact conceals the two alternatives of a power of distribution coupled with a trust to dispose of the undistributed surplus, by accumulation or otherwise, and a trust for distribution coupled with a power to withhold a portion and accumulate or otherwise dispose of it[1].

[307]

The objects of a discretionary non-exhaustive trust do not have concurrent interests in the income, nor do they have a group interest[2]. They all have individual rights: they are in competition with each other and what the trustees give to one is his alone. The reference to a class or group of objects under a discretionary trust is merely a convenient form of reference to indicate individuals who satisfy requirements to qualify as objects who may separately receive benefits under the exercise of the discretion. The separate 'interest' of each separate object is unquantifiable, and of a limited kind. What he has is a right to be considered as a potential beneficiary, a right to have his interest protected by a court of equity and a right to take and enjoy whatever part of the income the trustees choose to give him. He could accordingly go to court if the trustees refused to exercise their discretion at all, or exercised it improperly[3]. He has also, it has been said[4], a right to have the trust property properly managed and to have the trustee account for his management.

If trustees fail to execute a discretionary trust the court will do so in the manner best calculated to give effect to the settlor's or testator's intentions. It may do so by appointing new trustees, or by authorising or directing representative persons of the classes of beneficiaries to prepare a scheme of distribution, or even, should the proper basis for distribution appear, by itself directing the trustees so to distribute[5].

[308]

1   See *McPhail v Doulton* [1971] AC 424 at 448, [1970] 2 All ER 228 at 240, HL per Lord Wilberforce. The distinction between these alternatives does not appear to have been raised in *Gartside v IRC* [1968] AC 553, [1968] 1 All ER 121, HL, and it is submitted that it is only if the provision in question was construed in the latter sense that it should properly have been called a discretionary trust. In *Re Weir's Settlement Trusts, Macpherson and Viscount Weir v IRC* [1971] Ch 145 at 164, [1970] 1 All ER 297 at 300, CA Russell LJ referred to *Gartside v IRC* [1968] AC 553, [1968] 1 All ER 121 as 'a case of a non-exhaustive discretionary power or trust'. Cf *Pearson v IRC* [1981] AC 753, [1980] 2 All ER 479, HL.

2   *Gartside v IRC* [1968] AC 553, [1968] 1 All ER 121. See also *Re Weir's Settlement Trusts, Macpherson and Viscount Weir v IRC* [1971] Ch 145, [1970] 1 All ER 297; *Sainsbury v IRC* [1970] Ch 712, [1969] 3 All ER 919 in respect of exhaustive trusts. For the right of the beneficiaries acting together to end the trust see *Re Smith, Public Trustee v Aspinall* [1928] Ch 915.

3   *Tempest v Lord Camoys* (1882) 21 Ch D 571, CA; *Martin v Martin* [1919] P 283, CA; *Gartside v IRC* [1968] AC 553, [1968] 1 All ER 121. Discretionary dispositive powers involve selecting amongst the beneficiaries (ie they inevitably involve preferring one beneficiary over another). As to what is meant in this context by the duty to exercise such powers impartially: see *Edge v Pensions Ombudsman* [2000] Ch 602, [1999] 4 All ER 546, CA where, at p 567, Chadwick J commented as follows:

'Properly understood, the so-called duty to act impartially — on which the ombudsman placed such reliance — is no more than the ordinary duty which the law imposes on a person who is entrusted with the exercise of a discretionary power; that he exercises the power for the purpose for which it is given, giving proper consideration to the matters which are relevant and excluding from consideration matters which are irrelevant. If pension fund trustees do that, they cannot be criticised if they reach a decision which appears to prefer the claims of one interest — whether that of employers, current employers or pensioners — over others. The preference will be as a result of a proper exercise of the discretionary power.'

4   *Spellson v George* (1987) 11 NSWLR 300 at 316 per Powell J.

5   *McPhail v Doulton* [1971] AC 424, [1970] 2 All ER 228 at 456, 247 per Lord Wilberforce; and see *Re Londonderry's Settlement, Peat v Walsh* [1965] Ch 918, [1964] 3 All ER 855, CA.

[309]

125 Discretionary settlements

The most common form of settlement in circumstances where it is desired to benefit a large class of persons is the discretionary settlement[1]. This usually takes the form of a power conferred on the trustees or some other persons (usually two in number or a trust corporation) to appoint by deed the whole or any part of the income or capital of the trust fund[2]. This power is usually expressed in terms sufficiently wide to enable the trustees, if they think fit, to resettle the whole of the trust fund provided that the persons likely to benefit from such resettlement are limited to objects of the power. The power of appointment might never be exercised and the settlement will usually provide for the disposal of income and capital in default of appointment and such disposal may accord with the intentions of the trustees. If an object of the power releases his interest for valuable consideration, the trustees may no longer exercise their discretion in favour of that object[3]. The exercise of the power of appointment may be made conditional on the consent of the settlor[4] and the trustees are sometimes given power to release the trust fund from the power of appointment. The power of appointment and the interests created under it must be exercised or vest within the perpetuity period applicable to the settlement[5], or such shorter period as the settlement may prescribe. The power of appointment is sometimes expressed as a power overriding the prior trusts contained in the settlement.

[310]

In default of and subject to any exercise of the power of appointment, discretionary settlements usually provide for a discretionary trust of the income of the settled property[6]. The class of beneficiaries who will be entitled to benefit from this trust and the objects for which such money can be paid or applied (for example, maintenance) will be defined in the settlement[7]. The beneficiaries who are likely to benefit must be defined so as to include only those persons alive at the time the trustees are to exercise their discretion. Unless the discretionary power over income is a mere power (as where there is an individual or class specified to take in default of appointment), the class must be defined with certainty. If the power is a trust power and there is some uncertainty as to the objects, there may be a resulting trust to the settlor[8]. In the absence of a power or direction to accumulate[9], the trustees are usually bound to distribute the income of the settled property arising to them in any one year[10].

In so far as the capital of the property settled by a discretionary trust has not been appointed under any power contained in the settlement[11], it is usual to direct that, at the end of the perpetuity period applicable to the settlement[12] or at such earlier time as the settlement may provide, the capital shall be held on trust for the members of a specified class[13] alive at that date; it is usual to make membership of this class dependent on some additional qualification such as the attainment of a specified age or marriage under that age. The settlement should also provide for the event of there being no individuals fulfilling the requirements which allow them to take a vested interest in default of appointment, so that if there are none the settled property and the future income should vest absolutely in one or more individuals or their personal representatives. This will avoid any possibility of a resulting trust arising in favour of the settlor[14]. Care must be taken in defining the class to take in default of appointment. If the class of beneficiaries likely to benefit from the exercise of a power is a wide one (for example, including the wives or widows of remote issue of the settlor), the trusts which come into operation in default of appointment may allow persons who were far from the settlor's intention to benefit.

[311]

1 For a discretionary settlement see Form 4 [1081] post; and for a discretionary trust of land see vol 40(2) (2001 Reissue) TRUSTS AND SETTLEMENTS Part 8 [3501]. Discretionary trusts (or settlements containing similar wide powers) enjoy the advantage of flexibility in that, generally, the trust property can be resettled so as to secure benefits otherwise denied to it. Note *Blausten v IRC* [1972] Ch 256,

[1972] 1 All ER 41, CA, where under the settlement as originally drawn, the settlor's wife was a member of the discretionary class, a situation which had tax consequences adverse to the settlor. It was held that the trustees could properly exercise their power of appointment by (in effect) appointing the trust funds on discretionary trusts which were the same as before except that the wife was excluded from the discretionary class. Most discretionary settlements now give trustees power to exclude any person from all benefit under the trusts: see Form 4 clause 6 [1087] post.

2   The power will not be a 'trust power': see *McPhail v Doulton* [1971] AC 424, [1970] 2 All ER 228, HL. The trustees or other appointees will not be compelled to exercise their discretion: see, as to the distinction between trusts and powers, 48 Halsbury's Laws (4th Edn 2000 Reissue) para 511 et seq. In general it is desirable that, if the trustees are to have power to revoke any appointment which may be made under the power of appointment, they should be given specific power to do so. As to powers of appointment generally see vol 31 (1999 Reissue) POWERS OF APPOINTMENT Paragraph 3 [3005] et seq. Trustees to whom such a power is given may disclaim it by deed: Law of Property Act 1925 s 156(1) (37 Halsbury's Statutes (4th Edn) REAL PROPERTY).

3   *Re Gulbenkian's Settlement Trusts (No 2), Stephens v Maun* [1970] Ch 408, [1969] 2 All ER 1173. Whether the position would be the same in the case of a voluntary release not under seal was not decided: see *Re Gulbenkian's Settlement Trusts (No 2), Stephens v Maun* above at 418, 1179.

4   Or, in the case of offshore trusts, the consent of the protector. As to offshore trusts generally, see vol 40(2) (2001 Reissue) TRUSTS AND SETTLEMENTS Part 15 [8701].

5   As to the perpetuity period see further Paragraph 77 [183] et seq ante.

[312]

6   The trustees can be compelled, if they fail to exercise their discretion, to distribute the income in equal shares to all beneficiaries entitled to benefit: see *Re Allen-Meyrick's Will Trusts, Mangnall v Allen-Meyrick* [1966] 1 All ER 740, [1966] 1 WLR 499. It would be otherwise if the income was being accumulated by the trustees under an express trust or power contained in the settlement, at least if there was more than one person entitled to benefit: cf *Saunders v Vautier* (1841) Cr & Ph 240. The trustees must exercise their discretion as to income within a reasonable time, generally within the year in which the income arises. There may, however, be special circumstances which justify a postponement of the exercise of the discretion: see *Re Gulbenkian's Settlement Trusts (No 2) Stephens v Maun* [1970] Ch 408, [1969] 2 All ER 1173 at 419, 1180. It was held in *Re Locker's Settlement Trusts, Meachem v Sachs* [1978] 1 All ER 216, [1977] 1 WLR 1323 that where trustees had failed to discharge their duty by properly distributing the income in their discretion and now desired to do it, the court should encourage them to do so. *Re Allen-Meyrick's Will Trust, Mangnall v Allen-Meyrick* above and *Re Gulbenkian's Settlement Trusts (No 2), Stephens v Maun* above were distinguished as concerning permissive rather than obligatory discretionary powers.

7   If the income is to be applied for minors contingently on their attaining a specified age, the trustees may accumulate the balance of income not applied for the maintenance of those minors under the Trustee Act 1925 (48 Halsbury's Statutes (4th Edn) TRUSTS AND SETTLEMENTS): see the Trustee Act 1925 s 31(2) as amended by the Family Law Reform Act 1969 s 1(3), Sch 1 Pt I and the Trustee Act 2000 Sch 2 para 25. In the case of minors, the settlement will usually provide for the payment of income by the trustees to the parent or guardian of such minor.

8   As to the degree of certainty required see *Re Gulbenkian's Settlement Trusts (No 2), Stephens v Maun* [1970] Ch 408, [1969] 2 All ER 1173; *McPhail v Doulton* [1971] AC 424, [1970] 2 All ER 228, HL; *Re Baden's Deed Trusts (No 2)* [1973] Ch 9, [1972] 2 All ER 1304, CA; *Re Manisty's Settlement, Manisty v Manisty* [1974] Ch 17, [1973] 2 All ER 1203.

9   For the periods for which or objects for whom such accumulations may be directed, see Paragraph 83 [194] et seq ante.

10   See note 6 above.

11   The statutory power of advancement contained in the Trustee Act 1925 s 32 as amended by the Trusts of Land and Appointment of Trustees Act 1996 s 25(1), Sch 3 para 3(8) (see Paragraph 238 [573] post) may allow the trustees to advance capital to any beneficiary entitled to a vested or contingent interest under the settlement and may be varied: see Form 153 [1594] post. If the trustees are to have power to advance capital to a beneficiary absolutely, it is probably desirable (as a matter of form if not otherwise) to give them express power to do so.

12   As to the perpetuity period see Paragraph 77 [183] et seq ante.

13   This may be the class entitled to benefit from the exercise of the power or a more narrowly defined group.

14   As to the tax consequences of a resulting trust see Paragraph 292 [753] post.

[313]

126   Settlements on children, grandchildren and other members of the settlor's family

Settlements on children, grandchildren and other members of a settlor's family may take the form of discretionary trusts. Alternatively, the property may be settled on the beneficiary or beneficiaries contingently on the fulfilment of a particular requirement (for example, attaining a specified age or marrying) or otherwise[1]. In settlements incorporating contingent interests, it is desirable to provide for trusts in the event of a beneficiary dying without attaining a vested interest leaving issue, so that any children can take their parent's share (provided always that their shares vest within the perpetuity period applicable to the settlement)[2]. Care must be taken in drafting such settlements to ascertain precisely whom the settlor wishes to benefit and to adopt the form appropriate to such intentions. The rules of construction must be borne in mind; for example, the rule that the word 'children' or 'nephews' means children or nephews in being at the date of the settlement and does not extend to include after-born children or nephews, and the rule under which a class closes on the first member of that class attaining a vested interest[3]. If the settlor intends a beneficiary born after the first beneficiary attains a vested interest to take an interest in the fund, the settlement should provide specifically for this event[4].

It is probably desirable in such a settlement to give the trustees a power to resettle the trust property before a beneficiary attains a vested interest[5]. There may be tax and other advantages in a resettlement which, though not existing or apparent at the time of the settlement, arise or become apparent as the result of changes in the law or the circumstances of the beneficiaries[6]. It is probably also desirable to vary the statutory powers of maintenance and advancement[7] and to include, where necessary, an appropriate hotchpot provision[8].

As in the case of discretionary trusts, the settlement should also provide for the contingency of none of the beneficiaries attaining a vested interest[9].

[314]

1   This form of settlement (in the case of infant beneficiaries this is usually termed an 'accumulation and maintenance trust' see Paragraph 127 [316] post) may be preferred to discretionary trusts (see Paragraph 125 [310] ante) in circumstances where the class of persons it is intended to benefit is small or the trust is to be of short duration only.
2   As to the perpetuity period generally see further Paragraph 77 [183] et seq ante.
3   Ie under the rule in *Andrews v Partington* (1790) 2 Cox Eq Cas 223.
4   For a clause excluding the rule in *Andrews v Partington* (1790) 2 Cox Eq Cas 223 see Form 89 [1455] post.
5   For a power to resettle the trust fund for the benefit of the beneficiaries see Form 100 [1478] post.
6   A resettlement must, of course, comply with the various rules appertaining to the settlement such as remoteness and certainty of objects. It may also have adverse capital gains tax consequences: see Paragraph 342 [919] post.
7   Ie the powers contained in the Trustee Act 1925 ss 31, 32 as amended by the Trusts of Land and Appointment of Trustees Act 1996 s 25(1), Sch 3 para 3(8) (48 Halsbury's Statutes (4th Edn) TRUSTS AND SETTLEMENTS): see Paragraph 235 [568] et seq post. See also Form 152 [1592], Form 153 [1594] post.
8   As to hotchpot provisions see Paragraph 129 [320] post.
9   As to the contingency of none of the beneficiaries attaining a vested interest see Paragraph 125 [310] ante.

[315]

4: ACCUMULATION TRUSTS

(For a detailed consideration of accumulation and maintenance settlements together with precedents see vol 40(2) (2001 Reissue) TRUSTS AND SETTLEMENTS *Part 11 [6301].)*

127   Accumulation and maintenance settlements

These settlements are in effect the creation of the Inheritance Tax Act 1984 under which special taxation privileges are accorded to settlements which satisfy the requirements of Section 71 of that Act[1]. These requirements are that:

127.1   one or more persons ('the beneficiaries') will, on or before attaining a specified age, not exceeding 25 years, become beneficially entitled to the settled property or to an interest in possession in it[2];

127.2   no interest in possession subsists in the settled property and the income from it is to be accumulated so far as not applied for the maintenance, education or benefit of a beneficiary[3]; and

127.3   either not more than 25 years have elapsed since the creation of the settlement (or its conversion into an accumulation and maintenance settlement, if later), or all the beneficiaries are, or have been, grandchildren of a common grandparent, or children, widows or widowers of such grandchildren who died before attaining an interest under Paragraph 127.1[4].

It is possible to create highly flexible trusts which take advantage of these provisions.

[316]

---

1   As to the tax treatment of accumulation and maintenance settlements see vol 40(2) (2001 Reissue) TRUSTS AND SETTLEMENTS Part 11 [6301]. For examples of such trusts see vol 40(2) (2001 Reissue) TRUSTS AND SETTLEMENTS Part 11 [6501].

2   Inheritance Tax Act 1984 s 71(1)(a) (42–44 Halsbury's Statutes (4th Edn) TAXATION).

3   Inheritance Tax Act 1984 s 71(1)(b).

4   See the Inheritance Tax Act 1984 s 71(2). If more than 25 years have passed since the creation of the accumulation and maintenance settlement and not all the beneficiaries are the grandchildren of a common grandparent, the settlement will lose its inheritance tax status. The earliest accumulation and maintenance settlement to lose its status in this way will be one created on 15 April 1976, its status being lost on 15 April 2001. The settlement will revert back to being subject to the inheritance tax framework applicable to ordinary discretionary trusts. Also, when the 25-year period expires in the case of such accumulation and maintenance trusts, there is an inheritance tax charge of 21% of the value of the trust assets.

[317]

5: MARRIAGE SETTLEMENTS

(a) Trusts for Issue in Marriage Settlements

128   Beneficial interests of issue

In marriage settlements of personalty the settled fund or funds are frequently held by the trustees after the death of the survivor of the husband and the wife upon trust for the children or more remote issue of the marriage in such shares and for such interests as the husband and wife, by any deed with or without power of revocation, have jointly appointed[1], and in default of such appointment as the survivor by deed, revocable or irrevocable, or by will or codicil, has appointed. The extension of a power to more remote issue of a marriage is desirable in view of the inconvenience of a limitation to children of the marriage only, which precludes provision for grandchildren[2], so that the issue of a child predeceasing the parent might be left without provision, it being impossible to appoint either to the issue or to the personal representatives of the deceased child[3]. The power must be exercised within the limits prescribed by the rule against perpetuities[4].

A power of appointment among issue is usually expressed to be to appoint to one or more exclusively of the others or other of the children or issue, although every power is now prima facie exclusive[5].

A trust for children at such ages as the donee of the power appoints authorises an appointment to a child en ventre sa mère at the date of the appointment, and such a child can take by virtue of an appointment made under a power to appoint to issue born before the date of appointment[6].

The donee of the power is generally authorised to make provision for the maintenance, education and advancement of the objects of the power. The statutory powers of maintenance and advancement[7] are available in relation to interests taken by minors under a power of appointment. It is now common practice to vary the statutory powers of maintenance and advancement in order to allow the trustees a greater discretion in exercising their powers[8]. A power of appointment can be expressed in terms sufficiently wide so as to allow the donee of the power to vary the implied provisions of the interests.

A special power of appointment by will given to the survivor of a husband and wife is not validly exercised by an appointment made by the will of the actual survivor during the joint lives[9].

[318]

1   For the purposes of the rule against perpetuities a joint power has been held not to be a general power: *Re Churston's Settled Estates* [1954] Ch 334, [1954] 1 All ER 725. See further *Re Earl of Coventry's Indentures, Smith v Earl of Coventry* [1974] Ch 77, [1973] 3 All ER 1. As to the rule against perpetuities generally see Paragraph 77 [183] et seq ante.
2   *Alexander v Alexander* (1755) 2 Ves Sen 640.
3   *Maddison v Andrew* (1747) 1 Ves Sen 57.
4   As to the rule against perpetuities see Paragraph 77 [183] et seq ante.
5   See the Law of Property Act 1925 s 158(1) (37 Halsbury's Statutes (4th Edn) REAL PROPERTY).
6   *Fearon v Desbrisay* (1851) 14 Beav 635; *Re Farncombe's Trusts* (1878) 9 Ch D 652.
7   As to the statutory powers of maintenance and advancement see Paragraph 235 [568] et seq post.
8   See Forms 152 [1592] and 153 [1594] post.
9   *Re Moir's Settlement Trusts* (1882) 46 LT 723. A general power exercisable by the survivor may, however, be exercised by them jointly: *Macarmick v Buller* (1787) 1 Cox Eq Cas 357.

[319]

129   Hotchpot clauses

A hotchpot clause[1], is often inserted in settlements in order to preclude appointees[2] of a share of the fund from participating in the unappointed fund without treating the appointed shares as received in or towards satisfaction of the shares to which they would be entitled if the whole fund were to go in default of appointment[3]. The clause applies to appointments of life or reversionary interests[4]. A life interest must be brought into hotchpot on the basis of an actuarial calculation of its value on the date when it fell into possession, irrespective of subsequent events[5].

A hotchpot clause in a settlement will not normally, however, apply to advancements[6].

[320]

1   For a hotchpot clause see Form 82 [1445] post. As to hotchpot clauses in wills see vol 42(1) (1998 Reissue) WILLS AND ADMINISTRATION Paragraph 95 [225] et seq.

2   If the power of appointment extends to issue more remote than children, the hotchpot clause should be made expressly to apply to such issue: *Langslow v Langslow* (1856) 21 Beav 552; *Hewitt v Jardine* (1872) LR 14 Eq 58.

3   In the absence of a hotchpot clause the appointee of a share in a fund is entitled to share in the unappointed residue: *Wilson v Piggott* (1794) 2 Ves 351; *Alloway v Alloway* (1843) 4 Dr & War 380; *Wombwell v Hanrott* (1851) 14 Beav 143; *Foster v Cautley* (1855) 6 De GM & G 55; *Walmsley v Vaughan* (1857) 1 De G & J 114; *Close v Coote* (1880) 7 LR Ir 564, CA; *Re Alfreton's Trust Estates* (1883) 52 LJ Ch 745. The rule may, however, be excluded by clear expression of intention on the part of the appointor (*Fortescue v Gregor* (1800) 5 Ves 553; *Foster v Cautley* above), or by the appointee agreeing to take under the appointment in lieu of his share in the unappointed property (*Clune v Apjohn* (1865) 17 I Ch R 25; *Armstrong v Lynn* (1875) IR 9 Eq 186).

4   Where the interest appointed is a life interest with a general power of appointment by will in default of issue, only the life interest need be brought into hotchpot: *Re Gordon, Public Trustee v Bland* [1942] Ch 131, [1942] 1 All ER 59.

5   *Re Thomson Settlement Trusts, Robertson v Makepeace* [1953] Ch 414, [1953] 1 All ER 1139; see also *Re Heathcote, Trench v Heathcote* [1891] WN 10; *Re Westropp* (1903) 37 ILT 183; *Re North Settled Estates, Public Trustee v Graham* [1946] Ch 13; *Re Morton, Morton v Warham* [1956] Ch 644, [1956] 3 All ER 259; and cf *Re West, Denton v West* [1921] 1 Ch 533, where the life interests never fell into possession and a retrospective actuarial calculation was rejected.

6   *Re Fox, Wodehouse v Fox* [1904] 1 Ch 480. As to advancement see Paragraph 238 [573] et seq post.

[321]

130   Application of hotchpot clause where two settled funds

If two distinct funds are settled for the same purposes by two distinct deeds, each containing a hotchpot clause, each hotchpot clause applies only to the fund settled by the deed containing it[1]. Where a settlement declares express trusts of one fund, with a hotchpot clause referring to that fund, the hotchpot clause is not incorporated with reference to a second and distinct fund by a general reference to the trusts, powers, provisos and agreements expressed in reference to the former fund[2]. Where, however, it appears on the true construction of the settlement that the second fund is to be amalgamated with or treated as an accretion to the first fund, the hotchpot clause is applicable to both funds[3]. A settlement may, however, in the absence of express words contain a plain indication of intention that the hotchpot clause shall apply to all funds settled by it[4].

[322]

1   *Montague v Montague* (1852) 15 Beav 565; *Lady Wellesley v Earl of Mornington* (1855) 1 Jur NS 1202.

2   *Re Cavendish, Grosvenor v Butler* [1912] 1 Ch 794; *Re Wood, Wodehouse v Wood* [1913] 2 Ch 574, CA; cf *Re Campbell's Trusts, Public Trustee v Campbell* [1922] 1 Ch 551; (a case of a will); *Re Rydon's Settlement, Barclays Bank Ltd v Everitt* [1955] Ch 1, [1954] 3 All ER 1, CA.

3   *Re Fraser, Ind v Fraser* [1913] 2 Ch 224.

4   *Hutchinson v Tottenham* [1898] 1 IR 403; *Re Perkins, Perkins v Bagot* (1892) as reported in 67 LT 743 (a case of a will); cf *Stares v Penton* (1867) LR 4 Eq 40; *Middleton v Windross* (1873) LR 16 Eq 212.

[323]

131   Trusts in default of appointment

In default of and subject to any appointment, settled property is frequently, in settlements made on marriage, directed to go to all the children or any child of the marriage[1] who being sons or a son attain the age of majority[2], or being daughters or a daughter attain that age or marry under that age, and if more than one in equal shares[3]. A rule of construction has been established in the case of wills[4] that, where there is an immediate gift to members of a class to be paid on their attaining a specified age, the time of distribution is the death of the testator, if any member of the class has then attained that age, and, if not, the first occasion when a member attains that age; this rule applies also to inter vivos settlements, at any rate if made by voluntary deed[5], although as the parent will commonly have a prior life interest it is not normally called into play in relation to a marriage settlement, at least when the gift in default is to the children of the settlor, and the rule may be excluded by the use of appropriate words[6].

[324]

1   An ultimate trust for children of the intended husband includes children by a subsequent marriage, notwithstanding a limitation to him in default of children of the then intended marriage (*Isaac v Hughes* (1870) LR 9 Eq 191); and a trust in a post-nuptial settlement for children to be born of the marriage includes children in existence at the date of the settlement (*Slingsby v —* (1718) 10 Mod Rep 397; *Hewet v Ireland* (1718) 1 P Wms 426; and see *Cook v Cook* (1706) 2 Vern 545).

2   If a trust is made to take effect at an age exceeding 21 years and the settlement would therefore be rendered void for remoteness, the settlement will take effect as if the age nearest to the age which would have prevented the disposition from being void had been substituted for the age stated in the settlement: Perpetuities and Accumulations Act 1964 s 4(1) (33 Halsbury's Statutes (4th Edn) PERPETUITIES). See further Paragraph 79 [188] ante.

3   Where there was a trust for such a class of persons 'as being male shall have attained the age of 21 years or being female shall have married under that age' the trust was, on the construction of the settlement as a whole, given effect to as if it read 'or being female shall have attained the age of 21 years or shall have married under that age': *Re Hargraves' Trusts, Leach v Leach* [1937] 2 All ER 545. A reference to marriage without more means marriage during minority: *Lang v Pugh* (1842) 1 Y & C Ch Cas 718.

4   See eg *Andrews v Partington* (1791) 3 Bro CC 401.

5   *Re Knapp's Settlement, Knapp v Vassall* [1895] 1 Ch 91. It seems that it also applies to settlements for value: *Re Knapp's Settlement, Knapp v Vassall* above at 99; and see also *Re Wernher's Settlement Trusts, Lloyds Bank Ltd v Earl Mountbatten* [1961] 1 All ER 184, [1961] 1 WLR 136.

6   For a clause excluding the rule in *Andrews v Partington* (1791) 3 Bro CC 401 see Form 93 [1468] post.

[325]

132   Time of vesting in issue

If the settlement clearly and unequivocally throughout all its provisions makes the right of a child depend upon its surviving both its parents, the court has no authority to control that disposition[1]. If, however, the settlement is in any of its provisions ambiguously expressed, so as to leave it in any degree uncertain whether it was intended that the right of a child should depend upon the event of its surviving both its parents, then the court is bound by authority to declare, upon what may be called the presumed intention in marriage settlements, that the interest of a child, although not to take effect in possession until after the death of both parents, did, upon the limitations in the settlement, vest in the case of sons at the age of majority and of daughters at the age of majority or on marriage[2].

If limitations or trusts giving a vested interest at birth are employed, they are generally accompanied by an accruer clause, so that on the death of a child under the age of majority or, if a daughter, without having been married, his or her share devolves on the other children or child[3].

[326]

1   *Bright v Rowe* (1834) 3 My & K 316; *Jeffery v Jeffery* (1849) 17 Sim 26; *Lloyd v Cocker* (1854) 19 Beav 140; *Barnett v Blake* (1862) 2 Drew & Sm 117; *Beale v Connolly* (1874) IR 8 Eq 412; cf *Re Edgington's Trusts* (1855) 3 Drew 202 (where a gift over to children 'then living' was held to refer to the period at which the prior life interest determined). Cf the similar rule in relation to portions: see vol 40(2) (2001 Reissue) TRUSTS AND SETTLEMENTS Part 9 [4101].

2   *Perfect v Lord Curzon* (1820) 5 Madd 442; *Torres v Franco* (1830) 1 Russ & M 649; *Re Orlebar's Settlement Trusts* (1875) LR 20 Eq 711; *Martin v Dale* (1884) 15 LR Ir 345; cf *Bree v Perfect* (1844) 1 Coll 128. The court's policy is to accelerate, if possible, the period of vesting unless there is something in the document to show an intention to postpone enjoyment until the happening of some event personal to the parties interested themselves: *Darley v Perceval* [1900] 1 IR 129. Having regard to the provisions of the Family Law Reform Act 1969 s 1 (6 Halsbury's Statutes (4th Edn) CHILDREN) it is probable that the court would construe the right as vesting on the child attaining the age of 18 years.

3   Cross-remainders may sometimes be implied as a matter of construction: *Re Bickerton's Settlement, Shaw v Bickerton* [1942] Ch 84, [1942] 1 All ER 217; and see *Adamson v A-G* [1933] AC 257 at 279, HL. The court construes 'survivors' as 'others' if there is a sufficient context to enable this to be done (*Re Palmer's Settlement Trusts* (1875) LR 19 Eq 320; *Re Friend's Settlement, Cole v Allcot* [1906] 1 Ch 47), although otherwise the words must bear their grammatical meaning (*Cole v Sewell* (1848) 2 HL Cas 186). Survivorship has also been applied to the period of vesting (*Re Acott's Settlement* (1859) 28 LJ Ch 383), and of distribution (*Reid v Reid* (1862) 30 Beav 388).

[327]

133   Meaning of 'issue'

Where trusts are declared in favour of issue the question frequently arises whether the meaning of the word is confined to children, or whether and to what extent it includes grandchildren. The word 'issue' prima facie includes descendants in all degrees, unless the document negatives that construction[1]. If, however, issue are specified as persons to take with reference to the share of the parent a gift which with regard to the parent fails, they take on a quasi-representative principle, namely, the children of each parent whose share fails take the parent's share, but grandchildren are not admitted to take in competition with children[2]. There may also be sufficient indication of intention in a deed to cause the word 'issue' to be construed as children[3].

A substitutional gift in favour of the issue of a named parent, in the event of that parent dying in the settlor's lifetime, will not fail by reason only of the parent being dead at the date of the settlement[4].

[328]

1   *South v Searle* (1856) 2 Jur NS 390; *Harrison v Symons* (1866) 14 WR 959; *Re Warren's Trusts* (1884) 26 Ch D 208; as to male issue see *Re Du Cros' Settlement, Du Cros Family Trustee Co Ltd v Du Cros* [1961] 3 All ER 193, [1961] 1 WLR 1252. References to 'issue taking … their parent's share' indicated an intention to benefit issue through all degrees and references to the words 'parent's share' indicated an intention that such issue were to take per stirpes and not per capita: *Re Earle's Settlement Trusts, Reiss v Norrie* [1971] 2 All ER 1188, [1971] 1 WLR 1118.

         In any enactments passed, and in instruments made, after 4 April 1988, references to any relationship between two persons will, unless the contrary intention appears, be construed without regard to whether or not the father and mother of either of them, or the father and mother of any person through whom the relationship is deduced, have or had been married to each other at any time: Family Law Reform Act 1987 s 1(1) (6 Halsbury's Statutes (4th Edn) CHILDREN). References to any relationship between two persons in inter vivos dispositions made on or after 4 April 1988 and dispositions by will or codicil where the will or codicil is made on or after 4 April 1988, must be construed in accordance with the Family Law Reform Act 1987 s 1: see the Family Law Reform Act 1987 s 19(1).

2   *Robinson v Sykes* (1856) 23 Beav 40; *Marshall v Baker* (1862) 31 Beav 608; *Barraclough v Shillito* (1884) 53 LJ Ch 841.

3   As where a gift to issue was followed by a gift to one child if there should be but one (*Re Biron's Contract* (1878) 1 LR Ir 258, CA), or where a power of appointment given in the event of death without leaving lawful issue was followed by a gift over in default of appointment, in case there should be no children (*Re Heath's Settlement* (1856) 23 Beav 193; *Gordon v Hope* (1849) 3 De G & Sm 351).

4   *Barnes v Jennings* (1866) LR 2 Eq 448.

[329]

134   Effect of no trust in default of appointment

Where a settlement by which property is given to a class, contains no gift over in default of appointment, but gives a power to appoint in what shares and in what manner the members of that class shall take, the property vests, until the power is exercised, in all the members of the class, and they all take in default of appointment in equal shares, so that the personal representatives of a member of the class who dies in the lifetime of the donee of the power are entitled to participate in the property, even if the power is only testamentary[1].

If, however, the settlement does not contain a gift of the property to any class, but only a power to give it among the members of the class as the donee of the power may think fit, those only can take in default of appointment who might have taken under an exercise of the power, and in such a case the court may imply an intention to give the property in default of appointment to those only to whom the donee of the power might give it[2], so that the personal representatives are entitled to participate if the power is one which the donee could have exercised in his lifetime[3], but not if the power is purely testamentary[4].

It is desirable, in all cases where there may be uncertainty in the form of difficulty in ascertaining the objects of a power of appointment, that there should be a specific gift over in default, otherwise the settlement as a whole may fail for uncertainty, and there will be a resulting trust to the settlor[5].

[330]

1   *Lambert v Thwaites* (1866) LR 2 Eq 151.
2   *Lambert v Thwaites* (1866) LR 2 Eq 151; *Re Llewellyn's Settlement, Official Solicitor v Evans* [1921] 2 Ch 281; *Fenwick v Greenwell* (1847) 10 Beav 412. In a marriage settlement where the power is to appoint among issue, such an inference would be certain, but in other cases it is a question of construction whether or not there is an intention to benefit the class: see *Re Weekes' Settlement* [1897] 1 Ch 289. See further 36(2) Halsbury's Laws (4th Edn Reissue) para 209 et seq.
3   *Wilson v Duguid* (1883) 24 Ch D 244; but see *Re Llewellyn's Settlement, Official Solicitor v Evans* [1921] 2 Ch 281.
4   *Re Susanni's Trusts* (1877) 47 LJ Ch 65; *Walsh v Wallinger* (1830) 2 Russ & M 78; *Re Arnold, Wainwright v Howlett* [1947] Ch 131, [1946] 2 All ER 579.
5   See further Paragraph 125 [310] ante.

[331]

135   Provision for issue of subsequent marriage

Provision for issue of a subsequent marriage is usually made by the insertion of a power to appoint in favour of a subsequent spouse and the children of the subsequent marriage a portion of the trust fund, the amount being commonly made to depend on the number of children of the first marriage who become adult[1]. Such a power is sometimes made conditional on the making of a settlement on a subsequent marriage.

1   For powers of appointment to spouse and issue of a subsequent marriage see Form 118 [1521] et seq post.

[332]

(b)   Trusts in Default of Issue in Marriage Settlements

136   Usual trusts in default of issue

As a rule the aim of the trusts in default of issue contained in a marriage settlement is to return the settled property to the destination to which it would have gone if no settlement had been made[1]. Since it is usually the intention of settlors who are not parties to the marriage to divest themselves entirely of the property settled by them, the marriage settlement should provide for the ultimate destination of the property in default of issue.

The ordinary ultimate limitation of personal property settled by the husband is for the husband absolutely in default of issue[2].

The wife's fund may be settled in trust for the wife absolutely if the wife survives the husband[3], but, if the husband survives the wife, on such trusts as the wife by will or codicil appoints, and, in default of and subject to any such appointment, in trust for the person or persons who would have been entitled to it if the wife had died domiciled in England a widow and intestate and in the same shares and proportions[4].

[333]

1   Trusts in default of issue may arise on the dissolution of a marriage, there being no issue of the marriage:
       Bond v Taylor (1861) 2 John & H 473. A gift over on the death of issue under age was held to take effect
       on there being no issue of the marriage: *Osborn v Bellman* (1860) 2 Giff 593.
2   See Form 83 [1447] and Form 95 [1471] post. If and so long as the settled property or its income cannot
       become payable to the settlor except on:
       (a)   the death of a child of the settlor who had become beneficially entitled to the property at an age
              not exceeding 25 years;
       (b)   the bankruptcy of some person who is or may become beneficially entitled to the property; or
       (c)   an assignment of or charge on the property being made or given by some such person,
       an ultimate trust for the settlor will not be an interest retained by him within the Income and
       Corporation Taxes Act 1988 s 660A as inserted by the Finance Act 1995 s 74, Sch 17 para 1 (42–44
       Halsbury's Statutes (4th Edn) TAXATION): see further Paragraph 359 [1011] post.
3   A trust for such children of a future marriage as the wife, if she survives her husband, by will appoints
       does not interfere with her right to the trust funds under an absolute trust for her if she survives her
       husband and there is no issue of the intended marriage: *Hanson v Cooke and Hanson* (1825) 4 LJOS
       Ch 45.
4   See Form 84 [1448] post. As to rights on intestacy see vol 42(2) (1998 Reissue) WILLS AND
       ADMINISTRATION Paragraph 517 [3058] et seq.

[334]

137   Trusts for next of kin

A trust for the next of kin of a person, without more, is not a trust for the next of kin
according to the statutes which would have regulated the distribution of his property if
he had died intestate[1], but a trust for his nearest blood relations, so that brothers and
sisters take to the exclusion of the children of deceased brothers and sisters[2]. In the
absence of some indication to the contrary, such persons take as joint tenants[3]. A husband
is not next of kin to his wife[4], nor is a wife next of kin to her husband[5]. If the trust for
the next of kin of a person contains any reference, express or implied[6], to any statute
regulating the distribution of the estates of intestates[7], those persons take who would have
taken if he had died intestate and, in the absence of any provision to the contrary, they
take as tenants in common in the shares and manner in which they would have taken on
an intestacy[8]. Both husband and wife are entitled as statutory next of kin on a death
intestate since 1925[9].

In a marriage settlement, the ultimate trust of the wife's fund, in the event of the
husband surviving her, may be for the persons who would be her statutory next of kin
if she had survived the husband and died intestate. As a general rule, when a trust is
created in favour of persons who take under any statute, and the only hypothesis stated
is the death of some person intestate possessed of the personal property settled by the
instrument creating the trust, the persons who take are the persons determined by the
statute and ascertained at the time, that is to say, at the death of the person in question[10].
The trust may, however, be so worded as to show that the class of persons to be
ascertained is not to be ascertained at the time of the death, but at some other time, as if
the death had occurred at that other time[11]. The question in each case is one of
grammatical construction. In the case of the foregoing ultimate trust of a wife's fund, the
time for ascertaining the next of kin would probably be the date of the husband's death[12].

[335]

1   See the Administration of Estates Act 1925 ss 46, 47 as amended (17 Halsbury's Statutes (4th Edn)
       EXECUTORS AND ADMINISTRATORS). As to the regulation of the distribution of property on
       intestacy generally see vol 42(2) (1998 Reissue) WILLS AND ADMINISTRATION Paragraph 513 [3051]
       et seq.
2   *Elmsley v Young* (1835) 2 My & K 780; *Withy v Mangles* (1843) 10 Cl & Fin 215, HL; *Rook v A-G* (1862)
       31 Beav 313; *Re Gray's Settlement, Akers v Sears* [1896] 2 Ch 802.
3   *Withy v Mangles* (1843) 10 Cl & Fin 215, HL; *Lucas v Brandreth (No 2)* (1860) 28 Beav 274.
4   *Watt v Watt* (1796) 3 Ves 244; *Bailey v Wright* (1811) 18 Ves 49 (affd (1818) 1 Swan 39); *Grafftey v
       Humpage* (1838) 1 Beav 46 (affd (1839) 3 Jur 622).

5   *Worseley v Johnson* (1753) 3 Atk 758; *Garrick v Lord Camden* (1807) 14 Ves 372; *Cholmondeley v Lord Ashburton* (1843) 6 Beav 86; *Kilner v Leech* (1847) 10 Beav 362; *Re Fitzgerald* (1889) 58 LJ Ch 662.
6   A reference to intestacy in settlements executed at the present time will imply a reference to the statutory provisions referred to in note 1 above (as the case may require): see *Re Gray's Settlement, Akers v Sears* [1896] 2 Ch 802; following *Garrick v Lord Camden* (1807) 14 Ves 372; *Maclean v Smith* [1927] NI 109, CA (where the next of kin were held entitled to settled realty); *Re Jackson, Holliday v Jackson* (1943) 113 LJ Ch 78; and see *Cotton v Scarancke* (1815) 1 Madd 45. A reference to death unmarried, however, contains no such implication: *Halton v Foster* (1868) 3 Ch App 505; and see *Re Webber's Settlement* (1850) 19 LJ Ch 445.

[336]

7   See note 6 above. The Family Provision Act 1966 only affects the position in so far as the deceased leaves a surviving spouse.
8   *Re Ranking's Settlement Trusts* (1868) LR 6 Eq 601; *Re Nightingale, Bowden v Griffiths* [1909] 1 Ch 385; but see *Re Krawitz's Will Trusts, Krawitz v Crawford* [1959] 3 All ER 793, [1959] 1 WLR 1192.
9   See the Administration of Estates Act 1925 Part IV (ss 45—52) as amended: see the Administration of Estates Act 1925 s 50(1). See also *Re Gilligan* [1950] P 32, [1949] 2 All ER 401.
10   *Wheeler v Addams* (1853) 17 Beav 417; cf *Smith v Smith* (1841) 12 Sim 317; *Day v Day* (1870) 18 WR 417; and see *Wharton v Barker* (1858) 4 K & J 483; *Bullock v Downes* (1860) 9 HL Cas 1 (where the rule is stated with reference to wills).
11   *Re King's Settlement, Gibson v Wright* (1889) 60 LT 745, per Chitty J.
12   *Pinder v Pinder* (1860) 28 Beav 44; *Chalmers v North* (1860) 28 Beav 175; *Re King's Settlement, Gibson v Wright* (1889) 60 LT 745; *Clarke v Hayne* (1889) 42 Ch D 529; *Re Peirson's Settlement, Cayley v De Wend* (1903) 88 LT 794; but cf *Druitt v Seaward, Re Ainsworth, Ainsworth v Seaward* (1885) 31 Ch D 234; *Re Bradley, Brown v Cottrell* (1888) 58 LT 631.

[337]

138   Effect of phrase 'without having been married'

A trust for the statutory next of kin of the wife as if she had died intestate and 'without having been married', or 'without ever having been married', has been held to exclude the issue of the wife, whether issue of the intended marriage who fail to attain a vested interest, or issue of a former or subsequent marriage[1]. There may, however, be a context[2] or special circumstances in connection with the particular settlement that may lead to the conclusion that it cannot have been the intention to exclude children of the wife[3]. If the words used are 'as if she had died intestate and unmarried', the word 'unmarried', in the absence of any evidence of contrary intention, is taken to bear its primary meaning of 'never having been married'[4]. 'Unmarried' is, however, a word of flexible meaning, and may be construed according to the obvious intention of the persons using the word[5]. Accordingly, where the effect of giving the word its primary meaning would be to favour collaterals at the expense of lineals, the court has interpreted it as meaning 'not having a husband living at her death', thus admitting issue[6] and excluding a subsequent husband[7].

A trust for the wife's next of kin on the death or remarriage of the husband, who took an interest for life or until remarriage if he survived his wife, has been held to take effect on the cesser of the prior interests, and, the marriage having been terminated by divorce and the husband having remarried, the next of kin took on the death of the wife in the lifetime of her husband[8].

[338]

1   *Emmins v Bradford, Johnson v Emmins* (1880) 13 Ch D 493; *Hardman v Maffett* (1884) 13 LR Ir 499; *Re Brydone's Settlement, Cobb v Blackburne* [1903] 2 Ch 84, CA; *Boyce v Wasbrough* [1922] 1 AC 425, HL.
2   See eg *Wilson v Atkinson* (1864) 4 De GJ & Sm 455 (where the trust was followed by a declaration that an illegitimate daughter should for the purposes of the trust be deemed to be a lawful child of the wife, the settlement containing no express provision for children or issue). As to the position of illegitimate children see Paragraph 133 note 1 [329] ante.
3   Eg the absence of any provision for the children or issue of the marriage: see *Re Deane's Trusts, Dudley v Deane* [1900] 1 I R 332.
4   *Blundell v De Falbe* (1888) 57 LJ Ch 576; see also *Heywood v Heywood* (1860) 29 Beav 9; *Clarke v Colls* (1861) 9 HL Cas 601 at 612, 615.
5   *Maugham v Vincent* (1840) 9 LJ Ch 329; but see *Boyce v Wasbrough* [1922] 1 AC 425 at 445, 446, HL per Lord Sumner

6   *Maugham v Vincent* (1840) 9 LJ Ch 329; *Re Norman's Trust* (1853) 3 De GM & G 965 (where the expression 'without being married', was said to mean 'without having a husband at the time of death'); *Pratt v Mathew* (1856) 8 De GM & G 522; *Re Saunders' Trust* (1857) 3 K & J 152; *Clarke v Colls* (1861) 9 HL Cas 601; *Re Woodhouse's Trusts* [1903] 1 I R 126.

7   *Re Saunders' Trust* (1857) 3 K & J 152.

8   *Re Mathew's Trusts* (1876) 24 WR 960; but the decision in that case, in so far as it was held that the husband's interest was destroyed by his second marriage during the wife's lifetime, seems to be in conflict with *Re Pilkington's Settlement, Pilkington v Wright* (1923) 129 LT 629; and *Re Monro's Settlement, Monro v Hill* [1933] Ch 82. As to the acceleration of subsequent interests generally see Paragraph 122 [303] ante.

[339]

(c) Power to Withdraw Funds from Marriage Settlements

139   Power of partial revocation by surviving spouse on remarriage
Many marriage settlements disposing of a large portion of the wife's fortune, with a view to the contingency of the wife being left a widow and desiring to marry again, formerly contained a provision enabling her to liberate a certain portion of the trust funds from the trusts of the settlement and devote it to other objects. This provision has been adapted and extended so as to empower the surviving spouse, after the death of the other, to withdraw parts of the funds settled by him or her from the scope of the settlement made on their own marriage and to resettle them for the benefit of a subsequent husband or wife and issue of such a subsequent marriage. The merit of including such a provision must now, however, be considered somewhat doubtful in view of the regard to the tax implications[1].

1   As to the capital gains tax implications of a resettlement see further Paragraph 342 [919] post.

[340]

140   Power of revocation without subsequent remarriage
A settlor being a party to a marriage may think fit to provide that, if he or she survives the other spouse and there is one child or perhaps two or three children of the marriage and no more, he or she without having any subsequent marriage in prospect shall be at liberty to withdraw from the settlement a part of what he or she made subject to it. If this is a settlor's intention, the power given will be one capable of exercise at any time after the death of the other spouse, and will in substance be a power of revocation only. It will be convenient if the subject over which such a power may be exercised, is, or is made measurable by, a sum of money to be raised out of the settled fund or any part of it at the discretion of the trustees. A similar course may be taken where new marriage settlement trusts of the part of the fund withdrawn are to be created; but in those cases the appointment, as is more usual, of aliquot parts of the originally settled fund may be more convenient, as the whole of that fund will remain settled.

[341]

141   Power to withdraw where no issue
In some cases a power is desired to withdraw the fund or some part of it from the settlement if, after a specified period (for example, 30 years or after the wife has passed the age of child bearing)[1] there are no issue of the marriage, and such power will in general be advantageous especially where the fund is of no great amount.

1   As to the presumptions and evidence as to future parenthood see further Paragraph 78 [186] ante.

[342]

142   Power to withdraw in favour of spouse and children of remarriage only

Frequently, the power of withdrawal is made capable of exercise only in contemplation of, and in order to enable, a provision to be made for a marriage by the surviving spouse. The objects to be attained are those of enabling the donee of the power, on a second marriage, to make part of the income of the originally settled fund applicable for the benefit of a subsequent wife or husband who may survive the appointor, and a part of the capital applicable for the benefit of issue of a subsequent marriage. The insertion of such a power implies a judgment by the settlor when the settlement is made that in the events contemplated such a power may be usefully exercised. It could not be usefully exercised if the fund were very small. In considering how much of it should be made subject to the power, regard should be had to the age of the intended wife, if it is her fund, and in any case the amount of the fund relative to unsettled property of the settlor and to the position in life of the parties.

[343]

143   Objections to alternative methods of providing for subsequent marriage

In order to save the prospective cost of exercising a power, settlors have sometimes in their marriage settlements declared trusts of the funds they settle for children of the settlor, whether by the intended or any subsequent marriage. Provision for a subsequent husband or wife, if he or she survives the wife or husband of the second marriage, may never have been effected by declaration of trust in a settlement made on a previous marriage, but it would be as practicable and perhaps as reasonable as trusts for children of a subsequent marriage. Provision for either by way of trust should not be made in the first marriage settlement, because in point of art it is wrong, as being a trust outside the field within which the operation of a marriage settlement should be confined, and because the trust, whether for a spouse or child or a subsequent marriage, will not have the support of the consideration of marriage. Furthermore, either the subsequent spouse or the issue of the subsequent marriage may have wealth which preclude their need to participate in the benefit of the originally settled fund or of its yearly produce[1].

1   *Bathurst v Murray* (1802) 8 Ves 74 at 76, 78; *Birkett v Hibbert* (1834) 3 My & K 227 at 231.

[344]–[350]

(8) RIGHTS AND POSITION OF BENEFICIARIES

A: RIGHTS AS BETWEEN LIFE TENANT AND REMAINDERMAN

144   Rights of tenant for life and remainderman

A tenant for life of settled property is entitled ordinarily to the income of the property[1]. He will be entitled also to the casual profits which accrue during the subsistence of the life interest, but not to capital receipts[2], unless, in either instance, the settlement provides otherwise[3]. Money received under a policy of insurance against loss or damage to trust property is to be treated as capital whether or not the trustees have power to pay premiums out of income[4]. Receipts that accrue to settled property may be either casual profits, which belong to the tenant for life, or capital accretions[5] or substitutions[6]; and the answer to the question whether a particular receipt is capital or income may depend not merely on its nature but on the intention of the person from whom it comes[7] or on statutory provisions[8].

The rule that a tenant for life is entitled to the income of settled property applies in general to wasting assets settled by deed or specifically by will; therefore, apart from statute[9], a tenant for life is entitled to the income of wasting property such as leaseholds[10] or to the income of mines lawfully worked[11]. Whether a tenant for life may cut timber or open new mines depends, apart from statutory powers[12], on whether he is impeachable for waste. If he is unimpeachable for waste, he will be entitled to the rents and profits[13]; if he is impeachable for waste, but exercises the statutory power, he will be entitled beneficially to the proportion allowed him by statute[14].

[351]

1   See eg *Verner v General and Commercial Investment Trust* [1894] 2 Ch 239 at 258 (on appeal [1894] 2 Ch 260, CA); *Re Forster's Settlement, Forster v Custodian of Enemy Property for England* as reported in [1942] 1 All ER 180 at 184 (discretionary trust). The tenant for life's right to income extends to the income of a fund set aside to provide portions payable on his death, subject, of course, to a contrary provision in the settlement: see *Wellesley v Earl of Mornington* (1857) 27 LJ Ch 150; see also *Re Sneyd, Robertson-Macdonald v Sneyd* [1961] 1 All ER 744, [1961] 1 WLR 575 (interest on compensation for depreciation of land values apportionable over the period by reference to which it was calculated). 'Income' for their purposes means income receipts of the trust less outgoings properly set against income: see further *Carver v Duncan* [1985] AC 1082.

2   See eg *Re Wilson's Estate* (1863) 3 De GJ & Sm 410 (compulsory enfranchisement of copyholds on acquisition compulsorily by a railway company, no fines being payable to the lord of the manor who was tenant for life); cf *Brigstocke v Brigstocke* (1878) 8 Ch D 357 at 363, CA, in which it was considered that the fines payable on the renewal of perpetually renewable leaseholds were casual profits and should be paid to the tenant for life. See also the Trust Law Committee's Consultation Paper 'Capital and Income Trusts' (1999).

3   See *Simpson v Bathhurst, Shepherd v Bathhurst* (1869) 5 Ch App 193 (fines on renewal of leases given to the tenant for life). In the case of settlements of personalty the trustees are occasionally given power to decide whether a receipt is capital or income: see eg Form 174 [1651] post. Alternatively, the settlement may direct that a receipt is to be treated as capital (or as income). The effect of such provisions in the context of taxation is uncertain; any provision which could be considered to deprive a life tenant of income (decided in accordance with ordinary legal principles) might be considered to be detrimental to the existence of an interest in possession: see further the discussion of *Pearson v IRC* [1981] AC 753, [1980] 2 All ER 479, HL at Paragraphs 286.3 [727] and 287 [730] post.

       A provision in a settlement, giving power to trustees to decide conclusively in the case of dispute whether a receipt is capital or income, has been held to be void as an attempt to oust the jurisdiction of the court: see *Re Wynn's Will Trusts, Public Trustee v Newborough* [1952] Ch 271, [1952] 1 All ER 341.

4   See the Trustee Act 1925 s 20 as amended by the Trusts of Land and Appointment of Trustees Act 1996 s 25(1), Sch 3 para 3(5) and the Trustee Act 2000 s 34(2) (48 Halsbury's Statutes (4th Edn) TRUSTS AND SETTLEMENTS). In other cases in which the trustees are empowered to pay the premiums due under policies of insurance out of income it is desirable that the settlement should expressly provide that the proceeds of such policies should be treated as capital: see eg Form 191 [1684] post.

5   As to casual profits and capital receipts generally see 42 Halsbury's Laws (4th Edn Reissue) para 944 et seq.

6   The fact that money has, through fortuitous circumstances, been substituted for an interest in property affords no ground for effecting a substitution of beneficial interests; accordingly where war damage value payments were received in respect of settled leaseholds the payments were required to be applied in buying annuities for periods corresponding to the period of the leases, the annuities being themselves applied as the rents of the properties would have been applied: see *Re Scholfield's Will Trusts, Scholfield v Scholfield* [1949] Ch 341, [1949] 1 All ER 490.

[352]

7   Therefore, where a company makes a distribution, its intention may control whether the payment is capital or income: see eg *Re Whitehead's Will Trusts, Public Trustee v Whitehead* [1959] Ch 579 at 588, [1959] 2 All ER 497 at 501. For the recent debate concerning the nature of shares received by trustees on a corporate demerger see *Sinclair v Lee* [1993] Ch 497, [1993] 3 All ER 926. See further Paragraph 150 note 13 [367] post.

8   See eg the Coal Act 1938 Sch 3 para 21(2) (repealed) under which the compensation was applicable as a substitution, so as to give the beneficiaries the like benefits that they would have had from the property (cf the principle stated in note 6 above): see *Re Duke of Leeds, Duke of Leeds v Davenport* [1947] Ch 525, [1947] 2 All ER 200; *Re Lucas, Bethune v Lucas* [1947] Ch 558, [1947] 2 All ER 213n; *Re Blandy-Jenkins, Blandy-Jenkins v Public Trustee* [1948] Ch 322, [1948] 1 All ER 582; *Williams v Sharpe* [1949] Ch 593, [1949] 2 All ER 102, CA.

9   See the Settled Land Act 1925 ss 47 (capitalisation of part of mining rent), 66 (capitalisation of part of proceeds of sale of timber) (48 Halsbury's Statutes (4th Edn) TRUSTS AND SETTLEMENTS). See further Paragraphs 147 [358] and 178 [430] post.

10   *Milford v Peile* (1854) 17 Beav 602; *Hope v Hope* (1855) 1 Jur NS 770.

11   *Daly v Beckett* (1857) 24 Beav 114. As to mines generally see further Paragraph 147 [358] post.

12   As regards the statutory power to cut timber see Paragraph 178 [430] post; for the statutory power to grant mining leases see Paragraph 147 [358] post.

13   A provision that a tenant for life is unimpeachable for waste expresses an intention excluding the general rule that the price of land carried away and sold in the shape of minerals, stones or bricks, is treated as capital: see *Re Ridge, Hellard v Moody* (1885) 31 Ch D 504 at 508, CA; *Re Chaytor* [1900] 2 Ch 804 at 809. As regards the position of a tenant for life in relation to waste see generally Paragraph 176 [426] et seq post.

14   As to capitalisation of part of mining rent see Paragraph 147 [358] post. As to timber generally see Paragraph 178 [430] post.

[353]

145   Trust of land

Before 1997 the tenant for life was clearly entitled to the actual income in the case of settled land under the Settled Land Act 1925, and was equally clearly so entitled in the case of a trust for sale by virtue of the Law of Property Act 1925 Section 28(2). This section, which in effect made statutory the pre-existing law[1], was repealed by the Trusts of Land and Appointment of Trustees Act 1996[2], and although it has not been replaced, it is thought that there is little doubt but that a tenant for life of land that has been settled, whether by will or by deed, on a trust of land[3] is entitled, subject to any direction to the contrary in the disposition, to the net rents and profits of the land whether freehold or leasehold, after keeping down the cost of repairs and insurance and other outgoings[4].

[354]

1   See *Re Searle, Searle v Baker* [1900] 2 Ch 829 at 834; *Re Oliver, Wilson v Oliver* [1908] 2 Ch 74; *Re Woodhouse, Public Trustee v Woodhouse* [1941] Ch 332, [1941] 2 All ER 265.

2   Trusts of Land and Appointment of Trustees Act 1996 s 25(2), Sch 4 (37 Halsbury's Statutes (4th Edn) REAL PROPERTY).

3   For the meaning of a trust of land see Paragraph 108 [267] ante. For detailed commentary on the Trusts of Land and Appointment of Trustees Act 1996 see vol 40(2) (2001 Reissue) TRUSTS AND SETTLEMENTS Part 8 [3001].

4   As to the incidence of the burden of repairs etc see Paragraph 158 [385] et seq post. For the right of an interest in possession beneficiary to occupy trust land see Trusts of Land and Appointment of Trustees Act 1996 s 12.

[355]

146   Income of wasting assets, etc pending sale

The equitable rules[1], which provide for the sale of wasting and reversionary assets forming part of residuary personalty settled by will on persons in succession and for the apportionment of the income arising under them, have no application to settlements inter vivos of personalty unless there is an express trust for conversion[2] and, in the absence of a direction to the contrary, the trustees will not be obliged to sell or otherwise convert any part of the property transferred to them by the settlor, nor will they be obliged to apportion any part of the income to the life tenant or remainderman[3].

[356]

1   Ie the rules in *Howe v Earl of Dartmouth* (1802) 7 Ves 137 and *Re Earl of Chesterfield's Trusts* (1883) 24 Ch D 643, which is in fact a branch of the former rule: see also *Allhusen v Whittell* (1867) LR 4 Eq 295.

2   *Re Van Straubenzee, Boustead v Cooper* [1901] 2 Ch 779.

3   It is increasingly common to give trustees of settlements wide powers to meet expenses out of capital or income as they think fit and to allow them to determine whether a receipt is to be treated as capital or income: see eg Form 173 [1649], Form 174 [1651] post. In general trustees have a duty to hold the balance fairly between the person entitled to the income of the settled property and those entitled to the capital (remaindermen). If it is wished to exclude such a duty it is probably desirable, if only to resolve doubts, that specific provision be inserted: see the Society of Trust and Estate Practitioners' Standard Provisions paragraph 3(1)(b) at Form 3 [1065] post.

[357]

147   Mines and minerals

The general principle, apart from statute, is that as between tenant for life and remainderman, the price of minerals[1] gotten, that is paid by a mining lessee, is capital, as it is paid in respect of a part of the land that is carried away and sold; this rule yields, however, to an expression of contrary intention in the settlement and, if the mines were open mines when they were settled, such a contrary intention is inferred unless the inference is excluded by the settlement[2]. Accordingly, the tenant for life of a settled estate, where mines were opened[3], or contracted to be leased[4], by the settlor, is entitled to royalties payable in respect of minerals gotten; and the same applies where the mines were demised by trustees of the settlement in exercise of a power of leasing given by the settlor[5]. The principle extends (subject to statute) to stone[6], brickfields[7], and gravel[8].

Where, however, the statutory power of granting mining leases[9], or some additional or larger power conferred by the settlement[10], is exercised, a specific fraction of the rent[11] must be set aside as capital, whether the mines have or have not already been worked, unless a contrary intention is expressed in the settlement[12].

[358]

1   As to the grant of rights to work minerals see vol 26 (2000 Reissue) MINES, MINERALS AND LANDFILL Paragraph 40 [1857] et seq.

2   *Re Ridge, Hellard v Moody* (1885) 31 Ch D 504, CA at 508, CA per Lindley LJ; *Re Chaytor* [1900] 2 Ch 804 at 809 (the exception with regard to open mines rests on inference of the settlor's intention). The tenant for life is entitled to whatever the settlor, as owner in fee, would have taken as income, including the dead rent and royalties: see *Re Kemeys-Tynte, Kemeys-Tynte v Kemeys-Tynte* [1892] 2 Ch 211 at 215.

3   See *Brigstocke v Brigstocke* (1878) 8 Ch D 357 at 363, CA; *Re Canner, Bury v Canner* (1923) 155 LT Jo 211.

4   *Re Kemeys-Tynte, Kemeys-Tynte v Kemeys-Tynte* [1892] 2 Ch 211 at 215.

5   *Daly v Beckett* (1857) 24 Beav 114 at 123.

6   *Re Ridge, Hellard v Moody* (1885) 31 Ch D 504, CA at 508, CA per Lindley LJ.

7   *Miller v Miller* (1872) LR 13 Eq 263; *Leppington v Freeman* (1891) 40 WR 348, CA; *Re North, Garton v Cumberland* [1909] 1 Ch 625.

8   *Earl of Cowley v Wellesley* (1866) LR 1 Eq 656.

9   Ie the power conferred by the Settled Land Act 1925 s 41(ii) (48 Halsbury's Statutes (4th Edn) TRUSTS AND SETTLEMENTS).

10   See the Settled Land Act 1925 ss 108, 109.

11   Rent includes royalties: Settled Land Act 1925 s 117(1)(xxii).

12   See the Settled Land Act 1925 ss 47, 117(1)(xv) (minerals include 'substances').

[359]

148   Damages for breach of lessee's covenants

Money, not being rent, received by way of damages or compensation for breach of any covenant by a lessee or grantee contained in any lease or grant of settled land, whenever the lease or grant was made and whether it was made under the statutory powers or not, is, unless in any case the court on the application of the tenant for life or the trustees of the settlement otherwise directs, deemed to be capital money arising under the Settled Land Act 1925. Such money must be paid to or retained by the trustees of the settlement, or paid into court, and invested or applied, accordingly[1]. This provision applies only if and so far as a contrary intention is not expressed in the settlement and has effect subject to the terms of the settlement, and to any provisions contained in it, but a contrary intention is not deemed to be expressed merely by words negating impeachment for waste[2]. This provision does not apply to money received by way of damages or compensation for the breach of a covenant to repay to the lessor or grantor money laid out or expended by him, or to any case in which, if the money received was applied in making good the breach of covenant or the consequences of it, such application would not enure for the benefit of the settled land, or any buildings on it[3].

[360]

1   See the Settled Land Act 1925 s 80(1), (5) (48 Halsbury's Statutes (4th Edn) TRUSTS AND SETTLEMENTS). Capital money arising under the Settled Land Act 1925 means capital money arising under the powers and provisions of that Act, or the Acts replaced by it, and receivable for the trusts and purposes of the settlement, and includes securities representing capital money: Settled Land Act 1925 s 117(1)(ii). As to capital money arising otherwise than under the Act see the Settled Land Act 1925 s 81; and as to the application of money in the hands of trustees as if it were capital money see the Settled Land Act 1925 s 77.
2   Settled Land Act 1925 s 80(6).
3   Settled Land Act 1925 s 80(4).

[361]

149   Consideration for accepting surrender of leases

Since 1925 all money, not being rent[1] or a rentcharge, received on the exercise by a tenant for life of the statutory power to accept a surrender[2], is, unless the court[3], on an application made within six months after its receipt or within such further time as the court may in special circumstances allow, otherwise directs[4], capital money arising under the Settled Land Act 1925[5].

[362]

1   A tenant for life who bona fide accepts a surrender and grants a new lease at an increased rent is entitled to the increased rent during the unexpired part of the original term: Re Wix, Hardy v Lemon [1916] 1 Ch 279.
2   See the Settled Land Act 1925 s 52(1) (48 Halsbury's Statutes (4th Edn) TRUSTS AND SETTLEMENTS).
3   See the Settled Land Act 1925 s 113 as amended by the Courts Act 1971 s 56(4), Sch 11 Pt II, by the County Courts Act 1984 s 148(1), Sch 2 para 20 and by the Administration of Justice Act 1982 s 37, Sch 3 para 4.
4   There appears to be no reported case in which the court has given such a direction, but as to the principles which it might be expected to apply in directing apportionment between capital and income, see Cottrell v Cottrell (1885) 28 Ch D 628; Re Robinson's Settlement Trusts [1891] 3 Ch 129; Re Fullerton's Will [1906] 2 Ch 138; Re Duke of Westminster's Settled Estates, Duke of Westminster v Earl of Shaftesbury [1921] 1 Ch 585 (transaction regarded as cross-sales and purchase of the surrendered leases).
5   See the Settled Land Act 1925 s 52(1), (7). Capital money arising under the Settled Land Act 1925 means capital money arising under the powers and provisions of that Act, or the Acts replaced by it, and receivable for the trusts and purposes of the settlement, and includes securities representing capital money: Settled Land Act 1925 s 117(1)(ii). As to capital money arising otherwise than under the Act see the Settled Land Act 1925 s 81; and as to the application of money in the hands of trustees as if it were capital money see the Settled Land Act 1925 s 77.

[363]

150   Income of stocks and shares

If stocks or shares of a public company[1] are settled, the tenant for life or person entitled to the income of the settled property is entitled to all dividends declared out of current profits in respect of any period commencing and ending[2] during the continuance of his interest at whatever rate[3], and whether described as extraordinary or special dividends[4] or bonuses[5]. The rights of the tenant for life or such person to the entire dividend declared are not affected by the fact that the profits out of which the dividend is declared include money received by the company in respect of an old debt[6], or profits made in past years which have been put by under the name of a reserve fund[7], or that the amount declared covers arrears of a cumulative dividend[8]. Moreover, where, during the continuance of a life interest, arrears of dividend are satisfied by, for example, an issue of funding certificates or shares, or other property, the tenant for life is entitled to the property so issued[9].

Conversely, a tenant for life is not entitled to any part of dividends declared in a financial year of the company that falls wholly after the tenant for life's death, as there is no right to a dividend until it is declared; thus, where preference shares carry a right to a cumulative preferential dividend as and when the directors decide that one should be declared and the tenant for life of the shares dies while the preference dividends are in arrear, all future dividends (including any that might cover the arrears) in respect of periods after the death of the tenant for life belong to the remainderman[10]. The position is the same where preference shares carry a right to a fixed cumulative preferential dividend and, no dividends having been paid for some years before the death of the tenant for life, dividends are paid in financial years after his death to meet the arrears[11].

[364]

In general, a limited company that is not in liquidation cannot, except on a reduction of capital or reorganisation of capital, both of which require confirmation by the court, return capital to shareholders[12], and accordingly other distributions are by way of dividing profits, so that, when these are paid to the trustees of settled shares, they are received as income[13]; but other considerations apply where there is an increase of capital by way of capitalisation of profits[14]. In accordance with these principles, proper distributions of surplus assets to shareholders prior to the liquidation of a company are usually income[15], and, where trustees sell stock inflated in value by a contingent right to receive an income payment, the existence of such right makes the price in the hands of the trustees partially an income receipt[16].

A distribution out of money standing to the credit of a company's share premium account is to be regarded as a payment made in reduction of capital[17], whilst distributions to shareholders made in the liquidation of a limited company are also capital[18].

Where units in a fixed investment trust are settled, the trustees must inquire into the source of all distributions distributed by the investment trust as capital distributions, and must treat them as capital or income as if the trustees were the holders of the shares from which the sums distributed are derived[19].

Where shares have been purchased in breach of trust there is jurisdiction to apportion whatever may have been received by way of dividend distribution, or to allocate it to capital, so that beneficial rights are not altered[20].

[365]

---

1   See *Re White, Theobald v White* [1913] 1 Ch 231. There seems no reason why the principles considered in this paragraph should not apply also to private companies resident in this country. Particular difficulties may arise when trustees own shares (often a substantial majority holding) in a private company (often the settlor's family company). In such cases, it is thought that the trustees should adopt a dividend policy which is fair to all beneficiaries, although this may be easier said than done when it is realised that not only does this involve a consideration of the different requirements of tenant for life and remaindermen, but also of the company's commercial requirements. Including in the settlement a provision excluding the trustees from any duty to procure distributions in such cases should be considered: see further the Society of Trust and Estate Practitioners' Standard Provisions paragraph 3(4)(b) at Form 3 [1065] post.

2   See generally *Re Armitage, Armitage v Garnett* [1893] 3 Ch 337 at 346, CA, applied in *Re Sale, Nisbet v Philp* [1913] 2 Ch 697. As to the apportionment of dividends under the Apportionment Act 1870 (23 Halsbury's Statutes (4th Edn) LANDLORD AND TENANT) see Paragraph 157 [383] post. The rules may, of course, be modified by directions contained in the settlement: see eg Form 214 [1732] post.

3   *Barclay v Wainewright* (1807) 14 Ves 66; *Price v Anderson* (1847) 15 Sim 473.

4   *Re Hopkins' Trusts* (1874) LR 18 Eq 696.

5   *Preston v Melville* (1848) 16 Sim 163; *Johnson v Johnson* (1850) 15 Jur 714; *Dale v Hayes* (1871) 40 LJ
     Ch 244; cf *Re Tedlie, Holt v Croker* (1922) 91 LJ Ch 346.
6   *Maclaren v Stainton* (1861) 3 De GF & J 202; *Edmondson v Crosthwaite* (1864) 34 Beav 30.
7   *Re Alsbury, Sugden v Alsbury* (1890) 45 Ch D 237; *Re Northage, Ellis v Barfield* (1891) 60 LJ Ch 488.
8   *Re Wakley, Wakley v Vachell* [1920] 2 Ch 205, CA; *Re Marjoribanks, Marjoribanks v Dansey* [1923] 2 Ch
     307; *Re Joel, Johnson v Joel* [1936] 2 All ER 962; cf *First Garden City Ltd v Bonham-Carter* [1928] Ch 53.
9   *Re Pennington, Stevens v Pennington* [1915] WN 333; *Re Sandbach, Royds v Douglas* [1933] Ch 505; *Re
     MacIver's Settlement, MacIver v Rae* [1936] Ch 198; *Re Smith's Will Trusts* [1936] 2 All ER 1210. A cash
     bonus, however, paid in consideration of a release of preferential rights in respect of capital has been
     held to be capital: *Bates v Mackinley* (1862) 31 Beav 280; *Re Tedlie, Holt v Croker* (1922) 91 LJ Ch 346.
10   *Re Sale, Nisbet v Philp* [1913] 2 Ch 697, applying *Re Taylor's Trusts, Matheson v Taylor* [1905] 1 Ch 734;
     see also *Re Marjoribanks, Marjoribanks v Dansey* [1923] 2 Ch 307 (arrears of cumulative preference
     dividend, some of which had accrued before the testatrix's death, paid after her death, held to pass as
     income of her residuary estate).
11   *Re Grundy, Grundy v Holme* (1917) 117 LT 470; *Re Wakley, Wakley v Vachell* [1920] 2 Ch 205, CA.
12   As to alterations in share capital of a limited company generally see vol 10 COMPANIES (2001 Reissue)
     Paragraph 196 [1101] et seq. This is the case with companies registered under the Companies Act 1985
     (8 Halsbury's Statutes (4th Edn) COMPANIES) in the United Kingdom. If the assets comprised in the
     settlement include shares in overseas companies different considerations may apply.

[366]

13   See *Re Bates, Mountain v Bates* [1928] Ch 682; *Hill v Permanent Trustee Co of New South Wales Ltd* [1930]
     AC 720 at 731, PC; *Re Doughty, Burridge v Doughty* [1947] Ch 263 at 270, [1947] 1 All ER 207 at 211,
     CA; *Re Harrison's Will Trusts, Re Harrison's Settlement, Harrison v Milborne-Swinnerton-Pilkington* [1949]
     Ch 678. Therefore the fact that a company describes an income distribution as being capital does not
     alter its nature: see *Re Doughty, Burridge v Doughty* above at 272, 212. See also *Re Morris' Will Trusts,
     Public Trustee v Morris* [1960] 3 All ER 548, [1960] 1 WLR 1210.
         In *Sinclair v Lee* [1993] 3 All ER 926, Nicholls VC decided that shares received by trustees as a
     result of an 'indirect' demerger were capital and not income. The case of *Hill v Permanent Trustee Co of
     New South Wales Ltd* above was distinguished.
             'In the last analysis, the rationale behind the general principles enunciated in *Hill's* case is an
             endeavour by the law to give effect to the assumed intention of the testator or settlor in
             respect of a particular distribution to shareholders. When the inflexible application of these
             principles would produce a result manifestly inconsistent with the presumed intention of the
             testator or settlor, the court should not be required to apply them slavishly. In origin they
             were guidelines. They should not be applied in circumstances, or in a manner, which would
             defeat the very purpose they are designed to achieve.'
         The case leaves uncertain the position of direct demergers and of enhanced scrip dividends (as to
     the latter see Paragraph 151 note 5 [369] post). For the Inland Revenue's views on the current position
     see *Tax Bulletin 1994* p 164.
14   *Hill v Permanent Trustee Co of New South Wales Ltd* [1930] AC 720 at 731, PC. As to the effect of
     capitalisation of profits see Paragraph 151 [368] post.
15   See *Re Palmer, Palmer v Cassel* (1912) 28 TLR 301; *Re Tedlie, Holt v Croker* (1922) 91 LJ Ch 346. The
     following cases arose out of the distribution, as 'capital profits dividend', of a sum of British Transport
     Stock issued to a company as compensation on nationalisation: *Re Sechiari, Argenti v Sechiari* [1950] 1 All
     ER 417 (distribution treated as income); *Re Kleinwort's Settlement, Westminster Bank Ltd v Bennett* [1951]
     Ch 860, [1951] 2 All ER 328; *Re Rudd's Will Trusts, Wort v Rudd* [1952] 1 All ER 254.
16   *Thomson's Trustees v Thomson* 1955 SC 476 (trustees sold stock with the right attached to it, by
     resolution of the company, to receive a sum of government stock to be distributed by way of capital
     profits dividend to which the tenant for life would have been entitled (see note 15 above) if the stock
     had not been sold), distinguished in *Manclark v Thomson's Trustees* 1958 SC 147 (where the settlement
     was by will and the resolution had been passed before the testator's death).
17   See now the Companies Act 1985 s 130(3). See also *Re Duff's Settlements, National Provincial Bank Ltd
     v Gregson* [1951] Ch 923, [1951] 2 All ER 534, CA.
18   *Nicholson v Nicholson* (1861) 30 LJ Ch 617; *Re Armitage, Armitage v Garnett* [1893] 3 Ch 337, CA; *Re
     Palmer, Palmer v Cassel* (1912) 28 TLR 301; *IRC v Burrell* [1924] 2 KB 52, CA; *Hill v Permanent Trustee
     Co of New South Wales Ltd* [1930] AC 720 at 729, PC; cf *Re Pennington, Pennington v Pennington* [1914]
     1 Ch 203, CA (payments made in respect of debenture interest in a winding up were income). See also
     Re Morris' Will Trusts, Public Trustee v Morris [1960] 3 All ER 548, [1960] 1 WLR 1210.
19   *Re Whitehead's Will Trusts, Public Trustee v White* [1959] Ch 579, [1959] 2 All ER 497.
20   See *Re Maclaren's Settlement Trusts, Royal Exchange Assurance v Maclaren* [1951] 2 All ER 414 at 420; *Re
     Kleinwort's Settlements, Westminster Bank Ltd v Bennett* [1951] Ch 860 at 863, [1951] 2 All ER 328 at
     330; *Re Rudd's Will Trusts, Wort v Rudd* [1952] 1 All ER 254 at 258, 259.

[367]

151   Capitalisation of profits

A company which has the power of increasing its capital[1] can either distribute its profits as dividend or convert them into capital, and, if the company validly exercises this power, such exercise is binding on all persons interested in the shares under the settlement. Consequently what is paid by the company as dividend goes to the persons interested in the income, and what is paid by the company to the shareholder as capital, or appropriated as an increase of the capital stock in the concern, enures to the benefit of all interested in the capital[2].

A company has the power to determine conclusively against the world whether or not it will capitalise its profits[3], and it is a question of fact in each case whether a company has or has not done so.

If an option is given to the shareholder to take either a cash dividend or shares, the court determines from the scheme as a whole whether the profits dealt with are or are not capitalised[4]. In the latter case, however, the persons entitled to the income are not entitled to the entire value of the shares allotted in respect of dividend, but only to so much of the proceeds of realisation of such shares as represent the dividend (together with the relevant tax credit), and the balance ought to be applied as capital[5].

If the settlement contains an express declaration that bonuses shall be treated as income or as capital, the rights of the persons entitled to the income are governed by that declaration[6].

[368]

1   This power is possessed by all companies limited by shares or limited by guarantee and having a share capital, if authorised by their articles: see the Companies Act 1985 s 121 (8 Halsbury's Statutes (4th Edn) COMPANIES).

2   *Bouch v Sproule* (1887) 12 App Cas 385, HL. If the intention on the part of the company to capitalise is clear, the fact that the shareholders have an option to take cash or new shares does not affect the position as between the tenant for life and the remainderman: *Re Evans, Jones v Evans* [1913] 1 Ch 23. If the option in such a case is vested in trustees, there is no right to elect between them and their beneficiaries and they must take the dividend in the capitalised form: *Re Evans, Jones v Evans* above.

3   *IRC v Blott, IRC v Greenwood* [1921] 2 AC 171, HL; *IRC v Fisher's Executors* [1926] AC 395, HL; *Re Taylor, Waters v Taylor* [1926] Ch 923; *IRC v Wright* [1927] 1 KB 333, CA; cf *Re Schopperle's Trusts* [1932] IR 457 (where it was held that a similar determination by a foreign government was binding as between the tenant for life and remaindermen).

4   *Bouch v Sproule* (1887) 12 App Cas 385, HL; *Re Despard, Hancock v Despard* (1901) 17 TLR 478; *Blyth's Trustees v Milne* 1905 7 F (Ct of Sess) 799; *Re Evans, Jones v Evans* [1913] 1 Ch 23; *Re Hatton, Hockin v Hatton* [1917] 1 Ch 357; *Re Taylor, Waters v Taylor* [1926] Ch 923; *IRC v Wright* [1927] 1 KB 333, CA. The settlement may itself contain a direction as to how the distribution (whatever form it takes) is to be applied. In general, however, the character of the payment (ie whether it is to be treated as income or capital) will depend on rules of law (eg those appertaining to accumulations) applicable to settlements in general.

5   *Re Northage, Ellis v Barfield* (1891) 60 LJ Ch 488; *Re Tindal* (1892) 9 TLR 24; *Re Hume Nisbet's Settlement* (1911) 27 TLR 461; and see *Rowley v Unwin* (1855) 2 K & J 138. The recent spate of enhanced scrip issues has raised the question whether the shares taken instead of a dividend belong to the life tenant or remainderman. Although the law cannot be regarded as finally settled on this point, it is thought that the statement in the text represents the current state of the authorities. Unfortunately, *Sinclair v Lee* [1993] Ch 497, [1993] 3 All ER 926 provided no guidance on this point: see Paragraph 150 note 13 [367] ante. Reference should also be made to *Re Malam, Malam v Hitchens* [1894] 3 Ch 578; and for the Inland Revenue's view on the tax treatment of enhanced scrip dividends see Statement of Practice SP 4/94 (17 May 1994).

6   *Re Mittam's Settlement Trusts* (1858) 4 Jur NS 1077; cf *Plunkett v Mansfield* (1845) 2 Jo & Lat 344. The court may decide as a question of construction that bonuses paid out of current profits are not within a proviso in the settlement for the capitalisation of bonuses: *Hollis v Allan* (1866) 14 WR 980; *Re Baker, Ruddock v Baker* (1891) 8 TLR 7. In *Re Speir, Holt v Speir* [1924] 1 Ch 359, CA it was held that a trust to pay the 'dividends, bonuses, and income' of settled shares to a tenant for life did not cover a capital bonus: cf *Re Wright's Settlement Trusts, Wright v Wright* [1945] Ch 211, [1945] 1 All ER 587.

[369]

152   Options to take shares

Unless a settlement contains an express clause authorising the trustees to relinquish in favour of the persons entitled to the income of the settled property any preferential right to take new shares in a company that may accrue to them in respect of settled shares, they must exercise their option to take new shares on behalf of all their beneficiaries, and such new shares or any money received by sale of the option or the shares are capital[1]. If the calls on such new shares are paid out of income, the tenant for life has a lien on them for the amount so paid[2].

[370]

1   *Rowley v Unwin* (1855) 2 K & J 138; *Re Bromley, Sanders v Bromley* (1886) 55 LT 145; *Re Curtis, Hawes v Curtis* (1885) 1 TLR 332; *Re Malam, Malam v Hitchens* [1894] 3 Ch 578 at 586, 587.
2   *Rowley v Unwin* (1855) 2 K & J 138. If money is advanced by the tenant for life, at the request of the trustees, for payment of calls on shares, he has a lien on the shares for the repayment of the amount advanced with interest: *Todd v Moorhouse* (1874) LR 19 Eq 69.

[371]

153   Directors' fees accounted for by trustees

In a case where trustees are accountable to the trust for remuneration as directors of a company in which they hold shares subject to the trust (as they are where their appointment as directors is procured by virtue of the settled shares[1]) and they are not exempted from liability to account by the terms of the settlement[2], the sums accounted for are capital and not income[3].

[372]

1   *Re Francis, Barrett v Fisher* (1905) 74 LJ Ch 198; *Re Macadam, Dallow v Codd* [1946] Ch 73, [1945] 2 All ER 664. It is otherwise where the remuneration is received by the trustee independently of any use made by him of the trust holding by voting or refraining from voting: *Re Dover Coalfield Extension Ltd* [1908] 1 Ch 65, CA, as explained in *Re Gee, Wood v Staples* [1948] Ch 284, [1948] 1 All ER 498. *Re Gee, Wood v Staples* above was distinguished in *Re Orwell's Will Trusts* [1982] 3 All ER 177, [1982] 1 WLR 1337. A settlement should contain a provision allowing the retention by trustees of remuneration paid to them in circumstances where it is likely that the trustees will hold office as directors of companies by virtue of their holding of trust property. For a power to hold directorships and retain remuneration see Form 183 [1670] post.
2   Cf *Re Llewellin's Will Trusts, Griffiths v Wilcox* [1949] Ch 225, [1949] 1 All ER 487; *Re Northcote's Will Trusts, Northcote v Northcote* [1949] 1 All ER 442.
3   *Re Francis, Barrett v Fisher* (1905) 74 LJ Ch 198.

[373]

154   Partnerships

If a share in a partnership business[1] is settled, or if settled funds are properly employed in a partnership business, the question what is income and what is capital must be determined by the articles of partnership, and all that is divided between the partners as profit goes to the persons entitled to the income of the settled property[2]. What is properly retained as capital in the business is treated as capital, and belongs to the persons entitled to the capital, only the interest on it being payable to those entitled to income[3]. Where a tenant for life is entitled to the profits arising from a business carried on by the trustees, they may be justified in deducting a reasonable and proper annual sum for depreciation[4].

[374]

1   For clauses suitable for use where it is contemplated that trustees will or might carry on a business see Forms 179 [1660]–182 [1669] post. In general trustees should be expressly authorised by the settlement if they are to carry on a business.

2   *Stroud v Gwyer* (1860) 28 Beav 130; *Browne v Collins* (1871) LR 12 Eq 586; *Gow v Forster* (1884) 26 Ch D 672; *Re Robbins, Midland Bank Executor and Trustee Co Ltd v Melville* [1941] Ch 434, [1941] 2 All ER 601.

3   *Stroud v Gwyer* (1860) 28 Beav 130; *Straker v Wilson* (1871) 6 Ch App 503; *Re Robbins, Midland Bank Executor and Trustee Co Ltd v Melville* [1941] Ch 434, [1941] 2 All ER 601.

4   *Re Crabtree, Thomas v Crabtree* (1911) 106 LT 49, CA.

[375]

155   Right to emblements

Where a tenant for life has sown the land for crops which usually repay the sowing within the year, and dies before he has obtained the advantage of his expense and labour, his personal representatives are entitled to take the crops as emblements[1]; but he is not entitled to emblements if his estate determines in his lifetime by his own act[2].

1   Co Litt 55b. The sowing must be by or at the expense of the tenant for life himself: *Grantham v Hawley* (1615) Hob 132; 9 Vin Abr 369, Emblements (17). As to what crops are emblements and as to emblements generally see 1(2) Halsbury's Laws (4th Edn Reissue) para 382 and 17(2) Halsbury's Laws (4th Edn Reissue) para 349.

2   Eg where a widow, who holds during widowhood, remarries: *Oland's Case* (1602) 5 Co Rep 116a; Co Litt 55b.

[376]–[380]

B: APPORTIONMENT IN RESPECT OF TIME

156   Apportionment of payments in the nature of income

Unless the settlement expressly stipulates that no apportionment is to take place[1], all rents, annuities, dividends and other periodical payments in the nature of income are considered as accruing from day to day, and on the cesser of the interest of the tenant for life or person entitled for the time being to the income of the settled property, by death or otherwise[2] are apportionable accordingly[3] between him or his personal representatives and the remainderman[4].

Therefore, whenever there are periodical payments accruing when the event calling for apportionment occurs, the Apportionment Act 1870 must be applied, and when subsequently the accruing payments become due they must be distributed accordingly, the portion attributable to the period before the death of a tenant for life or other person entitled to the income being payable to his estate[5]. Moreover, if an investment on which a dividend is so accruing is transferred by trustees to a person absolutely entitled before the dividend is paid, the estate of the deceased tenant for life still remains entitled to the portion accruing prior to the tenant for life's death, and, accordingly, some arrangement should be made to secure payment to the estate of that amount[6]. A payment will not be apportionable unless it is declared or expressed to be made for or in respect of some definite period[7].

[381]

1   There must be either an express direction against apportionment or terms of gifts so clear as necessarily to exclude apportionment. As to apportionment generally see 42 Halsbury's Laws (4th Edn Reissue) para 957 et seq. For a clause excluding the application of the Apportionment Act 1870 (23 Halsbury's Statutes (4th Edn) LANDLORD AND TENANT) see Form 214 [1732] post.

2   *Re Jenkins, Williams v Jenkins* [1915] 1 Ch 46; and see *Re Joel's Will Trusts, Rogerson v Brudenell-Bruce* [1967] Ch 14, [1966] 2 All ER 482 (different presumptive share of capital a change of interest).

3   See the Apportionment Act 1870 ss 2, 7 as amended by the SLR (No 2) Act 1893.
4   *Re Cline's Estate* (1874) LR 18 Eq 213; *Pollock v Pollock* (1874) LR 18 Eq 329.
5   *Re Muirhead, Muirhead v Hill* [1916] 2 Ch 181 at 186.
6   *Re Henderson, Public Trustee v Reddie* [1940] Ch 368 at 378, [1940] 1 All ER 623 at 628.
7   *Re Jowitt, Jowitt v Keeling* [1922] 2 Ch 442; see also *Re Sneyd, Robertson-MacDonald v Sneyd* [1961] 1 All
ER 744, [1961] 1 WLR 575 (apportionment of interest on compensation for depreciation of land value
between two successive tenants for life). As to what sums are apportionable by the Apportionment Act
1870 see further 42 Halsbury's Laws (4th Edn Reissue) para 958.

[382]

157   Sale and purchase of investments

As a general rule, on a sale of investments, whether for purposes of reinvestment or
distribution, the court declines to make any apportionment between the persons entitled
to income or capital of the proceeds of sale on account of income accrued but not
payable at the time of sale, inasmuch as to do otherwise would be to impose a heavy
burden on trustees[1]. This rule is not affected by the Apportionment Act 1870, and it is
applied in cases where the tenant for life has died between the last payment of income
and the sale[2]. If a purchase of stock carries with it the right to receive dividends which
have been earned and declared but not paid, there is no question of apportionment, and
the tenant for life is not entitled to be paid the amount of such dividends by the trustees[3].

For income tax purposes, income from fixed-interest securities is taxable on the
accrual basis, not receipts basis, with certain exceptions[4].

[383]

1   *Scholefield v Redfern* (1863) 2 Drew & Sm 173; *Freman v Whitbread* (1865) LR 1 Eq 266; and see
Re Maclaren's Settlement Trusts, Royal Exchange Assurance v Maclaren [1951] 2 All ER 414.
2   *Bulkeley v Stephens* [1896] 2 Ch 241; *Re Firth, Sykes v Ball* [1938] Ch 517, [1938] 2 All ER 217.
Clauson J's decision in *Re Winterstoke's Will Trusts, Gunn v Richardson* [1938] Ch 158, [1937] 4 All ER
63 seems out of line with the other cases, and in *Re Ellerman's Settlement Trusts, Hitch v Ruegg* [1984]
LS Gaz 430 Nourse J said it was wrong and ought not to be followed.
3   *Re Peel's Settled Estates* [1910] 1 Ch 389.
4   For the accrued income scheme see the Income and Corporation Taxes Act 1988 ss 710–728 as
amended (42–44 Halsbury's Statutes (4th Edn) TAXATION).

[384]

C: ADJUSTMENT OF BURDENS BETWEEN CAPITAL AND INCOME

158   Outgoings payable out of income

In the absence of an express direction by a settlor to the contrary, it is presumed that the
settled property is intended to descend intact[1]. Income must, therefore, bear all ordinary
outgoings of a recurrent nature in respect of the property[2], such as rates and taxes[3], the
interest on charges and incumbrances on the property[4], rents reserved by the leases under
which settled leaseholds are held[5], and the expense of performing and observing all
continuing obligations, covenants and conditions on the part of the lessee[6]. The tenant
for life or person entitled to income is not required to bear the expense of insurance or
repairs which is not chargeable to income by the settlement or required by covenants
affecting the property[7]. The tenant for life must also bear the costs of legal proceedings
for his sole benefit in respect of his life interest, such as the costs of an application by the
tenant for life in respect of a fund which has been paid into court[8], including the costs of
the trustees if it is necessary for them to appear[9].

[385]

1   For a direction to the contrary see Form 173 [1649] post.
2   *Fountaine v Pellet* (1791) 1 Ves 337 at 342; *Shore v Shore* (1859) 4 Drew 501; *Re Copland's Settlement,*
     Johns v Carden [1900] 1 Ch 326; *Re Wynn, Public Trustee v Newborough* [1955] 2 All ER 865, [1955]
     1 WLR 940. Compensation to an outgoing tenant under a covenant in his lease has been held to be a
     current expense: *Mansel v Norton* (1883) 22 Ch D 769, CA.
3   *Fountaine v Pellet* (1791) 1 Ves 337 at 342; *Re Kingham, Kingham v Kingham* [1897] 1 IR 170;
     Re Redding, Thompson v Redding [1897] 1 Ch 876. Where the real value of property could only be
     ascertained and its real benefit enjoyed by means of a sale, the tenant for life has been held entitled to
     the income of the proceeds of sale without contributing to the charges accrued since the life interest
     came into possession: see *Earl of Lonsdale v Countess Berchtoldt* (1857) 3 K & J 185.
4   *Revel v Watkinson* (1748) 1 Ves Sen 93; *Whitbread v Smith* (1854) 3 De GM & G 727 at 741; *Marshall v*
     Crowther (1874) 2 Ch D 199; *Re Harrison, Townson v Harrison* (1889) 43 Ch D 55; *Honywood v Honywood*
     [1902] 1 Ch 347.
5   *Re Kingham, Kingham v Kingham* [1897] 1 IR 170; *Re Redding, Thompson v Redding* [1897] 1 Ch 876;
     Re Betty, Betty v A-G [1899] 1 Ch 821; *Re Gjers, Cooper v Gjers* [1899] 2 Ch 54. The same rule applies
     in the case of unsaleable leaseholds included in a residuary estate and any loss must be borne by the
     tenant for life: *Allen v Embleton* (1858) 4 Drew 226; *Re Owen, Slater v Owen* [1912] 1 Ch 519.
6   As to insurance see further 42 Halsbury's Laws (4th Edn Reissue) para 774. As to the application of fire
     insurance money where there is no express obligation to reinstate leased property see *Mumford Hotels*
     Ltd v Wheler [1964] Ch 117, [1963] 3 All ER 250.
7   As to capital outgoings see Paragraph 159 [387] post.
8   *Re Ingram's Trust* (1854) 2 WR 679; *Re Marner's Trusts* (1866) LR 3 Eq 432. As to payment into court
     under the Trustee Act 1925 s 63 as amended by the Administration of Justice Act 1965 s 36(4), Sch 3
     (48 Halsbury's Statutes (4th Edn) TRUSTS AND SETTLEMENTS) see 48 Halsbury's Laws (4th Edn 2000
     Reissue) para 809 et seq.
9   *Re Evans' Trusts* (1872) 7 Ch App 609. As to such costs see further 42 Halsbury's Laws (4th Edn
     Reissue) para 961.

[386]

159   Capital outgoings

The corpus of a trust estate must, in the absence of a specific direction to the contrary,
be resorted to for all costs, charges and expenses properly incurred for the benefit of the
whole estate such as:

159.1   the premiums on insurance policies forming part of the settled property[1];
159.2   the costs of legal proceedings for the administration and protection of the
               whole estate, for example the costs of paying the trust fund into court[2] and
               of actions by the trustees for the protection of the estate[3];
159.3   the costs of a yearly audit and stocktaking where capital is left in a business[4];
               and
159.4   the cost of appointing new trustees[5].

The costs of proceedings for the administration and protection of the settled property
are payable out of capital even though such costs are incurred by the tenant for life
primarily for his own benefit, as where the tenant for life applies to the court to decide
questions as to the proper investment of trust funds[6], incurs costs in settling a foreclosure
action brought by the mortgagees[7], or defends an action by a purchaser to recover a
deposit[8]. Where the sole question is one of apportionment between the tenant for life
and the remainderman, however, the costs may also be apportioned[9].

Costs which ought to be borne by capital may be retained out of income by the
trustees until they can be raised out of capital[10], but the tenant for life is entitled to have
such costs defrayed by an immediate sale[11].

Any capital gains tax payable on the disposal of assets forming part of the capital of
the trust estate is prima facie payable out of capital[12].

[387]

1   *Macdonald v Irvine* (1878) 8 Ch D 101, CA; *Re Sherry, Sherry v Sherry* [1913] 2 Ch 508; cf *Re Jones'
     Settlement, Stunt v Jones* [1915] 1 Ch 373 where a tenant for life was held not entitled to be repaid
     premiums paid voluntarily and without any request by the trustees. The Forms contained in this title
     usually provide for payment of such premiums out of the income or capital of the settled property: see
     eg Form 103 [1492] post.
2   *Re Staples' Settlement* (1849) 13 Jur 273; *Re Ingram's Trust* (1854) 2 WR 679; *Re Whitton's Trusts* (1869)
     LR 8 Eq 352.
3   *Stott v Milne* (1884) 25 Ch D 710, CA; *Re Ormrod's Settled Estate* [1892] 2 Ch 318; *Re Blake (a lunatic)*
     (1895) 72 LT 280. Expenses incurred by trustees in compelling lessees of settled land to perform their
     covenants to repair have, however, been directed to be raised by mortgage of the settled land, so that
     the tenant for life and the remainderman should bear them in fair proportion: *Re McClure's Trusts, Carr
     v Commercial Union Insurance Co* (1906) 76 LJ Ch 52. As to the costs of legal proceedings for the
     protection of the settled land see also 42 Halsbury's Laws (4th Edn Reissue) para 825.
4   *Re Bennett, Jones v Bennett* [1896] 1 Ch 778, CA. For clauses providing for audit see Form 230 [1763],
     Form 231 [1764] post.
5   Where the settlor has appointed a single trustee, the costs of appointing an additional trustee are payable
     out of corpus (*Re Ratcliff* [1898] 2 Ch 352; but see *Finlay v Howard* (1842) 2 Dr & War 490; *Re
     Brackenbury's Trusts* (1870) LR 10 Eq 45); and where trustees rightly retired in consequence of the acts
     of the tenant for life the costs were directed to be paid out of income (*Coventry v Coventry* (1837) 1
     Keen 758). As to the appointment of trustees see vol 40(2) (2001 Reissue) TRUSTS AND
     SETTLEMENTS Part 10 [5201]. For Forms of appointment see vol 40(2) (2001 Reissue) TRUSTS AND
     SETTLEMENTS Part 10 [5801] et seq.
6   *Beauclerk v Ashburnham* (1845) 8 Beav 322; *Hume v Richardson* (1862) 31 LJ Ch 713.
7   *More v More* (1889) 37 WR 414; and see *Selby v Selby* (1838) 2 Jur 106.
8   *Re Foster's Settled Estates* [1922] 1 Ch 348.
9   *Reeves v Creswick* (1839) 3 Y & C Ex 715; *Re Earl of Chesterfield's Trusts* (1883) 24 Ch D 643 at 654.
10   *Stott v Milne* (1884) 25 Ch D 710, CA. As to the rights of trustees to reimbursement and indemnity see
     generally Paragraph 200 [483] et seq post.
11   *Burkett v Spray* (1829) 1 Russ & M 113.
12   As to capital gains tax generally see further Paragraph 338 [896] et seq post.

[388]

160   Cost of repairs

Casual repairs should usually be paid out of income[1]. The trustees may pay for any repairs out of income, and if they do so the court will not interfere with their discretion[2]; but, if they think the repairs are such that they should not be paid for out of income, the trustees may apply to the court for a direction for payment out of capital[3]. Repairs amounting to structural reconstruction[4], and permanent improvements[5], should generally be borne by capital[6].

[389]

1   *Re Smith, Vincent v Smith* [1930] 1 Ch 88; *Re Earl of Berkeley, Inglis v Countess of Berkeley* [1968] Ch 744,
     [1968] 3 All ER 364, CA.
2   *Re Gray, Public Trustee v Woodhouse* [1927] 1 Ch 242.
3   *Re Jackson, Jackson v Talbot* (1882) 21 Ch D 786; *Re Robins, Holland v Gillam* [1928] Ch 721.
4   *Re Whitaker, Rooke v Whitaker* [1929] 1 Ch 662.
5   *Re Conquest, Royal Exchange Assurance v Conquest* [1929] 2 Ch 353; *Re Smith, Vincent v Smith* [1930] 1
     Ch 88.
6   If the trustees' powers overlap, they should be guided by the equitable principles laid down in *Re
     Hotchkys, Freke v Calmady* (1886) 32 Ch D 408, CA; see also *Re Robins, Holland v Gillam* above at 737;
     Re Conquest, Royal Exchange Assurance v Conquest [1929] 2 Ch 353.

[390]

161   Liability for incumbrances and interest on them

Apart from any question arising on the special terms of the instrument creating the settlement, a tenant for life is under no obligation to discharge any portion of the principal of paramount incumbrances[1]; but he is bound as between himself and the remainderman[2] to keep down the interest accruing during his lifetime to the extent of, and out of, the rents and profits received by him[3]. If the rents are at any time insufficient to keep down the interest, subsequent rents arising during the lifetime of the tenant for life are applicable to liquidate arrears accruing during his own life tenancy[4]. If part of the property is sold and principal, interest and costs due on the mortgage are then paid off out of the proceeds, the rents of the unsold portion subsequently received by the tenant for life remain liable as between himself and the remainderman to repay amounts paid out of capital in satisfaction of arrears of interest[5].

[391]

1   *Lord Penrhyn v Hughes* (1799) 5 Ves 99 at 107; *Kekewich v Marker* (1851) 3 Mac & G 311 at 328.
2   The obligation does not exist as between the tenant for life and the incumbrancers: *Re Morley, Morley v Saunders* (1869) LR 8 Eq 594.
3   *Revel v Watkinson* (1748) 1 Ves Sen 93; *Amesbury v Brown* (1750) 1 Ves Sen 477 at 480; *Earl of Peterborough v Mordaunt* (1760) 1 Eden 474; *Faulkner v Daniel* (1843) 3 Hare 199 at 207; and see *Syer v Gladstone* (1885) 30 Ch D 614 as explained in *Frewen v Law Life Assurance Society* [1896] 2 Ch 511 at 517.
4   *Revel v Watkinson* (1748) 1 Ves Sen 93; *Tracy v Viscountess Dowager Hereford* (1786) 2 Bro CC 128. This was applied to interest on unpaid instalments of estate duty: *Re Earl Howe's Settled Estates, Earl Howe v Kingscote* [1903] 2 Ch 69, CA; *Re Earl of Egmont's Settled Estates, Lefroy v Egmont* [1912] 1 Ch 251.
5   *Honywood v Honywood* [1902] 1 Ch 347.

[392]

162   Extent of tenant for life's obligation to keep down interest

The obligation of the tenant for life to keep down interest applies although there is an ultimate limitation to him in fee[1], or he has an absolute or general power of appointment, by reason of which he might make the estate his own[2]. A purchaser of the estate of the tenant for life, although himself the mortgagee, is bound to discharge the obligations[3].

The liability of the tenant for life is not personal[4], but is a charge on his life estate, and if he fails to keep down interest, future rents and profits payable during his tenancy for life are liable to be paid to the remainderman up to the full amount of his default[5], and he is not entitled to have any portion of the settled estates sold for the purposes of paying off interest and arrears[6]. He may, however, have an incumbrance paid off by sale if the rents are insufficient to keep down the interest[7].

[393]

1   *Burges v Mawbey* (1823) Turn & R 167.
2   As to the application of this rule generally see 42 Halsbury's Laws (4th Edn Reissue) para 967.
3   *Lord Penrhyn v Hughes* (1799) 5 Ves 99; *Raffety v King* (1836) 1 Keen 601.
4   *Honywood v Honywood* [1902] 1 Ch 347 at 351.
5   *Waring v Coventry* (1834) 2 My & K 406; *Fitzmaurice v Murphy* (1859) 8 I Ch R 363; *Makings v Makings* (1860) I De GF & J 355; *Lord Kilworth v Earl of Mountcashell* (1864) 15 I Ch R 565. The remedy of the remainderman is to apply to the court for the appointment of a receiver, whose costs must be borne by the tenant for life (*Shore v Shore* (1859) 4 Drew 501), and have the rents appropriated for the purpose of paying the accruing interest (*Hill v Browne* (1844) Drury temp Sug 426 at 434; *Coote v O'Reilly* (1844) I Jo & Lat 455 at 461; *Lord Kensington v Bouverie* (1859) 7 HL Cas 557 at 575; *Kirwan v Kennedy* (1869) IR 3 Eq 472 at 481).
6   *Hawkins v Hawkins* (1836) 6 LJ Ch 69; *Shore v Shore* (1859) 4 Drew 501.
7   *Lord Penrhyn v Hughes* (1799) 5 Ves 99; *Cooke v Cholmondeley* (1857) 4 Drew 244.

[394]

163   Rights of remainderman

The remainderman is entitled to be repaid arrears of interest out of the assets of a deceased tenant for life to the extent of the rents received during the life tenancy[1], subject to any set-off that there may be in respect of capital charges paid by the tenant for life[2]. He is not entitled, however, to have arrears of interest which have accrued during a previous life tenancy discharged by a subsequent tenant for life out of the rents and profits. Such arrears are primarily a charge on the inheritance[3], and if the subsequent tenant for life is forced to pay them they are repayable to him out of capital[4].

[395]

1   *Baldwin v Baldwin* (1856) 6 I Ch R 156; *Re Fitzgerald's Estate* (1867) IR 1 Eq 453; *Kirwan v Kennedy* (1869) IR 3 Eq 472 at 481; *Re Gore* (1874) IR 9 Eq 83. The remainderman will not, however, have a specific lien on rents collected or to be collected by a personal representative after the death of the tenant for life: *Dillon v Dillon* (1853) 4 I Ch R 102.

2   *Re Whyte* (1857) 7 I Ch R 61n; *Howlin v Sheppard* (1872) IR 6 Eq 497.

3   *Caulfield v Maguire* (1845) 2 Jo & Lat 141; *Sharshaw v Gibbs* (1854) Kay 333; *Kennedy v Daley* (1858) 7 I Ch R 445.

4   *Kirwan v Kennedy* (1869) IR 3 Eq 472. Where, however, the tenant for life has overpaid interest by mistake, this is not recoverable out of capital: see *Kirwan v Kennedy* above.

[396]

164   Several estates in one settlement

If several estates are included in the same settlement, the tenant for life is bound out of the whole rents and profits to keep down the interest on charges on all the estates[1], and, if a charge in respect of which arrears of interest have arisen is paid off by means of a sale of one of the estates, he remains liable to make good the arrears out of subsequent rents received by him from any of the estates[2].

1   *Tracy v Viscountess Dowager Hereford* (1786) 2 Bro CC 128; *Scholefield v Lockwood* (1863) 4 De GJ & Sm 22; *Frewen v Law Life Assurance Society* [1896] 2 Ch 511; *Honywood v Honywood* [1902] 1 Ch 347; and see *Re Hotchkys, Freke v Calmady* (1886) 32 Ch D 408 at 418, 419, CA.

2   *Honywood v Honywood* [1902] 1 Ch 347.

[397]

165   Annuities

On a gift of real estate charged with annuities, the tenant for life is, in the absence of provision to the contrary, bound to keep down the annuities[1], and, if he fails to do this, and the estate is sold to pay the arrears, the remainderman is entitled to have the arrears repaid out of interest on the surplus of the purchase money accruing during the life tenancy[2]. If, however, the income is insufficient to pay the annuities in full and the deficiency is raised out of capital, the remaindermen are not entitled to have the deficiency repaid out of future income accruing during the life tenancy[3]. Arrears unpaid at the death of a tenant for life become a charge upon and must be raised out of corpus, and the succeeding tenant for life is only bound to keep down the interest on them[4].

If the annuity charged on the settled estate is a debt of the settlor, the tenant for life and the remainderman must contribute to the annuity proportionately[5].

[398]

1   *Re Grant, Walker v Martineau* (1883) 52 LJ Ch 552; *Re Popham, Butler v Popham* (1914) 111 LT 524.

2   *Coote v O'Reilly* (1844) 1 Jo & Lat 455.

3   *Re Croxon, Ferrers v Croxton* [1915] 2 Ch 290.

4   *Playfair v Cooper, Prince v Cooper* (1853) 17 Beav 187.

5   As to the rules for ascertaining the respective liabilities of the tenant for life and the remainderman see 17(2) Halsbury's Laws (4th Edn Reissue) para 539. As to whether an annuity is payable out of the corpus or income of property charged see 39(2) Halsbury's Laws (4th Edn Reissue) para 830.

[399]

166   Discharge of interest

A tenant for life in possession of an estate subject to a charge bearing interest, who pays the interest, although the rents and profits are insufficient to enable him to do so, may make himself an incumbrancer[1] for the excess of his payments beyond the amount of the rents and profits; but, if he pays the interest during his life without any intimation that the rents and profits are insufficient, or that he has any intention of charging the corpus of the estate with any deficiency, his personal representatives cannot after his death set up any such charge[2]. If the charge is a continuing charge on income as well as a charge on the corpus, it is doubtful whether a tenant for life is entitled, until after the termination of his life interest, to repayment out of the corpus in respect of a deficiency, which he has made good out of his own money[3].

[400]

1   Cf *Fetherstone v Mitchell* (1846) 9 I Eq R 480.
2   *Dixon v Peacock* (1855) 3 Drew 288; *Lord Kensington v Bouverie* (1859) 7 HL Cas 557.
3   As to when a tenant for life is entitled to repayment out of the corpus see 42 Halsbury's Laws (4th Edn Reissue) para 971.

[401]

167   Discharge of capital charge by tenant for life

A tenant for life who pays off a capital charge on the settled property is prima facie entitled to that charge for his own benefit[1]; and the presumption applies equally in favour of a tenant for life in remainder[2], or in any case where the charge is paid off by the trustees out of rents and profits[3]. If successive tenants for life pay off a mortgage by instalments, the money must be repaid to them rateably in proportion to the payments made by them, and not divided among them in order of priority[4].

[402]

1   As to payment off of a capital charge by the tenant for life generally see 42 Halsbury's Laws (4th Edn Reissue) para 972.
2   *Re Chesters, Whittingham v Chesters* [1935] Ch 77.
3   *Re Harvey, Harvey v Hobday* [1896] 1 Ch 137, CA.
4   *Re Nepean's Settled Estate* [1900] 1 IR eq 298.

[403]

168   Evidence of intention

A tenant for life is under no obligation to prove his intention to pay off the charge for his own benefit[1]. The simple payment of the charge by him is sufficient to establish his prima facie right to have the charge raised out of the estate; he is under no obligation or duty to make any declaration, or to do any act demonstrating his intention[2]. In every case, however, the court must ascertain the intention of the person paying off the charge. In the absence of direct evidence the intention must be deduced from what it was in his interest to do, but any evidence to the contrary must be regarded[3], and the smallest demonstration that he meant to discharge the estate is sufficient[4]. Such a demonstration may be made by acts as well as by words of the tenant for life. The burden of proving an intention to exonerate the estate, however, lies on the remainderman[5], and evidence drawn from recitals in a deed, or the form of reconveyance, may be in its turn rebutted by a long series of acts consistent only with an intention to keep the charge alive[6], or by the personal evidence of the tenant for life[7].

The fact that the tenant for life who pays off the charge and the remainderman stand in the relationship of parent and child is material if there is anything else to rebut the presumption that the tenant for life paid the charge off for his own benefit, but is not by itself sufficient to rebut it[8].

[404]

1   *Lindsay v Earl of Wicklow* (1873) IR 7 Eq 192.
2   *Redington v Redington* (1809) 1 Ball & B 131; *Burrell v Earl of Egremont* (1844) 7 Beav 205; *Lord Kensington v Bouverie* (1859) 7 HL Cas 557 at 595; *Lindsay v Earl of Wicklow* (1873) IR 7 Eq 192; *Re Harvey, Harvey v Hobday* [1896] 1 Ch 137, CA.

3   *Pitt v Pitt* (1856) 22 Beav 294; *Williams v Williams-Wynn* (1915) 84 LJ Ch 801. For a case where there
     was a covenant to assign to the trustees of the settlement the benefit of charges paid off see *Cochrane v
     St Clair* (1855) 1 Jur NS 302.
4   *Jones v Morgan* (1783) 1 Bro CC 206 at 218; *Lord Kensington v Bouverie* (1859) 7 HL Cas 557; *Re
     Warwick's Settlement Trusts, Greville Trust Co v Grey* [1938] Ch 530, [1938] 1 All ER 639, CA. In the
     present state of the authorities, a tenant for life who wishes to keep a charge alive would be well advised
     to give express notice to the trustees whenever he makes a payment out of his own money.
5   *Re Harvey, Harvey v Hobday* [1896] 1 Ch 137, CA.
6   *Lindsay v Earl of Wicklow* (1873) IR 7 Eq 192.
7   *Lord Gifford v Lord Fitzhardinge* [1899] 2 Ch 32; *Williams v Williams-Wynn* (1915) 84 LJ Ch 801. On
     the other hand, an assignment of a charge to a trustee for the benefit of the tenant for life has been held
     not to keep the charge alive in the face of evidence contained in his will that he regarded it as
     extinguished: *Re Lloyd's Estate* [1903] 1 IR 144. For a case where an intention to keep a charge alive
     was evidenced by the will see *Lysaght v Lysaght* (1851) 4 Ir Jur 110.
8   *Re Harvey, Harvey v Hobday* [1896] 1 Ch 137, CA.

[405]

169   Extinction of charge by mistake

A tenant for life who extinguishes a charge on the estate in a mistaken belief as to his own rights is entitled on discovering his error to keep the charge alive against the settled property[1], and a vague intention of not requiring repayment, if he should find that he could conveniently do without it, will not convert the payment into a gift for the benefit of the estate[2].

1   *Burrell v Earl of Egremont* (1844) 7 Beav 205; *Conolly v Barter* [1904] 1 IR 130, CA. Apart from mistake,
     an intention to discharge the incumbrance cannot afterwards be changed: see *Lindsay v Earl of Wicklow*
     (1873) IR 7 Eq 192 at 209; but see *Lysaght v Lysaght* (1851) 4 Ir Jur 110.
2   *Cuddon v Cuddon* (1876) 4 Ch D 583.

[406]

170   Renewable leaseholds

Since 1925, perpetually renewable leases take effect as a demise for a term of 2,000 years, and perpetually renewable underleases take effect as a demise for a term less in duration by one day than the term out of which they are derived[1]. Leases and underleases may, however, still contain a provision for renewal for a term not exceeding 60 years from the termination of the lease or underlease[2] and, if such renewable leaseholds are included in the subject matter of a settlement, the settlement should make it clear whether an imperative trust for renewal is intended to be created. A direction to renew may be couched in discretionary terms in order to avoid placing the estate and the persons interested at the mercy of the lessor, and yet impose on the trustees a trust which the court will execute if they do not renew[3]. If there is a direction to renew, whether express or implied[4], it must be obeyed, and the persons whose duty it is to renew, whether the trustees or the tenant for life, are liable to compensate the remainderman for the loss occasioned by their default[5], or, if he himself renews, to repay him the amount of the fine, provided that it is reasonable[6].

In the absence of a direction to renew, the mere circumstance of there being limitations over imposes no necessity on the tenant for life, and he may renew or allow the term to expire[7]. If, however, a tenant for life in such circumstances chooses to renew, he is a trustee of the lease for all persons interested under the subsequent limitations, in accordance with the principle of equity that parties interested jointly with others in a lease cannot take to themselves the benefit of a renewal to the exclusion of the other parties interested with them[8].

[407]

The settlement should provide how and by whom the expenses of renewal are to be raised and borne. If there is no special direction in the settlement as to the raising of expenses of renewal[9], or the special direction is limited in amount[10], the expenses of renewal, or the excess of them over the limited sum, must be borne by the tenant for life and remainderman in proportion to their actual enjoyment of the renewed lease[11].

If the expenses of renewal are paid by the tenant for life, then, in the absence of an express provision in the settlement to the contrary, his estate has a lien upon the residue of the term for whatever should be paid by the remainderman in respect of the period of which the tenant for life has not had the enjoyment[12]. The tenant for life cannot, however, require repayment of the sum advanced in his lifetime[13]. The remainderman will be required to pay compound interest on the amount found due from him for the period down to the death of the tenant for life and simple interest from that date till payment[14].

[408]

1   See the Law of Property Act 1925 s 145, Sch 15 paras 1(1), 2(1), 5, 6(1), 7(1) (23 Halsbury's Statutes (4th Edn) LANDLORD AND TENANT).
2   See Law of Property Act 1925 s 145, Sch 15 para 7(2).
3   *Viscount Milsington v Earl Mulgrave* (1818) 3 Madd 491 (subsequent proceedings *Viscount Milsintown v Earl Portmore, Earl Mulgrave* (1821) 5 Madd 471); *Mortimer v Watts* (1852) 14 Beav 616.
4   *Lock v Lock* (1710) 2 Vern 666. The court is, however, slow on mere inference to impose an obligation on the tenant for life to renew: *Capel v Wood* (1828) 4 Russ 500.
5   *Lord Montfort v Lord Cadogan* (1810) 17 Ves 485 (varied (1816) 19 Ves 635); *Bennett v Colley* (1833) 2 My & K 225; and see *Hulkes v Barrow* (1829) Taml 264. The trustees have a right to be recouped by a tenant for life who has received the rents and profits that ought to have made good the fine (*Lord Montfort v Lord Cadogan* above); but, in a case where the estate of a tenant for life who neglected to renew was insolvent, the loss was required to be borne by capital and not by the tenant for life in remainder: *Wadley v Wadley* (1845) 2 Coll 11.
6   *Colegrave v Manby* (1826) 2 Russ 238.
7   *Stone v Theed* (1787) 2 Bro CC 243; *White v White* (1804) 9 Ves 554 at 561; *O'Ferrall v O'Ferrall* (1834) L & G *temp* Plunk 79. A tenant for life ought not, however, by surrendering a lease, to deprive himself of the option of renewing for the benefit of the parties in remainder: *Harvey v Harvey* (1842) 5 Beav 134.
8   As to this principle see 42 Halsbury's Laws (4th Edn Reissue) para 975.
9   If there is a power in the trustees to raise expenses of renewal either by sale or mortgage or out of rents and profits, and the trustees do not exercise their discretion, the court treats the case as one in which there is no direction binding the court: *Jones v Jones* (1846) 5 Hare 440 at 462; *Ainslie v Harcourt* (1860) 28 Beav 313; but see *Viscount Milsintown v Earl Portmore, Earl Mulgrave* (1821) 5 Madd 471.
10   *Plumtre v Oxenden* (1855) 25 LJ Ch 19.
11   As to liability for the expenses of renewal generally see 42 Halsbury's Laws (4th Edn Reissue) para 976.
12   *Adderley v Clavering* (1789) 2 Cox Eq Cas 192; *Jones v Jones* (1846) 5 Hare 440 at 465.
13   *Harris v Harris (No 3)* (1863) 32 Beav 333.
14   *Nightingale v Lawson* (1785) 1 Bro CC 440; *Giddings v Giddings* (1827) 3 Russ 241; *Cridland v Luxton* (1834) 4 LJ Ch 65; *Bradford v Brownjohn* (1868) 3 Ch App 711. As to the reimbursement of a remainderman see 42 Halsbury's Laws (4th Edn Reissue) para 977.

[409]–[415]

D: ADJUSTMENT OF LOSSES BETWEEN TENANT FOR LIFE AND REMAINDERMAN

171   Losses on authorised investments generally

A person entitled to income under an ordinary settlement of personal property is entitled to the whole income arising from authorised investments, notwithstanding any shrinkage or decrease of the capital value, but he is not entitled to share in any augmentation of the capital value[1]. If the settled property, therefore, produces a diminished or no income, any income loss must be borne by the person entitled to the income, and he has no claim to have it, or any portion of it, made good out of capital[2]. Similarly such person has no claim against capital in respect of loss of income by the reduction of dividends[3], or by the non-payment of interest where the covenant is to pay out of net earnings available, and no earnings are available, or by the non-payment of cumulative dividends until after the cesser of his interest[4]. Any loss arising from the misappropriation by a trustee of the rents of settled property must be borne by the person entitled to the income[5].

[416]

1   *Verner v General and Commercial Investment Trust* [1894] 2 Ch 239 at 258, 270, CA.
2   *Shore v Shore* (1859) 4 Drew 501 at 509; *Yates v Yates* (1860) 28 Beav 637; but cf *Re Carr's Settlement, Riddell v Carr* [1933] Ch 928 where settled annuities were redeemed under the Law of Property Act 1925 s 191 (repealed) and the income from the investments of the redemption money being insufficient to pay the annuities in full, the tenants for life were held entitled to have the deficiency made good out of the capital.
3   *Bague v Dumergue* (1853) 10 Hare 462.
4   *Re Sale, Nisbet v Philp* [1913] 2 Ch 697; *Re Grundy, Grundy v Holme* (1917) 117 LT 470; *Re Wakley, Wakley v Vachell* [1920] 2 Ch 205, CA.
5   *Solley v Wood* (1861) 29 Beav 482.

[417]

172   Losses on authorised mortgage investments

If the authorised investment is a security, such as a mortgage, not only for principal but also for interest, then, notwithstanding any payment of interest to the tenant for life or person entitled to the income, that person has a right as against the remainderman to have arrears of interest charged upon the security, and the proceeds of the insufficient security must be apportioned in the proportions which the amount due for capital and the amount due to the tenant for life or person entitled to the income for arrears of interest bear to one another[1]. This right to apportionment is not defeated by a provision that no property not actually producing income shall be treated as producing income[2]. Where the mortgagees enter into possession of the mortgaged property, the rents of the property, pending realisation, should be applied, in the absence of a contrary provision in the settlement, primarily in payment to the tenant for life or persons entitled to income of sums not exceeding the interest on the mortgages, and any excess should be applied as capital[3]. Interest on arrears of interest is not allowed[4], but, where a mortgage contains a proviso for reduction of interest on punctual payment, the arrears may be calculated on the full rate of interest[5].

If the equity of redemption becomes barred, either by virtue of the Limitation Act 1980[6], or of an order for foreclosure, or otherwise, the tenant for life or person entitled to income is then entitled to the actual net rents, even if they exceed the amount of the interest which was previously payable under the mortgage, but he is not entitled to have any subsequent deficiency repaid out of capital[7]. This does not, however, affect any right to apportionment which had accrued prior to the equity of redemption becoming barred[8].

[418]

1   See *Re Morris's Will Trusts, Public Trustee v Morris* [1960] 3 All ER 548, [1960] 1 WLR 1210.
2   *Re Hubbuck, Hart v Stone* [1896] 1 Ch 754, CA; *Re Lewis, Davies v Harrison* [1907] 2 Ch 296.
3   *Re Coaks, Coaks v Bayley* [1911] 1 Ch 171. In *Re Broadwood's Settlements, Broadwood v Broadwood* [1908] 1 Ch 115 where there were successive tenants for life, sums received as income were ordered to be distributed between the personal representatives of the deceased tenants for life and the remainderman in proportion to the amounts owing to them for arrears of interest when the particular sum was received. In *Re Southwell, Carter v Hungerford* (1915) 85 LJ Ch 70, rents distributed under a similar order had to be brought into hotchpot when the security was realised, the ultimate distribution being made on the principle laid down in *Re Atkinson, Barbers' Co v Grose-Smith* [1904] 2 Ch 160, CA. But cf *Re Ancketill's Estate, ex p Scottish Provident Institution* (1891) 27 LR Ir 331 (where a receiver had been appointed); *Re Godden, Teague v Fox* [1893] 1 Ch 292.

4   *Re Moore, Moore v Johnson* (1885) 54 LJ Ch 432.
5   *Re Atkinson, Barbers' Co v Grose-Smith* [1904] 2 Ch 160, CA.
6   See the Limitation Act 1980 s 16 (24 Halsbury's Statutes (4th Edn) LIMITATION OF ACTIONS).
7   See the Law of Property Act 1925 s 31 as amended by the Trusts of Land and Appointment of Trustees Act 1996 ss 5, 25(2) Sch 2 para 1, Sch 4 (37 Halsbury's Statutes (4th Edn) REAL PROPERTY). See also *Re Horn's Estate, Public Trustee v Garnett* [1924] 2 Ch 222.
8   *Re Horn's Estate, Public Trustee v Garnett* [1924] 2 Ch 222.

[419]

173   Losses on investments not immediately realisable

A loss arising on the ultimate realisation of a security covering both principal and interest, which for some time after entitlement to its possession could not be realised, must, in the absence of provision to the contrary, be shared between those entitled to income and those entitled to capital in the same way as they would have shared it if the loss had occurred when they first became entitled in possession to the fund, the principle being that neither shall gain an advantage over the other[1]. In such cases a calculation is made of what principal sum, if invested at the date when the conversion should have taken place, would, with interest, amount to the sum actually recovered. Interest on this principal sum, or, in other words, the difference between such principal sum and the amount actually recovered, goes to those entitled to the income and the rest is treated as principal[2].

[420]

1   *Cox v Cox* (1869) LR 8 Eq 343.
2   *Turner v Newport* (1846) 2 Ph 14; *Cox v Cox* (1869) LR 8 Eq 343. In both these cases the rate of interest was calculated at four per cent: cf *Re Beech, Saint v Beech* [1920] 1 Ch 40; *Re Baker, Baker v Public Trustee* [1924] 2 Ch 271; *Re Ellis, Nettleton v Crimmins* [1935] Ch 193; and see *Re Parry, Brown v Parry* [1947] Ch 23, [1946] 2 All ER 412. The same principle was applied in *Re Duke of Cleveland's Estate, Hay v Wolmer* [1895] 2 Ch 542, where money was paid away under an erroneous order of the court and subsequently recovered, but without interest.

[421]

174   Loss on conversion of authorised investment into unauthorised security

The same principle as in the case of investments not immediately realisable[1] has been applied to a case of a trustee wrongfully selling an authorised investment and investing the proceeds in an unauthorised equitable mortgage. The total amount of dividends that the person entitled to income would have received if the wrongful investment had not been made and the value of the authorised investment at the death of the person entitled to income, which was the proper time of distribution of the fund, were ascertained, and the loss was divided between the estate of that person and the remainderman in the proportion which the total dividends that the person entitled to income would have received bore to the value of the authorised investment at the death, the executor giving credit for interest actually received, but not being liable to refund any overpayment, as the person entitled to income was in no way responsible for, or aware of, the breach of trust[2]. If the person entitled to income in such a case was responsible for the breach of trust, the remainderman would have the right to have the income received refunded to capital[3].

[422]

1   As to losses on investments not immediately realisable see Paragraph 173 [420] ante.
2   *Re Bird, Re Evans, Dodd v Evans* [1901] 1 Ch 916, which is difficult to reconcile with *Re Grabowski's Settlement* (1868) LR 6 Eq 12, except that in the latter case the dividends actually received by the tenant for life were in excess of anything that could have been recovered on an apportionment.
3   *Raby v Ridehalgh* (1855) 7 De GM & G 104.

[423]

175   Losses on trust business

Where a business is vested in trustees in trust for successive tenants for life, losses incurred in carrying on the business must in ordinary cases be made good out of subsequent profits[1], but a direction to defray losses out of the estate throws them on capital[2], and, in a case where a share in a partnership was settled, the practice of the partnership was followed, and, accordingly, losses were written off against capital[3]. Where a business is only carried on temporarily until it can be sold profitably, and not pursuant to a direction in the settlement, it seems that any loss probably should be apportioned between capital and income[4].

[424]

1   *Upton v Brown* (1884) 26 Ch D 588.
2   *Re Millichamp, Goodale and Bullock* (1885) 52 LT 758; *Re Clapham, Rutter v Clapham* (1886) 2 TLR 424 (where it was held that the losses and profits on the working of several boats, part of the estate, should be set off against each other, and that the tenant for life should take the net income).
3   *Gow v Forster* (1884) 26 Ch D 672.
4   See *Re Hengler, Frowde v Hengler* [1893] 1 Ch 586 (a case on a will).

[425]

E: WASTE

176   Liability for waste

A tenant for life has the right to the full enjoyment of the land during the continuance of his estate subject to the duty of leaving it unimpaired for the remainderman; this duty is defined by the doctrine of waste[1]. Waste may be legal or equitable[2], and legal waste may be either voluntary[3] or permissive[4].

Whether a tenant for life[5] will be liable for voluntary waste will depend on the terms of the settlement; he will be liable unless, as is frequently the case, he is expressly made unimpeachable for waste[6]. A tenant for life, even though impeachable for waste, is not liable for permissive waste unless his estate is expressly made subject to the condition of maintaining the premises[7]. Every tenant for life, however, whether impeachable for waste or not, will be liable for equitable waste[8].

[426]

1   Co Litt 53a. Certain acts which are technically waste but which improve without injuring the settled property are sometimes known as meliorating waste: see further 42 Halsbury's Laws (4th Edn Reissue) para 993.
2   As to equitable waste see Paragraph 181 [436] post.
3   As to voluntary waste see Paragraph 177 [428] post.
4   As to permissive waste see Paragraph 180 [434] post.
5   An action for waste will lie against a tenant by the curtesy, tenant in dower, tenant for life, for years, or half a year: Co Litt 53a et seq. As to tenant by the curtesy and tenant in dower see 39(2) Halsbury's Laws (4th Edn Reissue) paras 157, 161. A tenant in tail cannot be impeached for waste, either legal or equitable. A tenant in tail after possibility of issue extinct, however, or a tenant in fee simple subject to an executory devise over, may be restrained from committing equitable, but not legal, waste: see further 42 Halsbury's Laws (4th Edn Reissue) para 997 et seq.
6   *Woodhouse v Walker* (1880) 5 QBD 404.
7   *Woodhouse v Walker* (1880) 5 QBD 404.
8   As to equitable waste see Paragraph 181 [436] post.

[427]

177   Voluntary waste

Voluntary waste is any act which is injurious to the settled property, either by diminishing the value of the estate or by increasing the burden upon it. Unless unimpeachable for waste[1], therefore, a tenant for life may not pull down buildings, even though ruinous, without rebuilding, or erect new buildings, or suffer such new buildings, if erected, to be wasted[2]. He may not open new mines, quarries, or clay-pits, or work old abandoned pits or mines[3], but he may work mines or pits which have been previously opened in the sense that they have been worked, not necessarily for profit, so long as such previous working or use was not limited to any special or restricted purpose, such as the purpose of fuel or repair to some particular tenements[4].

Apart from any statutory provision, however, a tenant for life, even though impeachable for waste, may cut timber necessary for repairs[5], and may also cut trees, with certain exceptions[6], other than timber trees[7] or trees which would be timber if they were over 20 years of age, but timber trees under 20 years of age may be cut down in the course of the proper management of the estate for the purpose of allowing the growth of other timber[8].

[428]

1   As to the privilege of a tenant for life who is unimpeachable for waste see Paragraph 179 [432] post.
2   Co Litt 53a.
3   *Viner v Vaughan* (1840) 2 Beav 466. As to the statutory power to grant mining leases see Paragraph 147 [358] ante.
4   As to the working of mines generally see 31 Halsbury's Laws (4th Edn Reissue) para 373 et seq. As to dispositions of mines and minerals see vol 26 MINES AND QUARRIES Paragraph 31 [1847] et seq.
5   Timber for repairs may not be cut in advance (*Gorges v Stanfield* (1597) Cro Eliz 593) or sold in order to pay the wages of men employed to do the repairs (Bro Abr Waste pl 112) or to purchase other timber with the proceeds (Co Litt 53b; *Simmons v Norton* (1831) 7 Bing 640).
6   Eg ornamental trees, underwood, trees planted for the protection of the house, and quickset fences of whitethorn, or fruit trees growing in a garden or an orchard, may not be cut by a tenant for life impeachable for waste: Co Litt 53a.
7   As to what trees are timber see vol 16(1) FORESTRY AND CONSERVATION Paragraph 24 [2151].
8   *Pidgeley v Rawling* (1845) 2 Coll 275; *Bagot v Bagot, Legge v Legge* (1863) 32 Beav 509 at 517; *Earl of Cowley v Wellesley* (1866) LR 1 Eq 656; *Honywood v Honywood* (1874) LR 18 Eq 306; cf *Dunn v Bryan* (1872) IR 7 Eq 143. As to licences for felling and as to timber generally see vol 16(1) FORESTRY AND CONSERVATION Paragraph 25 [2154] et seq.

[429]

178   Cutting and sale of timber

Where a tenant for life is impeachable for waste in respect of timber and there is on the settled land timber ripe and fit for cutting, the tenant for life, on obtaining the consent of the trustees of the settlement or an order of the court, may cut and sell that timber or any part of it[1]. He may also cut down and use timber and other trees, provided that they have not been planted or left standing for shelter or ornament[2], for the purpose of executing, maintaining or repairing any improvement authorised by the Settled Land Act 1925[3].

Where the cutting of timber is authorised at common law either under an order of the court, or otherwise[4], the proceeds follow the interests of the estate, in the absence of direction to the contrary, that is to say, they are invested and the income given to the tenant for life impeachable for waste in the first place[5]. On the death of such tenant for life, the proceeds become the property of the first tenant for life unimpeachable for waste[6], or the first absolute owner, whichever estate first comes into possession[7].

On any exercise of the statutory power to cut and sell timber, three-quarters of the net proceeds of sale must be set aside as capital money arising under the Settled Land Act 1925, and the other quarter goes as rents and profits[8].

A tenant for life impeachable for waste is entitled to the proceeds of sale of trees (not being timber) cut in the ordinary course of management[9]; but if he cuts and sells timber without authority, he does so at his peril, and may in no case be permitted to derive any advantage from his wrongful act[10].

Where timber is blown down in a storm, the rule is, in the absence of improper conduct on the part of the tenant for life, to treat the produce of such timber trees as capital and allow the income to the tenant for life[11].

[430]

1   Settled Land Act 1925 s 66(1) (48 Halsbury's Statutes (4th Edn) TRUSTS AND SETTLEMENTS).
2   As to the meaning of ornamental timber and rights to fell it see 42 Halsbury's Laws (4th Edn Reissue) para 998 et seq. If the tenant for life is to be permitted to cut ornamental timber, express provision in the settlement is desirable.
3   See the Settled Land Act 1925 s 89. As to improvements see vol 40(2) (2001 Reissue) TRUSTS AND SETTLEMENTS Part 9 [4101].
4   *Waldo v Waldo* (1841) 12 Sim 107; *Gent v Harrison* (1859) John 517.
5   As to the proceeds of timber and other trees properly cut generally see 42 Halsbury's Laws (4th Edn Reissue) para 990.
6   *Waldo v Waldo* (1841) 12 Sim 107; *Phillips v Barlow* (1844) 14 Sim 263; *Gent v Harrison* (1859) John 517; *Lowndes v Norton* (1877) 6 Ch D 139.
7   *Honywood v Honywood* (1874) LR 18 Eq 306.
8   Settled Land Act 1925 s 66(2). As to the application of any compensation for the refusal of a felling licence see vol 16(1) FORESTRY AND CONSERVATION Paragraph 29 [2209].
9   *Honywood v Honywood* (1874) LR 18 Eq 306; *Re Harker's Will Trusts, Harker v Bayliss* [1938] Ch 323, [1938] 1 All ER 145.
10 *Williams v Duke of Bolton* (1784) 1 Cox Eq Cas 72; *Seagram v Knight* (1867) 2 Ch App 628, CA. As to the persons entitled to such wrongfully cut timber or its produce see 42 Halsbury's Laws (4th Edn Reissue) para 991.
11 As to windfalls generally see 42 Halsbury's Laws (4th Edn Reissue) para 992.

[431]

179   Privilege of tenant for life unimpeachable for waste

If the tenant for life is, as is usual, unimpeachable for waste, he has the same power to commit legal waste as if he were tenant in tail[1] and is therefore not liable for voluntary waste[2]. He will, therefore, be entitled to open new mines, or pits, and to fell timber, but not, in the absence of express authorisation, except in proper thinning, trees planted as an improvement under the Settled Land Act 1925[3], and the produce of such minerals or timber will belong to him, whether severed from the estate by his act or not, but not until severance[4]. This remains the law[5] even though the sale is made not under a power contained in the settlement, but under the statutory powers[6] conferred by the Settled Land Act 1925. It follows that on a sale of the estate with timber he is not entitled to the produce of the timber[7].

The exemption from liability for waste of a tenant for life without impeachment for waste is a special power given to him to appropriate part of the settled property, and may be controlled or qualified, either impliedly or expressly, by special powers given to the trustees[8], or it may be restricted by exceptions, such as, for example, for pulling down houses[9], for voluntary waste[10], for wilful waste[11], for spoil or destruction[12], or permissive waste such as suffering buildings or houses to decay without repairing them.

[432]

1   *Bowles' Case* (1615) 11 Co Rep 79b; Co Litt 220a; and see *Re Hanbury's Settled Estates* [1913] 2 Ch 357. See also Paragraph 176 note 5 [427] ante.
2   *Lowndes v Norton* (1864) 33 LJ Ch 583; *Re Ridge, Hellard v Moody* (1885) 31 Ch D 504 at 507, CA; *Pardoe v Pardoe* (1900) 82 LT 547. As to voluntary waste generally see Paragraph 177 [428] ante.
3   See the Settled Land Act 1925 s 88(2) (48 Halsbury's Statutes (4th Edn) TRUSTS AND SETTLEMENTS). As to improvements see vol 40(2) (2001 Reissue) TRUSTS AND SETTLEMENTS Part 9 [4101].

4   *Re Hall, Hall v Hall* [1916] 2 Ch 488.
5   *Re Llewellin, Llewellin v Williams* (1887) 37 Ch D 317.
6   As to the statutory powers see Paragraph 178 [430] ante.
7   *Doran v Wiltshire* (1792) 3 Swan 699; *Wolf v Hill* (1806) 2 Swan 149n.
8   *Kekewich v Marker* (1851) 3 Mac & G 311; *Briggs v Earl of Oxford* (1851) 5 De G & Sm 156; see *Lord Lovat v Duchess of Leeds* (1862) 2 Drew & Sm 62 (where an overriding trust to discharge mortgages out of the rents and profits of the settled estates was held not to interfere with the rights of a tenant for life to cut timber).
9   *Aston v Aston* (1750) 1 Ves Sen 264.
10   *Garth v Cotton* (1753) 3 Atk 751.
11   *Wickham v Wickham* (1815) 19 Ves 419.
12   *Vincent v Spicer* (1856) 22 Beav 380 (where it was declared that the tenant for life was entitled to cut such timber (except ornamental) as the owner of an estate in fee simple, having not only a due regard to his own interest, but to the permanent advantage of the estate, might properly cut in due course of management).

[433]

180   Permissive waste

A tenant for life, whether or not made impeachable for waste, is not liable for permissive waste[1], that is, an omission by which damage results to the premises, such as suffering houses to fall into decay[2]. If, however, the settlor has imposed a condition that the tenant for life shall keep the premises in repair, there is a personal liability which can be enforced by the court[3], even in respect of dilapidations existing at the time when the settlement came into force[4].

A tenant for life of settled leaseholds is not liable to the remainderman for permissive waste in the absence of an express condition that he is to keep the settled leaseholds in repair. Nevertheless he, and every successive owner of the lease, is bound as between himself and the estate of the settlor to perform the covenants in the lease, including the covenant to repair, and indemnify the estate against any breach[5].

[434]

1   *Lord Castlemaine v Lord Craven* (1733) 22 Vin Abr 523 pl 11. See further 42 Halsbury's Laws (4th Edn Reissue) para 995. The principle applies equally in the case of land settled by the instrument creating the settlement and of land purchased under a direction contained in such instrument: *Re Freman, Dimond v Newburn* [1898] 1 Ch 28.
2   2 Co Inst 145.
3   *Caldwall v Baylis* (1817) 2 Mer 408. If on renewal of leaseholds the tenant for life covenants with the lessor to do repairs he is under the same personal liability if he neglects to perform the covenant: *Marsh v Wells* (1824) 2 Sim & St 87. A direction that trustees shall pay for repairs out of rents throws the cost of ordinary repairs on income (*Crowe v Crisford* (1853) 17 Beav 507; *Clarke v Thornton* (1887) 35 Ch D 307; *Re Baring, Jeune v Baring* [1893] 1 Ch 61; *Debney v Eckett* (1894) 43 WR 54; *Re Thomas, Weatherall v Thomas* [1900] 1 Ch 319 at 323), but not the cost of extraordinary repairs which would be equivalent to rebuilding (*Crowe v Crisford* above; *Cooke v Cholmondeley* (1858) 4 Drew 326); but where the tenant for life has power to direct the repairs, and the trustees' expenses in carrying out the repairs are charged on the estate, they are borne by capital (*Skinner v Todd* (1881) 46 LT 131).
4   *Cooke v Cholmondeley* (1858) 4 Drew 326; *Re Bradbrook, Lock v Willis* (1887) 56 LT 106. As to the damages recoverable from the estate of a deceased tenant for life see 42 Halsbury's Laws (4th Edn Reissue) para 995.
5   *Re Redding, Thompson v Redding* [1897] 1 Ch 876.

[435]

181   Equitable waste

A tenant for life, though made unimpeachable for waste, is not, unless expressly authorised by the settlement, entitled to commit what is termed equitable waste[1], namely, such an unconscientious or unreasonable use of his legal power as goes to the destruction of the thing settled[2]. Therefore the courts have restrained a tenant for life unimpeachable for waste from pulling down the mansion house[3], or other houses[4]. Fixtures which have become part of the settled property may not be removed by a limited owner without the commission of waste except in the case of trade fixtures and certain ornamental fixtures[5].

[436]

1   Law of Property Act 1925 s 135 (37 Halsbury's Statutes (4th Edn) REAL PROPERTY).
2   *Aston v Aston* (1750) 1 Ves Sen 264.
3   *Vane v Lord Barnard* (1716) 2 Vern 738.
4   *Abrahal v Bubb* (1679) Freem Ch 53; *Williams v Day* (1680) 2 Cas in Ch 32; *Cooke v Whaley* (1701) 1 Eq Cas Abr 221; *Cooke v Winford* (1701) 1 Eq Cas Abr 400. See also *Aston v Aston* (1750) 1 Ves Sen 264 (where it was said that the court would restrain the pulling down of farmhouses unless two were pulled down to make into one).
5   *Bain v Brand* (1876) 1 App Cas 762 at 767, HL; and see *Re Lord Chesterfield's Settled Estates* [1911] 1 Ch 237.

[437]–[450]

(9) DUTIES AND POSITION OF TRUSTEES

A: LIABILITY OF TRUSTEES

182   General duty to observe terms of trust

In administering the trust, the trustee has to perform a number of duties and exercise a number of powers or discretions. He will commit a breach of trust if he fails to do what his duty requires, or if he does something he is not entitled to do. The directions of the instrument creating the trust and the duties imposed by statute and the rules of equity must be strictly observed. Any such departure which results in loss may involve the trustee in liability to make good such loss[1]. In exercising his powers or discretions, a trustee must act honestly[2] and must use as much diligence as a prudent man of business would in dealing with his own private affairs[3]. A higher standard of care will be required from a paid professional trustee, in that he will be held to the standards of skill and expertise which he claims to possess[4].

[451]

1   See the review of the law in this area by Lord Browne-Wilkinson in *Target Holdings Ltd v Redferns (a firm)* [1996] AC 421, [1995] 3 All ER 785, HL. As to the extent to which a trustee may delegate responsibility see Paragraph 257 [632] et seq post; as to protection for trustees see Paragraph 193 [473] et seq post; as to indemnity for trustees see Paragraph 200 [483] et seq post; and as to a trustee's liability as a fiduciary see Paragraph 205 [490] et seq post. For indemnity and exoneration clauses see Form 220 [1747] et seq post and see vol 40(2) (2001 Reissue) TRUSTS AND SETTLEMENTS Part 20 [9821].
2   *Re Smith, Smith v Thompson* [1896] 1 Ch 71.
3   *Speight v Gaunt* (1883) 9 App Cas 1. The duty of a trustee is not to take such care only as a prudent man would take if he had only himself to consider; the duty, rather, is to take such care as an ordinary prudent man would take if he were minded to make an investment for the benefit of people for whom he felt morally bound to provide: *Re Whiteley, Whiteley v Learoyd* (1886) 33 Ch D 347 at 355, CA per Lindley LJ; affd sub nom *Learoyd v Whitely* (1887) 12 App Cas 727, HL. See also the statutory duty of care laid down in the Trustee Act 2000 ss 1, 2 (48 Halsbury's Statutes (4th Edn) TRUSTS AND SETTLEMENTS), which would appear to operate alongside the existing equitable rules. See Paragraph 183 [453] post.
4   *Bartlett v Barclays Bank Trust Co Ltd* [1980] Ch 515, [1980] 1 All ER 139.

[452]

183 Statutory duty of care

The Trustee Act 2000[1] establishes a 'duty of care' applicable to trustees when carrying out their functions under the Act (and equivalent functions under the express provisions of the trust deed). It does not, however, apply if or in so far as it appears from the trust instrument that it is not meant to apply[2].

Whenever the duty of care applies to a trustee, he must exercise such care and skill as is reasonable in the circumstances, having regard in particular:

183.1   to any special knowledge or experience that he has or holds himself out as having; and

183.2   if he acts as trustee in the course of a business or profession, to any special knowledge or experience that it is reasonable to expect of a person acting in the course of that kind of business or profession.

The new duty does not, however, alter the principles relating to the exercise of discretionary powers by trustees. The decision whether to exercise a discretion remains a matter for the trustee to determine. That decision is not subject to the duty of care. However, once trustees have decided to exercise a discretionary function which is subject to the new duty, the manner in which they exercise it is measured against the appropriate standard of care.

1   Trustee Act 2000 s 1(1), (2) (48 Halsbury's Statutes (4th Edn) TRUSTS AND SETTLEMENTS).
2   Trustee Act 2000 Sch 1 para 7. See Form 4 clause 17 [1092] post.

[453]

184 Functions to which the duty of care applies

The duty of care applies to a trustee in relation to the following matters:

184.1   Investment[1]:

    184.1.1   when exercising the general power of investment or any other power of investment, however conferred;

    184.1.2   when carrying out a duty[2] relating to the exercise of a power of investment or to the review of investments.

184.2   Acquisition of land[3]:

    184.2.1   when exercising the statutory power to acquire land[4];

    184.2.2   when exercising any other power to acquire land, however conferred;

    184.2.3   when exercising any power in relation to land so acquired.

184.3   Agents, nominees and custodians[5]:

    184.3.1   when entering into arrangements under which a person is authorised[6] to exercise functions as an agent;

    184.3.2   when entering into arrangements under which a person is appointed to act as a nominee[7];

    184.3.3   when entering into arrangements under which a person is appointed to act as a custodian[8];

    184.3.4   when entering into arrangements under which, under any other power, however conferred, a person is authorised to exercise functions as an agent or is appointed to act as a nominee or custodian;

    184.3.5   when carrying out his duties[9] in relation to the review of an agent, nominee or custodian.

For the above purposes, entering into arrangements under which a person is authorised to exercise functions or is appointed to act as a nominee or custodian includes, in particular[10]:

184.3.6   selecting the person who is to act;

184.3.7   determining any terms on which he is to act; and

184.3.8   if the person is being authorised to exercise asset management functions, the preparation of a policy statement[11].

184.4   Compounding of liabilities[12]:

184.4.1   when exercising the power under the Trustee Act 1925 Section 15 to do any of the things referred to in that section;

184.4.2   when exercising any corresponding power, however conferred.

184.5   Insurance[13]:

184.5.1   when exercising the statutory power to insure property[14];

184.5.2   when exercising any corresponding power, however conferred.

184.6   Reversionary interests, valuations and audit[15]:

184.6.1   when exercising the power under the Trustee Act 1925 Section 22(1) or (3)[16] to do any of the things referred to there;

184.6.2   when exercising any corresponding power, however conferred.

[454]

1   Trustee Act 2000 s 2, Sch 1 para 1 (48 Halsbury's Statutes (4th Edn) TRUSTS AND SETTLEMENTS). But not in relation to pension schemes: Trustee Act 2000 s 36(2).
2   Under the Trustee Act 2000 s 4 or 5.
3   Trustee Act 2000 Sch 1 para 2; but not in relation to pension schemes: Trustee Act 2000 s 36(2).
4   Trustee Act 2000 s 8.
5   Trustee Act 2000 Sch 1 para 3(1), qualified in relation to pension schemes: Trustee Act 2000 s 36(2). As to agents etc see Paragraph 246 [611] et seq post.
6   Under the Trustee Act 2000 s 11.
7   Under the Trustee Act 2000 s 16.
8   Under the Trustee Act 2000 s 17 or 18.
9   Under the Trustee Act 2000 s 22.
10   Trustee Act 2000 Sch 1 para 3(2).
11   Under the Trustee Act 2000 s 15.
12   Trustee Act 2000 Sch 1 para 4.
13   Trustee Act 2000 Sch 1 para 5.
14   Under the Trustee Act 1925 s 19 as substituted by the Trustee Act 2000 s 34; see Paragraph 259 [641] post.
15   Trustee Act 2000 Sch 1 para 6.
16   These subsections have been amended by the Trustee Act 2000 Sch 2 para 22 by substituting for the phrase 'in good faith' a reference to the duty of care in s 1(1) of the Trustee Act 2000.

[455]

185   Liability is personal

A trustee is essentially liable for his own acts and omissions and not for those of others, including any other trustee[1]. However, a trustee can still be liable for breaches committed by a co-trustee if he himself is at fault[2], although the burden of proof lies not on the trustee but on the person who alleges that any loss was due to the trustee's default[3].

1   See the Trustee Act 1925 s 30(1), repealed. See now the Trustee Act 2000 s 23 (48 Halsbury's Statutes (4th Edn) TRUSTS AND SETTLEMENTS) and Paragraph 254 [627] post.
2   Eg improperly allowing a co-trustee to receive property or have control over it.
3   In *Brier, Brier v Evison* (1884) 26 Ch D 238 it was said that the predecessor of the Trustee Act 1925 s 30 merely made statutory the pre-existing rule in equity.

[456]

186   Liability for acts of former trustees

A trustee is not liable for breaches of trust committed by former trustees since he is entitled to assume that they have performed their duties and got in the trust property[1]. However, a trustee who has notice to the contrary is under a duty to obtain satisfaction from the former trustees[2] unless such action would be futile[3].

1   *Re Strahan, ex p Geaves* (1856) 8 De GM & G 291.
2   See *Re Forest of Dean Coal Mining Co* (1878) 10 Ch D 450.
3   *Hobday v Peters (No 3)* (1860) 28 Beav 603.

[457]

187   Liability for acts of future trustees

A trustee is not liable for breaches of trust once he has retired from the trust unless he retired in order to enable the breach to be committed, since by such action he is failing in his duty to protect the trust property[1]. However, it is not enough to show that when he retired he knew some breach was likely or that a breach might be facilitated; it must be established that he retired in contemplation of the particular breach being committed[2].

1   *Head v Gould* [1898] 2 Ch 250.
2   *Webster v Le Hunt* (1861) 9 WR 918; *Head v Gould* [1898] 2 Ch 250.

[458]

188   Measure of liability

A defaulting trustee is, essentially, obliged to effect restitution to the trust estate[1]; in other words to account for what has been lost (or what might have been obtained in the case of an omission to act). He is not liable to pay damages[2]. If a trustee makes a profit from a breach of trust, the beneficiaries are entitled to it[3] even if it is the result of an unauthorised investment[4]. In the context of unauthorised investments, a profit made in one transaction cannot be set against a loss made in another such transaction[5] unless both transactions were part of the same wrongful course of conduct[6]. A trustee cannot set off, against the amount which he has to repay to the trust, the tax which would have been payable on that amount had it not been lost as a result of his breach[7].

The position is modified where the trusts have come to an end and the trustees hold the trust fund on a bare trust for a beneficiary absolutely entitled. In relation to a breach of trust in such a case there is no reason for compensating the breach of trust by way of an order for restitution and compensation to the trust fund as opposed to the beneficiary himself[8].

[459]

1   *Bartlett v Barclays Bank Trust Co Ltd* [1980] Ch 515, [1980] 1 All ER 139; *Target Holdings Ltd v Redferns (a firm)* [1996] AC 421, [1995] 3 All ER 785, HL.
2   See *Re Lake, ex p Dyer* [1901] 1 KB 710, CA; *Metall und Rohstoff AG v Donaldson Lufkin & Jenrette Inc* [1990] 1 QB 391, [1989] 3 All ER 14.
3   *Docker v Somes* (1834) 2 My & K 655.
4   As to the power of investment see Paragraph 241 [591] et seq post.
5   *Dimes v Scott* (1827) 4 Russ 195.
6   *Bartlett v Barclays Bank Trust Co Ltd* [1980] Ch 515, [1980] 1 All ER 139.
7   *Re Bell's Indenture* [1980] 3 All ER 425, [1980] 1 WLR 1217.
8   *Target Holdings Ltd v Redferns (a firm)* [1996] AC 421, [1995] 3 All ER 785, HL.

[460]

189   Liability to pay interest

A trustee who is liable to make good a loss must replace what has been lost with interest at the discretion of the court. At one time the rate of interest was 4%[1] save in special cases; for example, where the trustee had actually received more[2]. Nowadays, the courts usually award simple interest at the rate allowed from time to time on money in court on special account[3] or compound interest with yearly rests at 1% above the minimum lending rate[4].

Prima facie, the liability is for simple interest only, but compound interest may be awarded in cases where money has been obtained and retained by fraud, or where it has been withheld or misapplied by a trustee or anyone else in a fiduciary position, by way of recouping from such a defendant an improper profit made by him[5].

[461]

1   *Re Davy, Hollingsworth v Davy* [1908] 1 Ch 61, CA.
2   *Re Emmet's Estate, Emmet v Emmet* (1881) 17 Ch D 142. An inquiry may be ordered as to what use the defendant made of the trust money and what return on it he received: *Mathew v T M Sutton Ltd* [1994] 4 All ER 793, [1994] 1 WLR 1455.
3   See, eg, *Bartlett v Barclays Bank Trust Co Ltd (No 2)* [1980] Ch 515, [1980] 2 All ER 92 and see the Court Fund Rules 1987, SI 1987/821 r 26. The rate of interest is prescribed from time to time by direction of the Lord Chancellor: SI 1987/821 r 27(1).
4   *Wallersteiner v Moir (No 2)* [1975] QB 373, [1975] 1 All ER 849, CA. In *Re Evans, Evans v Westcombe* [1999] 2 All ER 777, a case 'involving the non-professional administrator of a small estate in times of more gentle inflation', 8% was awarded.
5   *Westdeutsche Landesbank Girozentrale v Islington London Borough Council* [1996] AC 669, [1996] 2 All ER 961, HL

[462]

190   Liability for costs

A trustee who is held liable for a breach of trust will be ordered to pay costs on the standard basis[1]. In exceptional circumstances, costs on the higher indemnity basis may be awarded[2]. Interest on costs runs from the date of judgment even though the trustee does not know what he has to pay until the costs have been taxed[3].

1   For costs of other actions by or against trustees see Paragraph 204 [489] post.
2   See *Bartlett v Barclays Bank Trust Co Ltd (No 2)* [1980] Ch 515, [1980] 2 All ER 92; *Bowen-Jones v Bowen-Jones* [1986] 3 All ER 163.
3   *Hunt v R M Douglas (Roofing) Ltd* [1990] 1 AC 398, HL (overruling *K v K* [1977] Fam 39, [1977] 1 All ER 576, CA, which was applied in *Bartlett v Barclays Bank Trust Co Ltd (No 2)* [1980] Ch 515, [1980] 2 All ER 92).

[463]

191   Impounding of trustee's beneficial interest

If a trustee has a beneficial interest under the trust, it is subject to an implied condition that it is dependent on the trustee properly performing his obligations[1]. Should the trustee be liable for a breach of trust, he will not be allowed to receive any part of the trust fund in which he is beneficially entitled until he makes good the breach[2]. The principle is that the trustee is to be regarded as having already received his share to the extent to which he is in default[3].

1   See *Morris v Livie* (1842) 1 Y & C Ch Cas 380; *Re Pain, Gustavson v Haviland* [1919] 1 Ch 38.
2   See *Re Dacre, Whitaker v Dacre* [1916] 1 Ch 344, CA.
3   See *Selangor United Rubber Estates Ltd v Cradock (No 4)* [1969] 3 All ER 965, [1969] 1 WLR 1773 for adjustments to be made as regards costs.

[464]–[470]

B: PROTECTION OF TRUSTEES

1: TRUSTEES IN GENERAL

192   Exemption clause in trust instrument

The efficacy of a trustee exemption clause was affirmed by the Court of Appeal in *Armitage v Nurse*[1] where a clause in a settlement provided that no trustee should be liable for any loss or damage to the fund or its income 'unless such loss or damage shall be caused by his own actual fraud'. It was held that the clause was effective no matter how indolent, imprudent, lacking in diligence, negligent or wilful he might have been, so long as he had not acted dishonestly[2]. It is not contrary to public policy to exclude liability for gross negligence by an appropriate clause clearly worded to that effect. Further a trustee does not lose the protection of an exemption clause by ceasing to be a trustee[3]. However, where there is a doubt on the construction of a trust whether a trustee would be exempted for breach of trust by a trustee exemption clause, such doubt should be resolved against the trustee and the clause construed so as not to protect him[4].

While the law is as stated above, a wide exemption clause should not be inserted as a matter of routine. In *Armitage v Nurse* Millett LJ said that 'the view is widely held that these clauses have gone too far, and that trustees who charge for their services and who, as professional men, would not dream of excluding liability for ordinary professional negligence, should not be able to rely on a trustee exemption clause excluding liability for gross negligence[5]. If, after full consideration with the settlor, an exemption clause is to be included consideration should be given to its extent[6], and to whether a distinction is to be drawn between professional and lay trustees'[7].

[471]

1   *Armitage v Nurse* [1998] Ch 241, [1997] 2 All ER 705, CA. See also *Bogg v Raper* [1998] CLY 4592, (1998) Times 22 April, CA. See Forms 220 [1747], 221 [1749] post.
2   As to the test of dishonesty see *Walker v Stones* [2000] 4 All ER 412, [2001] 2 WLR 623, CA. This case has been appealed to the House of Lords, whose judgement is expected shortly.
3   *Seifert v Pensions Ombudsman* [1997] 1 All ER 214, [1996] PLR 479, QBD, revsd [1997] 4 All ER 947, CA, but no doubt cast on point for which here cited.
4   *Wight v Olswang* (1998) Times 17 September, revsd (1999) Times 18 May, CA, on a question of construction without affecting this point.
5   *Armitage v Nurse* above at 255 and at 713.
6   Should it only deal with honest mistakes or should it encompass negligence, even gross negligence? See *Armitage v Nurse* above.
7   See the Standard Provisions of the Society of Trust and Estate Practitioners at Form 3 [1063] post, in which no protection is afforded to a professional trustee and only limited protection to a lay trustee. See also the Trust Law Committee Consultation Paper on Trustee Exemption Clauses, November 1998. The matter has now been referred to the Law Commission for consideration.

[472]

193   Protection by advertisement

Notwithstanding anything to the contrary in the trust instrument[1], trustees may, with a view to the conveyance or distribution of any real or personal property among the persons entitled, give notice by advertisement of their intention to make such conveyance or distribution, and requiring any person interested to send them within the time, being not less than two months, fixed in the notice (or, if more than one is given, the last notice) particulars of his claim. The notice must be made in the London Gazette and in a newspaper, circulating in the district in which the land is situated, and the trustees should also give such other like notices, including notices elsewhere than in England and Wales, as would, in any special case, have been directed by a court of competent jurisdiction in an action for administration[2].

At the expiration of the time, the trustees may convey or distribute the property having regard only to claims of which they then have notice, but this does not free the trustees from any obligation to make searches or obtain official certificates such as a purchaser would be advised to make[3]. Trustees must, however, give effect to claims of which they have notice otherwise than by replies to their advertisements.

[473]

1 Trustee Act 1925 s 27(3) (48 Halsbury's Statutes (4th Edn) TRUSTS AND SETTLEMENTS).
2 Trustee Act 1925 s 27(1) as amended by the Law of Property (Amendment) Act 1926 ss 7, 8(2), Schedule and by the Trusts of Land and Appointment of Trustees Act 1996 s 25(1), Sch 3 para 3(7). On a strict construction the section would appear not to apply to trustees of a personalty settlement where there is no trust for sale. If the trustees are in any doubt as to what notices should be given they should apply to the court for directions: see *Re Letherbrow, Hopp v Dean* [1935] WN 34, 48; *Re Holden, Isaacson v Holden* [1935] WN 52. For a notice to creditors and others to make their claims against the estate of a deceased person see vol 42(2) (1998 Reissue) WILLS AND ADMINISTRATION Form 719 [5001].
3 Trustee Act 1925 s 27(2). The trustees are not liable to a person of whose claim they did not have notice, but such person may follow the property, or any property representing it, into the hands of any person, other than a purchaser, who has received it: Trustee Act 1925 s 27(2)(a).
    In the case of registered land, account will need to be taken of any entries on the register which may hinder the intended transfer or distribution of the property (eg claims which are the subject of cautions against dealings, notices or restrictions).

[474]

194 Protection against rent and covenants

Where a trustee, liable as such for any rent, covenant or agreement under a lease (including an underlease)[1], or under a grant made in consideration of a rentcharge, or any indemnity given in respect of such rent, covenant or agreement, satisfies all liabilities which may have accrued and been claimed under it to date, and, where necessary, sets apart a sufficient fund to answer any future claim in respect of any fixed and ascertained sum which the lessee or grantee agreed to lay out on the property, the trustee may convey the property to a purchaser, legatee, devisee or other person entitled to call for a conveyance, and may afterwards distribute the trust estate (other than the fund, if any, set apart) among the persons entitled to it, and is not to be personally liable in respect of any subsequent claim under the lease or grant[2].

[475]

1 Trustee Act 1925 s 26(3) (48 Halsbury's Statutes (4th Edn) TRUSTS AND SETTLEMENTS).
2 Trustee Act 1925 s 26 as amended by the Law of Property (Amendment) Act 1926 ss 7, 8(2), Schedule. Where executors have rendered themselves personally liable by entering into possession of the leasehold property, the court will order a fund to be set aside: *Re Owers, Public Trustee v Death* [1941] Ch 389, [1941] 2 All ER 589. The section operates without prejudice to the right of the lessor or grantor to follow the trust property into the hands of the persons among whom it has been distributed and applies notwithstanding anything to the contrary in the trust instrument: Trustee Act 1925 s 26(2).
    Note the Trustee Act 1925 s 26(1A) as inserted by the Landlord and Tenant (Covenants) Act 1995 s 30(1), Sch 1 para 1 concerning authorised guarantee agreements entered into by a trustee.

[476]

195   Protection as to notice

A trustee acting in more than one trust is not, in the absence of fraud, to be affected by notice of anything in relation to a particular trust if he has obtained notice merely by acting in another trust[1].

1   Trustee Act 1925 s 28 (48 Halsbury's Statutes (4th Edn) TRUSTS AND SETTLEMENTS).

[477]

196   Protection by court authority

In certain cases, the court may authorise trustees to do what might otherwise constitute a breach of trust[1]. They may also pay into court any trust money or securities in their hands or under their control in cases where there is no other way of obtaining a discharge; for example where they cannot obtain a valid receipt[2].

1   Trustee Act 1925 s 57 (48 Halsbury's Statutes (4th Edn) TRUSTS AND SETTLEMENTS). See Form 4 clause 8.3 [1089] post for an express clause allowing the trustees to confer on themselves additional administrative powers.
2   Trustee Act 1925 ss 63(1), 68(17) as amended by the Administration of Justice Act 1965 s 36(4), Sch 3.

[478]

197   Protection on acquisition and disposal of securities

A trustee is not chargeable with breach of trust by reason only of the fact that he has, for the purpose of acquiring securities which he has power to acquire in connection with the trust, paid for securities under arrangements which provide for them to be transferred to him from a recognised clearing house, or a nominee of a recognised clearing house or of a recognised investment exchange, but not until after payment of the price[1]. Similarly, he is not chargeable by reason only of the fact that he has, for the purpose of disposing of securities which he has power to dispose of in connection with the trust, transferred them to such a clearing house or nominee under arrangements which provide that the price is not to be paid to him until after the transfer is made[2].

[479]

1   Stock Exchange (Completion of Bargains) Act 1976 s 5(1)(a) as amended by the Financial Services Act 1986 s 194(1), (2) (48 Halsbury's Statutes (4th Edn) TRUSTS AND SETTLEMENTS). The terms 'recognised clearing house' and 'recognised investment exchange' are defined by reference to the Financial Services Act 1986: Stock Exchange (Completion of Bargains) Act 1976 s 5(2) as inserted by the Financial Services Act 1986 s 194(2).
2   Stock Exchange (Completion of Bargains) Act 1976 s 5(1)(b) as amended by the Financial Services Act 1986 s 194(1), (2).

[480]

198   Protection by limitation of action

The period of limitation for actions for breach of trust (not being actions for which some other period is prescribed by the Limitation Act 1980) is six years, except where the trustee has been guilty of or privy to fraud or has retained trust property or converted it to his own use, in which case no period of limitation runs so as to protect him[1].

1   Limitation Act 1980 s 21(1) (24 Halsbury's Statutes (4th Edn) LIMITATION OF ACTIONS). As to settled land and land held on trust see the Limitation Act 1980 s 18 as amended by the Trusts of Land and Appointment of Trustees Act 1996 s 25(2), Sch 4. Where a trustee, who is also a beneficiary, receives or retains trust property as his share in a distribution, his liability in an action to recover trust property after the period of the limitation is limited to the excess over his proper share: Limitation Act 1980 s 21(2).

[481]

2: TRUSTEES UNDER THE SETTLED LAND ACT 1925

199   General

A number of provisions in the Settled Land Act 1925 give special protection to trustees of a settlement for the purposes of that Act[1].

1   See the Settled Land Act 1925 ss 97, 98 and 99 as amended by the Trustee Act 2000 Sch 2 para 13 (48 Halsbury's Statutes (4th Edn) TRUSTS AND SETTLEMENTS). For a detailed consideration of settlements under the Settled Land Act 1925 see vol 40(2) (2001 Reissue) TRUSTS AND SETTLEMENTS Part 9 [4101].

[482]

C: INDEMNITY OF TRUSTEES

200   Relief by the court

If it appears to the court that a trustee is or may be personally liable for any breach of trust, but has acted honestly and reasonably, and ought fairly to be excused for the breach of trust and for omitting to obtain the directions of the court in the matter in which he committed such breach, the court may relieve him either wholly or partly from personal liability for the breach[1]. The onus is on the trustee to show that he ought fairly to be excused[2], but the court is more loath to exercise its discretion in favour of a professional trustee than one who is unpaid[3].

[483]

1   Trustee Act 1925 s 61 (48 Halsbury's Statutes (4th Edn) TRUSTS AND SETTLEMENTS). The Companies Act 1985 s 727 (8 Halsbury's Statutes (4th Edn) COMPANIES) gives the court a similar power to relieve a director, officer, or auditor from liability for negligence or breach of trust. See *Re Evans* [1999] 2 All ER 777.
2   See *Re Windsor Steam Coal Co (1901) Ltd* [1929] 1 Ch 151, CA; *Holland v German Property Administrator* [1937] 2 All ER 807, CA. Acquiescence by a beneficiary does not necessarily relieve a trustee of liability if the Trustee Act 1925 s 61 does not apply: see *Re Pauling's Settlement Trusts, Younghusband v Coutts & Co* [1964] Ch 303, [1963] 3 All ER 1, CA; see also *Holder v Holder* [1968] Ch 353, [1968] 1 All ER 665, CA.
3   See *Re Windsor Steam Coal Co (1901) Ltd* [1929] 1 Ch 151, CA; *Re Waterman's Will Trusts, Lloyds Bank Ltd v Sutton* [1952] 2 All ER 1054; *Bartlett v Barclays Bank Trust Co Ltd* [1980] Ch 515, [1980] 1 All ER 139. The settlement may itself excuse the trustees and may extend the exemption to breaches in circumstances not covered by the Trustee Act 1925 s 61. See, eg, Form 4 clause 13 [1090] and the notes thereto. For an indemnity to trustees by joint settlors see Form 224 [1755] post and see the consultation paper of the Trust Law Committee 'Trustee Exemption Clauses' (June 1999).

[484]

201   Reimbursement

A trustee is entitled to be reimbursed from the trust funds[1], or may pay out of the trust funds, expenses properly incurred by him when acting on behalf of the trust[2]. This provision applies to a trustee who has been duly authorised[3] to exercise functions as an agent of the trustees, to act as a nominee or custodian, as it applies to any other trustee[4].

The above provisions apply:

'. . . in relation to . . . expenses incurred on or after their commencement on behalf of, trusts whenever created'[5].

These provisions are not made subject to any contrary provision in the trust instrument[6].

Decisions on corresponding words in earlier statutes continue to be relevant. Thus a trustee's rights extend to liability on the covenants of a lease and liabilities incurred by a trustee in properly carrying on a trade or business under the provisions of the settlement and to damages and costs recovered against him as legal owner of the trust property where the injury in respect of which they were recovered was not caused by his neglect or default[7]. As between the beneficiaries, a trustee's costs and expenses are generally recoverable out of capital[8]; and the trustee has a lien for them on both the capital and income of the trust in priority to the beneficiaries[9].

[485]

1   'Trust funds' means income or capital funds of the trust: Trustee Act 2000 s 39(1) (48 Halsbury's Statutes (4th Edn) TRUSTS AND SETTLEMENTS).

2   Trustee Act 2000 s 31(1). Unlike the wording of the Trustee Act 1925 s 30(2) (repealed) which it replaces, the word 'all' does not precede 'expenses', but it is not thought that this is significant. Nor is it thought that the addition of the word 'properly' changes the law, for this was, in effect, implied by the courts under the earlier legislation. Subject to an exception where the trustees pay off an interest-bearing debt of the estate, the court has no jurisdiction to award interest on expenses: *Foster v Spencer* [1996] 2 All ER 672.

3   Ie under a power conferred by the Trustee Act 2000 Pt IV (ss 11–27) or any other enactment or provision of subordinate legislation, or by the trust instrument: Trustee Act 2000 s 31(2).

4   Trustee Act 2000 s 31(2).

5   Trustee Act 2000 s 33(1). In so far as this section refers to services (whenever provided apparently) it is not applicable to the Trustee Act 2000 s 31, which refers only to expenses.

6   Contrast the other provisions contained in the Trustee Act 2000. Trustee Act 1925 s 30 was subject to the Trustee Act 1925 s 69(2).

7   As to covenants in a lease see *Matthews v Ruggles-Brice* [1911] 1 Ch 194. As to liabilities in carrying on a business see *Re Blundell, Blundell v Blundell* (1890) 44 Ch D 1 at 11, CA (creditors of the business have a right to be put in place of the trustee as against the trust estate).

8   *Powys v Blagrave* (1854) 4 De GM & G 448; *Re Bullock's Settled Estates, Lofthouse v Haggard* (1904) 91 LT 651; *Carver v Duncan (Inspector of Taxes)* [1985] AC 1082, [1985] 2 All ER 645, HL.

9   See *Re Spurling's Will Trusts, Philpot v Philpot* [1966] 1 All ER 745, [1966] 1 WLR 920. Where a trustee has mixed his own money with the trust fund, the beneficiaries have a first claim on the trust fund: *Re Tilley's Will Trusts, Burgin v Croad* [1967] Ch 1179, [1967] 2 All ER 303.

[486]

202   Beneficiary instigating breach of trust

If a trustee commits a breach of trust at the instigation or request or with the written consent of a beneficiary, the court may, if it thinks fit, make such order as it thinks just for impounding all or any part of the interest of the beneficiary by way of indemnity to the trustee[1].

1   Trustee Act 1925 s 62(1) as amended by the Married Woman (Restraint upon Anticipation) Act 1949 s 1(4), Sch 2 (48 Halsbury's Statutes (4th Edn) TRUSTS AND SETTLEMENTS).

[487]

203   Indemnity by beneficiary or settlor

A beneficiary (even if having only a limited interest in the trust property), or the settlor, may become liable to indemnify the trustees if he expressly or impliedly[1] contracts to do so.

1   *Jervis v Wolferstan* (1874) LR 18 Eq 18, distinguished in *Fraser v Murdoch* (1881) 6 App Cas 855, HL.

[488]

204   Cost of litigation

Where litigation appears to be prima facie proper and in the interests of the trust, the court will grant trustees leave to sue or defend (a 'Beddoe order')[1]. This leave, however the litigation results, will protect the trustees from claims by beneficiaries and entitle them to be reimbursed their costs out of the trust estate[2]. Without leave, they are still entitled to be reimbursed their costs if the action was properly brought or defended for the benefit of the trust estate[3].

1   *Re Beddoe, Downes v Cottam* [1893] 1 Ch 547, CA.
2   As to proceedings for the protection or recovery of settled land see the Settled Land Act 1925 s 92 (48 Halsbury's Statutes (4th Edn) TRUSTS AND SETTLEMENTS).
3   *Stott v Milne* (1884) 25 Ch D 710, CA.

[489]

D: TRUSTEE AS FIDUCIARY

205   General position

A trustee stands in a fiduciary position towards a beneficiary; ie it is a mark of their relationship that the trustee has been entrusted with an authority and a task which he is bound to exercise and perform in the best interests of the beneficiary. Failure to do so will result in the trustee being accountable for profits made and the return of property acquired.

In reaching decisions as to the exercise of their fiduciary powers, trustees have to weigh up competing factors, ones which are often incommensurable in character. In that sense they have to be fair[1].

1   *Scott v National Trust for Places of Historic Interest or Natural Beauty* [1998] 2 All ER 705, [1998] 1 WLR 226, from which it appears that it may be proper to take into account the legitimate expectations of potential beneficiaries; *Edge v Pensions Ombudsman* [2000] Ch 602, CA, [1999] 4 All ER 546, CA.

[490]

206   Duty to keep accounts and audit

Trustees[1] must keep accounts and produce them to the beneficiaries when required[2]. Trustees who fail to do so may be ordered to pay the costs of any application to the court made necessary by their default[3]. Trustees have a discretion to have their accounts examined or audited by an independent accountant once every three years (or more frequently if the nature of the trust or any specific dealings with trust property make a more frequent exercise of this right reasonable)[4].

[491]

1   As to personal representatives see the Administration of Estates Act 1925 s 25(b) as substituted by the Administration of Estates Act 1971 s 9 (17 Halsbury's Statutes (4th Edn) EXECUTORS AND ADMINISTRATORS).
2   See *Pearse v Green* (1819) 1 Jac & W 135.
3   *Re Skinner, Cooper v Skinner* [1904] 1 Ch 289.
4   Trustee Act 1925 s 22(4) (48 Halsbury's Statutes (4th Edn) TRUSTS AND SETTLEMENTS). For variations of this power see Forms 230 [1763], 231 [1764] post.

[492]

207   Duty to provide information

Trustees are obliged to give any beneficiary all reasonable information and explanations as to the nature of the trust property, the trust income, and as to how the trustees have been investing and distributing it[1]. In the absence of special circumstances, they must also allow a beneficiary to inspect all title deeds and trust documents[2]. These obligations extend to contingent beneficiaries and the objects of a discretionary trust[3]. However, trustees need not disclose why they have exercised discretionary powers in a particular way, and can refuse access to documents which may reveal such information, such as the minutes of their meeting[4]. Statute requires a trustee to produce to any person, subject to payment of costs, any notice of any dealing with the beneficiary's interest which he has received[5].

[493]

1   *Re Murphy's Settlements, Murphy v Murphy* [1998] 3 All ER 1, [1999] 1 WLR 282; *Re Dartnall, Sawyer v Goddard* [1895] 1 Ch 474, CA.
2   *Re Cowin, Cowin v Gravett* (1886) 33 Ch D 179; *O'Rourke v Darbishire* [1920] AC 581, HL; cf *Butt v Kelson* [1952] Ch 197, [1952] 1 All ER 167, CA.
3   *Re Murphy's Settlements, Murphy v Murphy* [1998] 3 All ER 1, [1999] 1 WLR 282; *Chaine-Nickson v Bank of Ireland, Brett and Lewis-Crosby* [1976] IR 393. It is not thought that such duties are owed to persons who are the object of a trustee's power.
4   *Re Londonderry's Settlement, Peat v Walsh* [1965] Ch 918, [1964] 3 All ER 855, CA. The principles of this case have been held applicable to pension fund trustees: *Wilson v Law Debenture Trust Corpn plc* [1995] 2 All ER 337. For a clause authorising the refusal of disclosure see Form 232 [1766] post.
5   Law of Property Act 1925 s 137(8) (37 Halsbury's Statutes (4th Edn) REAL PROPERTY).

[494]

208   Trustee must not profit from his trust

The rule, subject to certain exceptions, is that a trustee must not make a profit for himself out of his office. As a fiduciary, a trustee must not be allowed to put himself in a position where there is a conflict between his duty to the beneficiaries and his own personal interests, or where he may be able to take advantage of information gained as a trustee. The rule does not depend on fraud, dishonesty or bad faith on the part of the trustee but on the mere fact that a profit has been made[1]. It applies to all types of trustee and to other persons in a fiduciary position[2]. In the context of trustees the rule has been applied in the following circumstances:

208.1   Where a trustee obtains the renewal of a lease which has been devised to the trust[3]. It appears, however, that if a beneficiary, not being a trustee or otherwise in a fiduciary position, obtains a renewal, he can keep it for himself[4].

208.2   Where a trustee purchases the freehold reversion of a trust lease[5].

208.3   Where a trustee uses his position to appoint himself director of a company and so becomes accountable for directors' fees[6]. However, as with any application of the rule, it must be shown that there is a causal connection between the position and the profit which is claimed. Therefore, the rule does not apply where a trustee has already become a director before becoming a trustee[7] or where he would still have been elected director even if he had used the trust shares to vote against himself[8].

208.4   Where a trustee who is a stockbroker procures the employment of his firm to value trust investments[9].

208.5   Where a trustee uses information gained as a trustee to make a profit for himself[10].

It should be noted that the trust instrument may in fact authorise the trustee to retain profits, fees and remuneration[11].

[495]

1   *Regal (Hastings) Ltd v Gulliver (1942)* [1967] 2 AC 134n, [1942] 1 All ER 378, HL. For a recent illustration of the 'self dealing' rule see *Kane v Radley-Kane* [1999] Ch 274, [1998] 3 All ER 753.

2   Eg agents, solicitors, company directors, partners.

3   *Keech v Sandford* (1726) Cas *temp* King 61.

4   *Re Biss, Biss v Biss* [1903] 2 Ch 40, CA.

5   *Protheroe v Protheroe* [1968] 1 All ER 1111, [1968] 1 WLR 519, CA; *Thompson's Trustee in Bankruptcy v Heaton* [1974] 1 All ER 1239, [1974] 1 WLR 605.

6   *Re Macadam, Dallow and Moscrop v Codd* [1946] Ch 73, [1945] 2 All ER 664.

7   *Re Dover Coalfield Extension Ltd* [1908] 1 Ch 65, CA.

8   *Re Gee, Wood v Staples* [1948] Ch 284, [1948] 1 All ER 498.

9   *Williams v Barton* [1927] 2 Ch 9.

10   *Boardman v Phipps* [1967] 2 AC 46, [1966] 3 All ER 721, HL. Cf *Satnam Investments Ltd v Dunlop Heywood & Co Ltd* [1999] 3 All ER 652, CA. As to competing with the trust and using information generally see Paragraph 211 [500] post.

11   For a power to hold directorships and retain remuneration see Form 183 [1670] post and for a power to retain commissions and brokerages see Form 228 [1761] post. As to remuneration generally see Paragraph 212 [511] et seq post and see generally the Society of Trust and Estate Practitioners' Standard Provisions paragraph 9 at Form 3 [1070] post.

[496]

209   Trustee purchasing trust property

If a trustee purchases trust property, the transaction is voidable at the instance of any beneficiary[1] The trustee takes a voidable title which can be set aside by a beneficiary within a reasonable time of discovering the circumstances[2]. This right exists no matter how honest and fair the sale might be[3] and even if it was for a price higher than that obtainable on the open market or which is otherwise on terms which are generous to the trust estate[4]. The rule does not apply to a trustee who has been retired from the trust for a long time[5], nor to a trustee who acquires a right to buy the property before becoming a trustee[6]. The trust instrument may expressly authorise the purchase[7] and the Settled Land Act 1925 allows a tenant for life to purchase and otherwise deal with settled property which he holds on trust[8].

[497]

1   *Campbell v Walker* (1800) 5 Ves 678; and contrast *Holder v Holder* [1968] Ch 353, [1968] 1 All ER 665, CA. See also *Kane v Radley-Kane* [1998] 3 All ER 753 where it was held to be a breach of the self-dealing rule for a sole personal representative of an intestate estate to appropriate to herself unquoted shares in satisfaction of her statutory legacy, unless she had been authorised to do so by the other beneficiaries, or the court had sanctioned the appropriation.

2   *Beningfield v Baxter* (1886) 12 App Cas 167, PC. If some of the beneficiaries do not agree to the property reverting to the trust the court will order a resale: see *Holder v Holder* [1968] Ch 353, [1968] 1 All ER 665, CA. If the trustee's title is avoided, he is entitled to recoup his expenditure with interest: *Re Walters, Trevenen v Pearce* [1954] Ch 653, [1954] 1 All ER 893.

3   *Ex p James* (1803) 8 Ves 337; *Re Bulmer* [1937] Ch 499, [1937] 1 All ER 323, CA.

4   *Aberdeen Rly Co v Blaikie Bros* (1854) 1 Macq 461, HL; *Re Thompson's Settlement, Thompson v Thompson* [1986] Ch 99, [1985] 3 All ER 720. As to whether a purchase at public auction is within the rule see *Ex p Lacey* (1802) 6 Ves 625 and *Holder v Holder* [1968] Ch 353, [1968] 1 All ER 665, CA; see also *Re Thompson's Settlement, Thompson v Thompson* above.

5   *Re Boles and British Land Co's Contract* [1902] 1 Ch 244. In *Wright v Morgan* [1926] AC 788, PC the sale was set aside even though the trustee retired immediately before the transaction.

6   *Re Mulholland's Will Trusts, Bryan v Westminster Bank Ltd* [1949] 1 All ER 460 (option).

7   Eg by giving the trustee an option to purchase or right to bid at auction: see Form 188 [1676] and Form 220 [1743] post. And see Form 4 schedule paragraph 29 [1102] post.

8   See the Settled Land Act 1925 s 68 as amended by the Mental Health Act 1959 s 149, Sch 7 Pt I (48 Halsbury's Statutes (4th Edn) TRUSTS AND SETTLEMENTS); *Re Pennant's Will Trusts, Pennant v Rylands* [1970] Ch 75, [1969] 2 All ER 862.

[498]

210   Trustee purchasing beneficiary's interest

A trustee's purchase of trust property must be distinguished from his purchase of a beneficiary's interest. Whilst the former transaction is voidable at the instance of the beneficiary, the latter will only be set aside by the court if there is a suggestion that the trustee has abused his position or exercised undue influence over the beneficiary. The purchase is unimpeachable as long as the beneficiary entered into the contract of his own free will and provided there is no fraud, concealment, or advantage taken by the trustee of information acquired by him as a trustee[1].

1   *Coles v Trecothick* (1804) 9 Ves 234; *Wright v Carter* [1903] 1 Ch 27, CA. See, however, *Dougan v Macpherson* [1902] AC 197, HL where there was non-disclosure by the trustee of a valuation obtained *qua* beneficiary.

[499]

211   Trustee competing with trust and using information

In keeping with the basic principle that a trustee must not allow his duty to conflict with his personal interests, it is established that a trustee should not put himself in a position where he might gain for himself the benefit of any goodwill acquired by the trust or useful information. A trustee may be restrained from carrying on a business in competition with the trust[1] and will be accountable for all profits made by using information gained in his fiduciary capacity[2].

1   See *Bray v Ford* [1896] AC 44, HL; *Re Thomson, Thomson v Allen* [1930] 1 Ch 203.
2   *Boardman v Phipps* [1967] 2 AC 46, [1966] 3 All ER 721, HL where a trustee who acted in good faith and who used confidential information to make a profit for himself was held liable to account to the trust. The fact that his actions had also resulted in a large profit being made for the trust was held to be immaterial, although he was allowed remuneration on a *quantum meruit* for work done on behalf of the trust. As to the inherent jurisdiction of the court to authorise payment of remuneration see Paragraph 216 [518] post.

[500]–[510]

(10) REMUNERATION OF TRUSTEES

A: INTRODUCTION

212   General rule

As a general rule a trustee is not entitled to make any profit out of his office[1]. He may not charge for his loss of time whilst attending to the business of the trust, nor for professional services rendered[2]. However, he is generally entitled to reimbursement of expenses[3].

[511]

1   As to the principle that a trustee stands in a fiduciary position towards a beneficiary see Paragraph 205 [490] et seq ante. For the introduction of a statutory right to remuneration see the Trustee Act 2000 s 28 et seq (48 Halsbury's Statutes (4th Edn) TRUSTS AND SETTLEMENTS).

2   For the position in respect of director's fees where a trustee has been appointed a director of a company see *Re Macadam, Dallow and Moscrop v Codd* [1946] Ch 73, [1945] 2 All ER 664; *Re Llewellin's Will Trusts, Griffiths v Wilcox* [1949] Ch 225, [1949] 1 All ER 487; *Re Gee, Wood v Staples* [1948] Ch 284, [1948] 1 All ER 498. See also *Re French Protestant Hospital* [1951] Ch 567, [1951] 1 All ER 938. For a power to hold directorships and retain remuneration see Form 183 [1670] post.

3   Trustee Act 2000 s 31, and see Paragraph 201 [485] ante. Subject to an exception where the trustees pay off an interest-bearing debt of the estate, the court has no jurisdiction to award interest on expenses: *Foster v Spencer* [1996] 2 All ER 672.

[512]

B: WHERE REMUNERATION MAY BE ALLOWED

213   Authority in trust instrument

It has always been possible for the trust instrument to authorise the trustees to receive remuneration, and it has been common for a professional trustee, such as a solicitor, to be given authority to charge for his professional services[1].

The Trustee Act 2000 has introduced new rules for the construction of an express charging clause[2]. These rules apply in relation to services provided to or on behalf of trusts whenever created[3]. The rules apply where the trustee is a trust corporation or is acting in a professional capacity[4], provided that their application is not inconsistent with the terms of the trust instrument[5]. Reversing the old rules, a trustee is now to be treated as entitled under the trust instrument to receive payment out of the trust funds in respect of services even if they are services which are capable of being provided by a lay trustee[6]; and any payments to which a trustee is entitled in respect of services are to be treated as remuneration for services and not as a gift[7]. Accordingly, reversing the old rules, the benefit of a charging clause will not be lost if the trustee witnesses the will; and trustee charges become an expense of the administration for the purpose of the priority rules which determine the order of payments due from a deceased's estate. A person acts as a lay trustee if he is not a trust corporation and does not act in a professional capacity[8].

[513]

1   For such an authority see eg Form 233 [1769] post and note that the standard remuneration clause requires amendment if it is envisaged that a bank or corporation will be a trustee: see, for example, Form 4 clause 11 [1090] post. For a power to hold directorships and retain remuneration see Form 183 [1670] post.

2   Ie a provision in the trust instrument entitling him to receive payment out of the trust funds in respect of services provided by him to or on behalf of the trust: Trustee Act 2000 s 28(1)(a) (48 Halsbury's Statutes (4th Edn) TRUSTS AND SETTLEMENTS). 'Trust funds' means income or capital funds of the trust: Trustee Act 2000 s 39(1).

3   Trustee Act 2000 s 33(1). It seems that this provision has a retrospective effect: as to expenses see Trustee Act 2000 s 31 and Paragraph 201 [485] ante.

4   Trustee Act 2000 s 28(1)(b). A person acts in a professional capacity if he acts in the course of a profession or business which consists of or includes the provision of services in connection with the management or administration of trusts generally or a particular kind of trust, or any particular aspect thereof, where the services he provides to or on behalf of the trust fall within that description: Trustee Act 2000 s 28(5).

5   Trustee Act 2000 s 28(1).

6   Trustee Act 2000 s 28(2). This provision applies to a trustee of a charitable trust who is not a trust corporation only if he is not a sole trustee, and to the extent that a majority of the other trustees have agreed that it should apply to him: Trustee Act 2000 s 28(3).

7   Ie for the purposes of the Wills Act 1837 s 15 (gifts to attesting witnesses void), and the Administration of Estates Act 1925 s 34(3) (order in which estate is to be paid out): Trustee Act 2000 s 28(4). This does not affect the position in the case of deaths occurring before February 2001: Trustee Act 2000 s 33(2).

8   Trustee Act 2000 s 28(6).

[514]

214   Implied charging clause under Trustee Act 2000
There are new statutory provisions in the Trustee Act 2000 which apply where there is no provision (either for or against) about the entitlement of a trustee to remuneration in the trust instrument, or in any enactment or any provision of subordinate legislation[1]. The new rules do not apply where there is any such provision. It is now provided that a trustee who is a trust corporation, but who is not a trustee of a charitable trust, is entitled to receive reasonable remuneration out of the trust funds for any services it provides to or on behalf of the trust[2]. A trustee who acts in a professional capacity, but who is not a trust corporation, a trustee of a charitable trust or a sole trustee is likewise entitled, but in his case only if each other trustee has agreed in writing that he may be remunerated for the services[3]. 'Reasonable remuneration' means, in relation to the provision of services by a trustee, such remuneration as is reasonable in the circumstances for the provision of those services to or on behalf of that trust by that trustee[4]. These provisions apply in relation to services provided to or on behalf of trusts, whenever created[5].
    The above provisions apply even if the services in question could be provided by a lay trustee[6]; and they apply equally to a trustee who has been duly authorised[7] to exercise functions as an agent of the trustees, or to act as a nominee or custodian[8].
    The above provisions do not apply to trustees of charitable trusts. However, the Secretary of State has power to make regulations for the provision of remuneration of trustees of charitable trusts who are trust corporations or act in a professional capacity[9].

[515]

1   Trustee Act 2000 s 29(5) (48 Halsbury's Statutes (4th Edn) TRUSTS AND SETTLEMENTS).
2   Trustee Act 2000 s 29(1). 'Trust funds' means income or capital funds of the trust: Trustee Act 2000 s 39(1).
3   Trustee Act 2000 s 29(2).
4   Trustee Act 2000 s 29(3). It includes, in relation to the provision of services by a trustee who is an authorised institution under the Banking Act 1987 (4 Halsbury's Statutes (4th Edn) BANKING) and provides the services in that capacity, the institution's reasonable charges for the provision of such services: Trustee Act 2000 s 29(3).
5   Trustee Act 2000 s 33(1). It seems that this provision has retrospective effect: as to expenses see the Trustee Act 2000 s 31 and Paragraph 201 [485] ante. Nothing in the Trustee Act 2000 s 29 is to be treated as affecting the operation of the Wills Act 1837 s 15 or the Administration of Estates Act 1925 s 34(3) in relation to any death occurring before the commencement of s 29: Trustee Act 2000 s 33(2).
6   Trustee Act 2000 s 29(4).
7   Ie under a power conferred by the Trustee Act 2000 Part IV (ss 11–27) or the trust instrument.
8   Trustee Act 2000 s 29(6).
9   Trustee Act 2000 s 30. No regulations had been made by the date at which this volume sets out the law.

[516]

215   Agreement with beneficiaries
A trustee will be able to charge if, at the time of accepting the trust, he has made an agreement with the beneficiaries, being *sui juris*, to that effect[1]. It is necessary that the beneficiaries should freely and without unfair pressure assent, since such a contract by a trustee with beneficiaries providing for his remuneration is regarded jealously by the court[2].

1   *Re Sherwood* (1840) 3 Beav 338; *Douglas v Archbutt* (1858) 2 De G & J 148.
2   *Ayliffe v Murray* (1740) 2 Atk 58.

[517]

216   Inherent jurisdiction of the court

The court has an inherent jurisdiction both to authorise payment of remuneration to trustees in the absence of authority in the trust instrument[1] and to authorise an increase in the remuneration so authorised[2].

[518]

1   See eg *Boardman v Phipps* [1967] 2 AC 46, [1966] 3 All ER 721, HL (see further Paragraph 211 note 2 [500] ante); see also *O'Sullivan v Management Agency and Music Ltd* [1985] QB 428, [1985] 3 All ER 351, CA.
2   See *Re Duke of Norfolk's Settlement Trusts, Earl of Perth v Fitzalan-Howard* [1982] Ch 61, [1981] 3 All ER 220, CA.

[519]

217   Costs of a solicitor trustee in legal proceedings

In the absence of a charging clause in the trust instrument, a solicitor trustee is generally in no better position than a lay trustee with regard to remuneration, but to this rule there is an anomalous exception known as the rule in *Cradock v Piper*[1]. Under this rule, which will rarely be called into play since the enactment of the Trustee Act 2000 Section 29[2], the solicitor trustee is entitled to his profit costs if he acts as solicitor in an action or other legal proceedings on behalf of himself and his co-trustees jointly. The cost of appearing and acting for both parties must not have increased the expense, that is to say, the solicitor trustee must not have added to the expense which would have been incurred if he or his firm had appeared for his co-trustees alone.

Moreover, there is no objection to a solicitor trustee employing his partner to do any legal work in connection with the trust (and not merely in connection with legal proceedings) provided that the partner will be exclusively entitled to the profit costs for his own benefit[3]. If, however, he employs his firm to do the work, the firm's charges are not recoverable even if it is agreed that he will receive nothing himself[4].

[520]

1   *Cradock v Piper* (1850) 1 Mac & G 664. The rule in this case does not apply to a case where proceedings are brought by a solicitor liquidator and his co-liquidator: Insolvency Rules 1986, SI 1986/1925 r 4.128(3) as amended by SI 1991/2684.
2   See Paragraph 214 [515] ante.
3   *Clack v Carlon* (1861) 30 LJ Ch 639.
4   *Re Gates, Arnold v Gates* [1933] Ch 913; *Re Hill, Claremont v Hill* [1934] Ch 623, CA.

[521]

218   Trust property abroad

Where the trust property is abroad, and the law of the country where the property is situated allows payment, the trustees appear to be entitled to retain their emoluments[1].

1   *Re Northcote's Will Trusts, Northcote v Northcote* [1949] 1 All ER 442; cf *Re Sandys' Will Trusts, Sandys v Kirton* [1947] 2 All ER 302, CA.

[522]

219   Statutory authority

Where the court appoints a corporation other than the Public Trustee to be a trustee, it may authorise such remuneration as the court thinks fit[1]. The court can make an order that a judicial trustee is to be remunerated.

The Public Trustee has a statutory right to charge[2]. Likewise, corporations appointed custodian trustees are also entitled by statute to charge for their services[3].

Subject to the above provisions and the provisions of the Trustee Act 2000[4], it seems that a company acting as trustee cannot make any charge beyond that expressly provided for in the instrument appointing it[5], unless the company contracts with the beneficiaries for remuneration at the time of accepting the trusteeship.

[523]

1   Trustee Act 1925 s 42 (48 Halsbury's Statutes (4th Edn) TRUSTS AND SETTLEMENTS).
2   Public Trustee Act 1906 s 9 as amended by the Public Trustee (Fees) Act 1957 s 1(5) (48 Halsbury's Statutes (4th Edn) TRUSTS AND SETTLEMENTS).
3   Public Trustee Act 1906 s 4(3).
4   Trustee Act 2000 s 29 (48 Halsbury's Statutes (4th Edn) TRUSTS AND SETTLEMENTS) and see Paragraph 214 [515] ante.
5   *Bath v Standard Land Co Ltd* [1911] 1 Ch 618, CA.

[524]–[530]

(11) ADMINISTRATIVE PROVISIONS AND POWERS

A: INTRODUCTION

220   General

In addition to the dispositive clauses creating and determining the beneficial interests in the trust property, other provisions are required to make the management of the property possible throughout the duration of the trust. It is not necessary to set out every administrative provision in a trust, as the trustee has certain powers conferred on him by statute, but the extent of the powers so conferred varies with the kind of trust or settlement concerned. For the purposes of this title administrative provisions are considered in three groups, namely:

220.1   those relating to settlements of land by way of trust of land;
220.2   those affecting trusts and settlements generally (including settlements of land); and
220.3   those relating to settlements of land under the Settled Land Act 1925[1].

1   As to administrative powers relating to Settled Land Act settlements see vol 40(2) (2001 Reissue) TRUSTS AND SETTLEMENTS Part 9 [4101].

[531]

B: PROVISIONS RELATING TO TRUSTS OF LAND

(For a detailed commentary on the provisions of the Trusts of Land and Appointment of Trustees Act 1996 Parts I and III see further vol 40(2) (2001 Reissue) TRUSTS AND SETTLEMENTS *Part 8 [3001]. As to Part II of the Act see vol 40(2) Part 10 [5201].)*

221 General powers under Trusts of Land and Appointment of Trustees Act 1996

The Trusts of Land and Appointment of Trustees Act 1996[1] provides that trustees of land, for the purpose of exercising their functions as trustees, have in relation to the land subject to the trust all the powers of an absolute owner. This means the management powers such as letting and mortgaging, but if the land is sold the question becomes one of investing the sale proceeds which in general is outside the scope of this Act. Exceptionally, however, the Act[2] gives trustees of land power to acquire land under the power conferred by the Trustee Act 2000[3].

The powers referred to above[4] are subject to general equitable principles. It is expressly provided that in exercising these powers trustees shall have regard to the rights of the beneficiaries[5], and that the powers shall not be exercised in contravention of, or of any order made in pursuance of, any other enactment or any rule of law or equity[6].

[532]

1 Trusts of Land and Appointment of Trustees Act 1996 s 6(1) (37 Halsbury's Statutes (4th Edn) REAL PROPERTY). For a detailed consideration of the sections of this Act see further vol 40(2) (2001 Reissue) TRUSTS AND SETTLEMENTS Part 8 [3001].
2 Trusts of Land and Appointment of Trustees Act 1996 s 6(3), as amended by the Trustee Act 2000 Sch 2 para 45(1).
3 Trustee Act 2000 s 8 (48 Halsbury's Statutes (4th Edn) TRUSTS AND SETTLEMENTS).
4 Ie those under the Trusts of Land and Appointment of Trustees Act 1996 s 6(1), (3) as amended.
5 Trusts of Land and Appointment of Trustees Act 1996 s 6(5). 'Beneficiary' is defined in the Trusts of Land and Appointment of Trustees Act 1996 s 22.
6 Trusts of Land and Appointment of Trustees Act 1996 s 6(6). This includes an order of any court or of the Charity Commissioners: Trusts of Land and Appointment of Trustees Act 1996 s 6(7). See also the Trusts of Land and Appointment of Trustees Act 1996 s 6(8).

[533]

222 Power to convey land to beneficiaries

The Trusts of Land and Appointment of Trustees Act 1996[1] gives trustees of land power, where each of the beneficiaries interested in the land is a person of full age and capacity who is absolutely entitled to the land[2], to convey the land to the beneficiaries even though they have not been required by the beneficiaries to do so. Moreover the trustees are not under any duty to consult the beneficiaries in relation to the exercise of this power[3]. Where land is conveyed by virtue of this provision the beneficiaries must do whatever is necessary to secure that it vests in them, and, if they fail to do so, the court may make an order requiring them to do so[4].

[534]

1 Trusts of Land and Appointment of Trustees Act 1996 s 6(2) (37 Halsbury's Statutes (4th Edn) REAL PROPERTY).
2 It is thought that the power can only be exercised in cases where there is a single beneficiary absolutely entitled to the land or, in the case of more than one beneficiary, when those beneficiaries are together jointly entitled as either tenants in common or joint tenants.
3 Trusts of Land and Appointment of Trustees Act 1996 s 11(2)(c).
4 Trusts of Land and Appointment of Trustees Act 1996 s 6(2).

[535]

223   Power to partition

Trustees of land may, where beneficiaries of full age are absolutely entitled in undivided shares, partition the land, or any part of it, and provide for the payment of any equality money[1]. Subject to obtaining the consent of each of those beneficiaries[2], the trustees must give effect to any such partition by conveying the partitioned land in severalty, either absolutely or in trust, in accordance with the rights of those beneficiaries[3]. In the case of a minor, the trustees may act on his behalf and retain land or other property representing his share in trust for him[4].

[536]

1   Trusts of Land and Appointment of Trustees Act 1996 s 7(1) (37 Halsbury's Statutes (4th Edn) REAL PROPERTY): see further vol 40(2) (2001 Reissue) TRUSTS AND SETTLEMENTS Part 8 [3001]. Where a share in the land is affected by an incumbrance, the trustees may either give effect to it or provide for its discharge: Trusts of Land and Appointment of Trustees Act 1996 s 7(4). Incumbrance includes a legal or equitable mortgage and a trust for securing money, and a lien, and a charge of a portion, annuity, or other capital or annual sum: Law of Property Act 1925 s 205(1)(vii) (37 Halsbury's Statutes (4th Edn) REAL PROPERTY), incorporated by the Trusts of Land and Appointment of Trustees Act 1996 s 23(2).
2   Trusts of Land and Appointment of Trustees Act 1996 s 7(3).
3   Trusts of Land and Appointment of Trustees Act 1996 s 7(2).
4   Trusts of Land and Appointment of Trustees Act 1996 s 7(5).

[537]

224   Restriction and exclusion of powers

All the powers contained in the Trusts of Land and Appointment of Trustees Act 1996 Sections 6 and 7[1] can be restricted or excluded by an appropriate provision in the disposition creating the trust[2]. In particular if any consent is required to be obtained to the exercise of any power, it cannot be exercised without the consent being obtained[3]. However, if more than two consents are required, in favour of a purchaser[4], the consent of any two of them is sufficient[5]. If a person whose consent is required is a minor, in favour of a purchaser his consent is not required, but the trustees must obtain the consent of a parent who has parental responsibility for him[6] or a guardian of his[7].

[538]

1   As to these powers see Paragraph 221 [532] et seq ante. For a detailed consideration of these sections see vol 40(2) (2001 Reissue) TRUSTS AND SETTLEMENTS Part 8 [3001].
2   Trusts of Land and Appointment of Trustees Act 1996 s 8(1) (37 Halsbury's Statutes (4th Edn) REAL PROPERTY). 'Disposition' includes every assurance of property or of an interest in it by any instrument (other than a statute, unless the statute creates a settlement), and also a devise, bequest, or an appointment of property contained in a will: see the Law of Property Act 1925 s 205(1)(ii), (viii) (37 Halsbury's Statutes (4th Edn) REAL PROPERTY), incorporated by the Trusts of Land and Appointment of Trustees Act 1996 s 23(2). Trusts of Land and Appointment of Trustees Act 1996 s 8(1) does not apply in the case of charitable, ecclesiastical or public trusts: Trusts of Land and Appointment of Trustees Act 1996 s 8(3).
        In the case of registered land, trustees must apply for the restriction contained in the Land Registration Rules 1925, SR & O 1925/1093 rr 59A, 106A, 236, Sch 2 Form 11A as inserted by SI 1996/2975 to be entered on the register and beneficiaries may apply for a restriction or caution to protect their interests. There is no such facility for beneficiaries in the case of unregistered land, although it should be noted that under the Land Registration Act 1997 s 1 (37 Halsbury's Statutes (4th Edn) REAL PROPERTY) the range of dispositions inducing compulsory first registration has been greatly extended.
3   Trusts of Land and Appointment of Trustees Act 1996 s 8(2). Both the Trusts of Land and Appointment of Trustees Act 1996 ss 8(1) and 8(2) have effect subject to any enactment which prohibits or restricts such provisions (eg the Pensions Act 1995 s 35(4) (33 Halsbury's Statutes (4th Edn) PENSIONS AND SUPERANNUATION)): Trusts of Land and Appointment of Trustees Act 1996 s 8(4).

4   But not as between trustees and beneficiaries.
5   Trusts of Land and Appointment of Trustees Act 1996 s 10(1). This does not apply to charitable,
       ecclesiastical or public trusts: Trusts of Land and Appointment of Trustees Act 1996 s 10(2).
6   Within the meaning of the Children Act 1989 s 3(1) (6 Halsbury's Statutes (4th Edn) CHILDREN). As
       to parental responsibility for children see vol 16(2) (1996 Reissue) FAMILY.
7   Trusts of Land and Appointment of Trustees Act 1996 s 10(3).

[539]

225   Consultation with beneficiaries

Subject to any provision to the contrary in a disposition creating a trust of land[1], the
trustees must, in the exercise of any function relating to the land, so far as practicable,
consult the beneficiaries of full age and beneficially entitled to an interest in possession
in the land, and so far as consistent with the general interest of the trust, give effect to
the wishes of those beneficiaries or (in case of dispute) of the majority (according to the
value of their combined interests)[2]. The duty does not apply to the power to convey land
to beneficiaries[3], nor to a trust created or arising under a will made before 1 January
1997[4]. Furthermore, the duty does not apply to a trust created before 1 January 1997[5],
unless a provision that it is to apply is made by an irrevocable deed executed by the settlor
(being of full capacity) or, if more than one, by the survivor or survivors (being of
full capacity)[6].

[540]

1   Trusts of Land and Appointment of Trustees Act 1996 s 11(2)(a) (37 Halsbury's Statutes (4th Edn)
       REAL PROPERTY): see further Form 4 clause 9 [1089] post.
2   Trusts of Land and Appointment of Trustees Act 1996 s 11(1).
3   Trusts of Land and Appointment of Trustees Act 1996 s 11(2)(c). For the power to convey land to
       beneficiaries see Paragraph 222 [534] ante.
4   Trusts of Land and Appointment of Trustees Act 1996 s 11(2)(b).
5   Or after it by reference to such a trust.
6   Trusts of Land and Appointment of Trustees Act 1996 s 11(3), (4). For a deed pursuant to the Trusts
       of Land and Appointment of Trustees Act 1996 s 11(3) see vol 40(2) (2001 Reissue) TRUSTS AND
       SETTLEMENTS Part 8 [3501].

[541]

226   Trust for sale and the power to postpone

In the case of every trust for sale created by a disposition there is to be implied, despite
any provision to the contrary made therein, a power for the trustees to postpone sale of
the land; and the trustees will not be liable in any way for postponing sale of the land, in
the exercise of their discretion, for an indefinite period[1].

1   Trusts of Land and Appointment of Trustees Act 1996 s 4(1) (37 Halsbury's Statutes (4th Edn) REAL
       PROPERTY). The section applies whenever the trust was created or arose, but any liability incurred by
       trustees before 1 January 1997 is unaffected: Trusts of Land and Appointment of Trustees Act 1996
       s 4(2), (3). As to this section see vol 40(2) (2001 Reissue) TRUSTS AND SETTLEMENTS Part 8 [3001].

[542]

227   Delegation of powers

All the trustees of land acting jointly may, by power of attorney[1], delegate for any period
or indefinitely[2] to any beneficiary or beneficiaries of full age and beneficially entitled to
an interest in possession in land subject to the trust any of their functions as trustees which
relate to the land[3]. Unless expressed to be irrevocable, and to be given by way of security,
the power of attorney may be revoked by any one or more of the trustees[4].

Beneficiaries to whom functions have been delegated are, in relation to the exercise of the functions, in the same position as trustees (with the same duties and liabilities), but they are not to be regarded as trustees for any other purposes[5].

In favour of a person dealing in good faith with a person to whom the trustees have purported to delegate functions, it is presumed that the latter person is someone to whom the functions could be delegated, unless the person dealing with him had knowledge at the time of the transaction that this was not the case. Furthermore, it is to be conclusively presumed in favour of any purchaser whose interest depends on the validity of that transaction that that other person dealt in good faith and did not have such knowledge if that other person makes a statutory declaration to that effect before or within three months after the completion of the purchase[6].

The duty of care under the Trustee Act 2000[7] applies to trustees of land when exercising the powers conferred by the Trusts of Land and Appointment of Trustees Act 1996[8] and in particular in deciding whether to delegate any of their functions thereunder[9]. If a delegation is made and is not irrevocable, the trustees, while it continues:

227.1   must keep the delegation under review;

227.2   if circumstances make it appropriate to do so, must consider whether there is a need to exercise any power of intervention[10] that they have;

227.3   if they consider that there is a need to exercise such a power, must do so[11].

A trustee of land is not liable for any act or default of the beneficiary, or beneficiaries, unless the trustee fails to comply with the above duty of care in deciding to delegate any of the trustees' functions or in carrying out any duty referred to above[12].

[543]

---

1   It cannot, however, be an enduring power of attorney within the meaning of the Enduring Powers of Attorney Act 1985 (1 Halsbury's Statutes (4th Edn) AGENCY): Trusts of Land and Appointment of Trustees Act 1996 s 9(6) (37 Halsbury's Statutes (4th Edn) REAL PROPERTY). For powers for trustees to delegate see Form 316 [2194] et seq post.

2   Trusts of Land and Appointment of Trustees Act 1996 s 9(5).

3   Trusts of Land and Appointment of Trustees Act 1996 s 9(1), (3). Delegations effected before 1 January 1997 under the Law of Property Act 1925 s 29 (repealed) are unaffected: Trusts of Land and Appointment of Trustees Act 1996 s 9(9).

4   Trusts of Land and Appointment of Trustees Act 1996 s 9(3). This sub-section also provides that a power of attorney is revoked by the appointment as a trustee of a person other than those by whom it is given (although not by any of those persons dying or otherwise ceasing to be a trustee). As to the effect of a person to whom functions have been delegated ceasing to be a person beneficially entitled to an interest in possession in land subject to the trust, see Trusts of Land and Appointment of Trustees Act 1996 s 9(4).

5   Trusts of Land and Appointment of Trustees Act 1996 s 9(7). It is thought that the final bracketed phrase in this sub-section prevents an attorney from receiving capital money. Accordingly, the trustees themselves will need to join in any transfer or conveyance giving effect to any disposition by the beneficiary where capital money arises.

6   Trusts of Land and Appointment of Trustees Act 1996 s 9(2).

7   Trustee Act 2000 s 1: see Paragraph 183 [453] ante.

8   Ie those in the Trusts of Land and Appointment of Trustees Act 1996 s 9 as amended by the Trustee Act 2000 Sch 2 para 45(3).

9   Trusts of Land and Appointment of Trustees Act 1996 s 9A(1) inserted by the Trustee Act 2000 Sch 2 para 47. The Trustee Act 2000 does not affect the operation of any delegation effected before its commencement: Trusts of Land and Appointment of Trustees Act 1996 s 9A(4).

10   'Power of intervention' includes (a) a power to give directions to the beneficiary; and (b) a power to revoke the delegation: Trusts of Land and Appointment of Trustees Act 1996 s 9A(4).

11   Trusts of Land and Appointment of Trustees Act 1996 s 9A(2), (3). The duty of care applies to trustees in carrying out any duty under the Trusts of Land and Appointment of Trustees Act 1996 s 9A(3): s 9A(5).

12   Ie the duties under the Trusts of Land and Appointment of Trustees Act 1996 ss 9 and 9A(3): s 9A(6).

[544]

228   Right of beneficiaries to occupy trust land

Under the Trusts of Land and Appointment of Trustees Act 1996[1], a beneficiary who is beneficially entitled to an interest in possession of land subject to a trust of land has a right to occupy the land at any time when:

228.1   the purposes of the trust of land include making the land available for his occupation[2]; or

228.2   the land is held by trustees so as to be so available.

The Act does not, however, confer on a beneficiary a right to occupy land if it is either unavailable or unsuitable for occupation by him[3]. The Act does not appear to contemplate an express exclusion of its provisions by the trust instrument, but the settlement may contain a statement that it is not the intention of the settlor and that it is not the purpose of the settlement that any trust land should be occupied by or be available for occupation by any beneficiary or beneficiaries[4].

Where two or more beneficiaries are prima facie entitled to occupy land under these provisions, the trustees of land may exclude or restrict the entitlement of any one or more (but not all) of them[5]. The trustees of land may from time to time impose reasonable conditions on any beneficiary in relation to his occupation of land[6]. In particular, the conditions may require him to pay any outgoings or expenses in respect of the land or to assume any other obligation in relation to the land and activities conducted thereon[7]. Where the entitlement of any beneficiary has been excluded or restricted the conditions imposed on any other beneficiary may require the payment of compensation or foregoing of a benefit[8]. The trustees must not exercise their powers so as to prevent a person in occupation of land from continuing to occupy the land or in a manner likely to result in any such person ceasing to occupy the land, unless he consents or the court has given approval[9]. The court in determining whether to give such approval[10], and the trustees in exercising their power to impose conditions, and their powers of exclusion and restriction[11], must have regard to:

228.3   the intentions of the settlor(s);

228.4   the purposes for which the land is held; and

228.5   the circumstances and wishes of each of the beneficiaries with a prima facie right to occupy[12].

[545]

1   Trusts of Land and Appointment of Trustees Act 1996 ss 12, 13 (37 Halsbury's Statutes (4th Edn) REAL PROPERTY). See also Paragraph 73 [169] ante and, for a detailed consideration of these sections, see vol 40(2) (2001 Reissue) TRUSTS AND SETTLEMENTS Part 8 [3001].

2   Or the occupation of beneficiaries of a class of which he is a member, or of beneficiaries in general.

3   Trusts of Land and Appointment of Trustees Act 1996 s 12(2).

4   For a statement for inclusion in a settlement see vol 40(2) (2001 Reissue) TRUSTS AND SETTLEMENTS Part 8 [3501]. This may be backed up by a provision restricting the investment powers of trustees under the Trusts of Land and Appointment of Trustees Act 1996 s 6(1), (3) as amended by the Trustee Act 2000 Sch 2 para 45(1), so as to exclude buying land for beneficial occupation: see vol 40(2) (2001 Reissue) TRUSTS AND SETTLEMENTS Part 8 [3501].

5   Trusts of Land and Appointment of Trustees Act 1996 s 13(1). Under the Trusts of Land and Appointment of Trustees Act 1996 s 13(2) the trustees may not unreasonably exclude any beneficiary's entitlement to occupy land or restrict it to an unreasonable extent.

6   Trusts of Land and Appointment of Trustees Act 1996 s 13(3). For an agreement with a beneficiary for occupation of a trust property see vol 40(2) (2001 Reissue) TRUSTS AND SETTLEMENTS Part 8 [3501].

7   Trusts of Land and Appointment of Trustees Act 1996 s 13(5).

8   Trusts of Land and Appointment of Trustees Act 1996 s 13(6).

9   Trusts of Land and Appointment of Trustees Act 1996 s 13(7).

10   Trusts of Land and Appointment of Trustees Act 1996 s 13(8).

11   Ie under the Trusts of Land and Appointment of Trustees Act 1996 s 13(1), (2).

12   Trusts of Land and Appointment of Trustees Act 1996 s 13(4).

[546]

229 Purchaser protection

The Trusts of Land and Appointment of Trustees Act 1996 contains various provisions for the protection of a purchaser[1]. In the case of unregistered land, a purchaser is not concerned to see that in exercising their management powers the trustees have had regard to the rights of the beneficiaries[2], that the consent of beneficiaries has been obtained to a partition[3], or that due consultation[4] has been had with the beneficiaries[5]. A purchaser, unless he has actual notice, is unaffected by the failure of trustees to comply with applicable enactments or rules of law or equity[6]. Likewise, although the trustees are under a duty to take all reasonable steps to bring any limitations in the trust instrument on their powers[7] to the notice of a purchaser, a conveyance to him is not invalidated unless he has actual notice[8].

Where trustees convey land to persons they believe to be beneficiaries absolutely entitled to the land and of full age and capacity, they must (and if necessary can be ordered by the court to) execute a deed declaring that they are discharged from the trust in relation to that land[9]. A subsequent purchaser of that land is entitled to assume that as from the date of the deed the land is not subject to the trust, unless he has actual notice that the trustees were mistaken in their belief[10].

In the case of registered land subject to a trust of land, the land must be registered in the names of the trustees or in the name of a nominee appointed under Section 16 of the Trustee Act 2000[11], and there must also be entered on the register such restrictions as may be prescribed, or may be expedient, for the protection of the persons beneficially interested[12]. A purchaser of the registered land will have the usual protection[13]. Where the trustees have executed a deed declaring that they are discharged from the trust in relation to the land[14], the Registrar, on the same basis as a purchaser in the case of unregistered land[15], is entitled to assume that the land to which the deed relates is not subject to the trust[16].

[547]

1   Trusts of Land and Appointment of Trustees Act 1996 s 16 (37 Halsbury's Statutes (4th Edn) REAL PROPERTY). 'Purchaser' means a person who acquires an interest in or a charge on property for money or money's worth, and where the context so requires includes an intending purchaser: Law of Property Act 1925 s 205(1)(xxi) (37 Halsbury's Statutes (4th Edn) REAL PROPERTY), incorporated by the Trusts of Land and Appointment of Trustees Act 1996 s 23(1).

2   See Trusts of Land and Appointment of Trustees Act 1996 s 6(5) and Paragraph 221 [532] ante.

3   See Trusts of Land and Appointment of Trustees Act 1996 s 7(3) and Paragraph 223 [536] ante.

4   See Trusts of Land and Appointment of Trustees Act 1996 s 11 and Paragraph 225 [540] ante.

5   Trusts of Land and Appointment of Trustees Act 1996 s 16(1).

6   Trusts of Land and Appointment of Trustees Act 1996 s 16(2). See the Trusts of Land and Appointment of Trustees Act 1996 s 6(6), (8) and Paragraph 221 [532] ante.

7   See the Trusts of Land and Appointment of Trustees Act 1996 s 8 and Paragraph 224 [538] ante.

8   Trusts of Land and Appointment of Trustees Act 1996 s 16(3). This subsection and the Trusts of Land and Appointment of Trustees Act 1996 s 16(2) do not apply to land held on charitable, ecclesiastical or public trusts: Trusts of Land and Appointment of Trustees Act 1996 s 16(6).

9   Trusts of Land and Appointment of Trustees Act 1996 s 16(4).

10   Trusts of Land and Appointment of Trustees Act 1996 s 16(5).

11   Land Registration Act 1925 s 94(1) as substituted by the Trusts of Land and Appointment of Trustees Act 1996 s 25(1), Sch 3 para 5(8)(a) and amended by the Trustee Act 2000 Sch 2 para 26 (37 Halsbury's Statutes (4th Edn) REAL PROPERTY).

12   Land Registration Act 1925 s 94(4) as inserted by the Trusts of Land and Appointment of Trustees Act 1996 s 25(1), Sch 3 para 5(8)(c). Note the trustee restriction contained in the Land Registration Rules 1925, SR & O 1925/1093 rr 213, 236 (both substituted by SI 1996/2975), Sch 2 Form 62 (as substituted by SI 1989/801 and amended by SI 1996/2975).

     Where the powers of trustees of land are restricted or excluded under the Trusts of Land and Appointment of Trustees Act 1996 s 8 an application for first registration, or an application for registration of a disposition in favour of the trustees, should be accompanied by an application for the restriction contained in SR & O 1925/1093 rr 59A, 106A, Sch 2 Form 11A as inserted by SI 1996/2975. As to an application by a beneficiary for an appropriate restriction see SR & O 1925 r 236 as substituted by SI 1996/2975. See also SR & O 1925/1093 Sch 2 Forms 75, 76 as substituted by SI 1996/2975 and amended by SI 1997/3037 and SI 1998/128 (applications to register a restriction).

13   See the Land Registration Act 1925 s 20. In addition to taking subject to entries on the Register, he will take subject to any overriding interests.
14   Ie under the Trusts of Land and Appointment of Trustees Act 1996 s 16(4).
15   Trusts of Land and Appointment of Trustees Act 1996 s 16(5).
16   Land Registration Act 1925 s 94(5) as inserted by the Trusts of Land and Appointment of Trustees Act 1996 s 25(1), Sch 3 para 5(8)(c).

[548]

230   Applications to the court

In addition to a trustee of land any person who has an interest in property subject to a trust of land may apply to the court[1], and on such an application the court may make any such order relating to the exercise by the trustees of any of their functions, or declaring the nature or extent of a person's interest in property subject to the trust, as the court thinks fit[2]. The Trusts of Land and Appointment of Trustees Act 1996 specifically refers to an order relieving the trustees of any obligation to obtain the consent of, or to consult, any person in connection with the exercise of their functions. The court may not, however, under these provisions make an order as to the appointment or removal of trustees[3].

In determining an application matters to which the court is required to have regard include:

230.1   the intentions of the person or persons (if any) who created the trust;
230.2   the purposes for which the property subject to the trust is held;
230.3   the welfare of any minor who occupies or might reasonably be expected to occupy any land subject to the trust as his home; and
230.4   the interests of any secured creditor of any beneficiary[4].

In the case of an application relating to the exercise by trustees of land of their powers to exclude or restrict the right of the beneficiary to occupy trust land[5], the matters to which the court is to have regard also include the circumstances and wishes of each of the beneficiaries who is (or apart from any previous exercise by the trustees of their power would be) entitled to occupy the land[6]. In the case of any other application[7], the matters to which the court is to have regard also include the circumstances and wishes of any beneficiary of full age and entitled to an interest in possession in property subject to the trust or (in case of dispute) of the majority (according to the value of their combined interests)[8].

[549]

1   Trusts of Land and Appointment of Trustees Act 1996 s 14(1) (37 Halsbury's Statutes (4th Edn) REAL PROPERTY). District judges have jurisdiction to hear and dispose of proceedings under this section: *Practice Direction (family proceedings: allocation and costs)* [1999] 3 All ER 192, [1999] 1 WLR 1128. As to this section see further vol 40(2) (2001 Reissue) TRUSTS AND SETTLEMENTS Part 8 [3001].
2   Trusts of Land and Appointment of Trustees Act 1996 s 14(2). The court has these powers whether the application was made before or after the commencement of the Act: Trusts of Land and Appointment of Trustees Act 1996 s 14(4).
3   Trusts of Land and Appointment of Trustees Act 1996 s 14(3).
4   Trusts of Land and Appointment of Trustees Act 1996 s 15(1). The use of the word 'include' indicates that the matters specifically referred to are not exclusive: *TSB v Marshall* [1998] 2 FLR 769, [1998] Fam Law 596. The section does not apply in the case of an application by a trustee of a bankrupt's estate for an order for the sale of land: Trusts of Land and Appointment of Trustees Act 1996 s 15(4). There are special provisions for this situation in the Insolvency Act 1986 s 335A as inserted by the Trusts of Land and Appointment of Trustees Act 1996 s 25(1), Sch 3 para 23 (4 Halsbury's Statutes (4th Edn) BANKRUPTCY AND INSOLVENCY).
5   Trusts of Land and Appointment of Trustees Act 1996 s 13. As to the right of beneficiaries to occupy trust land see Paragraph 228 [545] ante.
6   Trusts of Land and Appointment of Trustees Act 1996 s 15(2).
7   Other than one relating to the power of trustees of land to convey it to the beneficiaries: see Trusts of Land and Appointment of Trustees Act 1996 s 6(2) and Paragraph 222 [534] ante.
8   Trusts of Land and Appointment of Trustees Act 1996 s 15(3).

[550]

231   Payment of proceeds of sale

Notwithstanding anything to the contrary in the instrument creating a trust of land or in any trust affecting the net proceeds of sale of the land if it is sold, the proceeds of sale or other capital money must not be paid to or applied by the direction of fewer than two persons as trustees, except where the trustee is a trust corporation[1].

1   See the Law of Property Act 1925 s 27(2) as substituted by the Law of Property (Amendment) Act 1926 s 7, Schedule and amended by the Trusts of Land and Appointment of Trustees Act 1996 s 25(1), Sch 3 para 4(8)(b) (37 Halsbury's Statutes (4th Edn) REAL PROPERTY). This provision does not prevent a single trustee for sale from selling, where under the instrument creating the trust the purchase-money is to be paid to two other persons as trustees: see *Re Wight and Best's Brewery Co Ltd's Contract* [1929] WN 11.

[551]–[560]

C: GENERAL STATUTORY POWERS OF TRUSTEES

1: SOURCES AND AVAILABILITY

232   Source of powers

All trustees have certain powers conferred on them by statute, in particular by the Trustee Act 1925 and the Trustee Act 2000. The powers conferred by the Trustee Act 1925 are in addition to any powers conferred by the instrument creating the trust, but, unless otherwise stated, apply if and so far only as a contrary intention is not expressed in that instrument and have effect subject to the terms of that instrument[1]. There are similar provisions in relation to powers conferred by the Trustee Act 2000[2].

[561]

1   See the Trustee Act 1925 s 69(2) (48 Halsbury's Statutes (4th Edn) TRUSTS AND SETTLEMENTS). As to the expression of a contrary intention see *Re Warren, Public Trustee v Fletcher* [1939] Ch 684, [1939] 2 All ER 599; *Re Rider's Will Trusts, Nelson v Rider* [1958] 3 All ER 135, [1958] 1 WLR 974.
2   See, as to the duty of care, Trustee Act 2000 Sch 1 para 7 (48 Halsbury's Statutes (4th Edn) TRUSTS AND SETTLEMENTS); as to the general power of investment, Trustee Act 2000 s 6(1); as to the acquisition of land, Trustee Act 2000 s 9; as to the power to employ agents and appoint nominees and custodians, Trustee Act 2000 s 26; and as to the remuneration of professional trustees, Trustee Act 2000 s 29(5). There is no such provision in relation to expenses, but in practice no trust instrument would deprive a trustee of his expenses and if it did it is barely conceivable that the trustee would accept the trust.

[562]

233   Miscellaneous powers

The powers conferred by the Trustee Act 1925 and the Trustee Act 2000 include the following:

233.1   Where a trustee has a duty or power to sell property, he may sell or concur with any other person in selling all or any part of the property, whether subject to prior charges or not, and either together or in lots, by public auction or by private contract, subject to any such conditions respecting title or evidence of title or other matters as the trustee thinks fit, with power to vary any contract for sale, and to buy in at any auction, or to rescind any contract for sale and to resell, without being answerable for any loss[1].

233.2   Where a duty or power of sale of land is vested in a trustee, power to sell or dispose of part of the land, whether the division is horizontal, vertical, or made in any other way[2].

233.3   Where trustees are authorised by the instrument creating the trust or by law to pay or apply capital money subject to the trust for any purpose or in any manner, power, which they are deemed always to have had, to raise the money required by sale, conversion, calling in, or mortgage of all or any part of the trust property for the time being in possession[3]. This provision applies notwithstanding anything to the contrary in the instrument creating the trust[4].

[563]

233.4   Power to insure any property which is subject to the trust against risks of loss or damage due to any event, and to pay the premiums out of trust funds[5].

233.5   Power to delegate trusts, powers and discretions for any reason for a period of 12 months[6].

233.6   Power to apply income for the maintenance of beneficiaries who are minors, and to make advancements out of capital[7].

233.7   Power to authorise any person to exercise any or all of their delegable functions as their agent[8].

233.8   Power to appoint a person to act as their nominee in relation to such of the assets of the trust as they determine[9].

233.9   Power to appoint a person to act as custodian in relation to such of the assets of the trust as they may determine[10].

[564]

1   See the Trustee Act 1925 s 12(1) as amended by the Trusts of Land and Appointment of Trustees Act 1996 s 25(1), Sch 3 para 3(2)(a) (48 Halsbury's Statutes (4th Edn) TRUSTS AND SETTLEMENTS). Trustees of land have power to leave part of the purchase money on mortgage: see the Trusts of Land and Appointment of Trustees Act 1996 s 6(1) (37 Halsbury's Statutes (4th Edn) REAL PROPERTY).
2   See the Trustee Act 1925 s 12(2) as amended by the Trusts of Land and Appointment of Trustees Act 1996 s 25(1), Sch 3 para 3(2)(b).
3   Trustee Act 1925 s 16(1).
4   See the Trustee Act 1925 s 16(2). The section does not apply to trustees of property held for charitable purposes, or to Settled Land Act trustees who are not also statutory owners: see the Trustee Act 1925 s 16(2). 'Statutory owner' means the trustees of the settlement or other persons who, during a minority, or at any other time when there is no tenant for life, have the powers of a tenant for life under the Settled Land Act 1925, but does not include the trustees of the settlement, where by virtue of an order of the court or otherwise, the trustees have power to convey the settled land in the name of the tenant for life: Settled Land Act 1925 s 117(1)(xxvi) (48 Halsbury's Statutes (4th Edn) TRUSTS AND SETTLEMENTS).
5   See the Trustee Act 1925 s 19(1) as substituted by the Trustee Act 2000 s 34. As to the application of the insurance money see the Trustee Act 1925 s 20 as amended by the Trusts of Land and Appointment of Trustees Act 1996 s 25(1), Sch 3 para 3(5) and the Trustee Act 2000 s 34(2). Trustees of land also have power to insure the land under the Trusts of Land and Appointment of Trustees Act 1996 s 6 but it would seem to be redundant.
6   See the Trustee Act 1925 s 25(1) as substituted by the Trustee Delegation Act 1999 s 5; and see further Paragraph 256 [630] post.
7   See the Trustee Act 1925 ss 31, 32 as amended by the Family Law Reform Act 1969 s 1(3), Sch 1 Pt I and as amended by the Trusts of Land and Appointment of Trustees Act 1996 s 25(1), Sch 3 para 3(8); and see Paragraph 235 [568] et seq post.
8   Trustee Act 2000 s 11(1) (48 Halsbury's Statutes (4th Edn) TRUSTS AND SETTLEMENTS); and see further Paragraph 246 [611] et seq post.
9   Trustee Act 2000 s 16(1); and see further Paragraph 249 [617] et seq post.
10 Trustee Act 2000 s 17(1); and see further Paragraph 249 [617] et seq post.

[565]

234   Power of the court to authorise dealings

Where in the management or administration of any property vested in trustees[1], any transaction, which is in the opinion of the court expedient, cannot be effected by reason of the absence of any power for that purpose vested in the trustees by the trust instrument or by law, the court may by order confer the necessary power on the trustees[2].

[566]

1   Other than trustees of a settlement for the purposes of the Settled Land Act 1925 (48 Halsbury's Statutes (4th Edn) TRUSTS AND SETTLEMENTS).

2   See the Trustee Act 1925 s 57(1) (48 Halsbury's Statutes (4th Edn) TRUSTS AND SETTLEMENTS). As to the extent of the jurisdiction conferred on the court by this section see eg *Municipal and General Securities Co Ltd v Lloyds Bank Ltd* [1950] Ch 212 at 223, 224, [1949] 2 All ER 937 at 944, 945. See further 48 Halsbury's Laws (4th Edn 2000 Reissue) para 957. As to the similar power under the Settled Land Act 1925 s 64 see vol 40(2) (2001 Reissue) TRUSTS AND SETTLEMENTS Part 9 [4101]. As to the inherent jurisdiction of the court to vary trusts and as to the statutory jurisdiction under the Variation of Trusts Act 1958 see 48 Halsbury's Laws (4th Edn 2000 Reissue) para 958 et seq.

Nothing in the Variation of Trusts Act 1958 s 1 as amended (48 Halsbury's Statutes (4th Edn) TRUSTS AND SETTLEMENTS) is to be taken as limiting the powers under the Trustee Act 1925 s 57. The settlement may itself confer on the trustees the power to add to their administrative powers: see Form 194 [1688] post.

[567]

2: POWERS OF MAINTENANCE

235   Statutory power of maintenance

The trust instrument may contain express powers for providing maintenance or education for, or otherwise benefiting, a beneficiary who is a minor[1]. Apart from any such express powers and subject to any contrary intention expressed in the trust instrument[2], where a trustee holds property in trust for any person for any interest whatsoever, whether vested or contingent, he has statutory power during the minority of that person, subject to any prior interests or charges affecting that property, at his discretion to pay to that person's parent or guardian, if any, or otherwise apply for or towards his maintenance, education or benefit the whole or such part, if any, of the income[3] of the property as may in all the circumstances be reasonable, and must accumulate any surplus income[4]. Once the beneficiary attains his majority, the trustees must pay a beneficiary's share of income to him even if his interest is still contingent under the terms of the trust[5].

[568]

1   As to the exercise of express powers of maintenance see Paragraph 237 [571] post. For specimen express powers of maintenance see Forms 151 [1590], 152 [1592] post; see also vol 40(2) (2001 Reissue) TRUSTS AND SETTLEMENTS Part 11 [6501] for a form which extends the maintenance period beyond the age of 18 years provided that there is a valid power to accumulate and with a final cut off at age 25 years (to preserve the accumulation and maintenance status of the trust).

2   See the Trustee Act 1925 s 69(2) (48 Halsbury's Statutes (4th Edn) TRUSTS AND SETTLEMENTS). A direction to accumulate income amounts to a contrary intention even if such a direction is invalid: see *Re Erskine's Settlement Trusts, Hollis v Pigott* [1971] 1 All ER 572, [1971] 1 WLR 162.

3   'Income' includes rents and profits: see the Trustee Act 1925 s 68(1), (10).

4   See the Trustee Act 1925 s 31 as amended by the Family Law Reform Act 1969 s 1(3), Sch 1 Pt I. The statutory power may be varied or extended: see Form 162 [1611] post.

5   *Re Jones' Will Trusts, Soames v AG* [1947] Ch 48, [1946] 2 All ER 281.

[569]

236   Disposal of accumulations

Where a minor, a member of a class, dies without attaining a vested interest, accumulations of income belonging contingently to that minor must be added to and afterwards dealt with as part of the entire capital of the trust fund[1].

1   *Re Joel's Will Trusts, Rogerson v Brudenell-Bruce* [1967] Ch 14, [1966] 2 All ER 482.

[570]

237   Express powers of maintenance

Any express trusts or powers for providing maintenance or education for, or otherwise benefiting, a minor, lawfully created by the settlement or will, are exercisable in respect of the property in which the minor is interested[1]. Where there is an imperative trust and not a mere power to apply the income, the trustees are not entitled to accumulate[2]. A power to apply income for the maintenance and support of a minor authorises its application for his education[3] and may be exercised during his father's lifetime in spite of the father's legal duty to maintain the minor[4], if the terms of the power so direct[5] or authorise[6]. A power to apply income for the benefit of a minor will include expenditure not strictly comprehended under maintenance or education[7]. If the power is discretionary, the court will not interfere with the donee's discretion so long as it is exercised in good faith[8]; having regard exclusively to the best interests of the minor[9], but if the opinion of the trustees is divided, the court may exercise the discretion for them[10].

Where the fund to be settled is small, it may be desirable to give the trustees a discretionary power to make advances for maintenance out of capital.

[571]

1   *Hall v Carter* (1742) 2 Atk 354; *King-Harman v Cayley* [1899] 1 IR 39. An account will not be ordered as to the mode in which the trust or power has been exercised: *Hora v Hora* (1863) 33 Beav 88.
2   *Re Peel, Tattersall v Peel* [1936] Ch 161.
3   *Re Breeds' Will* (1875) 1 Ch D 226 at 229.
4   Cf the statutory power; see the Trustee Act 1925 s 31(1)(i)(b) (48 Halsbury's Statutes (4th Edn) TRUSTS AND SETTLEMENTS).
5   *Mundy v Earl Howe* (1793) 4 Bro CC 223.
6   *Berkeley v Swinburne* (1834) 6 Sim 613; *Brophy v Bellamy* (1873) 8 Ch App 798; *Malcomson v Malcomson* (1885) 17 LR Ir 69, CA.
7   *Re Peel, Tattersall v Peel* [1936] Ch 161.
8   *Thompson v Griffin* (1841) Cr & Ph 317; *Re Lofthouse (an infant)* (1885) 29 Ch D 921, CA; *Re Bryant, Bryant v Hickley* [1894] 1 Ch 324.
9   *Fuller v Evans* [2000] 1 All ER 636 (not fatal that exercise of the power may confer an incidental and unintended benefit on some other person).
10   *Klug v Klug* [1918] 2 Ch 67.

[572]

3: POWERS OF ADVANCEMENT

238   Statutory power of advancement

Trustees, subject to any contrary intention expressed in the trust instrument and subject to the terms of that instrument[1], have a statutory power at their discretion to make advancements out of the capital of the trust property[2]. They may in their absolute discretion pay or apply capital money subject to the trust for the advancement or benefit of any person entitled to the capital of the trust property or any share of it, not exceeding altogether in amount half[3] the presumptive or vested share or interest of that person in the trust property, whether the person is entitled to the capital or a share of it absolutely or contingently on his attaining any specified age or on the occurrence of any other event or subject to a gift over on his death under any specified age or on the occurrence of any other event, and whether in possession or in remainder or reversion[4]. Such an advance may be made notwithstanding that the interest of that person is liable to be defeated by the exercise of a power of appointment or revocation or to be diminished by the increase of the class to which he belongs[5].

[573]

1   See the Trustee Act 1925 s 69(2) (48 Halsbury's Statutes (4th Edn) TRUSTS AND SETTLEMENTS); and see *IRC v Bernstein* [1961] Ch 399, [1961] 1 All ER 320, CA, where the statutory power of advancement was held to be impliedly excluded by the manifest intention of the settlor that there should be no distribution in his lifetime. Cf *Re Henderson's Trusts, Schreiber v Baring* [1969] 3 All ER 769, [1969] 1 WLR 651, CA. See also *Re Evans' Settlement, Watkins v Whitworth-Jones* [1967] 3 All ER 343, [1967] 1 WLR 1294 where it was held that, although an express power of advancement did not necessarily exclude the statutory power, the express power in that case, being limited to a stated sum, did so.

2   Ie powers under the Trustee Act 1925 s 32. For express provisions extending the statutory power see Forms 153 [1594]–157 [1611] post and for an express power to advance capital to the life tenant see vol 40(2) (2001 Reissue) TRUSTS AND SETTLEMENTS Part 11 [6501]. The Trustee Act 1925 s 32 does not apply to capital money arising under the Settled Land Act 1925 (48 Halsbury's Statutes (4th Edn) TRUSTS AND SETTLEMENTS): see the Trustee Act 1925 s 32(2) as amended by the Trusts of Land and Appointment of Trustees Act 1996 s 25(1), Sch 3 para 3(8). Assets may be transferred in specie: *Re Collard's Will Trusts, Lloyds Bank Ltd v Rees* [1961] Ch 293, [1961] 1 All ER 821.

3   Once the one-half limit is reached, no further advance can be made even if the retained half increases in value: *Re Marquess of Abergavenny's Estate Act Trusts, Marquess of Abergavenny v Ram* [1981] 2 All ER 643, [1981] 1 WLR 843.

4   See the Trustee Act 1925 s 32(1). The money advanced must be brought into account if the person advanced is or becomes absolutely and indefeasibly entitled to a share in the trust property: Trustee Act 1925 s 32(1) proviso (b). No advance may be made so as to prejudice any person entitled to any prior life or other interest, whether vested or contingent, in the money advanced unless that person is in existence and of full age and consents in writing to the advance being made: Trustee Act 1925 s 32(1) proviso (c) and see further Paragraph 240 [577] post.

5   See note 3 above.

[574]

239   Exercise of power of advancement

The word 'benefit' used in the statutory power is a word of wide meaning, unlike 'advancement' which contemplates some definite purpose for preferring the beneficiary in life[1]. The inclusion of the word 'benefit' does not, however, absolve the trustees from the duty to decide whether the payment in the particular manner which they contemplate is for the benefit of the beneficiary[2].

If the power of advancement is exercised for the benefit of the beneficiary, its exercise will not be made improper by the fact that other people may benefit incidentally as a result[3]. Great care is, however, required to ensure that in the exercise of such a power the person really benefiting from the exercise will be primarily the object of the power, and the power must not be exercised so as to procure a benefit to the trustees[4].

Trustees exercising a power of advancement may make settlements on objects of the power if the particular circumstance of the case warrant that course as being for the benefit of the objects of the power[5].

If the property advanced under the statutory power is settled by that advance, the interests created by such advancement must vest within the perpetuity period applicable to the settlement; the rule in this respect is similar to that applicable to the exercise of special powers of appointment[6].

[575]

1   See eg *Roper-Curzon v Roper-Curzon* (1871) LR 11 Eq 452 (providing a settled fund on marriage to yield income).

2   *Re Moxon's Will Trusts, Downey v Moxon* [1958] 1 All ER 386, [1958] 1 WLR 165; *Re Pauling's Settlement Trusts, Younghusband v Coutts & Co* [1964] Ch 303, [1963] 3 All ER 1, CA.

3   See *Pilkington v IRC* [1964] AC 612, [1962] 3 All ER 622, HL; and see *Re Clore's Settlement Trusts, Sainer v Clore* [1966] 2 All ER 272, [1966] 1 WLR 955 where an advancement was made to a charity of the beneficiary's choice. For a request for an advancement see Form 265 [1879] post.

4   See *Molyneux v Fletcher* [1898] 1 QB 648.

5   *Re Wills' Will Trusts, Wills v Wills* [1959] Ch 1, [1958] 2 All ER 472; *Pilkington v IRC* [1964] AC 612, [1962] 3 All ER 622, HL. See further Paragraph 18 note 4 [49] ante. Also, see Form 280 [1953] et seq post.

6   *Pilkington v IRC* [1964] AC 612, [1962] 3 All ER 622, HL. As to the application of the rule against perpetuities to special powers see Paragraph 77 note 3 [184] ante. See also *Re Hastings-Bass, Hastings-Bass v IRC* [1975] Ch 25, [1974] 2 All ER 193, CA; *Breadner v Granville-Grossman* [2001] Ch 523, [2000] 4 All ER 705 and see *Green v Cobham* (19 January 2000, unreported).

[576]

240   Consent to advancements

An advancement in pursuance of the statutory power requires the consent of any person in existence and of full age entitled to any prior life or other interest in the money paid or applied[1], and there are no circumstances which will justify non-compliance with this requirement[2]. The giving of consent to an advance under the statutory power or an express power by a person having the protected life interest under the statutory protective trusts[3] will not operate to cause a forfeiture of his protected interest[4], nor will the giving of consent by a person entitled to a protected life interest other than under the statutory protective trusts, where the advance is made under an express power conferred by the settlement[5]. The giving of consent by a person entitled to a protected life interest other than under the statutory protective trusts may, however, so operate, where the advance is made under the statutory power[6].

The objects of a discretionary trust or power are not persons entitled to a prior life or other interest, vested or contingent, so as to make their consent necessary[7].

[577]

1   See the Trustee Act 1925 s 32(1) proviso (c) (48 Halsbury's Statutes (4th Edn) TRUSTS AND SETTLEMENTS). For the consent of a beneficiary with a prior interest see Form 266 [1881] post.

2   *Re Forster's Settlement, Forster v Custodian of Enemy Property for England* [1942] Ch 199, [1942] 1 All ER 180. See also *Henley v Wardell* (1988) Times, 29 January where an 'absolute and uncontrolled discretion to advance' did not remove the requirement for consent.

3   As to statutory protective trusts generally see Paragraph 123 [305] ante.

4   See the Trustee Act 1925 s 33(1)(i).

5   See *Re Shaw's Settlement Trusts, Shaw v Shaw, Re Wisely's Settlement Trusts, Wisely v Public Trustee* [1951] Ch 833, [1951] 1 All ER 656; following *Re Hodgson, Weston v Hodgson* [1913] 1 Ch 34, and distinguishing *Re Stimpson's Trusts, Stimpson v Stimpson* [1931] 2 Ch 77.

6   *Re Stimpson's Trusts, Stimpson v Stimpson* [1931] 2 Ch 77.

7   *Re Beckett's Settlement, Re Beckett, Eden v Von Stutterheim* [1940] Ch 279.

[578]–[590]

4: POWERS OF INVESTMENT

241   The general power of investment under the Trustee Act 2000

Part II of the Trustee Act 2000[1] is revolutionary in that it replaces the previous system[2], under which a trustee was only permitted to make specified 'authorised' investments, by one under which a trustee can make any kind of investment that he could make if he were absolutely entitled to the assets of the trust. This is called the 'general power of investment[3]. The general power of investment does not, however, permit a trustee to make investments in land other than in loans secured on land[4], but there are special provisions in relation to the acquisition of land elsewhere in the Act, which are discussed below[5].

The general power of investment, which applies to trusts whenever created[6], is additional to any powers of investment conferred on trustees otherwise than by the Act[7], but is subject to any restriction or exclusion imposed by the trust instrument, or by any enactment or any provision of subordinate legislation[8].

There are exceptions to the new provisions. Part II does not apply to trustees of pension schemes[9], authorised unit trusts[10], or funds established under schemes made under the Charities Act 1993 Sections 24 or 25[11].

[591]

1 Trustee Act 2000 Pt II (ss 3–7) (48 Halsbury's Statutes (4th Edn) TRUSTS AND SETTLEMENTS). For transitional provisions following the repeal of the Trustee Act 1925 ss 8, 9, see the Trustee Act 2000 Sch 3 paras 2, 3. Also see the Trustee Act 2000 Sch 3 para 7 in relation to perpetual rentcharges.

2 See the Trustee Act 1925 Part I (ss 1–11) (48 Halsbury's Statutes (4th Edn) TRUSTS AND SETTLEMENTS) and the Trustee Investments Act 1961 (48 Halsbury's Statutes (4th Edn) TRUSTS AND SETTLEMENTS).

3 Trustee Act 2000 s 3(1), (2). The new statutory duty of care applies: Trustee Act 2000 s 1, Sch 1 para 1. But see the Trustee Act 2000 s 36(2) as to pension schemes.

4 Trustee Act 2000 s 3(3). A person invests in a loan secured on land if he has rights under any contract under which (a) one person provides another with credit, and (b) the obligation of the borrower to repay is secured on land: Trustee Act 2000 s 3(4). 'Credit' includes any cash, loan or other financial accommodation, and 'cash' includes money in any form: Trustee Act 2000 s 3(5), (6).

5 Trustee Act 2000 s 8.

6 Trustee Act 2000 s 7(1).

7 Trustee Act 2000 s 6(1)(a).

8 Trustee Act 2000 s 6(1)(b). In the Trustee Act 2000 'subordinate legislation' has the same meaning as in the Interpretation Act 1978: Trustee Act 2000 s 6(3). For the purposes of the Trustee Act 2000, an enactment or a provision of subordinate legislation is not to be regarded as being, or as being part of, a trust instrument: Trustee Act 2000 s 6(2). The Trustee Act 2000 s 7(2) prevents the provisions of a trust instrument made before 3 August 1961 from being treated as such a restriction or exclusion. In relation to trusts existing when the Trustee Act 2000 Part II (ss 3–7) came into force, a provision in a trust instrument which has effect under the Trustee Investments Act 1961 s 3(2) as a power to invest under that Act, or which confers a power to invest under that Act, is to be treated as conferring the general power of investment on a trustee: Trustee Act 2000 s 7(3). See Form 148 [1576] post for a clause excluding the power conferred under the Trustee Act 2000 s 3.

9 Trustee Act 2000 s 36(3).

10 Trustee Act 2000 s 37(1). 'Authorised unit trust' means a unit trust scheme in the case of which an order under the Financial Services Act 1986 s 78 is in force: Trustee Act 2000 s 37(2).

11 Trustee Act 2000 s 38. As to common investment schemes and common deposit schemes see the Charities Act 1993 ss 24, 25 (5 Halsbury's Statutes (4th Edn) CHARITIES) and 5(2) Halsbury's Laws (Reissue) paras 351, 352.

[592]

242 Standard investment criteria

The Trustee Act 2000 provides that in exercising any power of investment, whether arising under the Act or otherwise, and whenever created, a trustee must have regard to the standard investment criteria[1].

The standard investment criteria in relation to a trust are:

'(a) the suitability to the trust of investments of the same kind as any particular investment proposed to be made or retained and of that particular investment as an investment of that kind, and

(b) the need for diversification of investments of the trust, in so far as is appropriate to the circumstances of the trust[2]'

'Suitability' relates both to the kind of investment proposed and to the particular investment as an investment of that kind. It includes considerations as to the size and risk of the investment and the need to produce an appropriate balance between income and capital growth to meet the needs of the trust. It will also include any relevant ethical considerations as to the kind of investments which it is appropriate for the trust to make.

The Act also requires trustees to review the investments of the trust from time to time and to consider whether, having regard to the standard investment criteria, they should be varied[3].

1   Trustee Act 2000 ss 4(1), 7(1) (48 Halsbury's Statutes (4th Edn) TRUSTS AND SETTLEMENTS). It does
     not appear that this requirement can be excluded in the trust deed.
2   Trustee Act 2000 s 4(3).
3   Trustee Act 2000 s 4(2).

[593]

243   Duty to obtain advice before investing

The Trustee Act 2000 provides that before exercising any power of investment, whether arising under the Act or otherwise, a trustee must obtain and consider proper advice about the way in which, having regard to the standard investment criteria, the power should be exercised[1]. 'Proper advice' is the advice of a person who is reasonably believed by the trustee to be qualified to give it by his ability in and practical experience of financial and other matters relating to the proposed investment[2].

Likewise when reviewing the investments of the trust a trustee must obtain and consider proper advice about whether, having regard to the standard investment criteria, the investments should be varied[3].

The above duties apply whenever the trust was created[4].

By way of exception to the above requirements, it is provided that a trustee need not obtain such advice if he reasonably concludes that in all the circumstances it is unnecessary or inappropriate to do so[5].

[594]

1   Trustee Act 2000 s 5(1) (48 Halsbury's Statutes (4th Edn) TRUSTS AND SETTLEMENTS).
2   Trustee Act 2000 s 5(4).
3   See the Trustee Act 2000 s 5(2).
4   See the Trustee Act 2000 s 7(1).
5   See the Trustee Act 2000 s 5(3).

[595]

244   Acquisition of land

The Trustee Act 2000 Part III[1] provides that a trustee may acquire freehold or leasehold land in the United Kingdom:

244.1   as an investment;

244.2   for occupation by a beneficiary; or

244.3   for any other reason[2].

As with Part II of the Trustee Act 2000, the powers conferred by Part III are additional to any powers conferred on trustees otherwise than by the Act, but are subject to any restriction or exclusion imposed by the trust instrument or by any enactment or any provision of subordinate legislation[3].

For the purposes of exercising his functions as a trustee, a trustee who acquires land under these provisions has all the powers of an absolute owner in relation to the land[4].

The above provisions, which apply to trusts whenever created[5], are broadly modelled on the Trusts of Land and Appointment of Trustees Act 1996 Section 6(3), (4), but are in wider terms than that section as originally enacted, though the section has been amended by the Trustee Act 2000[6] so as to give trustees of land the powers conferred by the Trustee Act 2000 Section 8. Unlike the Trusts of Land and Appointment of Trustees Act 1996, the Trustee Act 2000 is not restricted to trustees of land but applies to trustees generally. The 1996 Act imposed an express duty on trustees to have regard to the interest of the beneficiaries in exercising their powers under Section 6[7]: there is no equivalent provision in the 2000 Act, but since that provision merely made statutory the equitable duty of trustees, it is thought that the obligations of trustees are no less under the 2000 Act.

The Trustee Act 2000 Part III does not apply to trustees of a settlement under the Settled Land Act 1925[8] or to trustees of trusts subject to the Universities and College Estates Act 1925[9]. Nor does it apply to trustees of pension schemes[10], authorised unit trusts[11], or funds established under schemes made under the Charities Act 1993 Section 24 or 25[12].

[596]

1   Trustee Act 2000 ss 8–10 (48 Halsbury's Statutes (4th Edn) TRUSTS AND SETTLEMENTS).
2   Trustee Act 2000 s 8(1). The new statutory 'duty of care' applies: Trustee Act 2000 s 1 Sch 1 para 2, but see the Trustee Act 2000 s 36(2) as to pension trustees. 'Freehold or leasehold land' is defined in the Trustee Act 2000 s 8(2): in relation to England and Wales it means a legal estate in land: Trustee Act 2000 s 8(2)(a). In relation to Scotland and Northern Ireland see the Trustee Act 2000 s 8(2)(b), (c).
3   Trustee Act 2000 s 9. See the Trustee Act 2000 s 6(2), (3) and Paragraph 241 note 8 [592] ante.
4   Trustee Act 2000 s 8(3).
5   Trustee Act 2000 s 10(2).
6   Trustee Act 2000 Sch 2 para 45. This paragraph also imposes on trustees of land the duty of care under the Trustee Act 2000 s 1 when exercising the powers conferred by the Trusts of Land and Appointment of Trustees Act 1996 s 6.
7   Trusts of Land and Appointment of Trustees Act 1996 s 6(5) (37 Halsbury's Statutes (4th Edn) REAL PROPERTY).
8   Trustee Act 2000 s 10(1)(a).
9   Trustee Act 2000 s 10(1)(b).
10   Trustee Act 2000 s 36(3).
11   Trustee Act 2000 s 37(1).
12   Trustee Act 2000 s 38. As to the Charities Act 1993 ss 24 and 25 see 5(2) Halsbury's Laws (Reissue) paras 351, 352.

[597]

245   Express powers of investment
Trustees have hitherto usually been given extended powers of investment by way of express provision in the trust instrument. This gave the trustees more flexibility in their choice of investment and avoided having to comply with the complex administrative provisions of the Trustee Investments Act 1961.

An express investment clause is now more likely to be thought desirable in order to restrict the wide statutory power of investment, for instance by prohibiting for ethical considerations investments of which the settlor disapproves[1].

[598]

1   Cowan v Scargill [1985] Ch 270, [1984] 2 All ER 750; Harries v Church Commrs for England [1993] 2 All ER 300, [1992] 1 WLR 1241. See Forms 147 [1575], 148 [1576] post. For a wider general power of investment see Form 4 schedule paragraph 1 [1092] post and see Form 4 note 31 [1106] post.

[599]–[610]

5: POWER TO EMPLOY AGENTS AND TO DELEGATE POWERS

246   Power to employ agents

The Trustee Act 2000 confers on trustees a power of collective delegation[1], whether the trust was created before or after the Act came into force[2]. This power is additional to any other powers the trustees may have, but is subject to any restriction or exclusion imposed by the trust instrument or by any enactment or provision of subordinate legislation[3].

The Trustee Act 2000[4] provides that trustees may authorise any person to exercise any or all of their delegable functions as their agent. A distinction is made between charitable and non-charitable trusts. In the case of the latter, the trustees' delegable functions consist of:

246.1   any function relating to whether or in what way any assets of the trust should be distributed;

246.2   any power to decide whether any fees or other payment due to be made out of the trust funds should be made out of income or capital;

246.3   any power to appoint a person to be a trustee of the trust; or

246.4   any power conferred by any other enactment or the trust instrument which permits the trustees to delegate any of their functions or to appoint a person to act as a nominee or custodian[5].

In the case of a charitable trust, the trustees' delegable functions are:

246.5   any function consisting of carrying out a decision that the trustees have taken[6];

246.6   any function relating to the investment of assets subject to the trust[7];

246.7   any function relating to the raising of funds for the trust otherwise than by means of profits of a trade which is an integral part of carrying out the trust's charitable purpose[8];

246.8   any other functions prescribed by an order[9] made by the Secretary of State[10].

None of the above provisions apply to trustees of authorised unit trusts[11], or to trustees managing a fund under a common investment scheme or a common deposit scheme under the Charities Act 1993[12]. They apply to trustees of a pension scheme, subject to certain restrictions[13].

[611]

1   Trustee Act 2000 s 11 (48 Halsbury's Statutes (4th Edn) TRUSTS AND SETTLEMENTS). As to delegation by individual trustees see the Trustee Act 1925 s 25 as substituted by the Trustee Delegation Act 1999 s 5(1), (2) (48 Halsbury's Statutes (4th Edn) TRUSTS AND SETTLEMENTS). For powers for trustees to delegate see Form 316 [2194] et seq post.

2   Trustee Act 2000 s 27. This Part of the Act applies in relation to a trust having a sole trustee: Trustee Act 2000 s 25(1).

3   Trustee Act 2000 s 26. See the Trustee Act 2000 s 6(2), (3) and Paragraph 241 note 8 [592] ante.

4   Trustee Act 2000 s 11(1). The new statutory duty of care applies: Trustee Act 2000 s 1 Sch 1 para 3, qualified as to pension schemes: Trustee Act 2000 s 36(2).

5   Trustee Act 2000 s 11(2)

6   Trustee Act 2000 s 11(3)(a).

7   Including, in the case of land acquired as an investment, managing the land and creating or disposing of an interest in land: Trustee Act 2000 s 11(3)(b).

8   Trustee Act 2000 s 11(3)(c). Note the Trustee Act 2000 s 11(4) which provides that for the purposes of the Trustee Act 2000 s 11(3)(c) a trade is an integral part of carrying out a trust's charitable purpose if, whether carried on in the United Kingdom or elsewhere, the profits are applied solely to the purposes of the trust and either (a) the trade is exercised in the course of actually carrying out a primary purpose of the trust; or (b) the work in connection with the trade is mainly carried out by beneficiaries of the trust.

9   Made by statutory instrument as prescribed by the Trustee Act 2000 s 11(5).
10   Trustee Act 2000 s 11(3)(d). For transitional provisions relating to agents appointed under the Trustee
        Act 1925 s 23 (repealed) see the Trustee Act 2000 Sch 3 paras 5, 6.
11   Trustee Act 2000 s 37.
12   Charities Act 1993 ss 24 and 25 respectively (5 Halsbury's Statutes (4th Edn) CHARITIES): Trustee Act
        2000 s 38.
13   Trustee Act 2000 s 36(4)–(7).

[612]

247   Persons who may act as agents

The only restrictions on whom the trustees can appoint as their agents are that they cannot authorise a beneficiary to exercise any function as their agent (even if the beneficiary is also a trustee)[1], and they cannot authorise two or more persons to exercise the same function unless they are to exercise it jointly[2]. The persons whom the trustees authorise to exercise functions as their agent may, however, include one or more of their number[3], and a person so authorised may also be appointed to act as their nominee or custodian[4].

The statutory duty of care[5] is limited to trustees. It does not apply to an agent in the performance of his agency, though such a person will owe a separate duty of care to the trust under the general law of agency. In particular an agent is subject to any specific duties or restrictions attached to the function. An example would be where trustees delegate their investment function. In such a case the agent must have regard to the standard investment criteria[6].

A duly authorised agent[7] is not subject to the requirement to obtain advice before exercising a power of investment[8] if he is the kind of person from whom it would have been proper for the trustees, in compliance with the requirement, to obtain advice[9].

Trustees of land are, by virtue of the Trusts of Land and Appointment of Trustees Act 1996[10], under duties to consult beneficiaries and give effect to their wishes. The Trustee Act 2000 provides that trustees must ensure that, in delegating any of their functions under the 2000 Act, they do so on terms that do not prevent them from complying with their duties under the 1996 Act[11]. However a duly authorised agent[12], who is authorised to exercise any function relating to land subject to the trust, is not subject to the duties under the Trusts of Land and Appointment of Trustees Act 1996 referred to above[13].

[613]

1   Trustee Act 2000 s 12(3) (48 Halsbury's Statutes (4th Edn) TRUSTS AND SETTLEMENTS). The
        restrictions may be considered unsatisfactory: see Form 317 [2196] post. In this subsection 'trustees'
        does not include a sole trustee: Trustee Act 2000 s 25(1): quaere whether this is an error for the Trustee
        Act 2000 s 12(4). Contrast the power of trustees of land under the Trusts of Land and Appointment of
        Trustees Act 1996 s 9 (37 Halsbury's Statutes (4th Edn) REAL PROPERTY). That power, however, is
        subject to restrictions which do not apply under the Trustee Act 2000 s 11. See Paragraph 227 [543]
        ante.
2   Trustee Act 2000 s 12(2).
3   Trustee Act 2000 s 12(1). In this subsection 'trustees' does not include a sole trustee: Trustee Act 2000
        s 25(1).
4   Trustee Act 2000 s 12(4). See note 1 above.
5   See the Trustee Act 2000 s 1 and Paragraph 183 [453] ante.
6   Trustee Act 2000 s 13(1).
7   Ie under the Trustee Act 2000 s 11.
8   Ie under the Trustee Act 2000 s 5. See Paragraph 243 [594] ante.
9   Trustee Act 2000 s 13(2).
10   Trusts of Land and Appointment of Trustees Act 1996 s 11(1).
11   Trustee Act 2000 s 13(3), (4).
12   Ie under the Trustee Act 2000 s 11.
13   Trustee Act 2000 s 13 (5).

[614]

248   Terms of agency

In general trustees are free to agree terms as to remuneration and other matters in relation to the appointment of an agent[1].

Certain terms, however, may only be agreed by the trustees where it is reasonably necessary for them to do so. These terms are:

248.1   a term permitting the agent to appoint a substitute;

248.2   a term restricting the liability of the agent or his substitute to the trustees or any beneficiary;

248.3   a term permitting the agent to act in circumstances capable of giving rise to a conflict of interest[2].

Further restrictions apply where trustees delegate any of their asset management functions. In this case the appointment must be made in writing or evidenced in writing[3]. Further, the trustees must first prepare a 'policy statement', giving guidance as to how the functions should be exercised, with a view to ensuring that the functions are exercised in the best interests of the trust. The agreement with the agent must include a term to the effect that the agent will secure compliance with the policy statement and any revision or replacement thereof[4]. The policy statement must be in or evidenced in writing[5].

The asset management functions of trustees are their functions relating to:

248.4   the investment of assets subject to the trust;

248.5   the acquisition of property which is to be subject to the trust; and

248.6   managing property which is subject to the trust and disposing of, or creating and disposing of an interest in, such property[6].

[615]

---

1   Trustee Act 2000 s 14(1) (48 Halsbury's Statutes (4th Edn) TRUSTS AND SETTLEMENTS). This is subject to the Trustee Act 2000 s 15(2) as discussed below, and to the Trustee Act 2000 ss 29–32 relating to remuneration: these last sections are considered in Paragraph 212 [511] et seq ante.

2   Trustee Act 2000 s 14(2), (3). Particular difficulties may arise in the case of fund managers as a result of Paragraph 248.3 above: see Form 319 [2200] post.

3   Trustee Act 2000 s 15(1).

4   Trustee Act 2000 s 15(2), (3).

5   Trustee Act 2000 s 15(4). There is no requirement for a policy statement where the trustees obtain investment advice but take decisions on investment matters themselves.

6   Trustee Act 2000 s 15(5).

[616]

249   Appointment of nominees and custodians

Trustees of a trust, whenever created[1], which does not have a custodian trustee, may appoint a person to act as their nominee in relation to such of the assets of the trust as they may determine, and take such steps as are necessary to secure that those assets are vested in the person so appointed[2]. The statutory power is additional to any other powers the trustees may have, but is subject to any restriction or exclusion imposed by the trust instrument or by any enactment or any provision of subordinate legislation[3]. The appointment must be in or evidenced in writing[4].

The trustees may also appoint a person to act as a custodian in relation to such of the assets of the trust as they may determine[5]. A person is a custodian in relation to assets if he undertakes the safe custody of the assets or of any documents or records concerning the assets[6]. The appointment must be in or evidenced in writing[7]. The section does not apply to any trust having a custodian trustee or in relation to any assets vested in the official custodian for charities[8].

If trustees retain or invest in securities payable to bearer, they have a duty (unless exempted by a provision in the trust instrument or any enactment or provision of subordinate legislation) to appoint a person to act as a custodian of the securities[9]. The appointment must be in or evidenced in writing[10].

The powers to appoint nominees and custodians do not apply to the trustees of a pension scheme[11], to trustees of an authorised unit trust[12], or to trustees managing a fund under a common investment scheme or a common deposit scheme under the Charities Act 1993[13].

[617]

1   Trustee Act 2000 s 27 (48 Halsbury's Statutes (4th Edn) TRUSTS AND SETTLEMENTS).
2   Trustee Act 2000 s 16(1), (3). The section applies in relation to a trust having a sole trustee: Trustee Act 2000 s 25(1). It does not apply in relation to settled land or in relation to any assets vested in the official custodian of charities: Trustee Act 2000 s 16(1), (3).
3   Trustee Act 2000 s 26. See the Trustee Act 2000 s 6(2), (3) and Paragraph 241 note 8 [592] ante.
4   Trustee Act 2000 s 16(2).
5   Trustee Act 2000 s 17(1). This section applies in relation to a trust having a sole trustee: Trustee Act 2000 s 25(1). For transitional provisions where a banker or banking company held documents deposited for safe custody under the Trustee Act 1925 s 21 (repealed) see the Trustee Act 2000 Sch 3 para 4.
6   Trustee Act 2000 s 17(2).
7   Trustee Act 2000 s 17(3).
8   Trustee Act 2000 s 17(4).
9   Trustee Act 2000 s 18(1), (2). The section does not impose a duty on a sole trustee if that trustee is a trust corporation: Trustee Act 2000 s 25(2). The section does not apply to a trust already having a custodian trustee, or in relation to any securities vested in the official custodian for charities: Trustee Act 2000 s 18(4). For transitional provisions where a banker or banking company held securities under the Trustee Act 1925 s 7(1) (repealed) see the Trustee Act 2000 Sch 3 para 1.
10   Trustee Act 2000 s 18(3).
11   Trustee Act 2000 s 36(8).
12   Trustee Act 2000 s 37.
13   Trustee Act 2000 s 38.

[618]

250   Persons who may be appointed as nominees or custodians

To be eligible for appointment as a nominee or custodian, one of the relevant conditions must be satisfied[1]. These are that:

250.1   the person carries on a business which consists of or includes acting as a nominee or custodian;

250.2   the person is a body corporate which is controlled by the trustees;

250.3   the person is a body corporate recognised under the Administration of Justice Act 1985 Section 9[2] .

The trustees may appoint one of their number, if that one is a trust corporation, or two (or more) of their number if they are to act as joint nominees or joint custodians[3].

The person appointed as nominee or custodian may also be appointed as custodian or nominee, as the case may be, or authorised to exercise functions as the trustees' agent[4].

Trustees of a charitable trust which is not an exempt charity must act in accordance with any guidance given by the Charity Commissioners in the selection of a nominee or custodian[5].

[619]

1   Trustee Act 2000 s 19(1) (48 Halsbury's Statutes (4th Edn) TRUSTS AND SETTLEMENTS). See Form 4 schedule paragraph 18 [1098] post for an unrestricted express power.
2   Trustee Act 2000 s 19(2). The question whether a body is controlled by trustees is determined in accordance with the Income and Corporation Taxes Act 1988 s 840 (42–44 Halsbury's Statutes (4th Edn) TAXATION): Trustee Act 2000 s 19(3).
3   Trustee Act 2000 s 19(5). This is subject to the Trustee Act 2000 s 19(1), (4). In the Trustee Act 2000 s 19(5) the reference to trustees does not include a sole trustee: Trustee Act 2000 s 25(1).
4   Trustee Act 2000 s 19(6), (7).
5   Trustee Act 2000 s 19(4).

[620]

251   Terms of appointment of nominees and custodians

In general the trustees may appoint a person to act as a nominee or custodian on such terms as to remuneration and other matters as they may determine[1]. They may not, however, appoint a person to act on any of three specified terms unless it is reasonably necessary for them to do so[2]. The specified terms are:

251.1   a term permitting the nominee or custodian to appoint a substitute;

251.2   a term restricting the liability of the nominee or custodian or his substitute to the trustees or to any beneficiary;

251.3   a term permitting the nominee or custodian to act in circumstances capable of giving rise to a conflict of interest[3].

[621]

1   Trustee Act 2000 s 20(1) (48 Halsbury's Statutes (4th Edn) TRUSTS AND SETTLEMENTS). This is subject to the Trustee Act 2000 ss 29–32 relating to remuneration: see Paragraph 213 [513] et seq ante.
2   Trustee Act 2000 s 20(2).
3   Trustee Act 2000 s 20(3).

[622]

252   Remuneration and expenses of agents, nominees and custodians

Where under a power conferred by the Trustee Act 2000[1] or by the trust instrument a person, other than a trustee, has been authorised to exercise functions as an agent of the trustees, or appointed to act as a nominee or custodian, there are provisions in relation to his remuneration and expenses[2].

Remuneration is payable to an agent, nominee or custodian out of trust funds[3] for services[4] if he was engaged on terms entitling him to be remunerated for those services, and the amount does not exceed such remuneration as is reasonable in the circumstances for the provision of those services by him to or on behalf of the trust[5].

Expenses[6] properly incurred by an agent, nominee or custodian in exercising his functions as such may be reimbursed out of the trust funds[7].

[623]

1   Trustee Act 2000 Part IV (ss 11–27) (48 Halsbury's Statutes (4th Edn) TRUSTS AND SETTLEMENTS) or under any other enactment or any provision of subordinate legislation.
2   Trustee Act 2000 s 32(1).
3   'Trust funds' means income or capital funds of the trust: Trustee Act 2000 s 39(1).
4   Ie services provided to or on behalf of the trust, whenever created. By contrast with expenses this appears retrospective: Trustee Act 2000 s 33(1).
5   Trustee Act 2000 s 32(2).
6   Ie expenses incurred on or after 1 February 2001 on behalf of trusts whenever created: Trustee Act 2000 s 33(1).
7   Trustee Act 2000 s 32(3). As to the meaning of trust funds see note 3 above.

[624]

253   Review of agents, nominees and custodians

Statutory provisions[1] for the review of agents, nominees and custodians apply where they were authorised or appointed under the statutory provisions[2] in the Trustee Act 2000[3]. The same provisions apply where trustees have under any power conferred on them by the trust instrument or by any enactment or any provision of subordinate legislation authorised a person to exercise functions as their agent, or appointed a person to act as a nominee or custodian[4]. The above provisions do not apply were they are inconsistent with the terms of the trust instrument or the enactment or provision of subordinate legislation[5].

So long as an agent, nominee or custodian continues to act for the trust the trustees:

253.1   have a duty to keep under review the arrangements under which the agent, nominee or custodian acts, and how those arrangements are being put into effect. This obligation means that the trustees must keep under review the question of whether the agent, nominee or custodian is a suitable person to act for the trust, and whether the terms of his appointment are appropriate;

253.2   if circumstances make it appropriate, they must consider whether there is a need to exercise any power of intervention that they have; and

253.3   if they consider that there is a need to exercise such a power, they must do so[6].

'Power of intervention' includes a power to give directions to the agent, nominee or custodian, and a power to revoke the authorisation or appointment[7].

If an agent has been authorised to exercise asset management functions[8] the duties referred to above include, in particular:

253.4   a duty to consider whether there is any need to revise or replace the policy statement[9];

253.5   if they consider that there is a need to revise or replace the policy statement, a duty to do so; and

253.6   a duty to assess whether the policy statement (as it has effect for the time being) is being complied with[10].

[625]

1   Ie those set out in the Trustee Act 2000 s 22 (48 Halsbury's Statutes (4th Edn) TRUSTS AND SETTLEMENTS).
2   Ie under the Trustee Act 2000 ss 11, 16, 17, or 18.
3   Trustee Act 2000 s 21(1).
4   Trustee Act 2000 s 21(2).
5   Trustee Act 2000 s 21(3). See the Trustee Act 2000 s 6(2), (3) and Paragraph 241 note 8 [592] ante.
6   Trustee Act 2000 s 22(1).
7   Trustee Act 2000 s 22(4).
8   See the Trustee Act 2000 s 15(5), and see Paragraph 248 [615] ante.
9   Ie that made under the Trustee Act 2000 s 15(2), and see Paragraph 248 [615] ante.
10   Trustee Act 2000 s 22(2). The Trustee Act 2000 s 15(3), (4) applies to the revision or replacement of a policy statement under the Trustee Act 2000 s 22: Trustee Act 2000 s 22(3).

[626]

254   Liability of trustees for agents, nominees and custodians

Statutory provisions[1] in respect of the liability of a trustee for any act or default of an agent, nominee or custodian apply where he was authorised or appointed under the statutory provisions[2] in the Trustee Act 2000[3]. The same provisions apply where trustees have under any power conferred on them by the trust instrument or by any enactment or any provision of subordinate legislation authorised a person to exercise functions as their agent, or appointed a person to act as a nominee or custodian[4]. The above provisions do not apply where they are inconsistent with the terms of the trust instrument or the enactment or provision of subordinate legislation[5].

A trustee is not liable for any act or default of an agent, nominee or custodian unless he has failed to comply with the statutory duty of care[6] applicable to him when entering into the arrangements under which the person acts as an agent, nominee or custodian; or when carrying out his duty to review[7].

If a trustee has agreed a term under which the agent, nominee or custodian is permitted to appoint a substitute, the trustee is not liable for any act or default of the substitute unless he has failed to comply with the duty of care applicable to him when agreeing the term[8], or when carrying out his duty to review in so far as they relate to the use of the substitute[9].

[627]

183 VOL 40(1): TRUSTS AND SETTLEMENTS

1 Ie those set out in the Trustee Act 2000 s 23 (48 Halsbury's Statutes (4th Edn) TRUSTS AND SETTLEMENTS).
2 Ie under the Trustee Act 2000 ss 11, 16, 17 or 18.
3 Trustee Act 2000 s 21(1).
4 Trustee Act 2000 s 21(2).
5 Trustee Act 2000 s 21(3). See the Trustee Act 2000 s 6(2), (3) and Paragraph 241 note 8 [592] ante.
6 As to the duty of care see the Trustee Act 2000 s 1 Sch 1 para 3 and Paragraph 183 [453] ante.
7 Trustee Act 2000 s 23(1). As to the duty to review see the Trustee Act 2000 s 22 and Paragraph 253 [625] ante.
8 As to the duty of care see note 1 above.
9 Trustee Act 2000 s 23(2). As to the duty to review see the Trustee Act 2000 s 22 and Paragraph 253 [625] ante.

[628]

255 Protection of third parties

A failure by the trustees to act within the limits of their statutory powers[1] in authorising a person to exercise a function of theirs as an agent, or in appointing a person to act as a nominee or custodian does not invalidate the authorisation or appointment[2]. The trustees will, of course, be liable for any loss to the trust estate.

1 Ie those conferred by the Trustee Act 2000 Part IV (ss 11–27) (48 Halsbury's Statutes (4th Edn) TRUSTS AND SETTLEMENTS).
2 Trustee Act 2000 s 24.

[629]

256 Power to delegate for a period not exceeding 12 months

A new Section 25 of the Trustee Act 1925 has been substituted for the original Section 25 (as amended) by the Trustee Delegation Act 1999[1]. As substituted it now provides that a trustee may, by power of attorney[2], delegate the execution or exercise of all or any of the trusts, powers and discretions vested in him as trustee either alone or jointly with any other person or persons[3]. The delegation may be for a period of 12 months (or any shorter period specified) commencing with the date of the instrument creating the power or such later date as may be specified[4]. The donee of the power may be a trust corporation[5]. The delegation may be by means of an enduring power of attorney under the Enduring Powers of Attorney Act 1985[6].

Before or within seven days of giving a power of attorney, the donor must give written notice containing specified information to each person, if any, having power to appoint a new trustee, and each of the other trustees, if any. Failure to comply with this requirement does not, however, in favour of a person dealing with the donee of the power, invalidate any act done or instrument executed by the donee[7].

The donor of the power is liable for the acts and defaults of the donee in the same manner as if they were his own acts and defaults[8]. The donee may exercise any of the powers conferred on the donor as trustee by statute or by the instrument creating the trust, including a power to delegate to an attorney the power to transfer any inscribed stock, but not including the power of delegation conferred by statute[9].

[630]

1 Trustee Delegation Act 1999 s 5 (48 Halsbury's Statutes (4th Edn) TRUSTS AND SETTLEMENTS). For powers for trustees to delegate see Form 316 [2194] et seq post.
2 The Trustee Delegation Act 1999 has effect in relation to powers of attorney created after its commencement on 1 March 2000: Trustee Delegation Act 1999 s 5(2). It applies notwithstanding any rule of law or equity to the contrary: Trustee Act 1925 s 25(1). The power of attorney must be executed as a deed by the donor: Powers of Attorney Act 1971 s 1, as amended by the Law of Property (Miscellaneous Provisions) Act 1989 s 1(8).

3   Trustee Act 1925 s 25(1) (48 Halsbury's Statutes (4th Edn) TRUSTS AND SETTLEMENTS). The Trustee Act 1925 s 25(5) introduces a standard form power of attorney (set out in the Trustee Act 1925 s 25(6): see Form 320 [2205] post) which may be used to delegate to a single attorney the execution and exercise of all the trusts, powers and discretions of the donor as trustee of the particular trust. See also Form 321 [2207] post.

4   Trustee Act 1925 s 25(2).

5   Trustee Act 1925 s 25(3). The prohibition in the corresponding provision in the original s 25 of delegation to a sole co-trustee has been removed and the objective obtained by other means: see the Trustee Delegation Act 1999 s 7 and Paragraph 258 [634] post.

6   See the Trustee Delegation Act 1999 s 6 repealing the Enduring Powers of Attorney Act 1985 s 2(8). It may thus continue after the incapacity of the donor, but the 12 months time limit applies.

7   Trustee Act 1925 s 25(4).

8   Trustee Act 1925 s 25(7).

9   Trustee Act 1925 s 25(8). See also the Trustee Act 1925 s 25(9).

[631]

257   Delegation under the Trustee Delegation Act 1999 Section 1

A new statutory exception has been created to the general rule that a trustee must exercise in person the functions vested in him as a trustee. It provides that where the donee of a power of attorney who is not otherwise authorised[1] to exercise trustee functions[2] by power of attorney, would only be prevented from doing an act because doing it would involve the exercise of a function of the donor as a trustee, the donee may nevertheless do that act if:

257.1   it relates to land[3], the capital proceeds of a conveyance[4] of land, or income from land; and

257.2   at the time when the act is done the donor has a beneficial interest in the land, proceeds or income[5].

The person creating the trust or the donor may, however, exclude or restrict this provision in the document creating the trust, or the power of attorney, as the case may be[6].

Subject to the provisions in the trust instrument, although a trustee is not liable for permitting the donee to exercise a function by virtue of the Trustee Delegation Act 1999 Section 1(1), he remains liable for the acts and defaults of the donee in exercising such function in the same manner as if they were the acts or defaults of the donor[7].

The fact that it appears that, in dealing with any shares or stock, the donee of the power of attorney is exercising a function by virtue of the Trustee Delegation Act 1999[8] does not affect with any notice of any trust a person in whose books the shares are, or stock is, registered or inscribed[9].

The above provisions are of particular benefit to co-owners of land who are essentially trustees for themselves. First, it enables them to delegate without having to comply with the restrictions which apply where trustees hold land only for third parties[10]. Secondly, it enables a co-owner of land to make effective provision for the disposal of the co-owned land if he becomes mentally incapable[11]. Finally, it ensures that the donee is able to deal with the proceeds of sale and income from the land as well as the land itself. It follows from the terms of Section 1(1) that a person dealing with a donee under that section needs to know whether that donee has a beneficial interest in the relevant property. To avoid the difficulties that might otherwise arise in investigating the title to the beneficial interest, it is provided that in favour of a purchaser[12] 'an appropriate statement', ie a signed statement by the donee, made when doing the act in question or within three months thereafter, that the donor has such a beneficial interest is conclusive evidence thereof[13].

[632]

1   Ie under a statutory provision or a provision in a trust instrument, under which the donor of the power
     is expressly authorised to delegate the exercise of all or any of his trustee functions by power of attorney:
     Trustee Delegation Act 1999 s 1(8) (48 Halsbury's Statutes (4th Edn) TRUSTS AND SETTLEMENTS).
2   References to a trustee function of the donor are to a function which the donor has as trustee (either
     alone or jointly with any other person or persons): Trustee Delegation Act 1999 s 1(2)(b).
3   Defined in the Trustee Delegation Act 1999 s 11(1) by reference to the Trustee Act 1925. Further, by
     the Trustee Delegation Act 1999 s 10(1)–(3), a reference to land in a power of attorney created after
     the commencement of the Act includes, subject to any contrary intention expressed in the instrument
     creating the power, a reference to any estate or interest of the donor of the power of attorney in the
     land at the time that the donee acts. In the few remaining cases where the doctrine of conversion
     continues to operate, a person who has a beneficial interest in the proceeds of sale of land is treated for
     the purposes of the Trustee Delegation Act 1999 ss 1, 2 as having a beneficial interest in the land:
     Trustee Delegation Act 1999 s 1(7). See Form 324 [2230] post.
4   Defined in the Trustee Delegation Act 1999 s 1(2)(a) by reference to the Law of Property Act 1925.
5   Trustee Delegation Act 1999 s 1(1). The provision applies to powers of attorney created after the
     commencement of the Trustee Delegation Act 1999 on 1 March 2000: Trustee Delegation Act 1999
     s 1(9). Exceptionally the Trustee Delegation Act 1999 s 1 applies to an enduring power created before
     the commencement of the Act from the time when (in accordance with the Trustee Delegation Act
     1999 s 4(2)–(5)) the Enduring Powers of Attorney Act 1985 s 3(3) ceases to apply to it: Trustee
     Delegation Act 1999 s 4(6). Note that the Trustee Delegation Act 1999 s 3 amends the Powers of
     Attorney Act 1971 s 10 so that a donee of a general power of attorney in the form prescribed by Section
     10 may by virtue of the Trustee Delegation Act 1999 s 1(1) exercise the trustee functions of the donor
     in relation to the relevant property. This reverses to this extent *Walia v Michael Naughton Ltd* [1985]
     3 All ER 673, [1985] 1 WLR 1115.
6   Trustee Delegation Act 1999 s 1(3), (5). See Form 326 [2234] post.
7   Trustee Delegation Act 1999 s 1(4), (5).
8   Trustee Delegation Act 1999 s 1(1).
9   Trustee Delegation Act 1999 s 1(6). Cf the Trustee Act 1925 s 25(9) as substituted by the Trustee
     Delegation Act 1999 s 5(1), and see Paragraph 256 [630] ante.
10   See the Trustee Act 1925 s 25 a substituted by the Trustee Delegation Act 1999 s 5(1) (48 Halsbury's
     Statutes (4th Edn) TRUSTS AND SETTLEMENTS), and Paragraph 256 [630] ante.
11   So assumed in the Explanatory Notes to the Bill, but a doubt has been raised as the Trustee Delegation
     Act 1999 s 1 does not actually refer in terms to an enduring power of attorney.
12   'Purchaser' has the same meaning as in the Law of Property Act 1925 Part I (ss 1–39): Trustee
     Delegation Act 1999 s 2(1).
13   Trustee Delegation Act 1999 s 2(1)–(3). If an appropriate statement is false, the donee is liable in the
     same way as he would be if the statement were contained in a statutory declaration: Trustee Delegation
     Act 1999 s 2(4). See Form 325 [2233] post.

[633]

258   Application of the 'two-trustee rules' to an attorney acting for a trust

The Trustee Delegation Act 1999 contains provisions intended to strengthen and clarify
the operation of the 'two-trustee rules'[1] in relation to an attorney acting for a trustee. It
is provided that these rules are not satisfied by money being paid to or dealt with as
directed by, or a receipt for money being given by, a 'relevant attorney' or by a
conveyance or deed being executed by such an attorney[2].

'Relevant attorney' is defined as meaning a person (other than a trust corporation
within the meaning of the Trustee Act 1925) who is acting either:

258.1   both as a trustee and as attorney for one or more other trustees; or

258.2   as attorney for two or more trustees;

and who is not acting together with any other person or persons[3].

[634]

1   Namely (a) that capital money be paid to, or dealt with as directed by, at least two trustees or that a
     valid receipt for capital money be given otherwise than by a sole trustee; or (b) that, in order for an
     interest or power to be overreached, a conveyance or deed be executed by at least two trustees. See
     the Settled Land Act 1925 ss 18(1)(c), 94(1) (48 Halsbury's Statutes (4th Edn) TRUSTS AND
     SETTLEMENTS), and the Law of Property Act 1925 s 27(1) (37 Halsbury's Statutes (4th Edn) REAL
     PROPERTY).

2   Trustee Delegation Act 1999 s 7(1) (48 Halsbury's Statutes (4th Edn) TRUSTS AND SETTLEMENTS).
3   Trustee Delegation Act 1999 s 7(2). The section applies whenever the power under which the relevant attorney is acting was created (but in the case of such an attorney acting under an enduring power created before the commencement of the Trustee Delegation Act 1999, without prejudice to the continuing application of the Enduring Powers of Attorney Act 1985 s 3(3), after that commencement in accordance with the Trustee Delegation Act 1999 s 4: Trustee Delegation Act 1999 s 7(3).

[635]–[640]

6: OTHER ANCILLARY STATUTORY POWERS

259   Power to insure

Section 19 of the Trustee Act 1925 as substituted by the Trustee Act 2000[1] confers power on all trustees, whenever the trust was created[2], to insure any trust property against such risks as they think fit, and to pay the premiums out of the income or capital funds of the trust[3]. Where property is held on a bare trust, however, this is subject to any direction given by the beneficiary (or each of them) that any specified property is not to be insured, or only insured on specified conditions[4]. Property is held on a bare trust if the beneficiary (each beneficiary if more than one) is of full age and (taken together if more than one) is absolutely entitled to the trust property[5]. To the extent that such directions are given the trustees may not delegate their power to insure[6].

The new Section 19 does not impose any duty to insure. It is thought that a failure by trustees to exercise a power to insure (whether statutory or express), in circumstances where a reasonable person would have done so, would constitute a breach of the trustees' paramount duty to act in the best interests of the beneficiaries[7]. Moreover the statutory duty of care[8] applies to a trustee when exercising the statutory power to insure, or any corresponding power, however conferred[9]. It will cover, for example, the selection of an insurer and the terms on which the insurance cover is taken out.

It will invariably be right to insert a clause imposing a duty on the trustees to insure against any risk in all the circumstances in which an ordinary prudent man of business would so insure; up to full replacement value where it would be sensible to do so, otherwise up to market value[10]. Premiums could be made payable out of capital as well as income, but in such a way as to maintain the balance between the tenant for life and the remainderman. Subject to the terms of the instrument, statute dictates how the trustees are to apply money received following a claim[11].

Statute does not empower the trustees to insure the lives of the settlor, or beneficiaries, and so express provision in the trust instrument is required[12]. Nor can the trustees insure themselves for their liability to the trust in the event of being liable for a breach of trust. Should the trustees wish to avail themselves of insurance cover, there is no reason why they should not do so, but they will have no recourse to the trust property by way of reimbursement of the premiums.

[641]

1   Trustee Act 2000 s 34 (48 Halsbury's Statutes (4th Edn) TRUSTS AND SETTLEMENTS).
2   Trustee Act 2000 s 34(3).
3   Trustee Act 1925 s 19(1), (5) as substituted by the Trustee Act 2000 s 34(1) (48 Halsbury's Statutes (4th Edn) TRUSTS AND SETTLEMENTS). So far as land is concerned trustees of land no longer need rely on the Trusts of Land and Appointment of Trustees Act 1996 s 6(1) which provides that trustees of land have in relation to the land all the powers of an absolute owner, which must include a power to insure.
4   Trustee Act 1925 s 19(2) as substituted by the Trustee Act 2000 s 34(1).
5   Trustee Act 1925 s 19(3) as substituted by the Trustee Act 2000 s 34(1).
6   Trustee Act 1925 s 19(4) as substituted by the Trustee Act 2000 s 34(1). This is so that the beneficiaries can ensure compliance with their directions.

7   The old case of *Bailey v Gould* (1840) 4 Y & C Ex 221 which suggests that trustees are not under a duty to insure trust property unless there is an obligation to insure imposed by the trust instrument is of doubtful authority in contemporary conditions.
8   Under the Trustee Act 2000 s 1: see Paragraph 183 [453] ante.
9   Trustee Act 2000 s 1 and Sch 1 para 5.
10   For an express power to insure see Form 212 [1730] post.
11   See the Trustee Act 1925 s 20 as amended by the Trusts of Land and Appointment of Trustees Act 1996 s 25(1) Sch 3 para 3(5) and the Trustee Act 2000 s 34(2). As to the application of insurance money see further 48 Halsbury's Laws (4th Edn 2000 Reissue) para 929.
12   There may be good reasons why the trustees would wish to do so in order to provide funds for a contingent liability to inheritance tax. For a power to insure the lives of the settlor and any of the beneficiaries see Form 109 [1504] and Form 191 [1684] post.

[642]

260   Power to give receipts

Statute provides that the receipt in writing of a trustee for any money, securities, investments or other personal property or effects payable, transferable, or deliverable to him under any trust or power is a sufficient discharge to the person paying, transferring, or delivering the same[1]. Consequently, a purchaser is not concerned with the application of the purchase money in the hands of the trustees. However, this provision does not enable a sole trustee, other than a trust corporation, to give a valid receipt for the proceeds of sale or other capital money arising under a trust of land or for capital money arising under the Settled Land Act 1925[2].

[643]

1   Trustee Act 1925 s 14(1) as amended by the Trustee Act 2000 Sch 2 para 19 (48 Halsbury's Statutes (4th Edn) TRUSTS AND SETTLEMENTS). Trustee Act 1925 s 14 applies notwithstanding anything to the contrary in the trust instrument: Trustee Act 1925 s 14(3). Nothing in the Trustee Act 1925 s 14 as amended by the Law of Property (Amendment) Act 1926 ss 7, 8(2), Schedule, by the Trusts of Land and Appointment of Trustees Act 1996 s 25(1), Sch 3 para 3(3) and the Trustee Act 2000 Sch 2 para 19 is thought to affect the principle that if there is more than one trustee, a receipt must be given by all of them if it is to be valid.
2   Trustee Act 1925 s 14(2) as amended by the Law of Property (Amendment) Act 1926 ss 7, 8(2), Schedule and by the Trusts of Land and Appointment of Trustees Act 1996 s 25(1), Sch 3 para 3(3). Capital money arising under the Settled Land Act 1925 (48 Halsbury's Statutes (4th Edn) TRUSTS AND SETTLEMENTS) means capital money arising under the powers and provisions of that Act, or the Acts replaced by it, and receivable for the trusts and purposes of the settlement, and includes securities representing capital money: Settled Land Act 1925 s 117(1)(ii). As to cases where two trustees are required see Paragraph 258 [634] ante as regards land held on a trust of land and vol 40(2) (2001 Reissue) TRUSTS AND SETTLEMENTS Part 9 [4101] as regards settled land. See also the Trustee Delegation Act 1999 s 7.

[644]

261   Power of compromise, compounding debts, apportionment and severance of funds etc

By statute, if and so far as a contrary intention is not expressed in the trust instrument[1], two or more trustees acting together, may, if and as they think fit:

261.1   accept any property, real or personal, before the time at which it is made transferable or payable;
261.2   sever and apportion any blended trust funds or property;
261.3   pay or allow any debt or claim on any evidence that he or they think sufficient;

261.4   accept any composition or any security, real or personal, for any debt or
            for any property, real or personal, claimed;
261.5   allow any time for payment of any debt; and
261.6   compromise, compound, abandon, submit to arbitration, or otherwise
            settle any debt, account, claim or thing whatever relating to the trust.

Similarly, subject to the statutory restrictions relating to receipts by a sole trustee not
being a trust corporation, a sole acting trustee, where, by the instrument, if any, creating
the trust, or by statute, a sole trustee is authorised to execute the trusts and powers
thereof, may, if and as he thinks fit, exercise these powers.

For any of those purposes, the trustees or trustee may enter into, give, execute and
do such agreements, instruments of composition or arrangement, releases and other
things as may seem expedient, without being responsible for any loss occasioned by any
act or thing so done by them or him if he has or they have discharged the duty of care
set out in the Trustee Act 2000 s 1(1)[2].

This power enables trustees to enter into compromises of a kind which they could
not safely have accepted independently of the power, as for example, where minors are
interested[3]. It is conceived that this statutory power does not authorise an arrangement
under which trustees compromise a debt due from one of themselves[4]. If such an
arrangement is proposed the other trustees would be well advised to surrender their
discretion to the court[5]. In exercising their discretion, the trustees should consider the
wishes of the beneficiaries but the final decision rests with the trustees once they have
considered all the circumstances[6]. They must exercise an active discretion, and not
merely fail to take proper steps[7].

[645]

1   Trustee Act 1925 s 69(2) (48 Halsbury's Statutes (4th Edn) TRUSTS AND SETTLEMENTS). For an
        express power to institute proceedings and compromise claims see Form 205 [1707] post.
2   See the Trustee Act 1925 s 15 as amended by the Trustee Act 2000 Sch 2 para 20.
3   See *Re Ezekiel's Settlement Trusts, National Provincial Bank Ltd v Hyam* [1942] Ch 230, [1942] 2 All ER
        224, CA; *Re Shenton* [1935] Ch 651.
4   A provision in a trust deed allowing trustees to act although personally interested may be sufficient to
        allow trustees to compromise a debt due from one of themselves under the Trustee Act 1925 s 15.
5   For a case in which the discretion was so surrendered see *Re Ezekiel's Settlement Trusts, National
        Provincial Bank Ltd v Hyam* [1942] Ch 230, [1942] 2 All ER 224, CA.
6   See *Re Ezekiel's Settlement Trusts, National Provincial Bank Ltd v Hyam* [1942] Ch 230, [1942] 2 All ER
        224, CA; *Re Earl of Strafford, Royal Bank of Scotland v Byng* [1980] Ch 28, [1979] 1 All ER 513, CA.
7   See *Re Greenwood, Greenwood v Firth* (1911) 105 LT 509.

[646]

262   Power to value trust property

Trustees are empowered to instruct duly qualified agents to ascertain and fix the value of
any trust property in such a manner as they think proper, and any valuation made is
binding on all persons interested under the trust if the trustees have discharged the duty
of care set out in the Trustee Act 2000 Section 1(1)[1]. This provision is not obligatory,
and the settlement may provide for valuation by persons other than duly qualified
agents[2].

[647]

1   See the Trustee Act 1925 s 22(3) as amended by the Trustee Act 2000 Sch 2 para 22(b) (48 Halsbury's
        Statutes (4th Edn) TRUSTS AND SETTLEMENTS).
2   For a power to employ persons to fix valuations on an appropriation see Form 165 clause 0.2 [1629]
        post.

[648]

263   Power to sell subject to depreciatory conditions

No sale made by a trustee may be impeached by any beneficiary upon the ground that any of the conditions subject to which the sale was made may have been unnecessarily depreciatory, unless it also appears that the consideration for the sale was thereby rendered inadequate[1]; nor may any sale made by a trustee be impeached as against the purchaser after the execution of the conveyance upon such grounds, unless it appears that the purchaser was acting in collusion with the trustee at the time when the contract for sale was made[2]. Furthermore, no purchaser, upon any sale made by a trustee, is at liberty to make any objection against the title upon any of these grounds[3].

[649]

1   Trustee Act 1925 s 13(1) (48 Halsbury's Statutes (4th Edn) TRUSTS AND SETTLEMENTS). It is increasingly common to free trustees from liability incurred as the result of sales which fall outside this exception.
2   See the Trustee Act 1925 s 13(2).
3   Trustee Act 1925 s 13(3).

[650]

264   Power to concur in dealings with undivided shares notwithstanding interest

Subject to any provisions in the settlement to the contrary, where an undivided share in any property is subject to a trust, the trustees may (without prejudice to the trust affecting the entirety of the land and the powers of the trustees in reference thereto) execute or exercise any duty or power vested in them in relation to such share in conjunction with the persons entitled to or having power in that behalf over the other share or shares. This applies notwithstanding that any one or more of the trustees may be entitled to or interested in any such other share, either in his or their own right or in a fiduciary capacity[1].

[651]

1   See the Trustee Act 1925 ss 24, 69(2) as amended by the Trusts of Land and Appointment of Trustees Act 1996 s 25(1), Sch 3 para 3(6) (48 Halsbury's Statutes (4th Edn) TRUSTS AND SETTLEMENTS). The power for trustees to act even though personally interested can, of course, be extended to transactions other than that under consideration here: see eg Form 188 [1676] post. Such an extension will be particularly desirable where the trustees are members of the family of the settlor and the assets of the trust fund are shares in a family company or similar assets.

[652]

265   Powers and duties as to property not in possession

Where trust property includes any share or interest in property not vested in the trustees, or the proceeds of sale of any such property, or any other thing in action, when the property falls into possession, or becomes payable or transferable, the trustees have statutory power to agree or ascertain the amount or value in any manner they think fit. They may also accept authorised investments in or towards satisfaction thereof, to allow reasonable deductions for costs and expenses, and execute releases without being responsible in any such case for any loss occasioned by any act or thing so done by them if they have discharged the duty of care set out in the Trustee Act 2000 Section 1(1)[1].

Similarly, trustees are not under any obligation (or chargeable with any breach of trust for any omission) to apply for a stop notice on securities or other property out of or on which such a share or interest or other thing in action is derived, payable or charged, or to take any proceedings for any act, default or neglect on the part of the persons in whom the property is or has at any time been vested, unless and until required to do so in writing by a beneficiary, or a guardian of a beneficiary. They may also require that due provision is made to their satisfaction for the payment of the costs of such proceedings. This does not, however, relieve trustees of the obligation to get in the property when it falls into possession[2].

This statutory limitation on the obligation of trustees is usually regarded as sufficient, but the provision is narrower than some currently in use in settlements, which, in the wider form of discretionary trusts, relieve a trustee from liability for any kind of loss to the trust estate, without adding any limitation in respect of the bona fides or otherwise of the trustees[3].

[653]

1   See the Trustee Act 1925 s 22(1) as amended by the Trustee Act 2000 Sch 2 para 22(a) (48 Halsbury's Statutes (4th Edn) TRUSTS AND SETTLEMENTS).
2   See the Trustee Act 1925 s 22(2).
3   A provision giving this wider protection is not included in this title, it being considered that settlors should be advised that protection to trustees should be limited to indemnity in the absence of actual dishonesty. For such an indemnity see Form 224 [1755] post.

[654]

266   Audit

Trustees have a statutory power, in their absolute discretion, to cause the trust accounts to be examined or audited by an independent accountant, and to direct payment of costs and fees out of the capital or income of the trust property, or partly in one way and partly in the other[1]. This power must not, however, be exercised more frequently than once in every three years unless the nature of the trust or any special dealings with the property make a more frequent exercise of the power reasonable[2]. This power may be adequate for most settlements, but special circumstances of a particular settlement may require a variation of the power[3].

[655]

1   See the Trustee Act 1925 s 22(4) (48 Halsbury's Statutes (4th Edn) TRUSTS AND SETTLEMENTS). In default of a direction by the trustees to the contrary, costs attributable to capital and those attributable to income are to be borne respectively by capital and income: Trustee Act 1925 s 22(4). For wider express powers see Forms 230 [1763], 231 [1764] post.
2   Trustee Act 1925 s 22(4).
3   Generally the trustees are required to keep accounts and produce them to a beneficiary if and when required to do so. Trustees of charitable trusts must comply with the accounting and audit requirements prescribed by regulation under the Charities Act 1993 (5 Halsbury's Statutes (4th Ed) CHARITIES). See vol 6(2) (2001 Reissue) CHARITIES AND CHARITABLE GIVING Paragraph 59 [305].

[656]–[660]

(12) VARIATION OF TRUSTS

A: GENERAL

267   Duty not to deviate from the terms of the trust

The fundamental principle is that a trustee must faithfully observe the directions contained in the trust instrument and, 'as a rule, the court has no jurisdiction to give, and will not give, its sanction to the performance by trustees of acts with reference to the trust estate which are not, on the face of the instrument creating the trust, authorised by its terms'[1]. The House of Lords has made it clear[2] that under the inherent jurisdiction the exceptions to this rule are very limited.

The cases under the inherent jurisdiction can be grouped under four heads[3]: the first three being cases in which the court has allowed the trustees of settled property to enter into some business transaction which was not authorised by the settlement; cases in which the court has allowed maintenance out of income which the settlor or testator directed to be accumulated; and cases in which the court has approved a compromise on behalf of minors and possible after-born beneficiaries. The fourth head, which is of limited practical importance today, comprises cases in which the court has effected changes in the nature of a minor's property; for example by directing investment of his personalty in the purchase of freeholds.

[661]

1   *Re New, Re Leavers, Re Morley* [1901] 2 Ch 534 at 544, CA per Romer LJ.
2   See *Chapman v Chapman* [1954] AC 429, [1954] 1 All ER 798, HL.
3   *Chapman v Chapman* [1954] AC 429, [1954] 1 All ER 798 at 451, 807, 808, HL per Lord Morton.

[662]

268   Circumstances in which application to court is required

If the beneficiaries are sui juris they can, if they think fit, terminate the trust[1] and, if they so choose, set up new trusts in respect of the trust property. If, however, the beneficiaries are not so qualified it is necessary that an application be made to the court for a variation of the trust. It is important to make a distinction for this purpose between two classes of variation by the court:

268.1   variations concerned with the management or administration of the trusts[2]; and

268.2   variations of the beneficial interests arising under the trusts[3].

[663]

1   As to the termination of trusts generally see 48 Halsbury's Laws (4th Edn 2000 Reissue) para 644 et seq.
2   As to variations concerned with the management or administration of the trusts see Paragraph 275 [686] et seq post.
3   As to variations of the beneficial interests see Paragraph 269 [665] et seq post.

[664]

B: VARIATION OF BENEFICIAL INTERESTS

269   Awarding of maintenance

Where a testator has made his disposition in such a way, for example, by a trust for accumulation, with the result that the immediate beneficiaries have no fund for their present maintenance, the court has an inherent power to award maintenance in disregard of the trusts[1]. An order for maintenance results in a variation of the beneficial interests.

1   *Havelock v Havelock, Re Allan* (1881) 17 Ch D 807; *Re Collins, Collins v Collins* (1886) 32 Ch D 229; *Re Downshire Settled Estates, Marquess of Downshire v Royal Bank of Scotland* [1953] Ch 218 at 238, [1953] 1 All ER 103 at 113, CA; affd sub nom *Chapman v Chapman* [1954] AC 429, [1954] 1 All ER 798, HL.

[665]

270   Compromise

The court has an inherent power to sanction a compromise on behalf of a minor, or unborn person. A compromise in this sense, however, refers only to a compromise of a disputed right[1]. This jurisdiction will not apply where there is no real dispute between the parties[2].

The court has no inherent jurisdiction to order payment of a minor's damages to trustees so as to postpone the minor's entitlement beyond the age of majority, but its jurisdiction to approve a compromise is founded on the original claim and not limited to the inherent jurisdiction, with the result that it could approve one for payment out of court 'in such manner as the judge may direct to or for the benefit of each child' although this gives the court power to postpone entitlement beyond majority[3].

Where a general dispute between the beneficiaries is being resolved by the beneficiaries, it is wrong for the trustees to include as one of the terms of the compromise a provision which has nothing to do with the dispute and is directly for the trustees' benefit[4].

[666]

1   There cannot be said to be any disputed right where there is merely an ambiguity in, for instance, an investment clause and it would be to the common advantage of all the beneficiaries to have a new clause substituted for it: *Re Powell-Cotton's Resettlement, Henniker-Major v Powell-Cotton* [1956] 1 All ER 60, [1956] 1 WLR 23, CA. Cf *Mason v Farbrother* [1983] 2 All ER 1078.
2   *Chapman v Chapman* [1954] AC 429, [1954] 1 All ER 798, HL.
3   *Allen v Distillers Co (Biochemicals) Ltd, Albrice v Distillers Co (Biochemicals) Ltd* [1974] QB 384, [1974] 2 All ER 365, distinguishing *Re Hooker's Settlement, Heron v Public Trustee* [1955] Ch 55 at 59, [1954] 3 All ER 321 at 323.
4   See *Re Barbour's Settlement, National Westminster Bank Ltd v Barbour* [1974] 1 All ER 1188, [1974] 1 WLR 1198, where a provision was sought to be included increasing the trustees' remuneration.

[667]

271   Jurisdiction under the Settled Land Act 1925

Any transaction[1] affecting or concerning the settled land, or any part of it (not being a transaction otherwise authorised by the Settled Land Act 1925, or by the settlement) which in the opinion of the court would be for the benefit of the settled land, or any part of it, or the persons interested under the settlement, may, under an order of the court, be effected by a tenant for life, if it is one which could have been validly effected by an absolute owner[2].

This jurisdiction enables the beneficial interests under a settlement to be remoulded and it is not, therefore, restricted to steps of an administrative character[3].

[668]

1   As to the meaning of transaction for this purpose see the Settled Land Act 1925 s 64(2) as amended by the Settled Land and Trustee Acts (Court's General Powers) Act 1943 s 2 and by the SL(R) Act 1969 (48 Halsbury's Statutes (4th Edn) TRUSTS AND SETTLEMENTS). For a detailed consideration of the Settled Land Act 1925 see vol 40(2) (2001 Reissue) TRUSTS AND SETTLEMENTS Part 9 [4101].

2   Settled Land Act 1925 s 64(1). Note that this subsection confers a larger jurisdiction than that conferred by the Trustee Act 1925 s 57 (48 Halsbury's Statutes (4th Edn) TRUSTS AND SETTLEMENTS): see further Paragraph 276 [688] post.

3   *Re Downshire Settled Estate, Marquess of Downshire v Royal Bank of Scotland* [1953] Ch 218, [1953] 1 All ER 103, CA; affd sub nom *Chapman v Chapman* [1954] AC 429, [1954] 1 All ER 798, HL. See also *Re Scarisbrick Resettlement Estates* [1944] Ch 229, [1944] 1 All ER 404; *Re Earl of Mount Edgcumbe* [1950] Ch 615, [1950] 2 All ER 242; *Raikes v Lygon* [1988] 1 All ER 884, [1988] 1 WLR 281; *Hambro v Duke of Marlborough* [1994] Ch 158, [1994] 3 All ER 332.

[669]

272   Power to authorise treatment of management expenses as capital outgoings

The Settled Land and Trustee Acts (Court's General Powers) Act 1943 as amended[1], extends the jurisdiction of the court under the Trustee Act 1925 Section 57[2], and the Settled Land Act 1925 Section 64(1)[3]. It gives the power to the court, taking all relevant circumstances into account[4], in certain cases of deficiency of income to authorise the expenses of action taken or proposed in or for the management of settled land or of land subject to a trust of land to be treated as a capital outgoing, notwithstanding that in other circumstances the expenses could not properly have been so treated[5].

The circumstances referred to are that the court is satisfied that the action taken or proposed was or would be for the benefit of the persons entitled under the settlement, or under the trust of land[6]; and either:

272.1   that the available income from all sources of a person who, as being beneficially entitled to possession or receipt of rents and profits of the land or to reside in a house comprised in it, might otherwise have been expected to bear the expenses has been so reduced as to render him unable to bear that expense, or unable to bear it without undue hardship[7]; or

272.2   where there is no such person, that the income available for meeting that expense has become insufficient[8].

[670]

1   See the Settled Land and Trustee Acts (Court's General Powers) Act 1943 s 1 as amended by the Emergency Laws (Miscellaneous Provisions) Act 1953 ss 9, 14, Sch 3 and by the Trusts of Land and Appointment of Trustees Act 1996 s 25(1), Sch 3 para 8 (48 Halsbury's Statutes (4th Edn) TRUSTS AND SETTLEMENTS). The Settled Land and Trustee Acts (Court's General Powers) Act 1943 was made permanent by the Emergency Laws (Miscellaneous Provisions) Act 1953 s 9.

2   As to the Trustee Act 1925 s 57 (48 Halsbury's Statutes (4th Edn) TRUSTS AND SETTLEMENTS) see Paragraph 276 [688] post. As to applications by the trustees and others to the court see vol 40(2) (2001 Reissue) TRUSTS AND SETTLEMENTS Part 19 [9751].

3   As to the Settled Land Act 1925 s 64(1) (48 Halsbury's Statutes (4th Edn) TRUSTS AND SETTLEMENTS) see Paragraph 271 [668] ante.

4   See the Settled Land and Trustee Acts (Court's General Powers) Act 1943 s 1(3) as amended by the Trusts of Land and Appointment of Trustees Act 1996 s 25(1), Sch 3 para 8(b).

5   See the Settled Land and Trustee Acts (Court's General Powers) Act 1943 s 1(1), (5) as amended by the Emergency Laws (Miscellaneous Provisions) Act 1953 ss 9, 14, Sch 3 and by the Trusts of Land and Appointment of Trustees Act 1996 s 25(1), Sch 3 para 8(a).

6   Settled Land and Trustee Acts (Court's General Powers) Act 1943 s 1(2)(a) as amended by the Trusts of Land and Appointment of Trustees Act 1996 s 25(1), Sch 3 para 8(b).

7   Settled Land and Trustee Acts (Court's General Powers) Act 1943 s 1(2)(b) as amended by the Emergency Laws (Miscellaneous Provisions) Act 1953 ss 9, 14, Sch 3.

8   Settled Land and Trustee Acts (Court's General Powers) Act 1943 s 1(2)(c) as amended by the Emergency Laws (Miscellaneous Provisions) Act 1953 ss 9, 14, Sch 3.

[671]

273   Jurisdiction under the Variation of Trusts Act 1958

The Variation of Trusts Act 1958[1] gives the court[2] a discretionary power[3], where real or personal property is held on trusts arising under any will, settlement or other disposition, to approve on behalf of any of four classes of persons any arrangement[4] varying or revoking all or any of the trusts upon which the property is held, or enlarging the powers of the trustees in managing or administering the property subject to the trust[5]. The Act enables, therefore, the court to sanction a variation of beneficial interest generally. The four classes of persons are:

273.1   any person having, directly or indirectly, an interest, whether vested or contingent, under the trusts who by reason of minority[6] or other incapacity is incapable of assenting[7];

273.2   any person (whether ascertained or not) who may become entitled[8], directly or indirectly, to an interest under the trusts as being at a future date or on the happening of a future event a person of any specified description or a member of any specified class of persons, so however that this provision shall not include any person who would be of that description, or a member of that class, as the case may be, if the said date had fallen or the said event had happened at the date of the application to the court[9];

273.3   any person unborn[10];

273.4   any person[11] in respect of any discretionary interest of his under protective trusts where the interest of the principal beneficiary has not failed or determined[12].

[672]

Except in the case of a person falling under Paragraph 273.4 above the court must not approve any arrangement on behalf of any person unless it would be for the benefit of that person[13]. Benefit is not restricted to financial benefit[14], but applies also to moral or social benefit[15], administrative benefit[16] or other benefit[17]. The word arrangement used in the Act has been widely construed to cover many classes of variations. It has been said that the word is deliberately used in the widest possible sense so as to cover any proposal which any person may put forward for varying or revoking the trusts[18]. It appears, however, to be established that the word does not extend to allow a completely new resettlement as opposed to a variation[19]. Furthermore, it is the arrangement itself, not the order of the court, which effects the variation[20].

Finally it should be noted that the court may make an order even though there may be persons with potential interests in the estate who are not parties and who will not be bound by the order. In such a case the trustees are not free, except at their own risk, to treat the trusts as effectively varied until they have obtained the consent of such persons[21].

[673]

1   It was because of the limited operation of the Trustee Act 1925 s 57 (48 Halsbury's Statutes (4th Edn) TRUSTS AND SETTLEMENTS) (see Paragraph 276 [688] post) and of the inherent jurisdiction of the court in its application to variations of beneficial interests that the Variation of Trusts Act 1958 (48 Halsbury's Statutes (4th Edn) TRUSTS AND SETTLEMENTS) was passed.

2   As to the relevant court see the Variation of Trusts Act 1958 s 1(3) as amended by the County Courts Act 1959 s 204, Sch 3, by the Mental Health Act 1959 s 149(1), Sch 7 Pt I and by the Mental Health Act 1983 s 148, Sch 4 para 14.

3   *Re Oakes' Settlement Trusts* [1959] 2 All ER 47n, [1959] 1 WLR 502; *Re Van Gruisen's Will Trusts, Bagger v Dean* [1964] 1 All ER 843n, [1964] 1 WLR 449.

4   The power to approve exists by whoever the arrangement is proposed and whether or not there is any other person beneficially interested who is capable of assenting to it: see the Variation of Trusts Act 1958 s 1(1).

5   See the Variation of Trusts Act 1958 s 1(1). Nothing in the Variation of Trusts Act 1958 s 1(1)–(3) as amended (see note 2 above) applies to trusts affecting property settled by the Act of Parliament: Variation of Trusts Act 1958 s 1(5). Nothing in the Variation of Trusts Act 1958 s 1 is to be taken to limit the powers conferred by the Settled Land Act 1925 s 64(1) (48 Halsbury's Statutes (4th Edn)

TRUSTS AND SETTLEMENTS) (see Paragraph 271 [668] ante) or the Trustee Act 1925 s 57 (see Paragraph 276 [688] post) or the powers of the authority having jurisdiction under the Mental Health Act 1983 Part VII (ss 93–113): Variation of Trusts Act 1958 s 1(6) as amended by the Mental Health Act 1959 s 149(1), Sch 7 Pt I and the Mental Health Act 1983 s 148, Sch 4 para 14.

6   As to the duty of the guardian ad litem of an infant beneficiary who is defendant to an application under the Variation of Trusts Act 1958 and as to the jurisdiction of the court to approve an arrangement on behalf of an infant beneficiary notwithstanding the absence of proper consideration by or positive consent of the guardian ad litem see *Re Whittall, Whittall v Faulkner* [1973] 3 All ER 35, [1973] 1 WLR 1027.

     The payment out of court to trustees of damages awarded to an infant is not the kind of trust contemplated by the 1958 Act and accordingly does not extend the court's inherent jurisdiction: see *Allen v Distillers Co (Biochemicals) Ltd, Albrice v Distillers Co (Biochemicals) Ltd* [1974] QB 384, [1974] 2 All ER 365.

7   Variation of Trusts Act 1958 s 1(1)(a).

[674]

8   A person who is entitled to a contingent interest under a trust, even if the interest is defeasible on the exercise of a testamentary power of appointment, is not a person 'who may become entitled' to an interest within the meaning of the Variation of Trusts Act 1958 s 1(1)(b): See *Knocker v Youle* [1986] 2 All ER 914, [1986] 1 WLR 934.

9   Variation of Trusts Act 1958 s 1(1)(b). See *Re Suffert's Settlement, Suffert v Martyn-Linnington* [1961] Ch 1, [1960] 3 All ER 561; *Knocker v Youle* [1986] 2 All ER 914, [1986] 1 WLR 934. See also *Re Moncrieff's Settlement Trusts* [1962] 3 All ER 838n, [1962] 1 WLR 1344.

10   Variation of Trusts Act 1958 s 1(1)(c).

11   This includes an unascertained or unborn person: *Re Turner's Will Trusts, Bridgman v Turner* [1960] Ch 122, [1959] 2 All ER 689. It appears that under this paragraph approval may be given on behalf of, and even against the wishes of, an adult ascertained beneficiary.

12   Variation of Trusts Act 1958 s 1(1)(d).

13   Variation of Trusts Act 1958 s 1(1) proviso. See *Re Clitheroe's Settlement Trusts* [1959] 3 All ER 789, [1959] 1 WLR 1159; *Re Cohen's Settlement Trusts, Eliot-Cohen v Cohen* [1965] 3 All ER 139, [1965] 1 WLR 1229. See also *Re Bristol's Settled Estates, Bristol v Jermyn* [1964] 3 All ER 939, [1965] 1 WLR 469.

14   The court, however, starts from the principle that the beneficiary should not be materially worse off as a result of the variation, whatever happens: *Re Robinson's Settlement Trusts, Heard v Heard* [1976] 3 All ER 61, [1976] 1 WLR 806 where the court considered some of the implications of the change from estate duty to capital transfer tax. But the court can give its approval on behalf of someone who gets no financial benefit at all from the arrangement: *Re CL* [1969] 1 Ch 587, [1968] 1 All ER 1104.

15   *Re T's Settlement Trusts* [1964] Ch 158, [1963] 3 All ER 759; *Re Holt's Settlement, Wilson v Holt* [1969] 1 Ch 100, [1968] 1 All ER 470; *Re Weston's Settlements, Weston v Weston* [1969] 1 Ch 223, [1968] 3 All ER 338, CA; *Re Windeatt's Will Trusts* [1969] 2 All ER 324, [1969] 1 WLR 692.

16   *Re Seale's Marriage Settlement* [1961] Ch 574, [1961] 3 All ER 136; *Re Windeatt's Will Trusts* [1969] 2 All ER 324, [1969] 1 WLR 692.

17   *Re Remnant's Settlement Trusts, Hooper v Wenhaston* [1970] Ch 560, [1970] 2 All ER 554.

18   See *Re Steed's Will Trusts* [1960] Ch 407 at 419, [1960] 1 All ER 487 at 492, CA per Evershed MR.

19   *Re T's Settlement Trusts* [1964] Ch 158, [1963] 3 All ER 759; *Re Ball's Settlement* [1968] 2 All ER 438, [1968] 1 WLR 899.

20   *Re Holt's Settlement, Wilson v Holt* [1969] 1 Ch 100, [1968] 1 All ER 470. See also *Re Viscount Hambleden's Will Trusts* [1960] 1 All ER 353n, [1960] 1 WLR 82; *IRC v Holmden* [1968] AC 685, [1968] 1 All ER 148, HL.

21   *Re Suffert's Settlement, Suffert v Martyn-Linnington* [1961] Ch 1, [1960] 3 All ER 561.

[675]

274   Power of court to vary ante-nuptial or post-nuptial settlement

The court has jurisdiction, after granting a decree of divorce or nullity of marriage or judicial separation, to vary for the benefit of the parties to the marriage and the children (if any) of the family or either or any of them any ante-nuptial or post-nuptial settlement (including such a settlement made by will or codicil) made on the parties to the marriage[1]. The jurisdiction extends to rearrangements of beneficial interests[2].

[676]

1   See currently the Matrimonial Causes Act 1973 s 24(1)(c) (27 Halsbury's Statutes (4th Edn) MATRIMONIAL LAW). See also the Matrimonial Causes Act 1973 s 21(2) as substituted by the Family Law Act 1996 s 15, Sch 2 para 2 from a day to be appointed. For the appropriate form of order where husband and wife are tenants in common see *Jones v Jones* [1972] 3 All ER 289, [1972] 1 WLR 1269.

2   See eg *Thomson v Thomson and Whitmee* [1954] P 384, [1954] 2 All ER 462.

[677]–[685]

C: VARIATIONS CONCERNING ADMINISTRATION, POWERS AND MANAGEMENT

275   Inherent jurisdiction of court

The court has an inherent jurisdiction to sanction departures from the terms of the trust, but it is established that this in general applies only to the management or administration of the trust[1]. It does not apply to rearrangement of the rights of the beneficiaries to a beneficial interest, with the exception only of certain cases of the award of maintenance[2] and of compromise[3], if it is to be assumed that compromise in the sense in which the word is used in this connection amounts to a variation[4]. The jurisdiction has been described as one to cover an emergency which has arisen in the administration of the trust, that is to say, something for which no provision was made in the trust and which could not have been foreseen or anticipated by the author of the trust[5].

[686]

1   As to interference by the court in the administration of the trust see generally 48 Halsbury's Laws (4th Edn 2000 Reissue) para 953 et seq. As to applications by the trustees and others to the court see vol 40(2) (2001 Reissue) TRUSTS AND SETTLEMENTS Part 19 [9751].

2   As to the award of maintenance see Paragraph 269 [665] ante.

3   As to compromise see Paragraph 270 [666] ante.

4   This is perhaps doubtful because it seems that the court's sanction does not result in a variation of the beneficial trusts, but only brings to an end any dispute about them: see further Paragraph 270 [666] ante.

5   *Re New, Re Leavers, Re Morley* [1901] 2 Ch 534, CA; *Re Tollemache* [1903] 1 Ch 955, CA. See also *Re Montagu, Derbishire v Montagu* [1897] 2 Ch 8, CA.

[687]

276   Jurisdiction under the Trustee Act 1925

The inherent jurisdiction of the court was largely superseded by the Trustee Act 1925 Section 57. This Section applies where in the management or administration of any property vested in trustees, any sale, lease, mortgage, surrender, release, or other disposition, or any purchase, investment, acquisition, expenditure, or other transaction, is in the opinion of the court expedient, but it cannot be effected by reason of the absence of any power for that purpose vested in the trustees by the trust instrument, if any, or by the law. In such cases the court may by order confer upon the trustees, either generally or in any particular instance, the necessary power for the purpose, on such terms, and subject to such provisions and conditions, if any, as the court may think fit. The court may also direct in what manner any money authorised to be expended, and the costs of any transaction, are to be paid or borne as between capital and income[1].

An application to the court[2] under this Section may be made by the trustees, or by any of them, or by any person beneficially interested under the trust[3].

[688]

The object of this Section is to secure that the trust property is managed as advantageously as possible in the interests of the beneficiaries. With that object in view, it authorises specific dealings with the property which the court may have felt itself unable to sanction under the inherent jurisdiction, either because no actual emergency has arisen or because of inability to show that the position which calls for intervention is one which the creator of the trust cannot reasonably have foreseen. However, it is no part of the legislative aim to disturb the rule that the court will not rewrite a trust[4]. This Section is accordingly limited to mere general supervision and control of trust property by trustees. Subject to this limitation, however, it is an overriding provision to be read into every trust[5].

This Section envisages an act:

276.1   unauthorised by a trust instrument[6],

276.2   to be effected by the trustees of the settlement,

276.3   in the management or administration of the trust property,

276.4   which the court will empower the trustees to perform if in its opinion the act is expedient for the trust as a whole[7].

The Section has been used for a variety of purposes, for example, to authorise the partitioning of land where the necessary consent could not be obtained[8] or the sale of a reversionary interest which the trustees had no power to sell under the trust instrument[9]. A transaction will not, however, be sanctioned if it could be effected without the help of the court under this Section[10].

[689]

---

1   Trustee Act 1925 s 57(1) (48 Halsbury's Statutes (4th Edn) TRUSTS AND SETTLEMENTS). As to applications by the trustees and others to the court see vol 40(2) (2001 Reissue) TRUSTS AND SETTLEMENTS Part 19 [9751].

2   Ie the High Court or, where the trust estate or fund does not exceed the specified county court limit, the county court: see the Trustee Act 1925 ss 63A (as inserted by the County Courts Act 1984 s 148(1), Sch 2 para 1) 67 (as amended by the Courts Act 1971 s 56, Sch 11 Pt II); see also the County Court Jurisdiction Order 1981, SI 1981/1123 as amended. There may be jurisdiction by agreement above the normal county court limit: see the County Courts Act 1984 s 24(1), (2)(b) as amended by the Courts and Legal Services Act 1990 s 125(3), Sch 18 para 49(3) (11 Halsbury's Statutes (4th Edn) COUNTY COURTS).

3   Trustee Act 1925 s 57(3); see *Rennie and Rennie v Proma Ltd & Byng* [1990] 1 EGLR 119, CA. This section does not apply to trustees of the settlement for the purpose of the Settled Land Act 1925: Trustee Act 1925 s 57(4).

4   *Re Downshire Settled Estates, Marquess of Downshire v Royal Bank of Scotland* [1953] Ch 218 at 248, [1953] 1 All ER 103 at 119, CA; affd sub nom *Chapman v Chapman* [1954] AC 429, [1954] 1 All ER 798, HL. See also *Re Earl of Strafford, Royal Bank of Scotland v Byng* [1980] Ch 28, [1979] 1 All ER 513, CA. As to the extension of jurisdiction under the Trustee Act 1925 s 57, in relation to the treatment of management expenses as capital outgoings see Paragraph 272 [670] ante.

5   *Re Mair, Richards v Doxat* [1935] Ch 562.

6   *Re Pratt's Will Trusts, Barrow v McCarthy* [1943] Ch 326, [1943] 2 All ER 375.

7   *Re Craven's Estate, Lloyd's Bank Ltd v Cockburn (No 2)* [1937] Ch 431, [1937] 3 All ER 33.

8   *Re Thomas, Thomas v Thompson* [1930] 1 Ch 194.

9   *Re Cockerell's Settlement Trusts, Cockerell v National Provincial Bank Ltd* [1956] Ch 372, [1956] 2 All ER 172. See also *Re Hope's Will Trust, Hope v Thorp* [1929] 2 Ch 136; *Re Beale's Settlement Trusts, Huggins v Beale* [1932] 2 Ch 15; *Re Salting, Baillie-Hamilton v Morgan* [1932] 2 Ch 57; *Re Harvey, Westminster Bank Ltd v Askwith* [1941] 3 All ER 284; *Re Forster's Settlement, Michelmore v Byatt* [1954] 3 All ER 714, [1954] 1 WLR 1450. If there is no express or statutory power to delegate the management of investments it is a relatively straightforward matter to obtain such power by application to the court under the Trustee Act 1925 s 57: see *Anker-Peterson v Anker-Peterson* [1991]16 LS Gaz R 32. This is preferable to an application under the Variation of Trusts Act 1958 in that consents of adult beneficiaries are not required and the matter is considered in private. An application will rarely be necessary with the coming into force of the Trustee Act 2000.

10   *Re Basden's Settlement Trusts, Basden v Basden* [1943] 2 All ER 11.

[690]

D: DISENTAILING ASSURANCES

1: BARRING THE ENTAIL

277   Introduction

For over 500 years it has been possible for the tenant in tail to vary the terms of a settlement by barring the entail. At first a tenant in tail who was seised of the land could suffer a common recovery which operated to defeat the claims not only of the tenant's issue but of all those entitled in remainder or reversion. The fee tail was enlarged into a fee simple estate. A tenant in tail in remainder could not[1], however, suffer a common recovery as he was not seised of the land. What he could do was to levy a fine. This was less efficacious as it operated only to defeat the claims of the issue; the estate created was known as a base fee[2].

Both fines and recoveries became mere formalities, but they were expensive and not infrequently failed because of the complexity of the law. The Fines and Recoveries Act 1833 was designed to simplify the procedure, while retaining the substance of the distinction between fines and recoveries. It remains the law, subject to modification by the Law of Property Act 1925. A distinction is now drawn between the case where the tenant in tail is, and is not, entitled in possession.

It should be noted that it has not been possible to create an entailed interest since 31 December 1996[3].

[691]

1   Unless the freeholder in possession was prepared to collaborate.
2   As to disentailing at common law generally see 39(2) Halsbury's Laws (4th Edn Reissue) para 121.
3   Trusts of Land and Appointment of Trustees Act 1996 s 2, Sch 1 para 5 (37 Halsbury's Statutes (4th Edn) REAL PROPERTY).

[692]

278   Tenant in tail in possession

A tenant in tail in possession and of full age can bar the entail under the Fines and Recoveries Act 1833 by any assurance, (that is any conveyance or other transfer) except a will, by which a fee simple estate may be disposed of. It is known as a disentailing assurance, and must be either made or evidenced by a deed. Since the Act requires an assurance, a mere declaration that the entail has been barred will not suffice[1]. If the tenant wishes to dispose of the land he makes the disentailing assurance in favour of the grantee; if he wishes to retain it he makes the disentailing assurance to trustees in trust for himself[2].

Since 1925 it has also been possible for a tenant in tail of full age to bar the entail by a will executed after 31 December 1925[3]. The will must refer specifically either to the property or to the instrument under which it was acquired or to entailed property generally[4].

Whether the entail is barred inter vivos or by will, the effect is that the grantee, devisee or legatee[5] obtains a legal estate derived from the grantor, but enlarged from an entail into a fee simple estate[6], or absolute interest in the case of personalty.

[693]

1   See the Fines and Recoveries Act 1833 s 40 as amended by the SLR (No 2) Act 1888 and the SL(R) Act 1969 (37 Halsbury's Statutes (4th Edn) REAL PROPERTY). See also *Green v Paterson* (1886) 32 Ch D 95 at 108, CA; *Carter v Carter* [1896] 1 Ch 62 at 67, 69, CA. For disentailing assurances see Form 300 [2101] et seq post.

2   This remains the usual practice, although by the Law of Property Act 1925 s 72(3) (37 Halsbury's
     Statutes (4th Edn) REAL PROPERTY) he can now convey land to himself. Prior to 1926 enrolment
     was necessary, but this is no longer required: Law of Property Act 1925 s 133 (repealed).
3   Or confirmed or republished by a codicil executed after that date: Law of Property Act 1925 s 176(4).
4   See Law of Property Act 1925 s 176(1).
5   Between 1925 and 1997 personalty could be entailed: Law of Property Act 1925 s 130(1) repealed by
     the Trusts of Land and Appointment of Trustees Act 1996 s 25(2), Sch 4 (37 Halsbury's Statutes
     (4th Edn) REAL PROPERTY).
6   *Lord Lilford v A-G* (1867) LR 2 HL 63.

[694]

279   Tenant in tail not entitled in possession

A tenant in tail not entitled in possession of full age can likewise bar the entail inter vivos,
but the effect will depend upon whether he has the consent of the protector of the
settlement, normally the owner of the prior life interest or of the first of several life
interests, or who would have been the owner had he not disposed of his beneficial
interest[1]. If he has that consent the effect will be a complete bar, as in the case of a tenant
in tail in possession. If the protector does not give his consent, the tenant in tail not in
possession can still bar the entail, but the effect will be to create only a base fee[2].

A tenant in tail not in possession cannot bar the entail by will.

[695]

1   See the Fines and Recoveries Act 1833 s 22 as amended by the SLR (No 2) Act 1888 (37 Halsbury's
     Statutes (4th Edn) REAL PROPERTY). See also the Fines and Recoveries Act 1833 s 33 as amended by
     the SLR (No 2) Act 1888, by the Mental Health Act 1959 s 149(1), Sch 7, by the Mental Health Act
     1983 s 148, Sch 4 para 1(a) and by the Criminal Law Act 1967 s 10, Sch 3 Pt I. See also *Re Darnley's
     Will Trusts, Darnley v Bligh* [1970] 1 All ER 319, [1970] 1 WLR 405. As to the protector of the
     settlement generally see 39(2) Halsbury's Laws (4th Edn Reissue) para 124 et seq. For disentailing
     assurances see Form 300 [2101] et seq post.
2   See the Fines and Recoveries Act 1833 s 34 as amended by the SLR (No 2) Act 1888.

[696]

280   Enlargement of base fee into fee simple

A base fee may be enlarged into a fee simple estate in any one of the following ways:

280.1   If the owner of the base fee acquires the immediate remainder or reversion
         in fee simple, the Fines and Recoveries Act 1833 provides that it is
         enlarged into a fee simple absolute[1].

280.2   The owner of a base fee can convert it into a fee simple absolute by means
         of a new disentailing assurance with the consent of the protector[2], or
         without it if the protectorship has come to an end[3]. He can do this even if
         he has parted with the base fee[4], but a purchaser of the base fee apparently
         has no power of enlargement.

280.3   Under the Limitation Act 1980 a base fee is enlarged into a fee simple if
         the person taking possession under the disentailing assurance, or any other
         person, is in possession of the land for 12 years from the time when the
         protectorship came to an end, and the tenant in tail was in a position to bar
         the entail completely[5].

280.4   The owner of a base fee in possession who has power to enlarge the base
         fee into a fee simple without the concurrence of any other person can
         enlarge the base fee by will in the same way as a tenant in tail in possession
         can bar his entail[6].

[697]

1   See the Fines and Recoveries Act 1833 s 39 as amended by the SLR (No 2) Act 1888 (37 Halsbury's Statutes (4th Edn) REAL PROPERTY).
2   See the Fines and Recoveries Act 1833 s 35 as amended (see note 1 above).
3   See the Fines and Recoveries Act 1833 s 19 as amended (see note 1 above).
4   *Bankes v Small* (1887) 36 Ch D 716, CA.
5   See the Limitation Act 1980 s 27 (24 Halsbury's Statutes (4th Edn) LIMITATION OF ACTIONS).
6   See the Law of Property Act 1925 s 176(1), (3) (37 Halsbury's Statutes (4th Edn) REAL PROPERTY).

[698]

2: UNBARRABLE ENTAILS

281   General

There are some special cases where the tenant in tail has no power to bar the entail at all. These are:

281.1   a tenant in tail after possibility of issue extinct;

281.2   where the estate tail was created by Parliament as a reward for services rendered, and the statute expressly provides that there is no right of disentailment; and

281.3   entails created by the Crown for services rendered to the Crown, the reversion being the Crown[1].

1   See the Fines and Recoveries Act 1833 s 18 as amended by the SLR (No 2) Act 1888 (37 Halsbury's Statutes (4th Edn) REAL PROPERTY). As to unbarrable entails generally see 39(2) Halsbury's Laws (4th Edn Reissue) para 132 et seq.

[699]–[710]

(13) TAXATION

A: INTRODUCTION

282   General

This section of commentary considers inheritance tax, capital gains tax and income tax, these being the three main taxes that affect trusts and settlements. Reference is made to stamp duty in the appropriate precedents, although in most cases this tax does not pose any problem.

[711]

B: INHERITANCE TAX

1: DEFINITIONS AND CLASSIFICATION

283   Meaning of 'settlement'

283.1   Statutory definition

'Settlement' is defined as follows for inheritance tax purposes[1]:

'(2)   … any disposition or dispositions of property, whether effected by instrument, by parol or by operation of law, or partly in one way and partly in another, whereby the property is for the time being:

(a)   held in trust for persons in succession[2] or for any person subject to a contingency, or

(b)   held by trustees on trust to accumulate the whole or part of any income of the property or with power to make payments out of that income at the discretion of the trustees or some other person, with or without power to accumulate surplus income, or

(c)   charged or burdened (otherwise than for full consideration in money or money's worth paid for his own use or benefit to the person making the disposition) with the payment of any annuity or other periodical payment payable for a life or any other limited or terminable period, ...

(3)   A lease of property which is for life or lives, or for a period ascertainable only by reference to a death, or which is terminable on, or at a date ascertainable only by reference to, a death, shall be treated as a settlement and the property as settled property, unless the lease was granted for full consideration in money or money's worth; and where a lease not granted as a lease at a rack rent is at any time to become a lease at an increased rent it shall be treated as terminable at that time.'

[712]

The ambit of this definition is illustrated in the following example:

Example 1

(1)   Property is settled on X for life remainder to Y and Z absolutely (this is a 'fixed' trust).

(2)   Property is held on trust for 'such of A, B, C, D, E and F as my trustees in their absolute discretion may select' (this is a 'discretionary' trust).

(3)   Property is held on trust 'for A contingent on attaining 18 years' (an accumulation and maintenance settlement).

(4)   Property is held on trust by A and B as trustees for Z absolutely (a bare trust, but for inheritance tax purposes there is no settlement and the property is treated as belonging to Z)[3].

(5)   A and B jointly purchase Blackacre. There is a statutory trust of land[4] with A and B holding the land on trust (as joint tenants) for themselves as either joint tenants or tenants in common in equity. For inheritance tax purposes there is no settlement and the property belongs to A and B equally[5].

(6)   A grants B a lease of Blackacre for B's life at a peppercorn rent. This is a settlement for inheritance tax purposes and A is the trustee of the property[6]. Under the Law of Property Act 1925 Section 149(6) the lease is treated as being for a term of 90 years which is determinable on the death of B.

---

[713]

1   Inheritance Tax Act 1984 s 43 (42–44 Halsbury's Statutes (4th Edn) TAXATION).
2   In *IRC v Lloyds Private Banking Ltd* [1998] STC 559, [1999] 1 FLR 147 the relevant terms of the deceased's will were as follows:
  '(1)   While my Husband Frederick Arthur Evans remains alive and desires to reside in the property and keeps the same in good repair and insured comprehensively to its full value with Insurers approved by my Trustee and pays and indemnifies my Trustee against all rates taxes and other outgoings in respect of the property my Trustee shall not make any objection to such residence

and shall not disturb or restrict it in any way and shall not take any steps to enforce the trust for sale on which the property is held or to realise my share therein or obtain any rent or profit from the property.

(2)   On the death of my said Husband Frederick Arthur Evans I devise and bequeath the said property known as Hillcroft Muzzy Hill, Astwood Bank, near Redditch to my daughter Kathleen Roberts-Hindle absolutely.'

The effect of this clause was that the deceased's husband was given a right of occupation in the property which was equivalent to an interest in possession, so that the property was settled within the Inheritance Tax Act 1984 s 43(2)(a). See also *Woodhall (personal representatives of Woodhall) v IRC* [2000] STC (SCD) 558.

3   For the (similar) capital gains tax position see Paragraph 339.2 [898] post.
4   Law of Property Act 1925 ss 34, 36 as amended by the Trusts of Land and Appointment of Trustees Act 1996 s 5, Sch 2 (37 Halsbury's Statutes (4th Edn) REAL PROPERTY).
5   For the (similar) capital gains tax position see Paragraph 339.4 [900] post.
6   Inheritance Tax Act 1984 s 45. As to the position where a lease is treated as a settlement see Paragraph 297 [765] post.

[714]

283.2   When is there a disposition creating a settlement?

As discussed below[1], difficulties have arisen in identifying, for capital gains tax purposes, when property has been resettled (ie when a new settlement has been created out of an existing settlement). Difficulties may also occur when it is necessary to determine whether the settlor has created one or more settlements. Similar problems may arise for inheritance tax and the definition of 'settlement', set out above, may not help to resolve these problems[2].

[715]

Example 2

Each year S creates a discretionary trust of £3,000 (thereby utilising his annual inheritance tax exemption) and his wife does likewise. Accordingly, at the end of five years there are ten mini-discretionary trusts. As a matter of trust law, and assuming that each settlement is correctly documented and constituted, there is no reason why this series should be treated as one settlement. So far as the inheritance tax legislation is concerned the settlements are not related settlements made on the same day[3]; the associated operations provisions would seem inapplicable[4]; and the principle in *WT Ramsay Ltd v IRC*[5] although of uncertain ambit, could only be applied with difficulty to a series of gifts. The trusts should be kept apart (there should be no pooling of property) and each settlement should be fully documented[6].

[716]

1   As to resettlements see Paragraph 342 [919] post.
2   See, for example, *Minden Trust (Cayman) Ltd v IRC* [1984] STC 434; affd [1985] STC 758, CA; and *Tax Bulletin*, February 1997.
3   See the Inheritance Tax Act 1984 s 62 (42–44 Halsbury's Statutes (4th Edn) TAXATION).
4   See Inheritance Tax Act 1984 s 268, but see also note 6 below.
5   *WT Ramsay Ltd v IRC* [1982] AC 300, [1981] 1 All ER 865, HL.
6   It is common for separate discretionary trusts to be created of substantial life insurance policies. Such trusts will normally be on identical terms, with the same trustees, but established on consecutive days. Each trust contains a separate item of property (a particular insurance policy). It is understood that the Capital Taxes Office take the view that such a series of settlements fall within the Inheritance Tax Act 1984 s 268 (associated operations) and so may be treated as a single settlement. It is not thought that this argument is correct.

[717]

284   Settlors and trustees

In the majority of cases it is not difficult to identify the settlor, because there is usually one settlor who has created a settlement by a 'disposition' of property (which may include a series of associated operations)[1]. If that settlor adds further property, this creates no problems in the interest in possession settlement, but difficulties may arise if the settlement is discretionary[2] with further complications if the original property was excluded property and the additional property was not, or vice versa.

Example 3

(1)   A and B create a settlement in favour of their neighbour C and his family.

(2)   B adds property to a settlement that had been created two years ago by A in favour of neighbour C and family.

---

[718]

The Inheritance Tax Act 1984 Section 44(2) states that: 'Where more than one person is a settlor in relation to a settlement and the circumstances so require, this Part of this Act (except section 48(4) to (6)) shall have effect in relation to it as if the settled property were comprised in separate settlements.' *Thomas v IRC*[3] indicates that this provision normally only applies where an identifiable capital fund has been provided by each settlor. The fund is then treated as two separate settlements in the case of discretionary trusts where both the incidence of the periodic charge and the amount of inheritance tax chargeable may be affected. 'Settlor' is defined (in terms similar to the income tax definition) as follows[4]:

> 'In this Act "settlor", in relation to a settlement, includes any person by whom the settlement was made directly or indirectly, and ... includes any person who has provided funds directly or indirectly for the purpose of or in connection with the settlement or has made with any other person a reciprocal arrangement for that other person to make the settlement.'[5]

[719]

A further problem arises where there is only one settlor who adds property to his settlement; is this one settlement or two? The question is significant in relation to discretionary trusts (especially with regard to timing and rate of the periodic and inter periodic charges) and where excluded property is involved in a settlement. As a matter of trust law, there is a single settlement where funds are held and managed by one set of trustees for one set of beneficiaries, so that such additions do not lead to the creation of separate settlements. If it would be advantageous to have two settlements for inheritance tax purposes, a separate settlement deed should be drawn up for the later property.

The ordinary meaning is given to the term 'a trustee', although it also includes any person in whom the settled property or its management is for the time being vested[6]. In cases where a lease for lives is treated as a settlement the landlord is the trustee.

[720]

---

1   Inheritance Tax Act 1984 s 272 (42–44 Halsbury's Statutes (4th Edn) TAXATION). See *Hatton v IRC* [1992] STC 140 and note 5 below.
2   As to discretionary settlements see Paragraph 316 [821] et seq post. As to added property see Paragraph 323.4 [854] post.
3   *Thomas v IRC* [1981] STC 382.
4   Inheritance Tax Act 1984 s 44(1).
5   In *Hatton v IRC* [1992] STC 140 Chadwick J considered the impact of the associated operations provisions of the Inheritance Tax Act 1984 s 268 on the question of multiple settlors. He concluded in that case that the first settlement was made with a view to enabling or facilitating the making of the

second (within the meaning of the Inheritance Tax Act 1984 s 268(1)(b)). Accordingly, there was a disposition by associated operations which was treated as a single disposition of property from the first settlor into the second settlement of which he therefore became a settlor. Given the nature of the property settled by these two settlors, the judge was then forced to conclude that both settlors had created a separate settlement of the entirety of the property in the second settlement. This approach (treating each settlor as having established a separate settlement of the entirety of the settled property) would, the judge suggested, also apply to reciprocal settlements. In a simple case A would settle property on X for a limited interest in possession and as a quid pro quo B would settle property on Y for similar interest. In both cases the reverter to settlor provisions would at first sight apply on the termination of X and Y's respective interests. Once it is accepted, however, that A is also a settlor of B's trust and vice versa (see the Inheritance Tax Act 1984 s 44(1)) that analysis does not hold good. Instead, because B is a settlor of 'A's settlement' on the termination of X's limited interest an inheritance tax charge may arise. The judge viewed the situation as one in which A and B were settlors of two separate settlements rather than accepting the view propounded by the Inland Revenue that B should be seen as 'a dominant settlor' of A's trust.

6   Inheritance Tax Act 1984 s 45.

[721]

285   Classification of settlements

Settlements for inheritance tax purposes must be divided into three categories:

285.1   *Category A.* An interest in possession settlement; eg where the property is held for a tenant for life who, by virtue of his interest, is entitled to the income and has 'an interest in possession'.

285.2   *Category B.* A settlement lacking an interest in possession, eg where trustees are given a discretion over the distribution of the income. At most, beneficiaries have the right to be considered by the trustees; the right to ensure that the fund is properly administered; and the right to join with all the other beneficiaries to bring the settlement to an end.

285.3   *Category C.* Into this category fall special or privileged trusts. They lack an interest in possession, but are not subject to the Category B regime. The main example is the accumulation and maintenance trust.

To place a particular trust into its correct category is important for two reasons. First, because the inheritance tax treatment of each is totally different both as to incidence of tax and as to the amount of tax charged; and secondly, because a change from one category to another normally gives rise to an inheritance tax charge. For example, if a life interest ceases, whereupon the fund is held on discretionary trusts, the settlement moves from Category A to Category B, and a chargeable occasion (the ending of a life interest) has occurred[1].

1   This event is not a potentially exempt transfer: see the limitation in the Inheritance Tax Act 1984 s 3A(1)(c) as inserted by the Finance Act 1986 s 101, Sch 19 para 1 (42–44 Halsbury's Statutes (4th Edn) TAXATION).

[722]

286   Meaning of an 'interest in possession'

286.1   Introduction

Normally trusts can easily be slotted into their correct category. Trusts falling within Category C[1] are carefully defined so that any trust not specifically falling into one of those special cases must fall into Category B. Problems are principally caused by the borderline between Categories A and B where the division is drawn according to whether the settlement has an interest in possession or not. In the majority of cases no problems will arise: at one extreme stands the life interest settlement; at the other the discretionary trust. What, however, of a settlement which provides for the income to be paid to A, unless the trustees decide to pay it to B, or to accumulate it; or where the property in the trust is enjoyed in specie by one beneficiary as the result of the exercise of a discretion (eg a beneficiary living in a dwelling house which is part of the assets of a discretionary trust)? To resolve these difficulties, the phrase an 'interest in possession' needs definition. The legislation does not assist; instead, its meaning must be gleaned from an Inland Revenue press notice[2] and the speeches of the House of Lords in *Pearson v IRC*[3] which largely endorsed the statements in that press notice.

[723]

1   As to the classification of settlements see Paragraph 285 [722] ante.
2   Inland Revenue Press Notice, 12 February 1976.
3   *Pearson v IRC* [1981] AC 753, [1980] 2 All ER 479, HL. The term 'interest in possession' is used in the Trusts of Land and Appointment of Trustees Act 1996 (37 Halsbury's Statutes (4th Edn) REAL PROPERTY) where it is assumed that it will bear the inheritance tax meaning.

[724]

286.2   Inland Revenue press notice
The Inland Revenue press notice reads as follows[1]:

> '... an interest in settled property exists where the person having the interest has the immediate entitlement (subject to any prior claim by the trustees for expenses or other outgoings properly payable out of income) to any income produced by that property as the income arises; but ... a discretion or power, in whatever form, which can be exercised after income arises so as to withhold it from that person negatives the existence of an interest in possession. For this purpose a power to accumulate income is regarded as a power to withhold it, unless any accumulation must be held solely for the person having the interest or his personal representatives.
>
> On the other hand the existence of a mere power of revocation or appointment, the exercise of which would determine the interest wholly or in part (but which, so long as it remains unexercised, does not affect the beneficiary's immediate entitlement to income) does not ... prevent the interest from being an interest in possession.'

[725]

The first paragraph of the notice is concerned with the existence of discretions or powers which might affect the destination of the income after it has arisen and which prevent the existence of any interest in possession (eg a provision enabling the trustees to accumulate income or to divert it for the benefit of other beneficiaries). The second paragraph concerns overriding powers which, if exercised, would terminate the entire interest of the beneficiary, but which do not prevent the existence of an interest in possession (eg the statutory power of advancement). Administrative expenses charged on the income can be ignored in deciding whether there is an interest in possession, so long as such payments are for 'outgoings properly payable out of income'. A clause in the settlement providing for expenses of a capital nature to be so charged is, therefore, not covered and the Inland Revenue considers the mere presence of such a clause fatal to the existence of any interest in possession.

1   Inland Revenue Press Notice, 12 February 1976.

[726]

286.3   *Pearson v IRC*[1]
Both capital and income of the trust fund were held for the settlor's three adult daughters in equal shares subject to three overriding trustee powers:

286.3.1   to appoint capital and income amongst the daughters, their spouses and issue;

286.3.2   to accumulate so much of the income as they should think fit; and

286.3.3   to apply any income towards the payment or discharge of any taxes, costs or other outgoings which would otherwise be payable out of capital.

The trustees had regularly exercised their powers to accumulate the income. What caused the disputed tax assessment was the irrevocable appointment of some £16,000 from the fund to one of the daughters. There was no doubt that, after the appointment, she enjoyed an interest in possession in the appointed sum; but did she already have an interest in possession in the fund? If so, no inheritance tax would be chargeable on the appointment[2]; if not, there would be a charge because the appointed sums had passed from a 'no interest in possession' to an 'interest in possession' settlement (Category B[3] to Category A).

[727]

The Inland Revenue argued that the existence of the overriding power to accumulate and the provision enabling all expenses to be charged to income deprived the settlement of any interest in possession. It was common ground that whether such powers had been exercised or not was irrelevant in deciding the case. The overriding power of appointment over capital and income was not seen as endangering the existence of any interest in possession (see the second paragraph of the press notice).

For the bare majority of the House of Lords the presence of the overriding discretion to accumulate the income was fatal to the existence of an interest in possession. 'A present right to present enjoyment' was how an interest in possession was defined and the beneficiaries did not have a present right. 'Their enjoyment of any income from the trust fund depended on the trustees' decision as to accumulation of income' (per Viscount Dilhorne). No distinction is to be drawn between a trust to pay income to a beneficiary (with an overriding power to accumulate), and a trust to accumulate (with a power to pay). Therefore, in the following examples there is no interest in possession:

286.3.4   to A for life but the trustees may accumulate the income for the benefit of others; and

286.3.5   the income shall be accumulated but the trustees may make payments to A.

[728]

1   *Pearson v IRC* [1981] AC 753, [1980] 2 All ER 479, HL.
2   As to advancements to a life tenant or absolute entitlement on the satisfaction of a contingency see Paragraph 300.5 [777] et seq post.
3   As to the classification of settlements see Paragraph 285 [722] ante.

[729]

287   Problems remaining after *Pearson v IRC*[1]

287.1   General
The test laid down by the majority in the House of Lords provides some certainty in a difficult area of law and the borderline between trusts with and without an interest in possession is reasonably easy to draw. Where there is uncertainty about the entitlement of a beneficiary to income, it is likely that the settlement will fall into the 'no-interest in possession' regime. In the light of the relatively favourable regime for taxing discretionary trusts introduced in 1982 that may be no bad thing for taxpayers. The following are some of the difficulties remaining after the case.

1   *Pearson v IRC* [1981] AC 753, [1980] 2 All ER 479, HL.

[730]

287.2   Dispositive and administrative powers

For there to be an interest in possession the beneficiary must be entitled to the income as it arises. Were this test to be applied strictly, however, even a trust with a life tenant receiving the income might fail to satisfy the requirement because trustees will always deduct management expenses from the gross income, so that few beneficiaries are entitled to all the income as it arises. This problem was commented on by Viscount Dilhorne in *Pearson v IRC*[1] as follows:

> '... Parliament distinguished between the administration of a trust and the dispositive powers of trustees ... A life tenant has an interest in possession but his interest only extends to the net income of the property, that is to say, after deduction from the gross income of expenses etc properly incurred in the management of the trust by the trustees in the exercise of their powers. A dispositive power is a power to dispose of the net income. Sometimes the line between an administrative and a dispositive power may be difficult to draw but that does not mean that there is not a valid distinction.'

[731]

In *Pearson v IRC* the trustees had an overriding discretion to apply income towards the payment of any taxes, costs or other outgoings which would otherwise be payable out of capital and the Inland Revenue took the view that the existence of this overriding power was a further reason for the settlement lacking an interest in possession. Was this power administrative (in which case its presence did not affect the existence of any interest in possession) or dispositive (fatal to the existence of such an interest)? Viscount Dilhorne decided that the power was administrative. Acceptable though this argument may be for management expenses, is it convincing when applied to other expenses and taxes (eg capital gains tax and inheritance tax) which would normally be payable out of the capital of the fund? In *Miller v IRC*[2] the Court of Session held that a power to employ income to make good depreciation in the capital value of assets in the fund was administrative. It must be stressed that the House of Lords did not have to decide whether the Inland Revenue's contention was correct or not; Viscount Dilhorne's observations are obiter dicta and the Inland Revenue still adheres to its press notice[3]. Would-be settlors should be advised not to insert such clauses.

[732]

1   *Pearson v IRC* [1981] AC 753, [1980] 2 All ER 479, HL.
2   *Miller v IRC* [1987] STC 108, Court of Sess.
3   Ie Inland Revenue Press Notice, 12 February 1976. See further Paragraph 286.2 [725] ante.

[733]

287.3   Power to allow beneficiaries to occupy a dwelling house

This power may exist both in settlements which otherwise have an interest in possession and in those without. The mere existence of such a power is to be ignored; problems may only arise if and when it is exercised. A statement of practice[1] indicates that if such a power is exercised to allow, for a definite or indefinite period, someone other than the life tenant to have exclusive or joint right of residence in a dwelling house as a permanent home, there would be an inheritance tax charge on the partial ending of that life interest. In the case of a fund otherwise lacking an interest in possession, the exercise of the power would result in the creation of an interest in possession and therefore an inheritance tax charge would arise. Whether this view is correct is arguable; in *Swales v IRC*[2] for instance, the taxpayer's argument that the mandating of trust income to a beneficiary was equivalent to providing a residence for permanent occupation (and accordingly created an interest in possession) was rejected by the court. In practice, any challenge could prove costly to the taxpayer, and trustees who possess such powers should think carefully before exercising them[3].

[734]

1   Ie Inland Revenue Statement of Practice SP10/79 (15 August 1979).
2   *Swales v IRC* [1984] 3 All ER 16.
3   For a power to allow beneficiaries to occupy a dwelling house see Form 4 schedule paragraph 22 [1100] post. See also the Trusts of Land and Appointment of Trustees Act 1996 ss 12, 13 (37 Halsbury's Statutes (4th Edn) REAL PROPERTY) and Paragraph 228 [545] ante.

[735]

287.4   Interest-free loans to beneficiaries

The Inland Revenue apparently took the view that an interest-free loan to a beneficiary created an interest in possession in the fund[1]. As that beneficiary became a debtor (to the extent of the loan), one wonders in what assets his interest subsists; the money loaned would appear to belong to him absolutely.

1   It is thought that this position has now been abandoned.

[736]

287.5   Position of the last surviving member of a discretionary class

If the class of beneficiaries has closed, the sole survivor must be entitled to the income as it arises so he enjoys an interest in possession. When the class has not closed, however, trustees have a reasonable time to decide how the accrued income is to be distributed and, if a further beneficiary could come into existence before that period has elapsed, the current beneficiary is not automatically entitled to the income as it arises so that there is no interest in possession[1]. Likewise, if the class has not closed and the trustees have a power to accumulate income.

1   *Re Trafford's Settlement: Moore v IRC* [1985] Ch 32, [1984] 1 All ER 1108.

[737]–[745]

2: CREATION OF SETTLEMENTS

288   Charge to tax

If a settlement is created inter vivos there is no immediate inheritance tax charge if the transfer is a potentially exempt transfer. This is the case if the trust contains an interest in possession (when the settlor will make a potentially exempt transfer to the relevant beneficiary) or is an accumulation and maintenance or disabled trust[1]. Nor does an inheritance tax charge arise in the circumstances set out in the following example.

Example 4

(1)   S settles £100,000 on trust for himself for life with remainder to his children. As S, the life tenant, is deemed to own the entire fund (and not simply a life interest in it) his estate has not fallen in value.

(2)   S settles £100,000 on trust for his wife for life, remainder to his children. S's wife is treated as owning the fund so that S's transfer is an exempt transfer to a spouse.

---

[746]

An immediate charge at half rates may, however, be imposed if a discretionary trust is created inter vivos. Normal rules apply to the creation of will trusts: generally tax is charged unless eg the spouse exemption applies (as in paragraph (2) of this example). Trusts established in the seven years before death may suffer an inheritance tax charge as a failed potentially exempt transfer or, when there was a tax charge on creation, a supplementary charge.

1   Inheritance Tax Act 1984 s 3A(1)(c) as inserted by the Finance Act 1986 s 101, Sch 19 para 1 (42–44 Halsbury's Statutes (4th Edn) TAXATION).

[747]

3: PAYMENT OF INHERITANCE TAX

289   Liability to tax[1]

If inheritance tax payable on creation of the trust is paid by the trustees (eg in the case of discretionary trusts) the settlor does not as a result retain an interest in the settlement for income tax purposes[2].

Primary liability for inheritance tax arising during the course of the settlement rests upon the trustees. Their liability is limited to the property which they have received or disposed of or become liable to account for to a beneficiary and such other property which they would have received but for their own neglect or default.

If trustees fail to pay, the Inland Revenue can collect tax from any of the following[3]:

289.1   Any person entitled to an interest in possession in the settled property. The liability of such person is limited to the value of the trust property, out of which he can claim an indemnity for the tax he has paid.

289.2   Any beneficiary under a discretionary trust up to the value of the property that he receives (after paying income tax on it) and with no right to an indemnity for the tax he is called upon to pay.

289.3   The settlor, where the trustees are resident outside the United Kingdom, because, if the trustees do not pay, the Inland Revenue cannot enforce payment abroad. If the settlor pays he has a right to recover the tax from the trust.

[748]

1   For the duty to deliver accounts and information see the Inheritance Tax Act 1984 s 216 as amended (42–44 Halsbury's Statutes (4th Edn) TAXATION) and for the reporting requirements when non-resident trusts are established see the Inheritance Tax Act 1984 s 218.
2   Inland Revenue Statement of Practice SP1/82 (6 April 1982). As to whether an agreement that the trustees should pay inheritance tax amounts to a reservation of benefit see (1987) 84 LS Gaz No 14, 1041.
3   See the Inheritance Tax Act 1984 s 201(1).

[749]

4: RESERVATION OF BENEFIT

290   General

The creation of inter vivos settlements can lead to problems in the reservation of benefit area and the matters set out below are especially worthy of note.

[750]

291   Settlor appoints himself a trustee

If the settlor appoints himself a trustee of his settlement, that appointment does not by itself amount to a reserved benefit. A settlor may therefore retain control over the settled property. If the terms of the settlement provide for his remuneration as trustee, however, there may be a reservation in the settled property[1]. One way of overcoming this is for the settlor/trustee to be paid by an annuity, as such an arrangement will not constitute a reserved benefit and the ending of that annuity will not lead to any inheritance tax charge[2].

Particular difficulties are caused if the settlor/trustee is a director of a company whose shares are held in the trust fund. The general rule of equity is that a trustee may not profit from his position and this means that he will generally have to account for any director's fees that he may receive. It is standard practice, however, for the trust deed to provide that a trustee need not in such cases account for those fees[3]. When the settlor/trustee is allowed to retain fees under the deed it is arguable that he has reserved a benefit in the trust assets within the ruling in *Oakes v Comr of Stamp Duties of New South Wales*. The Inland Revenue has, however, indicated that it will not take this point so long as the director's remuneration is on reasonable commercial terms.

[751]

1   *Oakes v Comr of Stamp Duties of New South Wales* [1954] AC 57, [1953] 2 All ER 1563, PC. It is understood that the Inland Revenue do not at present take this point: see *CTO Advanced Instruction Manual* para D 75.
2   Inheritance Tax Act 1984 s 90 (42–44 Halsbury's Statutes (4th Edn) TAXATION).
3   For a power to hold directorships and retain remuneration see Form 183 [1670] post.

[752]

292   Settlor reserves an interest for himself

If the settlor reserves an interest for himself under his settlement, whether he does so expressly or whether his interest arises by operation of law, there is no reservation of benefit and he is treated as making a partial gift.

Example 5

S created a settlement for his minor son, absolutely on attaining 21 years. No provision was made for what should happen if the son were to die before that age, and therefore there was a resulting trust to the settlor. The settlor died whilst the son was still a minor and was held to have reserved no benefit. Instead, he was treated as making a partial gift; ie a gift of the settled property less the retained remainder interest in it[1].

---

[753]

The position with regard to discretionary trusts is more problematic. It appears that if the settlor is one of the class of beneficiaries, he is not entirely excluded from the property. In view of the limited nature of a discretionary beneficiary's rights[2] it is unlikely that he can be treated as making a partial gift. The Inland Revenue considers, therefore, that if a settlor is a discretionary beneficiary he will be treated as having reserved a benefit in the entire settled fund despite the fact that he may receive no benefit from the fund[3]. Although there is some doubt about the correctness of this view, taxpayers face the familiar dilemma in that they would probably have to appeal to the House of Lords to overturn this argument. The insertion of the settlor's spouse as a discretionary beneficiary does not by itself result in a reserved benefit. Were that spouse to receive property from the settlement, however, which was then shared with or used for the benefit of the settlor, the Inland Revenue will argue that he has reserved a benefit.

[754]

---

1   *Stamp Duties Comr of New South Wales v Perpetual Trustee Co Ltd* [1943] AC 425, PC; see also *Cochrane v IRC* [1974] STC 335 where the settlor expressly reserved surplus income. For a general consideration of so-called 'shearing operations' see *Ingram (executors of Lady Ingram) v IRC* [1999] STC 37, [1999] 1 All ER 297, HL and vol 17(2) (2000 Reissue) GIFTS Paragraphs 131 [979], 131 [979].
2   See *Gartside v IRC* [1968] AC 553, [1968] 1 All ER 121, HL.
3   It is thought that a similar result arises if the settlor, although not a discretionary beneficiary, is capable of becoming such a beneficiary (eg under a power to add to the class of beneficiaries). For a clause excluding the settlor and spouse from any benefit under a discretionary trust see further Form 4 clause 14 [1091] post.

[755]

293   Gift to spouse

The reservation of benefit rules do not apply to an exempt gift to a spouse. Accordingly, it may be possible to channel a benefit through a spouse.

Example 6

A settles property on his wife B for life and subject to this on discretionary trusts for a class of beneficiaries which includes A. B's life interest terminates after six months. It is arguable that A has not reserved any benefit since the gift is spouse exempt although he is one of the objects of the discretionary trust. At the time of writing, a case is being brought to test the position.

---

[756]–[757]

5: TREATMENT OF INTEREST IN POSSESSION TRUSTS

(a) Treatment of Beneficiaries

294   General

The beneficiary entitled to income of a fund (usually the life tenant) is treated as owning that portion of the capital of the fund. This rule is a fiction since in no real sense is the life tenant the owner of the capital in the fund. For inheritance tax purposes, however, the capital forms part of his estate, so that on a chargeable occasion inheritance tax is charged on the trust fund at his rates. The settlement itself is not a separate taxable entity (contrast the rules for discretionary trusts)[1], although primary liability for any tax falls upon the trustees.

As the life tenant is treated as owning all the capital in the fund, other beneficiaries with 'reversionary interests' own nothing. Reversionary interest means:

> 'a future interest under a settlement, whether it is vested or contingent (including an interest expectant on the termination of an interest in possession which, by virtue of section 50 ... is treated as subsisting in part of any property)'[2].

[758]

Generally, reversionary interests are excluded property and can be assigned without charge to inheritance tax. It is unclear whether the term catches the interests of discretionary beneficiaries because such rights as they possess (to compel due administration, to be considered and jointly to wind up the fund) are present rights. Accordingly, their interests may be neither in possession nor in reversion.

1   As to the treatment of discretionary trusts see Paragraph 316 [821] et seq post.
2   Inheritance Tax Act 1984 s 47 (42–44 Halsbury's Statutes (4th Edn) TAXATION).

[759]

(b) Persons Treated as Owning the Fund

295   The interest in possession beneficiary

The beneficiary entitled to an interest in possession is treated as being the beneficial owner of the property, or an appropriate part of that property; if there is more than one, it is necessary to apportion the capital in the fund[1].

A beneficiary who has the right to the income of the fund for a period shorter than his lifetime (however short the period may be) is still treated for inheritance tax as owning the entire settled fund. If the settlement does not produce any income, but instead the beneficiary is entitled to use the capital assets in the fund, he is treated as owning those assets. If the use is enjoyed by more than one beneficiary, the value of the fund is apportioned in accordance with the 'annual value' of their respective interests[2]. Annual value is not defined.

Example 7

A and B, interest in possession beneficiaries under a trust of land, jointly occupy property which is worth £150,000. This capital value must be apportioned to A and B in proportion to the annual value of their respective interests. As their interests are equal the apportionment will be as to £75,000 each.

---

[760]

1   Inheritance Tax Act 1984 s 49(1) (42–44 Halsbury's Statutes (4th Edn) TAXATION).
2   Inheritance Tax Act 1984 s 50(5). It is a moot point whether the decision by trustees of land under the
        Trusts of Land and Appointment of Trustees Act 1996 s 13 (37 Halsbury's Statutes (4th Edn) REAL
        PROPERTY) to exclude an interest in possession beneficiary from occupying trust property changes the
        inheritance tax position: see [1997] LS Gaz 22 January, 30.

[761]

296   Beneficiary entitled to a fixed income

Difficulties may arise where one beneficiary is entitled to a fixed amount of income each year (eg an annuity) and the remaining income is paid to another beneficiary. If the amounts of income paid to the two were compared in the year when a chargeable event occurred, a tax saving could be engineered. Assume, for instance, that the annuity interest terminates so that inheritance tax is charged on its value. The proportion of capital attributable to that interest and, therefore, the inheritance tax would be reduced if the trustees invested in assets producing a high income in that year. As a result, a relatively small proportion of the total income would be payable to the annuitant who would be treated as owning an equivalently small portion of the capital. When a chargeable event affects the interest in the residue of the income (eg, through termination) the trustees could switch the assets into low income producers, thereby achieving a similar reduction in inheritance tax.

The Inheritance Tax Act 1984 Section 50(3) is designed to counter such schemes by providing that the Treasury may prescribe higher and lower income yields which take effect as limits beyond which any fluctuations in the actual income of the fund are ignored[1].

[762]

Example 8

The value of the settlement is £100,000; annual income £15,000. A is entitled to an annuity of £5,000 a year; B to the balance of the income. If there is a chargeable transfer affecting the annuity, A is not treated as owning £33,333 of the capital $\left(\frac{5,000}{15,000} \times 100,000\right)$ but instead a proportion of the Treasury prescribed higher rate yield.

Assume that the prescribed higher rate is 8% on the relevant date; the calculation is: Notional income = 8% of £100,000 = £8,000. A's annuity is £5,000; as a proportion of income it is £5,000 ÷ £8,000; A's share of the capital is, therefore, $\left(\frac{5,000}{8,000}\right)$ x £100,000 = £62,500.

---

[763]

This calculation is used whenever the actual income yield exceeds the prescribed higher rate. The calculation cannot lead to a charge in excess of the total value of the fund.

When a chargeable transfer affecting the interest in the balance of the income occurs, if the actual income produced falls below the prescribed lower rate, the calculation proceeds as if the fund yielded that rate. If both interests in the settlement are chargeable on the same occasion, the prescribed rates do not apply because the entire fund is chargeable.

1   See the Capital Transfer Tax (Settled Property Income Yield) Order 1980, SI 1980/1000.

[764]

297   Lease treated as a settlement
When a lease is treated as a settlement (eg a lease for life or lives not granted for full consideration), the tenant is treated as owning the whole of the leased property save for any part treated as belonging to the landlord. To calculate the landlord's portion it is necessary to compare what he received when the lease was granted with what would have been a full consideration for the lease at that time[1].

[765]

Example 9

(1)   Land worth £100,000 is let to A for his life. The landlord receives no consideration so that A is treated as owning the whole of the leased property (ie £100,000). The granting of the lease is a transfer of value by the landlord of £100,000.

(2)   As above, save that full consideration is furnished. The lease is not treated as a settlement[2]. No inheritance tax will be chargeable on its creation as the landlord's estate does not fall in value.

(3)   Partial consideration (equivalent to 40% of a full consideration) is furnished so that the value of the landlord's interest is 40% of £100,000 = £40,000. The value of the tenant's interest is £60,000 and the granting of the lease is a transfer of value of £60,000.

---

1   Inheritance Tax Act 1984 ss 50(6), 170 (42–44 Halsbury's Statutes (4th Edn) TAXATION).
2   As to the meaning of 'settlement' see Paragraph 283 [712] ante.

[766]

(c) When Inheritance Tax is Charged

298   General
Inheritance tax may be charged on the creation of the settlement and whenever an interest in possession terminates. These events may occur inter vivos or on death: in the former case the Finance Act 1986 limited the definition of the potentially exempt transfer[1] to exclude the creation of interest in possession settlements and chargeable occasions occurring during their lifetime. This limitation, which cuts across the principles of neutrality in the taxation of settlements and the fiction that the life tenant owned the fund, was inserted because of concern that the interest in possession trust would otherwise be used in a scheme for tax avoidance.

It was feared that an interest in possession trust would be set up by a potentially exempt transfer (thereby avoiding an immediate tax charge); quickly terminated (thereby triggering an inheritance tax charge but calculated according to the rates of the chosen life tenant who would be a 'man of straw'); and replaced by a discretionary trust. In this fashion the settlor would, in effect, create a discretionary trust by means of a potentially exempt transfer. The Finance (No 2) Act 1987 removed this limitation on the scope of potentially exempt transfers, but continuing fears that interest in possession trusts would be abused led to the introduction of complex anti-avoidance rules which are considered below.

[767]

Example 10

(1)   S settles property on his daughter D for life, remainder to charity. The creation of the trust is a potentially exempt transfer and there is no question of the anti-avoidance rules applying because the trust ends on D's death.

(2)   S settles property on a stranger, N, for life or until such time as the trustees determine and thereafter the property is to be held on discretionary trust for S's family and relatives. The creation of the trust is a potentially exempt transfer; a later termination of N's life interest will be a chargeable transfer and may trigger the anti-avoidance rules.

(3)   S settles property on D, his daughter, for life remainder to her twins at 21 years. D surrenders her life interest when the twins are (a) 17 years, (b) 18 years, (c) 21 years. The creation of the trusts is a potentially exempt transfer as is the surrender of D's life interest. If the life interest is surrendered at (a), the fund is then held for accumulation and maintenance trusts (a potentially exempt transfer); if surrendered at (b), the transfer is to the twins as interest in possession beneficiaries (a potentially exempt transfer); while finally, if surrendered at (c), the twins are absolutely entitled and so it will be an outright gift and a potentially exempt transfer.

---

[768]

1   As to potentially exempt transfers see the Inheritance Tax Act 1984 s 3A as inserted by the Finance Act 1986 s 101, Sch 19 para 1 and amended by the Finance (No 2) Act 1987 ss 96(1)–(3), 104(4), Sch 9 Pt III (42–44 Halsbury's Statutes (4th Edn) TAXATION).

[769]

299   Charge on death

As the assets in the settlement are treated as part of the property of the deceased life tenant at the time of his death, inheritance tax is charged on the settled fund at the estate rate appropriate to his estate. The tax attributable to the settled property is paid by the trustees. Notice that although the trustees pay this tax, the inclusion of the value of the fund in the deceased's estate may increase the estate rate, thereby causing a higher percentage charge on his free estate.

[770]

Example 11

A settlement consists of securities worth £100,000 and is held for A for life with remainder to B. A has just died and the value of his free estate is £300,000; he made chargeable lifetime transfers of £42,000. The tax rate on transfers up to £242,000 is 0%, thereafter 40% (tax year 2001–2002). Inheritance tax will be calculated as follows:

(1)   Chargeable death estate:
        £300,000 + £100,000 (the settlement) = £400,000.

(2)   Join table at £42,000 (point reached by lifetime transfers).

(3)   Calculate death inheritance tax:
        £200,000 at 0% and £200,000 at 40% = £80,000

(4)	Convert to estate rate:

$$\frac{tax}{estate} \text{ x } 100\text{: ie } \frac{80,000}{400,000} \text{ x } 100 = 20\%.$$

(5)	Inheritance tax attributable to settled property is 20% of £100,000 = £20,000.

[771]

300   Inter vivos terminations

300.1   General

An actual or deemed termination of an interest in possession which occurs during the life of the relevant beneficiary will be a potentially exempt transfer provided that the property is, after that event, held for one or more beneficiaries absolutely (so that the settlement is at an end), or for a further interest in possession or on accumulation and maintenance or disabled trusts. Accordingly, inheritance tax will only be payable in such cases if the former life tenant dies within seven years of the termination. If the above requirements are not satisfied (eg where after the termination the fund is held on discretionary trusts) there is an immediate charge to tax on the termination of the interest in possession and the anti-avoidance rules may be triggered[1].

1   As to the anti-avoidance provisions see Paragraph 301 [791] et seq post.

[772]

300.2   Actual terminations

A charge to inheritance tax may arise if the interest of the life tenant ceases. It is calculated on the basis that the life tenant had made a transfer of value at that time.

Example 12

£100,000 is held on trust for A for life or until remarriage and thereafter for B. If A remarries his life interest terminates and he makes a potentially exempt transfer. Accordingly, should he die within 7 years of that event, inheritance tax will be charged on the value of the fund at the time when his interest ended.

If A never remarried, but consented to an advancement of £50,000 to B, his interest ends in that portion of the fund and he makes a potentially exempt transfer. In the event of that potentially exempt transfer becoming chargeable, inheritance tax will be charged on £50,000. Assume that three years later, A surrenders his life interest in the fund, now worth £120,000. This is another potentially exempt transfer; inheritance tax may therefore be charged (if he dies in the following seven years) on £120,000. Notice that in all cases any tax charge is levied on a value transferred which is 'equal to the value of the property in which his interest subsisted'[1]. The principle of calculating loss to the donor's estate does not apply in these cases.

1   Inheritance Tax Act 1984 s 52(1) (42–44 Halsbury's Statutes (4th Edn) TAXATION).

[773]

300.3   Deemed terminations

If the beneficiary disposes of his beneficial interest in possession, that disposal 'is not a transfer of value, but shall be treated … as the coming to an end of his interest'[1]. The absence of gratuitous intent does not prevent an inheritance tax charge on the termination of beneficial interests in possession. As with actual terminations, the life tenant normally makes a potentially exempt transfer so that tax is only charged if he dies within seven years thereafter.

[774]

Example 13

(1)   A assigns by way of gift his life interest to C. Inheritance tax is charged as if that life interest had terminated. C becomes a tenant *pur autre vie* and when A dies C's interest in possession terminates so raising the possibility of a further inheritance tax charge, if he (ie C) dies within seven years of A. Both A and C have made potentially exempt transfers.

(2)   If, instead of gifting his interest, A sells it to C for £20,000 (full value) at a time when the fund was worth £100,000, A's interest terminates so that he has made a transfer of value of £100,000. However, as he has received £20,000, he has made a potentially exempt transfer equal to the fall in his estate of £80,000 (£100,000 − £20,000).

---

1   Inheritance Tax Act 1984 s 51(1) (42–44 Halsbury's Statutes (4th Edn) TAXATION).

[775]

300.4   Partition of the fund

A partition of the fund between life tenant and remainderman causes the interest in possession to terminate and inheritance tax may be charged (if the life tenant dies within seven years) on that portion of the fund passing to the remainderman[1].

Example 14

A (the life tenant) and B (the remainderman) partition a £100,000 fund in the proportions 40:60. A is treated as making a potentially exempt transfer of £60,000 (£100,000 − £40,000). Any tax payable will come out of the fund to be divided.

---

1   See the Inheritance Tax Act 1984 s 53(2) (42–44 Halsbury's Statutes (4th Edn) TAXATION).

[776]

300.5   Advancements to life tenant or satisfaction of a contingency

If all or part of the capital of the fund is paid to the interest in possession beneficiary, or if he becomes absolutely entitled to the capital, his interest in possession determines *pro tanto*, but no inheritance tax is charged because there is no fall in the value of his estate.

Example 15

Property is settled upon D contingent on his attaining the age of 30 years. At 18 years, he will be entitled to the income of the settlement[1]; an interest in possession will, therefore, arise. At 30 years, that interest terminates, but, as he is now absolutely entitled to the capital, no inheritance tax is chargeable.

---

[777]

1   Trustee Act 1925 s 31 as amended by the Family Law Reform Act 1969 s 1(3), Sch 1 Pt I and by the Trustee Act 2000 s 40(1), Sch 2 para 25 (48 Halsbury's Statutes (4th Edn) TRUSTS AND SETTLEMENTS). Up to the age of 18 years this will be an accumulation and maintenance trust (assuming that the conditions in the Inheritance Tax Act 1984 s 71 (42–44 Halsbury's Statutes (4th Edn) TAXATION) are satisfied). As to this section see Paragraph 127 [316] ante and see vol 40(2) (2001 Reissue) TRUSTS AND SETTLEMENTS Part 11 [6301].

[778]

300.6   Purchase of reversionary interest by life tenant[1]

As the life tenant owns the fund for inheritance tax purposes it follows that his potential tax bill could be reduced were he to purchase a reversionary interest in that settlement. To prevent this result, the reversionary interest is not valued as a part of the life tenant's estate at the time of its purchase (thereby ensuring that his estate has fallen in value); and the commercial bargains exemption[2] does not apply in this case thereby ensuring that the fall in value may be subject to charge even though there is no donative intent.

Assume, for instance, that B has £60,000 in his bank account and is the life tenant of a fund with a capital value of £100,000 (on his death the fund passes to C absolutely). For inheritance tax purposes B owns £160,000. If B were to purchase the reversionary interest in the settlement from C, however, for its market value of £60,000, the result would be as follows:

300.6.1   B's estate has not fallen in value. Originally it included £60,000; after the purchase it includes a reversionary interest worth £60,000 since, although excluded property, the reversionary interest must still be valued.

300.6.2   B's estate now consists of the settlement fund valued at £100,000 and has been depleted by the £60,000 paid for the reversionary interest so that a possible charge to inheritance tax on £60,000 has been avoided.

However, if the reversionary interest is not valued as part of B's estate, then by paying £60,000 for it B has made a potentially exempt transfer of £60,000 which will be taxed if he dies in the following seven years.

[779]

1   See the Inheritance Tax Act 1984 ss 10, 55(1) as amended by the Finance Act 1987 s 58, Sch 8 para 1 (42–44 Halsbury's Statutes (4th Edn) TAXATION).

2   As to dispositions not intended to confer gratuitous benefit see the Inheritance Tax Act 1984 s 10 as amended (see note 1 above).

[780]

300.7   Transactions reducing the value of the property

When the value of the fund is diminished by a depreciatory transaction entered into between the trustees and a beneficiary (or persons connected with him), tax is charged as if the fall in value were a partial termination of the interest in possession[1]. A commercial transaction lacking gratuitous intent is not caught by this provision. In *IRC v Macpherson*[2] the value of pictures held in a trust fund was diminished by an arrangement with a person connected with a beneficiary that, in return for taking over care, custody and insurance of the pictures, he was entitled to keep the pictures for some 14 years. Although this arrangement was a commercial transaction, lacking gratuitous intent when looked at in isolation, it was associated with a subsequent operation (the appointment of a protected life interest) which did confer a gratuitous benefit so that the exception for commercial transactions did not apply and the reduction in value of the fund was subject to charge.

[781]

Example 16

Trustees grant a 50-year lease of a property worth £100,000 at a peppercorn rent to the brother of a reversionary beneficiary. As a result the property left in the settlement is the freehold reversion worth only £20,000. The granting of the lease is a depreciatory transaction which causes the value of the fund to fall by £80,000 and, as it is made with a person connected with a beneficiary, inheritance tax may be levied as if the life interest in £80,000 had ended. (Contrast the position if the lease had been granted to the brother in return for a commercial rent.)

---

1   Inheritance Tax Act 1984 s 52(3) (42–44 Halsbury's Statutes (4th Edn) TAXATION).
2   *IRC v Macpherson* [1989] AC 159, [1988] 2 All ER 753, HL.

[782]–[790]

(d) Anti-avoidance

301   General

A non-interest in possession trust (typically a discretionary trust) cannot be set up by a potentially exempt transfer, and this prohibition cannot be circumvented by channelling property into such a trust via an interest in possession granted to a 'man of straw'.

[791]

302   When the anti-avoidance rules apply

The three prerequisites are that an interest in possession trust is set up by means of a potentially exempt transfer; it terminates either as a result of the life tenant dying or by his interest ceasing inter vivos; and at that time a non-interest in possession trust (other than an accumulation and maintenance settlement) arises. If the termination occurs within seven years of the creation of the original interest in possession trust and at a time when the settlor is still alive, the anti-avoidance rules apply[1].

---

1   See the Inheritance Tax Act 1984 ss 54A, 54B as inserted by the Finance (No 2) Act 1987 s 96(1), (6), Sch 7 para 1 (42–44 Halsbury's Statutes (4th Edn) TAXATION).

[792]

303   Operation of the rules[1]

The inheritance tax charge on the property at the time when the interest in possession ends is the higher of two calculations. First, the inheritance tax that would arise under normal charging principles: ie by taxing the fund as if the transfer had been made by the life tenant at the time of termination. The rates of charge will be either half rates (where there is an inter vivos termination) or full death rates when termination occurs because of the death of the life tenant. The second calculation deems the settled property to have been transferred at the time of termination by a hypothetical transferor who in the preceding seven years had made chargeable transfers equal in value to those made by the settlor in the seven years before he created the settlement. For the purpose of this second calculation half rates are used.

[793]

Example 17

Assume that in 1989 S settles £90,000 on trust for P for life or until remarriage and thereafter on discretionary trusts for S's relatives and friends. His cumulative total at that time is £140,000 and he has made potentially exempt transfers of £85,000. P remarries one year later at a time when she has made chargeable transfers of £50,000; potentially exempt transfers of £45,000; and when the settled property is worth £110,000.

(1)   The anti-avoidance provisions are relevant because the conditions for their operation are satisfied.

(2)   Inheritance tax, ignoring these provisions, would be calculated at P's rates: ie on a chargeable transfer from £50,000 to £160,000. Under these provisions, however, the tax may be calculated by taking a hypothetical transferor who has S's cumulative total at the time when he created the trust; therefore on this calculation the £110,000 will be taxed as a chargeable transfer from £140,000 to £250,000. In this example, the second calculation will be adopted because a greater charge to inheritance tax results. This tax must be paid by the trustees.

[794]

(3)   Assume that either S or P died after the termination of the interest in possession trust. This may result in a recalculation of the inheritance tax liability (in this example potentially exempt transfers made by that person in the seven years before death would become chargeable). So far as the anti-avoidance rules are concerned, however, there is no question of disturbing the basis on which the inheritance tax calculation was made in the first place. Therefore as was shown in (2) above, the greater tax was produced by taking the hypothetical transferor and, therefore, the subsequent death of P is irrelevant since it cannot be used to switch the basis of computation to P's cumulative total. By contrast, the death of S may involve additional inheritance tax liability since his potentially exempt transfers of £85,000 may now become chargeable and therefore included in the hypothetical transferor's total when the settlement was created.

---

1   See the Inheritance Tax Act 1984 ss 54A, 54B as inserted by the Finance (No 2) Act 1987 s 96(1), (6), Sch 7 para 1 (42–44 Halsbury's Statutes (4th Edn) TAXATION).

[795]

304   Escaping from the anti-avoidance rules[1]

The following points should be noted:

304.1   where the interest in possession continues for seven years the anti-avoidance rules do not apply;

304.2   the anti-avoidance rules are not in point if the settlement was created without an immediate interest in possession (eg if the settlor started with an accumulation and maintenance trust which subsequently turned into an interest in possession trust), or if the settlement was created by means of an exempt transfer (eg if a life interest was given to the settlor's spouse and that interest was subsequently terminated in favour of a discretionary trust);

304.3   trustees can prevent the anti-avoidance rules from applying if, within six months of the ending of the interest in possession, they terminate the discretionary trust either by an absolute appointment or by creating a further life interest; and

304.4   it is always possible to channel property into a discretionary trust by a potentially exempt transfer, if an outright gift is made to another individual (a potentially exempt transfer) who then settles the gifted property on the appropriate discretionary trusts (a chargeable transfer but taxed at his rates).

[796]

1   See the Inheritance Tax Act 1984 ss 54A, 54B as inserted by the Finance (No 2) Act 1987 s 96(1), (6), Sch 7 para 1 (42–44 Halsbury's Statutes (4th Edn) TAXATION). The immediate inheritance tax charge is the main reason why relatively few inter vivos discretionary trusts are created. Most that are involve transfers falling within the settlor's nil rate band. In other cases, schemes have been devised to produce the result that although the property settled exceeds the nil rate band of the settlor, because of rights which he retains under the settlement the loss to his estate remains relatively small. At the time of writing, such arrangements are being tested before the courts: see *Melville v IRC* [2000] STC 628.

[797]

(e) Exemptions and Reliefs

305   Reverter to settlor or spouse[1]

If, on the termination of an interest in possession, property reverts to the settlor, there is no charge to inheritance tax unless the settlor (or his spouse) had acquired his interest for money or money's worth. This exemption also applies when the property passes to the settlor's spouse or (if the settlor is dead) his widow or widower, so long as that reverter occurs within two years of his death.

Example 18

J creates a settlement of £100,000 in favour of K for life. When K dies and the property reverts to the settlor no inheritance tax is charged. Contrast the position, if the settlement provided that the fund was to pass to L on the death of the life tenant, but the settlor's wife had purchased that remainder interest and given it to her husband as a gift. On the death of the life tenant, although the property reverts to the settlor, the normal charge to inheritance tax applies.

---

[798]

1   See the Inheritance Tax Act 1984 s 53(3)–(5) (42–44 Halsbury's Statutes (4th Edn) TAXATION). For
     the capital gains tax position see the Taxation of Chargeable Gains Act 1992 s 73(1)(b) as amended by
     the Finance Act 1996 s 201, Sch 39 para 6(2), (4), (5) (42–44 Halsbury's Statutes (4th Edn)
     TAXATION). For the use of this provision in the context of providing for a surviving parent see
     Form 14 [1179] post.

[799]

306   Life tenant's exemptions

The spouse exemption is available on the termination of the interest in possession if the
person who then becomes entitled, whether absolutely or to another interest in
possession, is the spouse of the former life tenant. Furthermore, the life tenant's annual
exemption and the exemption for gifts in consideration of marriage may be available on
the inter vivos termination of an interest in possession if the life tenant so elects[1].

Although there is no duty to report the making of a potentially exempt transfer, the
life tenant should give the appropriate notice to the trustees indicating that he wishes the
transfer to be covered by his relevant exemption. If this procedure is carried out, should
the potentially exempt transfer become chargeable, the appropriate exemption will be
available.

1   See the Inheritance Tax Act 1984 s 57 (42–44 Halsbury's Statutes (4th Edn) TAXATION).

[800]

307   Estate duty—surviving spouse exemption

The continuation of the estate duty relief available when property was left on death to a
surviving spouse in such circumstances that the spouse was not competent to dispose of
it (eg was given a life interest) is preserved by the Inheritance Tax Act 1984[1]. The first
spouse must have died before 13 November 1974 and the relief ensures that tax is not
charged on the termination of the surviving spouse's interest in the property (whether
that occurs inter vivos or on death).

1   See the Inheritance Tax Act 1984 s 273, Sch 6 para 2 (42–44 Halsbury's Statutes (4th Edn)
     TAXATION).

[801]

308   Excluded property

If the settlement contains excluded property, inheritance tax is not charged on that
portion of the fund[1].

1   Inheritance Tax Act 1984 ss 5(1), 53(1) (42–44 Halsbury's Statutes (4th Edn) TAXATION).

[802]

309   Dispositions for maintenance of family

If the interest in possession is disposed of for the purpose of maintaining the disponer's
child or supporting a dependent relative, inheritance tax is not charged[1].

1   See the Inheritance Tax Act 1984 s 11 (42–44 Halsbury's Statutes (4th Edn) TAXATION).

[803]

310   Charities

Tax is not charged if on the termination of the interest in possession the property is held
on trust for charitable purposes.

[804]

311   Protective trusts

The forfeiture of a protected life interest is not chargeable[1].

1   As to protective trusts see the Inheritance Tax Act 1984 ss 73, 88 (42–44 Halsbury's Statutes (4th Edn) TAXATION) and Paragraph 123 [305] ante. For a detailed consideration see vol 40(2) (2001 Reissue) TRUSTS AND SETTLEMENTS Part 12 [6901].

[805]

312   Variations and disclaimers

Dispositions of the deceased (made by will, on intestacy or otherwise) may be redirected after death by means of an instrument of variation or disclaimer without incurring a second inheritance tax charge. Disclaimers are possible in the case both of settlements created by the deceased[1] and pre-existing settlements in which the death has resulted in a person becoming entitled to an interest in settled property[2]. Variations, on the other hand, are only permitted for settlements created on death by the deceased, not for settlements in which the deceased had been the beneficiary.

Example 19

If A leaves a life interest to his wife remainder to their daughter, Mrs A can accelerate the daughter's interest by a disclaimer of her life interest. Alternatively, if Mrs A has already received income from the interest (so that it is too late to disclaim), she may achieve the same result by a variation.

---

[806]

1   See the Inheritance Tax Act 1984 s 142 as amended by the Finance Act 1986 s 101(1), (3), Sch 19 para 24 (42–44 Halsbury's Statutes (4th Edn) TAXATION).
2   Inheritance Tax Act 1984 s 93.

[807]

313   Quick succession relief

This relief is similar to that for unsettled property. The first chargeable transfer may be either the creation of the settlement or any subsequent termination of an interest in possession (whether that termination occurs inter vivos or on death). Therefore, it can be voluntarily used by the life tenant surrendering or assigning his interest (contrast unsettled property when it is only available on a death[1].

1   See the Inheritance Tax Act 1984 s 141 (42–44 Halsbury's Statutes (4th Edn) TAXATION).

[808]

314   Reliefs for business and agricultural property

In a settlement containing business property that property is treated as belonging to the life tenant who must fulfil the conditions for relief[1]. Similar principles operate for agricultural relief: ie the life tenant must satisfy the conditions of two years' occupation or seven years' ownership (ownership by the trustees being attributed to the life tenant)[2].

[809]

1   As to business property relief see the Inheritance Tax Act 1984 ss 103–114 (42–44 Halsbury's Statutes (4th Edn) TAXATION).

2   Inheritance Tax Act 1984 ss 115–124. With the availability of relief at 100% it is crucial to ensure wherever possible that the qualifying conditions are met.

[810]

(f) Reversionary Interests

315 Taxation

As reversionary interests are generally excluded property their disposition does not lead to an inheritance tax charge. In the following cases, however, reversionary interests are not excluded property. This is to prevent their use as a tax avoidance device[1].

315.1   A sale of a reversionary interest to a beneficiary under the same trust, who is entitled to a prior interest[2].

315.2   A disposition of a reversionary interest which has at any time, and by any person, been acquired for a consideration in money or money's worth.

315.3   A disposition of a reversionary interest if it is one to which either the settlor or his spouse is, or has been, beneficially entitled.

315.4   The disposition of a reversionary interest where that interest is expectant upon the termination of a lease which is treated as a settlement. The result is that the landlord's reversion is treated in the same way as a reversionary interest purchased for money or money's worth so that on any disposition of it, inheritance tax may be charged.

[811]

1   See the Inheritance Tax Act 1984 s 48 as amended by the Finance Act 1996 s 154(7), (9), Sch 28 para 8 (42–44 Halsbury's Statutes (4th Edn) TAXATION).

2   As to the purchase of a reversionary interest by a life tenant see Paragraph 300.6 [779] ante.

[812]–[820]

6: TREATMENT OF SETTLEMENTS WITHOUT AN INTEREST IN POSSESSION

(a) Introduction and Terminology

316 General

The method of charging settlements lacking an interest in possession is totally different from that for settlements with such an interest. Instead of attributing the fund to one of the beneficiaries, it is the settlement itself which is the taxable entity for inheritance tax. Like an individual, it must keep a record of chargeable transfers made, although, unlike the individual, it will never die and so will only be taxed at half rates. For convenience this section discusses the taxing provisions by reference to the discretionary trust which is the most significant of the 'no interest in possession' settlements. In fact the category of non-interest in possession settlement is wider than discretionary trusts, catching for instance, the type of settlement in *Pearson v IRC*[1] and trusts where the beneficiaries' interests are contingent but which do not satisfy the requirement for an accumulation and maintenance trust.

[821]

Example 20

(1)   A fund of £100,000 is held upon trust for such of A, B, C, D, E and F as the trustees may in their absolute discretion (which extends over both income and capital) think appropriate. The trust is one without an interest in possession.

(2)   A father settles property on trust for his son contingent on his attaining 30 years. The son is aged 21 years at the date of the settlement and the income is to be accumulated until son attains 30 years. There is no interest in possession.

Inheritance tax is charged on 'relevant property'[2] defined as settled property (other than excluded property) in which there is no qualifying interest in possession, with the exception of property settled on accumulation and maintenance trusts and certain other special trusts considered below[3].

A qualifying interest in possession is one owned beneficially by an individual or, in restricted circumstances, by a company. If within one settlement there exists an interest in possession in a part only of the settled property, the charge to inheritance tax under the discretionary trust provisions is on the portion which lacks such an interest.

[822]

1   *Pearson v IRC* [1981] AC 753, [1980] 2 All ER 479, HL. See further Paragraph 286.3 [727] ante.
2   Inheritance Tax Act 1984 s 58(1) (42–44 Halsbury's Statutes (4th Edn) TAXATION).
3   As to accumulation and maintenance trusts see Paragraph 127 [316] ante and vol 40(2) (2001 Reissue) TRUSTS AND SETTLEMENTS Part 11 [6301]. As to special trusts see Paragraph 329 [873] et seq post.

[823]

(b)   Method of Charge

317   Main features

The central feature is the periodic or anniversary charge imposed upon discretionary trusts at ten-yearly intervals. The anniversary is calculated from the date on which the trust was created[1].

Example 21

(1)   S creates a discretionary trust on 1 January 1989. The first anniversary charge will fall on 1 January 1999; the next on 1 January 2009 and so on. If the trust had been created by will and he had died on 31 December 1988, that date marks the creation of the settlement[2].

(2)   S creates (in 1988) a settlement in favour of his wife A for life; thereafter for such of his three daughters as the trustees may in their absolute discretion select. A dies in 1989. For inheritance tax purposes the discretionary trust is created by A on her death[3]. The ten-year anniversary, however, runs from the creation of the original settlement in 1988[4].

Apart from the anniversary charge, inheritance tax is also levied (the 'exit charge') on the happening of certain events. In general, the tax then charged is a proportion of the last periodic charge. Special charging provisions operate for chargeable events which occur before the first ten-year anniversary when the first periodic charge is levied.

[824]

1   Inheritance Tax Act 1984 s 61(1) (42–44 Halsbury's Statutes (4th Edn) TAXATION).
2   Inheritance Tax Act 1984 s 83.
3   Inheritance Tax Act 1984 s 80.
4   Inheritance Tax Act 1984 s 61(2).

[825]

318   Creation of the settlement

The creation of the settlement will, generally, be a chargeable transfer of value by the settlor for inheritance tax purposes (it cannot be a potentially exempt transfer). The following matters should be noted:

318.1   If the settlement is created inter vivos, grossing-up applies unless the inheritance tax is paid out of the settled property.

318.2   The cumulative total of chargeable transfers made by the settlor is crucial because it forms part of the cumulative total of the settlement on all future chargeable occasions (ie his transfers do not drop out of the cumulative total after seven years). Therefore, in order to calculate the correct inheritance tax charge it is essential that the trustees know the settlor's cumulative total at the date when he created the trust. When, as a result of the settlor's fraud, wilful default or neglect, there is an underpayment of inheritance tax, the Inland Revenue may recover that sum from the trustees outside the normal six-year time limit. In such cases the time limit is six years from the date when the impropriety comes to the notice of the Inland Revenue[1]. Obviously a problem would arise for trustees if at the time when the underpayment came to light they held insufficient assets to discharge the extra inheritance tax because they could be made personally liable for the tax unpaid. The Inland Revenue has, however, stated that where the trustees have acted in good faith and hold insufficient settlement assets it will not seek to recover any unpaid tax from them personally[2].

[826]

318.3   A 'related settlement' is another settlement created by the same settlor on the same day as the discretionary trust (other than a charitable trust). Generally such settlements should be avoided.

318.4   Additions of property by the original settlor to his settlement should be avoided. If property is added by a person other than the original settlor, the addition is treated as a separate settlement.

Particular problems may arise for the trustees if the settlor dies within seven years of creating the trust. If this happens potentially exempt transfers made before the settlement was created and within seven years of his death become chargeable so that tax on creation of the settlement and the computation of any exit charge made during this period may need to be recalculated. If extra tax becomes payable this is primarily the responsibility of the settlement trustees and their liability is not limited to settlement property in their hands at that time. Given this danger it obviously is prudent for trustees who are distributing property from the discretionary trust within the first seven years to retain sufficient funds or take suitable indemnities to cover their contingent inheritance tax liability.

[827]

Example 22

S makes the following transfers of value:

(1)   May 1997; £250,000 to his sister B (a potentially exempt transfer).

(2)   May 1998; £80,000 to a family discretionary trust.

(3)   In May 2000 the trustees distribute the entire fund to the beneficiaries and in May 2001 S dies.

As a result of his death, the 1997 potentially exempt transfer is chargeable (the resultant inheritance tax is primarily the responsibility of B) and in addition tax on the creation of the settlement must be recalculated. When it was set up the potentially exempt transfer was ignored so that the transfer fell within S's nil rate band. With his death, however, inheritance tax must be calculated, at the rates in force in May 2001, on transfers from £250,000 to £330,000. In addition, no inheritance tax will have been charged on the distribution of the fund and therefore a recomputation is again necessary with the trustees being primarily accountable for the resulting bill.

[828]

1   Inheritance Tax Act 1984 s 240(3) (42–44 Halsbury's Statutes (4th Edn) TAXATION).
2   (1984) LS Gaz 3517.

[829]

319   Exit charges before the first ten-year anniversary

319.1   Arising of an exit charge

An exit charge arises whenever property in the settlement ceases to be relevant property[1]. Therefore, if the trustees appoint property to a beneficiary or if an interest in possession arises in any portion of the fund, there is an inheritance tax charge to the extent of the property ceasing to be held on discretionary trusts. A charge is also imposed if the trustees make a disposition as a result of which the value of relevant property comprised in the settlement falls (a 'depreciatory transaction'; notice that there is no requirement that the transaction be made with a beneficiary or with a person connected with him)[2].

If the resultant inheritance tax is paid out of the property that is left in a continuing discretionary trust, grossing-up applies.

The exit charge does not apply to a payment of costs or expenses (so long as fairly attributable to the relevant property), nor does it catch a payment which is income of any person for the purposes of income tax[3].

[830]

1   Inheritance Tax Act 1984 s 65(1) (42–44 Halsbury's Statutes (4th Edn) TAXATION).
2   In the case of interest in possession trusts cf Paragraph 300.7 [781] ante.
3   Inheritance Tax Act 1984 s 65(5).

[831]

319.2   Calculation of the settlement rate

The rate of inheritance tax to be charged is based upon half the full inheritance tax rates, even if the trust was set up under the will of the settlor. The rate of tax actually payable is then 30% of those rates applicable to a hypothetical chargeable transfer which is the sum of the following:

319.2.1   the value of the property in the settlement immediately after it commenced;

319.2.2   the value (at the date of the addition) of any added property; and

319.2.3   the value of property in a related settlement (valued immediately after it commenced)[1].

[832]

No account is taken of any rise or fall in the value of the settled fund and the value comprised in the settlement, and in any related settlement, can include property subject to an interest in possession.

Tax at half rates on this hypothetical transfer is calculated by joining the table at the point reached by the cumulative total of previous chargeable transfers made by the settlor in the seven years before he created the settlement. Other chargeable transfers made on the same day as the settlement are ignored and, therefore, if the settlement was created on death, other gifts made in the will or on intestacy are ignored[2].

The resultant tax is converted to an average rate (the equivalent of an estate rate) and 30% of that rate is then taken. The resultant rate (the 'settlement rate') is used as the basis for calculating the exit charge.

[833]

Example 23

J settles £200,000 on discretionary trusts on 1 April 2001. His total chargeable transfers immediately before that date stood at £60,000. The trustees pay the inheritance tax. If an exit charge arises before the first ten-year anniversary of the fund (1 April 2011) the settlement rate would be calculated as follows:

(1)   Calculate the hypothetical chargeable transfer. As there is no added property and no related settlement it comprises only the value of the property in the settlement immediately after its creation (ie £200,000).

(2)   Cumulate the £200,000 with the previous chargeable transfers of J (ie £60,000). Taking inheritance tax rates current at the time when the exit charge arises, tax on transfers between £60,000 and £260,000 is £3,600 (using tax year 2001–02 rates).

(3)   The tax converted to a percentage rate is 1.8%; 30% of that rate produces a settlement rate of 0.54%.

---

[834]

1   Inheritance Tax Act 1984 s 68(5) (42–44 Halsbury's Statutes (4th Edn) TAXATION).
2   See the Inheritance Tax Act 1984 s 68(4)(b) as amended by the Finance Act 1986 s 101(1), (3), Sch 19 para 18.

[835]

319.3   Tax charged

The charge is on the fall in value of the fund. To establish the rate of charge, a further proportion of the settlement rate must be calculated equal to one-fortieth of the settlement rate for each complete successive quarter that has elapsed from the creation of the settlement to the date of the exit charge. That proportion of the settlement rate is applied to the chargeable transfer (the 'effective rate').

[836]

Example 24

Assume in Example 23[1] that on 25 March 2003 there was an exit charge on £20,000 ceasing to be relevant property. The effective rate of inheritance tax is calculated as follows (using 2001–02 rates):

(1)   Take completed quarters since the settlement was created, ie seven.

(2)   Take 7/40ths of the 'settlement rate' (0.54%) to discover the effective rate = 0.0945%.

(3)   The effective rate is applied to the fall in value of the relevant property. The inheritance tax is, therefore, £18.90 if the tax is borne by the beneficiary; or £18.92 if borne by the remaining fund.

There is no charge on events that occur in the first three months of the settlement[2] nor, where the trust was set up by the settlor on his death, on events occurring within two years of that death[3].

[837]

1   Ie Example 23 [834] ante.
2   Inheritance Tax Act 1984 s 65(4) (42–44 Halsbury's Statutes (4th Edn) TAXATION).
3   Inheritance Tax Act 1984 s 144(2).

[838]

320   Charge on the first ten-year anniversary

320.1   Property that is charged

The charge is levied on the value of the relevant property comprised in the settlement immediately before the anniversary[1] and at first sight no distinction appears to be drawn between income and capital in the fund. The Inland Revenue accepts, however, that income only becomes relevant property, and therefore subject to charge, when it has been accumulated[2]. Pending accumulation the income is not subject to the anniversary charge and can, of course, be distributed free from any exit charge. The crucial question is, therefore, at what moment is income accumulated? Obviously accumulation occurs once an irrevocable decision to that effect has been taken by trustees, it may also occur after a reasonable time for distribution has passed[3]. The legislation gives no guidance on what property is treated as being distributed first: ie if an appointment is made by the trustees out of property comprised in the settlement, does it come out of the original capital or out of accumulations of income? As a reduced charge may apply to property which has been added to the trust (such as accumulated income) this is an important omission.

The assets in the fund are valued according to general principles and, if they include business or agricultural property, the reliefs appropriate to that property apply, subject to satisfaction of the relevant conditions. Any inheritance tax charged on such property is payable by instalments[4].

[839]

1   See the Inheritance Tax Act 1984 s 64 (42–44 Halsbury's Statutes (4th Edn) TAXATION).
2   See Inland Revenue Statement of Practice SP 8/86 (10 November 1986) and see [1989] *Capital Taxes News* vol 8, May 1989.
3   But see *Re Locker's Settlement Trusts, Meachem v Sachs* [1978] 1 All ER 216, [1977] 1 WLR 1323 where income which arose between 1965 and 1968 was still available for distribution in 1977.
4   See the Inheritance Tax Act 1984 ss 103–114, 115–124B, 227 as amended.

[840]

320.2   Calculation of the rate of inheritance tax

Half rates are used in calculating the inheritance tax rate and, as with the exit charge[1], the calculation depends upon a hypothetical chargeable transfer. The calculation is as follows:

320.2.1   Calculate the hypothetical chargeable transfer which is made up of the sum of the following:

320.2.1.1   the value of relevant property comprised in the settlement immediately before the anniversary;

320.2.1.2   the value, immediately after it was created, of property comprised in a related settlement; and

320.2.1.3   the value, at the date when the settlement was created, of any non-relevant property then in the settlement which has not subsequently become relevant property.

Normally the hypothetical chargeable transfer will be made up exclusively of property falling within Paragraph 320.2.1.1 above. Property within Paragraphs 320.2.1.2 and 320.2.1.3 above, affects the rate of inheritance tax to be charged without itself being taxed. Related settlements are included because transfers made on the same day as the creation of the settlement are normally ignored and, therefore, an inheritance tax advantage could be achieved if the settlor were to set up a series of small funds rather than one large fund. Non-relevant property in the settlement is included because the trustees could switch the values between the two portions of the fund.

[841]

320.2.2   Calculate tax at half rates on the hypothetical chargeable transfer by joining the table at the point reached by:

320.2.2.1   the chargeable transfers of the settlor made in the seven years before he created the settlement; and

320.2.2.2   chargeable transfers made by the settlement in the first ten years. Where a settlement was created after 26 March 1974 and before 9 March 1982, distribution payments (as defined by the inheritance tax charging regime in force between those dates) must also be cumulated[2].

Discretionary settlements therefore have their own total of chargeable transfers, with transfers over a ten-year period being cumulated (the seven-year period used for individuals is not employed for discretionary trusts). The unique feature of a settlement's cumulation lies in the inclusion (and they never drop out) of chargeable transfers of the settlor in the seven years before the settlement is created.

320.2.3   The inheritance tax is converted to a percentage and 30% of that rate is then taken and charged upon the relevant property in the settlement. For the tax year 2001–02 the highest rate of inheritance tax is 20% (half of 40%). The highest effective rate (anniversary rate) is, therefore, 30% of 20%, ie 6%. Where the settlement comprises business property qualifying for 50% relief, this effective rate falls to 3% and assuming that the option to pay in instalments is exercised, the annual charge over the ten-year period becomes a mere 0.3%.

[842]

Example 25

Take the facts of Example 24[3] (ie, original fund £200,000, exit charge on £20,000; previous transfers of settlor £60,000). In addition, assume J had created a second settlement of £15,000 on 1 April 2001. The fund is worth £205,000 at the first ten-year anniversary

(1)   Relevant property to be taxed is £205,000.

(2)   Calculate hypothetical chargeable transfer:

		£
(a)	Relevant property, as above	205,000
(b)	Property in related settlement	15,000
		£220,000

(3)   Settlement's cumulative inheritance tax total:

	£
Settlor's earlier transfers	60,000
Chargeable transfers of trustees in the preceding 10 years	20,000
	£80,000

(4)   Tax from the table (at half rates) on transfers from £80,000 to £300,000 (£220,000 + £80,000) = £11,600 (using 2001–02 rates) so that, as a percentage rate, inheritance tax is 5.27%.

(5)   The effective rate is 30% of 5.27% = 1.58%.

Tax payable is £205,000 x 1.58% = £3,239.

[843]–[844]

1   As to exit charges before the first ten-year anniversary see Paragraph 319 [830] ante.
2   Inheritance Tax Act 1984 s 66(6) (42–44 Halsbury's Statutes (4th Edn) TAXATION).
3   Ie Example 24 [837] ante.

[845]

321   Exit charges after the first anniversary charge and between anniversaries

The same events trigger an exit charge after the first ten-year anniversary as before it[1]. The inheritance tax charge is levied on the fall in value of the fund with grossing-up, if necessary. The rate of charge is a proportion of the effective rate charged at the first ten-year anniversary. That proportion is one-fortieth for each complete quarter from the date of the first anniversary charge to the date of the exit charge[2].

Example 26

Continuing Example 25[3], exactly 15 months later the trustees appoint £25,000 to a beneficiary. The inheritance tax (assuming no grossing up) will be:
£25,000 x 1.58% x 5/40 (five quarters since last ten year anniversary) = £49.37.

---

[846]

If the rates of inheritance tax have been reduced (including the raising of the rate bands) between the anniversary and exit charges, the lower rates apply to the exit charge and, therefore, the rate of charge on the first anniversary has to be recalculated at those rates[4]. So long as the inheritance tax rate band remains linked to rises in the retail prices index[5] recalculation is likely to be the norm.

No exit charge is levied if the chargeable event occurs within the first quarter following the anniversary charge.

[847]

1   As to exit charges before the first ten-year anniversary see Paragraph 319 [830] ante.
2   See the Inheritance Tax Act 1984 s 69 (42–44 Halsbury's Statutes (4th Edn) TAXATION).
3   Ie Example 25 [843] ante.
4   Inheritance Tax Act 1984 s 9, Sch 2 para 3 as amended.
5   See the Inheritance Tax Act 1984 s 8 as amended.

[848]

322   Later periodic charges

The principles that applied on the first ten-year anniversary operate on subsequent ten-year anniversaries[1]. So far as the hypothetical chargeable transfer is concerned the same items are included (so that the value of property in a related settlement and of non-relevant property in the settlement is always included). The cumulative total of the fund includes, as before, the chargeable transfers of the settlor made in the seven years before he created the settlement and the transfers out of the settlement in the ten years immediately preceding the anniversary (earlier transfers by the settlement fall out of the cumulative total). The remaining stages of the calculation are unaltered.

1   As to the charge on the first ten-year anniversary see Paragraph 320 [839] ante.

[849]

323   Technical problems

323.1   General

The basic structure of the charging provisions is relatively straightforward. The charge to inheritance tax is built upon a series of periodic charges with interim charges (where appropriate) which are levied at a fraction of the full periodic charge. A number of technical matters should be noted.

[850]

323.2   Reduction in the rate of the anniversary charge

If property has not been in the settlement for the entire preceding ten years (as will be the case when income is accumulated during that period) there is a proportionate reduction in the charge[1]. The reduction in the periodic rate is calculated by reference to the number of completed quarters which expired before the property became relevant property in the settlement. This proportionate reduction in the effective rate of the periodic charge does not affect the calculation of inheritance tax on events occurring after the anniversary; ie any exit charge is at the full effective rate.

The legislation does not contain provisions which enable specific property to be identified. Therefore, the reduction mentioned above applies to the value of the relevant property in the fund at the ten-year anniversary 'attributable' to property which was not relevant property throughout the preceding ten years. Presumably, therefore, some sort of proportionate calculation is necessary where the value of the fund has shown an increase. Furthermore, if accumulated income is caught by the anniversary charge, a separate calculation has to be made with regard to each separate accumulation, as being property which has not been in the settlement for the whole of the previous decade[2].

[851]

1   Inheritance Tax Act 1984 s 66(2) (42–44 Halsbury's Statutes (4th Edn) TAXATION).
2   See Inland Revenue Statement of Practice SP 8/86 (10 November 1986) and see Paragraph 323.1 [850] ante.

[852]

323.3   Transfers between settlements

Legislation prevents a tax advantage from switching property between discretionary settlements by providing that such property remains comprised in the first settlement. Accordingly, property cannot be moved out of a discretionary trust to avoid an anniversary charge; property cannot be switched from a fund with a high cumulative total to one with a lower total; and the transfer of a property from one discretionary fund to another is not chargeable[1].

1   Inheritance Tax Act 1984 s 81 (42–44 Halsbury's Statutes (4th Edn) TAXATION) and see [1989] *Capital Taxes News* vol 8 p 219.

[853]

323.4   Added property

Special rules operate if, after the settlement commenced (and after 8 March 1982), the settlor makes a chargeable transfer as a result of which the value of the property comprised in the settlement is increased[1]. Note that it is only additions by the settlor that trigger these provisions and that it is the value of the fund which must have increased and not necessarily the amount of property in that fund. A transfer which has the effect of increasing the value of the fund is ignored if it was not primarily intended to have that effect and did not in fact increase the value by more than 5%.

Example 27

S, the settlor, creates in 2001 a discretionary trust of stocks and share in S Ltd and the benefit of a life insurance policy on S's life.

(1)   Each year S adds to the settlement property equal to his annual inheritance tax exemption.

(2)   S continues to pay the premium on the life policy each year.

(3)   S transfers further shares in S Ltd.

> The special rules for added property do not apply in either case (1) or (2), because S is not making a chargeable transfer; the first transfer is covered by his annual exemption and the second by the exemption for normal expenditure out of income. The transfer of further shares to the fund, however, is caught by the provisions relating to added property[2].

[854]

If the added property provisions apply, the calculation of the periodic charge which immediately follows the addition is modified. For the purposes of the hypothetical chargeable transfer, the cumulative total of the settlor's chargeable transfers is the higher of the totals:

323.4.1   immediately before creating the settlement plus transfers made by the settlement before the addition; and

323.4.2   immediately before transferring the added property, deducting from this latter total the transfer made on creation of the settlement and a transfer to any related settlement.

Accordingly, the settlor should avoid additions because they may cause more inheritance tax to be charged at the next anniversary. It is, therefore, preferable to create a separate settlement.

[855]

1   Inheritance Tax Act 1984 s 67(1) (42–44 Halsbury's Statutes (4th Edn) TAXATION).
2   Inheritance Tax Act 1984 s 67 as amended by the Finance Act 1986 s 101(1), (3), Sch 19 para 17.

[856]

323.5   The timing of the exit charge

Assume that a discretionary trust has been in existence for nearly ten years and that the trustees now wish to distribute all or part of the fund to the beneficiaries. Are they better off doing so just before the ten-year anniversary or should they wait until just after that anniversary? Generally it is advantageous to distribute before an anniversary because the inheritance tax payable is calculated at rates then in force but on historic values; ie on the value of the fund when it was settled or at the last ten-year anniversary. By contrast, if the trustees delay until after the anniversary, inheritance tax (still at current rates) is then assessed on the present value of the fund. To this general proposition, one major exception exists which may well be the result of defective drafting in the legislation. It relates to a fund consisting of property qualifying for either business relief or agricultural relief at 50% when the fund was set up. In this situation, trustees should not break up the fund immediately before the first anniversary. (This problem does not arise if 100% relief is available on the anniversary.)

[857]–[865]

(c) Exemptions and Reliefs

324   Exemptions and reliefs

Many of the exemptions from inheritance tax do not apply to property in discretionary trusts; eg the annual exemption, the marriage exemption, and the exemption for normal expenditure out of income. There is also no exemption if the settled fund reverts to either the settlor or his spouse (and note that if the settlor is a beneficiary the reservation of benefit provisions apply). Business and agricultural property relief may, however, be available, provided that the necessary conditions for the relief are met by the trustees. There is no question of any aggregation with similar property owned by a discretionary beneficiary.

Exit charges are not levied in certain cases when property leaves the settlement, eg:

324.1   Property ceasing to be relevant property within three months of the creation of the trust, or of an anniversary charge, or within two years of creation (if the trust was set up on death)[1] is not subject to an exit charge.

324.2   Property may pass, without attracting an exit charge, to such privileged trusts as employee trusts[2]; maintenance funds for historic buildings[3]; charities (with no time limits)[4]; political parties in accordance with the exemption in the Inheritance Tax Act 1984 Section 24[5]; national heritage bodies[6]. There is no exemption in the case of property passing into an accumulation and maintenance trust.

If a discretionary fund includes excluded property, the periodic and exit charges do not apply to that portion of the fund.

[866]

1   In connection with discretionary trusts see *Frankland v IRC* [1996] STC 735.
2   Inheritance Tax Act 1984 s 75 (42–44 Halsbury's Statutes (4th Edn) TAXATION).
3   Inheritance Tax Act 1984 s 77, Sch 4 as amended by the Finance Act 1998 s 144(1).
4   Inheritance Tax Act 1984 s 76(1)(a), Sch 4 para 16.
5   Inheritance Tax Act 1984 s 76(1)(b), Sch 4 para 16 as amended by the Finance Act 1998 s 143(4)(a).
6   Inheritance Tax Act 1984 s 76(1)(c), Sch 3.

[867]

(d) Discretionary Trusts created before 27 March 1974

325   Introduction

Discretionary settlements created before 27 March 1974 are subject to special rules for the calculation of inheritance tax which generally result in less tax being charged.

[868]

326   Chargeable events occurring before first ten–year anniversary

As the settlement is treated as a separate taxable entity only transfers made by the settlement are cumulated. Such chargeable transfers were either distribution payments (if made under the regime in force from 1974 to 1982) or are chargeable events[1]. Once the cumulative total is known, the rate of tax is calculated at half rate and the charge is at 30% of that rate[2].

1   See the Inheritance Tax Act 1984 s 65 (42–44 Halsbury's Statutes (4th Edn) TAXATION).
2   See the Inheritance Tax Act 1984 s 68(6) as amended by the Finance Act 1986 s 101(1), (3), Sch 19 para 18.

[869]

327   First anniversary charge

No anniversary charge can apply before 1 April 1983. Therefore, the first discretionary trust to suffer this charge is one created on 1 April 1973 (or 1963, 1953, 1943 and so on). The amount subject to the charge is calculated in the normal way. In calculating the rate of charge, however, it is only chargeable transfers of the settlement in the preceding ten years that are cumulated (as the settlement predates capital transfer tax/inheritance tax the settlor obviously has no chargeable transfers to cumulate). Property in a related settlement and non-relevant property in the settlement are ignored. As before, the rate of charge is reduced if property has not been relevant property throughout the decade preceding the first anniversary[1]. The danger of increasing an inheritance tax bill by an addition of property by the settlor[2] is even greater with these old trusts. If such an addition has been made, the settlor's chargeable transfers in the seven-year period before the addition must be cumulated in calculating the rate of tax on the anniversary charge[3]. The effective rate of charge for the anniversary charge is (as for new trusts) 30% of the rate calculated according to half the table rates.

[870]

1   As to such reduction in the rate of the anniversary charge see Paragraph 323.2 [851] ante.
2   As to the addition of property by the settlor see Paragraph 323.4 [854] ante.
3   Inheritance Tax Act 1984 s 67(4) as amended by the Finance Act 1986 s 101(1), (3), Sch 19 para 17 (42–44 Halsbury's Statutes (4th Edn) TAXATION).

[871]

328   Chargeable events after the first anniversary charge

The position is the same as for new trusts[1]. The charge is based upon the rate charged at the last anniversary.

1   As to exit charges after the first anniversary charge and between anniversaries see Paragraph 321 [846] ante. As to later periodic charges see Paragraph 322 [849] ante.

[872]

7: SPECIAL TRUSTS

329   Accumulation and maintenance trusts

For a detailed treatment of accumulation and maintenance trusts see vol 40(2) (2001 Reissue) TRUSTS AND SETTLEMENTS Part 11 [6301].

[873]

330   Charitable trusts

If a trust is perpetually dedicated to charitable purposes, there is no charge to inheritance tax and the fund is not 'relevant property'[1]. Transfers to charities are exempt, whether made by individuals or by trustees of discretionary trusts[2]. The Inheritance Tax Act 1984 Section 70 is concerned with temporary charitable trusts which that section defines as 'settled property held for charitable purposes only until the end of a period (whether defined by date or in some other way)'[3] and ensures that when the fund ceases to be held for such purposes an exit charge arises. That charge (which is calculated in the same way as for accumulation and maintenance trusts)[4] will never exceed a 30% rate which is reached after 50 years.

[874]

1   Inheritance Tax Act 1984 s 58 (42–44 Halsbury's Statutes (4th Edn) TAXATION).
2   Inheritance Tax Act 1984 s 76 as amended by the Finance Act 1998 ss 143(4)(a), 165, Sch 27 Pt IV.
3   Inheritance Tax Act 1984 s 70(1).
4   As to the calculation of such inheritance tax see vol 40(2) (2001 Reissue) TRUSTS AND SETTLEMENTS
     Part 11 [6301].

[875]

331   Trusts for the benefit of mentally and other disabled persons[1]

These rules were recast in 1981. As from 10 March 1981, a qualifying trust for a disabled person has been treated as giving that person an interest in possession[2]. As a result the inheritance tax regime for no interest in possession trusts does not apply. The inter vivos creation of this trust by a person other than the relevant beneficiary is a potentially exempt transfer. There are no restrictions on the application of income which can therefore be used for the benefit of other members of the class of beneficiaries. This can be particularly useful where the application of income to the 'principal' disabled beneficiary could jeopardise his entitlement to state benefits. Obviously a charge to inheritance tax will arise on the death of the disabled person whose deemed interest in possession will aggregate with his free estate in the normal way[3].

[876]

1   As to the meaning of 'disabled person' for the purpose of tax see vol 42(1) (1998 Reissue) WILLS AND
     ADMINISTRATION Paragraph 372 [2254]. For disabled trusts see vol 40(2) (2001 Reissue) TRUSTS
     AND SETTLEMENTS Part 16 [9301].
2   Inheritance Tax Act 1984 s 89(2) (42–44 Halsbury's Statutes (4th Edn) TAXATION).
3   Although disabled trusts can also attract capital gains tax advantages (eg a full annual exemption for the
     trustees), to qualify the disabled beneficiary must be entitled to at least one half of the income. This
     could mean, however, that inheritance tax relief would be lost because no interest in possession is
     permitted. For further discussion of tax benefits in relation to disabled persons see vol 40(2) (2001
     Reissue) TRUSTS AND SETTLEMENTS Part 16 [9301] and see vol 42(1) (1998 Reissue) WILLS AND
     ADMINISTRATION Paragraph 371 [2253] et seq. As to the use and drafting of trusts for the making of
     financial provision see further vol 42(1) (1998 Reissue) WILLS AND ADMINISTRATION Paragraph 389
     [2287] et seq.

[877]

332   Pension funds

A superannuation scheme or pension fund approved by the Inland Revenue for income tax purposes is not subject to the rules for no interest in possession trusts. It is common practice for the death benefit to be settled[1].

[878]

1   As to the treatment of pension rights etc see the Inheritance Tax Act 1984 s 151 as amended by the
     Income and Corporation Taxes Act 1988 Sch 29 para 32 and by the Finance (No 2) Act 1987 s 98(4)
     (42–44 Halsbury's Statutes (4th Edn) TAXATION). For forms of pension policy trust see vol 40(2)
     (2001 Reissue) TRUSTS AND SETTLEMENTS Part 18 [9601].

[879]

333   Employee trusts

Employee trusts are not in law charitable unless they are directed to the relief of poverty amongst employees[1]. They may, however, enjoy considerable inheritance tax privileges. Their creation does not involve a transfer of value, whether made by an individual[2] or by a discretionary trust[3]. Once created, the fund is largely exempted from the inheritance tax provisions governing discretionary trusts, especially from the anniversary charge. To qualify for this treatment, the fund must be held for the benefit of persons employed in a particular trade or profession together with their dependants[4] or all employees etc of a particular employer[5].

[880]

1   See *Oppenheim v Tobacco Securities Trust Co Ltd* [1951] AC 297, [1951] 2 All ER 31, HL.

2   Inheritance Tax Act 1984 s 28 (42–44 Halsbury's Statutes (4th Edn) TAXATION).

3   Inheritance Tax Act 1984 s 75.

4   Inheritance Tax Act 1984 s 86(1).

5   For forms of employee trust see vol 40(2) (2001 Reissue) TRUSTS AND SETTLEMENTS Part 14 [8101].

[881]

334   Compensation funds

Trusts set up by professional bodies and trade associations for the purpose of indemnifying clients and customers against loss incurred through the default of their members are exempt from the rules for non-interest in possession trusts[1].

1   Inheritance Tax Act 1984 ss 58–63 (42–44 Halsbury's Statutes (4th Edn) TAXATION).

[882]

335   Newspaper trusts

The provisions relating to employee trusts[1] are extended to cover newspaper trusts[2].

1   As to employee trusts see Paragraph 333 [880] ante and vol 40(2) (2001 Reissue) TRUSTS AND SETTLEMENTS Part 14 [8101].

2   Inheritance Tax Act 1984 s 87 (42–44 Halsbury's Statutes (4th Edn) TAXATION).

[883]

336   Maintenance funds for historic buildings

Inheritance tax exemptions are available for maintenance funds where property is settled and the Treasury give a direction[1]. Once the trust ceases, for any reason, to carry out its specialised function, an exit charge occurs calculated in the same way as for accumulation and maintenance trusts[2].

[884]

1   Ie under the Inheritance Tax Act 1984 Sch 4 para 1 (42–44 Halsbury's Statutes (4th Edn) TAXATION). For a maintenance fund settlement for heritage property see vol 40(2) (2001 Reissue) TRUSTS AND SETTLEMENTS Part 13 [7501].

2   Inheritance Tax Act 1984 s 77, Sch 4 para 8.

[885]

337   Protective trusts

The special treatment accorded to certain protective trusts is considered in vol 40(2) (2001 Reissue) TRUSTS AND SETTLEMENTS Part 12 [6901].

[886]–[895]

C: CAPITAL GAINS TAX

338   Introduction

The capital gains tax provisions seek to tax the settled fund and not the value of the individual interests of the beneficiaries. Actual disposals by the trustees and certain deemed disposals may trigger a charge, but disposals of beneficial interests are normally exempt. The creation and termination of a settlement may lead to a capital gains tax charge.

[896]

339   Settled property

339.1   Definition

'Settlement' is not defined, but settled property is 'any property held in trust'[1] with the exception of certain trusts mentioned in the Taxation of Chargeable Gains Act 1992 Section 60. In the following three situations, although there is a trust of property, the property is not settled property and is treated as belonging to the beneficiary.

---

1   Taxation of Chargeable Gains Act 1992 s 68 (42–44 Halsbury's Statutes (4th Edn) TAXATION). For the purpose of the capital payment rules (relevant for trusts which are or have been non United Kingdom resident), the income tax definition of a settlement is adopted: see the Taxation of Chargeable Gains Act 1992 s 97(7) as amended by the Finance Act 1998 s 129(2) and by the Finance Act 2000 Sch 26 Pt II para 4.

[897]

339.2   Assets held by person as nominee or as trustee

Property is not settled where assets are held by a person as nominee for another person or as trustee for another person absolutely entitled as against the trustee. The provision covers both nomineeships and bare or simple trusts.

[898]

339.3   Property on trust for a minor or person under a disability

Property is not settled where it is held on trust for any person who would be absolutely entitled but for being a minor or other person under a disability.

Example 28

(1)   A and B hold property for C absolutely, aged 9 years. Because of his age C cannot demand the property from the trustees and the trust is not, therefore, simple or bare. For capital gains tax purposes, however, C is a person who would be absolutely entitled but for his minority and he is treated as owning the assets in the fund.

(2)   A and B hold property on trust for D, aged 9 years, contingent upon his attaining the age of 18 years. At first sight it would seem that there is no material difference between this settlement and that considered in (1) above because, in both, the beneficiary would be absolutely entitled were it not for his minority. D, however, is not entitled to claim the fund from the trustees because of the provisions of the settlement. Unlike (1) above, D's entitlement is contingent upon living to a certain age, so that, were he to ask the trustees to give him the property, they would refuse because he has not satisfied the contingency. This distinction would be more obvious if the settlement provided that the contingency to be satisfied by D was the attaining of (say) 21 years[1]. The fund in this example is, therefore, settled property for the purposes of capital gains tax.

---

1   See *Tomlinson v Glyns Executor and Trustee Co* [1970] Ch 112, [1970] 1 All ER 381, CA.

[899]

339.4   Fund held for two or more persons jointly absolutely entitled

Property is not settled where the fund is held for two or more persons who are or would be jointly absolutely entitled. The word 'jointly' is not limited to the interests of joint tenants, but applies to concurrent ownership generally. It does not apply to interests which are successive, but only covers more than one beneficiary concurrently entitled 'in the same interest'[1].

Example 29

(1)   A and B purchase Blackacre as tenants in common. The land is held on a trust of land pursuant to the Law of Property Act 1925 Sections 34 and 36[2], but for the purposes of capital gains tax the property is not settled and is treated as belonging to A and B equally[3].

(2)   T and his family hold 72% of the issued share capital in T Ltd (their family company). In 1989 they enter into a written agreement as a result of which the shares are transferred to trustees and detailed restrictions, akin to pre-emption provisions in private company articles, are imposed. The beneficial interests of T and his family are not, however, affected. Subsequently the shares are transferred out again to the various settlors. In such a 'pooling arrangement' the shares are treated as nominee property with the result that there is no disposal for capital gains tax purposes on the creation of the trust nor on its termination[4].

---

[900]

1   See *Kidson v MacDonald* [1974] Ch 339, [1974] 1 All ER 849; *Booth v Ellard* [1980] 3 All ER 569, [1980] 1 WLR 1443, CA; *IRC v Matthew's Executors* [1984] STC 386.
2   Law of Property Act 1925 ss 34, 36 as amended by the Trusts of Land and Appointment of Trustees Act 1996 ss 5, 25(2), Sch 2 paras 3, 4, Sch 4 (37 Halsbury's Statutes (4th Edn) REAL PROPERTY).
3   *Kidson v MacDonald* above.
4   Cf *Booth v Ellard* above; and see *Jenkins v Brown* [1989] 1 WLR 1163; *Warrington v Sterland* [1989] STC 577 in which a similar result was arrived at in the case of a pooling of family farms.

[901]

339.5   Absolute entitlement

The Taxation of Chargeable Gains Act 1992 Section 60(2) provides as follows:

'It is hereby declared that references in this Act to any asset held by a person as trustee for another person absolutely entitled as against the trustee are references to a case where that other person has the exclusive right, subject only to satisfying any outstanding charge, lien or other right of the trustees to resort to the asset for payment of duty, taxes, costs or other outgoings, to direct how that asset shall be dealt with.'

Example 30

J is entitled to an annuity of £1,000 a year payable out of a settled fund held in trust for X absolutely. The property is settled for capital gains tax purposes[1].

---

[902]

The Taxation of Chargeable Gains Act 1992 Section 60(2) does not offer any guidance on the question of when a beneficiary has the exclusive right to direct how the asset in the settlement shall be dealt with. Under general trust law, beneficiaries are not able to issue such directions unless they have the right to end the trust by demanding their share of the property[2]. Difficulties may arise when one of a number of beneficiaries is entitled to a portion of the fund.

Example 31

A fund is held for the three daughters of the settlor (A, B and C) contingent upon attaining 21 years and, if more than one, in equal shares. A, the eldest, is 21 years old and is, therefore, entitled to one-third of the assets. Whether she is absolutely entitled as against the trustees to that share depends upon the type of property held by the trustees. The general principle is that she is entitled to claim her one-third share, but not, in exceptional cases, when the effect of distributing that slice of the fund would be to damage the interests of the other beneficiaries. When the settled assets are land this will be the result because, the asset would often have to be sold to raise the necessary money[3]. If A is entitled to demand her share that proportion of the fund ceases to be settled (even though A leaves her share in the hands of the trustees)[4]. If the fund consists of land, A is not absolutely entitled; therefore, the settlement continues until all three daughters either satisfy the contingency or die before 21 years. Only then will the fund cease to be settled because one or more persons will, at that point, become jointly absolutely entitled[5].

Finally, it should be noted that a person can become absolutely entitled to assets without being 'beneficially' entitled.

[903]

1   *Stephenson v Barclays Bank Trust Co Ltd* [1975] 1 All ER 625.
2   See eg *Re Brockbank, Ward v Bates* [1948] Ch 206, [1948] 1 All ER 287.
3   See *Crowe v Appleby* [1976] 2 All ER 914, CA. The position is different in Scotland (see for example *Stenhouse's Trustees v Lord Advocate* [1984] STC 195, Court of Sess) and in Ireland. See further Inland Revenue Manual CG37510 et seq.
4   In practice it is understood that the Revenue will not apply this rule in cases where the trustees have an express power of appropriation. In such cases they will only treat A as absolutely entitled when the trustee exercises that power (and in respect of the assets so appropriated). If no appropriation is made the settlement continues until all beneficiaries are together absolutely entitled (in effect as if the fund were land).
5   For problems that can arise on a division of a controlling shareholding see *Lloyds Bank plc v Duker* [1987] 3 All ER 193, [1987] 1 WLR 1324. For a consideration of when beneficiaries become absolutely entitled in cases when because of incapacity further beneficiaries will not be born see *Figg v Clarke* [1997] STC 247.

[904]

340   Creation of a settlement

The creation of a settlement is a disposal of assets by the settlor whether the settlement is revocable or irrevocable, and whether or not the settlor or his spouse is a beneficiary[1]. If chargeable assets are settled, a chargeable gain or allowable loss results. As the settlor and his trustees are connected persons[2], any loss resulting from the transfer is only deductible from a subsequent disposal to those trustees at a gain. Only if the settled assets comprise business property, or if the creation of the trust involves a chargeable transfer for inheritance tax purposes, is it possible to postpone the payment of capital gains tax by means of a hold-over election[3].

[905]

1   See the Taxation of Chargeable Gains Act 1992 s 70 (42–44 Halsbury's Statutes (4th Edn) TAXATION).
2   Taxation of Chargeable Gains Act 1992 s 18(3). For a discussion of the connected person rule see the
     Inland Revenue *Tax Bulletin*, February 1993, p 56.
3   For a specimen hold-over election see Form 299 [2086] post. It is common practice for a discretionary
     trust to be set up with the value transferred falling within the settlor's nil rate band, so that a capital
     gains tax hold-over election can be made: see *Melville v IRC* [2000] STC 628.

[906]

341   Actual and deemed disposal by trustees

341.1   Introduction

A charge to capital gains tax may arise as a result of either actual or deemed disposals of
property by trustees. Notice, however, that where, on a change of trustees, trust property
is transferred from the old to the new trustees, there is no charge to capital gains tax
because they are treated as a single and continuing body[1]. Trust gains are taxed at a rate
of 34% unless the settlor has retained an interest, when tax is charged at his rate (ie either
at 10%, 20% or, more likely, 40%)[2]. Trustees are generally only entitled to one half of
the full capital gains tax annual exemption.

[907]

1   Taxation of Chargeable Gains Act 1992 s 69(1) (42–44 Halsbury's Statutes (4th Edn) TAXATION).
2   Ie for the tax year 2001-02: see the Taxation of Chargeable Gains Act 1992 s 4 as amended and for
     when a settlor reserves an interest for these purposes, see the Taxation of Chargeable Gains Act 1992
     s 77 as substituted by the Finance Act 1995 s 74, Sch 17 para 27 and as amended by the Finance Act
     1998 Sch 21 para 6(1).

[908]

341.2   Actual disposals by trustees

When chargeable assets are sold by trustees normal principles apply in calculating their
gain (or loss). If the disposal generates a loss it may be set-off against trustees' gains of the
same year or of future years. However, if the loss is still unrelieved at the end of the trust
period, it can no longer be transferred to a beneficiary who has become absolutely
entitled to all or part of the trust fund.

Only on the occasion where a beneficiary becomes absolutely entitled to trust assets
so that the trustees make a deemed disposal which produces a loss may that loss be passed
to the beneficiary, and it is then 'ring fenced' in his hands so that it can only be offset
against a future disposal of those trust assets[1].

As in the case of individuals, the introduction of taper relief (especially on business
assets) has profound implications for trustees. Three points in particular should be noted:

341.2.1   After full business taper relief, trustees are taxed at only 8.5% on disposals
           of business assets (34% x 25%).

341.2.2   Trusts can be used as an 'umbrella', in that a change of beneficial
           entitlement in a continuing trust does not affect the trustees' ownership
           period in respect of the trust assets.

341.2.3   Accrued taper relief is lost if a hold-over election is made (for example, on
           the creation or ending of a trust).

[909]

1   Taxation of Chargeable Gains Act 1992 s 71(2)-(2D) as inserted by the Finance Act 1999 s 75(1) (42–
     44 Halsbury's Statutes (4th Edn) TAXATION) with effect from 16 June 1999. Prior to that date
     unrelieved trust losses passed to a beneficiary who became absolutely entitled to trust property.

[910]

341.3 Exit charge[1]

There is a deemed disposal of the chargeable assets in the fund, whenever a person becomes absolutely entitled to the settled property ('exit charge'). A trust will end either because there is a transfer of assets to a beneficiary, or, if the fund is still held by the trustees, on the arising of a bare trust[2]. The assets of the fund are deemed to be sold by the trustees (so that it is trustee rates of capital gains tax which are relevant) for their market value at that date and immediately reacquired for the same value. The deemed reacquisition by the trustees is treated as the act of the person who is absolutely entitled to the fund.

Example 32

Shares in D Ltd are held by trustees for S absolutely, contingent upon attaining the age of 25 years. S has just reached 25 years and the shares are worth £100,000. The trustees' base costs are £25,000. S is now absolutely entitled to the fund and the trustees are deemed to sell the shares (for £100,000) and to re-acquire them (for £100,000). On the sale they have realised a chargeable gain of £75,000 (£100,000 –£25,000). The shares are now deemed to be S's property so that if he directs their sale and, say, £107,000 is raised, he has a chargeable gain of £7,000 (£107,000 – £100,000). (For simplicity this example ignores the possible impact of taper relief.)

---

[911]

1   Taxation of Chargeable Gains Act 1992 s 71(1) (42–44 Halsbury's Statutes (4th Edn) TAXATION).
2   Taxation of Chargeable Gains Act 1992 s 60(1).

[912]

341.4 Settlement ending on death of interest in possession beneficiary

The termination of an interest in possession because of the death of the beneficiary may result in a deemed disposal by the trustees. Despite this, no capital gains tax (or loss relief) is charged (or allowed) on any resultant gain (or loss)[1]. This corresponds to the normal capital gains tax principle that on death there is an uplift but no charge.

Example 33

Property consisting of shares in Z Ltd is held on trust for C for life, or until remarriage and thereafter to D absolutely.

(1)   If C dies there is a deemed disposal and reacquisition of the shares by the trustees, but capital gains tax is not charged. The property from then on belongs to D.

(2)   If C remarries his life interest ceases with the same consequences as in (1), save that capital gains tax may be chargeable.

---

[913]

If the life interest subsisted in part only of the fund, the death of the beneficiary results in an uplift of the appropriate portion of each asset in the fund without any capital gains tax charge thereon[2].

If the death of the beneficiary causes the property to revert to the settlor, the 'reverter to disponer' exception[3] applies. The death of the beneficiary in these circumstances does not lead to a charge to inheritance tax and, so, the normal uplift but no charge provisions of capital gains tax are modified to ensure that there is no double benefit. Therefore the death causes a deemed disposal and reacquisition, but for such a sum as ensures that neither gain nor loss accrues to the trustees (a no gain/no loss disposal)[4].

Hold-over relief is only permitted if the settled assets comprise business property or if the termination is a chargeable transfer for inheritance tax purposes (a similar position operates on the creation of the trust)[5].

Normally, a tax-free uplift occurs when the death of the beneficiary entitled to an interest in possession brings the trust to an end. This general rule is, however, subject to one limitation. If the settlor had made an election to hold over his gain when he created the settlement (eg where this occurred before 14 March 1989), that held-over gain may not be wiped out on the subsequent death. Instead, the held-over gain is chargeable at that time[6].

[914]

1   Taxation of Chargeable Gains Act 1992 s 73 as amended by the Finance Act 1996 Sch 39 para 6 (42–44 Halsbury's Statutes (4th Edn) TAXATION.
2   Taxation of Chargeable Gains Act 1992 s 73(2) as amended (see note 1 above).
3   As to this exemption see Paragraph 306 [800] ante. If the settlor has predeceased the exemption will apply if the reverter is to the settlor's widow or widower provided that the settlor died within two years of that event.
4   Taxation of Chargeable Gains Act 1992 s 73(1)(b) as amended by the Finance Act 1996 Sch 39 para 6 but note that if the property reverts on a life interest trust for the settlor, the inheritance tax exemption still applies but there is the normal capital gains tax uplift.
5   Taxation of Chargeable Gains Act 1992 ss 165, 260 as amended.
6   Taxation of Chargeable Gains Act 1992 s 74.

[915]

341.5   Termination of an interest on death when the settlement continues[1]

The death of a beneficiary entitled to an interest in possession, in cases where the settlement continues afterwards, results in a deemed disposal and reacquisition of the assets in the fund by the trustees at their then market value. Capital gains tax is not normally imposed, and the purpose of this provision is the familiar one of ensuring a tax-free uplift.

The termination of an interest in a part of the fund, where the settlement continues afterwards, results in a proportionate uplift in the value of all the assets[2].

Example 34

Property is held on trust for W for life and afterwards for his son V contingently on attaining 25 years. W dies when V is aged 22. The capital gains tax consequences are:

(1)   Death of W. There is a deemed disposal of the property; there is a tax-free uplift. The settlement continues because V has not attained 25.

(2)   V becomes 25 years. There is a further deemed disposal and capital gains tax is charged on any increase in value of the assets since W's death.

The full tax-free uplift on death does not apply to a gain held over on the creation of a settlement which does, therefore, become chargeable.

[916]

1   See the Taxation of Chargeable Gains Act 1992 s 72 as amended by the Finance Act 1996 Sch 39 para 5
     (42–44 Halsbury's Statutes (4th Edn) TAXATION).
2   See the Taxation of Chargeable Gains Act 1992 s 72(1) as amended by the Finance Act 1996 Sch 39
     para 5(2); note that similar rules apply if a beneficiary entitled to an interest in possession dies albeit that
     the interest continues (eg an estate pur autre vie) and to certain annuity interests: Taxation of
     Chargeable Gains Act 1992 s 72(3), (4) as amended (see note 1 above).

[917]

341.6   Conclusions on deemed disposals

When it is not possible to postpone payment of the tax (by a hold-over election), it may prove prohibitively expensive to end a settlement. This may be the case with a life interest settlement where it may be preferable to wait for the death: in the case of discretionary trusts, because there is a chargeable transfer for inheritance tax purposes, it remains possible to hold over chargeable gains. In cases where a settlement will end on the happening of an event (eg, when A becomes 25) and an exit charge will, therefore, arise (then trusts are sometimes referred to as 'time bomb' trusts) thought should be given to extending the life of the settlement, for instance by a settled advance[1].

1   See Form 257 [1854] post.

[918]

342   Resettlements

When property is transferred from one settlement to another different settlement, a capital gains tax charge may arise[1] because the trustees of the second settlement (who may be the same persons as the trustees of the original settlement) become absolutely entitled to that property as against the original trustees[2]. Exactly when a resettlement occurs is still a matter of some uncertainty[3].

In *Roome v Edwards*, Lord Wilberforce stressed that the question should be approached 'in a practical and common sense manner' and suggested that relevant indicia included separate and defined property, separate trusts and separate trustees, although he emphasised that such factors are helpful but not decisive and that the matter ultimately depends upon the particular facts of each case. He contrasted special powers of appointment which, when exercised, do not usually result in a resettlement of property, with wider powers (eg of advancement) which permit property to be wholly removed from the original settlement. An Inland Revenue Statement of Practice[4] gives some guidance on when the exercise of a power of advancement or appointment is not treated as creating a new settlement.

[919]

Example 35

A family trust was created in discretionary form in 1965, since when 90% of the assets have been irrevocably appointed on various interest in possession trusts, with the remaining 10% being appointed on accumulation and maintenance trusts for beneficiaries who are all minors. The various funds are administered by the original trustees of the 1965 discretionary trust. On these facts the property has remained comprised in the original settlement for capital gains tax purposes. Accordingly:

(1)   Even if separate trustees are appointed for, eg, part of the assets held on interest in possession trusts, the trustees of the original 1965 trust remain liable for any capital gains tax attributable to that portion of the assets.

(2)   Only one annual exemption is available for gains realised in any part of the settled fund.

(3)   Losses realised in one part of the fund may reduce the chargeable gains realised in the other part. Whether the trust deed should make any provision for 'compensating' that part of the fund which produced the capital loss is a matter which should be considered by the trust draftsman.

[920]

1   Taxation of Chargeable Gains Act 1992 s 71(1) (42–44 Halsbury's Statutes (4th Edn) TAXATION).
2   See *Hoare Trustees v Gardner* [1979] Ch 10, [1978] 1 All ER 791.
3   See especially *Roome v Edwards* [1982] AC 279, [1981] 1 All ER 736, HL; *Bond v Pickford* [1983] STC 517, CA; and *Swires v Renton* [1991] STC 490. See further Form 157 [1611] post.
4   See Inland Revenue Statement of Practice SP7/84 (11 October 1984).

[921]

343   Disposal of a beneficial interest

343.1   The basic rule

The basic rule is that there is no charge to capital gains tax when a beneficiary disposes of his interest[1]. The rationale is that there are rules taxing gains in the trust[2] so that to charge tax on the interest of a beneficiary would be a form of double taxation. There is, however, a growing list of exceptions, which is added to each year as tax avoidance schemes seek to exploit the basic exemption. If a trust is viewed as akin to a company, in which not only are the corporate gains taxed but also disposals of shares are chargeable, it may be thought that the rationale behind the general rule is misconceived.

[922]

1   Taxation of Chargeable Gains Act 1992 s 76(1) as amended by the Finance Act 1998 s 128(1)(a) (42–44 Halsbury's Statutes (4th Edn) TAXATION): cf the disposal of an interest in an unadministered estate.
2   See Paragraph 338 [896] et seq ante.

[923]

343.2   Position of a purchaser

Once a beneficial interest has been purchased for money or money's worth, a future disposal of that interest will be chargeable to capital gains tax. The consideration does not have to be 'full' or 'adequate': ie any consideration however small will turn the interest into a chargeable asset. An exchange of interests by beneficiaries under a settlement is not treated as a purchase so that a later disposal of either interest will not be chargeable.

When a life interest has been sold, the wasting rules may apply on a subsequent disposal of that interest by the purchaser.

[924]

Example 36

A is the remainderman under a settlement created by his father. He sells his interest to his friend B for £25,000. No capital gains tax is charged. If B resells the remainder interest to C for £31,000, B has made a chargeable gain of £6,000 (£31,000 – £25,000).

[925]

343.3   Purchaser becoming absolutely entitled to any part of the settled property

The termination of the settlement may result in the property passing to a purchaser of the remainder interest (of course, he may also become entitled to such property in other situations, eg if an advancement is made in his favour). As a result, that purchaser will dispose of his interest in return for receiving the property in the settlement[1]. The resultant charge that he suffers does not affect the deemed disposal by the trustees (and the possible capital gains tax charge)[2].

[926]

Example 37

Assume in Example 36 [925] above, that C becomes entitled to the settled fund which is worth £80,000. He has realised a chargeable gain of £49,000 (£80,000 − £ 31,000). In addition, the usual deemed disposal rules under Section 71(1) operate.

---

[927]

1   Taxation of Chargeable Gains Act 1992 s 76(2) (42–44 Halsbury's Statutes (4th Edn) TAXATION).
2   Under the Taxation of Chargeable Gains Act 1992 Section 71(1).

[928]

343.4   Disposal of an interest in a non-resident settlement

The Taxation of Chargeable Gains Act 1992 Section 85(1) provides that the disposal of an interest in a non-resident settlement is chargeable: the basic exemption conferred by Section 76(1) is therefore excluded in such cases although it is expressly provided that no charge arises under Section 76(2) if the beneficiary becomes absolutely entitled to any part of the trust fund (this charge is therefore restricted to a sale of the interest). When the trust was originally UK resident the appointment of non-resident trustees triggers an exit charge and some protection against a double charge if a beneficial interest is subsequently sold as provided by Section 85(3):

> 'For the purpose of calculating any chargeable gain accruing on the disposal of the interest, the person disposing of it shall be treated as having:
> (a)   disposed of it immediately before the relevant time; and
> (b)   immediately reacquired it,
> at its market value at that time.'

Although not happily drafted, the purpose of the subsection is to fix the acquisition cost of the disponor at the date when the trustees emigrated (ie his acquisition cost will take into account the gains then realised and subject to UK tax). On first reading, the provision might be thought to impose a second charge at that time but this is not thought to be the case.

An infelicity in the drafting is that the provision is said to be relevant for the purpose of calculating the chargeable gain of the disponor: it should also be relevant in arriving at any allowable loss which he may have suffered.

[929]

Example 38

The X trust was set up in 1988 with J being entitled to the residue of the trust on the death of his sister, K. The trustees became non-UK resident on 20 March 1996 and J sold his remainder interest shortly afterwards for £150,000.

(1)   J has made a chargeable disposal[1].

(2)   In order to compute his chargeable gain, if any, the market value of his interest when the trust became non-resident on 20 March needs to be ascertained.

The Taxation of Chargeable Gains Act 1992 Section 85 has been amended[2] to prevent what might be termed 'the in-and-out scheme'. Assume that a non-resident trust has stockpiled gains and is now a cash fund. UK trustees are appointed so that the trust becomes resident and subsequently it is exported (by the appointment of further non-resident trustees). On the latter event Section 85(3) would operate to increase the base costs of all the beneficial interests but, given that the nature of the assets then in the trust, there could be no exit charge. Accordingly, a beneficiary could sell his interest (effectively extracting stockpiled gains) tax free. From 21 March 2000[3] the disposal of a beneficial interest in a settlement which had stockpiled gains at 'the material time' (ie when it ceased to be UK resident) cannot benefit from the uplift in value under Section 85(3).

[930]

1   Taxation of Chargeable Gains Act 1992 s 85(1) (42–44 Halsbury's Statutes (4th Edn) TAXATION).
2   By the Finance Act 2000 s 95 (42–44 Halsbury's Statutes (4th Edn) TAXATION).
3   The amendment to the Taxation of Chargeable Gains Act 1992 s 85 applies where the material time, within the meaning of s 85(10), falls on or after 21 March 2000: Finance Act 2000 s 95(5).

[931]

344   Sale of an interest in a 'settlor-interested' trust[1]

344.1   The basic rule

The rules relating to the sale of an interest in a 'settlor interested' trust took effect from 21 March 2000 and when they apply the trustees, provided that they are UK resident, are treated as disposing and reacquiring trust assets at market value (ie there is a deemed disposal). Tax is then calculated at either the settlor rate (if the settlor is interested in the trust) or at the normal 34% and may be recovered by the trustees from the beneficiary who sold the interest.

1   Taxation of Chargeable Gains Act 1992 Sch 4A as inserted by the Finance Act 2000 Sch 24 (42–44 Halsbury's Statutes (4th Edn) TAXATION).

[932]

344.2   When is a settlor interested in his trust?

The normal rules of the Taxation of Chargeable Gains Act 1992 Section 77(2) apply. For the rules to apply the trust must either be a settlor-interested trust when the interest is sold or must contain property derived from a trust which had been settlor-interested at any time in the previous two years. Notice that the disposal can be by any beneficiary: the legislation is not limited to disposals by the settlor. The settlor must, however, be either resident or ordinarily resident in the UK.

[933]

344.3   The mischief under attack

The intention was to prevent exploiting the Taxation of Chargeable Gains Act 1992 Section 76(1) exemption by individuals who placed assets in trusts (instead of selling the assets) and retained an interest which was sold. However, the scope of the legislation was not so limited and could catch the wholly innocent.

[934]

Example 39

(1)   D put assets into a trust and makes a hold-over election to avoid the payment of any capital gains tax. He is absolutely entitled to those assets on attaining 35 (which is, say, in three month's time). He sells this interest to E and F, trustees of a settlement with realised capital losses. As a result:

(a)   under general principles the sale by D does not attract a capital gains tax charge[1];

(b)   when E and F become absolutely entitled a further hold-over election is available, and when they dispose of the assets they can offset the resultant gain with their unused trust losses.

In these circumstances the Taxation of Chargeable Gains Act 1992 Schedule 4A provides that when D sells his interest the trustees make a deemed disposal of the trust property and the tax charge (at D's rates) will be borne by him.

[935]

(2)   The Z estate was resettled in 1990 and X, the current life tenant, is therefore considered to be a settlor. His son, Y, is the remainderman but is tired of waiting for his inheritance and so sells his interest. The Taxation of Chargeable Gains Act 1992 Schedule 4A applies and Y suffers a wholly undeserved capital gains tax charge.

---

1   Taxation of Chargeable Gains Act 1992 s 76(1) as amended by the Finance Act 1998 s 128(1)(a) (42–44 Halsbury's Statutes (4th Edn) TAXATION).

[936]

345   Payment of capital gains tax

Capital gains tax attributable to both actual and deemed disposals of settled property is payable by the trustees. The rate applicable to trusts is 34%[1] (note that in exceptional cases the settlor's rate applies). If the tax is not paid within six months of the due date for payment, it may be recovered from a beneficiary who has become absolutely entitled to the asset (or proceeds of sale from it) in respect of which the tax is chargeable. The beneficiary may be assessed in the trustees' name for a period of two years after the date when the tax became payable[2].

In cases where on the ending of a trust hold-over relief is claimed[3], the trustees are at risk of the postponed tax if the beneficiary subsequently emigrates. Retaining assets, or taking an indemnity from the relevant beneficiary, is recommended.

[937]

1   Ie since 6 April 1999: Income and Corporation Taxes Act 1988 s 686(1A) as substituted by Finance
     (No 2) Act 1997 s 32(4), (11) (42–44 Halsbury's Statutes (4th Edn) TAXATION).
2   Taxation of Chargeable Gains Act 1992 s 69(4) (42–44 Halsbury's Statutes (4th Edn) TAXATION).
3   For a specimen hold-over election see Form 299 [2086] post.

[938]

346   Exemptions and reliefs

A number of exemptions and reliefs should be noted in the context of settled property.

346.1   Main residence exemption

Main residence exemption may be available in the case of a house settled on either
discretionary or interest in possession trusts[1].

1   Taxation of Chargeable Gains Act 1992 s 225 (42–44 Halsbury's Statutes (4th Edn) TAXATION); and
     see *Sansom v Peay* [1976] 3 All ER 375, [1976] 1 WLR 1073. It does not matter that the beneficiary
     pays a rent for use of the property: see Form 312 [2146] post.

[939]

346.2   Annual exemption

Trustees are generally entitled to half of the annual exemption appropriate to an
individual[1].

1   Trustees of a settlement for the physically or mentally disabled are entitled to a full allowance: Taxation
     of Chargeable Gains 1992 s 3(8), Sch 1 (as amended) (42–44 Halsbury's Statutes (4th Edn) TAXATION)
     and note the rules for qualifying settlements comprised in a group.

[940]

346.3   Death exemption

The tax-free uplift on death is available for trusts with a life interest, but not for
discretionary trusts.

[941]

346.4   Retirement relief

Retirement relief on disposals of a family business may be available for trusts with a life
interest: it is not available for discretionary trusts[1].

1   Taxation of Chargeable Gains Act 1992 ss 163, 164, Sch 6 as amended (42–44 Halsbury's Statutes
     (4th Edn) TAXATION). Note that this relief is being progressively phased out to nil in 2003–04:
     Finance Act 1998 s 140(2) (42–44 Halsbury's Statutes (4th Edn) TAXATION).

[942]

346.5   Roll-over relief

Roll-over relief on replacement of business assets is available only if the trustees are
carrying on an unincorporated business[1].

1   See the Taxation of Chargeable Gains Act 1992 ss 152–162 as amended (42–44 Halsbury's Statutes
     (4th Edn) TAXATION).

[943]

346.6   Deferral relief

Deferral relief for re-investment under the enterprise investment scheme is available in respect of all trusts provided that all the beneficiaries are either individuals or charities[1].

1   See the Taxation of Chargeable Gains Act 1992 Sch 5B as inserted by the Finance Act 1995 and as amended (42–44 Halsbury's Statutes (4th Edn) TAXATION).

[944]–[955]

D: INCOME TAX

1: LIABILITY OF TRUSTEES

347   Introduction

During the life of a trust the trustees are subject to basic or lower rate income tax under the appropriate Schedule on all the income produced by the fund[1]. They are not allowed to deduct their personal allowances (the trust income is, after all, not their property) nor those of any beneficiary. Expenses incurred in administering the fund may not be deducted and are, therefore, paid out of taxed income.

Example 40

The trustees run a business. The profits of that business are calculated in accordance with the normal rules under Case I of Schedule D and are subject to basic rate income tax in the trustees' hands. A change of trustees does not result in the discontinuance rules applying[2].

---

[956]

Trustees are not liable in cases where the trust income accrues directly to a beneficiary who is not liable to pay income tax. The scope of this exception is limited: it applies only where there is no liability to tax (for instance, because of non-residence or charitable status) and not where the income is untaxed merely because of the personal allowances of the beneficiary.

[957]

1   But note the exceptional charge, on certain trustees where a company redeems or purchases its own shares, under the Income and Corporation Taxes Act 1988 s 686A as inserted by the Finance (No. 2) Act 1997 s 32(9), (11) (42–44 Halsbury's Statutes (4th Edn) TAXATION). The tax treatment of dividends received by trustees is considered at Paragraph 348.3 [966] post.

2   Income and Corporation Taxes Act 1988 s 113(7).

[958]

348   Trusts where trustees are liable to the rate applicable to trusts

348.1   Charge imposed by ICTA 1988 s 686

Trustees are not liable to income tax at the higher rate because they are not individuals. There is, however, a special rate applicable to certain trusts[1] on income after deducting administrative expenses[2]. The trusts in question are those where there is income arising to trustees in any year of assessment so far as it:

348.1.1   is income which is to be accumulated or which is payable at the discretion of the trustees or any other person (whether or not the trustees have power to accumulate it)[3];

348.1.2   is not, before being distributed, either:

    348.1.2.1   the income of any person other than the trustees; or

    348.1.2.2   treated for any of the purposes of the Income Tax Acts[4] as the income of a settlor[5];

348.1.3   is not income arising under a trust established for charitable purposes only[6]; and

348.1.4   exceeds the income applied in defraying the expenses of the trustees in that year which are properly chargeable to income (or would be so chargeable but for any express provisions of the trust)[7].

Broadly, trusts which contain a power for trustees to accumulate income, and trusts which give the trustees a discretion over the distribution of the income, are caught.

[959]

Example 41

Trustees of a discretionary trust have (non-dividend) investment income of £10,000 and incur administrative expenses of £1,000. Their income tax liability (using tax year 2001–02 rates) is:

	£
Trust rate on £9,000 (34% of £9,000)	3,060
Tax on £1,000 (20% of £1,000)	200
Total tax liability	£3,260

The investment income of trustees commonly suffers the deduction of lower rate tax at source. The special rules for dividend income are considered at Paragraph 348.2 [963] post.

[960]

In *IRC v Berrill*[8] the settlor's son was entitled to the income from the fund unless the trustees exercised a power to accumulate it. Vinelott J held that the Income and Corporation Taxes Act 1988 Section 686 applied because the income was 'income … which is payable at the discretion of the trustees'. 'Discretion' is wide enough to cover a discretion or power to withhold income.

The phrase 'income which is to be accumulated' in the Income and Corporation Taxes Act 1988 Section 686(2)(a) presumably refers to income which the trustees are under a duty to accumulate. A mere power to accumulate is not sufficient, although it usually means that the income 'is payable at the discretion of the trustees' within Section 686(2)(a).

In *Carver v Duncan*[9] trustees paid premiums on policies of life assurance out of the income of the fund as they were permitted to do under the trust deed. The House of Lords held that the payments did not fall to be deducted under Section 686(2)(d) (see now Section 686 (2AA)(b)) which was limited to expenses properly chargeable to income under the general law. As the life assurance premiums were for the benefit of capital they should be borne by capital and accordingly the express authority in the instrument did not bring the sums within the section.

The trust rate does not apply to income which is treated as that of a person other than the trustees, for instance, where a beneficiary has a vested interest in the income (eg a life tenant); or where the anti-avoidance provisions of the Income Tax Acts[10] operate to deem the income to be that of a settlor. Presumably the type of settlement considered in *Pearson v IRC*[11], in which the income of a life tenant could be taken from him after it had arisen by the exercise of a power to accumulate it, would be subject to the special rate as the income still belongs to the trustees.

[961]

1   The 'additional rate' before the Finance Act 1993, now 'the rate applicable to trusts': see the Income and Corporation Taxes Act 1988 ss 686, 687 as amended (42–44 Halsbury's Statutes (4th Edn) TAXATION).

2   This rate is 34% for the tax year 2001–02: the Income and Corporation Taxes Act 1988 s 686(1A) as amended.

3   Income and Corporation Taxes Act 1988 s 686(2)(a).

4   As to the meaning of 'the Income Tax Acts' see the Income and Corporation Taxes Act 1988 s 831(1)(b).

5   Income and Corporation Taxes Act 1988 s 686(2)(b) as substituted by the Finance Act 1995 s 74, Sch 17 para 13.

6   Income and Corporation Taxes Act 1988 s 686(2)(c) as substituted by the Finance Act 1988 s 55(3) and as amended. Income produced by pension funds is likewise outside the charge.

7   Income and Corporation Taxes Act 1988 s 686(2AA) as inserted by the Finance Act 1997 Sch 7 para 12 and as amended by the Finance (No 2) Act 1997 s 32(6).

8   *IRC v Berrill* [1982] 1 All ER 867, [1981] 1 WLR 1449.

9   *Carver v Duncan* [1985] AC 1082, [1985] 2 All ER 645, HL.

10   As to the anti-avoidance provisions see Paragraph 355 [1001] et seq post.

11   See *Pearson v IRC* [1981] AC 753, [1980] 2 All ER 479, HL; and Paragraph 286.3 [727] ante.

[962]

348.2   Charge imposed by ICTA 1988 s 687

If trustees pay income under a discretion and it becomes as a result the income of the payee for income tax purposes (or they pay income to or for the benefit of an unmarried minor child of the settlor and it is therefore treated as the settlor's income[1]), the payment is treated as a net amount after deduction of income tax at the rate applicable to trusts[2], which is 34% in 2001–02.

The recipient (or settlor), if liable at a lower rate than 34%, can claim repayment of income tax. To protect the Inland Revenue, the trustees must account for the income tax deemed to be so deducted, but are credited with the tax they have suffered. Trustees have a running total of income tax suffered, less income tax treated as deducted from payments[3].

[963]

Example 42

On 6 April 2001 a discretionary trust had tax brought forward of £438. In 2001–02 the trust receives non-dividend income of £2,000 on which it pays tax at 34% = £680. During that year, the trustees exercise their discretion to distribute income of £1,584. This is treated as a gross sum of £1,584 x 100/66 = £2,400 from which income tax at 34% = £816 has been deducted. The trustees must account to the Inland Revenue for £816, but have a credit of £438 plus £680 = £1,118 so that no tax is payable and leaving £302 tax carried forward in the 'tax pool'.

---

[964]

1   See Paragraph 356 [1002] post and the Income and Corporation Taxes Act 1988 s 660B as inserted by the Finance Act 1995 s 74, Sch 17 para 1 and as amended by the Finance Act 1999 s 64 (42–44 Halsbury's Statutes (4th Edn) TAXATION).

2   Income and Corporation Taxes Act 1988 s 687 as amended.

3   This running total started on 5 April 1973 for a trust which then had income available for distribution. It is commonly referred to as the trust 'tax pool'.

[965]

348.3   Dividend income

When dividend income is received and then distributed by discretionary trustees the position is more complex:

348.3.1   that income, if received after 5 April 1999, is taxed at the Schedule F trust rate of 25%.

348.3.2   only tax actually paid by the trustees is credited to the trust tax pool: therefore for a cash dividend of £90 the tax pool is credited with £15 tax: see the Income and Corporation Taxes Act Section 687(3).

348.3.3   if the net income remaining is then distributed the rules of Section 687 apply so that the trustees are accountable for tax at 34% on the grossed up distribution in the normal way.

[966]

Example 43

This example illustrates the treatment of dividend income received by discretionary trustees after 5 April 1999.

	£
Dividend received	900.00
Tax credit (1/9th)	100.00
Gross income	1,000.00
Deduct: Tax @ 25%	250.00
Income after tax	£750.00
Tax due from trustees	250.00
Deduct: Tax credit	100.00
Additional tax due	£150.00
Amount credited to tax pool	£150.00

[967]

If the trustees accumulate the income there is no further income tax to pay and the sum becomes capital. But if the trustees distribute the income the position is as follows:

(1)   the non-repayable tax credit cannot be added to the tax pool, and so:

(2)   if the trustees distribute to a beneficiary the whole of the income after tax, the position is:

	£
Net income distribution to beneficiary	750.00
Addition for tax @ 34%	386.36
Gross income of beneficiary	£1,136.36
Tax due under the Income and Corporation Taxes Act 1988 Section 687	386.36
Deduct tax credited to tax pool	150.00
Shortfall	£236.36

In this situation, unless there is a balance in the tax pool brought forward in order to 'frank' the whole amount of the tax of £386.36, the shortfall has to be funded from other sources. In such cases the trustees may therefore have to adopt an alternative strategy. For instance they may take the view that the distribution to the beneficiary and the tax payable under Section 687 must be wholly met from the net of tax income received, £750 in the above example. To achieve this, the distribution to the beneficiary must be limited to 66% of the cash dividend received. Continuing the example above, the result would be:

[968]

	£
Distribution to beneficiary £900 x 66%	594.00
Addition for tax @ 34%	306.00
Gross income of beneficiary	£900.00
Tax due under the Income and Corporation Taxes Act 1988 Section 687	306.00
Deduct tax credited to tax pool	150.00
Balance paid by trustees	£156.00

This is met out of the cash balance held by the trustees of £750 less the net payment to the beneficiary of £594.

[969]

2: TAXATION OF BENEFICIARIES

349   Taxing a beneficiary entitled to trust income

A beneficiary who is entitled to the income of a trust as it arises (or is entitled to have it applied for his benefit) is subject to income tax for the year of assessment in which that income arises, even if none of the money is paid to him during that year[1]. The sum to which the beneficiary is entitled is that which is left in the trustees' hands after they have paid administration expenses and discharged their income tax liability. The beneficiary is, as a result, entitled to a net sum which must be grossed up in order to find the sum which enters his total income computation and to a credit for some of the income tax paid by the trustees; not, it should be noted, for the full amount in cases where management expenses have been deducted[2].

Depending on his other income and allowances, a beneficiary may be entitled to reclaim all or some of the tax paid by the trustees. Alternatively, he may be liable for tax at the higher rate. The income that he receives from the trust is not earned income even if it arises from a trade run by the trustees[3].

[970]

Example 44

Z is entitled to the income produced by a trust fund. In 2001–02 rental income of £6,000 is produced and the trustees incur administrative expenses of £1,000. The trustees are subject to tax at 22% on the income of £6,000. The balance of the income available for Z is:

	£	£
Gross income		6,000
Deduct tax	1,320	
Deduct expenses	1,000	2,320
		£3,680

[971]

Z is, therefore, taxed on £3,680 grossed up by tax at 22% ie:

$$\frac{3{,}608 \times 100}{78} \quad = \quad £4{,}717.95$$

Z is given a credit for that portion of the basic rate tax paid by the trustees which is attributable to £4,717.95; ie £1,037.95. Z does not receive a credit for the rest of the tax paid by the trustees (£1,320 − £1,037.95 = £282.05) and the result is that management expenses have been paid out of taxed income so that the total cost of these expenses is £1,282.05.

'Income' for these purposes does not include items which are capital under general trust law although income tax may have been charged on them in the hands of the trustees[4].

[972]

1   *Baker v Archer-Shee* [1927] AC 844, HL.
2   *Macfarlane v IRC* [1929] SC 453. When a beneficiary is entitled to savings income the value of the credit passed on to him by the trustees is at the lower rate of 20% by virtue of the Income and Corporation Taxes Act 1988 s 1A as inserted by the Finance Act 1996 s 73 and as amended (42–44 Halsbury's Statutes (4th Edn) TAXATION).
3   See *Fry v Shiel's Trustees* [1915] SC 159. See also the Income and Corporation Taxes Act 1988 s 833(4) as amended by the Finance Act 1988 Sch 3 para 21, Sch 14 Pts IV, VIII noting, however, that in *Baker v Archer-Shee* above it appears that if a beneficiary is entitled to the income as it arises he is taxed according to the rules of the Schedule appropriate to that source of income.
4   For example premiums treated as rent under the Income and Corporation Taxes Act 1988 s 34 as amended by the Finance Act 1995 Sch 29 Pt VIII(1) and by the Finance Act 1998 s 40, Sch 5 para 15, and capital sums received on a disposal of land under the Income and Corporation Taxes Act 1988 s 776 as amended by the Taxation of Chargeable Gains Act 1992 Sch 10 para 14(50).

[973]

350   Taxing an annuitant

An annuitant under a trust is not entitled to income of the trust as it arises; instead he is taxed under Case III of Schedule D on the income that he receives. The trustees deduct income tax from the annuity under the Income and Corporation Taxes Act 1988 Section 348[1] and the beneficiary is given credit for the basic rate tax deducted at source in the usual way.

1   See the Income and Corporation Taxes Act 1988 s 348 as amended (42–44 Halsbury's Statutes (4th Edn) TAXATION).

[974]

351   Taxing a discretionary beneficiary

A discretionary beneficiary has no right to a specific amount of income but is merely entitled to be considered. Any payments that he receives are charged as his income under Case III of Schedule D (they are annual payments because they may recur) and he receives a credit for the tax paid by the trustees and attributable to that payment. As the trust is discretionary, that tax is at the rate applicable to trusts (34% since 1996–97).

Once an irrevocable decision has been taken by the trustees to retain income as a part of the capital of the fund, the sum accumulated loses its character as income and is treated in the same way as the original fund, ie as capital. It follows, therefore, that the income tax suffered on that income (at 34%) is irrecoverable and that no further income tax will be charged on the accumulations when they are eventually paid out to the beneficiaries as capital (although such distributions have capital gains tax and inheritance tax consequences). In deciding whether it is more advantageous to accumulate income or to pay it out to beneficiaries under their discretionary powers, trustees need to consider, inter alia, the tax position of the individual beneficiaries[1].

[975]

Example 45

Trustees receive in 2001–02 non-dividend income of £10,000. A, B and C are three discretionary beneficiaries (all unmarried). A has no other income and has an unused personal allowance; B is a basic rate taxpayer; and C is subject to tax at a marginal rate of 40%. The trustees are deciding whether to pay income to any one or more of the beneficiaries or whether to accumulate it. The following tax consequences would ensue:

(1)   The trustees are subject to tax at 34% on the trust income (ie £3,400 tax).

(2)   If the trustees decide to pay all the net income of £6,600 (ignoring expenses) to A (who has no other income) he is entitled to a repayment of tax as follows:

	£
Income (Schedule D Case III) (£6,600 x 100/66)	10,000
Deduct: Single person's allowance	4,535
Income chargeable to tax	£5,465

	£
Income tax:	
£1,880 at 10%	188.00
£3,585 at 22%	788.70
	£976.70
Deduct: Tax treated as paid	3,400.00
Tax refund	£2,423.30

[976]

(3)   If the trustees pay the income to B (the basic rate taxpayer), he is not entitled to a refund of any tax at the basic rate, but, depending on the amount of his other income, may obtain a refund of the extra 12% tax paid by the trustees.

(4)   If the trustees pay the income to C (the higher rate taxpayer), further tax is due as follows:

		£
Income	10,000	
Tax at 40%		4,000
Deduct: Tax treated as paid		3,400
Further tax due		£600

(5)   If the trustees accumulate the income, the £3,400 tax paid is irrecoverable and the net income of £6,600 is converted into capital.

From a tax viewpoint, the trustees could avoid payments to C, consider paying all or part of the income to A and B, and accumulate any balance.

1   Under the Trustee Act 1925 s 31(2) as amended by the Family Law Reform Act 1969 s 1(3), Sch 1 Pt I
           and by the Trustee Act 2000 s 40(1), Sch 2 para 25 (48 Halsbury's Statutes (4th Edn) TRUSTS AND
           SETTLEMENTS) the trustees may apply accumulations of income in the maintenance of the relevant
           beneficiary: the tax treatment of these payments is obscure. The better view is that they are capital
           payments.

                                                                                                    [978]

352   Post 5 April 1999 dividends

Inevitably the position is more complex when the income distributed is post 5 April 1999
dividends. The rules, which came into effect on 6 April 1999, have resulted in a basic or
higher rate beneficiary being in a worse position if he receives such income via a
Section 686 trust than if he had personally owned the shares and hence directly received
the dividend[1].

Example 46

B, a higher rate taxpayer, receives a net dividend of £900 from the shares which he
owns in 'X' plc.

		£
Gross dividend	£1,000	
Tax at 32.5%		325
Deduct: Tax credit (10%)		100
Tax payable		£225

Net cash in hand £900 − £225 = £675

                                                                                                    [979]

If B had been a basic rate taxpayer he would have been left with cash in hand of £900.
But consider the position if the dividends had reached B via a discretionary trust under
which the trustees (because of the lack of any tax pool) had adopted the alternative
strategy of Example 43 [967] above.

(1)   If B is a higher rate taxpayer he receives a net distribution of £594 with a
           credit of £306 (representing the Section 687 tax at 34%).

		£
Gross income	£900	
Deduct: Tax credit at 40%		360
Less credit		306
Tax payable		54
Net cash in hand £594 − £54		£540

                                                                                                    [980]

(b) If B is a basic rate taxpayer:

		£
Gross income	£900	
Tax at 22%		198
Deduct: Tax credit		306
Repayment due		108
Net cash in hand £594 + £108 =		£702

By contrast the non-taxpayer is no worse off than if he had received the dividend direct: in both cases (using the above figures) he ends up with £900 cash in hand.

---

1   The life tenant under a fixed interest trust is in no worse position given that the tax treatment is essentially 'transparent'.

[981]

353   Dangers of supplementing income out of capital

Capital payments are not generally subject to income tax. If, however, a beneficiary is entitled to a fixed amount of income each year which is to be made up out of capital should the trust fail to produce the requisite amount of income, such topping up payments are taxed as income in his hands[1].

Example 47

(1)   The settlor's widow is given an annuity of £4,000 a year; the trustees are required to pay it out of the capital of the fund if the income is insufficient. The widow is liable to income tax on the payments that she receives whether paid out of income or capital because they are annual payments.

(2)   The settlor's widow is given an annuity of £4,000 a year and, in addition, the trustees have the power 'to apply capital for the benefit of the widow in such manner as they shall in their absolute discretion think fit'. Any supplements out of capital escape income tax because the widow has an interest in both income and capital, and payments out of capital are treated as advances of capital rather than as income payments.

[982]

The Inland Revenue has argued that payments made out of trust capital can still be taxed as income in the hands of the recipient beneficiary even when the payments are not paid in augmentation of an income interest: the income nature of the payment in the hands of the recipient can be discovered by looking at its size, recurrence, and purpose. In *Stevenson v Wishart*[2] discretionary trust income was paid out in full each year to a charity and capital sums were then paid to one of the beneficiaries who had suffered a heart attack. The purpose of the payments was to cover medical expenses and the cost of living in a nursing home. The Inland Revenue argument that these sums were paid out for an income purpose and were therefore subject to income tax was rejected both at first instance and by the Court of Appeal. Fox LJ stated that:

'There is nothing in the present case which indicates that the payments were of an income nature except their recurrence. I do not think that is sufficient. The trustees were disposing of capital in exercise of a power over capital. They did not create a recurring interest in property. If, in exercise of a power over capital, they chose to make at their discretion regular payments of capital to deal with the special problems of [the beneficiary's] last years rather than release a single sum to her of a large amount, that does not seem to me to create an income interest. Their power was to appoint capital. What they appointed remained capital.'

[983]

The Court of Appeal stressed the exceptional nature of nursing-home payments. Fox LJ, for instance, stated that such expenditure, although involving day-to-day maintenance, was emergency expenditure of very substantial amounts which would usually fall outside normal income resources. It may be, therefore, that if the expenditure was not of an emergency nature the court would consider the payments to be income.

It is understood that the Inland Revenue currently treat advances or appointments out of trust capital as capital in the hands of the recipient beneficiary unless:

353.1   the payments in question are designed to augment income[3];

353.2   the payments in question really amount to an annuity[4]; or

353.3   the trust instrument contains a provision authorising the use of capital to maintain a beneficiary in the same degree of comfort as had been the case in the past[5].

The present tax treatment of dividends in the hands of trustees may encourage trustees to accumulate the dividend income and then seek to provide for beneficiaries out of capital advances.

[984]

1   See *Brodie's Will Trustees v IRC* (1933) 17 TC 432; *Cunard's Trustees v IRC* [1946] 1 All ER 159, CA.
2   *Stevenson v Wishart* [1987] 2 All ER 428, [1987] 1 WLR 1204, CA.
3   See for example *Brodie's Will Trustees v IRC* above.
4   See *Jackson's Trustees v IRC* (1942) 25 TC 13.
5   See *Cunard's Trustees v IRC* above.

[985]

354   The effects of the Trustee Act 1925 Section 31[1]

The effects of the Trustee Act 1925 Section 31 (which may be excluded or modified by the trust instrument) may be stated in the following propositions:

354.1   If a minor has a vested interest in the capital of a fund and the income is retained by the trustees the income belongs to the minor. Therefore, the trust rate is inapplicable because the income is that of a person other than the trustee; were the minor to die, both capital and income accumulations would belong to his estate.

354.2   If a minor has a vested interest in income only (eg if the trust is to A for life when A is seven years old), the trustees may retain that income with the capital of the fund. Were the minor to die the accumulations would not pass to his estate. In this case Section 31 has a divesting effect and for income tax purposes the accumulating income is subject to the rate applicable to trusts because it does not belong to any particular beneficiary as it arises. In *Stanley v IRC*[2] it was stated that 'Section 31 has effected a radical change in the law. [The beneficiary] is, in fact, for all practical purposes in precisely the same position as if his interest in surplus income were contingent'.

354.3   If a beneficiary is contingently entitled to trust capital on attaining an age in excess of 18, Section 31 vests the income of that contingent interest in the beneficiary from the age of 18[3]. In this case the section has a 'vesting effect.' This provision needs to be borne in mind when drafting accumulation and maintenance trusts in which capital entitlement is deferred until age 25. The beneficiary will normally become entitled to income at 18 as a result of the operation of Section 31[4].

[986]

1   Ie the Trustee Act 1925 s 31 as amended by the Family Law Reform Act 1969 s 1(3), Sch 1 Pt I and by the Trustee Act 2000 s 40(1), Sch 2 para 25 (48 Halsbury's Statutes (4th Edn) TRUSTS AND SETTLEMENTS).
2   *Stanley v IRC* [1944] 1 All ER 230, CA.
3   Trustee Act 1925 s 31(1)(ii) as amended by the Family Law Reform Act 1969 s 1(3), Sch 1 Pt I.
4   For accumulation and maintenance trusts see vol 40(2) (2001 Reissue) Part 11 [6301].

[987]–[1000]

3: THE ANTI-AVOIDANCE PROVISIONS

355   Introduction

When the anti-avoidance rules operate, they deem the income of a settlement to be that of the settlor, but they also enable him to recover from the trustees any tax that he suffers on that income[1].

1   Income and Corporation Taxes Act 1988 s 660D as inserted by the Finance Act 1995 s 74, Sch 17 para 1 (42–44 Halsbury's Statutes (4th Edn) TAXATION). Note that a 'settlement' is widely defined for these purposes: see the Income and Corporation Taxes Act 1988 s 660G (1) as inserted by the Finance Act 1995 s 74, Sch 17 para 1. On 'arrangements' see *Butler v Wildin* [1989] STC 22, 61 TC 666. The Income and Corporation Taxes Act 1988 Chapter IA (ss 660A–660G) (liability of settlor) does not apply to any qualifying income which arises under a trust, the trustees of which are resident in the UK, if given by the trustees to a charity in the year of assessment in which it arises, or if it is income to which a charity is entitled under the trust: Finance Act 2000 s 44 (48 Halsbury's Statutes (4th Edn) TRUSTS AND SETTLEMENTS). However, the trustees of a discretionary trust should consider the inheritance tax consequences of appointing a fixed income interest to a charity.

[1001]

356   Payments to minor unmarried children of settlor

Income produced by a settlement which is paid during the settlor's lifetime to or for the benefit of the settlor's own minor unmarried child is normally treated as the income of the settlor. If income is accumulated under an irrevocable settlement of capital, however, the income is not treated as that of the settlor, but payments out of the fund are treated as the settlor's income up to the amount of the accumulations[1].

[1002]

Example 48

D settles shares for the benefit of his three children A, B and C in equal shares contingent on attaining the age of 21 years. They are all minors and unmarried. If the income of the fund is £10,000 a year the income tax position (for the tax year 2001–02) is as follows:

(1)   The trustees are liable for income tax at a rate of 34% (assuming that no dividend income is involved).

(2)   If the balance of the income (after the payment of tax) is accumulated, it is not treated as the income of the settlor. Therefore, so long as the income is retained in the trust no further income tax is payable.

(3)   If any of the income is paid to a child, it is treated as income of D. Say, for instance, that £1,320 is paid to, or for the benefit of, A. The result is that D's income is increased by £2,000 (£1,320 grossed up at 34%). He is given credit for the £680 tax paid by the trustees. If he is charged to further income tax on that sum, tax recovery provisions enable him to claim a refund from the trustees, or from any other person to whom the income is payable (in this case A, B and C, although recourse would only be had to the beneficiaries to the extent that they had received income). If D is subject to higher rate tax at 40% the result is:

[1003]

	£
Deemed income	2,000
D's tax (higher rate) at 40%	800
Deduct: Credit for tax paid at 34%	680
Tax owing at 6%	£120

(4)   If all the net income (£6,600) is distributed amongst the three beneficiaries (and, therefore, treated as D's income), any further distributions to the beneficiaries would be capital advancements.

(5)   This settlement is an accumulation and maintenance trust for inheritance tax purposes; but this does not confer any income tax advantages.

[1004]

Three other general matters should be noted, namely that:

356.1   income covenants by the settlor/parent in favour of trustees are caught as income settlements;

356.2   'child' is widely defined to include a stepchild, an illegitimate child[2], and an adopted child[3], but does not, presumably, include a foster child; and

356.3   the definition of settlement for these purposes includes a transfer of assets and an arrangement[4].

If the settlor is not the parent of the child beneficiary, the above provisions do not apply; grandparental settlements are, therefore, advantageous from an income tax point of view. Even if the settlor is the parent, so long as the income is accumulated, there is still an income tax saving if the parent is subject to income tax at the higher rate of 40%.

[1005]

1   Income and Corporation Taxes Act 1988 s 660B as inserted by the Finance Act 1995 s 74, Sch 17 para 1 and as amended by the Finance Act 1999 s 64 (42–44 Halsbury's Statutes (4th Edn) TAXATION). Note that there is de minimis provision whereby income paid to a child in a year of assessment is not taxed on the settlor provided that it does not exceed £100: Income and Corporation Taxes Act 1988 s 660B(5) as substituted by the Finance Act 1999 s 64(4).

2   Income and Corporation Taxes Act 1988 s 660B(6)(a) as inserted by the Finance Act 1995 s 74, Sch 17 para 1.

3   Income and Corporation Taxes Act 1988 s 832(5).

4   *Thomas v Marshall* [1953] AC 543, [1953] 1 All ER 1102, HL.

[1006]

357   Bare trusts

Prior to 9 March 1999 a settlor could obtain an income tax advantage if he established a bare trust for his infant child[1].

[1007]

Example 49

F's marginal rate of income tax for the tax year 1997–98 was 40%. He settled property which produced an income of £1,000, upon trust for his minor daughter absolutely. The income has been retained by the trustees.

(1)   If F had received the income, the income tax payable would have been £400, so that he would have been left with £600.

(2)   As the income is settled upon trust for his daughter absolutely, the income was treated as belonging to her so long as it was retained by the trustees. As a result, she was able to set her personal allowance against the income which resulted in no income tax being due. (The rate applicable to trusts did not apply because the income belonged to a beneficiary.) The sum of £1,000 was, therefore, retained in the settlement. Of course, there must be no payments out of the fund until the daughter attains 18 years (or marries under that age), otherwise the sums paid out would be taxed as F's income.

The position was altered by the Finance Act 1999[2] as from 9 March 1999 with the result that:

(1)   if such trusts are established on or after that date income is taxed on the settlor as it arises;

(2)   trusts already in existence are not affected although, if property is added to such trusts, income produced by the addition is taxed on the settlor.

[1008]

1   See Form 10 [1166] post.
2   Income and Corporation Taxes Act 1988 s 660B (1)(b) as amended by the Finance Act 1999 s 64(1)(5) (42–44 Halsbury's Statutes (4th Edn) TAXATION). There remain capital gains tax advantages in such bare trusts.

[1009]

---

358   Other points on settlements for infant children

There must be no power to terminate the trust in circumstances where the fund could revert to the settlor. It is of no import whether the power to terminate is given to the settlor or to a stranger. The settlement must be irrevocable. Furthermore, the income or assets from the fund must not be payable, according to the terms of the settlement, to or for the benefit of the settlor or his spouse except for payments made after the death of the child beneficiary or on the bankruptcy of the child, or on a purported charge or assignment of assets by the child. Therefore a settlement is irrevocable if the child is given a protected life interest under the standard trusts[1], and if the settlement is to revert to the settlor on the death of the child beneficiary. Finally, a settlement is not irrevocable if it can be determined by act or default of any person. For example, a settlement that will terminate if the settlor ceases to be employed in a specified employment is not irrevocable.

1   See the Trustee Act 1925 s 33 as amended by the Family Law Reform Act 1987 s 33(1), Sch 2 para 2 (48 Halsbury's Statutes (4th Edn) TRUSTS AND SETTLEMENTS).

[1010]

359   Settlements in which the settlor retains an interest

The Income and Corporation Taxes Act 1988 Section 660A[1] was introduced in the Finance Act 1995 and superseded many of the anti-avoidance provisions applicable to settlements. Income arising under a settlement during the settlor's lifetime is taxed as his for all income tax purposes unless the income arises from property in which he has no interest. A settlor has an interest in property if it is or will or may become payable to or applicable for his benefit or that of his spouse in any circumstances, including where the fund reverts to the settlor under a revocable settlement, or the settlor is a discretionary beneficiary[2].

[1011]

When does the settlor retain an interest in a settlement? Section 660A provides that the settlor shall not be deemed to have an interest in property if and so long as none of that property, and no derived property, can become payable to or applicable for the benefit of the settlor or the wife or husband of the settlor, except in the event of:

359.1   the bankruptcy of some person who is or may become beneficially entitled to the property or any derived property[3];

359.2   an assignment of or charge on the property or any derived property being made or given by some such person[4];

359.3   in the case of a marriage settlement, the death of both parties to the marriage and of all or any of the children of the marriage[5]; or

359.4   the death of a child of the settlor who had become beneficially entitled to the property or any derived property at an age not exceeding 25[6].

The tax charge on the settlor is levied under Case VI of Schedule D[7] and he can recover any tax paid, either from the trustees or from any person to whom the income is payable[8].

Accordingly, if there is a power to revoke the trusts (whoever possesses that power) and as a result the fund may revert to the settlor or his spouse, the income of the fund is treated by the Income and Corporation Taxes Act 1988 Section 660A as belonging to the settlor because the property 'will or may' become payable to or applicable for the benefit of the settlor or his spouse[9]. If, under the terms of a discretionary settlement, any person has, or may have, the power to pay that income or property to the settlor or his spouse, then the income arising under the settlement is treated as belonging to the settlor[10].

[1012]

Example 50

A creates a settlement in favour of his two adult daughters C and D, as concurrent life tenants, and he gives the trustees an overriding power to accumulate the income. Because he has not disposed of the remainder interest, A has retained an interest in the fund with the result that accumulated income is taxed as his.

[1013]

The nature of the interest which the settlor must retain has given rise to some discussion. A power to participate in the management of the trust is not a sufficient interest; likewise, the possibility that a beneficiary might make a gift back to the settlor is to be ignored; and the Inland Revenue accepts that if the trustees agree to pay the inheritance tax that arises on the creation of the settlement, this does not amount to the retention of an interest[11]. Furthermore, if the interest of the settlor is dependent upon the happening of the events set out in the Income and Corporation Taxes Act 1988 Section 660A(4), (5)[12], income is not deemed to be his.

If a settlement is made on the spouse of the settlor, income remains taxed as the settlor's unless the spouse is given an absolute interest in the property. Contrast the position where Mr A holds shares for Mrs A absolutely (income taxed on Mrs A), with Mr A holding the shares for Mrs A for life, remainder to their son (income taxed as Mr A's)[13].

[1014]

1   Income and Corporation Taxes Act 1988 s 660A as inserted by the Finance Act 1995 s 74, Sch 17 para 1 and as amended by the Finance Act 2000 s 41(6) Sch 13 para 26, (42–44 Halsbury's Statutes (4th Edn) TAXATION). Compare the similar capital gains tax rules in the Taxation of Chargeable Gains Act 1992 s 77 as substituted by the Finance Act 1995 s 74, Sch 17 para 27 and as amended by the Finance Act 1998 Sch 21 para 6(1) (42–44 Halsbury's Statutes (4th Edn) TAXATION).

2   For the definition of a 'spouse' for these purposes see the Income and Corporation Taxes Act 1988 s 660A(3) as inserted (see note 1 above): note especially the exclusion of a separated spouse.

3   Income and Corporation Taxes Act 1988 s 660A(4)(a) as inserted (see note 1 above).

4   Income and Corporation Taxes Act 1988 s 660A(4)(b) as inserted (see note 1 above).

5   Income and Corporation Taxes Act 1988 s 660A(4)(c) as inserted (see note 1 above).

6   Income and Corporation Taxes Act 1988 s 660A(4)(d) as inserted (see note 1 above). See Income and Corporation Taxes Act 1988 s 660A(5) preventing any charge if a person is alive and under 25 years and during whose life the property cannot become applicable for the benefit of the settlor (or his spouse) save in the event of bankruptcy, assignment or charge. The typical accumulation and maintenance trust with a long-stop provision for the settlor or his spouse is thus covered.

7   Income and Corporation Taxes Act 1988 s 660C as inserted by the Finance Act 1995 s 74, Sch 17 para 1 and as amended by the Finance (No 2) Act 1997 Sch 4 para 14.

8   Income and Corporation Taxes Act 1988 s 660D as inserted by the Finance Act 1995 s 74, Sch 17 para 1.

9   Income and Corporation Taxes Act 1988 s 660A(1), (2) as inserted (see note 1 above).

10   Income and Corporation Taxes Act 1988 s 660A(1), (2) as inserted (see note 1 above).

11   See Inland Revenue Statement of Practice SP1/82 (6 April 1982).

12   Income and Corporation Taxes Act 1988 s 660A(4), (5) as inserted (see note 1 above).

13   See the Income and Corporation Taxes Act 1988 s 660A(6) as inserted (see note 1 above): *Young v Pearce; Young v Scrutton* [1996] STC 743.

[1015]

360   Receipt of capital benefits

The Income and Corporation Taxes Act 1988 Section 677 contains provisions aimed at preventing the settlor obtaining any benefit from a settlement in which the income may be taxed at a lower rate than that which would have applied had the settlor retained it[1]. In effect, capital payments to the settlor (or his spouse) from the fund are matched with undistributed income of the fund and taxed as the settlor's income. The sum is grossed up at the 34% rate; the settlor is entitled to credit for tax paid by the trustees, but not to any repayment. There are no provisions enabling the settlor to recover tax that he has to pay.

[1016]

A 'capital sum' covers any sum paid by way of loan or a repayment of a loan and any sum paid otherwise than as income and which is not paid for full consideration in money or money's worth[2]. A capital sum is treated as paid to the settlor if it is paid to a third party at his direction or as a result of his assignment[3].

A capital sum is only caught to the extent that it is less than, or equals, the income available in the settlement; this means the undistributed income of the fund from any year of assessment. Any excess is not charged in the year of receipt, but it may be charged later if income becomes available in any of the next 11 years[4].

Example 51

The undistributed net income of a settlement is as follows:

	£
Year 1	10,000
Year 2	2,500
Year 3	15,000
Year 4	6,000
Year 5	7,000

In year 3, the trustees lend the settlor £45,000. That loan is a capital sum and, therefore, the settlor is charged to income tax in year 3 on that sum to the extent that it represents available income. As the available income is £27,500 (years 1–3) he is taxed on £27,500 grossed up at 34%; ie on £41,666.67. If he is liable to higher rate tax at 40% he is taxed at 6%. The remaining £17,500 is carried forward and taxed in succeeding years when income becomes available; in year 4, for instance, £6,000 is available. If the loan is repaid, there is no further charge on income in subsequent years, but any tax paid during the loan period cannot be recovered[5].

[1017]

The Income and Corporation Taxes Act 1988 Section 677 also applies to a capital sum received by the settlor from a body corporate connected with the settlement. Generally, a company is connected with a settlement if it is a close company and the participators include the trustees of the settlement[6]. The width of the provision and its somewhat capricious nature[7] means that settlements often contain a clause prohibiting the payment of capital sums to the settlor or his spouse.

[1018]

---

1   See the Income and Corporation Taxes Act 1988 ss 677, 678 as amended by the Finance Act 1989 s 109(4), by the Finance Act 1993 Sch 6 paras 7, 25(1) and by the Finance Act 1995 s 74, Sch 17 paras 9, 10 (42–44 Halsbury's Statutes (4th Edn) TAXATION).
2   Income and Corporation Taxes Act 1988 s 677(9)(a) as amended by the Finance Act 1995 s 74, Sch 17 para 9.
3   Income and Corporation Taxes Act 1988 s 677(10).
4   Income and Corporation Taxes Act 1988 s 677(1)(b).
5   Income and Corporation Taxes Act 1988 s 677(4).
6   Income and Corporation Taxes Act 1988 s 682A(2) as inserted by the Finance Act 1995 s 74, Sch 17 para 11.
7   See, for example, *De Vigier v IRC* [1964] 2 All ER 907, [1964] 1 WLR 1073, HL. As a result a settlor should not lend money to his settlement without first checking whether a repayment will be caught by these provisions.

[1019]–[1050]

PART 2: TAKING INSTRUCTIONS FOR A NEW SETTLEMENT AND STANDARD CONDITIONS

Forms and Precedents

A: TAKING INSTRUCTIONS

1: INTRODUCTION

Preparation to setting up a trust

When taking instructions it is normally advantageous to complete a checklist and, in cases where tax planning is involved, to ensure that the client completes an asset questionnaire. It is important to consider carefully the tax implications of any proposed settlement[1]. A draft settlement should then be produced and sent to the client for checking along with a summary of its main terms. In preparing the draft settlement, start from a suitable precedent: in some cases the precedent may require only minor amendment, in others substantial modification may be needed. Whatever the position, it is important that everything in the precedent is relevant and needed, and that nothing is included that is unclear. Anything that is unnecessary should be deleted and any insertions should fit in with the existing clauses in respect of style, numbering and definitions of terms. Insertions should not in any way conflict with the framework of the existing precedent[2].

[1051]

---

1   See *Estill v Cowling Swift and Kirchin* [2000] Lloyd's Rep PN 378, CD.
2   For a salutary example of a settlement that was internally inconsistent, see *Wight v Olswang* (1988) Times 17 September, revsd (1999) Times 18 May, CA.

[1052]

2: FORMS

1

Checklist before drafting

1   Settlor

Obtain the following information in respect of the settlor (or each settlor if more than one)[1]:

1.1   Full name.

1.2   Address.

1.3   Domicile and residence.

2   Beneficiaries

Obtain the following information in respect of each beneficiary:

2.1   Full name.

2.2   Address.

2.3   Age (where relevant).

3   Beneficiaries' interests

Obtain the following information from the settlor:

3.1   What is the nature of the interest to be taken by each of the beneficiaries: is the interest to be vested in possession, a future interest etc?

3.2   Who is to be the default beneficiary[2]?

4   Letter of wishes

In the event of the trustees possessing flexible powers (eg in a discretionary trust) ensure that the settlor prepares (and keeps under review) a letter of wishes[3].

5   Trust Fund

Obtain from the settlor details of the property to be settled[4].

6   Trustees

Obtain the following information from the settlor:

6.1   Names and addresses of the persons to act as trustees.

6.2   Details of the person having power to appoint new or replacement trustees[5].

7   Administrative powers

Consider whether standard powers are appropriate[6]. Are any special powers required[7]?

8   Mechanics[8]

How is the trust to be constituted?

1   As to commencement when the parties consist of joint settlors and trustees see Form 49 [1384] post. Normally, joint settlors should be avoided.

2   A living person should be chosen primarily to ensure that there can be no possibility of a resulting trust to the settlor. For the horrors that may otherwise occur, see the *Vandervell* trust litigation: *Vandervell v IRC* [1967] 2 AC 291, [1967] 1 All ER 1, HL; *Re Vandervell's Trusts (No 2), White v Vandervell Trustees Ltd* [1974] Ch 269, [1974] 3 All ER 205, CA. In the case of minor or charitable beneficiaries, an appropriate receipt clause should be included.

3   For letters of wishes see Form 252 [1841] et seq post. The settlor should consider whether the contents of the letter are confidential or whether they may be disclosed to the beneficiaries (if so, this should be made clear in the letter).

4   In practice this topic may require extensive discussion with the client. The tax consequences if a particular item of property is settled should be considered (eg does it qualify for inheritance tax business property relief, or is capital gains tax hold-over relief available?). It should be ascertained whether the settlor is to be excluded from all benefit (note problems such as reservation of benefit for inheritance tax purposes if he is not). The manner in which the asset is to be transferred or assigned also requires consideration: see Part 4 Introduction to Section B [1281] post and see Form 33 [1283] et seq post. In the case of land, the trusts should be kept off the title. It is common for the settlement to be established in 'pilot' form, namely with the payment of £10 as initial trust capital.

5   The identity of the trustees is a crucial decision for the settlor, especially if the trustees are to have wide dispositive powers. As to the appointment of new and additional trustees see vol 40(2) (2001 Reissue) TRUSTS AND SETTLEMENTS Part 10 [5201]. It should be considered whether the Trusts of Land and Appointment of Trustees Act 1996 Pt II (ss 19–21) (37 Halsbury's Statutes (4th Edn) REAL PROPERTY) should be excluded. In the case of offshore trusts, the use of a protector might be desirable: see vol 40(2) (2001 Reissue) TRUSTS AND SETTLEMENTS Part 15 [8701].

6   Eg the Society of Trust and Estate Practitioners' Standard Provisions: see Introduction to Section B [1061] post and see Form 3 [1063] post.

7   Eg will the trustees be required to run a business? If it is envisaged that the property will eventually be comprised in separate funds, the trustees should be given appropriate powers of appropriation/reappropriation.

8   The trust must be properly constituted: eg in the case of a pilot trust the nominal cash sum must be received by the trustees. The Inland Revenue should also be notified where appropriate: see eg the Inheritance Tax Act 1984 s 218 (42–44 Halsbury's Statutes (4th Edn) TAXATION).

[1054]

2

Simple asset/liability statement

	Approximate value		
Assets	You	Your spouse	Tick if owned jointly
House			
Contents			
Other real estate			
Jewellery			
Cash at bank/building society			
Quoted stocks and shares			
Partnership share			

Unquoted stocks and shares (eg in a private company)			
Other assets, including non UK (please specify)			
Liabilities			
Mortgage			
Other			

[1055]

Life Assurance Policies

Life Insurance Company	Policy Number	Sum Assured	Premiums	Purpose of Policy	Whether or not in trust

[1056]

Pension Death Benefits

Pension Scheme/Policy	Amount of Death Benefit	Widow's or Widower's Pension	Is Death Benefit in Trust?	Nomination Form Completed

[1057]–[1060]

B: STANDARD PROVISIONS OF THE SOCIETY OF TRUST AND ESTATE PRACTITIONERS

1: INTRODUCTION

The dangers of using standard provisions

These Standard Provisions were prepared by the Society of Trust and Estate Practitioners from whom copies may be obtained[1]. They are intended to deal with routine administration matters that will commonly be included in any will trust or inter vivos settlement. Opinions inevitably vary as to the use of standard forms: consider, for example, in company law the use of standard articles of association and in wills the statutory will forms[2].

The arguments in favour of use of standard forms include word saving, in that the final settlement or will trust will be a document substantially reduced in size. For the draftsman the use of standard provisions removes any risk of omissions and enables him to concentrate on the beneficial trusts.

[1061]

As against that:

1   Incorporation by reference of a separate document is never entirely satisfactory. For instance, unless that document is attached to the settlement deed or will trust there may be a problem in due course in locating a copy of it (and a particular difficulty if what was incorporated was (say) the first edition of the document which has then gone into subsequent editions).

2   There is a risk of the draftsman simply incorporating the document without ensuring that all the provisions are relevant to the particular settlement or will trust. Of course this problem is also present in the case of word processed documents generally, but if the draftsman has the entire document in the draft there is at least a chance that he will read it all through, deleting as appropriate!

3   The Standard Provisions purport to provide a comprehensive code of administrative provisions. This, however, presents two problems:

        3.1   The provisions require regular updating in the light of changes in law and practice. The Standard Provisions were not amended in the light of the Trusts of Land and Appointment of Trustees Act 1996, but the Society of Trust and Estate Practitioners recommended that the following incorporation clause be used:

                'The Standard Provisions of the Society of Trust and Estate Practitioners (1st Edition) shall apply with the deletion of paragraph 5. Section 11 Trusts of Land and Appointment of Trustees Act 1996 (consultation with beneficiaries) shall not apply.'

                It should be borne in mind that what will be incorporated is the edition of the Standard Provisions current at the time when the relevant document is signed or executed.

        3.2   Although the provisions purport to deal with administrative matters only, the line between administrative and dispositive powers is difficult to draw and in places the Standard Provisions stray beyond pure questions of administration (for instance the provisions as to remuneration of trustees and their indemnity; power to act notwithstanding a conflict of interest and modifications to the statutory provisions of maintenance and advancement). The powers appear to have been drafted from the standpoint of professional trustees who are given full discretionary powers with accompanying protection. So the provisions of paragraph 3 (notably those in 3(4)) might be considered inappropriate in a simple life interest/ absolute remainder trust.

What should the client be told? One view is that a detailed explanation is unnecessary and it suffices for him to be aware that these are relatively routine provisions that enable the trustees to manage the trust fund properly. As against that, the provisions do, for example, enable professionals to charge, deal with potential conflicts of interest and afford some protection for what would otherwise be breaches of trust. As a minimum, therefore, it is suggested that the client should be shown the Standard Provisions, that the more important ones should be explained to him and that he should be provided with a copy to take away.

1   For the address and internet address of the Society of Trust and Estate Practitioners see Information
     Binder: Addresses [1].
2   See the Law of Property Act 1925 s 179 (37 Halsbury's Statutes (4th Edn) REAL PROPERTY); and the
     Statutory Will Forms 1925, SI 1925/780. The forms are printed in vol 42(1) (1998 Reissue) WILLS
     AND ADMINISTRATION Form 4 [691].

[1062]

2: STANDARD PROVISIONS FORMS

3

Standard provisions of the Society of Trust and Estate Practitioners[1]

(Please note that the footnote markers, and footnotes, accompanying this Form do not comprise part of the Standard Provisions.)

1.   INTRODUCTORY

1(1)   These Provisions may be called the standard provisions of the Society of Trust and Estate Practitioners (1st Edition).

1(2)   These Provisions may be incorporated in a document by the words:
           The standard provisions of the Society of Trust and Estate Practitioners (1st Edition) shall apply[2]
           or in any manner indicating an intention to incorporate them.

[1063]

2.   INTERPRETATION

2(1)   In these Provisions, unless the context otherwise requires:
           (a)   **Income Beneficiary**, in relation to Trust Property, means a Person to whom income of the Trust Property is payable (as of right or at the discretion of the Trustees).
           (b)   **Person** includes a person anywhere in the world and includes a Trustee.

(c)   **The Principal Document** means the document in which these Provisions are incorporated.

(d)   **The Settlement** means any settlement created by the Principal Document and an estate of a deceased Person to which the Principal Document relates.

(e)   **The Trustees** means the personal representatives or trustees of the Settlement for the time being.

(f)   **The Trust Fund** means the property comprised in the Settlement for the time being.

(g)   **Trust Property** means any property comprised in the Trust Fund.

(h)   **A Professional Trustee** means a Trustee who is or has been carrying on a business which consists of or includes the management of trusts or the administration of estates[3].

2(2)   These Provisions have effect subject to the provisions of the Principal Document[4].

[1064]

3.   ADMINISTRATIVE POWERS

The Trustees shall have the following powers:

3(1)   *Investment*[5]

(a)   The Trustees may invest Trust Property in any manner as if they were beneficial owners. In particular the Trustees may invest in unsecured loans.

(b)   The Trustees may decide not to diversify the Trust Fund.

3(2)   *Management*[6]

The Trustees may effect any transaction relating to the management administration or disposition of Trust Property as if they were beneficial owners. In particular:

(a)   The Trustees may repair and maintain Trust Property.

(b)   The Trustees may develop or improve Trust Property.

3(3)   *Joint Property*

The Trustees may acquire property jointly with any Person[7].

3(4)   *Income and Capital*

The Trustees may decide not to hold a balance between conflicting interests of Persons interested in Trust Property. In particular:

(a)   The Trustees may acquire
    (i)   wasting assets and
    (ii)   assets which yield little or no income
for investment or any other purpose[8].

(b)   The Trustees may decide not to procure distributions from a company in which they are interested[9].

(c)   The Trustees may pay taxes and other expenses out of income although they would otherwise be paid out of capital[10].

[1065]

3(5)   *Accumulated Income*[11]

The Trustees may apply accumulated income as if it were income arising in the current year.

3(6)   *Use of Trust Property*[12]
The Trustees may permit an Income Beneficiary to occupy or enjoy the use of Trust Property on such terms as the Trustees think fit. The Trustees may acquire any property for this purpose.

3(7)   *Application of Trust Capital*[13]
The Trustees may:
(a)   lend money which is Trust Property to an Income Beneficiary without security, on such terms as they think fit,
(b)   charge Trust Property as security for debts or obligations of an Income Beneficiary, or
(c)   pay money which is Trust Property to an Income Beneficiary as his income, for the purpose of augmenting his income
Provided that:
(i)   the Trustees have power to transfer such Property to that Beneficiary absolutely; or
(ii)   the Trustees have power to do so with the consent of another Person and the Trustees act with the written consent of that Person.

3(8)   *Trade*[14]
The Trustees may carry on a trade, in any part of the world, alone or in partnership.

3(9)   *Borrowing*[15]
The Trustees may borrow money for investment or any other purpose. Money borrowed shall be treated as Trust Property.

[1066]

3(10)   *Insurance*[16]
The Trustees may insure Trust Property for any amount against any risk.

3(11)   *Delegation*[17]
A Trustee may delegate in writing any of his functions to any Person. A Trustee shall not be responsible for the default of that Person (even if the delegation was not strictly necessary or expedient) provided that he took reasonable care in his selection and supervision.

3(12)   *Deposit of Documents*[18]
The Trustees may deposit documents relating to the Settlement (including bearer securities) with any Person.

3(13)   *Nominees*[19]
The Trustees may vest Trust Property in any Person as nominee, and may place Trust Property in the possession or control of any Person.

3(14)   *Offshore administration*[20]
The Trustees may carry on the administration of the trusts of the Settlement outside the United Kingdom.

[1067]

3(15)   *Payment of tax*[21]
The Trustees may pay tax liabilities of the Settlement (and interest on such tax) even though such liabilities are not enforceable against the Trustees.

3(16)   Indemnities
The Trustees may indemnify any Person for any liability properly chargeable against Trust Property.

3(17)   Security[22]
The Trustees may charge Trust Property as security for any liability properly incurred by them as Trustees.

3(18)   Supervision of Company[23]
The Trustees are under no duty to enquire into the conduct of a company in which they are interested, unless they have knowledge of circumstances which call for enquiry.

3(19)   Appropriation[24]
The Trustees may appropriate Trust Property to any Person or class of Persons in or towards the satisfaction of their interest in the Trust Fund.

3(20)   Receipt by Charities[25]
Where Trust Property is to be paid or transferred to a charity, the receipt of the treasurer or appropriate officer of the charity shall be a complete discharge to the Trustees.

3(21)   Release of Powers[26]
The Trustees may by deed release any of their powers wholly or in part so as to bind future trustees.

3(22)   Ancillary Powers[27]
The Trustees may do anything which is incidental or conducive to the exercise of their functions.

[1068]

4.   POWERS OF MAINTENANCE AND ADVANCEMENT

Sections 31 and 32 of the Trustee Act 1925 shall apply with the following modifications:

(a)   The Proviso to section 31(1) shall be deleted.

(b)   The words one-half of in section 32 (1) (a) shall be deleted.

5.   TRUST FOR SALE[28]

The Trustees shall hold land in England and Wales on trust for sale.

6.   MINORS

6(1)   Where the Trustees may apply income for the benefit of a minor, they may do so by paying the income to the minor's parent or guardian on behalf of the minor, or to the minor if he has attained the age of 16. The Trustees are under no duty to enquire into the use of the income unless they have knowledge of circumstances which call for enquiry.

6(2)   Where the Trustees may apply income for the benefit of a minor, they may do so by resolving that they hold that income on trust for the minor absolutely[29] and:
  (a)   The Trustees may apply that income for the benefit of the minor during his minority.
  (b)   The Trustees shall transfer the residue of that income to the minor on attaining the age of 18.
  (c)   For investment and other administrative purposes that income shall be treated as Trust Property.

[1069]

7. DISCLAIMER[30]

A Person may disclaim his interest under the Settlement wholly or in part.

8. APPORTIONMENT

Income and expenditure shall be treated as arising when payable, and not from day to day, so that no apportionment shall take place.

9. CONFLICTS OF INTEREST[31]

9(1)   In this paragraph:
  (a)   **A Fiduciary** means a Person subject to fiduciary duties under the Settlement.
  (b)   **An Independent Trustee**, in relation to a Person, means a Trustee who is not:
    (i)   a brother, sister, ancestor, descendant or dependent of the Person;
    (ii)   a spouse of the Person or of (i) above; or
    (iii)   a company controlled by one or more of any of the above.

9(2)   A Fiduciary may:
  (a)   enter into a transaction with the Trustees, or
  (b)   be interested in an arrangement in which the Trustees are or might have been interested, or
  (c)   act (or not act) in any other circumstances
even though his fiduciary duty under the Settlement conflicts with other duties or with his personal interest;
Provided that:
    (i)   The Fiduciary first discloses to the Trustees the nature and extent of any material interest conflicting with his fiduciary duties, and
    (ii)   there is an Independent Trustee in respect of whom there is no conflict of interest, and he considers that the transaction arrangement or action is not contrary to the general interest of the Settlement.

9(3)   The powers of the Trustees may be used to benefit a Trustee (to the same extent as if he were not a Trustee) provided that there is an Independent Trustee in respect of whom there is no conflict of interest.

[1070]

10. POWERS OF TRUSTEES

The powers of the Trustees may be exercised:

(a)   at their absolute discretion; and

(b)   from time to time as occasion requires.

11. TRUSTEE REMUNERATION[32]

11(1)   A Trustee who is a solicitor or an accountant or who is engaged in a business may charge for work done by him or his firm in connection with the Settlement, including work not requiring professional assistance. This has priority to any disposition made in the Principal Document.

11(2)   The Trustees may make arrangements to remunerate themselves for work done for a company connected with the Trust Fund.

12.   LIABILITY OF TRUSTEES[33]

12(1)   A Trustee (other than a Professional Trustee) shall not be liable for a loss to the Trust Fund unless that loss was caused by his own fraud or negligence.

12(2)   A Trustee shall not be liable for acting in accordance with the advice of Counsel of at least five years standing, with respect to the Settlement, unless, when he does so:
  (a)   he knows or has reasonable cause to suspect that the advice was given in ignorance of material facts; or
  (b)   proceedings are pending to obtain the decision of the court on the matter.

[1071]

13.   APPOINTMENT AND RETIREMENT OF TRUSTEES[34]

13(1)   A Person may be appointed trustee of the Settlement even though he has no connection with the United Kingdom.

13(2)   A Professional Trustee who is an individual who has reached the age of 65 shall retire if:
  (a)   he is requested to do so by his co-trustees, or by a Person interested in Trust Property; and
  (b)   he is effectually indemnified against liabilities properly incurred as Trustee.

On that retirement a new Trustee shall be appointed if necessary to ensure that there will be two individuals or a Trust Corporation to act as Trustee.

In this sub-paragraph Trust Corporation has the same meaning as in the Trustee Act 1925.

This sub-paragraph does not apply to a Professional Trustee who is:
  (a)   a personal representative
  (b)   the settlor of the Settlement
  (c)   a spouse or former spouse of the settlor or testator.

14.   PROTECTION FOR INTEREST IN POSSESSION AND ACCUMULATION AND MAINTENANCE SETTLEMENTS[35]

These Provisions shall not have effect:

(a)   so as to prevent a Person from being entitled to an interest in possession in Trust Property (within the meaning of the Inheritance Tax Act 1984);

(b)   so as to cause the Settlement to be an accumulation or discretionary settlement (within the meaning of Section 5 of the Taxation of Chargeable Gains Act 1992);

(c)   so as to prevent the conditions of Section 71(1) of the Inheritance Tax Act 1984 from applying to Trust Property[36].

[1072]

1   This Form is the Society of Trust and Estate Practitioners' Standard Provisions: 1st Edition (1992). The Form is the copyright of STEP and James Kessler MA, FTII, Barrister of 24 Old Buildings, Lincoln's Inn, WC2A 3UP and is reproduced with their permission. The STEP Standard Provisions were originally drafted by James Kessler. For the address and internet address of the Society of Trust and Estate Practitioners see Information Binder: Addresses [1].

2   It is important to refer to the relevant edition of the Standard Provisions which has been incorporated. See also Introduction to this section [1061] ante where it is suggested that these terms are incorporated with the deletion of paragraph 5 and the exclusion of the Trusts of Land and Appointment of Trustees Act 1996 s 11 (37 Halsbury's Statutes (4th Edn) REAL PROPERTY).

3   The Trustee Act 2000 Pt V (ss 28–33) (48 Halsbury's Statutes (4th Edn) TRUSTS AND SETTLEMENTS) refers to a 'trustee [who] acts in a professional capacity' and this is defined in the Trustee Act 2000 s 28(5). 'Lay trustee' is correspondingly defined: see the Trustee Act 2000 s 28(6).

4   The terms set out in provision 2 [1064] should be added to and/or deleted as appropriate.

5   For the statutory powers of investment see Paragraph 241 [591] et seq ante, noting, in particular, the provisions of the Trustee Act 2000. The Standard Provisions (1st Edn) were drafted before the passage of the Trustee Act 2000: compare the Trustee Act 2000 s 3(1) with provision 3(1)(a) [1065]. The reference to unsecured loans is dictated by the Privy Council case of *Khoo Tek Keong v Ch'ng Joo Tuan Neoh* [1934] AC 529, PC.

      For the obligation to diversify see the Trustee Act 2000 s 4(3)(b) and note that the obligation is to consider diversification 'in so far as is appropriate to the circumstances of the trust'. Commonly, when a trust fund comprises (only) shares in the settlor's family company the trustees are expressly authorised to retain those shares. In exceptional cases, the trustees may be required to retain the shares and may only sell after obtaining the consent of the settlor during his life: Form 146 [1574] post. See also Form 4 Schedule paragraphs 1–4 [1093] post.

      This power is to 'invest' and therefore does not enable trustees to acquire property for use by a beneficiary: see *Re Power, Public Trustee v Hastings* [1947] Ch 572, [1947] 2 All ER 282. See, however, provision 3(6) [1066] which deals with this point and see the Trustee Act 2000 s 8(1) and the Trusts of Land and Appointment of Trustees Act 1996 s 6(3) as amended by the Trustee Act 2000 s 40(1), Sch 2 para 45(1).

6   With the passage of the Trusts of Land and Appointment of Trustees Act 1996 s 6 as amended (see note 5 above) these powers are in the main redundant. It is thought that the power to repair and maintain would be implied. For the allocation of expenses of repairs and improvements between income and capital see Paragraph 160 [389] ante.

7   Express authorisation was formerly necessary if the trustees are to acquire property jointly with others: *Webb v Jonas* (1888) 39 Ch D 660. The Trustee Act 2000 s 3(1) (the general power of investment) is sufficiently widely drafted to cover joint investment, but note that land is not included in this provision. Under the Trustee Act 2000 s 8(1) trustees are only given power to acquire a legal estate (or equivalent) in freehold or leasehold land, so that if they wish to jointly purchase land with a beneficiary it is important that legal title is transferred into the trustees' names.

8   This provision may be used by the trustees to favour the income beneficiary at the expense of the remainderman and vice versa. As such it arguably strays beyond matters of pure administration and it is suggested that the settlor's consent should be obtained before this provision is included.

9   It is, of course, a moot point whether trustees *qua trustees* can procure distributions in these circumstances.

10   For the implications for interest in possession settlements and accumulation and maintenance trusts see Paragraph 287.2 [731] ante and Form 4 note 39 [1106] post. For the danger that such a provision could result in an accumulation of income see *Re Rochford's Settlement Trusts, Rochford v Rochford* [1965] Ch 111, [1964] 2 All ER 177 and Underhill and Hayton *Law of Trusts and Trustees* (15th Edn, 1995) at p 181. The rules of equity prescribed which expenses fell to be set against income and capital and it is not thought that the Trustee Act 2000 s 31 (dealing with trustee expenses) has affected this position. Whilst the trustees may be reimbursed (and may pay) expenses out of funds available (whether income or capital), it is considered that appropriate adjustments then fall to be made to ensure that each expense is correctly allocated (for a contrary view, see Kessler *Drafting Trusts and Will Trusts: A Modern Approach* (5th Edn, 2000) para 18.29 note 53).

[1073]

11   Compare the Trustee Act 1925 s 31(2) as amended by the Family Law Reform Act 1969 s 1(3), Sch 1 Pt I and the Trustee Act 2000 s 40(1), Sch 2 para 25 (48 Halsbury's Statutes (4th Edn) TRUSTS AND SETTLEMENTS).

12   See note 5 above. Note that the Trusts of Land and Appointment of Trustees Act 1996 s 6(3) as amended by the Trustee Act 2000 s 40(1), Sch 2 para 45(1), permits the trustees of land to acquire land for occupation by a beneficiary. Further, in the case of a trust of land, interest in possession beneficiaries may have a right to occupy the trust land: see the Trusts of Land and Appointment of Trustees Act 1996 s 12 and see further Paragraph 228 [545] ante. Under the Trustee Act 2000 Pt III (ss 8–10), which applies from 1 February 2001 (see the Trustee Act 2000 (Commencement) Order 2001, SI 2001/49), all trustees have been given power to acquire land for occupation by a beneficiary. In neither case is the power limited to an income beneficiary, but it is thought that such a limitation would be implied, given that the power is not dispositive in nature. Even after the passage of this Act it is considered that provision 3(6) [1066] should be retained for the powers that it gives to the trustees to acquire assets other than land (eg chattels) for use by a beneficiary.

13   The three powers given to the trustees only apply in cases where there is a power to transfer trust capital to an income beneficiary; with life interest trusts being increasingly drafted in flexible form (see Form 5 [1107] post) this will commonly be the case. In the case of (c), care should be taken to ensure that this does not involve unacceptable tax consequences; eg will the money be subject to an income tax charge in the hands of the income beneficiary?

14   In practice, it is comparatively rare for trustees to trade. In cases where this might be appropriate, trustees will often prefer to form a limited company or, perhaps, a limited liability partnership for the purpose: see Forms 181 [1665], 182 [1669] post.

15   There is no general power to borrow for the purposes of investment: see *Re Suenson-Taylor's Settlement, Moores v Moores* [1974] 3 All ER 397, [1974] 1 WLR 1280.

16   Note the improvements made to the Trustee Act 1925 s 19 by the Trustee Act 2000 s 34(1) which means that this power can be dispensed with.

17   The Trustee Act 2000 Pt IV (ss 11–27) now gives trustees the wide power to delegate to an agent 'delegable functions' (defined in the Trustee Act 2000 s 11(2)). The restriction in the Trustee Act 2000 s 12 means that many draftsmen will continue to include an express delegation clause (see for instance Form 316 [2194] et seq post). This provision of the Standard Provisions (1st Edn) is something of a mystery in that it appears to be dealing with individual rather than corporate delegation. As such it ousts the Trustee Act 1925 s 25 (as substituted by the Trustee Delegation Act 1999 s 5(1), (2)) and removes the restraints in that section. But if this is correct, then the Standard Provisions (1st Edn) contain no provision dealing with the power of trustees as a body to delegate. It is suggested that anyone using the Standard Provisions (1st Edn) adds an express collective delegation clause along the lines of Form 316 [2194] post.

        See provision 3(13) [1067] which provides for the use of nominees. Note that this provision expressly imposes an obligation to exercise reasonable care in supervising the agent. It does not include any provision for payment: query whether the ancillary power in provision 3(22) [1068] can be used for this purpose.

18   This provision has been rendered largely obsolete by the Trustee Act 2000 Pt IV (ss 11–27) (power to appoint agents, nominees and custodians).

19   This provision has been rendered largely obsolete by the Trustee Act 2000 Pt IV (ss 11–27) (power to appoint agents, nominees and custodians).

20   For the appointment of non-UK resident trustees see vol 40(2) (2001 Reissue) TRUSTS AND SETTLEMENTS Part 15 [8701]. It is not thought that this provision is necessary.

21   There are restrictions on foreign taxes that may properly be paid by trustees: see *Re Lord Cable, Garratt v Waters* [1976] 3 All ER 417, [1977] 1 WLR 7.

[1074]

22   The enhanced power to borrow (see provision 3(9) [1066]) is backed up by this enhanced power to charge the trust fund. It also enables trustees to secure any indemnity given under provision 3(16) [1068].

23   For the problems that can arise when trustees own a controlling interest in a private company see *Re Lucking's Will Trusts, Renwick v Lucking* [1967] 3 All ER 726, [1968] 1 WLR 866; *Bartlett v Barclays Bank Trust Co Ltd* [1980] Ch 515, [1980] 1 All ER 139; and Underhill and Hayton *Law of Trusts and Trustees* (15th Edn 1995) p 554. Quaere whether this provision is appropriate in a standard form precedent.

24   For powers of appropriation (and reappropriation) see Paragraph 74 [170] ante and Forms 165 [1629], 166 [1631] post.

25   For an alternative see Form 4 schedule paragraph 27 [1102] post. For a receipts clause for a parent or guardian of an infant beneficiary see provision 6 [1069].

26   Fiduciary powers cannot be released in the absence of an express provision: *Re Wills' Trust Deeds, Wills v Godfrey* [1964] Ch 219, [1963] 1 All ER 390. In practice it will be rare for trustees to wish to release any of their powers.

27   The intention is to ensure that the earlier powers are not narrowly construed.

28   With the passage of the Trusts of Land and Appointment of Trustees Act 1996 this provision should be deleted. See Introduction to this section at [1062] ante where it is suggested that this is done in the clause in the trust deed incorporating the Standard Provisions (1st Edn). Trustees may acquire land on trust for sale if they consider this to be desirable, but it should not be a requirement.

29   For trusts created before 9 March 1999 this could confer an income tax advantage where the settlor was the infant's parent. See Paragraph 357 example 49 [1008] ante.

30   For the inheritance tax consequences of the disclaimer of an interest under a settlement see the Inheritance Tax Act 1984 s 93 (42–44 Halsbury's Statutes (4th Edn) TAXATION). Although the position is far from clear, it is widely thought that in the absence of an express authorisation in the trust instrument a beneficiary cannot disclaim part only of his entitlement. See also *Guthrie v Walrond* (1883) 22 Ch D 573.

31   This provision permits transactions which might be avoided under the general rules of equity applicable to fiduciaries, provided that there is at least one independent trustee. Provision 9(3) [1070] may prove impractical and indeed the whole provision assumes the existence of an independent trustee.

32   For the remuneration of trustees see Paragraph 212 [511] et seq ante.

33   The liability of trustees is considered at Paragraph 182 [451] et seq ante. This provision is in striking contrast to Form 4 clause 12 [1090] post.

34   For the appointment of trustees consider the impact of the Trusts of Land and Appointment of Trustees Act 1996 Pt II (ss 19–21) and see, generally, vol 40(2) (2001 Reissue) TRUSTS AND SETTLEMENTS Part 10 [5201]. Provision 13(2) [1072] (mandatory retirement for a professional trustee) should not be included without careful consideration and discussion with the settlor.

35   This provision has apparently been inserted out of abundant caution and may be omitted.

36   In the light of the Trusts of Land and Appointment of Trustees Act 1996 it may be desirable to include provisions excluding the Trusts of Land and Appointment of Trustees Act 1996 s 11, excluding the Trusts of Land and Appointment of Trustees Act 1996 Pt II (ss 19–21) and restricting beneficial rights of occupation. See further vol 40(2) (2001 Reissue) TRUSTS AND SETTLEMENTS Part 10 [5201].

[1075]–[1080]

PART 3: COMPLETE TRUST DEEDS

Forms and Precedents

(For other complete trust precedents see vol 40(2) (2001 Reissue) TRUSTS AND SETTLEMENTS, *including: discretionary trust of land (see vol 40(2) Part 8 [3501]), employee trusts (see vol 40(2) Part 14 [8101]), offshore trusts (see vol 40(2) Part 15 [8701]), disabled trusts (see vol 40(2) Part 16 [9301]), personal injury compensation trusts (see vol 40(2) Part 17 [9451]) and pension policy trusts (see vol 40(2) Part 18 [9601]).)*

4

Discretionary settlement[1]

THIS SETTLEMENT is made the …… day of ………

BETWEEN:

(1)   *(settlor)* of *(address)* ('the Settlor') and

(2)   *(original trustees)* of *(addresses)* ('the Original Trustees')

WHEREAS

(1)   The Settlor wishes to make the settlement contained below for the benefit of the beneficiaries mentioned below and has paid to the Original Trustees the sum of £… cash to be held on and with and subject to the following trusts powers and provisions

(2)   Further assets may in the future be paid or transferred to the Trustees (as defined below) to be held on and with and subject to such trusts powers and provisions[2]

[(3)   It is intended that this settlement shall be irrevocable][3]

[(4)   The Original Trustees have agreed to act as the first trustees of the settlement][4]

[1081]

NOW THIS DEED WITNESSES as follows:

1   Definitions and interpretation

1.1   In this settlement the following expressions have where the context permits the following meanings:

　　　　1.1.1   'the Trustees' means the Original Trustees or other the trustees or trustee for the time being of this settlement and 'Trustee' means each and any of the Trustees

　　　　1.1.2   'the Trust Fund' means the sum of £… cash paid by the Settlor to the Original Trustees as recited above all assets at any time added to it by way of further settlement accumulation of income capital accretion or otherwise and all property from time to time representing the same

1.1.3   'the Discretionary Beneficiaries'[5] means (subject to the provisions of clause 6) the following persons:

    1.1.3.1   the Settlor's [widow *or* widower]

    1.1.3.2   the issue (whether present or future) of the Settlor's grandfather *(name of settlor's grandfather)* but other than and excluding the Settlor

    1.1.3.3   any spouse for the time being and any widow or widower (whether or not for the time being remarried) of the individuals referred to in clause 1.1.3.2 above (but other than any spouse of the Settlor)

    and 'Discretionary Beneficiary' has a corresponding meaning

[1082]

1.1.4   'the Accumulation Period' means the period of 21 years commencing with the date of this deed[6]

1.1.5   'the Specified Period' means the period beginning at the date of this deed and enduring for 80 years and the said number of years shall be the perpetuity period applicable to this settlement[7]

1.1.6   'Charitable' means charitable (and exclusively charitable) according to the law for the time being of England and Wales

1.1.7   'Charity' means a trust or corporation association society or other institution established only for Charitable purposes and 'Charities' have a corresponding meaning

[1.2   The provisions of this settlement shall be construed as though the Children Act 1989 the Legitimacy Act 1976 the Adoption Act 1976 and the Family Law Reform Act 1987 Sections 1 and 19 or any re-enactment of them had not been enacted][8]

[1.3   References in this settlement to the income of the Trust Fund shall (without any allocation or apportionment in favour of the Settlor) extend to any interest or other income now accrued or accruing but not yet actually payable in respect of the property paid by the Settlor to the Original Trustees as recited above][9]

[1083]

2   Principal trusts[10]

2.1   The Trustees shall stand possessed of the Trust Fund and the income from it on such trusts and with and subject to such charges powers and provisions whatever in favour or for the benefit of all or any one or more exclusively of the others or other of the Discretionary Beneficiaries as the Trustees (being at least 2 in number or a trust corporation) in their absolute discretion shall at any time or times during the Specified Period by any deed or deeds revocable or irrevocable appoint (regard being had to the law relating to remoteness)

2.2   Subject as stated above and subject also as is provided in clause 2.3 below any trust appointed under the power contained in clause 2.1 above may be mandatory or discretionary and may create any interest or interests whatever whether absolute or limited and whether vested or contingent and whether in possession or reversion and may divide the property subject to it or the income from it into any shares and may provide for the accumulation of the whole or any part of the income subject to it during the Accumulation Period (or during any other permissible period) and any discretionary trust or power may by such appointment be conferred on any person or persons (not necessarily being or including the Trustees) and any such trusts or powers so conferred may authorise the delegation to an unlimited extent of any discretion

2.3   PROVIDED always that:

2.3.1   no exercise of the power of appointment conferred by clause 2.1 above shall affect any capital or income of the Trust Fund (or any share or part of it) previously paid transferred or applied (except merely by accumulation) to or for the benefit of any person under the other provisions of this settlement or any income (except accumulated income) of the Trust Fund (or any share or part of it) accruing prior to such appointment

2.3.2   the Trustees (being at least 2 in number or a trust corporation) may at any time or times before the expiration of the Specified Period by deed or deeds extinguish (or restrict the future exercise of) the power conferred by clause 2.1 above

[1084]

3   Trusts of income

3.1   In default[11] of and until and subject to any and every appointment made under the power or powers conferred by clause 2.1 above the income of the Trust Fund shall during the Specified Period be held by the Trustees upon trust to pay or apply or (in the case of a minor) allocate the same to or for the maintenance support or otherwise for the benefit in any manner of all or any one or more exclusively of the others or other of the Discretionary Beneficiaries for the time being in existence and if more than one in such shares and in such manner in all respects as the Trustees shall in their absolute discretion [without being liable in any such case to account for the exercise of such discretion[12]] think fit

3.2   PROVIDED always that the Trustees shall not be bound to apply or allocate the whole or any part of the income accruing to the Trust Fund during the Accumulation Period but may during the Accumulation Period pay apply or allocate only so much of the income as the Trustees shall in their absolute discretion think fit and shall accumulate the surplus (if any) of such income at compound interest by investing the same and the resulting income from it in any of the investments authorised by this settlement and shall hold such accumulations as an accretion to (and as one fund with) the capital of the Trust Fund

[1085]

4   Trust on expiry of the Specified Period

In default[13] of and subject to any and every appointment made under the power or powers conferred by clause 2.1 above the Trust Fund and the future income from it shall from and after the end of the Specified Period be held upon trust absolutely for such of the Discretionary Beneficiaries as are living at the end of the Specified Period in equal shares[14]

5   Ultimate trust

Subject to all the trusts powers and provisions of this settlement and if and so far as (for any reason whatever) not wholly disposed of by it the Trust Fund and the income from it shall be held upon trust for *(name)*[15]

[1086]

6   Alteration of class of beneficiaries[16]

6.1   Subject to clause 6.2 below:

6.1.1   the Trustees (being at least 2 in number or a trust corporation) shall have power by any deed or deeds revocable or irrevocable executed during the Specified Period to declare that any individual or individuals (not being the Settlor or any spouse of the Settlor) whether or not then born or ascertained or any Charity or Charities (other than any individual then a Trustee and other than any individual or Charity previously excluded under the power set out in clause 6.1.2 below) shall from such time and (subject to any future exercise of the power contained in clause 6.1.2 below) either permanently or for such period or periods as shall be specified in any such deed or deeds be included in the class of the Discretionary Beneficiaries defined in clause 1.1.3 above

6.1.2   the Trustees (being not less than 2 in number or a trust corporation) shall also have power by any deed or deeds revocable or irrevocable executed during the Specified Period to declare that any individual or individuals whether or not born or ascertained or any Charity or Charities who or which is or are a member or members (or eligible to be added as a member or members) of the class of the Discretionary Beneficiaries immediately prior to the execution of such deed or deeds shall from such time and either permanently or for such period or periods as shall be specified in any such deed or deeds cease to be a member or members (or eligible to become a member or members) of such class

[1087]

6.2   PROVIDED always that:

6.2.1   no such deed made in exercise of the power conferred by clause 6.1 above shall affect the validity or effect of:

6.2.1.1   any distribution previously made to or for the benefit of any beneficiary under or pursuant to any power or discretion

6.2.1.2   any transmissible interest (whether vested or contingent) previously conferred on any beneficiary either by clauses 4 and 5 above or under or pursuant to any irrevocable exercise of the power of appointment conferred by clause 2 above or

6.2.1.3   any future distribution to any beneficiary consequent on the absolute vesting in possession of any such interest as is mentioned in clause 6.2.1.2 above

6.2.2   the Trustees (being not less than 2 in number or a trust corporation) may at any time or times during the Specified Period by deed or deeds extinguish (or restrict the future exercise of) the power (but not any of the restrictions applicable to the same) conferred by clause 6.1 above

7   Exclusion of apportionment

Where under the trusts for the time being affecting the same there is a change in the person or persons beneficially or prospectively beneficially entitled to the income of any part of the Trust Fund (whether due to the birth or death of any person or for any other reason whatever) the provisions of the Apportionment Act 1870 shall not apply and no apportionment shall be made of income accruing or accrued or of outgoings being expended on the occasion of such change in beneficial entitlement but rather the same shall be treated as having accrued due or become a proper liability on the day of actual receipt or expenditure (as the case may be)[17]

[1088]

8   Administrative provisions[18]

8.1   Subject to clauses 8.2 and 8.3 below the Trustees shall during the Specified Period and during such further period (if any) as the law may allow have the additional powers set out in the schedule

8.2   PROVIDED always that the Trustees (being not less than 2 in number or a trust corporation) may at any time or times during the Specified Period by deed or deeds extinguish (or restrict the future exercise of) all or any of the powers (but not any of the restrictions applicable to them) conferred by clause 8.1 above

[8.3   If in the administration of the Trust Fund any transaction is in the opinion of the Trustees expedient but the same cannot be effected by reason of the absence of any sufficient power for that purpose conferred by this deed or by law (or by any earlier exercise of the present power) then the Trustees may by deed confer upon themselves either generally or for the purpose of any particular transaction or transactions the necessary power and from the execution of such a deed the Trustees shall have such power as if it had been conferred by this deed [provided that before executing any such deed the Trustees shall obtain the written opinion of a counsel of at least ten years' standing practising in trust law that the possession by the Trustees of such power is desirable in the interests of the beneficiaries]]

[9   Consultation

The provisions of the Trusts of Land and Appointment of Trustees Act 1996 Section 11(1) shall not apply to any land situated in England and Wales which may at any time be subject to the trusts of this settlement or any trusts appointed or arising under it[19]

10   Trustees' charges and remuneration[20]

10.1   Any of the Trustees who shall be an individual engaged in any profession or business either alone or in partnership shall be entitled to charge and be paid and to retain all professional or other proper charges for any business done or time spent or services rendered by him or his firm in connection with the trusts powers and provisions of this settlement and shall also be entitled to retain any share of brokerage or commission paid to him or his firm by any broker agent or insurance office in connection with any acquisition of or dealing with any investments or property or the effecting or payment of any premium on any policy of insurance subject or intended to become subject to the trusts of this settlement or any such assurance

10.2   None of the Trustees holding any directorship or other office or employment or retainer in relation to any company all or any of whose shares stock or securities shall at any time be subject to any trusts of this settlement shall be accountable for any remuneration received in connection with such directorship office employment or retainer

10.3   Notwithstanding anything contained in this clause neither the Settlor nor any spouse of the Settlor who may be for the time being one of the Trustees shall be entitled to charge or be paid or retain any or any share of any professional or other charges by reason of this clause or be relieved thereby from any liability to account as a trustee for any money or assets[21]

[1089]

11   Corporate Trustees

11.1   A corporation (whether or not a trust corporation) may at any time be appointed to be one of the Trustees on such reasonable terms as to remuneration and charging and otherwise however as shall be agreed at the time when the appointment is made between the person or persons making the appointment on the one hand and the corporation on the other

11.2   The provisions of the Trustee Act 1925 Section 37 in their application to this settlement shall be varied so that for each reference to 'a trust corporation' there shall be substituted a reference to 'a corporation (whether or not a trust corporation)'[22]

12   Exclusion of self-dealing

Any of the Trustees may exercise or concur in exercising any powers and discretions given by this settlement or by law notwithstanding that he has a direct or other personal interest in the mode or result of any such exercise but any such Trustee may abstain from acting except as a merely formal party in any matter in which he may be so personally interested and may allow his co-trustees or co-trustee to act alone in relation thereto[23]

13   Protection of Trustees

13.1   In the professed execution of the trusts and powers of this settlement none of the Trustees (being an individual) shall be liable for any loss arising by reason of any improper investment made in good faith or the retention of any improper investment or any failure to see to the insurance of or preservation of any chattels or the making or revising of any inventory of them or for the negligence or fraud of any agent employed by him or by any other of the Trustees (although the employment of such agent was not strictly necessary or expedient) or by reason of any other matter or thing whatever except wilful and individual fraud or wrongdoing on the part of that one of the Trustees who is sought to be made liable[24]

13.2   The Trustees shall not be bound or required to interfere in the management or conduct of the affairs or business of any company in respect of which the Trustees shall hold or control the whole or a majority or any part of the shares carrying the control of the company or other the voting rights of the company and so long as there shall be no notice of any act of dishonesty or misappropriation of money on the part of the directors having the management of such company the Trustees shall be at liberty to leave the conduct of its business (including the payment or non-payment of dividends) wholly to such directors

[1090]

14   Exclusion of the Settlor and spouse from benefit

Notwithstanding anything in this settlement expressed or implied no money or other assets subject to the trusts of this settlement shall in any circumstances whatever be paid or transferred beneficially (except for full consideration) to or lent to or applied (whether directly or indirectly) for the benefit of the Settlor or any spouse of the Settlor[25]

15   Appointment of new Trustees

15.1   The power of appointing a new Trustee or new Trustees shall (subject to clause 15.3 below) be vested in the Settlor during the life of the Settlor[26]

15.2   Any individual or corporation may be appointed as a Trustee notwithstanding that such individual or corporation is resident domiciled or incorporated outside the United Kingdom and notwithstanding that as a result of such appointment (or any retirement occurring in connection with it) all or a majority of the Trustees are persons resident domiciled or incorporated outside the United Kingdom

15.3   It is declared (for the avoidance of any doubt) that the Settlor may at any time or times by deed release (or restrict the future exercise of) the power conferred on the Settlor by clause 15.1 above and it is further declared that the provisions of the Trustee Act 1925 Section 36 in their application to this settlement shall be varied so that it shall not be a ground for the appointment of a new Trustee that an existing Trustee has remained out of the United Kingdom for more than 12 months

[15.4   The provisions of the Trusts of Land and Appointment of Trustees Act 1996 Section[s] 19 [and 20] shall not apply to this settlement or to the trusts of this settlement or to any trusts appointed or arising under it][27]

[1091]

16   Exclusion of the Trustee Delegation Act 1999 Section 1

The provisions of the Trustee Delegation Act 1999 Section 1(1) shall not apply to any Trustee or Trustees for the time being of this settlement[28]

[17   Exclusion of the duty of care

The duty of care contained in the Trustee Act 2000 Section 1 shall not apply to the Trustees in the exercise of any of the powers conferred on them by this settlement nor to any duties relating to the exercise of such powers nor to the exercise by the Trustees of any powers contained in or duties imposed by the Trustee Act 2000, the Trustee Act 1925, the Trusts of Land and Appointment of Trustees Act 1996 or any other statute where the duty of care is expressed to be applicable[29]]

[18   Clause headings

The headings to the clauses and paragraphs of this settlement are for the purposes of information only and are not part of and shall not be used in the construction of this settlement or any part of it][30]

IN WITNESS etc

SCHEDULE

Administrative Powers

(When these powers are used with other settlements care should be taken to amend the powers selected so that they fit in with the definitions and terminology used in that other settlement, and with the fact that it may not be a discretionary settlement)

1   Application of money requiring investment[31]

Power as regards any money for the time being subject to the provisions of this settlement and requiring investment to invest or lay out the same in the purchase or otherwise in the acquisition of or at interest upon the security of any shares stocks funds securities policies of insurance or other investments or property (movable or immovable) of whatever nature and wherever situated and whether or not productive of income and whether involving liability or not or upon such personal credit with or without security in all respects as the Trustees shall in their discretion think fit to the intent that the Trustees shall have the same full and unrestricted powers of investing and transposing investments and dealing with trust money and buying or selling property in all respects as if they were absolutely entitled beneficially and so that:

1.1   the acquisition with trust money of property with a view to its enjoyment in kind by a Discretionary Beneficiary or Discretionary Beneficiaries in accordance with the provisions of paragraph 22 below shall for the purpose of this settlement be deemed to be an investment of trust money

1.2   nothing contained in this paragraph shall exclude limit or restrict the power to invest in a legal estate in any land in the United Kingdom conferred by the Trusts of Land and Appointment of Trustees Act 1996 Section 6(3) and the Trustee Act 2000 Section 8(1)

1.3   without prejudice to the generality of paragraph 1 the Trustees shall not be under any obligation to diversify the investments of the Trust Fund

1.4   any immovable property situated anywhere other than in England and Wales which may be acquired for any of the purposes of this settlement (including its enjoyment in kind) shall be conveyed to the Trustees either with or without any trust for sale as the Trustees think fit but nevertheless with power to sell the same[32]

[1092]

2   Retention of assets

Power to accept or acquire and retain any assets subject or to be subject to the trusts declared by this settlement (including any uninvested money) in their actual state and condition for any period even although the whole or a substantial part of the assets so subject may be producing no or little income or may consist of shares or securities of a single company[33]

3   Transposition of investments

Power at any time or times to sell or convert or call in any investments or other property for the time being comprised in the Trust Fund or to transpose or convert the same into any other investments or property the acquisition of which with money subject to this settlement is by this settlement authorised

4   Improvements to land

Power at any time or times to apply any money subject to the trusts of this settlement in making improvements to or otherwise developing or using any land or buildings or in erecting enlarging repairing decorating making alterations to or improvements in or pulling down and rebuilding any buildings which shall be subject to the same trusts

[1093]

5   Leases and mortgaging

Power to lease let licence mortgage and charge and to grant tenancies and licences and to accept surrenders of leases tenancies and licences and to enter into and carry into effect any grants agreements or arrangements whatever of or relating to and generally to manage and deal with any land or buildings which shall for the time being be subject to any trusts of this settlement in all respects as if the Trustees were an absolute beneficial owner of such land or buildings and so that no mortgagee or chargee or intending mortgagee or chargee dealing with the Trustees in regard to any such land or buildings shall be concerned to see for what purpose any money is raised or as to the application of such money PROVIDED that nothing in this paragraph shall affect or restrict any power conferred on the Trustees in respect of land situated in England and Wales conferred by the Trusts of Land and Appointment of Trustees Act 1996 Section 6(1) and by the Trustee Act 2000 Section 8(3)

6   Hiring of chattels

Power to hire out or lend or bail any movable chattels for any period or periods and for any consideration whatever

7   Mortgaging of chattels etc

In relation to any property other than land and buildings the like powers of mortgaging charging and entering into and carrying into effect any agreements or arrangements whatever as are given by paragraph 5 above in regard to land and buildings

[1094]

8   Borrowing

Power to borrow or raise money for the purposes of mere investment or for acquiring any property either without security or on the security of the whole or part of the Trust Fund and any property so acquired

9   Guarantees

Without prejudice to the generality of paragraphs 5 and 7 of this schedule power to effect any mortgage or charge under those paragraphs as collateral security for or to guarantee money payable in respect of any loan to a Discretionary Beneficiary or Discretionary Beneficiaries upon such terms in all respects as the Trustees shall in their absolute discretion think fit PROVIDED that this power shall not be exercised except in conformity with the beneficial trusts for the time being governing the Trust Fund (or the part of it affected by such mortgage charge or guarantee) and the income from it

10   Arbitration

Power to refer to arbitration or to the determination of any expert:

10.1   the amount of the money to be received or paid on any sale or purchase or exchange

10.2   the amount of the rent or other payment to be reserved by any lease tenancy agreement or licence in respect of the whole or any part of the term or currency of such lease and the covenants and provisions to be contained in any such lease tenancy agreement or licence

10.3   the terms for the surrender or other termination of any lease tenancy or licence and

10.4   all disputes between any tenant or licensee and the reversioner or licensor

[1095]

11   Appropriation

Power from time to time to set such a value upon any investments or other property forming part of the Trust Fund as the Trustees shall think fit and to appropriate if they shall think fit any such investments or property at such value in or towards satisfaction of any share or interest under the trusts affecting the same[34]

12   Valuation

Power at any time or times to have any assets valued for any purpose in such manner as the Trustees shall in their discretion think fit

13   Promotion of companies

Power to promote or form or join in promoting or forming any company or corporation for the purpose of acquiring or taking on lease or hire for any estate or interest all or any of the assets which are held on the trusts of this settlement or for any other purpose whatever connected with any assets which (or the net proceeds of sale of which) are subject or are to become subject to any of those trusts

[1096]

14   Subscription for shares etc

Power to subscribe for all or any of the shares debentures or other securities of any such company or corporation as is mentioned in paragraph 13 above

15   Sales etc for paper consideration

Power to sell transfer let or hire out for any estate or interest any assets which are subject to any of the trusts of this settlement in consideration of the issue or transfer to the Trustees or their nominees of any stock shares debentures or other securities

16   Rights attached to investments

Power to exercise or refrain from exercising (either themselves or by proxy) the rights attached to any investments subject to any of the trusts of this settlement in any manner whatever and in particular (without prejudice to the generality of the above) to wind up or dissolve or join in winding up or dissolving any company or corporation and to alter or join in altering any of those rights or any rights attached to any other investments or property

[1097]

17   Power to carry on a business

Power from time to time to carry on whether by themselves or in partnership with any other individual or corporation (whether or not such individual shall be beneficially entitled under the trusts of this settlement) any trade or business which they consider to be for the benefit of the beneficiaries under this settlement and in connection with any such trade or business the Trustees may:

17.1   employ all or any part of the capital of the Trust Fund

17.2   be indemnified out of the Trust Fund against any liability which they may incur in connection with the setting up carrying on or dissolution of such trade or business

17.3   use for the purposes of the trade or business any land or buildings which are subject to the trusts of this settlement

17.4   exercise in relation to any such trade or business and the assets thereof any of the administrative powers conferred on the Trustees by this deed or by law including (but without prejudice to the generality of the foregoing) powers of borrowing and charging and of delegation

17.5   employ or join in employing on such terms as to remuneration and otherwise as they shall think fit any manager and other employees[35]

18   Nominees

Power to put or leave any shares stocks securities insurance policies or other property whatever (including money) in the name or names of any nominee or nominees for the Trustees and to put or leave any movable chattels for safe keeping in the possession or custody of any person or persons without being responsible for any loss or damage and on such terms and subject to such conditions including remuneration of any such nominee or custodian (other than the Settlor or any spouse of the Settlor) as the Trustees shall think fit and so that any such nominees or custodians may be or include any one or more of the Trustees [The Trustee Act 2000 Sections 16 and 17 shall not apply to this deed] [The provisions of the Trustee Act 2000 Section 22 shall not apply to any nominee or custodian appointed by the Trustees pursuant to this power][36]

[1098]

19   Insurance

19.1   Power to effect maintain and deal with any insurance or insurances upon the life of any person or of all or any assets subject to any trusts of this settlement against any risk or risks which the Trustees may consider proper to cover PROVIDED:

　　19.1.1   that the Trustees shall be under no obligation to insure any such assets to their full value or at all

　　19.1.2   that the Trustees may pay all premiums and other costs relating to insurance out of the income or the capital of any property held upon the same trusts under this settlement as such assets [(save that in the case of life insurance the same shall be paid solely out of such capital and not out of income)][37] and

　　19.1.3   that nothing in this paragraph shall authorise any accumulations of income within the Law of Property Act 1925 Section 164

19.2   All the powers of an absolute owner in respect of any policy or policies forming part of the Trust Fund including the power to surrender convert or otherwise deal with any such policy or policies or any bonuses attaching to them or part of them in such manner as the Trustees shall consider most beneficial to the persons beneficially interested under these trusts

19.3   Power [(subject to the restrictions in paragraphs 19.1.2 and 19.1.3 above)] to apply any money subject to the trusts of this settlement in or towards payment of the premiums or other amounts (if any) necessary for keeping on foot or restoring any policy or policies forming part of the Trust Fund

20   Maintenance etc of chattels

Power to maintain repair improve and alter any movable chattels and to take such steps as they may consider proper for the preservation of any movable chattels or other assets subject to any trusts of this settlement

[1099]

21   Delegation

Power to delegate all or any of the powers of the Trustees contained in this schedule (including this power) and any administrative power conferred by law (and all or any of the duties and discretions of the Trustees relating to the exercise of such powers) to any person or persons (not being the Settlor or any spouse of the Settlor) subject to such conditions (if any) and upon such terms (including remuneration and so that in the case of a delegation to two or more persons such delegates may be authorised to act jointly and severally) as the Trustees shall think fit (without being liable for the acts or defaults of any such delegate) and to revoke or modify any such delegation or conditions [the Trustee Act 2000 Section 11 shall not apply to this deed] [The provisions of the Trustee Act 2000 Section 22 shall not apply to any delegate or agent appointed by the Trustees pursuant to the foregoing power][38]

22   Use of property in kind

Power (subject as provided below) to permit a Discretionary Beneficiary or Discretionary Beneficiaries (either alone or concurrently or successively) to occupy use or enjoy personally any movable or immovable property which may for the time being be comprised in the Trust Fund upon any terms or conditions whatever which the Trustees may think fit PROVIDED that this power shall not be exercised except in conformity with the beneficial trusts powers and provisions for the time being governing the Trust Fund (or the part of it in which such movable or immovable property is so comprised) and the income from it[39] and (without prejudice to the generality of the above) at any time when a Discretionary Beneficiary is (or would if of sufficient age be) entitled to an interest in possession in the property (or proceeds) in question such power shall only be exercisable (as regards that property or proceeds) in favour of that Discretionary Beneficiary alone

23   Loans to Discretionary Beneficiaries

Power (subject as provided below) to lend any money with or without security to a Discretionary Beneficiary or Discretionary Beneficiaries with or without payment of interest and upon such terms as to repayment and otherwise in such manner in all respects as the Trustees shall in their absolute discretion think fit PROVIDED that this power shall not be exercised except in conformity with the beneficial trusts powers and provisions for the time being governing the Trust Fund (or the part of it from which such loan is to be made) and the income from it[40] and (without prejudice to the generality of the above) at any time when a Discretionary Beneficiary is (or would if of sufficient age be) entitled to an interest in possession in the money in question such power shall only be exercisable (as regards that money) in favour of that Discretionary Beneficiary

[1100]

24   Transactions with other trustees

Power from time to time in their absolute discretion to enter into any agreement or transaction with the trustee or trustees of any other settlement or will (being an agreement or transaction which apart from this present provision the Trustees could properly have entered into if one or more of them had not also been a trustee of such other settlement or will) notwithstanding that the Trustees or one or more of them may also be trustees or a trustee or the sole trustee of such other settlement or will and in like manner in all respects as if none of the Trustees were a trustee of such other settlement or will

25   Power to sign cheques

Power to permit any one or more of the Trustees to sign cheques on any bank account in the names of the Trustees and generally to sign orders and authorities to any bank on behalf of the Trustees

26   Additions

Power (if the Trustees think fit) to accept any assets which may be transferred or otherwise given to the Trustees as an addition to the capital of the Trust Fund on terms that any capital transfer tax or inheritance tax that is payable in consequence of such transfer or gift shall be payable out of and borne by the Trust Fund and not by the transferor or donor personally and also power (if the Trustees think fit) to pay any capital transfer tax or inheritance tax that may from time to time be levied on the Trust Fund or any part of it notwithstanding that some other person or persons may also be liable to pay such tax

[1101]

27   Receipts

27.1   Where the Trustees are authorised or required to pay or apply any capital money or income to or for the benefit of any person who does not have the capacity to give a valid receipt for it the Trustees may pay the same to any parent or guardian of such person for the benefit of such person without seeing to the application of it or themselves apply the same for the benefit of such person as may be directed in writing by such parent or guardian and the receipt of such parent or guardian shall be a sufficient discharge to the Trustees

27.2   The receipt of the person professing to be the treasurer or other proper officer of any charity to which any capital or income may be payable or transferable under this settlement shall be a sufficient discharge to the Trustees

29   Exclusion of the self-dealing rule[41]

Power for any of the Trustees (a) to purchase or acquire from or sell or let to the Trustees themselves any property liable to be sold let disposed of or acquired or purchased under the Settlement or any statute at such price or rent and upon such terms as the Trustees shall think fit or approve without being liable to account for any profit and (b) to be employed and remunerated as a director or other officer or employee or as agent or advisor of any company or other corporation or undertaking or firm whatsoever at any time in any way connected with the Trust Fund or dealing with or acquiring any property from or selling or letting any property to the Trustees and (c) to retain as his absolute property (and without being liable to account therefor) any remuneration fees or profits received by him in any such capacity notwithstanding that his situation or office as such director officer employee agent or advisor may have been obtained or may be held or retained in right or by means or by reason of his position as one of the Trustees or any shares stock property rights or powers belonging to or connected with the Trust Fund

(signatures of the parties)[42]

(signatures of witnesses)

[1102]

1   As to stamp duty see Information Binder: Stamp Duties [1] Table of Duties (Declaration of trust). This Form contains a discretionary trust for a wide range of beneficiaries both named and by way of class and is capable of lasting for at least 80 years. The settlor should supplement the trust deed with a letter of wishes which he should review from time to time. For specimen letters of wishes see Form 252 [1841] et seq post.

2   It is common for the settlement to be constituted by the transfer of a nominal cash sum to the trustees and for property to be added later by the settlor. When a number of such trusts are created on consecutive days (for instance a series of life insurance settlements) the Inland Revenue has contended that, for inheritance tax purposes, they should be treated as a single settlement. It is thought that this approach in many cases is misconceived and should be resisted. See Paragraph 283.2 [716] ante.

3   This provision is declaratory: settlements are irrevocable unless the deed of settlement provides to the contrary.

4   This provision is declaratory: the trustees agree to act by executing the deed. Similarly clause 18 [1092] is declaratory.

5   Discretionary beneficiaries are commonly defined to include the settlor's issue and spouses of such issue but to expressly exclude both the settlor and his spouse. If this exclusion is not made then, not only may income tax and capital gains tax problems arise but, in addition, the Inland Revenue may argue that the settlor has reserved a benefit in his settlement for inheritance tax purposes. Including the widow (or widower) of the settlor does not give rise to any of these difficulties: *Lord Vestey's Executors v IRC* [1949] 1 All ER 1108. As to the reservation of benefit rules see Paragraph 290 [749] et seq ante. In deciding how wide the class of beneficiaries should be the draftsman should bear in mind the right to information which all beneficiaries normally possess. Hence a definition which includes remote collaterals, who are unlikely to benefit but who may create problems for the trustees, should be avoided. In this precedent the beneficial class can always be changed if the need arises: see clause 6 [1087]. For the right to information concerning the trust, see Paragraph 207 [493] ante.

6   Exceptionally it will be appropriate to select another accumulation period, for instance in the case of a trust of a pension policy: see vol 40(2) (2001 Reissue) TRUSTS AND SETTLEMENTS Part 18 [9601]. For the available periods see Paragraph 83 [194] ante.

7   A 'Specified Period' (sometimes 'Trust Period') is not the same as the perpetuity period and will frequently end before the longest period which could have been chosen for perpetuity purposes. In this case it is expressly provided that the two are to be the same.

8   This clause excludes (so far as their benefits depend on description through relationship) all persons who are legitimated, adopted, or illegitimate and any person who traces a relationship through them. Consequently, this clause should be included only after express instructions have been taken from the settlor.

9   This clause will not be relevant in cases where a cash sum is settled: contrast the position if the settled property is eg land subject to a lease where the rent produced would require apportionment.

10   This clause gives the trustees wide discretionary powers over the capital (and income) of the fund. It does not give the trustees power to transfer the trust assets to trustees of another settlement; for such a power see Form 5 clause 3.2.2 [1112] post.

[1103]

11   The default clause operates with regard to the income of the trust fund pending exercise by the trustees of the dispositive powers in clause 2 [1084]. The accumulation period is defined as a period of 21 years running from the date of creation of the settlement. If desired one of the alternative periods set out in the Law of Property Act 1925 s 164 as modified by the Perpetuity and Accumulations Act 1964 s 13 (37 Halsbury's Statutes (4th Edn) REAL PROPERTY) may be employed.

We have pleasure in sending you this volume

The Encyclopaedia of
FORMS AND PRECEDENTS
Fifth Edition
Volume 40(2)
TRUSTS AND SETTLEMENTS
2002 Reissue

Volume 40(2) (2002 Reissue) supersedes volume 40(2) (1997 Reissue) which should now be discarded.

If you are unsure of what to keep or what to discard please call our subscriber help-line on (020) 7400 2648.

For current information on the titles published in the Encyclopaedia, subscribers should refer to the *List of Titles*, in the Information Binder of the Service, which will always represent the most recent position of titles.

The title TRUSTS AND SETTLEMENTS is concerned with the law relating to the creation of trusts and settlements, their administration, their variation and their taxation. Volume 40(1) deals with establishment and administration generally, whilst this volume is concerned with areas of a more specialised nature.

Full account is taken of the major legislative changes that have occurred in this area. First is the Trusts of Land and Appointment of Trustees Act 1996 (which is considered in detail in Part 8 of this volume); followed by the Trustee Delegation Act 1999 (which is considered in detail in volume 40(1)) and finally the Trustee Act 2000. The Trustee Act 2000 has meant that the administrative provisions have been rethought throughout. In the event, the contributors have concluded that the 2000 Act is unlikely to result in a significant shortening of the standard express trust deed.

The text and precedent sections have been reviewed, expanded and redrafted to ensure that the title reflects the changes introduced by these Acts, and the title has been thoroughly updated to incorporate other legislative and case law developments. In view of the fact that more dispositions involve registered land, full account has been taken of the Land Registration Act 1997 and the Land Registration Rules 1997–2001. All transfers of land have been redrafted to reflect changes to the Land Registry prescribed forms.

Volume 40(1) (2001 Reissue) includes:

- A substantial commentary setting out the current law and practice on trusts and settlements and explaining the taxation factors that practitioners should take into account in setting up or modifying trusts and settlements;

- The standard provisions of the Society of Trust and Estate Practitioners which are intended to deal with routine administration matters commonly included in both will trusts and inter vivos settlements;

- A collection of complete precedents (together with full explanatory footnotes) including both flexible and fixed interest trusts;

- A selection of administrative powers and typical beneficial trusts;

- Ancillary documentation such as letters of wishes and trustee resolutions, as well as precedents relating to the exercise by trustees of their dispositive powers;

- Delegation of their functions by trustees.

This volume contains an in-depth treatment of trusts of land (including a section by section analysis of the Trusts of Land and Appointment of Trustees Act 1996 and precedents), as well as retaining coverage of strict settlements. There is a substantial section on change of trustees (including the provisions contained in Part II of the 1996 Act) and a consideration of the following:

- Trusts for minors and older children (including accumulation and maintenance trusts);

- Protective trusts and asset protection;

- Non-charitable purpose trusts;

- Employee trusts (with a consideration of the relevant tax factors);

- Offshore trusts (with a precedent Jersey trust);

- Trusts for the disabled;

- Personal injury compensation trusts;

- Pension policy trusts;

- Miscellaneous court applications by trustees;

- Releases and indemnities of trustees.

Extensive cross-references to the location of commentary and forms contained in volume 40(1) and the SALE OF LAND volumes 35–38(2) are also provided.

The law stated in this volume is in general that in force on 1 December 2001 although later developments have been noted wherever possible.

12   Although the words in square brackets are commonly included it is not possible to oust the jurisdiction of the court to review the exercise of the trustees' dispositive powers. For the distinction between administrative and dispositive powers, see Part 5, Introduction to Section H [1586] post.

13   The default provision will apply (subject to any exercise of the powers given to the trustees in clause 2 [1084]) at the end of the specified period.

14   Default trusts sometimes include a stirpital addition along the following lines:

'PROVIDED that if any of them shall have died during the Specified Period leaving issue living at the end of the Specified Period such issue shall take by substitution and if more than one in equal shares per stirpes the share of such part of the Trust Fund as stated above which the person so dying would have taken if he or she had survived until the end of the Specified Period but so that no issue shall take whose parent is alive at the end of the Specified Period and capable of taking'.

This would produce a most confusing situation in cases like this where the discretionary beneficiaries are defined as being all the issue of the settlor's grandfather. If a discretionary beneficiary therefore dies leaving children and grandchildren, those children and grandchildren themselves will be discretionary beneficiaries and therefore there could be a multiple claim: an individual might claim as being both a discretionary beneficiary living at the end of the specified period, and also by substitution of part of a parent's share and/or part of a grandparent's share.

15   This clause is a long-stop clause. It is important that the beneficiary named is living at the date of the settlement (or is a charity).

16   This clause enables the trustees to include or exclude, either permanently or for a specified period, any person (or charity) from the beneficial class. The exercise of this power does not affect the validity of anything which has already occurred. For the validity of powers to add beneficiaries, see *Re Manisty's Settlement, Manisty v Manisty* [1974] Ch 17, [1973] 2 All ER 1203 and Paragraph 31 [76] ante.

[1104]

17   It is usual to exclude apportionment calculations (which can be complex) under the Apportionment Act 1870 (23 Halsbury's Statutes (4th Edn) LANDLORD AND TENANT).

18   The powers set out in the schedule supplement those already possessed by the trustees: eg under the Trustee Act 1925 (48 Halsbury's Statutes (4th Edn) TRUSTS AND SETTLEMENTS). As to administrative provisions and powers generally see Paragraph 220 [531] et seq ante.

19   As to the consultation provisions see Paragraph 225 [540] ante. For a detailed consideration see vol 40(2) (2001 Reissue) TRUSTS AND SETTLEMENTS Part 8 [3001].

20   This provision is intended to circumvent the conflict of interest rules developed by the courts: see further *Snell's Equity* (30th Edn, 2000) para 11-87. For a consideration of the drafting of remuneration clauses after the Trustee Act 2000, see Paragraph 214 [515] ante. See also Form 233 [1769] and Form 226 [1758] post.

21   Neither the settlor nor his spouse may obtain any remuneration from the trust; this provision is important to avoid any argument that the inheritance tax reservation of benefit rules could apply. See note 5 above.

22   The amendment made to the wording of the Trustee Act 1925 s 37 as amended by the Trusts of Land and Appointment of Trustees Act 1996 s 25(1), Sch 3 para 3(12) is designed to avoid the difficulties that may arise if it is decided to export the trust. On the export of trusts see further clauses 15.2 [1091], 15.3 [1091]; and see generally vol 40(2) (2001 Reissue) TRUSTS AND SETTLEMENTS Part 15 [8701].

23   For the self-dealing rule see note 20 above. Although it may be argued that a trustee selected by the settlor, who is also a beneficiary, should be free to make appointments in his own favour, this clause is intended to put the matter beyond doubt.

24   This clause offers wide protection to trustees who have not committed wilful and individual fraud or wrongdoing. Express instructions from the settlor should be taken before including this clause. For further exoneration and indemnity clauses see Form 220 [1747] et seq post, see vol 40(2) TRUSTS AND SETTLEMENTS Part 20 [9821] and see Paragraph 182 [451] et seq ante and contrast Form 3 clause 12 [1071] ante of the STEP Standard Provisions. See also the Consultation Paper 'Trustee Exemption Clauses' (June 1999) of the Trust Law Committee. At the time of writing the Law Commission is looking at the matter.

In *Armitage v Nurse* [1998] Ch 241, [1997] 2 All ER 705, CA the following trustee exemption clause was considered by the Court of Appeal:

'No trustee shall be liable for any loss or damage which may happen to [the Trust Fund] or any part thereof or the income thereof at any time or from any cause whatsoever unless said loss or damage shall be caused by his own actual fraud...'

The court held:

(a)   that the clause was valid and did not breach the irreducible trust core;

(b)   the trustees were protected against honest mistakes and against negligence (and in English law gross negligence does not exist as a separate category);

(c)   'loss or damage' does not include breach of self-dealing rules;

(d)   fraud in this context meant dishonesty: an intention on the part of the trustee to pursue a course of action either knowing that it is contrary to the interests of the beneficiaries, or being recklessly indifferent whether it is contrary to their interests or not.

For other recent cases on exclusion clauses see *Bogg v Raper* [1998] CLY 4592, (1998) Times 22 April, CA; *Wight v Olswang* (1998) Times 17 Sept, reversed on a question of construction (1999) Times 18 May, CA and *Walker v Stones* [2000] 4 All ER 412, [2001] 2 WLR 623, CA. At the time of writing the case of *Walker v Stones* has been appealed to the House of Lords whose judgment is expected shortly.

25   The exclusion of the settlor and his spouse from benefiting is dictated by tax considerations. See note 5 above and see *IRC v Botnar* [1999] STC 711, CA.

26   The settlor should consider giving the main beneficiary the power to appoint new trustees after his death. For further clauses see Form 234 [1781] et seq post.

27   For the operation of the Trusts of Land and Appointment of Trustees Act 1996 ss 19, 20 (48 Halsbury's Statutes (4th Edn) TRUSTS AND SETTLEMENTS) see, generally, vol 40(2) (2001 Reissue) TRUSTS AND SETTLEMENTS Part 8 [3001]. Although Part II of the Act does not apply to the trust in its present form, the settlor may wish to exclude it in case the beneficiaries in the future fall within the terms of the Trusts of Land and Appointment of Trustees Act 1996 s 19(1)(b).

28   The provisions of the Trustee Delegation Act 1999 s 1 (48 Halsbury's Laws (4th Edn) TRUSTS AND SETTLEMENTS) are considered to be unsatisfactory in their application to continuing trusts (they are intended for co-ownership of land). See further Paragraph 257 [632] ante.

29   The duty of care imposed on Trustees by the Trustee Act 2000 Pt I (ss 1–2) (48 Halsbury's Statutes (4th Edn) TRUSTS AND SETTLEMENTS) can be excluded: see the Trustee Act 2000 Sch 1 para 7. Exclusion should only be with the knowledge and approval of the settlor. As an alternative, trustees may be protected by an exculpation clause: see clause 13 [1090] ante.

For a consideration of when the duty of care applies, see Paragraph 184 [454] ante. For a discussion of exemption clauses, see Paragraph 192 [471] et seq ante. For a clause excluding the duty of care under the Trustee Act 2000 s 1 and for exoneration of trustees clauses, see Form 219 [1745] et seq post.

30   This provision is optional given that even in the event of a conflict between the heading and the clause, it is not thought that the heading would override the express terms of the clause. In other cases (eg when the clause contains some ambiguity), the draftsman might consider that using the heading for the purpose of resolving such ambiguity was sensible.

[1105]

31   An express power of investment has been retained. It enables the trustees to acquire:
(a)   assets (including land) which are not income producing;
(b)   assets, irrespective of where such assets are situated; and
(c)   assets (including but not limited to land) for use by a Discretionary Beneficiary.

The provisions of the Trustee Act 2000 Pt II (ss 3–7) and Pt III (ss 8–9) apply to supplement this paragraph, eg, to enable land to be acquired for a purpose other than as an investment or for beneficial occupation.

For the general investment powers of trustees see Paragraph 241 [591] et seq ante.

32   The Trusts of Land and Appointment of Trustees Act 1996 applies to land situated in England and Wales: Trusts of Land and Appointment of Trustees Act 1996 s 27(3). In such cases it is likely that the acquisition will be on the basis of a simple trust of land since there will no longer be any reason (or justification) for using a trust for sale. For other land (and trustees in this Form have power to invest in land anywhere in the world) there may be specific reasons for employing a trust for sale; hence the inclusion of this provision. The actual trusts for sale should be set out in the conveyance to the trustees of any land that is purchased: see, eg, Form 45(1) [1309] post.

33   This paragraph affords some protection for trustees who do not wish to diversify (or who cannot diversify) the trust fund, eg, when it contains only land or shares in the settlor's private company. For the effect of the Trustee Act 2000 ss 4, 5 in such cases, see further Paragraphs 242 [593], 243 [594] ante.

34   The power of appropriation given in the Administration of Estates Act 1925 s 41 as amended (17 Halsbury's Statutes (4th Edn) EXECUTORS AND ADMINISTRATORS) does not extend to trustees. For further appropriation clauses see Form 165 [1629] et seq post.

35   Trustees cannot carry on a trade or business without express authorisation: see *Re Berry* [1962] Ch 97, [1961] 1 All ER 529. A wide investment power does not allow trustees to 'invest' in a business. 'Business' is a wider word than 'trade'. For alternative powers to be used when the relevant business involves the managing of a farm or woodlands, see Form 178 [1659] post. For a sub-clause permitting the formation of limited liability partnerships, see Form 182 [1669] post.

36   For the power to put property into the names of custodians and trustees given by the Trustee Act 2000, see Paragraph 111 [272] ante. An express power may still be preferred since the choice of nominees is not then restricted, as the statutory power is by the Trustee Act 2000 s 19. If an express power is to be relied upon, it is suggested that the statutory power be excluded, so that there can then be no doubt that the Trustees are acting under the express power. The duty to review contained in the Trustee Act 2000 s 22 can be excluded in the case of express powers: see the Trustee Act 2000 s 22(1). On the question of excluding the obligations laid on trustees in the Trustee Act 2000, see generally Paragraph 254 [627].

37   The optional wording in square brackets here, and in paragraph 19.3 of the schedule [1099], should only be included in the case of an accumulation and maintenance trust where the beneficiaries concerned do not take absolute interests on attaining the age of 25 years: see vol 40(2) (2001 Reissue) TRUSTS AND SETTLEMENTS Part 11 [6301]. It has been suggested that in the case of a purported accumulation and maintenance type trust where the beneficiaries on attaining 25 years do not take an absolute interest, but only a limited interest, the existence of a power to pay life insurance premiums out of income prevents the settlement from qualifying as an accumulation and maintenance type trust under the Inheritance Tax Act 1984 s 71 (42–44 Halsbury's Statutes (4th Edn) TAXATION): see *Dymond's Capital Taxes* vol 2 para 21.368.

        Note that this paragraph covers:

(a)   life insurance, eg, on the life of the settlor or of a beneficiary; and

(b)   insurance of trust assets.

        The latter is dealt with by the Trustee Act 1925 s 19 as substituted by the Trustee Act 2000 s 34(1) and is generally considered to provide trustees with a suitably wide power. Hence there will be draftsmen who consider that making express provision for the insurance of trust assets is no longer necessary. This paragraph has been retained, however, on the basis that the revised section 19 fails to deal with the question of whether there is a duty to insure (see further Paragraph 259 [641] ante). Paragraph 19.1.1 of the schedule [1099] puts this matter beyond doubt.

        So far as life insurance is concerned, this would generally be an investment falling within the general power of investment given by the Trustee Act 2000 s 3. An express clause may still be needed to deal with the payment of premiums and it will often be desirable to provide that the insurance proceeds are to be held on separate trusts (notably if it is the life tenant's life which is insured): for an appropriate clause see Form 109 [1504] post. This is not a relevant consideration when the trust is discretionary in form.

38   Despite the statutory power to appoint agents contained in the Trustee Act 2000 Pt IV (ss 11–27) the use of an express power may be considered desirable primarily to overcome the restrictions in the Trustee Act 2000 s 12 that such a delegate cannot be a beneficiary and that the appointment of more than one agent must be on the basis that the agents are to act jointly. See further Paragraph 246 [611] et seq ante for a consideration of the statutory power. The duty to review contained in the Trustee Act 2000 s 22 can be excluded, see the Trustee Act 2000 s 21(3). See further note 36 above.

39   The trustees must exercise considerable care to ensure that any such exercise will not result in the beneficiary obtaining an interest in possession in the relevant property: see *Sansom v Peay* [1976] 3 All ER 375, [1976] 1 WLR 1073; Inland Revenue Statement of Practice SP 10/79 (15 August 1979); and Paragraph 287.3 [734] ante. The right to occupy provisions in the Trusts of Land and Appointment of Trustees Act 1996 ss 12, 13 do not apply to a trust in discretionary form.

40   The Inland Revenue have in the past contended that the making of a loan creates an interest in possession and thereby triggers an exit charge for the purposes of inheritance tax. It is thought that they have now abandoned this view.

41   The self-dealing rules are considered at Paragraph 209 [497] ante.

42   As to the statutory requirements for the valid execution of a deed see vol 12 (1994 Reissue) DEEDS, AGREEMENTS AND DECLARATIONS.

[1106]

5

Life interest settlement with overriding powers[1]

THIS SETTLEMENT is made the …… day of ………

BETWEEN:

(1)   *(settlor)* of *(address)* ('the Settlor') and

(2)   *(original trustees)* of *(addresses)* ('the Original Trustees')

WHEREAS

The Settlor wishes to make the settlement contained below for the benefit of *(name)* ('the Principal Beneficiary') and has paid or transferred into the joint names or under the joint control of the Original Trustees the assets described in the first schedule to be held on and with and subject to the following trusts powers and provisions

[1107]

NOW THIS DEED WITNESSES as follows:

1   Definitions and interpretation

1.1   In this settlement the following expressions have where the context permits the following meanings:

    1.1.1   'the Trustees' means the Original Trustees or other the trustees or trustee for the time being of this settlement and 'Trustee' means each and any of the Trustees

    1.1.2   'the Trust Fund' means the assets described in the first schedule all assets at any time added by way of further settlement accumulation of income capital accretion or otherwise and all property from time to time representing the same

    1.1.3   'the Discretionary Beneficiaries' means (subject to the provisions of clause 5 of this settlement) the Principal Beneficiary the [wife] of the Principal Beneficiary all the issue (whether present or future) of the Principal Beneficiary and all the wives and husbands and widows and widowers (whether or not for the time being remarried) of such issue and 'Discretionary Beneficiary' has a corresponding meaning

    1.1.4   'the Ultimate Date' means the day on which shall expire the period of 20 years commencing with the death of the last survivor of:

        1.1.4.1   the Principal Beneficiary

        1.1.4.2   the children actually born before the date of this deed of the Principal Beneficiary and

        1.1.4.3   the issue (whether children or more remote) actually born before the date of this deed of His Late Majesty King George the Fifth

[1108]

    1.1.5   'Charitable' means charitable (and exclusively charitable) according to the law for the time being of England and Wales

    1.1.6   'Charity' means a trust or corporation association society or other institution established only for Charitable purposes and 'Charities' has a corresponding meaning

    1.1.7   references to a 'beneficiary' or to 'beneficiaries' include references to a person or persons who are the object of any dispositive power or discretion

    1.1.8   the expression 'interest in possession' has the same meaning as is now given to such expression for the purposes of inheritance tax

[1.2   This settlement shall be construed as though the Family Law Reform Act 1987 Sections 1 and 19 had not been enacted (but for the avoidance of any doubt it is declared that the respective provisions of the Children Act 1989 the Legitimacy Act 1976 and the Adoption Act 1976 shall apply)][2]

[1109]

2   Principal trusts

2.1   The Trustees shall stand possessed of the Trust Fund and the income of it upon trust to pay such income to the Principal Beneficiary during [his] life

2.2   Subject to clause 2.1 above the Trustees shall pay the income of the Trust Fund to the Principal Beneficiary's [widow] during [her] life[3]

2.3   Subject to clauses 2.1 and 2.2 above the Trustees shall stand possessed of the Trust Fund upon trust until the Ultimate Date to pay or apply or (in the case of a minor) allocate the income of the Trust Fund to or for the maintenance support or otherwise for the benefit in any manner of all or any one or more exclusively of the others or other of the Discretionary Beneficiaries for the time being in existence and if more than one in such shares and in such manner in all respects as the Trustees shall in their absolute discretion without being liable in any such case to account for the exercise of such discretion think fit

2.4   From and after the Ultimate Date the Trustees shall stand possessed of the Trust Fund (as to both capital and income) for such of the children of the Principal Beneficiary as are living on the Ultimate Date and if more than one in equal shares absolutely PROVIDED that if any of such children shall have died before the Ultimate Date leaving issue living at the Ultimate Date such issue shall take by substitution and if more than one in equal shares per stirpes the share of such part of the Trust Fund which his or her or their parent would have taken if such parent had survived to the Ultimate Date but so that no issue shall take whose parent is alive at the Ultimate Date and capable of taking

[1110]

3   Overriding powers

Notwithstanding the trusts powers and provisions declared and contained above[4] the Trustees shall have the following powers and so that such powers shall be exercisable without the necessity of obtaining the consent of the Principal Beneficiary or the [widow] of the Principal Beneficiary although he or she may for the time being be entitled to the income of the Trust Fund or the part of it affected by the exercise of the power:

3.1   power (the Trustees being at least 2 in number or a trust corporation) in their absolute discretion at any time or times before the Ultimate Date to apply the whole or any part or parts of the capital of the Trust Fund for any purpose which the Trustees may think to be for the benefit of any one or more of the Discretionary Beneficiaries for the time being in existence or to transfer or pay the whole or any part or parts of the capital of the Trust Fund to any one or more of the Discretionary Beneficiaries (including the Principal Beneficiary and the [wife] of the Principal Beneficiary) for the time being in existence (being of full age) for his her or their absolute use and benefit freed and discharged from the trusts of this settlement

3.2   power (the Trustees being not less than 2 in number or a trust corporation) at any time or times before the Ultimate Date by any deed or deeds revocable or irrevocable to revoke all or any of the trusts powers and provisions declared and contained in clause 2 above in respect of the whole or any part or parts of the Trust Fund and the income of it for the purpose only of appointing (and so that the Trustees shall by the same deed appoint) in respect of such whole or part or parts of the Trust Fund and the income of it (or so much of it as is affected by the revocation) such trusts powers and provisions for the benefit of all or any one or more of the Discretionary Beneficiaries (including if thought fit powers of appointment powers of maintenance and advancement and administrative and other powers and provisions) as the Trustees in their absolute discretion shall think fit and:

[1111]

3.2.1   any trust appointed under the power of revocation and new appointment contained in clause 3.2 may be mandatory or discretionary and may create any interest or interests whatsoever whether absolute or limited and whether vested or contingent and whether in possession or reversion and may divide the property subject to it or the income of it into any shares and may provide for the accumulation of the whole or any part of the income of it during any permissible period and any discretionary trust or power may by such revocation and new appointment be conferred on any person or persons (not necessarily being or including the Trustees) and any such trusts or powers so conferred may authorise the delegation to an unlimited extent of any discretion[5]

3.2.2   without prejudice to the generality of the above any appointment under the power of revocation and new appointment contained in clause 3.2 may (if the Trustees in their absolute discretion think fit) include in such appointment a trust or trusts immediately to pay or transfer any income or capital of the Trust Fund or any part or parts of it to the trustees of any other trust or settlement wherever established or existing under which any one or more of the Discretionary Beneficiaries is or are beneficially interested (whether or not such one or more of the Discretionary Beneficiaries is or are the only person or persons interested or capable of benefiting under such trust or settlement) so long as neither the Settlor nor any spouse of the Settlor shall be interested or capable of benefiting under such other trust or settlement[6]

PROVIDED always that no revocation and new appointment under the power conferred by clause 3.2 shall affect any capital or income of the Trust Fund (or any share or part of it) previously paid transferred or applied (except merely by accumulation) to or for the benefit of any person under the other provisions of this settlement or any income (except accumulated income) of the Trust Fund (or any share or part of it) accruing prior to such revocation and appointment

3.3   The Trustees (being not less than 2 in number or a trust corporation) may at any time or times before the Ultimate Date by deed or deeds extinguish (or restrict the future exercise of) either or both of the powers conferred by clauses 3.1 and 3.2 above

[1112]

4   Ultimate trust

Subject to all the trusts powers and provisions of this settlement and if and so far as (for any reason whatever) not wholly disposed of by it the Trust Fund and the income of it shall be held (as to both capital and income) upon trust for *(name)* absolutely[7]

[1113]

5   Alteration of class of beneficiaries[8]

5.1   Subject to clause 5.2 below:

5.1.1   the Trustees (being not less than 2 in number or a trust corporation) shall have power by any deed or deeds revocable or irrevocable executed before the Ultimate Date to declare that any individual or individuals (not being the Settlor or the spouse of the Settlor) whether or not then born or ascertained or any Charity or Charities (other than any individual then a trustee of the settlement and other than any individual or Charity previously excluded under the power set out in clause 5.1.2 below) shall from such time and (subject to any future exercise of the power set out in clause 5.1.2 below) either permanently or for such period or periods as shall be specified in any such deed or deeds be included in the class of the Discretionary Beneficiaries defined in clause 1.1.3 above and

5.1.2   the Trustees (being not less than 2 in number or a trust corporation) shall also have power by any deed or deeds revocable or irrevocable executed before the Ultimate Date to declare that any individual or individuals whether or not born or ascertained or any Charity or Charities who or which is or are a member or members (or eligible to be added as a member or members) of the class of the Discretionary Beneficiaries immediately prior to the execution of such deed or deeds shall from such time and either permanently or for such period or periods as shall be specified in any such deed or deeds cease to be a member or members (or eligible to become a member or members) of such class

[1114]

5.2   PROVIDED always that:

      5.2.1   no such deed made in exercise of either of the powers conferred by clause 5.1 above shall affect the validity or effect of:

           5.2.1.1   any distribution previously made to or for the benefit of any beneficiary under or pursuant to any power or discretion

           5.2.1.2   any transmissible interest (whether vested or contingent) previously conferred on any beneficiary either by clause 4 above or under or pursuant to any irrevocable exercise of the power of revocation and new appointment conferred by clause 3.2 above or

           5.2.1.3   any future distribution to any beneficiary consequent on the absolute vesting in possession of any such interest as is mentioned in clause 5.2.1.2 above and

      5.2.2   the Trustees (being not less than 2 in number or a trust corporation) may at any time or times before the Ultimate Date by deed or deeds extinguish (or restrict the future exercise of) both or either of the powers (but not any of the restrictions applicable to them) conferred by clause 5.1 above

6   Administrative powers

6.1   Subject to clauses 6.2 and 6.3 below the Trustees shall until the Ultimate Date and during such further period (if any) as the law may allow have the powers of investment and other additional administrative powers set out in the second schedule

6.2   PROVIDED always that the Trustees (being not less than 2 in number or a trust corporation) may at any time or times before the Ultimate Date by deed or deeds extinguish (or restrict the future exercise of) all or any of the powers (but not any of the restrictions applicable to them) conferred by clause 6.1 above

[6.3   If in the administration of the Trust Fund any transaction is in the opinion of the Trustees expedient but the same cannot be effected by reason of the absence of any sufficient power for that purpose conferred by this deed or by law (or by any earlier exercise of the present power) then the Trustees may by deed confer upon themselves either generally or for the purpose of any particular transaction or transactions the necessary power and from the execution of such a deed the Trustees shall have such power as if it had been conferred by this deed [provided that before executing any such deed the Trustees shall obtain the written opinion of a counsel of at least ten years' standing practising in trust law that the possession by the Trustees of such power is desirable in the interests of the beneficiaries]]

7   Exclusion of apportionment

Where under the trusts for the time being affecting the same there is a change in the person or persons beneficially or prospectively beneficially entitled to the income of any part of the Trust Fund (whether due to the birth or death of any person or for any other reason whatever) the provisions of the Apportionment Act 1870 shall not apply and no apportionment shall be made of income accruing or accrued or of outgoings being expended on the occasion of such change in beneficial entitlement but rather the same shall be treated as having accrued due or become a proper liability on the day of actual receipt or expenditure (as the case may be)[9]

[1115]

[8   Consultation

The provisions of the Trusts of Land and Appointment of Trustees Act 1996 Section 11(1) shall not apply to any land situated in England and Wales which[10] may at any time be subject to the trusts of this settlement or any trusts appointed or arising under it][11]

9   Trustees' charges and remuneration

9.1   Any of the Trustees who shall be an individual engaged in any profession or business either alone or in partnership shall be entitled to charge and be paid and to retain all professional or other proper charges for any business done or time spent or services rendered by him or his firm in connection with the trusts powers and provisions of this settlement and shall also be entitled to retain any share of brokerage or commission paid to him or his firm by any broker agent or insurance office in connection with any acquisition of or dealing with any investments or property or the effecting or payment of any premium on any policy of insurance subject or intended to become subject to the trusts of this settlement or any such assurance

9.2   None of the Trustees holding any directorship or other office or employment or retainer in relation to any company all or any of whose shares stock or securities shall at any time be subject to any trusts of this settlement shall be accountable for any remuneration received in connection with such directorship office employment or retainer

9.3   Notwithstanding anything contained in this clause neither the Settlor nor any spouse of the Settlor who may be for the time being one of the Trustees shall be entitled to charge or be paid or retain any or any share of any professional or other charges by reason of this clause or be relieved thereby from any liability to account as a trustee for any money or assets[12]

[1116]

10   Corporate Trustees

10.1   A corporation (whether or not a trust corporation) may at any time be appointed to be one of the Trustees on such reasonable terms as to remuneration and charging and otherwise however as shall be agreed at the time when the appointment is made between the person or persons making the appointment on the one hand and the corporation on the other

10.2   The provisions of the Trustee Act 1925 Section 37 in their application to this settlement shall be varied so that for each reference to 'a trust corporation' there shall be substituted a reference to 'a corporation (whether or not a trust corporation)'[13]

11   Exclusion of self-dealing

Any of the Trustees may exercise or concur in exercising any powers and discretions given by this settlement or by law notwithstanding that he has a direct or other personal interest in the mode or result of any such exercise but any such Trustee may abstain from acting except as a merely formal party in any matter in which he may be so personally interested and may allow his co-trustees or co-trustee to act alone in relation thereto[14]

12   Protection of Trustees

12.1   In the professed execution of the trusts and powers of this settlement or of any assurance of immovable property upon trust such that the property is to be held on the trusts of this settlement none of the Trustees (being an individual) shall be liable for any loss arising by reason of any improper investment made in good faith or the retention of any improper investment or any failure to see to the insurance of or preservation of any chattels or the making or revising of any inventory of them or for the negligence or fraud of any agent employed by him or by any other of the Trustees (although the employment of such agent was not strictly necessary or expedient) or by reason of any other matter or thing whatever except wilful and individual fraud or wrongdoing on the part of that one of the Trustees who is sought to be made liable[15]

12.2   The Trustees shall not be bound or required to interfere in the management or conduct of the affairs or business of any company in respect of which the Trustees shall hold or control the whole or a majority or any part of the shares carrying the control of the company or other the voting rights of the company and so long as there shall be no notice of any act of dishonesty or misappropriation of money on the part of the directors having the management of such company the Trustees shall be at liberty to leave the conduct of its business (including the payment or non-payment of dividends) wholly to such directors

[1117]

13   Exclusion of the Settlor and spouse from benefit

Notwithstanding anything in this settlement expressed or implied no money or other assets subject to the trusts of this settlement shall in any circumstances whatever be paid or transferred beneficially (except for full consideration) to or lent to or applied (whether directly or indirectly) for the benefit of the Settlor or any spouse of the Settlor[16]

14   Appointment of new Trustees

14.1   The power of appointing a new Trustee or new Trustees shall (subject to clause 14.3 below) be vested in the Settlor during the life of the Settlor[17]

14.2   Any individual or corporation may be appointed as a Trustee notwithstanding that such individual or corporation is resident domiciled or incorporated outside the United Kingdom and notwithstanding that as a result of such appointment (or any retirement occurring in connection with it) all or a majority of the Trustees are persons resident domiciled or incorporated outside the United Kingdom

14.3   It is declared (for the avoidance of any doubt) that the Settlor may at any time or times by deed release (or restrict the future exercise of) the power conferred on the Settlor by clause 14.1 above and it is further declared that the provisions of the Trustee Act 1925 Section 36 in their application to this settlement shall be varied so that it shall not be a ground for the appointment of a new Trustee that an existing Trustee has remained out of the United Kingdom for more than 12 months

[14.4 The provisions of the Trusts of Land and Appointment of Trustees Act 1996 Section[s] 19 [and 20] shall not apply to this settlement or to the trusts of this settlement or to any trusts appointed or arising under it[18]]

15 Exclusion of the Trustee Delegation Act 1999 Section 1

The provisions of the Trustee Delegation Act 1999 Section 1(1) shall not apply to any Trustee or Trustees for the time being of this settlement[19]

[16 Exclusion of the duty of care

The duty of care contained in the Trustee Act 2000 Section 1 shall not apply to the Trustees in the exercise of any of the powers conferred on them by this settlement nor to any duties relating to the exercise of such powers nor to the exercise by the Trustees of any powers contained in or duties imposed by the Trustee Act 2000, the Trustee Act 1925, the Trusts of Land and Appointment of Trustees Act 1996 or any other statute where the duty of care is expressed to be applicable[20]]

[17 Clause headings

The headings to the clauses and paragraphs of this settlement are for the purposes of information only and are not part of and shall not be used in the construction of this settlement or any part of it][21]

IN WITNESS etc

FIRST SCHEDULE

Assets

(describe assets referred to in the recital)

SECOND SCHEDULE

Administrative powers

(Select from administrative powers set out in Form 4 schedule [1092] ante as required amending as appropriate. Care should be taken to amend the powers selected so that they fit in with the definitions and other terminology used in this settlement)[22]

(signatures of the parties)[23]
(signatures of witnesses)
[1118]

1   As to stamp duty see Information Binder: Stamp Duties [1] Table of Duties (Declaration of trust). This Form is a flexible life interest trust which enables the trustees to terminate the interest in possession which arises under clause 2 [1110] and apply capital and income for the benefit of one or more of the discretionary class including the life tenant (see clause 3 [1111]). The mere existence of this power to terminate the life tenancy does not prevent there being an interest in possession for inheritance tax purposes. Under present legislation the termination of the interest in possession will be a potentially exempt transfer (by the life tenant) for inheritance tax purposes, provided that the trust fund is not

afterwards held on trusts lacking an interest in possession: see further Paragraph 298 [767] et seq ante. No capital gains tax charge will be incurred until the settlement comes to an end: see the Taxation of Chargeable Gains Act 1992 s 71 as amended by the Finance Act 1999 s 75(1), (2) (42–44 Halsbury's Statutes (4th Edn) TAXATION), Paragraph 342 [919] ante and notes 5 and 6 below. This type of settlement can be used instead of the traditional protective trust (see vol 40(2) (2001 Reissue) TRUSTS AND SETTLEMENTS Part 12 [6901]). As with any flexible trust, the settlor should give his trustees a signed letter of wishes. For specimen letters of wishes see Form 252 [1841] et seq post.

2   Express instructions should be taken before this clause is included. See Form 4 note 8 [1103] ante.

3   The inclusion of this clause means that if the life tenant were to die (without the overriding power of appointment in clause 3 [1111] having been exercised) the spouse exemption will apply to ensure that no inheritance tax will be payable. Alternative clauses include:
   (a)   one which gives the spouse a power to appoint a life interest to any surviving spouse (usually capable of being exercised by deed or will): see Forms 118 [1521], 119 [1522] post.
   (b)   one under which the interest of the surviving spouse is to terminate on remarriage or, in a few cases, on cohabitation: see Form 69 [1418] post.
       In this Form the existence of the overriding power means that the trustees can achieve this result by execution of that power.

4   The opening words make it clear that the power contained in this clause can be exercised to bring to an end the interests declared in clause 2 [1110] (ie it can terminate an existing interest in possession). It is not necessary to obtain the consent of a beneficiary with an interest in possession and hence there can be no question that if the trustees exercise this power the beneficiary has made a 'gift' of any property. Of course, the termination of an interest in possession involves a transfer of value for inheritance tax purposes (normally this will be a potentially exempt transfer), but the reservation of benefit rules depend upon the making of a gift and hence cannot apply to trust property in which the beneficiary contrives to enjoy a benefit even after his interest in possession has been terminated.

5   In exercising this power the trustees should have regard to the capital gains tax position. In most cases any revocation and appointment onto new trusts does not result in a deemed disposal for capital gains tax purposes. However, exceptionally the Inland Revenue may contend that a deemed disposal under the Taxation of Chargeable Gains Act 1992 s 71 as amended (see note 1 above) has occurred: see further Paragraph 342 [919] ante.

6   The transfer of assets on to a separate trust is a disposal for capital gains tax purposes and may therefore result in a charge to tax. As to capital gains tax in relation to resettlements see Paragraph 342 [919] ante. See also *IRC v Botnar* [1999] STC 711: the express exclusion of any benefit to the settlor or his spouse ensures that the problem that arose in that case cannot apply if this power is exercised.

7   This clause is a long-stop clause. It is important that the beneficiary named is living at the date of the settlement (or is a charity).

8   This clause enables the trustees to include or exclude, either permanently or for a specified period, any person (or charity) from the beneficial class. The exercise of this power does not affect the validity of anything which has already occurred.

9   It is usual to exclude apportionment calculations (which can be complex) under the Apportionment Act 1870 (23 Halsbury's Statutes (4th Edn) LANDLORD AND TENANT).

10   This wording caters for the situation where the trustees subsequently acquire land on trust for sale.

11   As to the consultation provisions see Paragraph 225 [540] ante. For a detailed consideration see vol 40(2) (2001 Reissue) TRUSTS AND SETTLEMENTS Part 8 [3001].

12   See Form 4 note 21 [1105] ante.

13   See Form 4 note 22 [1105] ante.

14   See Form 4 note 23 [1105] ante.

15   See Form 4 note 24 [1105] ante.

16   See Form 4 note 25 [1105] ante.

17   See Form 4 note 26 [1105] ante.

18   As to the provisions of the Trusts of Land and Appointment of Trustees Act 1996 ss 19, 20 see vol 40(2) (2001 Reissue) TRUSTS AND SETTLEMENTS Part 10 [5201]. See further Form 4 note 27 [1105] ante.

19   See Form 4 note 28 [1105] ante.

20   See Form 4 note 29 [1105] ante.

21   See Form 4 note 30 [1105] ante.

22   It is desirable for the trustees to have the largest number of administrative powers. The powers set out in this schedule supplement those already possessed by the trustees: eg under the Trustee Act 2000 (48 Halsbury's Statutes (4th Edn) TRUSTS AND SETTLEMENTS).

23   As to the statutory requirements for valid execution of a deed see vol 12 (1994 Reissue) DEEDS, AGREEMENTS AND DECLARATIONS.

6

Life insurance settlement[1]

THIS SETTLEMENT is made the ...... day of ....

BETWEEN:

(1)   *(settlor)* of *(address)* ('the Settlor') and

(2)   *(original trustees)* of *(addresses)* ('the Original Trustees')

WHEREAS

(1)   The Settlor is absolutely entitled to the life insurance policy ('the Policy') the particulars of which are contained in the first schedule

(2)   The Settlor wishes to assign the Policy to the Original Trustees to be held by them upon the trusts and with and subject to the powers and provisions contained in this settlement

[1120]

NOW THIS DEED WITNESSES as follows:

1   Definitions and interpretation

1.1   In this settlement the following expressions have where the context permits the following meanings:

    1.1.1   'the Trustees' means the Original Trustees or other the trustee or trustees for the time being of this settlement whether original additional or substituted and 'Trustee' means each and any of the Trustees

    1.1.2   'the Trust Fund' means:

        1.1.2.1   all that interest of the Settlor in the Policy assigned below to the Original Trustees and all money assured by or to become payable under or by virtue of it and all benefits and advantages of it

        1.1.2.2   any money investments or property in the future paid or transferred to the Trustees as additions to the Trust Fund and

        1.1.2.3   the investments and property from time to time representing the Policy or the proceeds of it or additions to the Trust Fund

[1121]

    1.1.3   'the Beneficiaries' means (subject to the provisions of clause 8 below) the following persons namely:

        1.1.3.1   the Settlor's [widow]

        1.1.3.2   the Settlor's children and any future issue of the Settlor (whether children or more remote) and

        1.1.3.3   any spouse for the time being and any widow or widower (whether or not for the time being remarried) of the individuals referred to in clause 1.1.3.2

    and 'Beneficiary' has a corresponding meaning[2]

1.1.4   'the Accumulation Period' means the period of 21 years commencing with the date of this deed[3]

1.1.5   'the Ultimate Date' means the day on which shall expire the period of 80 years from the date of this deed which period shall be the perpetuity period applicable[4]

1.1.6   'Charitable' means charitable (and exclusively charitable) according to the law for the time being of England and Wales

1.1.7   'Charity' means a trust or corporation association society or other institution established only for Charitable purposes and 'Charities' has a corresponding meaning

1.1.8   references to a 'beneficiary' or to 'beneficiaries' include references to a person or persons who are the object of any dispositive power or discretion

[1.2   This settlement shall be construed as though the Family Law Reform Act 1987 Sections 1 and 19 had not been enacted (but for the avoidance of any doubt it is now declared that the respective provisions of the Children Act 1989 the Legitimacy Act 1976 and the Adoption Act 1976 shall apply][5]

[1122]

2   Assignment

The Settlor as beneficial owner now assigns the Policy and all benefits and advantages of and all rights arising under and all money assured by or to become payable under or by virtue of it and any policy or policies substituted for it to the Original Trustees to hold the same unto the Original Trustees upon the trusts and subject to the powers and provisions declared and contained below

3   Power to retain or convert

The Trustees shall stand possessed of the Trust Fund upon trust either to retain the same in its present form of investment for so long as they think fit or to convert the same into money and invest the proceeds in any investments now authorised with power at their discretion to vary or transpose such investments for or into others of a like nature[6]

[1123]

4   Trusts of income

4.1   The Trustees shall stand possessed of the Trust Fund upon trust until the Ultimate Date (subject however to the provisions contained below) to pay or apply or (in the case of a minor) allocate the income of the Trust Fund to or for the maintenance support or otherwise for the benefit in any manner of all or any one or more exclusively of the others or other of the Beneficiaries for the time being in existence and if more than one in such shares and in such manner in all respects as the Trustees shall in their absolute discretion without being liable in any such case to account for the exercise of such discretion think fit

4.2   PROVIDED always that the Trustees shall not be bound to pay apply or allocate as provided in clause 4.1 above the whole or any part of the income accruing to the Trust Fund during the Accumulation Period but shall during the Accumulation Period pay apply or allocate only so much of such income as the Trustees shall in their absolute discretion think fit and shall accumulate the surplus (if any) of such income at compound interest by investing the same and the resulting income of it in any of the investments authorised by this settlement and shall hold such accumulations as an accretion to (and as one fund with) the capital of the Trust Fund

[1124]

5   Principal trusts

5.1   Notwithstanding the trusts powers and provisions contained above (but subject to the proviso contained in clause 5.2 below) the Trustees (being not less than 2 in number or a corporation) shall have power exercisable in their absolute discretion at any time or times before the Ultimate Date to apply the whole or any part or parts of the capital of the Trust Fund for any purpose whatever which the Trustees may think to be for the benefit of any one or more of the Beneficiaries for the time being in existence or to transfer or pay the whole or any part or parts of the capital of the Trust Fund to any one or more of the Beneficiaries for the time being in existence (being of full age) for his her or their absolute use and benefit freed and discharged from the trusts of this settlement

5.2   PROVIDED always that the Trustees (being not less than 2 in number or a corporation) may at any time or times before the Ultimate Date by deed or deeds extinguish (or restrict the future exercise of) the power (but not any of the restrictions applicable to it) conferred by clause 5.1 above

[1125]

6   Overriding powers of revocation and new appointment

6.1   Notwithstanding the above trusts powers and provisions of this settlement (but subject as is provided in clause 6.3 below)[7] the Trustees (being not less than 2 in number or a corporation) shall have power at any time or times before the Ultimate Date by any deed or deeds revocable or irrevocable to revoke all or any of the trusts powers and provisions declared and contained in clauses 4 and 5 [and clauses regarding receipts and administrative powers] of this settlement in respect of the whole or any part or parts of the Trust Fund and the income of it for the purpose only of appointing (and so that the Trustees shall by the same deed appoint) in respect of such whole or part or parts of the Trust Fund and the income of it (or so much of it as is affected by the revocation) such trusts powers and provisions for the benefit of all or any one or more of the Beneficiaries (including if thought fit powers of appointment powers of maintenance and advancement and administrative and other powers and provisions) as the Trustees in their absolute discretion shall think fit

6.2   Subject to clause 6.1 above and subject also as is provided in clause 6.3 below:
        6.2.1   any trust appointed under the power of revocation and new appointment contained in clause 6.1 above may be mandatory or discretionary and may create any interest or interests whatsoever whether absolute or limited and whether vested or contingent and whether in possession or in reversion and may divide the property subject to it or the income of it into any shares and may provide for the accumulation of the whole or any part of the income subject to it during the Accumulation Period (or during any other permissible period) and any discretionary trust or power may by such revocation and new appointment be conferred on any person or persons (not necessarily being or including the Trustees) and any such trusts or powers so conferred may authorise the delegation to an unlimited extent of any discretion and

[1126]

6.2.2   without prejudice to the generality of the above any appointment under the power of revocation and new appointment contained in clause 6.1 above may (if the Trustees in their absolute discretion think fit) include in such appointment a trust or trusts immediately to pay or transfer any income or capital of the Trust Fund or any part or parts of it to the trustees of any other trust or settlement wherever established or existing under which any one or more of the Beneficiaries is or are beneficially interested (whether or not such one or more of the Beneficiaries is or are the only person or persons interested or capable of benefiting under such trust or settlement) so long as the Settlor shall not be interested or capable of benefiting under such other trust or settlement and so long as any spouse of the Settlor shall not be interested or capable of benefiting under such other trust or settlement during the Settlor's lifetime

6.3   PROVIDED always that:

6.3.1   no revocation and new appointment under the power conferred by clause 6.1 above shall affect any capital or income of the Trust Fund (or any share or part of it) previously paid transferred or applied (except merely by accumulation) to or for the benefit of any person under the other provisions of this settlement or any income (except accumulated income) of the Trust Fund (or any share or part of it) accruing prior to such revocation and appointment and

6.3.2   the Trustees (being not less than 2 in number or a corporation) may at any time or times before the Ultimate Date by deed or deeds extinguish (or restrict the future exercise of) the power conferred by clause 6.1 above

[1127]

7   Ultimate Trust

Subject to all the trusts powers and provisions of this settlement and if and so far as (for any reason whatever) not wholly disposed of by it the Trust Fund and the income of it shall be held (as to both capital and income) upon trust for *(name)*[8]

8   Alteration of class of beneficiaries[9]

8.1   Subject to clause 8.2 below:

8.1.1   the Trustees (being not less than 2 in number or a corporation) shall have power by any deed or deeds revocable or irrevocable (executed before the Ultimate Date) to declare that any individual or individuals (not being the Settlor or any spouse of the Settlor) whether or not then born or ascertained or any Charity or Charities (other than any individual then a trustee of this settlement and other than any individual or Charity previously excluded under the power contained in clause 8.1.2 below) shall from that time and (subject to any future exercise of the power contained in clause 8.1.2 below) either permanently or for such period or periods as shall be specified in any such deed or deeds (not extending beyond the Ultimate Date) be included in the class of the Beneficiaries defined in clause 1.1.3 above and

8.1.2   the Trustees (being not less than 2 in number or a corporation) shall also have power by any deed or deeds revocable or irrevocable (executed before the Ultimate Date) to declare that any individual or individuals whether or not born or ascertained or any Charity or Charities who or which is or are a member or members (or eligible to be added as a member or members) of the class of the Beneficiaries immediately prior to the execution of such deed or deeds shall from that time and either permanently or for such period or periods as shall be specified in any such deed or deeds cease to be a member or members (or eligible to become a member or members) of such class

[1128]

8.2   PROVIDED always that:

8.2.1   no such deed made in exercise of either of the powers conferred by clause 8.1 above shall affect the validity or effect of:

8.2.1.1   any distribution previously made to or for the benefit of any Beneficiary under or pursuant to any power or discretion

8.2.1.2   any transmissible interest (whether vested or contingent) previously conferred on any Beneficiary either by clause 7 above or under or pursuant to any irrevocable exercise of the power of revocation and new appointment conferred by clause 6 above or

8.2.1.3   any future distribution to any Beneficiary consequent on the absolute vesting in possession of any such interest as is mentioned in clause 8.2.1.2 above and

8.2.2   the Trustees (being not less than 2 in number or a corporation) may at any time or times by deed or deeds executed before the Ultimate Date extinguish (or restrict the future exercise of) both or either of the powers (but not any of the restrictions applicable to them) conferred by clause 8.1 above

[1129]

9   Policy premiums

9.1   Neither the Settlor nor the Trustees shall be under any obligation to keep up any insurance policy or policies for the time being forming part of the Trust Fund but the Trustees may in their discretion apply any income or capital of the Trust Fund or any sum borrowed in keeping up any such policy or policies

9.2   If the Settlor shall pay any further premium in respect of the Policy as mentioned in the first schedule or any policy or policies substituted for it the Settlor shall not thereby acquire any lien or charge in or over the Policy or any such substituted policy or policies or over the Trust Fund or any property comprised in it

10   Administrative powers

10.1   Subject to clauses 10.2 and 10.3 below the Trustees shall have the additional powers set out in the second schedule

10.2   PROVIDED always that the Trustees (being not less than 2 in number or a trust corporation) may at any time or times by deed or deeds executed before the Ultimate Date extinguish (or restrict the future exercise of) all or any of the powers (but not any of the restrictions applicable to them) conferred by clause 10.1 above

[10.3   If in the administration of the Trust Fund any transaction is in the opinion of the Trustees expedient but the same cannot be effected by reason of the absence of any sufficient power for that purpose conferred by this deed or by law (or by any earlier exercise of the present power) then the Trustees may by deed confer upon themselves either generally or for the purpose of any particular transaction or transactions the necessary power and from the execution of such a deed the Trustees shall have such power as if it had been conferred by this deed [provided that before executing any such deed the Trustees shall obtain the written opinion of a counsel of at least ten years' standing practising in trust law that the possession by the Trustees of such power is desirable in the interests of the beneficiaries]]

[1130]

11   Exclusion of apportionment

Where under the trusts for the time being affecting the same there is a change in the person or persons beneficially or prospectively beneficially entitled to the income of any part of the Trust Fund (whether due to the birth or death of any person or for any other reason whatever) the provisions of the Apportionment Act 1870 shall not apply and no apportionment shall be made of income accruing or accrued or of outgoings being expended on the occasion of such change in beneficial entitlement but rather the same shall be treated as having accrued due or become a proper liability on the day of actual receipt or expenditure (as the case may be)[10]

[12   Consultation

The provisions of the Trusts of Land and Appointment of Trustees Act 1996 Section 11(1) shall not apply to any land situated in England and Wales which may at any time be subject to the trusts of this settlement or any trusts appointed or arising under it or to any assurance of immovable property situated in England and Wales such that the property is held on the trusts of this settlement][11]

[1131]

13   Trustees' charges and remuneration[12]

13.1   Any of the Trustees who shall be an individual engaged in any profession or business either alone or in partnership shall be entitled to charge and be paid and to retain all professional or other proper charges for any business done or time spent or services rendered by him or his firm in connection with the trusts powers and provisions of this settlement or of any assurance of immovable property upon trust such that the property or the net proceeds of sale are to be held on the trusts of this settlement and shall also be entitled to retain any share of brokerage or commission paid to him or his firm by any broker agent or insurance office in connection with any acquisition of or dealing with any investments or property or the effecting or payment of any premium on any policy of insurance subject or intended to become subject to the trusts of this settlement or any such assurance

13.2   None of the Trustees holding any directorship or other office or employment or retainer in relation to any company all or any of whose shares stock or securities shall at any time be subject to any trusts of this settlement shall be accountable for any remuneration received in connection with such directorship office employment or retainer

13.3   Notwithstanding anything contained in this clause neither the Settlor nor any spouse of the Settlor who may be for the time being one of the Trustees shall be entitled to charge or be paid or retain any or any share of any professional or other charges by reason of this clause or be relieved thereby from any liability to account as a trustee for any money or assets[13]

[1132]

14   Corporate Trustees

14.1   A corporation (whether or not a trust corporation) may at any time be appointed to be one of the Trustees on such reasonable terms as to remuneration and charging and otherwise however as shall be agreed at the time when the appointment is made between the person or persons making the appointment on the one hand and the corporation on the other

14.2   The provisions of the Trustee Act 1925 Section 37 in their application to this settlement shall be varied so that for each reference to 'a trust corporation' there shall be substituted a reference to 'a corporation (whether or not a trust corporation)'[14]

15   Exclusion of self-dealing

Any of the Trustees may exercise or concur in exercising any powers and discretions given by this settlement or by law notwithstanding that he has a direct or other personal interest in the mode or result of any such exercise but any such Trustee may abstain from acting except as a merely formal party in any matter in which he may be so personally interested and may allow his co-trustees or co-trustee to act alone in relation thereto[15]

16   Protection of Trustees

16.1   In the professed execution of the trusts and powers of this settlement or of any assurance of immovable property upon trust such that the property are to be held on the trusts of this settlement none of the Trustees (being an individual) shall be liable for any loss arising by reason of any improper investment made in good faith or the retention of any improper investment or any failure to see to the insurance of or preservation of any chattels or the making or revising of any inventory of them or for the negligence or fraud of any agent employed by him or by any other of the Trustees (although the employment of such agent was not strictly necessary or expedient) or by reason of any other matter or thing whatever except wilful and individual fraud or wrongdoing on the part of that one of the Trustees who is sought to be made liable[16]

16.2   The Trustees shall not be bound or required to interfere in the management or conduct of the affairs or business of any company in respect of which the Trustees shall hold or control the whole or a majority or any part of the shares carrying the control of the company or other the voting rights of the company and so long as there shall be no notice of any act of dishonesty or misappropriation of money on the part of the directors having the management of such company the Trustees shall be at liberty to leave the conduct of its business (including the payment or non-payment of dividends) wholly to such directors

17   Exclusion of the Settlor and spouse from benefit

Notwithstanding anything in this settlement expressed or implied no money or other assets subject to the trusts of this settlement shall in any circumstances whatever be paid or transferred beneficially (except for full consideration) to or lent to or applied (whether directly or indirectly) for the benefit of the Settlor or any spouse of the Settlor[17]

[1133]

18   Appointment of new Trustees

18.1   The power of appointing a new Trustee or new Trustees shall (subject to clause 18.3 below) be vested in the Settlor during the life of the Settlor[18]

18.2   Any individual or corporation may be appointed as a Trustee notwithstanding that such individual or corporation is resident domiciled or incorporated outside the United Kingdom and notwithstanding that as a result of such appointment (or any retirement occurring in connection with it) all or a majority of the Trustees are persons resident domiciled or incorporated outside the United Kingdom

18.3   It is declared (for the avoidance of any doubt) that the Settlor may at any time or times by deed release (or restrict the future exercise of) the power conferred on the Settlor by clause 18.1 above and it is further declared that the provisions of the Trustee Act 1925 Section 36 in their application to this settlement shall be varied so that it shall not be a ground for the appointment of a new Trustee that an existing Trustee has remained out of the United Kingdom for more than 12 months

[18.4   The provisions of the Trusts of Land and Appointment of Trustees Act 1996 Section[s] 19 [and 20] shall not apply to this settlement or to the trusts of this settlement or to any trusts appointed or arising under it][19]

19   Exclusion of the Trustee Delegation Act 1999 Section 1

The provisions of the Trustee Delegation Act 1999 Section 1(1) shall not apply to any Trustee or Trustees for the time being of this settlement[20]

20   Stamp duty certificate

It is hereby certified that this instrument falls within category N in the Schedule to the Stamp Duty (Exempt Instruments) Regulations 1987[21]

[21   Clause headings

The headings to the clauses and paragraphs of this settlement are for the purposes of information only and are not part of and shall not be used in the construction of this settlement or any part of it][22]

IN WITNESS etc

FIRST SCHEDULE

The Policy

(specify insurance company and policy number)

SECOND SCHEDULE

Administrative powers

(Select from administrative powers set out in Form 4 schedule [1092] ante as required amending as appropriate. Care should be taken to amend the powers selected so that they fit in with the definitions and other terminology used in this settlement)[23]

(signatures of the parties)[24]

(signatures of witnesses)

[1134]

1   As to stamp duty see Information Binder: Stamp Duties [1] Table of Duties (Declaration of trust) and (Voluntary disposition). In essence this settlement is an assignment of policy together with a declaration of trust (the trusts being discretionary). For inheritance tax purposes, it is usually desirable for a person to settle the benefit of any policy of life insurance which he takes out on his life. Failure to do so results in it forming part of his estate on death and therefore being subject to charge. Even when the policy is to pass to the deceased's surviving spouse, so that inheritance tax does not arise, it may still be advantageous to settle the policy so as to obtain immediate payment of the proceeds ahead of the grant of representation to the estate. Where the policy is charged as security for the repayment of a debt incurred by the life assured it may be impracticable to effect a settlement of what is, in effect, the equity of redemption. Trusts of term assurance are commonly set up to protect against the seven-year charge on failed potentially exempt transfers.

        The assignment of the benefit of the policy is unlikely to lead to inheritance tax problems. The value transferred is the higher of the surrender value of the policy and the premium paid: see the Inheritance Tax Act 1984 s 167 as amended by the Finance Act 1986 s 114(6), Sch 23 Pt X (42–44 Halsbury's Statutes (4th Edn) TAXATION). Although note the Inheritance Tax Act 1984 s 167(3) which excludes from this provision the standard seven-year term policy (such policies usually have a nil surrender value). Future premiums may continue to be paid by the settlor who will not add property to his discretionary trust provided that either the premiums fall within his annual exempt amount or are normal expenditure out of his income. The Inland Revenue accepts that the first premium paid before the assignment can fall within the normal expenditure exemption.

        There is no capital gains tax charge on the disposal of a life insurance policy unless the settlor had acquired the benefit of the policy for money or money's worth: Taxation of Chargeable Gains Act 1992 s 210(2) (42–44 Halsbury's Statutes (4th Edn) TAXATION).

        Notification of the assignment should be given to the relevant insurer (see Form 298 [2084] post) and as with all discretionary trusts the settlor should draw up a letter of wishes (see Form 252 [1841] et seq post). Different considerations apply when it is desired to settle the death benefit payable under a pension policy: see vol 40(2) (2001 Reissue) TRUSTS AND SETTLEMENTS Part 18 [9601].

2   See Form 4 note 5 [1103] ante.

3   See Form 4 note 6 [1103] ante.

4   See Form 4 note 7 [1103] ante.

5   Express instructions should be taken before this clause is included. See also Form 4 clause 1.2 [1083] ante.

6   This is a case where the trustees should not be under a duty to diversify the assets held in trust: cf Trustee Act 2000 s 4(3)(b).

7   The opening words make it clear that the power contained in this clause can be exercised to terminate an existing interest in possession. It is not necessary to obtain the consent of a beneficiary with an interest in possession and hence there can be no question that if the trustees exercise this power the beneficiary has made a 'gift' of any property. Of course, the termination of an interest in possession involves a transfer of value for inheritance tax purposes (normally this will be a potentially exempt transfer), but the reservation of benefit rules depend upon the making of a gift and hence cannot apply to trust property in which the beneficiary contrives to enjoy a benefit even after his interest in possession has been terminated.

8   See Form 4 note 15 [1104].

9   See Form 4 note 16 [1104] ante.

10   See Form 4 note 17 [1105] ante.

11   As to the consultation provisions see Paragraph 225 [540] ante.

12   See Form 4 note 20 [1105] ante.

13   See Form 4 note 21 [1105] ante.

14   See Form 4 note 22 [1105] ante.

15   See Form 4 notes 20 and 23 [1105] ante.

16   See Form 4 note 24 [1105] ante.

17   See Form 4 note 25 [1105] ante.
18   See Form 4 note 26 [1105] ante.
19   As to the provisions of the Trusts of Land and Appointment of Trustees Act 1996 ss 19, 20 see vol 40(2) (2001 Reissue) TRUSTS AND SETTLEMENTS Part 8 [3001] et seq See further Form 4 note 27 [1105] ante.
20   See Form 4 note 28 [1105] ante.
21   A conveyance or transfer of property, operating as a voluntary disposition inter vivos within Category N in the Schedule to the Stamp Duty (Exempt Instruments) Regulations 1987, SI 1987/516 as inserted by SI 1999/2539, is exempt from stamp duty under the provisions specified in SI 1987/516 reg 2(2) as amended by SI 1999/2539, if certified in accordance with SI 1987/516 reg 3.
22   See Form 4 note 30 [1105] ante.
23   The powers set out in this schedule supplement those already possessed by the trustees: eg under the Trustee Act 1925 (48 Halsbury's Statutes (4th Edn) TRUSTS AND SETTLEMENTS).
24   As to the statutory requirements for valid execution of a deed see vol 12 (1994 Reissue) DEEDS, AGREEMENTS AND DECLARATIONS.

[1135]

7

Marriage settlement[1]

THIS SETTLEMENT is made the …… day of ………

BETWEEN:

(1)   *(intended husband)* of *(address)* ('the Settlor')

(2)   *(intended wife)* of *(address)* ('the Wife') and

(3)   *(trustees)* of *(addresses)* ('the Original Trustees')

WHEREAS

(1)   A marriage ('the Marriage') is intended shortly to be solemnised between the Settlor and the Wife (together referred to as 'the Spouses')

(2)   The Settlor is entitled for his own benefit in possession absolutely to the investments described in the first schedule ('the Investments')

(3)   Upon the treaty for the Marriage it was agreed that the Settlor should settle the Investments in the manner appearing below

(4)   In part performance of the agreement mentioned above the Settlor has transferred the Investments to the Original Trustees

[1136]

NOW THIS DEED WITNESSES as follows:

1   Definitions and interpretation

In this settlement the following expressions have where the context permits the following meanings:

1.1   'the Trustees' means the Original Trustees or other the trustees or trustee for the time being of this settlement and 'Trustee' means each and any of the Trustees

1.2   'the Trust Fund' means the Investments all assets at any time added by way of further settlement accumulation of income capital accretion or otherwise and all property from time to time representing the same

2   Trusts for the Settlor and the Wife

The Trustees shall hold the Trust Fund and the income from it upon the following trusts and subject to the following powers and provisions declared concerning the same:

2.1   until the Marriage in trust for the Settlor absolutely

2.2   from and after the Marriage the Trustees shall pay the income of the Trust Fund to the Settlor during his life

2.3   after the death of the Settlor the Trustees shall pay the income of the Trust Fund to the Wife during the residue of her life so long as she shall remain a widow

2.4   if the Wife shall marry again then from and after such subsequent marriage the Trustees shall pay one-half of the income of the Trust Fund to the Wife during the residue of her life

[1137]

3   Trusts for issue etc of marriage

Subject to the trusts declared in clause 2 above the Trustees shall hold the Trust Fund and the income of it or so much of it respectively as shall not have been applied in exercise of any power by this settlement or by any statute created upon the following trusts:

3.1   in trust as to both capital and income for all or such one or more exclusively of the others or other of the children or remoter issue of the Marriage at such ages or times and if more than one in such shares and with such provisions for their respective maintenance education advancement and benefit generally (at the discretion of the Trustees or any other person or persons) as the Spouses shall by deed or deeds revocable or irrevocable (regard being had to the law relating to remoteness) appoint and in default of and until and subject to any and every such joint appointment as above as the survivor of the Spouses shall by deed or deeds revocable or irrevocable or by will or codicil appoint[2]

3.2   in default of and subject to any such appointment in clause 3.1 above in trust for all the children or any the child of the Marriage who [being sons or a son] shall attain the age of 18 years or [being daughters or a daughter shall attain that age or] marry under that age and if more than one in equal shares absolutely PROVIDED that unless the Spouses or the survivor of them shall in the manner above appoint the contrary no child of the Marriage to whom or to whose issue any part of the Trust Fund shall have been so appointed shall be entitled to any share of the unappointed part of the Trust Fund without bringing the part so appointed into hotchpot and accounting for the same accordingly

3.3   subject to all the trusts powers and provisions of this settlement and if and so far as (for any reason whatever) not wholly disposed of by it the Trust Fund and the income from it shall be held (as to both capital and income) upon trust for *(beneficiary)*[3]

[1138]

4   Powers of maintenance and advancement

The trusts contained in clause 3 above shall carry the intermediate income and the statutory powers of maintenance accumulation and advancement contained in the Trustee Act 1925 Sections 31 and 32 (as amended) shall apply to this settlement but with the following modifications:

4.1   in the case of the said Section 31 the substitution in subsection (1)(i) of the words 'the trustees in their absolute discretion think fit' for the words 'may in all the circumstances be reasonable' and the omission of the proviso to subsection (1) and

4.2   in the case of the said Section 32 the omission of the words 'one-half of' from proviso (a) to subsection (1) and the insertion of a further proviso to the effect that in any case where the said statutory power of advancement contained in the said Section is exercised so as to apply capital money for the advancement or benefit of a person who immediately prior to such exercise does not have an interest in possession in the capital money in question then such capital money must be vested either absolutely or for an interest in possession in the person in question immediately upon such application being made or (if such person is then under the age of 25 years) before he or she shall have attained the age of 25 years and in such manner that conditions (a) and (b) of the Inheritance Tax Act 1984 Section 71(1) shall be satisfied[4]

[1139]

5   Exclusion of apportionment

Where under the trusts for the time being affecting the same there is a change in the person or persons beneficially or prospectively beneficially entitled to the income of any part of the Trust Fund (whether due to the birth or death of any person or for any other reason whatever) the provisions of the Apportionment Act 1870 shall not apply and no apportionment shall be made of income accruing or accrued or of outgoings being expended on the occasion of such change in beneficial entitlement but rather the same shall be treated as having accrued due or become a proper liability on the day of actual receipt or expenditure (as the case may be)[5]

6   Administrative provisions

6.1   Subject to clauses 6.2 and 6.3 below the Trustees shall during such period as the law may allow have the additional powers set out in the second schedule

6.2   PROVIDED always that the Trustees (being not less than 2 in number or a trust corporation) may at any time or times during such period as the law may allow by deed or deeds extinguish (or restrict the future exercise of) all or any of the powers (but not any of the restrictions applicable to them) conferred by clause 6.1 above

[6.3   If in the administration of the Trust Fund any transaction is in the opinion of the Trustees expedient but the same cannot be effected by reason of the absence of any sufficient power for that purpose conferred by this deed or by law (or by any earlier exercise of the present power) then the Trustees may by deed confer upon themselves either generally or for the purpose of any particular transaction or transactions the necessary power and from the execution of such a deed the Trustees shall have such power as if it had been conferred by this deed [provided that before executing any such deed the Trustees shall obtain the written opinion of a counsel of at least ten years' standing practising in trust law that the possession by the Trustees of such power is desirable in the interests of the beneficiaries]]

[1140]

[7   Consultation

The provisions of the Trusts of Land and Appointment of Trustees Act 1996 Section 11(1) shall not apply to any land situated in England and Wales which may at any time be subject to the trusts of this settlement or any trusts appointed or arising under it or to any assurance of immovable property situated in England and Wales such that the property is held on the trusts of this settlement][6]

8   Trustees' charges and remuneration

8.1   Any of the Trustees who shall be an individual engaged in any profession or business either alone or in partnership shall be entitled to charge and be paid and to retain all professional or other proper charges for any business done or time spent or services rendered by him or his firm in connection with the trusts powers and provisions of this settlement also be entitled to retain any share of brokerage or commission paid to him or his firm by any broker agent or insurance office in connection with any acquisition of or dealing with any investments or property or the effecting or payment of any premium on any policy of insurance subject or intended to become subject to the trusts of this settlement or any such assurance

8.2   None of the Trustees holding any directorship or other office or employment or retainer in relation to any company all or any of whose shares stock or securities shall at any time be subject to any trusts of this settlement shall be accountable for any remuneration received in connection with such directorship office employment or retainer

[1141]

9   Corporate Trustees

9.1   A corporation (whether or not a trust corporation) may at any time be appointed to be one of the Trustees on such reasonable terms as to remuneration and charging and otherwise however as shall be agreed at the time when the appointment is made between the person or persons making the appointment on the one hand and the corporation on the other

9.2   The provisions of the Trustee Act 1925 Section 37 in their application to this settlement shall be varied so that for each reference to 'a trust corporation' there shall be substituted a reference to 'a corporation (whether or not a trust corporation)'[7]

[1142]

10   Protection of Trustees

10.1   In the professed execution of the trusts and powers of this settlement none of the Trustees (being an individual) shall be liable for any loss arising by reason of any improper investment made in good faith or the retention of any improper investment or any failure to see to the insurance of or preservation of any chattels or the making or revising of any inventory of them or for the negligence or fraud of any agent employed by him or by any other of the Trustees (although the employment of such agent was not strictly necessary or expedient) or by reason of any other matter or thing whatever except wilful and individual fraud or wrongdoing on the part of that one of the Trustees who is sought to be made liable[8]

10.2   The Trustees shall not be bound or required to interfere in the management or conduct of the affairs or business of any company in respect of which the Trustees shall hold or control the whole or a majority or any part of the shares carrying the control of the company or other the voting rights of the company and so long as there shall be no notice of any act of dishonesty or misappropriation of money on the part of the directors having the management of such company the Trustees shall be at liberty to leave the conduct of its business (including the payment or non-payment of dividends) wholly to such directors

[1143]

11   Exclusion of self-dealing

Any of the Trustees may exercise or concur in exercising any powers and discretions given by this settlement or by law notwithstanding that he has a direct or other personal interest in the mode or result of any such exercise but any such Trustee may abstain from acting except as a merely formal party in any matter in which he may be so personally interested and may allow his co-trustees or co-trustee to act alone in relation thereto[10]

12   Appointment of new Trustees

12.1   The power of appointing a new Trustee or new Trustees shall (subject to clause 12.3 below) be vested in the Settlor during the life of the Settlor[11]

12.2   Any individual or corporation may be appointed as a Trustee notwithstanding that such individual or corporation is resident domiciled or incorporated outside the United Kingdom and notwithstanding that as a result of such appointment (or any retirement occurring in connection with it) all or a majority of the Trustees are persons resident domiciled or incorporated outside the United Kingdom

12.3   It is declared (for the avoidance of any doubt) that the Settlor may at any time or times by deed release (or restrict the future exercise of) the power conferred on the Settlor by clause 12.1 above and it is further declared that the provisions of the Trustee Act 1925 Section 36 in their application to this settlement shall be varied so that it shall not be a ground for the appointment of a new Trustee that an existing Trustee has remained out of the United Kingdom for more than 12 months

[12.4   The provisions of the Trusts of Land and Appointment of Trustees Act 1996 Section[s] 19 [and 20] shall not apply to this settlement or to the trusts of this settlement or to any trusts appointed or arising under it[12]]

13   Exclusion of the Trustee Delegation Act 1999 Section 1

The provisions of the Trustee Delegation Act 1999 Section 1(1) shall not apply to any Trustee or Trustees for the time being of this settlement[13]

[14   Exclusion of the duty of care

The duty of care contained in the Trustee Act 2000 Section 1 shall not apply to the Trustees in the exercise of any of the powers conferred on them by this settlement nor to any duties relating to the exercise of such powers nor to the exercise by the Trustees of any powers contained in or duties imposed by the Trustee Act 2000, the Trustee Act 1925, the Trusts of Land and Appointment of Trustees Act 1996 or any other statute where the duty of care is expressed to be applicable[14]]

15   Settlement conditional on marriage

If the Marriage shall not be solemnised within **[6]** months from the date of this deed this settlement shall be void and the Trust Fund shall be held in trust for the Settlor absolutely

[16   Clause headings

The headings to the clauses and paragraphs of this settlement are for the purposes of information only and are not part of and shall not be used in the construction of this settlement or any part of it[15]**]**

IN WITNESS etc

FIRST SCHEDULE

The Investments

(describe the Investments)

SECOND SCHEDULE

Administrative Powers

(Select from administrative powers set out in Form 4 schedule [1092] ante as required amending as appropriate. Care should be taken to amend the powers selected so that they fit in with the definitions and other terminology used in this settlement)[16]

(signatures of the parties)[17]
(signatures of the witnesses)
[1144]

1   As to stamp duty see Information Binder: Stamp Duties [1] Table of Duties (Declaration of trust). The creation of this trust does not involve a transfer of value for inheritance tax purposes because the husband (the settlor) retains an interest in possession in the trust property. There is, however, a disposal (at market value) for capital gains tax purposes: see the Taxation of Chargeable Gains Act 1992 s 60 (42–44 Halsbury's Statutes (4th Edn) TAXATION). Although, until marriage, the husband remains entitled to the trust property absolutely, it is not considered that he is 'absolutely entitled as against the trustees' for the purposes of the Taxation of Chargeable Gains Act 1992 s 60. Since he has retained an interest, capital gains of the trust will be taxed on the husband: see the Taxation of Chargeable Gains Act 1992 ss 77, 78 as substituted by the Finance Act 1995 s 74, Sch 17 para 27, as amended by the Finance Act 1998 s 121(3), Sch 21 para 6(1) and as amended by the Finance Act 1995 s 74, Sch 17 para 28).

On the termination of the husband's initial life interest, there will be an inheritance tax exempt transfer to his surviving spouse. Her interest is (in part) determinable on subsequent remarriage: in that event, she will make a potentially exempt transfer in favour of the beneficiaries in clause 3 [1138]. As to absolute entitlement see Paragraph 339.5 [902] ante. For the negotiation of marriage settlements and considerations peculiar to marriage settlements see Paragraphs 56 [136], 57 [137] ante.

2   This is a relatively restricted class of beneficiaries, for example, it does not include spouses of issue.

3   See Form 4 note 15 [1104] ante.

4   The restrictions on the operation of the Trustee Act 1925 s 32 as amended by the Trusts of Land and Appointment of Trustees Act 1996 s 25(1), Sch 3 para 3(8) (48 Halsbury's Statutes (4th Edn) TRUSTS AND SETTLEMENTS) are intended to ensure that the requirements for a valid accumulation and maintenance trust are not broken.

5   It is usual to exclude apportionment calculations (which can be complex) under the Apportionment Act 1870 (23 Halsbury's Statutes (4th Edn) LANDLORD AND TENANT).

6   As to the consultation provisions see Paragraph 225 [540] ante.

7   See Form 4 note 22 [1105] ante.

8   See Form 4 note 24 [1105] ante.

10   See Form 4 notes 20 and 23 [1105] ante.

11   See Form 4 note 26 [1105] ante.

12   As to the provisions of the Trusts of Land and Appointment of Trustees Act 1996 ss 19, 20 see vol 40(2) (2001 Reissue) TRUSTS AND SETTLEMENTS Part 10 [5201]. See further Form 4 note 27 [1105] ante.

13   See Form 4 note 28 [1105] ante.

14   See Form 4 note 29 [1105] ante.

15   See Form 4 note 30 [1105] ante.

16   The powers set out in this schedule supplement those already possessed by the trustees: eg under the Trustee Act 1925.

17   As to the statutory requirements for valid execution of a deed see vol 12 (1994 Reissue) DEEDS, AGREEMENTS AND DECLARATIONS.

[1145]–[1160]

PART 4: DECLARATIONS OF TRUST, AND ASSIGNMENTS AND TRANSFERS TO TRUSTEES

Forms and Precedents

A: DECLARATIONS OF TRUST

1: INTRODUCTION

Using declarations of trust

A settlor may declare himself to be a trustee of property that he already owns, in which case no formalities for the transfer of that property are required[1].

In some cases a declaration of trust is the only available vehicle through which the owner of the property can achieve his goals. In the case of personal pension policies, the benefit of the pension is non-assignable but it is desirable to ensure that any death benefit does not form part of the individual's estate in the event that he dies before taking a pension. Given that the pension contract is indivisible, the only way of solving this particular problem is for the individual concerned to declare a trust of the entire pension contract, reserving all rights, including the pension, for himself except for the death benefit which is settled on appropriate trusts. Further trustees of the death benefit can then be appointed in due course[2]. Similarly, in the situation where the articles of association of a company restrict the transfer of shares, if an individual wishes to dispose of his shares, whether by gift or sale, consideration should be given to the use of a trust which can vest equitable interests in others whilst leaving the legal title to the shares with the original shareholder, so that the relevant article is not infringed[3].

In the majority of cases trusts are set up by the establishment of a 'pilot' settlement (usually to contain £10) into which property is subsequently transferred. Bear in mind that:

1   until the trustees transfer the property (of whatever form) the trust has not been constituted; and

2   if it is intended to establish a series of 'pilot' trusts on different days, the practitioner should ensure that the nominal property (£10 in the above example) is vested in the trustees on those days.

A voluntary disposition of property is not subject to duty, provided that the instrument which transfers that property contains a declaration along the following lines:

'It is certified that this instrument falls within Category 'L' in the Schedule to the Stamp Duty (Exempt Instruments) Regulations 1987'[4].

This declaration will be appropriate in all cases where property is assigned or transferred to trustees by a written instrument. It is, of course, irrelevant where the settlor declares himself to be trustee of property which he already owns. Given that the current practice is to establish the trust in 'pilot' form and subsequently to transfer or assign property to it, a stamp duty certificate will not be appropriate in the settlement, which does not effect any transfer of property, but will be appropriate in the instrument which vests the property in the trustees.

As a separate matter, declarations of trust are themselves dutiable at a fixed rate of duty[5]. Hence the settlement, whether established by declaration or involving third party trustees, should always be presented for stamping. In the rare case where the settlement involves a transfer of property (for instance when it effects the assignment of an equitable interest) as well as declaring trusts then it should contain an appropriately worded certificate and also be stamped at the fixed rate[6]. The one exception is when a life policy is assigned to trustees and a settlement deed then recites the trusts. In this case it would appear that duty is not charged on the declaration of trust provided that the deed is certified as Category N[7].

[1161]

1   Although in the case of land suitable entries will need to be made at the Land Registry to reflect the fact that the property is now held on trust.
2   For forms of trust of pension policies, see vol 40(2) (2001 Reissue) TRUSTS AND SETTLEMENTS Part 18 [9601].
3   See Forms 9 [1164], 10 [1166] post.
4   Stamp Duty (Exempt Instruments) Regulations 1987, SI 1987/516 reg 2, Schedule as amended by SI 1999/2539. Stamp duty is not chargeable on gifts inter vivos: Finance Act 1985 s 82(1) (42–44 Halsbury's Statutes (4th Edn) TAXATION). See also Information Binder: Stamp Duties [1] Table of Duties (Voluntary disposition).
5   For the current rate of stamp duty, prescribed by the Finance Act 1999 Sch 13 para 17(1) (42–44 Halsbury's Statutes (4th Edn) TAXATION), see Information Binder: Stamp Duties [1] Table of Duties (Declaration of Trust). Interest is not payable on this sum: Stamp Act 1891 s 15A(1)(a) as substituted by Finance Act 1999 s 109(1); although a penalty (currently £300) can be charged: Stamp Act 1891 s 15B as substituted by Finance Act 1999 s 109(1) (42–44 Halsbury's Statutes (4th Edn) TAXATION). This does not apply if the trust is established in a will: Finance Act 1999 Sch 13 para 17(2).
6   See note 5 above. See further *Sergeant and Sims on Stamp Duties* (2000) A [734].
7   SI 1987/516 reg 2, Schedule category N as inserted by SI 1999/2539 applies to: 'the declaration of any use or trust of or concerning a life policy, or property representing, or benefits arising under, a life policy'.

[1162]

2: GENERAL FORMS

8

Declaration of trust of existing life assurance policy[1]

The {Settlor} now declares that as and from the date of this deed the {Settlor} shall hold the {Policy} and all benefits and advantages of and all rights arising under and all money assured by or to become payable under or by virtue of it and any policy or policies substituted for it upon the trusts and with and subject to the powers and provisions declared and contained below

1   When this clause is inserted in a document the defined terms in { } must be altered to suit those used in the document. For a power enabling trustees to take out life insurance and to hold the policy on separate trusts, see Form 109 [1504] post.

[1163]

9

Declaration of trust of controlling shareholding[1]

WHEREAS

(1)   The Settlor is a registered owner of *(number)* ordinary shares ('the Shares') in the capital of *(name of company)*

(2)   The Settlor now wishes to declare himself trustee of the shares on the following trusts and subject to the provisions of this deed

NOW THIS DEED WITNESSES as follows:

1   Declaration of trust

As and from the date of this deed the Settlor shall hold the shares and all dividends accrued or to accrue upon trust for *(continue as appropriate: eg 'such of the Settlor's children as attain the age of 25 years and if more than one in equal shares')*[2]

[1164]

---

1   As to stamp duty see Introduction to this section [1161] ante and, for current rates of duty, see Information Binder: Stamp Duties [1] Table of Duties (Declaration of trust).
         The Finance (No 2) Act 1992 (42–44 Halsbury's Statutes (4th Edn) TAXATION) provides for 100% business property relief from inheritance tax where the value transferred by a transfer of value is attributable to shares which gave the donor control of a qualifying company immediately before the transfer. This was extended in subsequent Finance Acts to include minority shareholdings. As a result, there is no longer the same incentive to give away such shares during lifetime: see the Inheritance Tax Act 1984 s 104 as amended by the Finance Act 1987 s 58, Sch 8 para 4 and by the Finance (No 2) Act 1992 s 73, Sch 14 para 1 (42–44 Halsbury's Statutes (4th Edn) TAXATION). Retention of the shares until death results in an uplift in value for capital gains tax purposes. However, there is no guarantee that 100% relief will continue to be available in the event of a change in government policy. Consequently, this Form may be used as the basis for a controlling shareholder divesting himself of a majority shareholding. It is assumed that the settlor is and will continue to be a director, in which case care must be taken to avoid being caught by the reservation of benefit provisions: as to which see Paragraph 290 [749] et seq ante). With the improved capital gains tax taper relief rules from 6 April 2000, the loss of accrued taper as a result of the making of a hold-over election should be discussed with the settlor: see Paragraph 341.2 [909] ante.
         For a declaration of trust of stocks and shares by a person in whose name they have been registered see Form 23 [1211] post and for a simple form of voting trust in relation to shares see Form 24 [1216] post.

2   In determining the beneficial interests the following points should be borne in mind:
         (a)   Ignoring exemptions, if the trust contains an interest in possession or is an accumulation, maintenance or disabled settlement, the settlor will make a potentially exempt transfer.
         (b)   In cases other than (a) above, there will be a chargeable transfer.
         (c)   In (a) above, capital gains tax hold-over relief will be available if the shares are in a company carrying on a trade: Taxation of Chargeable Gains Act 1992 s 165 as amended by the Finance Act 1993 s 87, Sch 7 para 1(1), by the Finance Act 1998 ss 140(4), 165, Sch 27 Pt III and by the Finance Act 2000 s 90(1),(3),(4) (42–44 Halsbury's Statutes (4th Edn) TAXATION).
         (d)   In (b) above, hold-over relief will be available in all cases since there is an immediate charge to inheritance tax on the creation of the settlement: Taxation of Chargeable Gains Act 1992 s 260 as amended by the Finance Act 1998 s 165, Sch 27, Pt III, Pt IV and Finance Act 2000 s 90(2), (5).
         (e)   Business property relief can be lost in the event of the transferee ceasing to own the shares before the donor's death, should this occur within seven years of the gift. If the shares are transferred to an accumulation and maintenance settlement, the 'transferee' will be the trustees and it is thought that the trustees will no longer own the shares once a beneficiary becomes entitled to the shares or to an interest in possession in them: Inheritance Tax Act 1984 s 113A(8) as inserted by the Finance Act 1986 s 101(1), (3), Sch 19 Pt I para 21. It is advisable for any accumulation and maintenance settlement to continue for at least seven years to ensure that business property relief is not lost because of this technicality.
         (f)   In defining the beneficiaries, the reservation of benefit rules should be borne in mind. As to the reservation of benefit rules, see Paragraph 290 [750] et seq ante.

[1165]

10

Declaration of bare trust for a minor[1]

THIS DECLARATION OF TRUST is made the ...... day of .... by *(settlor)* of *(address)* ('the Settlor')

WHEREAS

The Settlor wishes to make provision for ('the Beneficiary') by declaring himself trustee of the property described in the schedule ('the Trust Fund')[2]

[1166]

NOW THIS DEED witnesses as follows:

1   Declaration of trust

The Settlor holds the Trust Fund and any income of it from the date of this deed on trust for the Beneficiary absolutely

2   Administrative provisions

Until the Beneficiary attains the age of 18 years the powers and provisions contained below shall apply to the Trust Fund and the income of it[3]
(continue with required administrative powers and provisions: eg investment; delegation; receipts clause; extended powers of maintenance and advancement)[4]

[1167]

---

1   As to stamp duty see Introduction to this section [1161] ante and, for current rates of duty, see Information Binder: Stamp Duties [1] Table of Duties (Declaration of Trust). One use of this Form prior to 9 March 1999 was to enable a parent to avoid paying income tax on income derived from property settled on his minor child. For the income tax consequences of parental settlements in favour of minor unmarried children, see Paragraph 356 [1002] ante. If a parent settles property on a minor unmarried child then the income is deemed to be that of the settlor, unless the income is accumulated during the child's minority: Income and Corporation Taxes Act 1988 s 660B as inserted by the Finance Act 1995 s 74, Sch 17 para 1 and amended by the Finance Act 1999 s 64 (42–44 Halsbury's Statutes (4th Edn) TAXATION). However, in the latter case, the Income and Corporation Taxes Act 1988 s 686 as amended imposes a charge at the 'trust rate' of 34% so that the tax saving for a 40% tax payer is merely 6% (tax year 2001–02 rates): see further Paragraph 348 [959] ante.
    One way to avoid these problems prior to 9 March 1999 was for the parent to create a bare trust for the minor child, the effect of which was that the child was absolutely entitled to both the capital and income of the trust. Since the child was entitled at the outset to the income (although not able to give a valid receipt), the Income and Corporation Taxes Act 1988 s 686 as amended did not apply. Consequently, income tax was charged at the lower and basic rates after taking account of the child's personal allowances.
    New bare trusts, created on or after 9 March 1999, do not have these income tax advantages and the income is taxed, as it arises, as that of the settlor parent: see the Finance Act 1999 s 64 amending the Income and Corporation Taxes Act 1988 s 660B. These provisions only apply to a settlor who is the parent of the infant beneficiary and so bare trusts may be created without adverse income tax consequences by grandparents. Note that these provisions apply to new bare trusts only and existing trusts are unaffected save in respect of added property. Remember also that, since the trust property is treated as owned by the child for capital gains tax purposes, the child's annual exemption will be applied in the event of a disposal of trust assets and this remains an advantage of such trusts when created by the parent of the infant. Such trusts are considered advantageous from a parent's point of view, provided the trustees do not invest in income producing assets and realise sufficient gains each year to use up the children's capital gains tax annual exemption, which is twice the amount available to trustees.
    This Form may also be used to meet cases where a donor wants to transfer the property immediately but there are formalities which will delay the passing of legal title; eg obtaining consent from, or giving notice to, a third party. By using this Form, the beneficial interest can effectively be transferred to the donee immediately, legal title to follow later.

2   If the fund includes registered land, the minor's interest should be protected on the register by entry of the trustee restriction contained in the Land Registration Rules 1925, SR & O 1925/1093 rr 213, 236 (both substituted by SI 1996/2975 and amended by SI 1997/3037), Sch 2 Form 62 (as substituted by SI 1989/801 and amended by SI 1996/2975). This may be supplemented with a restriction prohibiting a disposition of the land without the consent of the minor's parent or guardian, if the settlor is not himself the father of the minor. A bare trust falls within the definition of a trust of land in the Trusts of Land and Appointment of Trustees Act 1996 s 1(2)(a) (37 Halsbury's Statutes (4th Edn) REAL PROPERTY).

3   The statutory power of maintenance in the Trustee Act 1925 s 31 as amended by the Family Law Reform Act 1969 s 1(3), Sch 1 Pt I and by the Trustee Act 2000 s 40(1), Sch 2 para 25 (48 Halsbury's Statutes (4th Edn) TRUSTS AND SETTLEMENTS) will apply to this trust.

4   It is desirable to include the normal administrative powers and an express power to pay income or capital to a parent or guardian on behalf of any infant beneficiaries. It is thought that the default provisions of the Trustee Act 2000 (48 Halsbury's Statutes (4th Edn) TRUSTS AND SETTLEMENTS) apply to bare trusts. As to the tax advantages of bare trusts, see Paragraph 357 [1007] ante.

[1168]

11

Declaration of trust by spouses as to beneficial entitlement to income producing assets—assets owned jointly[1]

THIS DECLARATION OF TRUST is made the ...... day of ....

BETWEEN:

(1)   *(husband)* of *(address)* ('the Husband') and

(2)   *(wife)* also of *(address)* ('the Wife')

WHEREAS

(1)   The Husband and the Wife are the legal owners of the property described in the schedule ('the Property') the beneficial interest in which has since its acquisition been held by the Husband and the Wife as stated in the schedule

(2)   The Husband and the Wife have agreed that as from the date of this deed their beneficial interests in the Property shall be varied in accordance with the following provisions

[1169]

NOW THIS DEED WITNESSES as follows:

1   Declaration of trust

As from the date of this deed the Husband and the Wife declare that they hold the Property and the income of it as beneficial tenants in common in the following proportions:

1.1   as to ... % for the Husband and

1.2   as to ... % for the Wife

[2   Application to Land Registry

The Husband and the Wife will make such application to the Land Registry and execute and do all such documents acts and things as may be necessary to procure that the appropriate restriction and other necessary entries shall be entered in the register of the title referred to in the schedule for the purpose of giving effect to this deed[2]]

IN WITNESS etc

SCHEDULE

The Property

(describe the Property (setting out title number where registered land) indicating whether it is held beneficially as joint tenants or tenants in common, and in the latter case, the respective proportions prior to the execution of the deed)

(signatures of the parties)[3]

(signatures of witnesses)

[1170]

1   As to stamp duty see Introduction to this section [1161] ante and, for current rates of duty, see Information Binder: Stamp Duties [1] Table of Duties (Declaration of trust). This Form may be used to displace the so-called '50:50 rule' which applies to the income from assets held jointly by husband and wife: Income and Corporation Taxes Act 1988 s 282A as inserted by the Finance Act 1988 s 34 (42–44 Halsbury's Statutes (4th Edn) TAXATION). The rule is that such income is generally treated as belonging to the husband and wife equally and taxed accordingly (even if they have contributed to the acquisition of the asset in unequal shares). In appropriate cases, the parties may wish to declare that a greater share of the income goes to the spouse paying income tax at a lower rate than the other. If so, the declaration must relate to both the income and the capital, since the income cannot be shared in different proportions to the capital (but see Form 12 note 1 [1174] post). Where the declaration is made for income tax purposes, a notice must be given to the appropriate tax inspector within the period of 60 days beginning with the date of the declaration and must be made on the prescribed form (Inland Revenue Form 17). Any such declaration and notice made for income tax purposes will have a corresponding effect for capital gains tax purposes.

2   Where registered land is currently held by the parties as tenants in common, the appropriate restriction should already be on the register of title. If a beneficial joint tenancy is being converted into a tenancy in common by the declaration, then application should be made for the restriction contained in the Land Registration Rules 1925, SR & O 1925/1093 rr 213, 236 (both substituted by SI 1996/2975 and amended by SI 1997/3037), Sch 2 Form 62 (as substituted by SI 1989/801 and amended by SI 1996/2975) to be entered. For an application to register a restriction see vol 25(1) (1999 Reissue) LAND REGISTRATION Form 77 [3591].

3   As to the statutory requirements for valid execution of a deed see vol 12 (1994 Reissue) DEEDS, AGREEMENTS AND DECLARATIONS.

[1171]

12

Declaration of trust by husband and wife as to beneficial entitlement to income producing assets—assets owned by one party only[1]

THIS DECLARATION OF TRUST is made the ...... day of ....

BETWEEN:

(1)   *(husband)* of *(address)* ('the Husband') and

(2)   *(wife)* also of *(address)* ('the Wife')

WHEREAS

(1)   The Husband is the sole legal and beneficial owner of the property described in the schedule ('the Property')

(2)   As from the date of this deed the Husband wishes to hold the Property on trust for both himself and the Wife in accordance with the following provisions

[1172]

NOW THIS DEED WITNESSES as follows:

1 Declaration of trust

As from the date of this deed the Husband will hold the Property [and the income of it][2] upon trust for the Husband and the Wife as beneficial tenants in common in the following proportions[3]:

1.1   as to … % for the Husband and

1.2   as to … % for the Wife

[2 Application to Land Registry

The Husband and the Wife will make such application to the Land Registry and execute and do all such documents acts and things as may be necessary to procure that the appropriate restriction and other necessary entries shall be entered in the register of the title referred to in the schedule for the purpose of giving effect to this deed][4]

IN WITNESS etc

SCHEDULE

The Property

(describe the Property and set out title number where registered land)

(signatures of the parties)[5]
(signatures of witnesses)
[1173]

1   As to stamp duty see Introduction to this section [1161] ante and, for current rates of duty, see Information Binder: Stamp Duties [1] Table of Duties (Declaration of trust). This Form might be used in a case where the spouses wish the '50:50' rule to apply when the asset is in fact held in different proportions. For example, a wife owning a substantial asset in her sole name could transfer it into the joint names of herself and her husband in the proportions of 99% and 1% respectively. Provided that no unequal shares declaration is made on Inland Revenue Form 17, the husband will be taxed on 50% of the income while his wife retains beneficial ownership of 99% of the asset. See Form 11 note 1 [1171] ante.

2   The words in square brackets should be omitted if it is intended to rely on the '50:50' rule: see note 1 above and see Form 11 note 1 [1171] ante.

3   This Form assumes that the spouse owning the property will remain the sole trustee of the newly declared beneficial interests. If it is intended, as would seem desirable in most cases, for the other spouse to become a co-trustee, then the appropriate steps will need to be taken to vest the legal title in both spouses. For a suitable form of Transfer see vol 37 (2001 Reissue) SALE OF LAND Form 230 [1633]. It is compulsory to apply for first registration of unregistered property: Land Registration Act 1997 s 1 (37 Halsbury's Statutes (4th Edn) REAL PROPERTY).

4   In the case of registered land the beneficial interests should be protected on the register by entry of the trustee restriction contained in the Land Registration Rules 1925, SR & O 1925/1093 rr 213, 236 (both substituted by SI 1996/2975 and amended by SI 1997/3037), Sch 2 Form 62 (as substituted by SI 1989/801 and amended by SI 1996/2975). For an application to register a restriction see vol 25(1) (1999 Reissue) LAND REGISTRATION Form 77 [3591]. The effect of the restriction will be to prevent the sole proprietor (in this case the sole trustee) from selling or mortgaging the land in the future: see the wording of Form 62 and the effect of the 'two-trustee rule' under the Law of Property Act 1925 s 27(2) (37 Halsbury's Statutes (4th Edn) REAL PROPERTY). In the event of a sale or mortgage the trustee will, therefore, need to consider the appointment of a co-trustee.

5   As to the statutory requirements for valid execution of a deed see vol 12 (1994 Reissue) DEEDS, AGREEMENTS AND DECLARATIONS.

[1174]

3: SPECIFIC CASES

13

Declaration of trust in favour of cohabitant by the beneficial owner of land— the land to remain solely owned[1]

THIS DECLARATION OF TRUST is made the ...... day of ....

BETWEEN:

(1)   *(name)* of *(address)* ('the Trustee') and

(2)   *(name)* of *(address)* ('the Beneficiary')

NOW THIS DEED WITNESSES as follows:

1   Recitals

1.1   The Trustee is the [estate owner *or* registered proprietor] of the freehold property known as *(describe property)* [and registered at HM Land Registry under title number *(title number)*] ('the Property')

1.2   The Property is subject to a mortgage dated *(date)* in favour of *(lender)* ('the Mortgage') and the amount outstanding at the date of this deed is £...

1.3   The Trustee acknowledges that the Beneficiary has [been contributing towards the Mortgage payments *or* paid for repairs and improvements to the Property *or* contributed to the purchase price and costs of purchase]

1.4   The Trustee has agreed with the Beneficiary that [he] will hold the Property on trust for [himself] and the Beneficiary in the following manner

[1175]

2   Declaration of trust for sale[2]

The Trustee declares that as from the date of this deed [he] will hold the Property and the net proceeds of sale and net income until sale upon trust for sale for [himself] and the Beneficiary as tenants in common in the proportions set out in clause 4 below

3   Proceeds of sale

In the event of a sale the net sale proceeds shall be determined by deducting from the sale price the amount outstanding under the Mortgage legal fees agents' commission and valuers' fee (if any)

4   Floating shares

4.1   The net sale proceeds will be divided between the Trustee and the Beneficiary in proportion to the contributions made by each of them to:
4.1.1   the Mortgage capital repayments
4.1.2   the Mortgage interest repayments
4.1.3   any Mortgage linked endowment policy premiums and
4.1.4   any repairs and improvements to the Property

4.2   The shares shall be calculated as follows:
        4.2.1   totalling the contributions of the Trustee and the Beneficiary to arrive at the total contribution of the Trustee and the total contribution of the Beneficiary
        4.2.2   adding together the total contribution of the Trustee and the total contribution of the Beneficiary to arrive at the combined contributions
        4.2.3   dividing the net proceeds of sale by the combined contributions to arrive at the surplus
        4.2.4   multiplying the total contribution of each party by the surplus to arrive at the share

[1176]

5   Pre-emption rights

5.1   If either the Trustee or the Beneficiary wishes to bring to an end the trusts relating to the Property he or she must give to the other party written notice and the Trustee and the Beneficiary agree that except with the consent of both the Trustee and the Beneficiary there shall be no sale of the Property until the expiry of 3 months from the date of such notice

5.2   Within 6 weeks of receipt of a notice served in accordance with clause 5.1 above either the Trustee or the Beneficiary may give notice to the other party of his or her desire to purchase the share of the other party at the current market value such value to be agreed or in default of agreement fixed by an independent valuer appointed by agreement or in default of agreement on the application of either the Trustee or the Beneficiary to [the President for the time being of the Royal Institute of Chartered Surveyors *or* the President for the time being of the *(local)* Law Society]

5.3   If no notice under clause 5.2 above is served then the Property must be sold and the Trustee and the Beneficiary agree to use their best endeavours to achieve a sale as soon as possible

5.4   If a notice under clause 5.2 above is served then the Trustee and the Beneficiary agree that the purchase of the share will be completed within 2 months of the service of the notice[3]

[6   Restriction[4]

The Trustee covenants with the Beneficiary that [he] will make such application to the Land Registry and execute and do all such documents acts and things as may be necessary to procure that the appropriate restriction and other necessary entries shall be entered in the register of the title for the purpose of giving effect to this deed]

IN WITNESS etc

(signatures of the parties)[5]
(signatures of witnesses)
[1177]

1   As to stamp duty see Introduction to this section [1161] ante and, for current rates of duty, see Information Binder: Stamp Duties [1] (declaration of trust).
2   After the Trusts of Land and Appointment of Trustees Act 1996 (37 Halsbury's Statutes (4th Edn) REAL PROPERTY) beneficial co-ownership does not result in the imposition of a trust for sale: instead, the property is held on a trust of land. Nevertheless, it is suggested that an express trust for sale should be included so as to ensure: (a) that there is an overriding duty to sell; and (b) that the shares can be quantified by reference to net proceeds of sale on the basis of respective contributions. This reflects the fact that the rights of a cohabitee will in practice be of most significance on the breakdown of the

relationship at which time it will frequently be desirable for the property to be sold. In the event of either party dying, it will be necessary to value that person's interest in the property taking into account this declaration and then apply the appropriate discount: see *Wight v IRC* [1984] RVR 163; *Charkham v IRC* [2000] RVR 7, Lands Tribunal.

3   In the event that the parties both wish to retain the property and wish to serve notices upon each other, it may be advisable to include a provision that the trustee as sole legal owner has an overriding right to buy out the beneficiary.

4   If title to the property is registered, application should be made for entry of the restriction contained in the Land Registration Rules 1925, SR & O 1925/1093 r 213 (substituted by SI 1996/2975 and amended by SI 1997/3037) by the trustee, or SR & O 1925/1093 r 236 (substituted by SI 1996/2975) by the beneficiary. In both cases the form used is set out in SR & O 1925/1093, Sch 2 Form 62 (as substituted by SI 1989/801 and amended by SI 1996/2975). This may be supplemented with a restriction prohibiting a disposition of the land without the consent of the beneficiary. For an application to register a restriction see vol 25(1) (1999 Reissue) LAND REGISTRATION Form 76 [3591]. If the trustee fails to apply for the requisite restriction, the beneficiary will be able to apply for it himself.

5   As to the statutory requirements for valid execution of a deed see vol 12 (1994 Reissue) DEEDS, AGREEMENTS AND DECLARATIONS.

[1178]

14

Provisions for insertion in declaration of trust by which child of testator settles family residence on trust for surviving parent[1]

(1)   By his will dated *(date)* and duly proved on *(date)* in the [Principal Registry of the Family Division of the High Court *or (name)* District Probate Registry] *(testator)* late of *(address)* who died on *(date)* left the freehold property described in the schedule ('the Property') to the Settlor absolutely

(2)   The Settlor now wishes to declare trusts of the Property as set out below

[1179]

NOW THIS DEED WITNESSES as follows:

1   Declaration of trust

The Settlor holds the Property upon the following trusts:

1.1   for *(surviving parent)* of *(address)* ('the Principal Beneficiary') for life and

1.2   subject to clause 1.1 for the Settlor absolutely[2]

2   Residence

The Settlor or other the trustee or trustees of the trusts created by this deed shall permit the Principal Beneficiary to reside in the Property during [her] lifetime and no sale shall be effected during that period without the consent in writing of the Principal Beneficiary[3]

[3   Consultation

The provisions of the Trusts of Land and Appointment of Trustees Act 1996 Section 11(1) shall not apply to the Property or to any other land situated in England and Wales which may at any time be subject to the trusts of this deed]

4   Appointment

The power of appointing new trustees is vested in the Settlor during [his] lifetime

(continue with desired administrative powers and provisions: eg powers of insurance; powers of investment including a power to purchase land anywhere in the world as a residence for the Principal Beneficiary)

[1180]

1   As to stamp duty see Introduction to this section [1161] ante and, for current rates of duty, see Information Binder: Stamp Duties [1] Table of Duties (Declaration of trust). This Form enables a child of a testator to confer security on a surviving parent by granting a life interest in the family home which has been devised to the child. The creation of the trust is a potentially exempt transfer for inheritance tax purposes. On the termination of the life interest due to death, there may be no charge to inheritance tax due to the reverter to settlor exemption: Inheritance Tax Act 1984 s 53(3) (42–44 Halsbury's Statutes (4th Edn) TAXATION). For the capital gains tax position see the Taxation of Chargeable Gains Act 1992 s 73(1)(b) as amended by the Finance Act 1996 s 201, Sch 39 para 6(2), (4), (5) (42–44 Halsbury's Statutes (4th Edn) TAXATION). See note 2 below.

        In most cases, the child could enter into a post death variation in favour of the parent to achieve the same objective: see, for example, vol 42(2) (1998 Reissue) WILLS AND ADMINISTRATION Form 740 [5190]. If the usual election to read back is made, there will be no transfer of value (and therefore no potentially exempt transfer) by the child. Whether there is a reduction in the inheritance tax payable on the testator's death by reason of the spouse exemption depends on the circumstances (eg the devise of the house to the child may have been nil-rated anyway). However, on the subsequent death of the parent, there will be the usual charge on the termination of an interest in possession. Increasing property values might make a post death variation less attractive.

        The Form creates a trust of land: the trust for sale that would have been imposed prior to 1 January 1997 is no longer considered appropriate. It is likely that the Trusts of Land and Appointment of Trustees Act 1996 s 12 (37 Halsbury's Statutes (4th Edn) REAL PROPERTY) will confer a right of occupation on the principal beneficiary: this is reinforced by the wording of clause 2 [1247]. As to this section see Paragraph 228 [545] ante.

2   Consider whether, for capital gains tax purposes, the settlor should retain an interest in possession only, since this will mean that on the surviving parent the usual capital gains tax death uplift will apply (if the child is absolutely entitled the uplift is prevented by the Taxation of Chargeable Gains Act 1992 s 73(1)(b) as amended by the Finance Act 1996 s 201, Sch 39 para 6(2), (4), (5) and see vol 42(1) (1998 Reissue) WILLS AND ADMINISTRATION Paragraph 252 [1711]).

3   If title to the property is registered, application should be made for entry of the restriction contained in the Land Registration Rules 1925, SR & O 1925/1093 rr 213, 236 (both substituted by SI 1996/2975 and amended by SI 1997/3037), Sch 2 Form 62 (as substituted by SI 1989/801 and amended by SI 1996/2975). The effect of the restriction will be to prevent the sole proprietor from selling or mortgaging the land in the future: see the wording of Form 62 and the effect of the 'two-trustee rule' under the Law of Property Act 1925 s 27(2) (37 Halsbury's Statutes (4th Edn) REAL PROPERTY). In the event of a sale or mortgage the trustee will, therefore, need to consider the appointment of a co-trustee. Where the trust deed contains a limitation on the trustees powers of disposition (such as is found in clause 2 [1247]), then in addition the restriction contained in SR & O 1925/1093 rr 59A, 106A, 236, Sch 2 Form 11A as inserted by SI 1996/2975 and as amended by SI 2001/619 is required. For an application to register a restriction see vol 25(1) (1999 Reissue) LAND REGISTRATION Form 77 [3591]. In the event of supervening incapacity in the later years of the surviving parent, it is suggested that an enduring power of attorney should be granted by the parent to overcome difficulties in obtaining consent. For an enduring power of attorney see vol 31 (1999 Reissue) POWERS OF ATTORNEY Form 137 [4601].

[1181]

15

Declaration of trust of property given by will on half-secret trust[1]

THIS DECLARATION OF TRUST is made the …… day of ……… by *(declarants)* of *(addresses)* ('the Declarants')

WHEREAS

(1)   *(testator)* of *(address)* has by his will ('the Will') intended to be executed shortly after the execution of this declaration devised [and bequeathed] certain property ('the Property') to the Declarants to be held on trusts which he has communicated to them

(2)   The Declarants acknowledge that they do not hold the Property for their own absolute use and benefit but upon the trusts declared below

(3)   The Property is described in the schedule[2]

[1182]

NOW THIS DEED WITNESSES as follows:

Declaration of trust

If and when the Will shall become effective in law and the Property shall be vested in the Declarants the Property shall be held by the Declarants upon the following trusts: *(continue with required trusts: eg 'upon trust for X for life [secret mistress] remainder to the testator's children in equal shares'. Consider also what administrative powers need to be included.)*

IN WITNESS etc

SCHEDULE

The Property

(describe the property)

(signatures of the parties)[3]

(signatures of witnesses)

[1183]

1   As to stamp duty see Introduction to this section [1161] ante and, for current rates of duty, see Information Binder: Stamp Duties [1] Table of Duties (Declaration of trust). In the case of a half-secret trust, the terms of the trust must have been communicated to and accepted by the declarants at the time when the will was executed and the communication must not contain any provision for the alteration or revision of the trusts: see *Re Keen, Evershed v Griffiths* [1937] Ch 236, [1937] 1 All ER 452, CA; *Re Jones, Jones v Jones* [1942] Ch 328, [1942] 1 All ER 642; *Re Bateman's Will Trusts, Brierley v Perry* [1970] 3 All ER 817, [1970] 1 WLR 1463. Contrast the fully secret trust which is based upon the acquiescence or agreement of the trustee given at any time before the death of the testator. See further Paragraph 26 [68] ante and *Snell's Equity* (30th Edn, 2000) para 7-15.

2   At this stage (the testator is still alive) the trust is not constituted since no property is vested in the declarants subject to the terms of the trust.

3   As to the statutory requirements for valid execution of a deed see vol 12 (1994 Reissue) DEEDS, AGREEMENTS AND DECLARATIONS.

[1184]

16

Declaration of trust of property purchased in breach of trust[1]

THIS DECLARATION OF TRUST is made the ...... day of .... by *(trustees)* of *(addresses)* ('the Trustees')

WHEREAS

(1)   **[By a settlement ('the Settlement') dated *(date)* and made between *(parties)* a fund (in the Settlement and in this deed referred to as 'the *(name)* Fund') was settled upon the trusts then declared but the Settlement contained no power for the trustees to invest in land

or

By the will ('the Will') of *(testator)* late of *(address)* made on *(date)* and duly proved by the executors named in it on *(date)* in the [Principal Registry of the Family Division of the High Court *or (name)* District Probate Registry] *(testator)* settled a fund (in the Will and in this deed referred to as 'the *(name)* Fund') upon the trusts then declared but the Will contained no power for the trustees to invest in land]

[1185]

(2)   The Trustees are the present trustees of the [Settlement *or* Will]

(3)   By a [conveyance *or* transfer] dated *(date)* and made between (1) *(seller)* and (2) the Trustees the land described in the schedule ('the Land') was [conveyed *or* transferred] to the Trustees in fee simple

(4)   The purchase price for the Land was raised out of the *(name)* Fund

(5)   The Trustees wish to set out the trusts on which the Land is held by them

NOW THIS DEED WITNESSES as follows:

Declaration of trust

The Trustees declare that they hold the Land upon the trusts declared by the [Settlement *or* Will] and applicable to the *(name)* Fund so far as the same are still subsisting and capable of taking effect

IN WITNESS etc

SCHEDULE

The Land

(describe the Land)

(signatures of the parties)[2]

(signatures of witnesses)

[1186]

1   As to stamp duty see Introduction to this section [1161] ante and, for current rates of duty, see Information Binder: Stamp Duties [1] Table of Duties (Declaration of trust). As to such land being held on a trust of land consider *Power v Banks* [1901] 2 Ch 487 in the light of the Trusts of Land and Appointment of Trustees Act 1996 (37 Halsbury's Statutes (4th Edn) REAL PROPERTY). As to the power of trustees to give receipts see also the Trustee Act 1925 s 14(1) as amended by the Trustee Act 2000 s 40(1), Sch 2 para 19 (48 Halsbury's Statutes (4th Edn) TRUSTS AND SETTLEMENTS). This declaration should so far as possible be kept off the title. Since 1 February 2001, all trustees have the power to invest in land under the Trustee Act 2000 Pt II (ss 3–7) (48 Halsbury's Statutes (4th Edn) TRUSTS AND SETTLEMENTS), subject to a contrary indication in the trust instrument.

2   As to the statutory requirements for valid execution of a deed see vol 12 (1994 Reissue) DEEDS, AGREEMENTS AND DECLARATIONS.

[1187]

17

Declaration of trust in respect of customers payments[1]

The {Settlor} declares that as and from the date of this deed the {Settlor} will pay all sums received from mail order customers into account number *(number)* with *(bank)* of *(address)* which account is designated 'The Customer Trust Deposit Account' and further declares that money so deposited shall be held on trust for the absolute benefit of the customer until such time as that customer is supplied with the goods that he has ordered whereupon such money shall be withdrawn from the account and become the absolute property of the {Settlor}

1   As to stamp duty see Introduction to this section [1161] ante and, for current rates of duty, see Information Binder: Stamp Duties [1] Table of Duties (Declaration of trust). This Form is based on *Re Kayford* [1975] 1 All ER 604, [1975] 1 WLR 279 and illustrates the increasing use of trusts in commercial cases as a means of ensuring that trust property does not, in the event of insolvency, form part of the assets available to satisfy the settlor's creditors. See also *Barclays Bank Ltd v Quistclose Investments Ltd* [1970] AC 567, [1968] 3 All ER 651, HL and *Aluminium Industrie Vaassen BV v Romalpa Aluminium Ltd* [1976] 2 All ER 552, [1976] 1 WLR 676, CA. A trust can be established even though its existence is known only to the settlor: *Middleton v Pollock, ex p Elliott* (1876) 2 Ch D 104.

When this clause is inserted in a document the defined terms in { } must be altered to suit those used in the document.

[1188]

4: PERSONS HOLDING PROPERTY AS NOMINEE

(In the following section of Forms the existence of the nominee is ignored for the purposes of taxation and the property is treated as owned by the purchaser. The nominee will hold any land under a trust of land: see the Trusts of Land and Appointment of Trustees Act 1996 Section 1 and Paragraph 108 [267] ante.)

18

Declaration of trust of freehold property by a person in whose name it has been purchased—by a supplemental deed[1]

THIS DECLARATION OF TRUST is made the ...... day of .... by *(trustee)* of *(address)* ('the Trustee')

WHEREAS

(1)   This declaration is supplemental to a transfer dated *(date)* ('the Transfer') and made between *(parties)* being a transfer of the freehold property ('the Property') known as *(name)* and more particularly described in the Transfer to the Trustee in consideration of the sum of £... stated in the Transfer to have been paid by the Trustee to *(seller)*

(2)   The above mentioned sum of £... was provided by *(buyer)* of *(address)* ('the Buyer') and the Property has been held by the Trustee as trustee for the Buyer as the Trustee acknowledges

[1189]

NOW THIS DEED WITNESSES as follows:

Declaration of trust

The Trustee declares that he holds the Property in trust for the Buyer in fee simple and agrees that he will at the request and cost of the Buyer transfer the Property to such person or persons at such time and in such manner or otherwise deal with the same as the Buyer shall direct or appoint and will make such applications to the Land Registry and execute and do all such documents acts and things as may be necessary to procure the appropriate registration or entry in the register to give effect to any such transfer or dealing or if so required to enable the interest of the Buyer to be protected

IN WITNESS etc

(signature of the trustee)[2]
(signatures of witnesses)
[1190]

1   As to stamp duty see Introduction to this section [1161] ante and, for current rates of duty, see Information Binder: Stamp Duties [1] Table of Duties (Declaration of trust). Since the Form presumes a recent acquisition on sale to the trustee, following which the declaration is made, the Land Registration Act 1925 ss 1, 123, 123A as substituted by the Administration of Justice Act 1982 s 66(1) and substituted and inserted by the Land Registration Act 1997 s 1 (37 Halsbury's Statutes (4th Edn) REAL PROPERTY) will apply to require that an application be made for first registration of the land by the trustee if it is not already registered. This will require the use of a transfer usually in form TR1 or TP1. For a suitable form of transfer see vol 37 (2001 Reissue) SALE OF LAND Form 23 [223]. The interest of the real buyer should be protected on the register by entry of the trustee restriction contained in Land Registration Rules 1925, SR & O 1925/1093 r 213 (as substituted by SI 1996/2975 and amended by SI 1997/3037) where application is made by the trustee, or S R & O 1925/1093 r 236 (as substituted by SI 1996/2975) where application is made by the beneficiary. In both cases the form used is set out in SR & O 1925/1093, Sch 2 Form 62 (as substituted by SI 1989/801 and amended by SI 1996/2975). This may be supplemented with a restriction prohibiting a disposition of the land without the real buyer's consent: see vol 37 (2001 Reissue) SALE OF LAND Form 182 [1351].

2   As to the statutory requirements for valid execution of a deed see vol 12 (1994 Reissue) DEEDS, AGREEMENTS AND DECLARATIONS.

[1191]

19

Declaration of trust of registered freehold land by person to whom it has been transferred as nominee of real buyer[1]

THIS DECLARATION OF TRUST is made the …… day of ……… by *(trustee)* of *(address)* ('the Trustee')

WHEREAS

(1)   This declaration is supplemental to a transfer dated *(date)* and made between *(parties)* under which the freehold property known as *(describe property)* registered at HM Land Registry under title number *(title number)* ('the Property') was transferred to the Trustee in consideration of the sum of £… stated in such transfer to have been paid by the Trustee to *(seller)*

(2)   The above mentioned sum of £… was provided by *(buyer)* of *(address)* ('the Buyer') and the Property was transferred to the Trustee as trustee for the Buyer as the Trustee acknowledges

[1192]

NOW THIS DEED WITNESSES as follows:

Declaration of trust

The Trustee declares that he holds the Property in trust for the Buyer and agrees that he will at the request and cost of the Buyer transfer the Property to such person or persons at such time or times and in such manner or otherwise deal with the same as the Buyer shall direct or appoint and will make such applications to the Land Registry and execute and do all such documents acts and things as may be necessary to procure the appropriate registration or entry in the register of the above title to give effect to any such transfer or dealing or if so required to enable the interest of the Buyer to be protected

IN WITNESS etc

(signature of the trustee)[2]
(signatures of witnesses)
[1193]

1   As to stamp duty see Introduction to this section [1161] ante and, for current rates of duty, see Information Binder: Stamp Duties [1] Table of Duties (Declaration of trust). This declaration will take effect off the register: see the Land Registration Act 1925 s 101 (37 Halsbury's Statutes (4th Edn) REAL PROPERTY). References to trusts are required, so far as possible, to be excluded from the register: the Land Registration Act 1925 s 74. The interest of the real buyer should be protected on the register by entry of the trustee restriction contained in the Land Registration Rules 1925, SR & O 1925/1093 rr 213, 236 (both substituted by SI 1996/2975 and amended by SI 1997/3037), Sch 2 Form 62 (as substituted by SI 1989/801 and amended by SI 1996/2975); this may be supplemented with a restriction prohibiting a disposition of the land without his consent.

2   If an indemnity covenant is added (see Form 35 clause 2 [1285] post), the real buyer should also be made a party to execute this deed. As to the statutory requirements for valid execution of a deed see vol 12 (1994 Reissue) DEEDS, AGREEMENTS AND DECLARATIONS.

[1194]

20

Declaration of trust of registered leasehold land by person to whom the lease has been granted or assigned as nominee of real tenant who has joined to give indemnity[1]

THIS DECLARATION OF TRUST is made the ...... day of ....

BETWEEN:

(1)   *(trustee)* of *(address)* ('the Trustee') and

(2)   *(real tenant)* of *(address)* ('the Beneficiary')

WHEREAS

(1)   This declaration is supplemental to a lease dated *(date)* and made between *(parties)* ('the Lease') being a lease of *(describe property)* ('the Property') for a term of *(number)* years from *(date)* [and a transfer dated *(date)* and made between *(parties)*]

(2)   The title to the Property is registered at HM Land Registry in the name of the Trustee as proprietor with [absolute leasehold *or* good leasehold] title under title number *(title number)*

(3)   The Lease was [granted *or* transferred] to the Trustee on payment of [a premium *or* the sum] of £... which was provided by the Beneficiary and the Property was [leased *or* transferred] to the Trustee as trustee for the Beneficiary as the Trustee acknowledges

[1195]

NOW THIS DEED WITNESSES as follows:

1   Declaration of trust

The Trustee declares that he holds the Property in trust for the Beneficiary and agrees that he will at the request and cost of the Beneficiary [and subject to obtaining the landlord's consent (which the Trustee will use his best endeavours to obtain)] assign the Property to such person or persons at such time or times and in such manner or otherwise deal with the same as the Beneficiary shall direct or appoint and will make such applications to the Land Registry and execute and do all such documents acts and things as may be necessary to procure the appropriate registration or entry in the register of the above title to give effect to any such assignment or dealing or if so required to enable the interest of the Beneficiary to be protected

2   Indemnity

The Beneficiary covenants with the Trustee that so long as the Property is vested in the Trustee as trustee for him he will pay the rent reserved by the Lease at the times and in the manner in which the same is payable and will perform and observe the covenants on the part of the tenant contained in the Lease[2] and will discharge all outgoings of or in any way relating to the Property and will indemnify the Trustee in respect of the same

IN WITNESS etc

(signatures of the parties)[3]

(signatures of witnesses)

[1196]

1   As to stamp duty see Introduction to this section [1161] ante and, for current rates of duty, see Information Binder: Stamp Duties [1] Table of Duties (Declaration of trust). This deed will take effect off the register: see Form 19 note 1 [1194] ante. The interest of the real tenant should be protected on the register by entry of the trustee restriction contained in the Land Registration Rules 1925, SR & O 1925/1093 r 213 (substituted by SI 1996/2975 and amended by SI 1997/3037) where application is made by the trustee, or SR & O 1925/1093 r 236 (substituted by SI 1996/2975) where application is made by the beneficiary. In both cases the form used is set out in SR & O 1925/1093, Sch 2 Form 62 (as substituted by SI 1989/801 and amended by SI 1996/2975). This may be supplemented with a restriction prohibiting a disposition of the land without the real tenant's consent.

        Caution may be needed where, as in the case of some leases, there is a covenant not only against assignment of the lease, but also against parting with possession of the premises, without the landlord's consent. A declaration of trust may not be a breach of a covenant not to assign, but it could involve a breach of the covenant not to part with possession if the fact that the nominee tenant (the trustee) holds on trust for the beneficiary means that the beneficiary will be occupying the premises. In some very restrictive forms of lease the covenant against alienation may even prevent the tenant holding on trust for another.

2   Note that with regard to leases granted on or after 1 January 1996 (and not in pursuance of an agreement or court order preceding that date) no indemnity covenants are implied on a permitted assignment and tenants are released from continuing liability under covenants on their part in the lease on such an assignment. Thus, in the absence of an authorised guarantee agreement, there will be no need in practice to consider indemnity covenants in relation to the disposal of such leases: Landlord and Tenant (Covenants) Act 1995 ss 5, 14 (23 Halsbury's Statutes (4th Edn) LANDLORD AND TENANT). If an indemnity covenant is required the wording in Form 21 clause 2 [1199] post should be followed.

3   As to the statutory requirements for valid execution of a deed see vol 12 (1994 Reissue) DEEDS, AGREEMENTS AND DECLARATIONS.

[1197]

21

Declaration of trust of freehold property by nominee—real buyer joining to give indemnity[1]

THIS DECLARATION OF TRUST is made the ...... day of ....

BETWEEN:

(1)   *(trustee)* of *(address)* ('the Trustee') and

(2)   *(buyer)* of *(address)* ('the Buyer')

WHEREAS

(1)   This declaration is supplemental to a [conveyance *or* transfer][2] dated *(date)* and made between *(parties)* being a [conveyance *or* transfer] of [certain freehold property therein described *or* the freehold property known as *(describe property)*

registered at HM Land Registry under title number *(title number)*³] ('the Property') to the Trustee in fee simple [subject to the tenancies therein mentioned] in consideration of the sum of £... paid by the Trustee to *(seller)*

(2)   The above mentioned sum of £... was provided by the Buyer and the Property was [conveyed *or* transferred] to the Trustee as trustee for the Buyer as the Trustee acknowledges

[1198]

NOW THIS DEED WITNESSES as follows:

1   Declaration of trust

The Trustee declares that he holds the Property in trust for the Buyer in fee simple and agrees that he will at the request and cost of the Buyer transfer the Property to such person or persons at such time or times and in such manner or otherwise deal with the same as the Buyer shall direct or appoint and will make such applications to the Land Registry and execute and do all such documents acts and things as may be necessary to procure the appropriate registration or entry in the register to give effect to any such transfer or dealing or if so required to protect the interest of the Buyer⁴

2   Indemnity

The Buyer covenants with the Trustee that he will keep the Trustee indemnified from all costs damages expenses claims and demands in respect of the Property and any tenancies or licences to which it may from time to time be subject

3   Expenditure

The Trustee shall not be required to incur any expenditure in respect of the Property unless and until money shall have been provided by the Buyer for that purpose

IN WITNESS etc

*(signatures of the parties)*⁵
(signatures of witnesses)
[1199]

1   As to stamp duty see Introduction to this section [1161] ante and, for current rates of duty, see Information Binder: Stamp Duties [1] Table of Duties (Declaration of trust). An express indemnity is not essential in such circumstances, but nominal buyers sometimes ask for it. For the general right of a trustee to be reimbursed out of trust property or by a beneficiary against expenses properly incurred see the Trustee Act 2000 s 31 (48 Halsbury's Statutes (4th Edn) TRUSTS AND SETTLEMENTS) and Paragraph 201 [485] ante. See the Trustee Act 2000 s 32(3) for circumstances in which trustees are entitled to reimburse agents etc for expenses properly incurred.

2   As the transaction, following which the declaration is made, is a recent acquisition on sale, the Land Registration Act 1925 ss 123 and 123A as substituted and inserted by the Land Registration Act 1997 s 1 (37 Halsbury's Statutes (4th Edn) REAL PROPERTY) will apply, in the case of unregistered land, to require that an application be made for first registration of the land by the trustee. For appropriate forms of transfer and conveyance see vol 37 (2001 Reissue) SALE OF LAND Forms 182 [1351]–186 [1362]. Whether the property before its transfer to the trustee was previously registered or unregistered, the interest of the real buyer should be protected on the register by entry of the trustee restriction contained in the Land Registration Rules 1925, SR & O 1925/1093 r 213 (as substituted by SI 1996/2975 and amended by SI 1997/3037) where application is made by the trustee, or SR & O 1925/1093 r 236 (as substituted by SI 1996/2975) where application is made by the beneficiary. In both cases the form used is set out in SR & O 1925/1093, Sch 2 Form 62 (as substituted by SI 1989/801 and amended by SI 1996/2975). This may be supplemented with a restriction prohibiting a disposition of the land without the real buyer's consent.

3   As this deed will take effect off the register (see Form 19 note 1 [1194] ante), it seems preferable, in the case of registered land, to define the property.

4   See note 2 above.

5   As to the statutory requirements for valid execution of a deed see vol 12 (1994 Reissue) DEEDS, AGREEMENTS AND DECLARATIONS.

[1200]

22

Declaration of trust where freehold property has been transferred to nominee of persons purchasing as tenants in common[1]

THIS DECLARATION OF TRUST is made the ...... day of ....

BETWEEN:

(1)   *(nominee)* of *(address)* ('the Nominee') and

(2)   *(tenants in common)* of *(addresses)* ('the Buyers')

WHEREAS

(1)   This declaration is supplemental to a transfer[2] dated *(date)* and made between (1) *(seller)* and (2) the Nominee under which [the freehold property therein described *or* the freehold property known as *(describe property)* registered at HM Land Registry under title number *(number)*[3]] ('the Property') was transferred to the Nominee in fee simple in consideration of the sum of £... therein stated to be paid by the Nominee to *(seller)*

(2)   The above mentioned consideration of £... was provided by the Buyers in equal shares and the Property was transferred to the Nominee as the nominee of the Buyers as the Nominee acknowledges

[1201]

NOW THIS DEED WITNESSES as follows:

1   Declaration of trust

The Nominee declares that he holds the Property in trust for the Buyers in fee simple and agrees that he will at the request and cost of the Buyers transfer the same to such person or persons at such time or times and in such manner or otherwise deal with the Property as the Buyers shall [in writing][4] direct or appoint and will make such applications to the Land Registry and execute and do all such documents acts and things as may be necessary to procure the appropriate registration or entry in the register to give effect to any such transfer or dealing or if so required to protect the interest of the Buyers[5]

2   Shares

The Buyers declare that the Property and the income from it shall be held in trust for them as tenants in common in equal shares and that all expenditure incurred in respect of the Property shall be borne by them in equal shares

[1202]

3   Indemnity

The Buyers jointly and severally covenant with the Nominee that they will at all times keep the Nominee indemnified against all costs damages expenses claims proceedings and demands in respect of the Property and any dealing with it authorised by them but although so far as the Nominee is concerned the Buyers shall be jointly and severally liable under this covenant each Buyer shall as between himself and the other Buyers be liable only for [one-third *or (specify other fraction according to the number of buyers)*] share of the sums payable under this covenant

4   Expenses

The Nominee shall not be required to incur any expenditure in respect of the Property except in so far as money in respect of it shall have been provided by the Buyers or some or one of them for that purpose and any Buyer providing more than [one-third *or (specify other fraction)*] share of such expenditure shall be entitled to contribution from the other Buyers on the footing that such expenditure is to be borne equally by all the Buyers

IN WITNESS etc

(signatures of the parties)[6]
(signatures of witnesses)
[1203]

1   As to stamp duty see Introduction to this section [1161] ante and, for current rates of duty, see Information Binder: Stamp Duties [1] Table of Duties (Declaration of trust).
2   If the transfer, following which the declaration is made, is a recent transfer on sale of unregistered land, the Land Registration Act 1925 ss 123, 123A as substituted and inserted by the Land Registration Act 1997 s 1 (37 Halsbury's Statutes (4th Edn) REAL PROPERTY) will apply, to require that an application be made for first registration of the land by the nominee. Whether the title is already registered, or is to be registered for the first time, the interest of the real buyers should be protected on the register by entry of the trustee restriction contained in the Land Registration Rules 1925, SR & O 1925/1093 r 213 (as substituted by SI 1996/2975 and amended by SI 1997/3037) where application is made by the trustee, or SR & O 1925/1093 r 236 (as substituted by SI 1996/2975) where application is made by the beneficiary. In both cases the form used is set out in SR & O 1925/1093, Sch 2 Form 62 (as substituted by SI 1989/801 and amended by SI 1996/2975). This may be supplemented with a restriction prohibiting a disposition of the land without the real buyers' consent.
3   As this deed will take effect off the register (see Form 19 note 1 [1194] ante), it seems preferable, in the case of registered land, to define the property.
4   It is probably better not to omit the words in square brackets as the nominee may find himself in difficulties if he contracts to sell on instructions from one tenant in common and another tenant in common does not wish the sale to proceed. The nominee would be well advised to obtain written directions from all the tenants in common before committing himself to any transaction.
5   See note 2 above.
6   As to the statutory requirements for valid execution of a deed see vol 12 (1994 Reissue) DEEDS, AGREEMENTS AND DECLARATIONS.

[1204]–[1210]

23

Declaration of trust of shares by person in whose name they have been registered[1]

THIS DECLARATION OF TRUST is made the ...... day of ....

BETWEEN:

(1)   *(trustee)* of *(address)* ('the Trustee') and

(2)   *(person beneficially entitled to investments purchased)* of *(address)* ('the Beneficiary')

WHEREAS

(1)   The Beneficiary has lately transferred or caused to be transferred into the name of the Trustee the shares specified in the [first and second] schedule[s] ('the Investments')

[(2)   The shares specified in the second schedule are not fully paid up]

(3)   All the above transfers were made to the Trustee as a nominee of the Beneficiary and it was agreed prior to the date of such transfers that the Trustee should execute the following declaration of trust

[1211]

NOW THIS DEED WITNESSES as follows:

1   Declaration of trust

The Trustee declares that he holds the Investments and all dividends and interest accrued or to accrue upon the same or any of them upon trust for the Beneficiary and his successors in title and agrees to transfer pay and deal with the Investments and the dividends and interest payable in respect of the same in such manner as he or they shall from time to time direct

2   Meetings of shareholders

The Trustee [will [at the request of the Beneficiary or his successors in title] attend all meetings of shareholders or otherwise which he shall be entitled to attend by virtue of being the registered proprietor of the Investments or any of them and will vote at every such meeting *or* will vote at all meetings of shareholders or otherwise which as registered proprietor of the Investments he may attend][2] in such manner as the Beneficiary or his successors in title shall have previously directed in writing and in default of and subject to any such direction at the discretion of the Trustee and further will if so required by the Beneficiary or his successors in title execute all proxies or other documents which shall be necessary or proper to enable the Beneficiary his personal representatives or assigns of his or their nominees to vote at any such meeting in the place of the Trustee

[1212]

3   Indemnity

The Beneficiary will at all times indemnify and keep indemnified the Trustee his personal representatives estate and effects against all liabilities which the Trustee or they may incur by reason of the Investments or any of them being so registered in the name of the Trustee as stated above and in particular will punctually pay all calls and other demands which the Trustee or his personal representatives may be or become liable to pay in respect of [any of the shares specified in the second schedule or in respect of] any shares or securities for which pursuant to any conditional or preferential right offered to the Trustee in respect of the Investments or any of them the Trustee may in his discretion subject as mentioned below think fit to subscribe and all costs and expenses incurred by the Trustee in the execution of the trusts of this deed

4   Exercise of options etc[3]

If any conditional or preferential right to subscribe for shares or securities in any company or any other option shall be offered to the Trustee as holder of the Investments or any of them or otherwise in respect of them or any call be made upon [the shares specified in the second schedule or] any shares and securities so offered to and subscribed for by the Trustee or other payment demanded in respect of them the Trustee shall so soon as conveniently may be give notice of such offer call or demand to the Beneficiary by letter sent through the post to his last address in the United Kingdom known to the Trustee and if not less than one week before the expiration of the time allowed for the exercise of such option or making such payment the Trustee shall receive any direction in writing from the Beneficiary and the Beneficiary shall pay or provide for any money required to be paid to comply with such direction the Trustee shall act on such direction but if no such direction shall be received or the money required to be provided for such action shall not be received or sufficient money to the satisfaction of the Trustee shall not be received before the time stated above the Trustee shall act in his discretion in the matter and such action shall be binding on the Beneficiary

[1213]

5   Charge for money paid

If the Trustee shall pay any money for calls or other demands in respect of [the shares specified in the second schedule or in respect of] any shares or securities so offered to and subscribed for by the Trustee such money together with interest on it at …% per year until payment shall be and remain a charge in favour of the Trustee upon the Investments

6   Trusts of new shares

The Trustee shall hold all and any shares or securities so offered to the Trustee in respect of the Investments and subscribed for by him upon the trusts and subject to the powers and provisions now declared concerning the Investments as if the same were an accretion to them

[7   Remuneration

During the continuance of the trust now declared the Beneficiary will pay to the Trustee the sum of £… [per year *or* in respect of each meeting which he shall attend at such request as stated above] as remuneration for his services as such trustee]

[1214]

8   New trustee

The power to appoint a new trustee of this deed is vested in the Beneficiary during his life

IN WITNESS etc

[FIRST] SCHEDULE
(list fully paid shares)

[SECOND SCHEDULE
(list partly paid shares)]

(signatures of the parties)[4]
(signatures of witnesses)

1   As to stamp duty see Introduction to this section [1161] ante and, for current rates of duty, see Information Binder: Stamp Duties [1] Table of Duties (Declaration of trust).

2   The second alternative wording in square brackets should be used if an obligation to attend all meetings is thought too onerous.

3   Trustee Act 1925 ss 10(4), 11 as amended by the Trustee Investments Act 1961 s 9(1) formerly dealt with rights issues and calls: both sections were repealed by the Trustee Act 2000 (48 Halsbury's Statutes (4th Edn) TRUSTS AND SETTLEMENTS). The trustees provisos in this regard are contained in the Trustee Act 2000 Pt II (ss 3–7). The Trustee Act 2000 s 3 introduces the 'general power of investment' as if the trustee were the absolute owner: see Paragraph 241 [591] ante.

4   As to the statutory requirements for valid execution of a deed see vol 12 (1994 Reissue) DEEDS, AGREEMENTS AND DECLARATIONS.

[1215]

24

Simple form of voting trust in relation to shares[1]

I *(shareholder)* of *(address)* [as the holder of *or* admit and declare that I hold] *(number and class of shares)* of *(nominal value)* each in the capital of *(company)* [upon trust for *(name and address of person to whom undertaking is given)*] [and] undertake that [subject to *(specify any consideration for the undertaking, special conditions or time limit which is to apply)*] I will [sell transfer or otherwise deal with the same and] exercise all rights of voting and other privileges attached to them [or to any of the above shares of which for the time being I remain the holder] in such manner as *(person to whom undertaking is given)* shall direct [and in the event of my selling transferring or otherwise disposing of any of the above shares I will procure that the person or persons to whom any such shares are sold transferred or disposed of shall enter into an undertaking in like terms]

Dated *(date)*

(signature of shareholder)

1   As to stamp duty see Introduction to this section [1161] ante and, for current rates of duty, see Information Binder: Stamp Duties [1] Table of Duties (Declaration of trust).

[1216]

5: JOINT TENANTS, TENANTS IN COMMON AND PARTNERS

25

Declaration of express trust for sale by joint tenants for the purpose of severing the joint tenancy in equity[1]

THIS DECLARATION OF TRUST is made the ...... day of ....

BETWEEN:

(1)   *(first joint tenant)* of *(address)*

(2)   *(second joint tenant)* of *(address)* and

(3)   *(third joint tenant)* of *(address)* (and the parties to this deed are together referred to as 'the Joint Tenants')[2]

WHEREAS

(1)   By virtue of [a [conveyance *or* transfer] dated *(date)* and made between *(parties)* or a settlement dated *(date)* and made between *(parties) or* an assent dated *(date)* and made [by *(personal representative)* or between *(personal representatives)* and the Joint Tenants]] [and in the events which have happened] the property described in the schedule ('the Property') is vested in the Joint Tenants at law and beneficially as joint tenants[3] in fee simple [and is registered in their names as registered proprietors at HM Land Registry under the title number referred to in the schedule]

(2)   The rents and profits of the Property have up to the date of this deed been collected paid and applied in accordance with the directions and to the satisfaction of the Joint Tenants

(3)   The Joint Tenants desire to sever the joint tenancy in equity at present subsisting in the Property upon the terms appearing below

[1217]

NOW THIS DEED WITNESSES as follows:

1   Declaration of trust

The Joint Tenants shall continue to hold the Property as joint tenants at law but on trust that they or the survivors or survivor of them or the personal representatives of the last survivor or other the trustees for the time being of this deed ('the Trustees') shall sell the same in such manner as they may be advised with full power to postpone such sale so long as they shall think fit unless and until some one or more of the Joint Tenants or persons claiming under him or them shall deliver or send by post to the Trustees such notice as is provided below

2   Trust for the Joint Tenants equally

The Trustees shall hold the net proceeds of sale after payment of the costs of and incidental to the sale and the net rents and profits of the Property until sale as from the date of this deed in trust for the Joint Tenants in equal shares

3   Death of a Joint Tenant

If any of the Joint Tenants shall die before the whole of the Property shall be sold and the net proceeds of it shall be distributed his personal representatives or assigns shall be entitled to receive the share in the trust property or the net proceeds of sale of the Property to which that one of the Joint Tenants so dying was entitled and to give to the Trustees a valid discharge for the same

[1218]

4   Notice

Any one of the Joint Tenants or those claiming under him may give to the Trustees a notice in writing requiring the Trustees to sell the Property and upon which the Trustees shall use their best endeavours to effect a sale of the Property so soon as circumstances admit

5   Enlargement of powers

The Trustees shall have the following powers[4]:

5.1   they may cause the accounts of the trust estate for the time being undistributed to be audited yearly or otherwise [by a professional accountant *or* by any person whether a professional accountant or not] whom they may select and may pay the cost of such audit out of the income of the trust estate and such accounts when signed by the Trustees and such [accountant *or* person] shall be binding on all persons claiming under this deed

5.2   they may cause a valuation of any part of the Property remaining unsold to be made by such person as they may believe to be an able practical surveyor and appoint for the purpose and in accordance with such valuation may make partition[5] of that part of the Property remaining unsold or any part of it and provide for the payment of equality money out of any money or investments (such investments to be taken at the market value of them as ascertained by the certificate of a banker or stockbroker) representing the proceeds of sale of any part of the Property that has been sold and any such partition shall be binding on all parties claiming under this deed

5.3   they may pay any of the Trustees who is a solicitor for any business done by him or his firm in relation to the trusts of this deed whether such business be of a professional character or not and

5.4   they may invest any proceeds of sale which they may determine not to distribute immediately in any investments authorised by law for the investment of trust funds and shall divide the income of them equally between the parties entitled to the shares of the Property and may from time to time vary such investments for others of a like nature[6]

[1219]

6   Appointment of new trustees

The power of appointing new trustees of this deed is vested in [the Trustees *or* the persons for the time being entitled in equity to two undivided one-third parts of or shares in the Property or the proceeds of sale of it]

[7   Application to Land Registry

The Joint Tenants will make such application to the Land Registry and execute and do all such documents acts and things as may be necessary or convenient to procure that the appropriate restriction and any other necessary entries and registrations shall be entered or registered in the register of the title referred to in the schedule for the purpose of giving effect to this deed and the exercise of the trusts and powers contained in it]

IN WITNESS etc

SCHEDULE
(describe the Property and set out title number where registered)

(signatures of the parties)[7]

(signatures of witnesses)

[1220]

1   As to stamp duty see Introduction to this section [1161] ante and, for current rates of duty, see Information Binder: Stamp Duties [1] Table of Duties (Declaration of trust). No severance of a joint tenancy of a legal estate, so as to create a tenancy in common, is permissible: Law of Property Act 1925 s 36(2) as amended by the Law of Property (Amendment) Act 1926 s 7, Schedule and by the Trusts of Land and Appointment of Trustees Act 1925 s 5(1), Sch 2 para 4 (37 Halsbury's Statutes (4th Edn) REAL PROPERTY). A joint tenant may, however, release his interest to the others or sever his equitable interest; provided that, where a legal estate (not being settled land) is vested in joint tenants beneficially, and any tenant desires to sever the joint tenancy in equity, he gives to the other joint tenants a notice in writing of such desire or does such other acts or things as would, in the case of personal estate, have been effectual to sever the tenancy in equity.
       Prior to 1 January 1997, the result was that, under the trust for sale which affected the land (under the Law of Property Act 1925 s 36(1)), the net proceeds of sale, and the net rents and profits until sale, were held upon the trusts which would have been requisite to give effect to the beneficial interests if there had been an actual severance. With the passage of the Trusts of Land and Appointment of Trustees Act 1996 (37 Halsbury's Statutes (4th Edn) REAL PROPERTY) a statutory trust for sale is no longer imposed (the land is held on a trust of land): see Paragraph 108 [267] ante. This Form is retained as an illustration of the procedure to be followed if an express trust for sale is to be imposed.

For shorter Forms where the joint tenancy is severed by the service of a notice see Forms 292 [2071] and 293 [2073] post. Nothing in the Law of Property Act 1925 affects the right of a survivor of joint tenants who is solely and beneficially interested to deal with the legal estate as if it were not held in trust: Law of Property Act 1925 s 36(2) as amended.

2   Where a husband and wife hold property as beneficial joint tenants, it may in some circumstances be desirable to convert the beneficial joint tenancy into a beneficial tenancy in common for the purpose of mitigating liability to inheritance tax on the death of the survivor of the spouses. If the beneficial interest is so converted, the share of the first spouse to die will not pass automatically to the survivor, but may be gifted to chargeable persons (such as children or grandchildren) to take advantage of the spouse's inheritance tax nil rate band. As to liability for inheritance tax, see Paragraph 283 [712] ante.

[1221]

3   The survivor of two or more joint tenants (and the personal representatives of such survivor) is, in favour of a purchaser of the legal estate, deemed to be solely and beneficially interested if the conveyance includes a statement that he is so interested; but not if, at any time before the date of the conveyance:

(a)   a memorandum of severance (ie a note or memorandum signed by the joint tenants or one of them and recording that the joint tenancy was severed in equity on a date therein specified) has been indorsed on or annexed to the conveyance by virtue of which the legal estate was vested in the joint tenants: Law of Property (Joint Tenants) Act 1964 s 1(1)(a) as amended by the Law of Property (Miscellaneous Provisions) Act 1994 s 21(1), (2), Sch 1 para 3, Sch 2, by the Insolvency Act 1985 s 235, Sch 8 para 13 and by the Insolvency Act 1986 s 437, Sch 11 (37 Halsbury's Statutes (4th Edn) REAL PROPERTY); or

(b)   a bankruptcy order made against any of the joint tenants, or a petition for such an order, has been registered under the Land Charges Act 1972, being an order or petition of which the purchaser has notice, by virtue of the registration, on the date of the conveyance by the survivor: Law of Property (Joint Tenants) Act 1964 s 1(1)(b) as amended by the Law of Property (Miscellaneous Provisions) Act 1994 s 21(1), (2), Sch 1 para 3, Sch 2, by the Insolvency Act 1985 s 235, Sch 8 para 13 and by the Insolvency Act 1986 s 437, Sch 11.

'Conveyance' for this purpose includes every assurance of property or an interest therein by any instrument except a will: see the Law of Property Act 1925 s 205(1)(ii); the Law of Property (Joint Tenants) Act 1964 s 4(1). Accordingly, in the case of unregistered land, a memorandum of the severance effected by this deed should be indorsed on the assurance by virtue of which the property is vested in the parties.

The Law of Property (Joint Tenants) Act 1964 does not apply to registered land: Law of Property (Joint Tenants) Act 1964 s 3. In the case of registered land which is held by joint proprietors on trust for themselves as tenants in common, the inability of the survivor to give a valid receipt for capital money is reflected by the entry of a restriction which the Registrar is under a statutory obligation to place on the register: see the Land Registration Act 1925 s 58(3) (37 Halsbury's Statutes (4th Edn) REAL PROPERTY); Land Registration Rules 1925, SR & O 1925/1093 rr 213, 236 (both as substituted by SI 1996/2975 and amended by SI 1997/3037), Sch 2 Form 62 (as substituted by SI 1989/801 and amended by SI 1996/2975). Where the land is held by joint proprietors on trust for themselves as joint tenants, no such restriction is entered and the survivor can transfer the land on sale without the need for any inquiry by the purchaser as to whether severance has taken place. When, however, severance does take place, an application should at once be made for the entry of the Form 62 restriction under SR & O 1925/1093 r 213(4). For an application to register a restriction see vol 25(1) (1999 Reissue) LAND REGISTRATION Form 77 [3591].

4   For the general powers of trustees of land see the Trusts of Land and Appointment of Trustees Act 1996 s 6 as amended by the Trustee Act 2000 s 40(1), Sch 2 para 45 (37 Halsbury's Statutes (4th Edn) REAL PROPERTY) and Paragraph 221 [532] ante.

5   The trustees could also make a partition under Trusts of Land and Appointment of Trustees Act 1996 s 7. The power under that section is limited, and it is, therefore, preferable to include an express power: see Paragraph 223 [536] ante.

6   The trustees enjoy the wide power of investment conferred by the Trustee Act 2000 Pt II (ss 3–7) (48 Halsbury's Statutes (4th Edn) TRUSTS AND SETTLEMENTS), and can acquire land under the Trustee Act 2000 Pt III (ss 8–10). Accordingly it is not considered that further express powers are required.

7   As to the statutory requirements for valid execution of a deed see vol 12 (1994 Reissue) DEEDS, AGREEMENTS AND DECLARATIONS.

[1222]

26

Declaration of express trust for sale where joint tenancy is severed after one tenant has expended his own money on improving the property[1]

THIS DECLARATION OF TRUST is made the ...... day of ....

BETWEEN:

(1)   *(first joint tenant)* of *(address)* and

(2)   *(second joint tenant)* of *(address)* (together referred to as 'the Joint Tenants')

WHEREAS

(1)   By a [conveyance *or* transfer] dated *(date)* and made between (1) *(seller)* and (2) the Joint Tenants the property described in the first schedule ('the Property') was [conveyed *or* transferred] to the Joint Tenants in fee simple as beneficial joint tenants [and is registered in their names as registered proprietors at HM Land Registry under the title number referred to in the first schedule]

(2)   *(first joint tenant)* has out of his own money expended £... on the improvement of the Property short particulars of which improvements are set out in the second schedule

(3)   Having regard to such expenditure the Joint Tenants have agreed that the Property shall as from the date of this deed be held by them upon trust for sale and to hold the proceeds of sale upon trust for the Joint Tenants as tenants in common in the shares mentioned below

                                                           [1223]

NOW THIS DEED WITNESSES as follows:

1   Severance of joint tenancy

As from the date of this declaration the Joint Tenants will hold the Property in fee simple upon trust to sell the same and to hold the net proceeds of such sale and the net income until sale upon trust as to *(specify)* equal *(specify)* parts of it for *(first joint tenant)* and as to the remaining *(specify)* equal *(specify)* parts of it for *(second joint tenant)* as tenants in common[2]

[2   Restriction

The Joint Tenants will make such application to the Land Registry and execute and do all such documents acts and things as may be necessary or convenient to procure that the appropriate restriction[3] and any other necessary entries may be entered or registered in the register of the title referred to in the first schedule for the purpose of giving effect to this declaration]

IN WITNESS etc

FIRST SCHEDULE
(describe the Property and set out title number where registered)

SECOND SCHEDULE
(give details of improvements)

                                     (signatures of the parties)[4]
                                     (signatures of witnesses)
                                                [1224]

1   As to stamp duty see Introduction to this section [1161] ante and, for current rates of duty, see Information Binder: Stamp Duties [1] Table of Duties (Declaration of trust). This declaration should avoid the difficulty of quantifying the value of improvements effected to the property: for the right of a co-owner to an account for such improvements, see *Snell's Equity* (30th Edn, 2000) para 44-10.

As to the indorsing of a memorandum of severance on the assurance by virtue of which the property is vested in the parties see Form 25 note 3 [1222] ante.

2   Although a trust for sale is not required, it has been included on the basis that this is likely to correspond to the intentions of the parties. As a trust of land is created the trustees enjoy the wide powers conferred by the Trusts of Land and Appointment of Trustees Act 1996 s 6 as amended by the Trustee Act 2000 s 40(1), Sch 2 para 45 (37 Halsbury's Statutes (4th Edn) REAL PROPERTY) including power to sell, lease and mortgage: see Paragraph 221 [532] ante.

3   As to the necessary restriction in the case of registered land see Form 25 note 3 [1222] ante. This deed itself takes effect off the register: see the Land Registration Act 1925 s 74 (37 Halsbury's Statutes (4th Edn) REAL PROPERTY).

4   As to the statutory requirements for valid execution of a deed see vol 12 (1994 Reissue) DEEDS, AGREEMENTS AND DECLARATIONS.

[1225]

27

Declaration of simple trust of land on severance of joint tenancy of property subject to a mortgage[1]

THIS DECLARATION OF TRUST is made the ...... day of ....

BETWEEN:

(1)   *(first joint tenant) of (address)* and

(2)   *(second joint tenant) of (address)* (together referred to as 'the Joint Tenants')

WHEREAS

(1)   By a [conveyance *or* transfer] dated *(date)* and made between (1) *(seller)* and (2) the Joint Tenants the property described in the schedule ('the Property') was [conveyed *or* transferred] to the Joint Tenants in fee simple as beneficial joint tenants [and is registered in their names as registered proprietors at HM Land Registry under the title number referred to in the schedule]

(2)   By a mortgage ('the Mortgage') dated *(date)* and made between (1) the Joint Tenants and (2) *(lender)* ('the Lender') the Property was [demised *or* charged] to the Lender to secure the payment to the Lender of the sum of £... and interest on it as mentioned in the Mortgage and the payment of such principal and interest was to be made by equal monthly instalments of £... during a period of *(number)* years from *(date)*

[1226]

(3)   The Joint Tenants have agreed that as from the date of this deed such joint tenancy shall be severed and the Property subject to the Mortgage shall be held by them as tenants in common in equal shares and they have further agreed to the other terms appearing below

NOW THIS DEED WITNESSES as follows:

1   Tenancy in common

As from the date of this deed the Joint Tenants will hold the Property in fee simple subject to the Mortgage in trust for the Joint Tenants as tenants in common in equal shares

2   Indemnity

The Joint Tenants covenant with each other that each will pay one-half of the instalments and any other money payable under the Mortgage and each will at all times in future keep the other and his or her estate and effects indemnified from all actions costs claims and demands on account of such half of such instalments and other money

[3   Restriction

The Joint Tenants will make such application to the Land Registry and execute and do all such documents acts and things as may be necessary or convenient to procure that the appropriate restriction² and any other necessary entries may be entered or registered in the register of the title referred to in the schedule for the purpose of giving effect to this declaration]

IN WITNESS etc

SCHEDULE

(describe the Property and set out title number where registered)

(signatures of the parties)³
(signatures of witnesses)
[1227]

1   As to stamp duty see Introduction to this section [1161] ante and, for current rates of duty, see Information Binder: Stamp Duties [1] Table of Duties (Declaration of trust). As to stamp duty on partition see the Finance Act 1999, Sch 13 para 21 (41 Halsbury's Statutes (4th Edn) STAMP DUTIES) and see vol 29 PARTITION Paragraph 16 [1537]. As to the indorsement of a memorandum of severance on the assurance by virtue of which the property is vested in the parties see Form 25 note 3 [1222] ante. As a trust of land is created the trustees enjoy the wide powers conferred by the Trusts of Land and Appointment of Trustees Act 1996 s 6 as amended by the Trustee Act 2000 s 40(1), Sch 2 para 45 (37 Halsbury's Statutes (4th Edn) REAL PROPERTY) including power to sell, lease and mortgage: see Paragraph 221 [532].

2   As to the necessary restriction in the case of registered land see Form 25 note 3 [1222] ante. This deed itself takes effect off the register: see the Land Registration Act 1925 s 74 (37 Halsbury's Statutes (4th Edn) REAL PROPERTY).

3   As to the statutory requirements for valid execution of a deed see vol 12 (1994 Reissue) DEEDS, AGREEMENTS AND DECLARATIONS.

[1228]

28

Declaration of express trust of sale by husband and wife on occasion when they have contributed unequally in purchase of residence—provision for payments for improvements and mortgage instalments¹

THIS DECLARATION OF TRUST is made the ...... day of ....

BETWEEN:

(1)   *(husband)* of *(address)* ('the Husband') and
(2)   *(wife)* of *(address)* ('the Wife') (together referred to as 'the Joint Tenants')

WHEREAS

(1)   By a transfer² of even date with this deed but executed before this deed and made between (1) *(seller)* and (2) the Joint Tenants and in consideration of the payment by the Joint Tenants to *(seller)* of the sum of £... the property described in the schedule ('the Property') was transferred to the Joint Tenants free from incumbrances

[1229]

(2)   By a mortgage ('the Mortgage') of even date with this deed but also executed before this deed the Joint Tenants charged the Property to *(lender)* ('the Lender') to secure the payment to the Lender of the sum of £... with interest on it at the rate and by the instalments and subject to the terms and conditions set out in the Mortgage

(3)   The purchase money paid to *(seller)* in consideration of the transfer was provided as to £... by the Husband and as to £... by the Wife and as to the balance being the above sum of £... borrowed by the Joint Tenants from the Lender on the security of the Mortgage

(4)   It has been agreed between the Joint Tenants that they shall hold the Property jointly as trustees for sale with power to postpone sale and that they shall hold the proceeds of such sale upon trust for themselves as tenants in common in the shares in which they have each contributed to the purchase of the Property and to the payments of the instalments due under the Mortgage and to such extension and improvements to the Property (if any) as may from time to time be jointly agreed between the Joint Tenants in so far as such extensions and improvements involve the expenditure of money

[1230]

NOW THIS DEED WITNESSES as follows:

1   Trusts

The Joint Tenants shall hold the Property on trust to sell the same with power to postpone sale and shall hold the net proceeds of sale (after deducting out of them the balance of any money due under the Mortgage) on trust for themselves as tenants in common in the proportions mentioned below[3]

2   Husband's share of proceeds

The Husband shall be entitled to such share of the total of the net proceeds of sale as shall be calculated by multiplying such total by the total of the sum of £...[4] paid by the Husband together with all such further sums paid by the Husband in respect of the Property whether by the way of payment of instalments due under the Mortgage or for any extensions and improvements to the Property which the Joint Tenants may from time to time jointly agree and dividing the product of such multiplication by the total of all sums paid by the Joint Tenants with the agreement of one another in respect of the Property

[1231]

3   Wife's share of proceeds

The Wife shall be entitled to such share of the total of the net proceeds of sale as shall be calculated by multiplying such total by the total of the sum of £...[5] paid by the Wife together with all such further sums paid by the Wife in respect of the Property whether by way of payment of instalments due under the Mortgage or for any extensions and improvements to the Property which the Joint Tenants may from time to time jointly agree and dividing the product of such multiplication by the total of all sums paid by the Joint Tenants with the agreement of one another in respect of the Property

IN WITNESS etc

SCHEDULE
(describe the Property and set out title number where registered)

(signatures of the parties)[6]
(signatures of witnesses)
[1232]

1   As to stamp duty see Introduction to this section [1161] ante and, for current rates of duty, see Information Binder: Stamp Duties [1] Table of Duties (Declaration of trust). An express trust setting out the shares of the couple is always desirable since otherwise considerable difficulties may arise. For instance, this Form negatives the presumption of advancement which arises when a husband purchases property in the name of his wife or (as in the case contemplated in this Form) the property is purchased in the names of the husband and wife. The presumption does not normally extend to mortgage repayments (*Outram v Hyde* (1875) 24 WR 268), but these are mentioned for the purpose of clarity. On the presumption, see *Snell's Equity* (30th Edn, 2000) para 9-11 et seq.

By virtue of the Matrimonial Proceedings and Property Act 1970 s 37 (27 Halsbury's Statutes (4th Edn) MATRIMONIAL LAW) if a husband or wife makes a substantial contribution in money or money's worth to the improvement of property in which either or both of the spouses has or have a beneficial interest, then he or she, subject to any contrary agreement between them, is to be treated as having acquired a share or enlarged share in the beneficial interest of such an extent as may have been agreed or, in default of agreement, as to the court may seem just.

2   If the transfer, following which the declaration is made, is a recent transfer on sale of unregistered land, the Land Registration Act 1925 ss 1, 123, 123A as substituted by the Administration of Justice Act 1982 s 66(1) and substituted and inserted by the Land Registration Act 1997 s 1 (37 Halsbury's Statutes (4th Edn) REAL PROPERTY) will apply, to require that an application be made for first registration of the land. Whether the title is already registered, or is to be registered for the first time, the interests of the declarants should be protected on the register by entry of the trustee restriction contained in the Land Registration Rules 1925, SR & O 1925/1093 r 213 (as substituted by SI 1996/2975 and amended by SI 1997/3037) where application is made by the trustee, or SR & O 1925/1093 r 236 (as substituted by SI 1996/2975) where application is made by the beneficiary. In both cases the form used is set out in SR & O 1925/1093, Sch 2 Form 62 (as substituted by SI 1989/801 and amended by SI 1996/2975).

3   The imposition of a trust for sale is considered to be the likely wish of the parties in this situation. If not required the property may be held on a simple trust of land. As a trust of land is created, the trustees have the wide powers conferred by the Trusts of Land and Appointment of Trustees Act 1996 s 6 as amended by the Trustee Act 2000 s 40(1), Sch 2 para 45 (37 Halsbury's Statutes (4th Edn) REAL PROPERTY) including power to sell, lease and mortgage: see Paragraph 221 [532] ante.

4   The sum referred to here should be that mentioned in recital (3) [1230]. So as to avoid uncertainty any share attributable to extensions and improvements should be limited to those which result from the actual expenditure of money for which receipts may be made available.

5   See note 4 above.

6   As to the statutory requirements for valid execution of a deed see vol 12 (1994 Reissue) DEEDS, AGREEMENTS AND DECLARATIONS.

[1233]–[1240]

29

Declaration that property held by trustees for themselves as tenants in common be held for themselves as joint tenants[1]

THIS DECLARATION OF TRUST is made the ...... day of .... BY *(tenants in common)* of *(addresses)* ('the Trustees')

WHEREAS

(1)   [By a [conveyance *or* transfer] dated *(date)* and made between *(parties)* the property described in the schedule ('the Property') was [conveyed *or* transferred] in fee simple to the Trustees *or* The Trustees as registered proprietors of the property described in the schedule ('the Property') hold the Property] upon trust for themselves as tenants in common in equal shares

(2)   Each of the Trustees holds his beneficial interest in the Property for his own absolute use and benefit free from incumbrances and subsidiary trusts

(3)   The Trustees desire that as from the date of this deed they shall hold the Property as beneficial joint tenants

[1241]

NOW THIS DEED WITNESSES as follows:

Declaration of trust

The Trustees declare that as from the date of this deed they will hold the Property upon trust for themselves as beneficial joint tenants [and will make such application to the Land Registry and execute and do all such documents and things as may be necessary or convenient to procure the cancellation of the restriction entered on *(date)*[2] on the register of the title referred to in the schedule]

IN WITNESS etc

SCHEDULE

(describe the Property and set out title number where registered)

(signatures of the parties)[3]

(signatures of witnesses)

[1242]

1   As to stamp duty see Introduction to this section [1161] ante and, for current rates of duty, see Information Binder: Stamp Duties [1] Table of Duties (Declaration of trust). The property is held under a trust of land.

2   This will be the restriction entered pursuant to the Land Registration Act 1925 s 58(3) (37 Halsbury's Statutes (4th Edn) REAL PROPERTY) when the trustees were registered as proprietors: see the Land Registration Rules 1925, SR & O 1925/1093 r 213 (as substituted by SI 1996/2975 and amended by SI 1997/3037) where application is made by the trustee, or SR & O 1925/1093 r 236 (as substituted by SI 1996/2975) where application is made by the beneficiary. In both cases the form used is set out in SR & O 1925/1093, Sch 2 Form 62 (as substituted by SI 1989/801 and amended by SI 1996/2975). Where application is made to cancel the restriction referred to on the basis of the declaration, the Registrar may also call for evidence to satisfy him that neither of the tenants in common has dealt with his share in the land prior to the declaration in any way which might be incompatible with the conversion of their tenancy in common into a joint tenancy.

3   As to the statutory requirements for valid execution of a deed see vol 12 (1994 Reissue) DEEDS, AGREEMENTS AND DECLARATIONS.

[1243]

30

Declaration of trust of leasehold property subject to a mortgage by two persons who have purchased on behalf of themselves and others

30(1) Trust for sale[1]

THIS DECLARATION OF TRUST is made the ...... day of ....

BETWEEN:

(1)   *(trustee purchasers)* of *(addresses)* ('the Trustees') and

(2)   *(first co-purchaser)* of *(address)* and *(second co-purchaser)* of *(address)* ('the Co-Purchasers')

WHEREAS

(1)   By an assignment dated *(date)* and made between *(parties)* in consideration of £... paid by the Trustees as mentioned in such instrument the property[2] described in the schedule ('the Leasehold Property') was assigned to the

Trustees for the residue of a term of **[99]** years granted by a lease ('the Lease') dated *(date)* and made between *(parties)* at the rent and subject to the covenants on the part of the tenant and conditions reserved and contained by and in the Lease

[1244]

(2) By a mortgage ('the Mortgage') dated *(date)* and made between *(parties)* in consideration of £... paid to them by *(mortgagees)* ('the Mortgagees') the Trustees demised the Leasehold Property by way of legal mortgage to the Mortgagees to secure the payment to the Mortgagees of the sum of £... together with interest thereon [and also covenanted with the Mortgagees for the payment to them of such sum of £... and interest]

(3) The Trustees hold the Leasehold Property upon the trusts declared below as they admit

NOW THIS DEED WITNESSES as follows:

1   Trust for sale

The Trustees declare that they will hold the Leasehold Property upon trust and that they shall with the consent in writing of the Co-Purchasers[3] sell the same or any part of it in such manner as they shall from time to time think fit with power to postpone sale so long as they shall think fit [until otherwise requested in writing by the Co-Purchasers]

2   Payment of mortgage money

The Trustees shall apply the net proceeds of sale after payment of the cost of the same in payment or part payment of the money for the time being owing on the Mortgage subject as mentioned below

[1245]

3   Residue

The Trustees shall hold the residue of the net proceeds of sale upon the trusts declared by a deed of the same date and made between the same parties in the same order as this deed or on such other trusts as the same ought to be held from time to time

4   Powers on sale of part

On any sale of part only of the Leasehold Property the Trustees shall have the following powers:

4.1   they may agree with the Mortgagees that the whole or some part only of the net proceeds of sale shall be applied in payment or reduction of the money for the time being owing on the Mortgage and if any part of the net proceeds be not so applied the same shall be held on the trusts declared above concerning the residue of the net proceeds of sale

4.2   they may with or without the concurrence of the landlord apportion the rent payable in respect of the part or parts sold and the parts retained and for that purpose may if they think fit effect any such sale by subdemise or by assignment and acceptance of a subdemise and make such other provision for the apportionment of the rent and for securing payment of the apportioned parts of the same and the performance and observance of the covenants contained in the lease and otherwise as the Trustees may think fit[4]

[1246]

5   Transfer of mortgage

Until the whole of the Leasehold Property shall be sold the Trustees may arrange for or concur in a transfer of the Mortgage and may pay off or arrange for the payment of any mortgage debt and make such further or other mortgage of the Leasehold Property as they think proper

6   Restriction on trustee powers

[The provisions of the Trusts of Land and Appointment of Trustees Act 1996 Sections *(specify)* shall not apply to the land which is at any time subject to the trusts of this deed

or

The provisions of the Trusts of Land and Appointment of Trustees Act 1996 Sections *(specify)* shall apply with the following modification to the land which is at any time subject to the trusts of this deed: *(continue as appropriate)*[5]]

[7   Appointment of new trustees

The statutory power of appointing new trustees of this deed is vested in [a majority of] the Trustees and the Co-Purchasers and the survivor or survivors of them][6]

IN WITNESS etc

SCHEDULE

(date of and parties to the Lease and description of the Leasehold Property)

(signatures of the parties)[7]
(signatures of witnesses)
[1247]

1   As to stamp duty see Introduction to this section [1161] ante and, for current rates of duty, see Information Binder: Stamp Duties [1] Table of Duties (Declaration of trust). Normally the property will be assigned by the vendor to trustees with, if desired, the co-purchasers as parties of the third part. For limitation of the number of trustees see vol 40(2) (2001 Reissue) TRUSTS AND SETTLEMENTS Part 10 [5201]. In this Form, it is assumed that an assignment has been made to the two trustees vesting the property in them as joint tenants. Although there is no longer a statutorily implied trust for sale, in this case an express trust for sale has been included on the basis that this will correspond to the intentions of the parties. Caution may be needed where, as in the case of some leases, there is a covenant not only against assignment of the lease, but also against parting with possession of the premises, without the landlord's consent: see Form 20 note 1 [1197] ante.

   This Form modifies the powers of the trustees under the trust of land. As the Form deals also with the legal interest in the land, it will be referred to on the registered title. A simple declaration of trust of the proceeds of sale (Form 30(2) [1250] post) will not be referred to on the registered title, being merely a statement of the rights of the parties among themselves. Under the assignment to them as joint tenants, the trustees have full power to sell the property, since the register contains no notice of the trust and, in many cases, it will be possible to dispense with this Form and merely to regulate the rights of the parties by Form 30(2) [1250] post. Separate deeds will not be necessary if the title to the land is registered.

2   Where the lease is registered (and compulsory registration will apply where there has been a recent assignment on sale or grant and the term or remaining term exceeds 21 years), consideration should be given to protecting the co-purchasers' interests by means of a restriction which, for example, prohibits any dispositions without the consent of the co-purchasers or their respective personal representatives. This is because the normal joint proprietor restriction (which the Registrar will be required to enter under the Land Registration Act 1925 s 58(3) (37 Halsbury's Statutes (4th Edn) REAL PROPERTY)) will not prevent the registration of a disposition by the trustee proprietors where there are two or more of them, even a disposition which prejudices their interests: see *City of London Building Society v Flegg* [1988] AC 54, [1987] 3 All ER 435, HL. The practitioner should consider whether the co-purchasers in such circumstances should be independently advised.

[1248]

3   If there are more than two co-purchasers, so far as a purchaser of the property is concerned, only two of them need consent: Trusts of Land and Appointment of Trustees Act 1996 ss 8, 10 (37 Halsbury's Statutes (4th Edn) REAL PROPERTY). It will be preferable to name the two, or, if they do not exceed three, say 'a majority of the co-purchasers'. In many cases, as where the greater part of the purchase money is contributed by the trustees, or the co-purchasers may be likely to be abroad or not readily accessible, it may be best to omit the words requiring consent altogether. This is a case where it is anticipated that the parties would wish to include an express trust for sale rather than to rely on the statutory trust of land.

4   Where the leasehold land is severed, the landlord may distrain for the whole rent on any part of the land, but can recover by action against an assignment of part of the land only an apportioned part of the rent: *Stevenson v Lambard* (1802) 2 East 575. As to the statutory remedies for apportioned rents see the Law of Property Act 1925 s 190(3)–(8) (37 Halsbury's Statutes (4th Edn) REAL PROPERTY). As to contribution by the tenant of an apportioned part to the tenant of the other part, see *Whitham v Bullock* [1939] 2 KB 81, [1939] 2 All ER 310, CA.

5   For powers conferred on trustees of land in England and Wales see the Trusts of Land and Appointment of Trustees Act 1996 s 6 as amended by the Trustee Act 2000 s 40(1), Sch 2 para 45. See also Paragraph 221 [532] ante. The Trustee Act 2000 Pt II (ss 3–7) (48 Halsbury's Statutes (4th Edn) TRUSTS AND SETTLEMENTS) now provides wide powers of investment in the event of land being sold.

6   The power of appointing new trustees must conform to that contained in the trust deed of the proceeds of sale.

7   As to the statutory requirements for valid execution of a deed see vol 12 (1994 Reissue) DEEDS, AGREEMENTS AND DECLARATIONS.

[1249]

30(2) Declaration of trust of proceeds of sale[1]

THIS DECLARATION OF TRUST is made the ...... day of ....

BETWEEN:

(1)   *(trustee purchasers)* of *(addresses)* ('the Trustees') and

(2)   *(first co-purchaser)* of *(address)* and *(second co-purchaser)* of *(address)* ('the Co-Purchasers')

WHEREAS

(1)   This deed is supplemental to a deed ('the Trust for Sale') of the same date and made between the same parties in the same order as this deed under which the Trustees agreed that they would hold certain leasehold property ('the Leasehold Property') described in the Trust for Sale subject to a mortgage mentioned in the Trust for Sale ('the Mortgage') for securing the sum of £... and interest upon trust that they should with the consent of the Co-Purchasers sell the same with power to postpone the sale as mentioned in the Trust for Sale and would hold the residue of the net proceeds of sale after payment of the costs of the same and of all money for the time being owing on the Mortgage upon the trusts declared by a deed described in the Trust for Sale and meaning this deed

[1250]

(2)   The Leasehold Property was purchased and mortgaged as stated above by the Trustees on behalf of themselves and the Co-Purchasers and the purchase money paid for the Leasehold Property namely the sum of £... was provided as to £... part by the parties to this deed in the following shares and proportions namely one half by the Trustees in equal shares out of their own money one quarter by *(first co-purchaser)* and the remaining one quarter by *(second co-purchaser)*[2] and as to £... balance by means of the sum of £... borrowed on the Mortgage as stated above and which it is intended shall be repaid by the parties to this deed in the like shares and proportions in which they contributed to such purchase money respectively

NOW THIS DEED WITNESSES as follows:

1 Trust of net proceeds

The Trustees shall hold the net residue of the proceeds of sale of the Leasehold Property after payment of the money due on the Mortgage upon trust to divide the same into four equal parts and shall hold one such quarter of such proceeds in trust for each of the Trustees and the Co-Purchasers or their respective personal representatives[3]

[1251]

2 Interim investment

Until the whole of the Leasehold Property shall have been sold the Trustees may in their discretion [unless they and the Co-Purchasers shall otherwise agree] instead of immediately distributing any capital money which may be received in respect of the Leasehold Property invest the same and such investments shall be held for and the income of such investments shall be paid to the Trustees and the Co-Purchasers in the proportions to which they are entitled to the net residue of the proceeds of sale of the Leasehold Property[4]

3 Covenants

Each of the Trustees and the Co-Purchasers covenants with the others and each of them as follows:

3.1 to pay or contribute his due proportion of the rent reserved by the lease described in the Trust for Sale and of the expenses incurred or to be incurred in performing and observing the covenants on the part of the tenant and conditions contained in such lease

3.2 to pay or contribute his due proportion of the principal money and interest secured by the Mortgage or by any other mortgage or incumbrance for the time being affecting the Leasehold Property as and when required so to do

3.3 to pay or contribute his due proportion of all rates taxes premiums of insurance and other outgoings payable in respect of the Leasehold Property

3.4 to pay or contribute his due proportion of all costs charges and expenses of or incidental to the purchase and the assurance of the Leasehold Property to the Trustees and the negotiation and completion of the Mortgage the Trust for Sale and this deed already incurred and of all costs charges and expenses which may in future be incurred by the Trustees in relation to the same or in the execution of the trusts of this deed

3.5 to keep indemnified every other party to this deed from all actions claims and demands incurred or to be incurred by such last-mentioned party by reason of any default on the part of the covenanting party in performing his obligations under this clause

[1252]

4 Meaning of due proportion

The due proportion which each party to this deed shall be liable to pay or contribute to in accordance with the provisions of this deed shall be in the case of each of the Trustees and each of the Co-Purchasers one quarter of the aggregate sum required[5] and all payments or contributions shall be made to the Trustees

5   Restriction on trustee powers

[The provisions of the Trusts of Land and Appointment of Trustees Act 1996 Sections *(specify)* shall not apply to the land which is at any time subject to the trusts of this deed

or

The provisions of the Trusts of Land and Appointment of Trustees Act 1996 Sections *(specify)* shall apply with the following modification to the land which is at any time subject to the trusts of this deed: *(continue as appropriate)*][6]

6   Charging clause

Any trustee for the time being of this deed being a solicitor or other person engaged in a profession or business may be employed in and paid for all business done or time occupied by him or his firm in relation to the trusts of this deed whether or not such business is of a professional character[7]

[1253]

7   Appointment of new trustees

The power of appointing new trustees of this deed is vested in [a majority of] the Trustees and the Co-Purchasers and the survivor or survivors of them

8   Interpretation clause

Every reference in this deed to the Trustees shall where the context admits include the trustees or trustee for the time being of this deed and every reference to the parties to this deed or to any one or more of them shall unless the context otherwise requires be deemed to include a reference to the personal representatives and assigns of such parties or party

IN WITNESS etc

(signatures of the parties)[8]
(signatures of witnesses)
[1254]

1   As to stamp duty see Introduction to this section [1161] ante and, for current rates of duty, see Information Binder: Stamp Duties [1] Table of Duties (Declaration of trust). See Form 30(1) note 1 [1248] ante.
2   See note 3 below.
3   If the purchase money was not contributed equally the trust should be altered accordingly. In such circumstances recital (2) [1251] and clause 4 [1253] must be altered so as to reflect the contributions.
4   Capital monies may be invested in accordance with the wide powers given to trustees in the Trustee Act 2000 Pts II (ss 3–7) and III (ss 8–10) (48 Halsbury's Statutes (4th Edn) TRUSTS AND SETTLEMENTS).
5   See note 3 above.
6   For powers conferred on trustees of land in England and Wales see the Trusts of Land and Appointment of Trustees Act 1996 s 6 as amended by the Trustee Act 2000 s 40(1), Sch 2 para 45 (37 Halsbury's Statutes (4th Edn) REAL PROPERTY). See also Paragraph 221 [532] ante.
7   For a fuller form of charging clause see Form 226 [1687] post. As to the remuneration of trustees generally see Paragraph 212 [511] et seq ante.
8   As to the statutory requirements for valid execution of a deed see vol 12 (1994 Reissue) DEEDS, AGREEMENTS AND DECLARATIONS.

[1255]

30(3) Incorporating a declaration as to beneficial entitlement[1]

THIS DECLARATION OF TRUST is made the ...... day of ....

BETWEEN:

(1)   *(trustee purchasers)* of *(addresses)* ('the Trustees') and

(2)   *(first co-purchaser)* of *(address)* and *(second co-purchaser)* of *(address)* ('the Co-Purchasers')

WHEREAS

(1)   By an assignment dated *(date)* and made between *(parties)* in consideration of £... paid by the Trustees as mentioned in such instrument the property[2] described in the schedule ('the Leasehold Property') was assigned to the Trustees for the residue of a term of [99] years granted by a lease ('the Lease') dated *(date)* and made between *(parties)* at the rent and subject to the covenants on the part of the tenant and conditions reserved and contained by and in the Lease

[1256]

(2)   By a mortgage ('the Mortgage') dated *(date)* and made between *(parties)* in consideration of £... paid to them by *(mortgagees)* ('the Mortgagees') the Trustees charged the Leasehold Property by way of legal mortgage to the Mortgagees to secure the payment to the Mortgagees of the sum of £... together with interest thereon [and also covenanted with the Mortgagees for the payment to them of such sum of £... and interest]

(3)   The Leasehold Property was purchased and mortgaged as stated above by the Trustees on behalf of themselves and the Co-Purchasers and the purchase money paid for the Leasehold Property namely the sum of £... was provided as to £... part by the parties to this deed in the following shares and proportions namely one half by the Trustees in equal shares out of their own money one quarter by *(first co-purchaser)* and the remaining one quarter by *(second co-purchaser)*[3] and as to £... balance by means of the sum of £... borrowed on the Mortgage as stated above and which it is intended shall be repaid by the parties to this deed in the like shares and proportions in which they contributed to such purchase money respectively

(4)   The Trustees hold the Leasehold Property upon the trusts declared below as they admit

NOW THIS DEED WITNESSES as follows:

1   Trust for sale

The Trustees declare that they will hold the Leasehold Property upon trust and that they shall with the consent in writing of the Co-Purchasers[4] sell the same or any part of it in such manner as they shall from time to time think fit with power to postpone sale so long as they shall thing fit [until otherwise requested in writing by the Co-Purchasers]

2   Payment of mortgage money

The Trustees shall apply the net proceeds of sale after payment of the cost of the same in payment or part payment of the money for the time being owing on the Mortgage subject as mentioned below

[1257]

3   Residue

The Trustees shall hold the residue of the net proceeds of sale upon trust to divide the same into [four equal] parts and shall hold [one such quarter] of such proceeds in trust for each of the Trustees and the Co-Purchasers or their respective personal representatives[5]

4   Powers on sale of part

On any sale of part only of the Leasehold Property the Trustees shall have the following powers:

4.1   they may agree with the Mortgagees that the whole or some part only of the net proceeds of sale shall be applied in payment or reduction of the money for the time being owing on the Mortgage and if any part of the net proceeds be not so applied the same shall be held on the trusts declared above concerning the residue of the net proceeds of sale

4.2   they may with or without the concurrence of the landlord apportion the rent payable in respect of the part or parts sold and the parts retained and for that purpose may if they think fit effect any such sale by subdemise or by assignment and acceptance of a subdemise and make such other provision for the apportionment of the rent and for securing payment of the apportioned parts of the same and the performance and observance of the covenants contained in the lease and otherwise as the Trustees may think fit[6]

[1258]

5   Transfer of mortgage

Until the whole of the Leasehold Property shall be sold the Trustees may arrange for or concur in a transfer of the Mortgage and may pay off or arrange for the payment of any mortgage debt and make such further or other mortgage of the Leasehold Property as they think proper

6   Interim investment

Until the whole of the Leasehold Property shall have been sold the Trustees may in their discretion [unless they and the Co-Purchasers shall otherwise agree] instead of immediately distributing any capital money which may be received in respect of the Leasehold Property invest the same and such investments shall be held for and the income of such investments shall be paid to the Trustees and the Co-Purchasers in the proportions to which they are entitled to the net residue of the proceeds of sale of the Leasehold Property[7]

7   Covenants

Each of the Trustees and the Co-Purchasers covenants with the others and each of them as follows:

7.1   to pay or contribute his due proportion of the rent reserved by the lease described in the Trust for Sale and of the expenses incurred or to be incurred in performing and observing the covenants on the part of the tenant and conditions contained in such lease

7.2   to pay or contribute his due proportion of the principal money and interest secured by the Mortgage or by any other mortgage or incumbrance for the time being affecting the Leasehold Property as and when required so to do

7.3   to pay or contribute his due proportion of all rates taxes premiums of insurance and other outgoings payable in respect of the Leasehold Property

7.4   to pay or contribute his due proportion of all costs charges and expenses of or
        incidental to the purchase and the assurance of the Leasehold Property to the
        Trustees and the negotiation and completion of the Mortgage the Trust for Sale
        and this deed already incurred and of all costs charges and expenses which may
        in future be incurred by the Trustees in relation to the same or in the execution
        of the trusts of this deed

7.5   to keep indemnified every other party to this deed from all actions claims and
        demands incurred or to be incurred by such last-mentioned party by reason of
        any default on the part of the covenanting party in performing his obligations
        under this clause

[1259]

8   Meaning of due proportion

The due proportion which each party to this deed shall be liable to pay or contribute
pursuant to the provisions of this deed shall be in the case of each of the Trustees and
each of the Co-Purchasers one quarter of the aggregate sum required[8] and all payments
or contributions shall be made to the Trustees

9   Restriction on trustee powers

[The provisions of the Trusts of Land and Appointment of Trustees Act 1996 Sections
(specify) shall not apply to the land which is at any time subject to the trusts of this deed

or

The provisions of the Trusts of Land and Appointment of Trustees Act 1996 Sections
(specify) shall apply with the following modification to the land which is at any time
subject to the trusts of this deed: *(continue as appropriate)*][9]

10   Charging clause

Any trustee for the time being of this deed being a solicitor or other person engaged in
a profession or business may be employed in and paid for all business done or time
occupied by him or his firm in relation to the trusts of this deed or the Trust for Sale
whether or not such business is of a professional character[10]

[1260]

11   Appointment of new trustees

The power of appointing new trustees of this deed is vested in [a majority of] the
Trustees and the Co-Purchasers and the survivor or survivors of them

12   Interpretation clause

Every reference in this deed to the Trustees shall where the context admits include the
trustees or trustee for the time being of this deed and every reference to the parties to
this deed or to any one or more of them shall unless the context otherwise requires be
deemed to include a reference to the personal representatives and assigns of such parties
or party

IN WITNESS etc

(signatures of the parties)[11]
(signatures of witnesses)
[1261]

1   As to stamp duty see Introduction to this section [1161] ante and, for current rates of duty, see Information Binder: Stamp Duties [1] Table of Duties (Declaration of trust). Normally the property will be assigned by the vendor to trustees with, if desired, the co-purchasers as parties of the third part. For limitation of the number of trustees see vol 40(2) (2001 Reissue) TRUSTS AND SETTLEMENTS Part 10 [5201]. In this Form, it is assumed that an assignment has been made to the two trustees vesting the property in them as joint tenants. Although there is no longer a statutorily implied trust for sale, in this case an express trust for sale has been included on the basis that this will correspond to the intentions of the parties. Caution may be needed where, as in the case of some leases, there is a covenant not only against assignment of the lease, but also against parting with possession of the premises, without the landlord's consent: see Form 20 note 1 [1197] ante.

      This Form modifies the powers of the trustees under the trust of land and will be referred to on the title. A simple declaration of trust of the proceeds of sale (see Form 30(2) [1250] ante) will not be on the title, being merely a statement of right of the parties among themselves.

2   Where the lease is registered (and compulsory registration will apply where there has been a recent assignment on sale or grant and the term or remaining term exceeds 21 years) consideration should be given to protecting the co-purchasers' interests by means of a restriction which, for example, prohibits any dispositions without the consent of the co-purchasers or their respective personal representatives. This is because the normal joint proprietor restriction, which the Registrar will be required to enter under the Land Registration Act 1925 s 58(3) (37 Halsbury's Statutes (4th Edn) REAL PROPERTY), will not prevent the registration of a disposition by the trustee proprietors where there are two or more of them, even a disposition which prejudices their interests: see *City of London Building Society v Flegg* [1988] AC 54, [1987] 3 All ER 435, HL. The practitioner should consider whether the co-purchasers in such circumstances should be independently advised.

3   See note 5 below.

4   If there are more than two co-purchasers, so far as a purchaser of the property is concerned, only two of them need consent: Trusts of Land and Appointment of Trustees Act 1996 ss 8, 10 (37 Halsbury's Statutes (4th Edn) REAL PROPERTY). It will be preferable to name the two, or, if they do not exceed three, say 'a majority of the co-purchasers'. In many cases, as where the greater part of the purchase money is contributed by the trustees, or the co-purchasers may be likely to be abroad or not readily accessible, it may be best to omit the words requiring consent altogether. Again, this is a case where it is anticipated that the parties would wish to include an express trust for sale rather than to rely on the statutory trust of land.

5   Recital (3) [1257] and clause 8 [1260] must be amended to reflect:

      (a)   the actual contributions made by the trustees and the beneficiaries and the proportions they bear to the whole price; and

      (b)   any agreement between the trustees and the beneficiaries that the proportions to which they are to be entitled are not to correspond to the proportions in which each contributed to the price.

6   Where the leasehold land is severed, the landlord may distrain for the whole rent on any part of the land, but can recover by action against an assignment of part of the land only an apportioned part of the rent: *Stevenson v Lambard* (1802) 2 East 575. As to the statutory remedies for apportioned rents see the Law of Property Act 1925 s 190(3)–(8) (37 Halsbury's Statutes (4th Edn) REAL PROPERTY). As to contribution by the tenant of an apportioned part to the tenant of the other part, see *Whitham v Bullock* [1939] 2 KB 81, [1939] 2 All ER 310, CA.

7   The trustees' investment powers in this Form are regulated this form by the Trustee Act 2000 Pts II (ss 3–7) and III (ss 8–10) (48 Halsbury's Statutes (4th Edn) TRUSTS AND SETTLEMENTS) and there are no express powers. Express powers could be included.

8   See note 5 above.

9   For powers conferred on trustees of land in England and Wales see the Trusts of Land and Appointment of Trustees Act 1996 s 6 as amended by the Trustee Act 2000 s 40(1), Sch 2 para 45 (37 Halsbury's Statutes (4th Edn) REAL PROPERTY). See also Paragraph 221 [532] ante.

10   For a fuller form of charging clause see Form 233 [1769] post. As to the remuneration of trustees generally see Paragraph 212 [511] et seq ante.

11   As to the statutory requirements for valid execution of a deed see vol 12 (1994 Reissue) DEEDS, AGREEMENTS AND DECLARATIONS.

31

Declaration of trust by two partners of leasehold property in trust for a firm on change of partnership—variations where the term has only a short time to run and where the land is registered[1]

THIS DECLARATION OF TRUST is made the ...... day of ....

BETWEEN:

(1)   *(retiring partner)* of *(address)* and *(continuing partner)* of *(address)* ('the Trustees')

(2)   *(continuing partner)*

(3)   *(first new partner)* of *(address)* and

(4)   *(second new partner)* of *(address)*

WHEREAS

(1)   By a lease ('the Lease') dated *(date)* and made between (1) *(landlord)* and (2) the Trustees the property described in the schedule ('the Leasehold Property') was demised to the Trustees for the term of **[28]** years from *(date)* at the yearly rent of £... and subject to the covenants on the part of the tenants and conditions contained in the Lease [and the Trustees are registered as the proprietors with a good leasehold title of the Leasehold Property under title number *(number)*]

[1263]

(2)   The Trustees have for some time past carried on business in partnership together on the Leasehold Property as [general merchants] under the style or firm name of *(name of firm)* and the Leasehold Property forms part of the partnership property

(3)   The partnership between the Trustees has recently been determined and *(continuing partner)* and *(new partners)* (together referred to as 'the Present Partners') have agreed to carry on the same business as partners on the terms of a partnership agreement entered into between the Present Partners under the same name as the old partnership

NOW THIS DEED WITNESSES as follows:

1   Declaration of trust

The Trustees declare that they will hold the Leasehold Property upon trust to sell the same[2] (with power to postpone the sale) and to stand possessed of the net proceeds of any such sale upon the trusts and with and subject to the powers and provisions applicable to the same as part of the partnership property of the firm *(name of firm)* ('the Firm') carried on by the Present Partners

2   Rent

The Present Partners shall duly pay the rent reserved by the Lease at the times and in the manner in which the same is payable and shall perform and observe the covenants on the part of the tenants contained in the Lease and discharge all outgoings of or in any way relating to the Leasehold Property and will indemnify the Trustees in respect of the same

[1264]

3 Indemnity

The Present Partners jointly and severally covenant with *(retiring partner)* ('the Retiring Partner') that they and each of them will indemnify and keep indemnified the Retiring Partner from all rent and other money payable under the Lease and from all costs damages expenses claims and demands under or in respect of the same or of this deed or of the Leasehold Property or any of them or which may arise on the termination of the Lease

[4 Application to Land Registry

The Trustees agree to make such application to the Land Registry and execute and do all such documents acts and things as may be necessary or convenient to procure the entry of the appropriate restrictions on the register of the title above referred to for the purpose of protecting the interest of the Firm and of the partners in it][3]

[5 Provision as to new lease

The Retiring Partner agrees with the Present Partners that on the expiration or sooner determination of the Lease he will use his best endeavours to procure a new lease of the Leasehold Property to be granted to the Present Partners on the terms of the Lease for a further term of *(number)* years or on such other terms and conditions as may be agreed][4]

[6 Certificate of value

(certificate of value if appropriate)]

IN WITNESS etc

SCHEDULE
(describe the Leasehold Property)

(signatures of the parties)[5]
(signatures of witnesses)
[1265]

1   As to stamp duty see Introduction to this section [1161] ante. This Form will be dutiable at a fixed rate of duty (see Information Binder: Stamp Duties [1] Table of Duties (Declaration of trust)); unless, on the change of partnership, purchase money was attributable to the beneficial interests in the property declared by this trust deed and stamp duty on it was not paid on another deed, such as a deed of dissolution or a new deed of partnership. In such circumstances see Information Binder: Stamp Duties [1] Table of Duties (Conveyance or transfer) and consider whether clause 6 [1265] of this Form should be included. For capital gains tax purposes the retiring partner will dispose of his share in the business on which retirement relief may be available: see the Taxation of Chargeable Gains Act 1992 ss 163, 164, Sch 6 as amended (42–44 Halsbury's Statutes (4th Edn) TAXATION). Caution may be needed where, as in the case of some leases, there is a covenant not only against assignment of the lease, but also against parting with possession of the premises, without the landlord's consent.

2   As to the nature of partnership property note that the Partnership Act 1890 s 22 which had imposed a trust for sale was repealed by the Trusts of Land and Appointment of Trustees Act 1996 s 25(2), Sch 4 (37 Halsbury's Statutes (4th Edn) REAL PROPERTY). However, it remains uncertain whether or not there was a pre-existing equitable rule that there should be a trust for sale on the basis that on a dissolution the land would have to be sold. The matter is discussed by Pettit in [1997] LQR at p 207. A trust for sale has been expressly included in this Form on the basis that it will correspond (in the majority of cases) to the intentions of the parties.

3   For an application to register a restriction see vol 25(1) (1999 Reissue) LAND REGISTRATION Form 77 [3591]. The normal form of partnership restriction will be one where dispositions are prohibited without the consent of the non-proprietor partners or his/their respective personal representatives.

4   If the lease has only a short time to run, it may be as well to insert this clause in order to show the intention of the parties.

5   As to the statutory requirements for valid execution of a deed see vol 12 (1994 Reissue) DEEDS, AGREEMENTS AND DECLARATIONS.

[1266]

32

Declaration of trust of leaseholds by former partner on sale of partnership assets to a registered company[1]

THIS DECLARATION OF TRUST is made the …… day of ………

BETWEEN:

(1)   *(tenant)* of *(address)* ('the Tenant')

(2)   *(present partners)* of *(addresses)* ('the Partners') and

(3)   *(company)* whose registered office is at *(address)* ('the Company')

WHEREAS

(1)   By a lease ('the Lease') dated *(date)* and made between (1) *(landlord)* ('the Landlord') and (2) the Tenant the property described in the schedule ('the Leasehold Property') was demised to the Tenant for the term of [28] years from *(date)* at the yearly rent of £… and subject to the performance and observance of the covenants on the part of the Tenant and to the conditions contained in the Lease and the Lease contained a covenant against assignment of the Leasehold Property without the consent in writing of the Landlord[2] [and the Tenant is registered as proprietor of the Leasehold Property with a good leasehold title under title number *(number)*]

[1267]

(2)   The Partners have for some time past carried on business in partnership together upon the Leasehold Property under the style or firm of *(name of firm)* ('the Firm')

(3)   The Tenant was formerly a partner in the Firm and by a deed dated *(date)* and made between (1) the Tenant and (2) the Partners on his retirement the Tenant agreed to hold the Leasehold Property in trust for the Partners as part of the partnership assets of the Firm and the Partners agreed to pay the rent and perform and observe the covenants on the part of the Tenant contained in the Lease and to indemnify the Tenant against all claims in respect of such rent and other outgoings of the Leasehold Property and any breach of such covenants

(4)   The Company was incorporated on *(date)* under the Companies Act 1985 with a capital of £… divided into *(number)* shares of £… each

(5)   The Partners have agreed with the Company to sell to it their above mentioned business and the assets of the partnership as a going concern as from *(date)* ('the Appointed Day')

[(6)   It is intended that the Leasehold Property shall ultimately be [assigned *or* transferred] to the Company provided that the consent of the Landlord can be obtained to such [assignment *or* transfer] but some time may elapse before such consent can be obtained]

[1268]

NOW THIS DEED WITNESSES as follows:

1   Declaration of trust

The Tenant declares that as from the Appointed Day he holds the Leasehold Property in trust for the Company and that he will deal with the same as the Company shall from time to time in writing direct

2   Covenant to pay

(where the lease being assigned does not create a new tenancy within the meaning of the Landlord and Tenant (Covenants) Act 1995 Section 1(3))

With the object of affording to the Tenant and also to the Partners a full and sufficient indemnity but not further or otherwise the Company covenants with the Tenant and with the partners that the Company will:

2.1   during the Term pay the rents reserved in the lease and perform all the covenants

2.2   keep the Tenant and the Partners indemnified against all actions, claims, demands, losses, costs, damages or liabilities whatsoever by reason of any future breach of the Covenants

[1269]

3   Tenant to procure assignment

The Tenant will at the request and cost of the Company use his best endeavours to procure the consent of the Landlord in writing to an [assignment *or* transfer] of the Leasehold Property to the Company for the residue of the above term [and will do all things necessary to protect the interest of the Company under this deed on the register of the title above referred to and to secure the registration of the Company on such title as proprietor]³

[4   Certificate of value

(certificate of value if appropriate)]

IN WITNESS etc

SCHEDULE
(describe the Leasehold Property)

*(signatures of the parties)*⁴
(signatures of witnesses)
[1270]

1   As to stamp duty see Introduction to this section [1161] ante and, for current rates of duty, see Information Binder: Stamp Duties [1] Table of Duties (Declaration of trust); but if a portion of the price payable by the company is attributable to this deed, then ad valorem conveyance on sale duty is payable. As to such duty see Information Binder: Stamp Duties [1] Table of Duties (Conveyance or transfer) and consider whether the certificate of value in clause 4 [1270] of this Form shall be included.

2   It is assumed that the covenant extends to assignment or assignment and subdemise only, and does not extend to parting with possession of the property. A declaration of trust, followed by a parting with possession, will be a breach of the covenant not to part with possession. Circumstances may, however, be such that there is even no breach of the tenant's covenant not to part with possession of the property or any part of it; eg where he merely permits a company in which he is interested to use the property: *Chaplin v Smith* [1926] 1 KB 198, CA.

3   The wording in square brackets is required in the case of registered land. Compulsory registration will apply in the case of an assignment where the remaining term exceeds 21 years. By reason of the Land Registration Act 1997 s 1 (37 Halsbury's Statutes (4th Edn) REAL PROPERTY) such an assignment will be subject to first registration under the Land Registration Act 1925 s 123 as substituted by the Land Registration Act 1997 s 1 and amended by the Greater London Authority Act 1999 s 219(1), (8) (37 Halsbury's Statutes (4th Edn) REAL PROPERTY) whether or not it is made for valuable consideration.

4   As to the statutory requirements for valid execution of a deed see vol 12 (1994 Reissue) DEEDS, AGREEMENTS AND DECLARATIONS.

[1271]–[1280]

B: ASSIGNMENT AND TRANSFERS TO TRUSTEES

1: INTRODUCTION

Voluntary settlements

The term 'voluntary settlement' is usually applied to any settlement, other than one made for valuable consideration such as marriage. Consequently, virtually all the settlements in this title are voluntary settlements. Such a settlement is fully constituted when the instrument declaring the trusts has been executed and everything which is necessary has been done by the settlor, according to the nature of the property, to transfer it to the trustees. Until then, the settlement and any covenants in it are unenforceable against the settlor[1]. An incompletely constituted settlement made for valuable consideration will be treated by the court as a contract to transfer the property which the settlor covenanted to transfer and the court will enforce it[2].

In practice, the forms of property most often assigned *in a settlement itself* are interests in other settlements (frequently reversionary interests) and insurance policies. Very occasionally debts are so assigned. Land is normally transferred by a separate conveyance[3] or transfer[4], so that parcels clauses in relation to land will rarely be used in a settlement itself. So far as registered land is concerned, it is always necessary to transfer the land to trustees by separate transfer.

If a voluntary settlement contains an assignment of property, no stamp duty is payable in respect of the assignment provided that the settlement contains the appropriate certificate. If it is a marriage settlement and the assignment is in consideration of marriage, Category G of the Stamp Duty (Exempt Instruments) Regulations 1987[5] should be included; otherwise, Category L.

Whenever a trust is created (whether by transfer or assignment of property or by a declaration), the settlor may consider making a declaration of solvency[6].

[1281]

1   See *Re Rose, Midland Bank Executor and Trustee Co Ltd v Rose* [1949] Ch 78, [1948] 2 All ER 971; *Re Rose, Rose v IRC* [1952] Ch 499, [1952] 1 All ER 1217, CA.
2   See *Pullan v Koe* [1913] 1 Ch 9.
3   For a transfer for use with a voluntary settlement of freehold property on trust for sale see Form 45(1) [1309] post.
4   For a transfer for use with a voluntary settlement of registered land see Form 44(1) [1295] post.
5   Ie the Stamp Duty (Exempt Instruments) Regulations 1987, SI 1987/516 as amended by SI 1999/2539. As to the inclusion of such a certificate see Information Binder: Stamp Duties [1] Table of Duties (Exempt Instruments Regulations). As to stamp duty on voluntary dispositions, see generally Information Binder: Stamp Duties [1] Table of Duties (Voluntary disposition).
6   For a declaration of solvency see Form 46 [1314] post.

[1282]

2: ASSIGNMENT OF PROPERTY

(For an assignment of a reversionary interest on trust see Form 310 [2142] post.)

33

Voluntary assignment of life insurance policy[1]

The {Assignor} now assigns the {Policy} and all benefits and advantages of rights arising and money assured by or to become payable under or by virtue of such policy and any policy or policies substituted for it to the {Trustees} to hold the same to the {Trustees} upon the trusts and subject to the powers and provisions declared and contained below

1   For a notice of assignment see Form 298 [2084] post. For a complete life insurance settlement see Form 6 [1120] ante. When this clause is inserted in a document the defined terms in { } must be altered to suit those used in the document.

[1283]

34

Assignment pursuant to marriage agreement[1]

In pursuance of the above agreement and in consideration of the [above marriage *or* marriage intended shortly to be solemnised between the {Husband} and the {Wife}] ('the Marriage') the [{Husband} *or* {Wife}] with the approbation of the [{Wife} *or* {Husband}] now conveys to the {Trustees} ALL THAT *(describe property)* to hold the same to the {Trustees} [in fee simple *or* for the residue of the term for which the same is held *or* absolutely] [in trust for the [{Husband} *or* {Wife}] until the Marriage and afterwards] upon the trusts and subject to the powers and provisions set out below

1   For a complete marriage settlement see Form 7 [1136] ante. When this clause is inserted in a document the defined terms in { } must be altered to suit those used in the document.

[1284]

35

Assignment of chattels to trustees[1]

THIS DEED OF GIFT is made the ...... day of ....

BETWEEN:

(1)   *(donors)* both of *(address)* ('the Donors') and

(2)   *(trustees)* of *(addresses)* ('the Trustees')

WHEREAS

(1)   The Donors are the joint owners of the assets listed in the schedule ('the Assets') which are situated in or about the dwelling house of the Donors at *(address)*

(2)   The Trustees are the present trustees of a settlement ('the Settlement') made on even date and between the same parties as this deed

NOW THIS DEED WITNESSES as follows:

1   Assignment

The Donors assign to the Trustees by way of gift all the Assets to be held by the Trustees in accordance with the terms of the Settlement

2   Tax indemnity

The Donors jointly and severally indemnify the Trustees and each of them and their successors as trustees and their respective personal representatives and estates against any liability to inheritance tax properly chargeable occasioned by the death of the Donors or either of the Donors in respect of the gift of the Assets

3   Stamp duty certificate

It is certified that this instrument falls within category 'L' in the Schedule to the Stamp Duty (Exempt Instruments) Regulations 1987[2]

IN WITNESS etc

SCHEDULE

The Assets

(list the Assets)

(signatures of the parties)[3]
(signatures of witnesses)
[1285]

1   As to stamp duty see Introduction to this section [1281] ante and see Information Binder: Stamp Duties [1] Table of Duties (Voluntary disposition). It is envisaged that the donors will retain possession and enjoyment of the chattels, and this may create two problems:

(a)   An assignment of personal chattels by way of gift falls within the definition of 'a bill of sale' for the purpose of the Bills of Sale Act 1878 s 4 (5 Halsbury's Statutes (4th Edn) BILLS OF SALE) and, therefore, is subject to the provisions of that Act with regard to registration and attestation: see the Bills of Sale Act 1878 ss 10, 11 and vol 4(1) (2000 Reissue) BILLS OF SALE Paragraph 6 [2009]. Unless these provisions are complied with, the assignment is, as regards any chattels remaining in the possession or apparent possession of the donor, void against the persons specified in the Bills of Sale Act 1878; namely, trustees or assignees in the donor's bankruptcy, or under any assignment for the benefit of his creditors, and the sheriff's officers and other persons seizing chattels under execution against the donor and every person on whose behalf such process has been issued: see the Bills of Sale Act 1878 s 8. A registered bill of sale has priority over an unregistered bill. Failure to register does not affect validity as between donor and recipient: *Davis v Goodman* (1880) 5 CPD 128, CA.

(b)   Continued use of the chattels by the donors will involve a reservation of benefit for inheritance tax purposes unless full consideration is furnished for that use: see the Finance Act 1986 s 102, Sch 20 para 6(1)(a) as amended by the Finance Act 1989 s 171(5), (6) and the Finance Act 1998 s 165, Sch 27, Pt IV (42–44 Halsbury's Statutes (4th Edn) TAXATION) and see Paragraph 290 [749] et seq ante. To fall within this provision an arm's length bailment agreement must be negotiated involving either the payment of a full rent incorporating review clauses, or the payment of a commercial premium on grant of the bailment. As to bailment generally see vol 3(1) (1999 Reissue) BAILMENT.

2   A conveyance or transfer of property, operating as a voluntary disposition inter vivos within Category L in the Schedule to the Stamp Duty (Exempt Instruments) Regulations 1987, SI 1987/516, is exempt from stamp duty under the provisions specified in SI 1987/516 reg 2(2) as amended by SI 1999/2539, if certified in accordance with SI 1987/516 reg 3.

3   As to the statutory requirements for valid execution of a deed see vol 12 (1994 Reissue) DEEDS, AGREEMENTS AND DECLARATIONS.

[1286]

3: PARCELS CLAUSES

36

Clause for vested share and possible accretions[1]

ALL THAT the *(specify)* equal part or share or other the part or share to which the {Settlor} is entitled in the residuary estate of the {Testator}[2] and the property for the time being representing the same [and all other if any the share shares or interest to which the {Settlor} may in future become entitled by accruer or otherwise in the residuary estate [or under the will and codicils of the {Testator}]]

1   When this clause is inserted in a document the defined terms in { } must be altered to suit those used in the document.

2   Care should be taken before an assignment is made of an interest in a residuary estate if the residue has not at the relevant time been ascertained. This is because the legal right of a residuary legatee to compel the personal representatives to administer the estate is regarded, during the course of that administration, as a chose in action with no base value for capital gains tax purposes. It is therefore arguable that a disposal by the legatee of part or all of his interest in the residuary estate could result in a substantial capital gains tax liability arising. This contrasts with the position if administration of the estate has been completed when the residuary estate vests in the legatee who acquires the relevant assets at their probate value.

[1287]

37

Clause for remainder interest in settled legacy[1]

ALL THAT the share or interest whatsoever the same may be or become of the {Settlor} of and in the legacy of £... settled by the will and codicils of the {Testator} now represented by the property described in the schedule subject to the prior life interests subsisting in the same by virtue of the said will and codicils

1   In this clause the property is a reversionary interest as defined for inheritance tax purposes: Inheritance Tax Act 1984 s 47 (42–44 Halsbury's Statutes (4th Edn) TAXATION). It is (normally) excluded property and can be assigned without any inheritance tax liability. See the Inheritance Tax Act 1984 s 48 as amended by the Finance Act 1996 s 154, Sch 28 para 8. For capital gains tax purposes, no chargeable gain accrues on the gratuitous disposal by a beneficiary of an interest in a trust unless that beneficiary had acquired it for a consideration in money or money's worth or unless the settlement was at any time non resident or had received property from such a settlement: Taxation of Chargeable Gains Act 1992 s 76(1) as amended by the Finance Act 1998 s 128 (42–44 Halsbury's Statutes (4th Edn) TAXATION).

        When this clause is inserted in a document the defined terms in { } must be altered to suit those used in the document.

[1288]

38

Clause for reversionary share under settlement and appointment[1]

ALL THAT the *(specify)* equal part or share or other the part share or interest to which the {Settlor} is entitled or may afterwards become entitled by accruer or otherwise under the settlement dated *(date)* and made between *(parties)* ('the Settlement') subject to the life interest in the same of *(tenant for life)* in the property subject to the trusts of the Settlement

1　See Form 37 note 1 [1288] ante. When this clause is inserted in a document the defined terms in { } must be altered to suit those used in the document.

[1289]

39

Clause for policy of insurance[1]

ALL THAT the policy of insurance on the life of the {Settlor} issued by *(insurers)* dated *(date)* and numbered *(number)* for the sum of £... [with profits] under the yearly premium of £... and all money to become payable under it and all benefits secured by it

1　When this clause is inserted in a document the defined terms in { } must be altered to suit those used in the document.

[1290]

40

Clause for several policies of insurance by reference to schedule[1]

ALL THAT the several policies of insurance on the life of the {Settlor} particularly described in the schedule and all money to become payable under the same policies respectively and all rights and remedies for the recovery of the same and all benefits secured by such policies respectively

1　When this clause is inserted in a document the defined terms in { } must be altered to suit those used in the document.

[1291]

41

Clause for rentcharge[1]

ALL THAT the perpetual yearly rentcharge of £... payable [half-yearly on *(date)* and *(date)* in each year *or* on the usual quarter days] [granted to *or* limited to *or* in trust for] the {Settlor} [in fee simple] by [[a conveyance *or* a settlement *or* *(specify)*] dated *(date)* and made between *(parties)* *or* [the conveyance *or* the settlement *or* *(specify)*] recited above] and charged upon and issuing out of [*(describe land charged)* or the lands described in the above conveyance] and all powers and remedies for recovering the same when in arrear together with the benefit of all covenants and conditions on the part of the grantor and those deriving title under him to be observed and performed

1   It should be noted that a rentcharge created out of a registered title must be registered if the rentcharge owner is to get the legal estate: see the Land Registration Act 1925 ss 18(1)(b), 19(2), 20 as amended by the Greater London Authority Act 1999 s 219(1), (4) and by the Land Registration Act 1986 s 4(3), (5) (37 Halsbury's Statutes (4th Edn) REAL PROPERTY). Where a rentcharge has been registered, it is appropriate to refer to it by reference to its title number. When this clause is inserted in a document the defined terms in { } must be altered to suit those used in the document.

[1292]

42

Parcels clause for several rentcharges by reference to schedule[1]

ALL THAT the several rentcharges for the several yearly sums mentioned in the schedule payable for the periods and on the dates and created by the deeds and charged upon and issuing out of the land stated in the several columns of the schedule

SCHEDULE

Amount of rentcharge	Period during which rentcharge is payable	Deed creating rentcharge	Date instalments become payable	Property charged with rentcharge
(amount)	*(years)*	*(date and parties)*	*(date)*	*(describe)*

1   It should be noted that where a rentcharge has been registered, it is appropriate to refer to it by reference to its title number. See Form 41 note 1 [1292] ante.

[1293]

43

Clause for furniture and personal chattels[1]

[All the furniture plate and other articles of domestic use or ornament belonging to the {Settlor} in or about the dwelling house *(describe property)* or its outbuildings gardens and curtilage

or

All the furniture chattels and effects specified in [the schedule *or* an inventory signed by the {Settlor} and the {Trustees} and intended to be annexed to this settlement]

or

All the diamonds pearls and other jewels and chattels described in the schedule]

1   When this clause is inserted in a document the defined terms in { } must be altered to suit those used in the document.

[1294]

4: COMPLETE VOLUNTARY SETTLEMENTS

44

Voluntary settlement of registered land of which the settlor is the registered proprietor

44(1) Transfer[1]

Use Land Registry Form TR1, for which see vol 37 (2001 Reissue) SALE OF LAND Form 1 [51], and insert the wording shown below in the panels specified

Panel 1 Stamp Duty

It is certified that this instrument falls within category 'L' in the Schedule to the Stamp Duty (Exempt Instruments) Regulations 1987

Panel 11 Declaration of trust

The Transferees are to hold the property upon the trusts declared by a deed dated *(date)* made between *(parties)*[2]

Panel 12 Additional provisions

The Transferees apply to the Registrar for entry of the following restriction[s] on the register:

[12.1   No disposition by a sole proprietor of the land (not being a trust corporation) under which capital money arises is to be registered except under an order of the Registrar or of the court][3]

[12.2   Except under an order of the Registrar no [disposition *(or specify type of disposition limited by the trust deed)*] by the proprietors of the land is to be registered unless they make a statutory declaration, or their solicitor or licensed conveyancer certifies, that the disposition is in accordance with a deed dated *(date)* made between *(parties)* or some variation thereof referred to in the declaration or certificate][4]

[1295]

1   As to stamp duty see Introduction to this section [1281] ante and see Information Binder: Stamp Duties [1] (Conveyance or transfer). A conveyance or transfer of property, operating as a voluntary disposition inter vivos within the Stamp Duty (Exempt Instruments) Regulations 1987, SI 1987/516, Schedule Category L is exempt from stamp duty under the provisions specified in SI 1987/516 reg 2(2) as amended by SI 1999/2539, if certified in accordance with SI 1987/516 reg 3.

2   No copy of the trust deed need be lodged with the application since neither the Registrar nor any other person dealing with a registered estate or charge is affected with notice of any trust and, so far as possible, such trusts are to be excluded from the register: see the Land Registration Act 1925 s 74 (37 Halsbury's Statutes (4th Edn) REAL PROPERTY).

3   This restriction is appropriate where the transferees hold the land as trustees of land as prescribed by the Land Registration Rules 1925, SR & O 1925/1093 r 213 as substituted by SI 1996/2975, Sch 2 Form 62 as substituted by SI 1989/801 and amended by SI 1996/2975. Application for this restriction in the transfer is optional because the survivor of the transferees, as trustees of land, are unable to give a valid receipt for capital money and the Registrar is, therefore, obliged to enter the restriction in any event: see the Land Registration Act 1925 s 58(3). It may, however, be convenient to include the application where further restrictions are sought (see note 4 below) and to provide a reminder to the transferees of the limitation imposed on their holding of the land. As to the restriction generally see vol 35 (1997 Reissue) SALE OF LAND Paragraph 983.1 [1287].

4   This restriction is appropriate where the separate trust deed imposes an express limitation on the trustees' power of disposition, eg where the deed requires the consent of a beneficiary to any disposition, or prohibits dispositions until a certain event, such as an occupying beneficiary attaining the age of majority, so that the trustees are under a duty to apply for entry on the register of this prescribed form of restriction: see SR & O 1925/1093 rr 59A, 106A as inserted by SI 1996/2975, Sch 2 Form 11A as inserted by SI 1996/2975.

As the transaction, following which the declaration is made, is a recent acquisition on sale, the Land Registration Act 1925 ss 123 and 123A as substituted and inserted by the Land Registration Act 1997 s 1 will apply, in the case of unregistered land, to require that an application be made for first registration of the land by the trustee. For appropriate forms of transfer and conveyance see vol 37 (2001 Reissue) SALE OF LAND Forms 182 [1351]–186 [1362]. Whether the property before its transfer to the trustee was previously registered or unregistered, the interest of the real buyer should be protected on the register by entry of the trustee restriction contained in SR & O 1925/1093 r 213 (as substituted by SI 1996/2975 and amended by SI 1997/3037) where application is made by the trustee, or SR & O 1925/1093 r 236 (as substituted by SI 1996/2975) where application is made by the beneficiary. In both cases the form used is set out in SR & O 1925/1093, Sch 2 Form 62 (as substituted by SI 1989/801 and amended by SI 1996/2975). This may be supplemented with a restriction prohibiting a disposition of the land without the real buyer's consent.

[1296]–[1305]

44(2) Trust deed[1]

THIS SETTLEMENT is made the …… day of ………

BETWEEN:

(1)   *(settlor)* of *(address)* ('the Settlor') and
(2)   *(trustees)* of *(addresses)* ('the Trustees')

WHEREAS

By a transfer bearing even date the Settlor has transferred to the Trustees the freehold land registered at HM Land Registry with absolute title under title number *(title number)* ('the Property') and wishes to declare the following trusts

[1306]

NOW THIS DEED WITNESSES as follows:

1   Trust of land

The Trustees shall hold the Property on the trusts of this settlement and all property for the time being representing the same ('the Trust Fund') on the following trusts

2   Trusts

(set out the beneficial interests: eg upon trust for the settlor's daughter for life with remainder to the settlor's grandchildren on accumulation and maintenance trusts)

3   Residence

The trusts declared by clause 2 above shall be sufficiently performed by allowing *(beneficiary)* to reside in the Property[2]

(continue with required administrative provisions and administrative powers: in this case a full range of powers may be desirable as may a trustee charging and indemnity clause)

IN WITNESS etc

(signatures of the parties)[3]
(signatures of witnesses)
[1307]

1   As to stamp duty see Information Binder: Stamp Duties [1] (Declaration of trust). See also Introduction to this section [1281] ante and Introduction to Section A [1161] ante.
2   For the right of a beneficiary entitled to an interest in possession to occupy trust land see the Trusts of Land and Appointment of Trustees Act 1996 ss 12, 13 (48 Halsbury's Statutes (4th Edn) TRUSTS AND SETTLEMENTS) and see Paragraph 228 [545] ante.
3   As to the statutory requirements for valid execution of a deed see vol 12 (1994 Reissue) DEEDS, AGREEMENTS AND DECLARATIONS.

[1308]

45

Voluntary settlement of freehold property on trust for sale by owner wishing to provide for an improvident person

45(1) Transfer of the whole of registered or unregistered freehold land to trustees of land to be held on the trusts of a separate deed[1]

Use Land Registry Form TR1, for which see vol 37 (2001 Reissue) SALE OF LAND Form 1 [51], and insert the wording shown below in the panels specified

Panel 1 Stamp duty
It is certified that this instrument falls within category 'L' in the Schedule to the Stamp Duty (Exempt Instruments) Regulations 1987

Panel 11 Declaration of trust
The Transferees are to hold the property upon the trusts declared by a deed dated *(date)* made between *(parties)*[2]

Panel 12 Additional provisions
The Transferees apply to the Registrar for entry of the following restriction[s] on the register:

[12.1   No disposition by a sole proprietor of the land (not being a trust corporation) under which capital money arises is to be registered except under an order of the Registrar or of the court][3]

[12.2   Except under an order of the Registrar no [disposition *(or specify type of disposition limited by the trust deed)*] by the proprietors of the land is to be registered unless they make a statutory declaration, or their solicitor or licensed conveyancer certifies, that the disposition is in accordance with a deed dated *(date)* made between *(parties)* or some variation thereof referred to in the declaration or certificate][4]

[1309]

1   As to stamp duty see Introduction to this section [1281] ante and see Information Binder: Stamp Duties [1] (Conveyance or transfer). A conveyance or transfer of property, operating as a voluntary disposition inter vivos within Category L in the Schedule to the Stamp Duty (Exempt Instruments) Regulations 1987, SI 1987/516, is exempt from stamp duty under the provisions specified in SI 1987/516 reg 2(2) as amended by SI 1999/2539, if certified in accordance with SI 1987/516 reg 3.
2   No copy of the trust deed need be lodged with the application since neither the Registrar nor any other person dealing with a registered estate or charge is affected with notice of any trust and, so far as possible, such trusts are to be excluded from the register: see the Land Registration Act 1925 s 74 (37 Halsbury's Statutes (4th Edn) REAL PROPERTY).
3   This restriction is in the usual form appropriate where transferees hold the land as trustees of land as prescribed by The Land Registration Rules 1925, SR & O 1925/1093 r 213 as substituted by SI 1996/2975, Sch 2 Form 62 as substituted by SI 1989/801 and amended by SI 1996/2975. Application for this restriction in the transfer is optional because the survivor of the transferees, as trustees of land, are unable to give a valid receipt for capital money and the Registrar is, therefore, obliged to enter the restriction in any event: see the Land Registration Act 1925 s 58(3). It may, however, be convenient

to include the application where further restrictions are sought (see note 4 below) and to provide a reminder to the transferees of the limitation imposed on their holding of the land. As to the restriction generally see vol 35 (1997 Reissue) SALE OF LAND Paragraph 983.1 [1287]. As the transaction, following which the declaration is made, is a recent acquisition on sale, the Land Registration Act 1925 ss 123 and 123A as substituted and inserted by the Land Registration Act 1997 will apply to require that an application be made for first registration of the land by the trustee. For appropriate forms of transfer and conveyance see vol 37 (2001 Reissue) SALE OF LAND Forms 182 [1351]–186 [1362].

    Whether the property before its transfer to the trustee was previously registered or unregistered, the interest of the real buyer should be protected on the register by entry of the trustee restriction contained in SR & O 1925/1093 r 213 (as substituted by SI 1996/2975 and amended by SI 1997/3037) where application is made by the trustee, or SR & O 1925/1093 r 236 (as substituted by SI 1996/2975) where application is made by the beneficiary. In both cases the form used is set out in SR & O 1925/1093, Sch 2 Form 62 (as substituted by SI 1989/801 and amended by SI 1996/2975). This may be supplemented with a restriction prohibiting a disposition of the land without the real buyer's consent.

4   This restriction will be appropriate where the separate trust deed imposes an express limitation on the trustees' power of disposition, eg where the deed requires the consent of a beneficiary to any disposition or prohibits dispositions until a certain event, such as an occupying beneficiary attaining the age of majority, so that the trustees are under a duty to apply for entry on the register of this prescribed form of restriction: see SR & O 1925/1093 rr 59A, 106A both as inserted by SI 1996/2975, Sch 2 Form 11A as inserted by SI 1996/2975.

[1310]

45(2) Trust deed[1]

THIS SETTLEMENT is made the ...... day of ....

BETWEEN:

(1)   *(settlor)* of *(address)* ('the Settlor') and
(2)   *(trustees)* of *(addresses)* ('the Trustees')

WHEREAS

This settlement is supplemental to a transfer ('the Transfer') of even date but executed before this deed by which the property known as *(describe property)* ('the Property') was transferred to the Trustees in fee simple on trust for sale with the consent of the Settlor during his life and afterwards at their discretion with power to postpone the sale as mentioned in the Transfer and to hold the net proceeds of sale on the trusts to be declared by a settlement of the same date and between the same parties in the same order as the Transfer

[1311]

NOW THIS DEED WITNESSES as follows:

1   Trust for sale

The Trustees shall hold the Property on trust for sale with power to postpone sale and the net rents and profits until sale and shall hold the net proceeds of sale on trust and shall invest the same when received in any investments authorised by this settlement and shall hold the proceeds and investments and any other property later directed or otherwise transferred to the Trustees to be held on the trusts of this settlement and all property for the time being representing the same ('the Trust Fund') on the following trusts and shall apply the income (income including any rents due and unpaid at the date of this settlement) of the Property until sale as though it were income of the Trust Fund
(set out required beneficial interests, administrative provisions etc)

IN WITNESS etc

(signatures of the parties)[2]
(signatures of witnesses)
[1312]

1   As to stamp duty see Information Binder: Stamp Duties [1] (Declaration of trust). See also Introduction
     to this section [1281] ante and Introduction to Section A [1161] ante. One option is for the settlor to
     create a protective trust. For examples of protective trusts see vol 40(2) (2001 Reissue) TRUSTS AND
     SETTLEMENTS Part 12 [6901]. For the inheritance tax advantages of protective trusts see the
     Inheritance Tax Act 1984 s 88 (42–44 Halsbury's Statutes (4th Edn) TAXATION) and vol 40(2) (2001
     Reissue) TRUSTS AND SETTLEMENTS Part 12 [6901]. As an alternative, a discretionary trust can be
     created adopting the appropriate provisions in Form 4 [1081] ante. Although the latter will be taxed as
     a settlement with no interest in possession, it has the advantage that the trustees have complete control
     of any income from the outset, whilst with a protective trust the principal beneficiary has the right to
     income until his interest is forfeited. A further possibility would be a revocable life interest for the
     principal beneficiary: eg see Form 5 [1107] ante.
2   As to the statutory requirements for valid execution of a deed see vol 12 (1994 Reissue) DEEDS,
     AGREEMENTS AND DECLARATIONS.

[1313]

46

Statutory declaration of solvency prior to making a voluntary settlement of assets—incorporating certificate by accountants[1]

I *(settlor)* of *(address)* do solemnly and sincerely declare as follows:

I have examined my financial situation as at *(date of execution of the settlement)* by reference to my aggregate assets and liabilities and have formed the opinion that:

1   I am now able to pay my debts as they fall due and the amount of my assets is
     not less than the amount of my liabilities, taking into account my contingent
     and prospective liabilities and

2   In consequence of the execution of the settlement I will not be unable to pay
     my debts as they fall due and the value of my assets will not be less than the
     amount of my liabilities, taking into account my contingent and prospective
     liabilities

AND I make this solemn declaration etc[2]

[1314]

ACCOUNTANTS REPORT

We *(chartered accountants)* of *(address)* have inquired into the financial situation of *(settlor)* and we are not aware of anything to indicate that the opinion expressed by *(settlor)* in his declaration dated *(date)* to which this is attached as to the matters mentioned in it is unreasonable in all the circumstances

Dated: *(date)*

(signature of the accountants)

1   As to commissioner's fees see Information Binder: Fees [1]. Solvency immediately before and after
     making an undervalue transaction is important (once two years have elapsed from the making of the
     settlement) in preventing the setting aside of that settlement: see the Insolvency Act 1986 ss 339,
     341(1)–(3) (4 Halsbury's Statutes (4th Edn) BANKRUPTCY AND INSOLVENCY) and Paragraph 90
     [216] ante. In practice it is highly unusual for a settlor to enter into such a declaration.
2   For the formal parts of a statutory declaration see vol 12 (1994 Reissue) DEEDS, AGREEMENTS AND
     DECLARATIONS.

[1315]–[1380]

PART 5: GENERAL CLAUSES FOR USE IN SETTLEMENTS

Forms and Precedents

A: PARTIES

1: INTRODUCTION

Common misconceptions

There are a surprising number of misconceptions concerning the standard opening words used in trust deeds: for instance:

1   It is not necessary for the trustees to be parties to the deed of settlement. The main advantage of including them is that by executing the deed they will accept the trusteeship (and so cannot disclaim)[1] and they will be familiar with the terms of the trust.

2   Full names and addresses are for identification purposes only and do not affect the validity of the settlement.

3   Although it is desirable for a date to be inserted its absence will not affect validity. Of course a trust only comes into effect (whatever date may be inserted) when the trustees are holding property in accordance with its terms. It is common practice to establish a 'pilot' settlement for (say) £10 to which the property is subsequently added. It should be remembered that until the £10 has been received by the trustees no trusts will come into existence (which may be of importance: eg for inheritance tax purposes).

4   Offshore trusts frequently involve a protector[2]. As with trustees he may be (although he does not have to be) a party to the settlement deed.

Modern trust drafting tends to define terms by the use of brackets and quotation marks. Defined terms will have a capital letter (eg 'the Property') which should be used throughout the settlement when the defined term is intended. The use of words such as 'hereinafter referred to as "the Original Trustees"' has fallen out of fashion.

---

1   As to disclaimer of trusts see vol 40(2) (2001 Reissue) TRUSTS AND SETTLEMENTS Part 10 [5201].
2   As to the use of a protector and for a Jersey trust incorporating a protector see vol 40(2) (2001 Reissue) TRUSTS AND SETTLEMENTS Part 15 [8701].

2: FORMS

47

Parties consisting of a settlor and trustees

THIS SETTLEMENT is made the ...... day of ....

BETWEEN:

(1) *(settlor)* of *(address)* ('the Settlor') and

(2) *(original trustees)* of *(addresses)* ('the Original Trustees')

[1382]

48

Parties consisting of a settlor and trustees—the settlor being one of the trustees[1]

THIS SETTLEMENT is made the ...... day of ....

BETWEEN:

(1) *(settlor)* of *(address)* ('the Settlor') and

(2) The Settlor and *(other original trustee)* of *(address)* ('the Original Trustees')

1 This wording is for use where one party is involved in two capacities: in this case the settlor is also one of the trustees. It is only necessary for the settlor to execute the deed once; he does not need to sign twice, once for each capacity.

[1383]

49

Parties consisting of joint settlors and trustees[1]

THIS SETTLEMENT is made the ...... day of ....

BETWEEN:

(1) *(settlor)* of *(address)* and *(settlor)* of *(address)* ('the Settlors') and

(2) *(original trustees)* of *(addresses)* ('the Original Trustees')

1 This wording is for use where there are joint settlors. A person may also become a settlor by adding property to an existing settlement, albeit that he was not a party to the original deed.

[1384]

50
Declaration of trust by trustee—the identity of the settlor not being disclosed[1]

THIS DECLARATION OF TRUST is made the ...... day of .... by *(trustee)* of *(address)* ('the Original Trustee')

1   This wording is for use where property is transferred to the trustee who then declares the trusts. Accordingly, the settlor does not appear as a party and will not be named in the deed: see, for example, the Jersey trust precedent in vol 40(2) (2001 Reissue) TRUSTS AND SETTLEMENTS Part 15 [8701].

[1385]

B: RECITALS

1: INTRODUCTION

The purpose of recitals

Recitals do not have legal effect and are inserted before the operative part of the deed to explain the background and purpose: for example in the context of the Trusts of Land and Appointment of Trustees Act 1996, a recital that it is not the purpose of the settlement that any land subject to its trust should be occupied as a residence by a beneficiary[1]. In the light of the Trustee Act 2000 a recital may be included to the effect that the settlement has been established for the express purpose of holding shares in the family company[2]. In the case of a non-UK domiciled settlor, a recital may be included indicating where he is domiciled. In the past, recitals along the lines of 'the settlor out of natural love and affection wishes to make provision for his family' were common; these add nothing and should be omitted.

1   For a recital for inclusion in a settlement as to the purposes of the settlement, having regard to the beneficiary's right to occupy under the Trusts of Land and Appointment of Trustees Act 1996 s 12(1) (37 Halsbury's Statutes (4th Edn) REAL PROPERTY), see vol 40(2) (2001 Reissue) TRUSTS AND SETTLEMENTS Part 8 [3501].
2   See Form 146 [1574] post.

[1386]

2: FORMS

51
Title to a settlement[1]

This settlement shall be known as '......... Settlement'

1   Whilst there is no requirement to include a recital of title it is useful for reference purposes. The Inland Revenue commonly gives a name to any trust or settlement and in the case of a settlor who creates a number of settlements it is helpful to distinguish them: eg 'John Smith's 1997 Discretionary Trust', 'John Smith's 1998 Discretionary Trust' etc. If a number of settlements are to be created in a single year they can be titled 'John Smith No 1 Discretionary Trust' etc.

[1387]

52

Principal beneficiaries[1]

The {Settlor} has the following children namely:

(0.1)   *(child)* born on *(date)*

(0.2)   *(child)* born on *(date)* and

(0.3)   *(child)* born on *(date)*

1   When this clause is inserted in a document the defined terms in { } must be altered to suit those used in the document.

[1388]

53

Irrevocability of settlement[1]

This settlement shall be irrevocable

1   Although not necessary as the courts consider a settlement to be irrevocable unless the contrary is provided for, this recital may be thought advantageous in stressing to the settlor the irreversible nature of what he is doing in setting up the trust. Revocable settlements are today a rarity, largely because of the tax regime (although see *Melville v IRC* [2000] STC 628).

[1389]

54

Consent of trustees[1]

The {Original Trustees} have consented to act as the trustees of this settlement

1   This recital is superfluous given that the trustees have executed the deed. When this clause is inserted in a document the defined terms in { } should be altered to suit those used in the document.

[1390]

55

Intended marriage[1]

A marriage ('the Marriage') is intended to be solemnised between the {Husband} and the {Wife}

1   As to marriage settlements generally see Paragraph 128 [318] et seq ante. For a form of marriage settlement see Form 7 [1136] ante. When this clause is inserted in a document the defined terms in { } must be altered to suit those used in the document.

[1391]

56

Settlement pursuant to marriage articles[1]

The {Husband} and {Wife} ('the Spouses') were married on *(date)* and by articles made before and in contemplation of the marriage ('the Marriage') it was agreed that such settlement should be made as appears below

1   As to marriage settlements generally see Paragraph 128 [318] et seq ante. For a form of marriage settlement see Form 7 [1136] ante. When this clause is inserted in a document the defined terms in { } must be altered to suit those used in the document.

[1392]

57

Effect of settlement and disentailing deed of freehold property[1]

Under or by virtue of a settlement ('the Settlement') created by *(give particulars of instruments, date and parties etc)* and a disentailing deed dated *(date)* and made between *(parties)* and certain appointments and other deeds acts and events the freehold property by this deed settled now stands limited to [the father *or (other tenant for life)*] in fee simple subject [to the charges and incumbrances mentioned below and] to the estates and charges prior to and the powers overreaching the estate tail of the said *(name)* discharged from all estates tail [male or in tail] upon such trusts and subject to such powers as [the father and the son *or (other tenant for life and tenant in tail)*] should by deed jointly appoint and in default of such appointment upon trust for [the father] during [his] life without impeachment of waste in restoration of [his] life interest under the Settlement and with the powers annexed to it and subject to it upon the trusts mentioned in the same

1   The Trusts of Land and Appointment of Trustees Act 1996 (37 Halsbury's Statutes (4th Edn) REAL PROPERTY) provides that no new settlement under the Settled Land Act 1925 (48 Halsbury's Statutes (4th Edn) TRUSTS AND SETTLEMENTS) can be created, or will be deemed to arise: Trusts of Land and Appointment of Trustees Act 1996 s 2(1). This recital would, however, be relevant in the event of a resettlement of settled land.
     As to disentailing assurances see Paragraph 277 [691] et seq ante and for forms of disentailing assurance see Form 300 [2101] et seq post.

[1393]

58

Dealings with settled property[1]

0.1   Since the date of the {Settlement} various sales and exchanges of [and other dealings with] parts of the freehold and leasehold estates and property originally comprised in or which have since become subject to the trusts of the {Settlement} have from time to time taken place under powers contained in the {Settlement} or conferred by statute and certain capital money has arisen under such sales exchanges or dealings and various purchases have from time to time been made out of such capital money [and parts of such capital money have been applied in improvements authorised by the {Settlement} or by statute]

0.2   The land and property [remaining undisposed of at the date of this deed *or* which was immediately before the execution of the disentailing deed mentioned above subject to the {Settlement}] is specified in the schedule and such capital money then remaining unapplied or undisposed of is represented by the stocks funds and securities and cash at *(name)* Bank now standing in the names of *(name)* and *(name)* the present trustees of the {Settlement} as the same are specified in the schedule

1   The Trusts of Land and Appointment of Trustees Act 1996 (37 Halsbury's Statutes (4th Edn) REAL PROPERTY) provides that no new settlement under the Settled Land Act 1925 (48 Halsbury's Statutes (4th Edn) TRUSTS AND SETTLEMENTS) can be created, or will be deemed to arise: Trusts of Land and Appointment of Trustees Act 1996 s 2(1). This recital would, however, be appropriate on a resettlement of settled land.

   When this clause is inserted in a document the defined terms in { } must be altered to suit those used in the document.

[1394]

59
Disentailing assurance[1]

By a disentailing assurance dated *(date)* and made between *(parties)* the settled land [and capital money and investments representing the same] was assured by the [{Tenant for Life} and] {Tenant in Tail} to the {Trustees} in fee simple or absolutely subject to the incumbrances mentioned below and to the estates and powers prior to and overreaching the estate [tail *or* in tail male] of the {Tenant for Life} [other than the estate or interest of the {Tenant for Life} but] discharged from all estates [tail *or* in tail male] or entailed interests in equity of the {Tenant in Tail} and all estates rights interests and powers to take effect after the determination or in defeasance of such estates [tail *or* in tail male] or entailed interests [upon trust for the {Tenant in Tail} absolutely *or* upon such trusts and subject to such powers and provisions as the {Tenant for Life} and {Tenant in Tail} should thereafter by deed revocable or irrevocable from time to time jointly appoint and in default of appointment upon trust for the {Tenant for Life} and [his] assigns during [his] life without impeachment of waste in restoration of [his] life interest under the *(settlement as referred to in the previously existing settlement)* with remainder upon the trust mentioned in the same]

1   The parts of this recital in square brackets will generally be suitable where the disentailing assurance is made by a tenant for life and tenant in tail with a view to a resettlement. As to disentailing assurances see Paragraph 277 [691] et seq ante and for forms of disentailing assurance see Form 300 [2101] et seq post.

   When this clause is inserted in a document the defined terms in { } must be altered to suit those used in the document.

[1395]

60
Transfer of property specified in schedule to trustees[1]

The {Settlor} has transferred to the {Original Trustees} the property specified in the [first] schedule to be held subject to the following trusts powers and provisions

1   When this clause is inserted in a document the defined terms in { } must be altered to suit those used in the document.

[1396]

61

Transfer of assets to trustees of personalty settlement for benefit of settlor's children[1]

The {Settlor} wishing to make provision for [his] children *(name)* who was born on *(date)* and *(name)* who was born on *(date)* [and any further children born to the {Settlor} after this settlement] [has transferred *or* is about to transfer][2] into the joint names of the {Original Trustees} the [investments specified in the schedule *or* sum of £... in cash] to be held by the {Trustees} upon the trusts declared below of and concerning the same

1   When this clause is inserted in a document the defined terms in { } must be altered to suit those used in the document.

2   A voluntary settlement is fully constituted when the instrument declaring the trusts has been executed and everything has been done, according to the nature of the property comprised in the settlement, to transfer the property to the trustees: see Paragraph 22 [61] ante. Where such a recital is included and the transfer is not in fact made, the settlement may itself operate as an effective disposition of the equitable interest of the settlor, which the court will enforce as to the legal estate: see *Re Wale, Wale v Harris* [1956] 3 All ER 280, [1956] 1 WLR 1346. As to equitable assignment generally see *Snell's Equity* (30th Edn, 2000) p 81 et seq.

[1397]

62

Conveyance or transfer of even date of freehold to trustees of settlement on trust for benefit of settlor's children[1]

The {Settlor} wishing to make provision for [his] children *(name)* who was born on *(date)* and *(name)* who was born on *(date)* [and any further children born to the {Settlor} after this settlement] has by a [conveyance or transfer] of even date with this settlement [but executed immediately before this settlement] and made between the same parties as are parties to this settlement and in the same order conveyed the freehold property known as *(describe property)* to the {Original Trustees} in fee simple upon the trusts and with and subject to the powers and provisions declared of and concerning the same by the settlement referred to in it (being this settlement)

1   If the land is registered the land will be transferred, rather than conveyed: the creation of a trust is an occasion of first registration. When this clause is inserted in a document the defined terms in { } must be altered to suit those used in the document.

[1398]

63

Title to property and transfer to the trustees of marriage settlement pursuant to agreement where the settled property consists of investments or cash[1]

The {Husband} is absolutely entitled to the property specified in the [first] schedule [and the {Wife} is absolutely entitled to the property specified in the [second] schedule] and on the treaty for the {Marriage} it was agreed that such property should be settled in the manner appearing below and such property has accordingly been transferred to or otherwise vested in the {Trustees}

1   As to marriage settlements generally see Paragraph 128 [318] et seq ante. For a form of marriage settlement see Form 7 [1136] ante. When this clause is inserted in a document the defined terms in { } must be altered to suit those used in the document.

[1399]

64

Settlor's title to share in a testator's residuary estate[1]

The {Settlor} is absolutely entitled[2] to a one [quarter] share of the residuary estate of *(testator)* who died on *(date)* and whose will dated *(date)* was on *(date)* proved by *(executors)* in the [Principal Registry of the Family Division of the High Court *or (name)* District Probate Registry]

1   When this clause is inserted in a document the defined terms in { } should be altered to suit those used in the document.

2   Where the interest is reversionary the words 'subject to the prior life interests of *(name)* and *(name)* therein', or as the case may require, should be inserted. For the capital gains tax implications of assigning such property to trustees see Paragraph 340 [905] ante.

[1400]–[1410]

C: TESTATUM

65

Testatum[1]

NOW THIS DEED WITNESSES as follows:

1   The testatum leads on to the operative body of the deed: arguably it serves no useful purpose. 'Witnesseth', although used in the 1925 property legislation, should not be used. Some draftsmen use the heading 'Operative Part'.

[1411]

D: COMMON BENEFICIAL TRUSTS

1: INTRODUCTION

Scope of this section

This section provides common form trusts over income both in the form of fixed and discretionary trusts. In addition to the forms in this section, reference should be made to:

1   Form 5 [1107] ante which creates a life interest trust with overriding powers (so that life interest is revocable);

2   Form 7 [1136] ante which creates a marriage settlement with successive life interests for husband and wife (whilst the wife remains a widow);

3   Vol 40(2) (2001 Reissue) TRUSTS AND SETTLEMENTS Part 16 [9301] for a disabled trust designed to satisfy the inheritance tax requirements in the Inheritance Tax Act 1984 s 89 as amended;

4   Vol 40(2) (2001 Reissue) TRUSTS AND SETTLEMENTS Part 11 [6501] for trusts for the benefit of minors including accumulation and maintenance trusts;

5   Vol 40(2) (2001 Reissue) TRUSTS AND SETTLEMENTS Part 12 [6901] for protective trusts.

There are also forms for use when disposing of both income and capital and these include a selection of default trusts: see Forms 94 [1470]–97 [1473] post and Form 85 [1450] post (accruer clause).

It is rare nowadays for an annuity interest to be created: for a consideration of such interests see vol 42(1) (1998 Reissue) WILLS AND ADMINISTRATION Form 170 [1181] et seq.

[1412]

2: TRUSTS OF INCOME

66

Income of fund—successive life interest for husband and wife

The {Trustees} shall pay the income of the {Trust Fund} ('the Husband's Fund') to the {Husband} during his life[1] and after his death shall [hold the same upon protective trusts[2] for the benefit of the {Wife} during her life *or* pay or apply the same to or for the benefit of the {Wife} during her life]

[1413]

1   If the property is settled by someone other than the husband, a protective trust for the benefit of the husband may be declared as the first trust of the husband's fund. As to the effect of bankruptcy on the life interest of a settlor see Paragraph 123 [305] ante. In the event that the husband wishes to give up his life interest inter vivos, a surrender is not appropriate; it is necessary to assign the benefit of the life interest in trust to the wife who will then hold an estate pur autre vie. In this event, no capital gains tax uplift is available on the death of the autre vie. An alternative would be to delete 'after his death' inserting instead 'subject thereto'. This would then enable the husband's life interest to be surrendered. On the termination of the husband's life interest, the inheritance tax exemption for inter-spouse transfers is available: Inheritance Tax Act 1984 s 18 (42–44 Halsbury's Statutes (4th Edn) TAXATION).

When this clause is inserted in a document the defined terms in { } must be altered to suit those used in the document.

2   As to statutory protective trusts generally see Paragraph 123 [305] ante and vol 40(2) (2001 Reissue) TRUSTS AND SETTLEMENTS Part 12 [6901].

[1414]

67

Income of fund—annuity to one spouse, balance to other spouse during joint lives and provision on first death

The {Trustees} shall hold the income of the {Trust Fund} upon trust during the joint lives of the {Husband} and {Wife} to pay out of it an annuity of £... to the {Wife} [such annuity to be deemed to accrue from day to day][1] and to commence from the date of this deed and to be payable by equal quarterly instalments [on the usual quarter days in each year] and subject to this shall pay the income to the {Husband} during his life and after his death shall [hold the income of the {Trust Fund} upon protective trusts[2] for the benefit of the {Wife} during her life *or* pay or apply the same to or for the benefit of the {Wife} during her life]

[1415]

1   All annuities are to be considered as accruing from day to day and are apportionable in respect of time in the absence of an express stipulation that no apportionment is to take place: Apportionment Act 1870 ss 2, 7 as amended by the SLR (No 2) Act 1893 (23 Halsbury's Statutes (4th Edn) LANDLORD AND TENANT). When this clause is inserted in a document the defined terms in { } must be altered to suit those used in the document.

2   As to statutory protective trusts generally see Paragraph 123 [305] ante and vol 40(2) (2001 Reissue) TRUSTS AND SETTLEMENTS Part 12 [6901].

[1416]

68

Division of trust fund into two equal parts—life interest with power to appoint interest to spouse—referential trusts of second share[1]

The {Trustees} shall divide the {Trust Fund} into 2 equal half-shares or moieties and shall stand possessed of the same and the income upon the following trusts and with and subject to the following powers and provisions:

0.1   as regards one such half-share or moiety of the {Trust Fund}:

     0.1.1   the Trustees shall pay the income of such moiety of the {Trust Fund} to *(first beneficiary)* during [his] life

     0.1.2   *(first beneficiary)* shall have power to appoint by any deed or deeds revocable or irrevocable executed before the expiry of the {Trust Period} or by will or codicil taking effect (due to the death of *(first beneficiary)*) before the expiry of the {Trust Period} to or for the benefit of [his] [widow] in the event of [his] dying before the expiry of the {Trust Period} an interest for the life of such [widow] or any less period in the whole or any part of the income of such moiety of the {Trust Fund} and such appointment may (due regard being had to the law concerning remoteness) be made upon protective trusts or otherwise for the benefit of such [widow] and subject to any conditions which *(first beneficiary)* may think proper

[1417]

     0.1.3   the {Trustees} (being at least 2 in number or a trust corporation) may at any time or times during the lifetime of *(first beneficiary)* and before the expiry of the {Trust Period} as to the whole or any part of such moiety of the {Trust Fund} to the income of which *(first beneficiary)* is for the time being entitled under the trust contained in sub-clause [0.1.1] transfer or pay the same to or for the absolute use and benefit of *(first beneficiary)* or raise and apply the same for the advancement or otherwise for the benefit of *(first beneficiary)* in such manner in all respects as the {Trustees} shall in their absolute discretion think fit PROVIDED that the {Trustees} (being at least 2 in number or a trust corporation) may at any time or times before the expiry of the {Trust Period} by deed or deeds extinguish (or restrict the future exercise of) this power

     0.1.4   from and after the death of *(first beneficiary)* such moiety of the {Trust Fund} (or so much of the same as shall not have been paid transferred or applied in sub-clause [0.1.3] or any statutory power applicable) and the income from it shall (subject to sub-clause [0.1.2]) be held upon the trusts and with and subject to the powers and provisions declared and contained in this deed concerning the {Trust Fund}

0.2   the {Trustees} shall stand possessed of the remaining half-share or moiety of the {Trust Fund} upon the like trusts and with and subject to the like powers and provisions in favour of *(second beneficiary)* as are in clause **[**0.1**]** declared and contained concerning the first moiety of the {Trust Fund} as if such trusts powers and provisions were herein repeated with the substitution of the name of *(second beneficiary)* for that of *(first beneficiary)* and any necessary consequential alterations

1   Note the wording of clause 0.2 above which incorporates the same trusts for the benefit of a second beneficiary. When establishing separate parts of a trust fund it will be desirable for the trustees to have an express power of appropriation (and perhaps of reappropriation): see generally Paragraph 74 [170] ante. When this clause is inserted in a document the defined terms in { } must be altered to suit those used in the document.

[1418]

69

Proviso cutting down surviving spouse's life interest in income on remarriage[1]

PROVIDED always that if after the death of the {Settlor} **[**his**]** surviving spouse shall remarry **[**and if there shall be any issue of the {Settlor} and **[**his**]** spouse living at the date of such remarriage**]** then as from the date of such remarriage the {Trustees} shall hold the income of one half only of the {Trust Fund} **[**on protective trusts for the benefit of the surviving spouse during **[**her**]** life *or* to pay or apply the same to or for the benefit of the surviving spouse during **[**her**]** life**]** and shall hold the other half of the {Trust Fund} and the income of it upon trusts for *(beneficiary)*

[1419]

1   Draftsmen are sometimes asked to insert a proviso terminating the interest in the event of subsequent cohabitation by the surviving spouse. Defining 'cohabitation' with any degree of precision is far from easy and it is therefore suggested that a revocable life interest supplemented by a detailed letter of wishes to the trustees is more satisfactory. For a statutory definition of cohabitation see the Inheritance (Provision for Family and Dependants) Act 1975 s 1(1A) as inserted by the Law Reform (Succession) Act 1995 s 2(3) (17 Halsbury's Statutes (4th Edn) EXECUTORS AND ADMINISTRATORS). The termination of a spouse's life interest (in part) will normally be a potentially exempt transfer for inheritance tax purposes and will not lead to any capital gains tax liability.

    When this clause is inserted in a document the defined terms in { } must be altered to suit those used in the document.

[1420]

70

Overriding power of appointment in favour of a surviving spouse[1]

PROVIDED always that *(beneficiary)* shall have power by any deed revocable or irrevocable or by will or codicil to appoint to any **[**husband *or* wife**]** who may survive **[**him *or* her**]** for the residue of **[**his *or* her**]** life or for any less period the whole or any part of the income of the {Trust Fund} and after the death of *(beneficiary)* the trusts declared above of and concerning the {Trust Fund} shall take effect subject to any such appointment

1   This clause is intended for use in circumstances in which it is considered that the surviving spouse may have insufficient means. To the extent that this power is exercised, the inheritance tax exemption for inter-spouse gifts will apply on the death of the beneficiary and this will usually provide a good reason for the power to be exercised since (a) it will avoid inheritance tax on the death of the appointer, and (b) even if the surviving spouse has no need of the income the appointment may be revocable and when revoked will result in the survivor making a potentially exempt transfer for inheritance tax purposes.

This clause provides for considerable flexibility: all or part of the income can be appointed and the appointment may be for a limited period or may determine (eg on remarriage).

When this clause is inserted in a document the defined terms in { } must be altered to suit those used in the document.

[1421]

71

Life interest in income in personalty settlement[1]

The {Trustees} shall hold the income of the {Trust Fund} upon trust to pay the same to *(beneficiary)* during [his] life

1   When this clause is inserted in a document the defined terms in { } must be altered to suit those used in the document.

[1422]

72

Successive protective life interests[1]

The {Trustees} shall hold the income of the {Trust Fund} upon protective trusts for the benefit of *(first beneficiary)* during [his *or* her] life and after [his *or* her] death [upon protective trusts for the benefit of *(second beneficiary)* during the remainder of [his *or* her] life *or* shall pay the same to *(second beneficiary)* during the remainder of [his *or* her] life]

1   As to statutory protective trusts generally see Paragraph 123 [305] ante and vol 40(2) (2001 Reissue) TRUSTS AND SETTLEMENTS Part 12 [6901]. When this clause is inserted in a document the defined terms in { } must be altered to suit those used in the document.

[1423]

73

Protective life interest—no forfeiture if prior consent of trustees[1]

As to income upon protective trusts for the benefit of the {Settlor} during [his] life PROVIDED always that the primary trust of the income for the {Beneficiary} shall not be determined by or in consequence of [him] doing or suffering any act or thing done or suffered with the previous consent in writing of the {Trustees} and PROVIDED ALSO that if any act or event shall cause the determination during [his] lifetime of the said trusts in [his] favour the {Trustees} shall not be responsible for continuing to pay income to the {Beneficiary} unless and until they have notice of it

[1424]

1   As to statutory protective trusts generally see Paragraph 123 [305] ante and vol 40(2) (2001 Reissue) TRUSTS AND SETTLEMENTS Part 12 [6901]. When this clause is inserted in a document the defined terms in { } must be altered to suit those used in the document.

[1425]

74

Protective trusts of income in marriage settlement[1]

As to such of the above income as shall accrue after the {Marriage} upon protective trusts for the benefit of the {Husband} during [his] life

1   As to statutory protective trusts generally see Paragraph 123 [305] ante and vol 40(2) (2001 Reissue) TRUSTS AND SETTLEMENTS Part 12 [6901]. When this clause is inserted in a document the defined terms in { } must be altered to suit those used in the document.

[1426]

75

Protective trusts of income in settlement other than on marriage[1]

The {Trustees} shall hold the income of the {Trust Fund} upon protective trusts for the benefit of *(beneficiary)* during [his] life

1   This clause incorporates the statutory protective trusts set out in the Trustee Act 1925 s 33 as amended by the Family Law Reform Act 1987 s 38(1), Sch 2 para 2, Sch 3 para 1 (48 Halsbury's Statutes (4th Edn) TRUSTS AND SETTLEMENTS): as to these trusts see Paragraph 123 [305] ante and vol 40(2) (2001 Reissue) TRUSTS AND SETTLEMENTS Part 12 [6901]. When this clause is inserted in a document the defined terms in { } must be altered to suit those used in the document.

[1427]

76

Protective trusts with power for trustees to enlarge interest into absolute life interest[1]

The income of the [{Wife's Fund} *or* {Trust Fund} *or* appointed share] shall be held upon protective trusts for the benefit of [the {Wife} *or* *(beneficiary)*] during [her *or* his] life PROVIDED always that the {Trustees} may at any time or times by any deed appoint that the protective trusts shall immediately be terminated with regard either to the whole or to any part of the income of the [{Wife's Fund} *or* {Trust Fund} *or* appointed share] and that the income shall afterwards be paid or applied to or for the benefit of [the {Wife} *or* *(beneficiary)*] during [her *or* his] life

[1428]

1   This clause is intended to obviate the disadvantage of a protective trust which results from the fact that the tenant for life cannot dispose of his interest or part of it without bringing the statutory discretionary trusts into operation. If exercised the power will not lead to any capital gains tax or inheritance tax charges. As to statutory protective trusts generally see Paragraph 123 [305] ante and vol 40(2) (2001 Reissue) TRUSTS AND SETTLEMENTS Part 12 [6901].

     When this clause is inserted in a document the defined terms in { } must be altered to suit those used in the document.

[1429]

77

Discretionary trusts of income[1]

The {Trustees} shall hold the {Trust Fund} and the income of it upon trust during the lifetime of the {Settlor} (or during the minority of the {Beneficiaries} now living) to receive the income of it and to apply the same as they shall in their absolute and uncontrolled discretion determine for the maintenance and benefit of any one or more of the {Beneficiaries} for the time being under the age of 18 years and so that the {Trustees} shall have an absolute and uncontrolled discretion as to how much (if any at all) of such income they will apply for the maintenance or benefit of any of the {Beneficiaries} but so that in each year the whole income shall subject to such discretion be applied to or for the maintenance or benefit of the {Beneficiaries} for the time being under the age of 18 years

[1430]

1   For a discretionary settlement see Form 4 [1081] ante and for a discretionary trust of land see vol 40(2) (2001 Reissue) TRUSTS AND SETTLEMENTS Part 8 [3501]. Because the whole of the income has to be paid out each year, the conditions for an accumulation and maintenance trust are not met: see the Inheritance Tax Act 1984 s 71(1)(b) (42–44 Halsbury's Statutes (4th Edn) TAXATION). When this clause is inserted in a document the defined terms in { } must be altered to suit those used in the document.

[1431]

78

Discretionary trusts of income in default of appointment[1]

In default of and subject to any such appointment as stated above the {Trustees} shall during the {Trust Period} pay or apply the income of the {Trust Fund} to or for the maintenance education and support or otherwise for the benefit of all or any one or more exclusively of the others or other of the {Beneficiaries} for the time being living in such shares and manner and upon such conditions as the {Trustees} think fit PROVIDED that:

0.1   the {Trustees} shall have power to pay any such income to the parents guardian or guardians (not being the {Settlor} or any spouse of the {Settlor}) of any Beneficiary of this trust being a minor for the maintenance education or benefit of such minor and shall not themselves be personally bound to see to the application of the same

[1432]

0.2   the {Trustees} may delegate to any persons or corporations in any manner the execution of the trusts contained in this clause and the power conferred in that behalf [2]

0.3   in the execution of the above trusts the {Trustees} may permit any one or more of the {Beneficiaries} from time to time and at any time during the {Trust Period} either alone or together with other or others of the {Beneficiaries} to occupy use or enjoy personally any land or other immovable property and any chattels which (or the proceeds of sale of which) are for the time being subject to the trusts of this settlement rent free or on such terms as to rent and insurance rates and other charges and otherwise as the {Trustees} in their absolute discretion think fit[3]

[0.4   *(specify any other powers required; eg to accumulate income or to effect insurance policies)*][4]

[1433]

1   For a discretionary settlement see Form 4 [1081] ante and for a discretionary trust of land see vol 40(2)
     (2001 Reissue) TRUSTS AND SETTLEMENTS Part 8 [3501]. When this clause is inserted in a document
     the defined terms in { } must be altered to suit those used in the document.
2   It is unusual for the trustees to be given power to delegate the exercise of a dispositive discretion: cf the
     definition of 'delegable functions' in the Trustee Act 2000 s 11 (48 Halsbury's Statutes (4th Edn)
     TRUSTS AND SETTLEMENTS).
3   For the inheritance tax consequences of exercising this power see Paragraph 287.3 [734] ante. The
     statutory power in the Trustee Act 2000 Pt III (ss 8–10) only extends to land in the UK.
4   For a power to accumulate income see Form 150 [1588] post; and for a power to effect insurance
     policies see Form 191 [1684] post.

[1434]–[1440]

3: TRUSTS OF CAPITAL AND TRUSTS OF INCOME AND CAPITAL CLAUSES

79

Final trusts after determination of life interests in a marriage settlement[1]

After the death of the survivor of the {Husband} and {Wife} the {Trustees} shall hold
the {Husband's Fund} and the {Wife's Fund} (together referred to as 'the Trust Fund')
and the future income of such funds on the following trusts:

(specify trusts)

1   When this clause is inserted in a document the defined terms in { } must be altered to suit those used
     in the document.

[1441]

80

Power of appointment among children and issue[1]

Upon trust for all or such one or more of the children or remoter issue of the {Marriage}[2]
such children and remoter issue to take vested interests within [21 years from the death
of the survivor of the {Husband} and {Wife} *or* the period ending 80 years from the date
of the execution of this deed which period shall be the perpetuity period applicable to
this settlement][3] as the {Husband} and {Wife} may by any deed with or without power
of revocation jointly appoint and in default of and subject to any such appointment as
the survivor of them shall by any deed will or codicil appoint

[1442]

1   As to beneficial interests of issue see Paragraph 128 [318] ante. When this clause is inserted in a
     document the defined terms in { } must be altered to suit those used in the document.
2   For the exemption from inheritance tax for inter vivos gifts made in consideration of marriage see the
     Inheritance Tax Act 1984 s 22 (42–44 Halsbury's Statutes (4th Edn) TAXATION).
3   As to the power to specify a perpetuity period not exceeding 80 years see Paragraph 77 [183] ante.

[1443]

81

Trust for children in default of appointment[1]

In default of and subject to any such appointment [and any appointment under any other power contained in this settlement] in trust for all the children or any the child of *(name)* who [being male] shall attain the age of [18] years [or being female shall attain that age] or marry under that age if more than one in equal shares absolutely

1   The settlor should consider making the shares of sons as well as of daughters vest on marriage under the age of 18 years (which can be effected by omitting the words in the second and fourth set of square brackets) for instance if it is considered that there is a possibility of the power not being exercised. It is, however, still more usual to retain the words in these brackets, and the court regards them as 'usual': see *Re Hargraves' Trusts, Leach v Leach* [1937] 2 All ER 545.

[1444]

82

Hotchpot[1]

In default of appointment to the contrary no child shall be entitled to any share of the unappointed part of [the {Trust Fund} *or* the {Settled Property} *or* the property now settled or agreed to be settled] [or any accretions to it] without bringing into hotchpot any share or shares appointed to such child [or his or her issue][2] under [the power stated above *or* any power contained in this settlement] and accounting for the same accordingly

[1445]

1   As to hotchpot clauses see Paragraph 129 [320] ante. When this clause is inserted in a document the defined terms in { } must be altered to suit those used in the document.

2   The words in square brackets will only be required if there is a substituting clause in the original gift in default of appointment.

[1446]

83

Trusts in default of issue—separate funds in a marriage settlement[1]

If no child or remoter issue of the {Marriage} shall attain a vested interest under the trusts contained in this settlement the {Trustees} shall hold the {Trust Fund} and any accretions to it as regards the {Husband's Fund} and any accretions to such fund in trust for the {Husband} absolutely and as regards the {Wife's Fund} and any accretions to such fund in trust for the {Wife} absolutely

1   As to marriage settlements generally see Paragraph 128 [318] et seq ante. For a marriage settlement see Form 7 [1136] ante. When this clause is inserted in a document the defined terms in { } must be altered to suit those used in the document.

[1447]

84

Alternative trusts in default of issue where fund settled for one spouse in a marriage settlement[1]

If no child or remoter issue of the {Marriage} shall attain a vested interest under the trusts contained in this settlement the {Trustees} shall hold the {Trust Fund} and any accretions to it if the {Wife} shall survive the {Husband} for the {Wife} absolutely but if the {Husband} shall survive the {Wife} in trust for such persons or purposes as she shall by will or codicil appoint and in default of and subject to any such appointment in trust for the persons who would have been entitled to the same if the {Wife} had died domiciled in England a widow and intestate[2] and in the same shares and proportions

[1448]

---

1   As to marriage settlements generally see Paragraph 128 [318] et seq ante. For a marriage settlement see Form 7 [1136] ante. When this clause is inserted in a document the defined terms in { } must be altered to suit those used in the document.
2   Under this clause if the wife is a widow with children by a previous marriage they would be entitled to share. Illegitimate children of the wife or their issue will have the same rights as if they were legitimate children: see the Family Law Reform Act 1987 ss 1, 18 (6 Halsbury's Statutes (4th Edn) CHILDREN).

[1449]

85

Accruer of a share of the trust fund, the trusts of which have failed, to other shares

SUBJECT to the trusts declared and contained in clause *(specify)* of this deed if and so far as the share in the {Trust Fund} of a [named beneficiary *or* {Selected Grand-Child}] is not wholly disposed of by such trusts the share (and every additional share accruing by virtue of this provision) shall (subject to all prior trusts whilst subsisting):

0.1   accrue for all purposes to the share or shares (whether presumptive or vested) in the {Trust Fund} of the other [named beneficiaries *or* members of the class of the {Selected Grand-Children}] the trusts of which are then subsisting and if more than one in equal shares per capita and

0.2   be held upon the trusts and with and subject to the powers and provisions contained in this settlement concerning the original share or shares

---

1   When this clause is inserted in a document the defined terms in { } must be altered to suit those used in the document.

[1450]

86

Ultimate trust for the beneficiaries under another settlement by transfer to the trustees of that settlement[1]

Upon failure or determination of the trusts declared above the {Trustees} shall hold the {Trust Fund} or so much of it as shall not have been applied under any of the above trusts upon trust after payment or satisfaction of their costs charges and expenses out of the assets for the time being forming part of the {Trust Fund} to pay or transfer the same or the residue of it to the trustees for the time being of a settlement *(give details)* dated *(date)* and made between *(parties)* to be held by the trustees of such settlement upon the trusts declared in it concerning the trust fund settled by it or upon such of the trusts of the same as are subsisting and capable of taking effect and as one fund therewith for all purposes

[1451]

1   This clause involves the transfer of the fund to other trustees who will hold it as one fund with their own assets. When including an ultimate trust in this form in a marriage settlement, it should be borne in mind that it may well be outside the marriage consideration and therefore that the persons taking under it will be volunteers. Furthermore, the inclusion of this clause may lose the exemption from inheritance tax: see the Inheritance Tax Act 1984 s 22(4) (42–44 Halsbury's Statutes (4th Edn) TAXATION). The perpetuity period applicable to the other settlement should not exceed that applicable to the settlement in which ultimate trusts of this kind are included. For capital gains tax purposes the transfer of the trust fund to another settlement will be a deemed disposal within the Taxation of Chargeable Gains Act 1992 s 71(1) (42–44 Halsbury's Statutes (4th Edn) TAXATION): see further Paragraph 342 [919] ante. For a power to make such a transfer see Form 98 [1474] and for a transfer made pursuant to an express power see Form 288 [1991] post.
      When this clause is inserted in a document the defined terms in { } must be altered to suit those used in the document.

[1452]

87

Contingent trust to individual on obtaining a specific age

The {Trustees} shall hold the {Trust Fund} and the income of it in trust for the {Beneficiary} contingently upon [his] attaining the age of *(specify age)*[1] years [or marrying under that age] and afterwards in trust for the {Beneficiary} absolutely

1   If advantage is to be taken of the accumulation and maintenance regime for inheritance tax purposes either the income or the capital (and income) must vest at an age not exceeding 25 years. Accordingly capital may vest at (say) 30 provided that income vests no later than age 25. In the absence of any indication to the contrary, the beneficiary of a contingent gift will become entitled to the income at 18 years by virtue of the Trustee Act 1925 s 31(1)(ii) as amended by the Family Law Reform Act 1969 s 1(3), Sch 1 Pt I (48 Halsbury's Statutes (4th Edn) TRUSTS AND SETTLEMENTS) thereby satisfying the accumulation and maintenance requirements. For capital gains tax purposes, given the restrictions on hold-over relief, it may be desirable to ensure that the accumulation and maintenance trust ends with a beneficiary becoming absolutely entitled to income and capital at the same time, thereby enabling any gain to be held over: see the Taxation of Chargeable Gains Act 1992 s 260(2)(d) (42–44 Halsbury's Statutes (4th Edn) TAXATION).
      As to accumulation and maintenance trusts generally see Paragraph 127 [316] ante and see vol 40(2) (2001 Reissue) TRUSTS AND SETTLEMENTS Part 11 [6301].
      When this clause is inserted in a document the defined terms in { } must be altered to suit those used in the document.

[1453]

88

Contingent trust to a class

The {Trustees} shall hold the {Trust Fund} and the income of it in trust for such of the {Beneficiaries} now living or to be born after this deed as shall attain the age of *(specify age)*[1] years [or [being female] shall marry under that age] and if more than one in equal shares absolutely

1   In the case of gifts to a class in futuro in which the beneficiaries are unnamed (eg, 'the issue' or 'the beneficiaries') care should in all cases be taken to ensure that the gift is so worded that those persons who are intended to take at that time do in fact take. Under this form, the class taking will close when the first child in it attains the specified age or marries under the rule in *Andrews v Partington* (1790) 2 Cox Eq Cas 223 (ie no person born after the first child to achieve the qualifying condition can take). This rule of construction can be excluded by the use of suitable words: see further Form 89 note 1 [1456] post. In practice the definition clause will normally define beneficiaries so that it does not include any person born after the first beneficiary to do so attains the specified age. Care should also be taken in defining the class if it is desired to include after-born persons. References in a settlement to 'the children of the settlor' prima facie mean the children in being at the date of the settlement. On the other hand references to 'children' of a particular person will, if no child exists, include all after-born children.

        When this clause is inserted in a document the defined terms in { } must be altered to suit those used in the document.

[1454]

89

Contingent trust to a class—rule in *Andrews v Partington* excluded[1]

Subject to and in default of any such appointment the {Trustees} shall stand possessed of the {Trust Fund} and the income of it upon trust for all or any the children or child of *(name)* who shall attain the age of 18 years or marry under that age (whether living or to be born after the first such event to happen)[2] before the day on which shall expire the period of 80 years from the date of this deed (which period will be the perpetuity period applicable to this deed) and if more than one in equal shares absolutely

[1455]

1   Under the rule in *Andrews v Partington* (1790) 2 Cox Eq Cas 223 (see further 50 Halsbury's Laws (4th Edn) para 492), when a class gift is made contingent on the attainment of some specified age or the happening of some event, the class is treated as closed at the time of the attainment of the specified age by the first such child to do so or on the happening of such event and after-born children cannot take. The rule was established in the case of wills, but applies also to settlements, at any rate to voluntary settlements (see *Re Knapp's Settlement, Knapp v Vassall* [1895] 1 Ch 91; *Re Wernher's Settlement Trusts, Lloyds Bank Ltd v Earl Mountbatten* [1961] 1 All ER 184, [1961] 1 WLR 136) and also, it seems, to settlements for value (*Re Knapp's Settlement, Knapp v Vassall* above at 99) although by reason of the previous life interest in the parent, the rule is not normally called into play in relation to a marriage settlement.

        As a rule of construction, it may be excluded expressly and also by implication from the context showing a sufficient contrary intention: see *Re Wernher's Settlement Trusts, Lloyds Bank Ltd v Earl Mountbatten* [1961] 1 All ER 184 at 188, 189, [1961] 1 WLR 136 at 141; *Re Henderson's Trusts, Schreiber v Baring* [1969] 3 All ER 769 at 771, 776, [1969] 1 WLR 651 at 655, 660, CA. In *Re Wernher's Settlement* above, the inclusion of the words 'whether now living or hereafter to be born' in delineating the class of children of the settlor entitled to benefit on attaining a particular age or marrying, was held not to be sufficient to exclude the rule, as the words could equally well refer to children born between the date of the settlement and the date the class closed under the operation of the rule: cf *Re Edmondson's Will Trusts, Baron Sandford of Banbury v Edmondson* [1972] 1 All ER 444, [1972] 1 WLR 183, CA; *Re Tom's Settlement, Rose v Evans* [1987] 1 All ER 1081, [1987] 1 WLR 1021.

        It seems that the surrender or release of a life interest with the intention of accelerating the interests of remaindermen, where under the usual application of the rule the class would close on the determination of the prior life interest, because a beneficiary had during the currency of that life interest attained a vested interest, will not operate to close the class before the death of the life tenant: see *Re Kebty-Fletcher's Will Trusts, Public Trustee v Swan* [1969] 1 Ch 339, [1968] 3 All ER 1076; *Re Harker's Will Trusts, Kean v Harker* [1969] 3 All ER 1, [1969] 1 WLR 1124.

        When this clause is inserted in a document the defined terms in { } must be altered to suit those used in the document.

2   The inclusion of the words in round brackets will allow afterborn children to take.

[1456]–[1460]

90

Contingent trust to a class—vesting within period allowed by perpetuity rules

Subject as stated above the {Trustees} shall hold the capital and income of the {Trust Fund} upon trust for such of the {Beneficiaries} as shall attain the age of *(specify age)*[1] years [or [being female] shall marry under that age] before the [end of the {Trust Period} *or* expiration of the period of 80 years from the date of the execution of this settlement (which period shall be the perpetuity period applicable to this deed)][2] and if more than one in equal shares absolutely

[1461]

1   In this clause the class will close as soon as the first of the beneficiaries attains the specified age or marries see Form 89 note 1 [1456] ante. When this clause is inserted in a document the defined terms in { } must be altered to suit those used in the document.

2   As to the power to specify a perpetuity period not exceeding 80 years see Paragraph 77 [183] ante. In appropriate cases a settlor may wish beneficiaries to take a share even if they have not attained the specified age or married, provided that they are alive at the end of the Trust Period.

[1462]

91

Discretionary trusts (capital and income)—wide form[1]

The {Trustees} shall hold the capital and income of the {Trust Fund} upon such trusts for [all or any one or more to the exclusion of the others or other of the {Beneficiaries} *or (specify)*] at such age or time or respective ages or times if more than one in such shares and with such trusts for their respective benefit and such provisions for their respective advancement maintenance education or benefit and all such other dispositions charges and powers whether contained in or conferred by this settlement or by law of or in relation to the capital and income of the {Trust Fund} or any part of it as an absolute owner beneficially entitled to the same could lawfully make or confer of or in relation to the same as the {Trustees} not being less than 2 in number or a trust corporation[2] may at any time or from time to time before the expiration of the {Trust Period} by any deed with or without power of revocation (without infringing the rule against perpetuities)[3] appoint and in particular and without prejudice to the generality of the above provision the {Trustees} not being less than 2 in number or a trust corporation[4] may by any deed do the following:

[0.1   delegate in any manner and to any extent to any persons or corporations whatsoever or wheresoever resident or situated the exercise at any time within the {Trust Period} of the power of appointment conferred by this clause]

[1463]

0.2   extinguish or otherwise restrict in any way and to any extent the future exercise of all or any of the powers contained in this clause PROVIDED that such extinguishment or restriction shall in no way operate by itself so as to invalidate any past performance or exercise of any of the trusts or powers contained in this settlement [and PROVIDED also that during the lifetime of the {Settlor} the {Trustees} may not exercise the power conferred by this sub-clause without the consent of the {Settlor} in writing]

0.3   provide for the appointment or remuneration of trustees or nominees in any parts of the world upon any terms and conditions

0.4   create any protective discretionary or other trusts and powers to be executed or exercised in favour of any one or more of the {Beneficiaries} by any like persons or corporations

[0.5   transfer or cause to be transferred to any like persons or corporations as the {Trustees} or to the trustees of any other settlement in which any of the {Beneficiaries} may for the time being be entitled to benefit (whether or not persons or objects other than the {Beneficiaries} are also entitled to benefit under them) the capital and income of the {Trust Fund} or any part or parts of it and so that the receipt of any such other trustees shall be a good discharge to the {Trustees}]⁵

PROVIDED that no exercise of any power contained in or conferred by this clause shall operate to make ineffective any prior payment or application of the capital or income of the {Trust Fund} whether made by this deed or by law

[1464]

1   For a discretionary settlement see Form 4 [1081] ante and for a discretionary trust of land see vol 40(2) (2001 Reissue) TRUSTS AND SETTLEMENTS Part 8 [3501]. When this clause is inserted in a document the defined terms in { } must be altered to suit those used in the document.

2   The requirement that there must be either two trustees or a trust corporation is commonly included. If there was to be a single trustee who was also a beneficiary could he appoint the entire property to himself? There are concerns that in such a case the 'self-dealing' rule could be invoked by any beneficiary to have such an appointment set aside (as to whether any such claim would succeed, see Paragraph 209 [497] ante. Of course, the same issue would arise even if the beneficiary-trustee joined in the appointment with a co-trustee. To avoid such concerns it is desirable to include, as a standard form, a provision enabling the trustee to join in an appointment which has the effect of conferring a benefit on him. There is a further question, namely if he failed to make such an appointment, has he omitted to exercise a right for inheritance tax purposes: see the Inheritance Tax Act 1984 s 3(3) (42–44 Halsbury's Statutes (4th Edn) TAXATION)? It is thought not on the basis that the power of appointment is held by him *qua* fiduciary.

3   For the application of the rule against perpetuities to the exercise of special powers of appointment see Paragraph 77 note 3 [184] ante. In general the rule does not extend to invalidate acts outside the period (or which might possibly take place outside it) which appertain solely to the management or administration of the trust property. An order made under the Variation of Trusts Act 1958 (48 Halsbury's Statutes (4th Edn) TRUSTS AND SETTLEMENTS) may be a relevant disposition for the purpose of deciding when the perpetuity period should run and, therefore, it may be possible by applying to the court under that Act to obtain an extension of the time in which any discretion as to the beneficial interests under the trusts might be exercised: *Re Holt's Settlement, Wilson v Holt* [1969] 1 Ch 100, [1968] 1 All ER 470. Cf *Spens v IRC* [1970] 3 All ER 295 at 300, 301, [1970] 1 WLR 1173 at 1183, 1184 (agreement of the beneficiaries varies the trusts and not the order of the court). The perpetuity period for the purposes of the settlement should be separately defined. In this clause it is assumed that the perpetuity period is defined by reference to the 'Trust Period'.

4   See note 2 above.

5   This provision may need to be omitted if it is desired to preserve the limited exemption from inheritance tax of gifts inter vivos in consideration of marriage. In the absence of an express provision of this type, trustees do not have the power to transfer property into another settlement. Note that it is only necessary for any one or more of the beneficiaries to be capable of benefiting under that settlement. A settlor may, of course, require the beneficial class of that other settlement to be *identical*: see also Form 98 [1474] post.

[1465]

92

Discretionary trusts of income and capital in default of appointment[1]

In default of and until and subject to any such appointment as stated above:

0.1   the {Trustees} shall during the {Trust Period} pay or apply the income of the {Trust Fund} to or for the maintenance education or support or otherwise for the benefit of all or any to the exclusion of the others or other of [the {Beneficiaries} *or (name of class intended to benefit)*] for the time being living in such shares and manner as the {Trustees} think fit with power for the {Trustees} to pay any such income to the guardian or guardians (not being the {Settlor} or any wife of the {Settlor}) of any object of this trust being a minor for the maintenance education or benefit of such minor so that the receipt of such parent or parents guardian or guardians shall be a good discharge to the {Trustees}

[1466]

0.2   from and after the expiration of the {Trust Period} the {Trustees} shall hold the capital and income of the {Trust Fund} upon trust for such of the {Beneficiaries} as shall be living at the expiration of the {Trust Period} and if more than one in equal shares but so that if any issue of any of the {Beneficiaries} then deceased are living at the expiration of the {Trust Period} then such issue shall take through all degrees according to their stocks in equal shares if more than one the share which his her or their parents would have taken if living at the expiration of the {Trust Period} and so that no issue shall take whose parent is then living and so capable of taking

0.3   in the event of the total failure or determination of the above trusts and subject to them the {Trustees} shall hold the capital and income of the {Trust Fund} in trust for the {Beneficiaries} in equal shares absolutely

1   For a discretionary settlement see Form 4 [1081] ante and for a discretionary trust of land see vol 40(2) (2001 Reissue) TRUSTS AND SETTLEMENTS Part 8 [3501]. When this clause is inserted in a document the defined terms in { } must be altered to suit those used in the document.

[1467]

93

Trusts to accumulate income and for accumulated income and capital in default of appointment

In default of and subject to any such appointment as stated above the {Trustees} shall stand possessed of the capital and income of the {Trust Fund} upon the following trusts:

0.1   for the period of 21 years from the date of this settlement the {Trustees} shall accumulate the income of the {Trust Fund} at compound interest by investing the same and the resultant income in any of the investments authorised below and shall hold the same as an accretion to the capital of the {Trust Fund} upon the trusts declared below and as one fund with it for all purposes[1]

[1468]

0.2   at the expiration of the period of 21 years or from and after such earlier date as the {Trustees} may at any time (but during the life of the {Settlor} only with [his] written consent in writing) by any deed declare the above trust for accumulation shall cease as regards the whole or any part of the {Trust Fund} and subject as stated above the {Trustees} shall stand possessed of the {Trust Fund} until the {Vesting Day} upon the following trusts namely the {Trustees} shall pay the income or such part of it as shall not have been accumulated under the trusts set out in clause [0.1] within 12 months of the receipt of such income to or for the benefit of all or such one or more to the exclusion of the other or others of the {Beneficiaries} for the time being in existence and in such shares if more than one and in such manner as the {Trustees} shall in their absolute discretion think fit PROVIDED always that the income or any part of it not expressly appropriated under the present power shall be paid to or applied for the benefit of [the {Children} *or* any living {Beneficiary}] or their issue and if more than one in equal shares per stirpes

0.3   on the {Vesting Day} the {Trustees} shall stand possessed of the {Trust Fund} upon trust for the children and remoter issue of the {Settlor} then living if more than one in equal shares per stirpes

0.4   subject as stated above the {Trustees} shall stand possessed of the {Trust Fund} and the income of it upon trust for *(specify person(s))* absolutely

PROVIDED always that no child who or whose issue shall take any part of the capital of the {Trust Fund} under an appointment by virtue of the power contained above shall in default of appointment to the contrary be entitled to any share of the unappointed part of it without bringing the share or shares appointed to him or her or to his or her issue into hotchpot and accounting for the same accordingly[2]

1   During this period the trustees will have no discretion as to the income of the trust fund: it must be accumulated. When this clause is inserted in a document the defined terms in { } must be altered to suit those used in the document.
2   As to hotchpot clauses see Paragraph 129 [320] ante.

[1469]

94

Longstop default trust of capital and income[1]

Subject as stated above the {Trustees} shall stand possessed of the capital and income of the {Trust Fund} for [*(beneficiaries)* in equal shares absolutely]

1   It is important in any settlement for there to be a default clause or longstop provision. Such a clause will take effect if all other beneficiaries die or all other trusts fail for any reason. The beneficiary should be one or more living individuals or a named charity. In the event that the sole named individual has died when property passes under the default clause, it will belong to his estate and pass under his will or intestacy. A clause providing for the trust fund to pass to an individual if he is then living, is not a true default trust since if he were dead at the relevant time a lacuna in the beneficial ownership would arise. If no default clause were included, on failure of the trusts the property would result to the settlor under a resulting trust. Because this takes effect automatically, it cannot be excluded by a provision to the effect that under no circumstances shall the settlor receive any benefit under his settlement. The fact that the settlor could benefit under a resulting trust has adverse tax consequences: see, for example, *Vandervell v IRC* [1967] 2 AC 291, [1967] 1 All ER 1, HL.
      When this clause is inserted in a document the defined terms in { } must be altered to suit those used in the document.

[1470]

95

Ultimate trust on failure of previous trusts[1]

Upon failure or determination of the trusts declared above the {Trustees} shall hold the {Trust Fund} and any accretions to it and the income of it or so much of it as shall not have become absolutely vested or been applied under the above trusts or powers in trust for *(name)* absolutely

1   When this clause is inserted in a document the defined terms in { } must be altered to suit those used in the document.

[1471]

96

Trusts of capital in default of appointment and on failure of beneficiaries[1]

Subject as stated above and in default of any such appointment the {Trustees} shall hold the capital of the {Trust Fund} upon trust for such of the {Beneficiaries} as shall be living on the {Vesting Day} and if more than one in equal shares absolutely and if none of the {Beneficiaries} shall be so living upon trust for *(specify named beneficiaries or class of beneficiaries)*

1   When this clause is inserted in a document the defined terms in { } must be altered to suit those used in the document.

[1472]

97

Trusts to take effect at end of period in which appointment might be exercised

On the {Vesting Day} the {Trustees} shall hold the {Trust Fund} or such part or parts of it as shall not have been paid transferred or applied under any trust or power contained or conferred in this settlement upon trust for such of the {Beneficiaries} as are then living in such shares if more than one as the {Trustees} shall on or before the {Vesting Day} determine and in default of such determination in equal shares

1   When this clause is inserted in a document the defined terms in { } must be altered to suit those used in the document.

[1473]

98

Power to transfer trust fund to another settlement[1]

The {Trustees} shall have power to pay or transfer all or any part of the {Trust Fund} to the trustees of any settlement existing at the date of such payment or transfer under which any one or more of the {Beneficiaries} is beneficially interested and under which neither the {Settlor} nor any spouse of the {Settlor} has any beneficial interest[2] (the receipt of such trustees to afford a good and sufficient discharge to the {Trustees} without themselves being responsible for seeing to the application of the assets so paid or transferred)

[1474]

1   Cf Form 86 [1451] and Form 91 [1463] ante. Care should be taken to ensure that the interests under such other settlement vest within the perpetuity period applicable to the settlement in which this power is inserted. The exercise of this power involves a disposal for capital gains tax purposes if both settlements are discretionary. Hold-over relief is only available if the property transferred comprises 'business assets' and for inheritance tax purposes the property remains comprised in the original settlement: see further Paragraph 341.3 [911] ante. For a transfer of property on to the trusts of a new settlement pursuant to an express power see Form 288 [1991] post.

    When this clause is inserted in a document the defined terms in { } must be altered to suit those used in the document.

2   As to the exclusion of the settlor and any spouse see Paragraph 62 [145] ante and see *IRC v Botnar* [1999] STC 711, CA.

[1475]

99

Discretionary power of variation to provide for spouses etc of beneficiaries[1]

Notwithstanding the trusts stated above the {Trustees} (being at least 2 in number or a trust corporation) may at such time or times as they shall in their absolute discretion think fit within the {Trust Period} by any deed with or without power of revocation vary the provisions contained in this settlement by revoking wholly or partially all or any of such provisions and substituting such new or modified limitations powers charges or provisions whatever concerning the {Trust Fund} and the income of it in favour or for the benefit of all or any one or more exclusively of *(beneficiaries including a reference to their children or other issue if appropriate)* and their respective wives and husbands and widows and widowers (whether or not for the time being remarried or until remarriage) of them as they may think fit without infringing the rule against perpetuities[2] and so that the {Trustees} shall have power to create protective or discretionary trusts or powers operative or exercisable at the discretion of any persons or corporations and generally to make or confer in favour or for the benefit of all or any of the above objects all such dispositions charges or powers of or in relation to the {Trust Fund} or the income of it or any part or parts of it as they could lawfully make or confer of or in relation to any property belonging to them absolutely and beneficially without infringing the rule against perpetuities and PROVIDED:

0.1   that the above powers shall not extend to any accumulations made pursuant to the statutory power of accumulation or in respect of any part of them that may then have been paid or applied under any other provision of this settlement and

0.2   that the {Trustees} may in their like discretion at any time or times by deed or deeds wholly or partially release or extinguish the above power or enter into any contract restricting their right to exercise the same

[1476]

1   This will be the equivalent of a special power of appointment and the exercise of such a power must comply with the rules (eg the perpetuity rules) applicable to special powers. The power should always be limited to conferring a benefit on a specified class of persons. If it is not so limited it may be treated as a general power. In the case of discretionary trusts it is common to give trustees power to add to (and remove from) the class of beneficiaries: see Form 4 clause 6 [1087] ante.

    When this clause is inserted in a document the defined terms in { } must be altered to suit those used in the document.

2   Any interests created under any power of appointment must vest within the perpetuity period applicable to the settlement.

[1477]

100

Power to resettle trust fund for benefit of beneficiaries[1]

The {Trustees} shall have power at any time or times [during the {Trust Period} *or* before the expiration of 80 years from the execution of this deed which period shall be the perpetuity period applicable to this settlement] by any deed revocable or irrevocable to resettle for the benefit of such one or more of the {Beneficiaries} such parts of the capital of the {Trust Fund} and the income of it and on such trusts together with such (if any) conditions limitations provisions for maintenance education advancement or benefit protective and discretionary trusts powers of appointment and other powers to be carried out or exercised at the discretion of the {Trustees} or any other person or persons (except the {Settlor} or any spouse of the {Settlor})[2] as the {Trustees} may in their absolute discretion think fit

---

1   For a discretionary power of variation to provide for spouses etc of beneficiaries see Form 99 [1476] ante. When this clause is inserted in a document the defined terms in { } must be altered to suit those used in the document.
2   As to the exclusion of the settlor and any spouse see Paragraph 62 [145] ante.

[1478]–[1486]

E: TRUSTS OF INSURANCE POLICIES

1: INTRODUCTION

Scope of this section

A complete insurance policy settlement is included in this title: see Form 108 [1502] post. For a complete life insurance settlement see Form 6 [1120] ante. For an express power enabling the trustees to effect life insurance see Form 4 schedule paragraph 19 [1099] ante and Form 191 [1684] post. For an assignment of life policy see Form 33 [1283] ante and for a notice of assignment see Form 298 [2084] post.

In some of the following clauses it is envisaged that the policy forms part of a marriage settlement; suitable amendments will be necessary if such a clause is to be used in other contexts. When the policy is taken out on the life of the interest in possession beneficiary (eg to cover the inheritance tax payable on that person's death), it will not be sensible for the policy to be held on the same trusts (ie so that the interest in possession beneficiary will have an interest in the policy which will accordingly be brought into charge to inheritance tax on that person's death). In this case the trustees should be given power to hold the benefit of the policy on trusts from which that beneficiary is excluded: see vol 40(2) (2001 Reissue) TRUSTS AND SETTLEMENTS Part 18 [9601].

[1487]

2: FORMS

101

Trusts of policy money[1]

The {Trustees} shall hold all money which shall be received by them in respect of the [{Policy} *or* policies set out in the schedule] or of any substituted policy or policies including bonuses profits and money received on the sale or surrender of the same or any of them upon trust that they shall invest the same in any investments [authorised by this settlement *or* authorised by law][2] and shall hold such money and investments upon the trusts declared below that is to say upon trust [*(set out the appropriate trusts) or* that they shall with such consent or at such discretion as provided in the case of the {Trust Fund} invest the same in any investments [by this settlement *or* by law] authorised and shall hold such money and investments and the income of them upon the trusts and subject to the powers and provisions by this settlement declared in respect of the {Trust Fund} and the income of it save that in case no child or remoter issue of the {Marriage} shall attain a vested interest in the {Trust Fund} then subject to the prior trusts by this settlement declared and to the exercise of any powers by this settlement or by law vested in the {Trustees} the {Trustees} shall hold the above mentioned policy money and investments and the income of them in trust for *(name)* absolutely]

1   When this clause is inserted in a document the defined terms in { } must be altered to suit those used in the document.
2   The second alternative wording should be used if there is no investment clause. As to the statutory powers of investment see Paragraph 241 [591] et seq ante.

[1488]

102

Covenants to maintain policy and trusts of substituted policies[1]

0.1   The {Settlor} covenants with the {Trustees} as follows:

0.1.1   not to do or suffer anything by which the [{Policy} *or* {Policies}] or any substituted policy or policies shall become void or voidable or by which the {Trustees} may be prevented from receiving any money payable under [it *or* them] or on the sale or surrender of [it *or* them]

0.1.2   to pay punctually all premiums and other money necessary for keeping on foot the [{Policy} *or* {Policies}] and any substituted policy or policies and [on demand] to deliver to the {Trustees} the receipts for the same[2]

[1489]

0.1.3   if the [{Policy} *or* {Policies} or any of them] or any substituted policy or policies shall become void or voidable immediately at the {Settlor's} own cost to effect a new policy or policies on [his] life in an office approved by the {Trustees} which shall either be effected in their names or shall be assigned to them in form and manner approved by them and shall be of such amount as would together with accrued bonuses or profits have become payable under the void or voidable policy or policies if the {Settlor} had died at the time of effecting such substituted policy or policies and such void or voidable policy or policies had remained on foot

0.1.4   not to do or suffer anything by which the {Trustees} may be prevented from recovering or receiving any money payable under the [{Policy} *or* {Policies}] or any substituted policy or policies

0.2   Every policy which shall be substituted for the [{Policy} *or* {Policies} or any of them] now settled and all money including bonuses payable under them shall be held upon trusts and with and subject to the powers and provisions declared in this settlement concerning the [{Policy} *or* {Policies}] now settled

[1490]

1   These clauses are suitable for a marriage settlement containing inter alia the benefit of the insurance policy. When this clause is inserted in a document the defined terms in { } must be altered to suit those used in the document.
2   Payment of premiums by the settlor will, given that he is wholly excluded from the beneficial class, result in a transfer of value for inheritance tax purposes. In most cases that transfer will be neither chargeable, nor potentially chargeable, either because it represents normal expenditure out of income (Inheritance Tax Act 1984 s 21 as amended by the Income and Corporation Taxes Act 1988 Sch 29 para 32 (42–44 Halsbury's Statutes (4th Edn) TAXATION)) or because it falls within the settlor's annual exempt amount (Inheritance Tax Act 1984 s 19 as amended by the Finance Act 1986 Sch 19 para 5). In other cases, the payments will be potentially exempt if the trust contains an interest in possession. If the trust is an accumulation and maintenance settlement this will only be the case if the money is given to the trustees who are responsible for making the payments. Where the trusts are discretionary, the payment (however arranged) cannot be potentially exempt. There is no capital gains tax liability when the policy matures and the trustees become entitled to the proceeds: Taxation of Chargeable Gains Act 1992 s 210(2) (42–44 Halsbury's Statutes (4th Edn) TAXATION).

[1491]

103

Power of trustees to pay premiums and exoneration of trustees[1]

0.1   The {Trustees} may if they shall think fit to do so at any time or times apply any part of the income or any part of the capital of either the {Husband's Fund} or the {Wife's Fund} in or towards payment of the annual premium or premiums or other the money necessary for keeping in force or restoring the [{Policy} *or* {Policies}] or any such future policy or policies as stated above[2]

0.2   The {Husband} will on demand pay to the {Trustees} all such money as shall have been so applied in or towards payment of any premium or premiums or money necessary for keeping in force or restoring the [{Policy} *or* {Policies}] or any such future policy or policies as stated above and the {Trustees} shall apply the money so paid to them in the manner upon and in which the money so applied by the {Trustees} would but for the payment have been applicable[3]

0.3   Any money so applied by the {Trustees} out of income or capital not belonging to the {Husband} if not previously discharged by him shall be recouped out of any income or capital payable to or becoming vested in the {Husband} or those claiming under him

[1492]

0.4   If the {Trustees} shall apply any money subject to the trusts declared of the {Wife's Fund} in or towards payment of any money which the {Husband} has covenanted to pay for maintenance or renewal of the [{Policy} *or* {Policies}] and neither he nor his personal representatives shall in performance of his covenant so to do repay the same to the {Trustees} then and in every such case if and when under the trusts declared in this settlement the {Wife's Fund} and the {Husband's Fund} shall become subject to different trusts so much of the {Husband's Fund} as shall be equivalent to the money so applied by the {Trustees} shall be applied by the {Trustees} upon the trusts then applicable to the {Wife's Fund}

[0.5   It shall not be obligatory on the {Trustees} to enforce any of the covenants contained above in relation to the [{Policy} *or* {Policies}] or to apply any of the above mentioned income or capital in payment of the annual premiums or sums of money necessary for keeping in force or restoring the [{Policy} *or* {Policies} or any of them] or to see to the [{Policy} *or* {Policies} or any of them] being kept in force or to recover from the {Husband} any trust money expended by them in payment of any premiums or premium and no omission to do any of the things specified above by the {Trustees} nor any of them [not being the {Husband}] nor the personal representatives of any {Trustee} [not being the {Husband}] shall be answerable for the [{Policy} *or* {Policies} or any of them] becoming void through any means whatsoever or for any money paid by the {Trustees} for a premium or premiums not being recovered]

[1493]

1   This clause is suitable for use when the policy is contained in a marriage settlement and the husband has covenanted to pay the premiums. For such a covenant see Form 102 [1489] ante. When this clause is inserted in a document the defined terms in { } must be altered to suit those used in the document.
2   For trusts of substituted policies see Form 102 [1489] ante.
3   Even in the absence of this express covenant by the husband the trustees can recover from him any premiums which they have paid as damages for breach of his covenant to pay them: *Schlesinger and Joseph v Mostyn* [1932] 1 KB 349.

[1494]

104

Power of trustees to borrow money on security of policy for payment of premiums[1]

If and whenever the {Settlor} shall make default in payment of any annual premium or other sum necessary for keeping on foot or restoring the [{Policy} *or* {Policies}] or in effecting or keeping on foot any substituted policy as provided above[2] the {Trustees} may borrow the amount required for such keeping on foot restoration or substitution from *(name of insurance company)* or otherwise at interest on the security of the [{Policy} *or* {Policies}] or such substituted policy

[1495]

1   This clause is suitable for use when the policy is contained in a settlement and the settlor has covenanted to pay the premiums. For such a covenant see Form 102 [1489] ante. For a general power to borrow see Form 168 [1641] post. When this clause is inserted in a document the defined terms in { } must be altered to suit those used in the document.
2   For trusts of substituted policies see Form 102 [1489] ante.

[1496]

105

Covenant by trustees to pay premiums[1]

The {Trustees} shall apply any part of the income or any part of the capital of the {Trust Fund} in or towards payment of the annual premium or premiums or other the money necessary for keeping in force or restoring the [{Policy} *or* {Policies}] or any future policy or policies as stated above[2]

[1497]

1   Usually trustees are given a power to pay premiums and are not put under an obligation to do so, the settlor often covenanting to pay the premiums direct. This clause is intended to be used in conjunction with Form 106 [1499] post so that the trustees have an obligation to pay the premiums but then have a right of reimbursement from the settlor. This may be beneficial for inheritance tax if the trust were to be in accumulation and maintenance form because, if the settlor paid the premiums direct, each payment would not fall within the definition of a potentially exempt transfer and reliance would have to be placed on the normal expenditure out of income exemption: see further Form 102 note 2 [1491] ante. If the funds are channelled through the trustees, however, then the sums involved are capable of being potentially exempt transfers. For the inheritance tax consequences of a power enabling trustees to pay premiums out of income or capital see *Carver v Duncan* [1985] AC 1082, [1985] 2 All ER 645, HL.

   When this clause is inserted in a document the defined terms in { } must be altered to suit those used in the document.

2   For trusts of substituted policies see Form 102 [1489] ante.

[1498]

106

Covenant by settlor to pay further sums to trustees to fund premium payments[1]

The {Settlor} will on demand pay to the {Trustees} all such money as shall have been applied by the {Trustees} in or towards payment of any premium or premiums or money necessary for keeping in force or restoring the [{Policy} *or* {Policies}] or any such future policy or policies as stated above[2]

1   See Form 105 note 1 [1498] ante. When this clause is inserted in a document the defined terms in { } must be altered to suit those used in the document.

2   For trusts of substituted policies see Form 102 [1489] ante.

[1499]

107

Power of appointment in trust of a life assurance policy which excludes the settlor and spouse from class of objects and in default confers interests in possession[1]

0.1   for the benefit of all or such one or more exclusively of the other or other of the children and remoter issue of [the {Settlor} *or (specify other defined class or named beneficiaries)*] in such shares as the {Trustees} may by deed or deeds revocable or irrevocable appoint and in default of and subject to any such appointment for the absolute benefit of [*(name)* and *(name)* in equal shares]

[0.2   Beneficial interests in default of appointment shall carry the right to intermediate income and all income accruing in the hands of the {Trustees} shall be paid to or applied for the benefit of the beneficiaries entitled to it and shall not be accumulated][2]

[1500]

1   This clause is based on one originally prepared by R Robertson Esq, LLB. When this clause is inserted in a document the defined terms in { } must be altered to suit those used in the document.
2   This addition is required where beneficiaries entitled in default of appointment are under the age of 18 years.

[1501]

108

Discretionary trust of a life assurance policy

108(1) Discretionary trust of a life assurance policy—settlor as appointor[1]

… for the benefit of all or such one or more exclusively of the others or other of *(members of the beneficial class)* ('the Beneficiaries') in such shares and subject to such conditions as the {Settlor} may by deed or deeds revocable or irrevocable or by will or codicil appoint and in default of and subject to any such appointment as the {Trustees} may by deed or deeds revocable or irrevocable executed after the death of the {Settlor} appoint provided that no appointment shall be made nor any power of revocation exercised on or after [the 21st anniversary of the death of the {Settlor} *or* the 21st anniversary of the death of the last to die of the {Settlor} and *(named spouse)* or the 21st anniversary of the death of the life assured under the {Policy} *or* the 21st anniversary of the death of the last to die of the lives assured under the {Policy} *or* the 18th anniversary of the date of this settlement] (which anniversary shall be 'the Vesting Day') and in default of and subject to any such appointment by the {Settlor} or {Trustees}:

0.1   the {Trustees} may in the {Trustees}' absolute discretion accumulate all or part of the income of the {Trust Fund} accruing during the lifetime of the {Settlor} and subject to this shall distribute the income of the {Trust Fund} to the Beneficiaries in such shares as the {Trustees} may determine and

0.2   the {Trustees} shall hold the {Trust Fund} for the Beneficiaries who shall be living on the Vesting Day and if more than one in equal shares but if none of them shall be living for the absolute benefit of the last of them to die

1   This clause is based on one originally prepared by R Robertson Esq, LLB. When this clause is inserted in a document the defined terms in { } must be altered to suit those used in the document.

[1502]

108(2) Discretionary trust of a life assurance policy—trustee as appointor[1]

… for the benefit of all or such one or more exclusively of the others or other of *(members of the beneficial class)* ('the Beneficiaries') in such shares and subject to such conditions as the {Trustees} (being at least 2 in number or a trust corporation) shall by deed or deeds revocable or irrevocable appoint PROVIDED that no appointment shall be made nor any power of revocation exercised on or after [the 21st anniversary of the death of the

{Settlor} *or* the 21st anniversary of the death of the last to die of the {Settlor} and *(named spouse) or* the 21st anniversary of the death of the life assured under the {Policy} *or* the 21st anniversary of the death of the last to die of the lives assured under the {Policy} *or* the 18th anniversary of the date of this settlement] (which anniversary shall be 'the Vesting Day') and in default of and subject to any such appointment:

0.1　　the {Trustees} may in the {Trustees}' absolute discretion accumulate all or part of the income of the {Trust Fund} accruing during the lifetime of the {Settlor} and subject to this shall distribute the income of the {Trust Fund} to the Beneficiaries in such shares as the {Trustees} may determine

0.2　　the {Trustees} shall hold the {Trust Fund} for the Beneficiaries who shall be living on the Vesting Day and if more than one in equal shares but if none of them shall be living for the absolute benefit of the last of them to die

---

1　　This clause is based on one originally prepared by R Robertson Esq, LLB. When this clause is inserted in a document the defined terms in { } must be altered to suit those used in the document.

[1503]

109

Power to effect life assurance and appoint the policies on trust[1]

0.1　　The {Trustees} shall have power to effect maintain and deal with any insurance or insurances upon the life of any person or persons and so that:

　　0.1.1　　the {Trustees} may pay all premiums and other costs relating to such insurance and any amounts necessary for keeping on foot or reinstating such policy or policies out of [the income or] the capital of the {Trust Fund}[2]

　　[0.1.2　　nothing in this clause shall authorise any accumulations of income within the Law of Property Act 1925 Section 164[3]]

0.2　　The {Trustees} shall in respect of any policy or policies effected under the power conferred by the preceding sub-clause [0.1] have all the powers of an absolute owner including power to surrender convert or otherwise deal with any such policy or policies or any bonuses attaching thereto or part of them in such manner as the {Trustees} shall consider most beneficial to the persons beneficially interested therein

0.3　　The {Trustees} (being at least 2 in number or a trust corporation or a trust corporation) shall have power at any time during the {Trust Period} to appoint that any policy effected on the life of any person or persons under the power contained in the preceding sub-clause [0.2] shall be held on such trusts and with and subject to such powers and provisions (including if thought fit protective and discretionary trusts and powers exercisable at the discretion of the {Trustees} or of any other person or persons and authorising the delegation of any discretion) in favour or otherwise for the benefit of all or any one or more of the {Discretionary Beneficiaries} as the {Trustees} in their absolute discretion (due regard being had to the law concerning remoteness) think fit. Provided that the {Trustees} (being at least 2 in number) may at any time or times during the {Trust Period} by deed or deeds extinguish (or restrict the future exercise of) the power conferred by this sub-clause.

[1504]

1   This clause is intended for use in an interest in possession trust where the trustees might wish, in particular, to insure the life of the life tenant but ensure that the resulting policy is held on different trusts in which he does not have a life interest. When this clause is inserted in a document the defined terms in { } must be altered to suit those used in the document.

2   It might be considered preferable to exclude the ability to pay premiums etc out of income lest this prevents the settlement qualifying as an interest in possession trust for the purposes of inheritance tax: see *Pearson v IRC* [1981] AC 753, [1980] 2 All ER 479, HL. If the words in brackets are excluded, para 0.1.2 of this sub-clause should be omitted.

3   There is some uncertainty as to whether payment of premiums out of income amounts to an accumulation of income. The better view is that being an administrative power it does not.

[1505]

110

Exercise of options as to bonuses or profits[1]

In every case (if any) in which by virtue of any policy for the time being subject to trusts declared by this settlement or otherwise the {Trustees} shall become entitled to any benefit other than that constituted by the contingent contract to pay the sum insured under it the {Trustees} [shall be entitled to that benefit in trust for the {Husband} absolutely and if they may at their option receive the same benefit in one or other of several forms they shall exercise their option in such manner as the {Husband} shall direct *or* shall be entitled to that benefit upon the trusts of this settlement and if they may at their option accept it in one of several forms they shall exercise their option as they in their own discretion shall think most beneficial to the objects of this settlement generally]

1   When this clause is inserted in a document the defined terms in { } must be altered to suit those used in the document.

[1506]

111

Application of bonuses or profits in redemption of premiums at discretion of trustees[1]

Any bonus or profit declared in respect of any policy now settled or any substituted policy may (if the insurance office permit) at the discretion of the {Trustees} be applied wholly or in part in redemption of the premiums payable on such policy and subject to and in default of the exercise of such option shall be added to the money insured by such policy and become subject to the trusts of the same

1   This clause contemplates that the insurance company will pay a bonus in cash or permit a bonus to be used for a premium. When this clause is inserted in a document the defined terms in { } must be altered to suit those used in the document.

[1507]

112
Power of trustees to surrender policy[1]

The {Trustees} may at any time if they shall think fit surrender the [{Policy} *or* {Policies}] or any other policy or policies which may then be subject to the trusts declared by this settlement to *(insurance company)* or to the company for the time being bound by the obligations of the [{Policy} *or* {Policies}] for such price and upon such terms as the {Trustees} shall think fit and shall hold the money representing the price when received upon the trusts and with and subject to the powers and provisions declared by this settlement concerning the money to become payable by virtue of the [{Policy} *or* {Policies}]

---

1   No chargeable gain for capital gains tax purposes accrues on the disposal of rights under any policy of insurance on the life of any person, or of an interest in any such rights, except when the person making the disposal is not the original beneficial owner and acquired the rights or interest for a consideration in money or money's worth: Taxation of Chargeable Gains Act 1992 s 210(2) (42–44 Halsbury's Statutes (4th Edn) TAXATION). When this clause is inserted in a document the defined terms in { } must be altered to suit those used in the document.

[1508]

113
Power of trustees to sell policy[1]

0.1   If at any time after the {Marriage} and during the life of the {Husband} the {Trustees} shall think it expedient so to do they may sell or dispose of the {Policy} or any substituted policy or policies (and any such sale or disposition may be by way of surrender to the insurance company)

0.2   In the event of and after any and every such sale or disposition the {Trustees} although the {Husband} shall still be living shall stand possessed of the net money produced by the sale or disposition upon the trusts and with and subject to the powers expressly or by reference declared above concerning the money insured by the policy or policies so sold or disposed of and to take effect after the death of the {Husband}

---

1   This clause contemplates that the policy forms part of a marriage settlement. When this clause is inserted in a document the defined terms in { } must be altered to suit those used in the document.

[1509]

114
Power of trustees to auction policy[1]

If at any time after the {Marriage} and during the life of the {Husband} the {Trustees} shall think it expedient so to do they may sell or dispose of the {Policy} or any substituted policy or policies (and any such sale or disposition may be by way of surrender to the insurance company or by auction)

---

1   In recent years, sums obtained through auctioning life policies have often yielded an amount of up to 35% more than that offered by way of surrender. Trustees would appear to be in breach of trust if they fail to obtain the best price when realising trust property. While a simple power to sell inevitably includes a sale by auction, an express reference to this mode of sale serves to remind the trustees that this option is available. When this clause is inserted in a document the defined terms in { } must be altered to suit those used in the document.

[1510]

115

Power of trustees to surrender or accept variation of policy[1]

If at any time during the life of the {Husband} the {Trustees} shall be of opinion that the maintenance in force of any policy or policies for the time being subject to any trusts declared by this settlement by payment from time to time of the sums of money which shall be needed for that purpose is either impossible or likely to be more burdensome than profitable to the {Beneficiaries} the {Trustees} may at their sole discretion surrender that policy or those policies or any of them to the company or society bound by every or any such policy or may negotiate with such company or society for and accept from that company or society any variation of the same policy or any substituted policy (whether term endowment or whole life insurance) and if the {Trustees} shall obtain the immediate payment of any money as the consideration or part of the consideration for any such surrender variation or substitution they [may at their sole discretion treat the same either as capital to which they are entitled in possession as part of the {Husband's Fund} or] may pay or apply the same to or for the benefit of the {Beneficiaries} in such manner as the {Trustees} may think fit and though such manner of payment or application may directly benefit one or more of the {Beneficiaries} more than or exclusively of others or another of them

1   This clause contemplates that the policy forms part of a marriage settlement. When this clause is inserted in a document the defined terms in { } must be altered to suit those used in the document.

[1511]

116

Power of settlor to redeem policy[1]

The {Husband} shall be entitled at any time during his life to redeem the {Policy} or any substituted policy upon payment to the {Trustees} of the sum of £... and if he shall do so the {Trustees} shall immediately at the cost and expense of the {Husband} assign the {Policy} or substituted policy to him freed and discharged from all trusts powers and provisions contained in this settlement and shall hold such sum of £... paid to them by the {Husband} upon the trusts and with and subject to the powers and provisions declared by this settlement concerning the money to become payable by virtue of the {Policy}

1   This clause contemplates that the policy forms part of a marriage settlement. When this clause is inserted in a document the defined terms in { } must be altered to suit those used in the document.

[1512]

117

Trustees to have powers of absolute owners as regards policies[1]

The {Trustees} shall in respect of the [{Policy} *or* {Policies}] have all the powers of an absolute owner of [it *or* them] and may deal with the same or any money to be received on mortgage surrender maturity or otherwise in respect of [it *or* them] in such manner as they shall consider most beneficial to the persons beneficially interested under the trusts contained in this settlement

1   This clause contemplates that the policy forms part of a marriage settlement. When this clause is inserted in a document the defined terms in { } must be altered to suit those used in the document.

[1513]–[1520]

F: PROVISION FOR FUTURE MARRIAGE AND FOR REVOCATION

118

Power of appointment to spouse and issue of subsequent marriages[1]

0.1   Subject to and in default of any appointment or advance made under or by virtue of the trusts and powers contained above the survivor of the {Spouses} may by any deed or by will or codicil appoint that such proportion as is mentioned below of the {Husband's Fund} if the husband is the appointor or of the {Wife's Fund} if the wife is the appointor be held after the death of the appointor upon trust to pay the income of such proportion or any part of it to any subsequent spouse of the appointor for life or any less period and subject to this upon such trusts for the issue of any future marriages of such appointor or any of such issue upon such terms and with and subject to such powers and provisions as the appointor may think fit (regard being had to the law relating to remoteness)

[1521]

0.2   The proportion of such funds which may be withdrawn from this settlement and appointed as stated above are:

0.2.1   if there is one child only of the present marriage who shall attain a vested interest under the above trust then two-thirds of such fund

0.2.2   if there are 2 or 3 such children and no more then one-half of such fund and

0.2.3   if there are 4 or more such children then one-quarter of such fund and such power of appointment may be exercised on any future marriages and notwithstanding that the proportion that may be appointed is still uncertain

---

1   The document envisages the remarriage of the survivor and permits that person to appoint a life interest to a surviving spouse (which will ensure that inheritance tax is not charged on the appointor's death) with an additional power to appoint a part of the fund to the children of such subsequent marriage. See also Form 119 [1523] post. When this clause is inserted in a document the defined terms in { } must be altered to suit those used in the document.

[1522]

119

Power to spouse to appoint part of trust fund to other spouse and issue of subsequent marriages[1]

PROVIDED nevertheless that notwithstanding and in derogation of the preceding trusts it shall be lawful for the {Wife} if she is the survivor by any deed or by will or codicil to make the following provisions for the spouse and issue of any subsequent marriages to take effect out of the proportion mentioned below of the {Trust Fund} namely:

0.1   to appoint to the issue of any such subsequent marriage or any of them (and in such shares and subject to such conditions as she shall think fit) any part of the {Trust Fund} not exceeding a fraction of the whole the numerator of which shall be the number of children of such subsequent marriage or marriages who [being male] shall live to attain the age of 18 years [or being female shall live to attain that age] or previously marry and the denominator of which shall be the total number of the children of the {Wife} who [being male] shall live to attain the age of 18 years [or being female shall live to attain that age] or previously marry

0.2   to appoint a life or lesser interest to any husband who may survive her in the same part or fraction of the {Trust Fund} last referred to [or if that part is less than one-third of the whole {Trust Fund} then in one-third of the {Trust Fund}]

and the above powers may be exercised in favour of a husband or issue of any such subsequent marriage notwithstanding that it is uncertain what proportion of the fund dealt with shall or may ultimately fall within such power and any appointment shall take effect according to the event

[1523]

---

1   This clause does not provide for the occasion of divorce. For the power of the court to vary marriage settlements see currently the Matrimonial Causes Act 1973 s 24 as substituted with savings by the Family Law Act 1996 s 15, Sch 2 para 6 and amended by the Welfare Reform and Pensions Act 1999 s 19, Sch 3 paras 1, 3 (27 Halsbury's Statutes (4th Edn) MATRIMONIAL LAW) and see also the Matrimonial Causes Act 1973 s 21(2) as substituted by the Family Law Act 1996 s 15, Sch 2 para 2 as amended by the Welfare Reform and Pensions Act 1999 s 84(1), Sch 12 paras 64, 65(1)–(8). When this clause is inserted in a document the defined terms in { } must be altered to suit those used in the document.

[1524]

120

Power to revoke if wife childless at specified age[1]

If the {Wife} shall attain the age of [55] years and if there shall be no issue of the {Marriage} then living it shall be lawful for the {Spouses} jointly by deed to revoke this settlement [(notwithstanding that the {Wife}'s income is directed above to be held on protective trusts for her benefit)] and then the {Trustees} shall transfer the {Husband's Fund} to the {Husband} and the {Wife's Fund} to the {Wife} absolutely and freed and discharged from all the trusts powers and provisions declared and contained in this settlement

[1525]

---

1   This clause is particularly suitable when the wife at the date of the settlement is unlikely to have any children or when the spouses anticipate they will wish to provide out of capital for their old age. For presumptions and evidence as to future parenthood see the Perpetuities and Accumulations Act 1964 s 2 (33 Halsbury's Statutes (4th Edn) PERPETUITIES) and Paragraph 78 [186] ante. It is thought that the effect of this clause in the case where the settlement has been created by the parties to the marriage is that they remain taxed on income and capital gains whilst the power remains capable of exercise: the Income and Corporation Taxes Act 1988 s 660A(1) as inserted by the Finance Act 1995 s 74, Sch 17 para 1 and the Taxation of Chargeable Gains Act s 77(2) as substituted by the Finance Act 1995 s 74, Sch 17 para 27. For inheritance tax purposes the right will remain part of their estates: compare *Melville v IRC* [2000] STC 628. Of course, these consequences do not apply if the settlor is, eg, the bride's father. When this clause is inserted in a document the defined terms in { } must be altered to suit those used in the document.

[1526]

121

Spouse's power to withdraw part of trust fund for appointment to other spouse and issue of subsequent marriage[1]

0.1   Notwithstanding anything else contained in this settlement the {Wife} shall have power ('the Power of Withdrawal') at any time or times after the termination of the {Marriage} and either in contemplation of or after any future marriage of hers by any deed with or without power of revocation or by will or codicil (but without prejudice to any appointment under the power contained in this settlement or any payment or application or capital under the provisions of the Trustee Act 1925 Section 32[2] as modified in this settlement which may previously have been made) to appoint that such part as is mentioned in clause **[0.4]** below or any less part of the {Trust Fund} shall be withdrawn wholly or partially as the case may be from the operation of this present settlement and be held upon such trusts and with and subject to such powers exercisable by such person or persons and generally subject to such provisions as shall be declared in such appointment for the benefit of the subsequent husband of the {Wife} and the issue (whether children or more remote) of such future marriage but so that such subsequent husband shall not take any interest exceeding a life interest (which may be appointed to trustees on protective trusts for his benefit or on discretionary trusts for the benefit of him and such other persons as shall be named for such purpose in such appointment) and so that no child or remoter issue of such subsequent marriage shall (except by the exercise of a power of advancement or some similar power) take an interest vesting before his or her eighteenth birthday or earlier marriage and so that no such appointment shall be made so as to infringe the rule against perpetuities

[1527]

0.2   Subject and without prejudice to any exercise of the Power of Withdrawal and to any trusts and powers appointed in exercise of the same so far as the same shall be capable of taking effect the property thereby appointed and the income of the same shall be held upon such of the trusts and with and subject to such of the powers and provisions therein declared and contained of and concerning the same as shall for the time being be subsisting and capable of taking effect

0.3   If the {Wife} shall marry more than once after the termination of the {Marriage} and if by the effect of any appointments made under the Power of Withdrawal more than such part as is mentioned in clause **[0.4]** below of the capital of the {Trust Fund} would but for this clause become vested in or payable to or charged in favour of any persons (other than the issue of the {Marriage}) the appointments so made shall be void to the extent of such excess and shall as between themselves have priority according to their respective dates

0.4   The part of the {Trust Fund} which may be appointed under the Power of Withdrawal shall not exceed in value the following proportion of it (that is to say):
        0.4.1   if there shall be 3 or more children of the {Marriage} who attain the age of 18 years or marry under that age then one equal half part
        0.4.2   if there shall be only 2 such children of the {Marriage} then two equal third parts
        0.4.3   if there shall be only one such child of the {Marriage} then three equal fourth parts and
        0.4.4   if there shall be no child of the {Marriage} then the whole of it

but so that for the purposes of this clause the {Trust Fund} on the occasion of any exercise of the Power of Withdrawal shall be deemed to include all parts of it previously appointed under any power (including the Power of Withdrawal) contained in this settlement or previously paid or applied under the provisions of the Trustee Act 1925 Section 32 (as extended above) and that any part of the {Trust Fund} previously so appointed or so paid or applied shall be brought into account for such purposes at such value as the {Trustees} shall in the circumstances consider fair and PROVIDED always that if and so long as after any appointment made in exercise of the Power of Withdrawal any child of the {Marriage} shall be living and under the age of 18 years without having married such appointment shall take effect only to the extent (if any) to which it would have taken effect if every such child of the {Marriage} had reached the age of 18 years

[1528]

1   For the inheritance tax exemption for gifts in consideration of marriage see the Inheritance Tax Act 1984 s 22(4)(c) (42–44 Halsbury's Statutes (4th Edn) TAXATION). When this clause is inserted in a document the defined terms in { } must be altered to suit those used in the document.

2   Ie the Trustee Act 1925 s 32 as amended by the Trusts of Land and Appointment of Trustees Act 1996 s 25(1), Sch 3 para 3(8) (48 Halsbury's Statutes (4th Edn) TRUSTS AND SETTLEMENTS).

[1529]

122

Power of spouse to appoint to other spouse and issue of subsequent marriages if no issue of first[1]

0.1   If no child of the {Marriage} shall attain a vested interest under the trusts declared above and if the {Wife} shall survive the {Husband} the {Trustees} shall hold the [{Trust Fund} *or* {Wife's Fund} *or (specify)*] upon such (if any) trusts and with and subject to such (if any) powers as either in contemplation of or after any subsequent marriage or marriages which the {Wife} may make after the death of the {Husband} she may by any deed either with or without power of revocation and new appointment or by will or codicil and in either case without transgressing the rule against perpetuities at any time or times appoint but only so that all the beneficial interests created by every or any such appointment shall be for the benefit of all or some or one of the members of a class constituted by the {Wife} her future husband and her issue and so that no interest which shall be so appointed for the benefit of the {Wife} shall endure longer than her life and no interest which shall be so appointed for the benefit of any future husband of the Wife shall endure longer than his life and so that no issue of the {Wife} shall take under any appointment made in exercise of this power unless that issue [being male] shall attain the age of 18 years [or being female shall attain that age] or shall marry

[1530]

0.2   PROVIDED also that if there shall not be any such child of the {Marriage} as mentioned above then subject to the power given above and to every or any exercise of it and to all other the trusts and powers contained above and to every or any exercise of any of those powers the {Trustees} shall hold the [{Trust Fund} *or* {Wife's Fund} *or (specify)*] and the income from it in trust for such if any child or children of the {Wife} as shall attain the age of 18 years or [being female shall attain that age or] marry under that age and if there shall be more than one such child in equal shares absolutely and subject as above (whether the {Wife} shall survive the {Husband} or die in his lifetime but subject to any and every trust and power and to every or any exercise of any such power) the {Trustees} shall hold the [{Trust Fund} *or* {Wife's Fund} *or (specify)*] in trust for all or such one or more exclusively of the other members or member of the class of persons consisting of *(names)* the [brothers] and *(names)* the [sisters] of the {Wife} and the issue of *(names of brothers and sisters)* respectively at such age or time or ages or times and if more than one in such shares and subject to such terms and limitations for the benefit of *(names of brothers and sisters)* and issue or of some or one of them and with such provisions for the maintenance education advancement accumulation of income during minority and benefit of all or any of such issue at the discretion of either the {Trustees} or any other persons and upon such conditions and with such restrictions and in such manner as the {Wife} by any deed with or without power of revocation and new appointment or by will or codicil and in either case without transgressing the rule against perpetuities shall at any time or times appoint and in default of and until any and subject to any and every such appointment in trust for *(names of brothers and sisters)* [if more than one] in equal shares absolutely

1   This clause is narrower than that contained in Form 121 [1527] ante, in that it is more restrictive of the manner in which the power may be exercised. Express provision should be made if it is desired to give the wife a power to create protective or discretionary trusts: see *Re Boulton's Settlement Trust, Stewart v Boulton* [1928] Ch 703; *Re Hunter's Will Trusts, Gilks v Harris* [1963] Ch 372, [1962] 3 All ER 1050. When this clause is inserted in a document the defined terms in { } must be altered to suit those used in the document.

[1531]

123

Power of revocation with consent of trustees[1]

The {Settlor} may at any time with the consent of the {Trustees} which they may in their absolute discretion give or withhold by deed to which the {Trustees} shall be parties for the purpose of giving their consent wholly or in part revoke the trusts declared by this settlement and declare other trusts of the {Trust Fund} in favour of [any spouse child children or issue of the {Settlor} *or* the persons beneficially entitled under the trusts of this settlement] with or without a like power of revocation [PROVIDED that this power shall not be exercised in such a manner that the {Trust Fund} or the income of it or any part or parts of it shall or may under or by virtue of any such exercise on declaration become vested in payable to or applicable for the benefit of the {Settlor} or any spouse of the {Settlor} in any circumstances whatsoever][2]

[1532]

1   This clause enables the settlor during his life to revoke and resettle part of the trust fund and is not specifically limited to marriage settlements. For capital gains tax purposes the exercise of this power will result in a deemed disposal of the relevant property given that it will revoke the existing trusts: Taxation of Chargeable Gains Act 1992 s 71 as amended by the Finance Act 1999 s 75(1) (42–44 Halsbury's Statutes (4th Edn) TAXATION). When this clause is inserted in a document the defined terms in { } must be altered to suit those used in the document.

2   Although the trustees have to consent to the exercise of this power, and the beneficial class who may be appointed excludes the settlor and any spouse, it may be feared that the mere existence of the power may lead to tax complications: consider the wording of the Taxation of Chargeable Gains Act 1992

s 77 (as substituted by the Finance Act 1995 s 74, Sch 17 para 27) and of the Income and Corporation Taxes Act 1988 s 660A (as inserted by the Finance Act 1995 s 74, Sch 17 para 1 and amended by the Finance Act 2000 s 41(b), Sch 13 para 26) (42–44 Halsbury's Statutes (4th Edn) TAXATION). Hence, although the inclusion of this proviso is common, it should only be incorporated after careful consideration of all the likely consequences, for instance:

(a)   Will the exercise trigger a capital gains tax charge under the Taxation of Chargeable Gains Act 1992 s 71 as amended by the Finance Act 1999 s 75(1)?

(b)   How should the trustees act when asked to consent to such an exercise?

An alternative would be to give the settlor a power of appointment or to make his consent necessary to the exercise of an appointment by the trustees.

[1533]–[1540]

G: INVESTMENT CLAUSES AND APPLICATION OF CAPITAL MONEY

1: INTRODUCTION

Powers of investment under the Trustee Act 2000 Part II

The Trustee Act 2000 Part II[1] has, since its commencement on 1 February 2001[2], revolutionised the investment powers of trustees. The 'general power of investment' given under Section 3(1) of that Act is akin to the wide express powers of investment that have been used by trust draftsmen for many years and may be thought to render redundant such clauses[3]. The draftsman should, however, bear in mind the following matters:

1   An 'investment' is not defined in the Trustee Act 2000.

2   Investments in land are dealt with specifically in the Trustee Act 2000 Part III[4] which specifically authorises the acquisition of freehold or leasehold land in the UK for investment, for occupation by a beneficiary or 'for any other reason'[5].

3   There is no statutory power to invest in land outside the UK, nor to acquire it for any of the other purposes set out in the Trustee Act 2000 Section 8. In a 'family trust' an express power to acquire land outside the UK may be desirable.

4   Although UK land can be acquired for occupation by a beneficiary, there is no power in the Trustee Act 2000 for other assets (eg chattels) to be so acquired. An express power may be desirable.

5   The statutory powers will apply in addition to the powers given in the trust instrument but may be excluded or restricted. A settlor may, for instance, wish his trustees to pursue some form of 'ethical' investment policy[6].

6   The Trustee Act 2000 Sections 4 and 5 impose on all trustees standard investment criteria and a requirement to take advice which must be observed by trustees when investing or reviewing the trust investments. These Sections apply to all trustees whether exercising the statutory power or any express power and they cannot, it appears, be excluded in the trust instrument. Note in particular Section 4(3)(b) which refers to the need for diversification 'in so far

as is appropriate to the circumstances of the trust'. This provision needs careful consideration when establishing a trust to hold a simple asset, eg shares in the settlor's private company or real property (eg his residence).

A selection of investment powers follow: in some cases the settlor will wish to limit the trustees' discretion to what is authorised expressly, in others he may wish to emphasise that a particular investment is open to the trustees without limiting their wide powers under the Trustee Act 2000 Part II. In the case of all the clauses it is important, if they are used, to consider their relationship to the new statutory powers. In some cases power is being conferred on trustees which is not given by the Trustee Act 2000: see, for instance, Form 140 [1564] and Form 143 [1571] post.

[1541]

1   The Trustee Act 2000 Pt II (ss 3–7) (48 Halsbury's Statutes (4th Edn) TRUSTS AND SETTLEMENTS) is discussed at Paragraph 241 [591] et seq ante.
2   Trustee Act 2000 (Commencement Order) 2001, SI 2001/49 art 2.
3   For a wide express power, see Form 4 schedule paragraph 1 [1092] ante.
4   Trustee Act 2000 Pt III (ss 8–10); see specifically the Trustee Act 2000 s 8(1)(a).
5   The Trustee Act 2000 Pt III (ss 8–10) is discussed at Paragraph 244 [596] ante.
6   See Forms 147 [1575]–149 [1577] post.

[1542]

2: MISCELLANEOUS POWERS PERMITTING THE ACQUISITION OF STOCKS AND SHARES

124

Securities transferred to the trustees in specie[1]

The {Trustees} may allow any securities transferred to them on the trusts of this settlement to remain in their present state of investment or may [with the consent of *(name)* during [his] lifetime and afterwards] at the discretion of the {Trustees} realise the same or any part of them and shall invest the proceeds of such realisation and any cash transferred to them on the trusts of this settlement [with the same consent or] at the same discretion in any investments authorised by this settlement or authorised by law with power to vary or transpose investments for or into others of a nature so authorised

1   For a Form giving power to retain securities which are not producing income see Form 184 [1671] post. It is thought that this clause would be a 'circumstance' to be taken into account under the Trustee Act 2000 s 4(3)(b) (48 Halsbury's Statutes (4th Edn) TRUSTS AND SETTLEMENTS) (the 'standard investment criteria' diversification). When this clause is inserted in a document the defined terms in { } must be altered to suit those used in the document.

[1543]

125

Authorised investments by reference to schedule[1]

Any money liable to investment under the trusts of this settlement may [with the consent of *(name)* during [his] lifetime and afterwards] at the discretion of the {Trustees} be invested in any of the investments set out in the schedule ('the Authorised Investments')

1   Direction to invest in particular investments will not exclude the statutory power under the Trustee Act 2000 (48 Halsbury's Statutes (4th Edn) TRUSTS AND SETTLEMENTS): *Re Warren, Public Trustee v Fletcher* [1939] Ch 684, [1939] 2 All ER 599 (a decision on the Trustee Act 1925 s 69(2) (48 Halsbury's Statutes (4th Edn) TRUSTS AND SETTLEMENTS)). But that power is excluded by a direction to invest in certain specified securities 'but not otherwise': *Re Rider's Will Trusts, Nelson v Rider* [1958] 3 All ER 135, [1958] 1 WLR 974.

     When this clause is inserted in a document the defined terms in { } must be altered to suit those used in the document.

[1544]

126

Government and local authority securities

Government securities of Great Britain Northern Ireland the Channel Islands and the Isle of Man [or any local authority of such] *(add such other countries as desired)* being fixed-interest [and dated] securities

[1545]

127

Deposits in banks and building societies

Deposits in the National Savings Bank or in any of the following banks *(names of banks)* or deposits or shares in any [of the following building societies *(names of building societies)* *or* building society within the meaning of the Building Societies Act 1986 as amended]

[1546]

128

Unit trusts[1]

The units of any authorised unit trust within the meaning of the Financial Services Act 1986

1   This clause substantially reproduces the (now-repealed) Trustee Investments Act 1961 s 1, Sch 1 Pt III para 3 as substituted by the Financial Services Act 1986 s 212(2), Sch 16 para 2(b) (48 Halsbury's Statutes (4th Edn) TRUSTS AND SETTLEMENTS). As to authorised unit trusts schemes generally see the Financial Services Act 1986 ss 77–86 (30 Halsbury's Statutes (4th Edn) MONEY).

[1547]

129

Investment in company securities, including companies incorporated in Commonwealth countries, subject to capital requirements and dividend record[1]

In the debentures or debenture stock or preference or preferred ordinary or ordinary or deferred shares or stock of any limited liability company incorporated in the United Kingdom the Isle of Man the Republic of Ireland or in a Commonwealth country of which the total issued and paid up share capital is not less than [ten million pounds sterling] (or the equivalent in the currency of the country in which the company is incorporated) and which has in each of the [5] years immediately preceding the calendar year in which the investment is made paid a dividend on all shares issued by the company excluding any shares issued after the dividend was declared and any shares which by the terms of their issue did not rank for dividend for that year

[1548]

1   The qualification as to paid up share capital in the (now-repealed) Trustee Investments Act 1961 s 1, Sch 1 Pt IV para 3(a) (48 Halsbury's Statutes (4th Edn) TRUSTS AND SETTLEMENTS) relating to securities issued by United Kingdom companies was one million pounds. The wide investment power conferred by the Trustee Act 2000 Pt II (ss 3–7) (48 Halsbury's Statutes (4th Edn) TRUSTS AND SETTLEMENTS) contains no such restriction but this is a matter on which a settlor might wish to impose restraints: if this clause were adopted, it is likely that the Trustee Act 2000 Pt II (ss 3–7) should be excluded, or at least modified.

[1549]

130

Securities of companies in, and of governments of, the European Union and of the United States of America

[With the advice of a member of The Stock Exchange[1]] [in *or* In] the shares of a corporation with limited liability incorporated in a country which is a member of the European Union [or incorporated in the United States of America] [or in the [dated] securities issued by any of the governments of such countries]

1   For the meaning of 'stock exchange' see the Stock Transfer Act 1963 s 4(1) (30 Halsbury's Statutes (4th Edn) MONEY) and note that The Stock Exchange, London has now been amalgamated with other members of the Federation of Stock Exchanges in Great Britain and Ireland into a single organisation known as 'The Stock Exchange'. This is now the only recognised stock exchange: see the Stock Transfer (Recognition of Stock Exchanges) Order 1973, SI 1973/536.

[1550]

131

Listed stock exchange securities including foreign and no par value securities[1]

0.1   Any investments of whatever nature which at the date of purchase are or on allotment will be dealt in or listed on The Stock Exchange *(add if desired and where applicable specific references to over-the-counter markets, or, if desired, by reference to stock exchanges of countries which are members of the European Union)*

[1551]

[0.2   PROVIDED always that no money part of the {Trust Fund} shall be invested in:

0.2.1   government securities of any country not part of Her Majesty's dominions or a Commonwealth country [except the United States of America or any of its States]

0.2.2   partly paid-up shares except shares of banking and insurance companies incorporated in the United Kingdom and

0.2.3   any securities of a company unless at the time of investment it has a paid-up capital of at least £... or its equivalent at the rate of exchange current at the time of the investment [and so that in the case of a company having shares of no par value the equivalent of such paid-up capital shall be the capital sum (other than capital surplus) appearing in the company's published accounts in respect of such shares]]

[1552]

1   For the meaning of 'stock exchange' see the Stock Transfer Act 1963 s 4(1) (30 Halsbury's Statutes (4th Edn) MONEY) and note that The Stock Exchange, London has now been amalgamated with other members of the Federation of Stock Exchanges in Great Britain and Ireland into a single organisation known as 'The Stock Exchange'. This is now the only recognised stock exchange: see the Stock Transfer (Recognition of Stock Exchanges) Order 1973, SI 1973/536.

Consider whether the Trustee Act 2000 Pt II (ss 3–7) (48 Halsbury's Statutes (4th Edn) TRUSTS AND SETTLEMENTS) should be excluded or suitably modified: this is a matter on which the settlor's instructions should be taken.

When this clause is inserted in a document the defined terms in { } must be altered to suit those used in the document.

[1553]

132

Securities on the Alternative Investment Market with advice[1]

With the advice of a member of The Stock Exchange[2] in any investments of whatever nature which at the date of purchase are or on allotment will be dealt with in or listed on the Alternative Investment Market

1   See the Trustee Act 2000 ss 4 (standard investment criteria) and 5 (duty to take advice) (48 Halsbury's Statutes (4th Edn) TRUSTS AND SETTLEMENTS).

2   For the meaning of 'stock exchange' see the Stock Transfer Act 1963 s 4(1) (30 Halsbury's Statutes (4th Edn) MONEY) and note that The Stock Exchange, London has now been amalgamated with other members of the Federation of Stock Exchanges in Great Britain and Ireland into a single organisation known as 'The Stock Exchange'. This is now the only recognised stock exchange: see the Stock Transfer (Recognition of Stock Exchanges) Order 1973, SI 1973/536.

[1554]

133

Government privatisation and floatation issues with advice[1]

With the advice of a member of The Stock Exchange in any securities which are offered for sale by or on behalf of Her Majesty's Government or in any other securities offered for sale by subscription on the occasion of an application for listing on the Official List of The Stock Exchange

1   See the Trustee Act 2000 ss 4 (standard investment criteria) and 5 (duty to take advice) (48 Halsbury's Statutes (4th Edn) TRUSTS AND SETTLEMENTS). As to the meaning of 'stock exchange' see Form 130 note 1 [1550] ante.

[1555]

134

Authority to accept offers of additional shares[1]

If the {Trustees} shall as holders of any shares or stock for the time being subject to the trusts of this settlement become entitled to take or subscribe for any new or other shares or stock (whether in the same or any other company formed for acquiring its assets) then they may if they think fit avail themselves of such right to take or subscribe for any or any part of such shares or stock as stated above and to dispose of or transfer the same or the title to them and shall hold or apply any premium or profit produced upon any such disposition or transfer upon the same trusts and in the same manner in all respects as if the same were [capital of the {Trust Fund} or income then yielded by that portion of the {Trust Fund} in respect of which the right to the shares or stock subscribed for and disposed of as stated above shall have accrued] and this power shall apply notwithstanding that they may not be otherwise than by this declaration authorised so to do or that the state of the {Trust Fund} may not enable them or that they may not consider it convenient or fitting to take and hold such new or other shares or stock as an investment for the purposes of this settlement

1   This clause enables trustees to accept shares or stock which they may consider or be advised are saleable at an enhanced price. It is thought that the trustees would already have this power under the statutory 'general power of investment': see the Trustee Act 2000 s 3 (48 Halsbury's Statutes (4th Edn) TRUSTS AND SETTLEMENTS). When this clause is inserted in a document the defined terms in { } must be altered to suit those used in the document.

[1556]

135

Shares in named company or any company which may acquire its business

The shares or securities of *(name of company)* or any company [incorporated in Great Britain] which on an amalgamation reconstruction or otherwise shall acquire the business now carried on by *(name of company)*

[1557]

136

Shares in company which acquires family business

The shares or securities of any company incorporated in Great Britain formed or to be formed in future which shall purchase or otherwise acquire or carry on the family business of *(specify)*

[1558]

137

Discretionary investment management scheme[1]

The {Trustees} may delegate their powers under clause *(number of clause containing investment powers)* and any other powers conferred by this settlement or the general law relating to the choice of investments and the management or administration of trust money or other trust property to any person or body carrying on the business of investment management [provided such person or body is authorised under the provisions of the Financial Services Act 1986][2] to any extent for any period on any terms and in such manner as they think fit and may remunerate such person or body and vest trust money or trust property in such person or body as their nominee

[1559]

1   This clause is intended to allow trustees to place trust funds in the hands of an investment fund manager who will then invest the funds on behalf of the trustees. The Trustee Act 2000 Pt IV (ss 11–27) (48 Halsbury's Statutes (4th Edn) TRUSTS AND SETTLEMENTS) permits delegation in such circumstances but note the restriction on this power in the Trustee Act 2000 s 12(2) (cannot delegate to more than one agent except jointly), s 12(3) (cannot delegate to a beneficiary) and the Trustee Act 2000 s 14 (terms of agency), in particular s 14(3)(c). For convenience it is likely that express powers will continue to be used although the trustees will be subject to the Trustee Act 2000 s 15 in exercising such a power to appoint a fund manager. The appointment should, therefore, be in writing and the trustees should draw up a 'policy statement': see further Forms 318 [2198], 319 [2200] post.

When this clause is inserted in a document the defined terms in { } must be altered to suit those used in the document.

2   As to authorised persons see the Financial Services Act 1986 Chapter III (ss 7–34) (30 Halsbury's Statutes (4th Edn) MONEY).

[1560]

138

Senior trustee on share register for voting purposes[1]

Where any investments [in *(name of company)* or in any limited company which shall purchase its business] are registered in the names of the {Trustees} *(senior trustee)* shall so long as [he] so wishes be named first in the register of shareholders

1   The Companies (Tables A to F) Regulations 1985, SI 1985/805 Schedule, Table A reg 55) provides that in the case of joint holders the vote of the senior who tenders a vote, whether in person or by proxy, must be accepted to the exclusion of the votes of the other joint holders; and for this purpose seniority is determined by the order in which the names stand in the register of members. This clause will be of particular importance where the settlor desires to secure the voting rights to a particular individual without a dispute arising (eg in the case of a family controlled company); this can only be achieved if SI 1985/805 Schedule, Table A reg 55 has been adopted by the company, or a regulation having the same effect has been included in the articles of the company.

In the case of a company which has adopted Table A, this clause will not be necessary if it is merely desired to ensure that notices and other official communications (including dividend vouchers if no other arrangements are made) are sent to the first-named trustee, as these will automatically be sent by a company to the address of the first-named trustee (see SI 1985/805 Schedule, Table A reg 112 as amended by SI 2000/3373); the settlor should bear this in mind when naming his trustees.

As a matter of trust law the senior trustee is not free to vote as he pleases. Like all trustee decisions this requires unanimity in the absence of any provision in the trust instrument to the contrary.

When this clause is inserted in a document the defined terms in { } must be altered to suit those used in the document.

[1561]

3: POWERS TO ACQUIRE PROPERTY OTHER THAN STOCKS AND SHARES

139

Freehold or leasehold property[1]

The purchase of any land or property of freehold tenure or of leasehold tenure [held for a term of which at least [60] years shall be unexpired] whether subject to leases or tenancies or not and the {Trustees} shall be indemnified not only out of the property purchased and the proceeds of sale of the same but out of all the property subject to this settlement against all liability in respect of any rent covenants conditions or outgoings to which the property so purchased or any part of it may be subject

[1562]

---

1   Trustees are given wide powers to purchase land in the UK including power to purchase land as an investment and for use as a residence for a beneficiary: see the Trustee Act 2000 s 8 (48 Halsbury's Statutes (4th Edn) TRUSTS AND SETTLEMENTS) and see also the Trusts of Land and Appointment of Trustees Act 1996 s 6(3) as amended by the Trustee Act 2000 s 40(1), Sch 2 para 45(1) (37 Halsbury's Statutes (4th Edn) REAL PROPERTY).

     It is possible to limit the wide power given in the Trustee Act 2000 s 8 by, for example, requiring in the case of leasehold property that there shall be a term of at least 60 years unexpired: see Form 142 [1568] post. An express power enabling trustees to 'invest' in land does not extend to the acquisition of a dwelling house for a beneficiary to live in: see *Re Power, Public Trustee v Hastings* [1947] Ch 572, [1947] 2 All ER 282. It is considered that this power (indeed all the powers in this section of Forms) is administrative and not dispositive in nature. Accordingly, whilst trustees can purchase property for a beneficiary to live in when that person is the life tenant or otherwise entitled to an interest in possession in the trust fund, it is not considered that they could do so for the remainderman. In the case of a discretionary trust (when trustees have a discretion as to the payment of income and capital) it is thought that a residence may be purchased for any of the discretionary objects.

     When this clause is inserted in a document the defined terms in { } must be altered to suit those used in the document.

[1563]

140

Purchase of holiday residence or timeshare[1]

The purchase of a residential property or an interest in a timeshare scheme (whether villa apartment or otherwise) ('the Property') situated in any of the following countries *(specify countries)* and in making such purchase the {Trustees} shall not be liable for any loss incurred as a result of the exercise of this power and the {Trustees} may expend trust capital [or income][2] on the improvement or maintenance of the Property and may either let the Property for such period on such conditions and at such rent as they think fit (and for that purpose may employ agents abroad) or may permit any one or more of the {Beneficiaries} to occupy the same as a holiday residence on such terms and conditions as they shall think proper and at all times the {Trustees} shall be indemnified out of the trust capital [or income][3] subject to this settlement against all liability in respect of any rent fee covenants conditions taxes or outgoings to which the Property or any interest in such may be subject

[1564]

1   This clause may be used to enable the trustees to buy property abroad or in the United Kingdom for use of the beneficiaries on holiday.

       The settlor could himself spend a holiday at the property without endangering the position as to inheritance tax on his death so long as he paid a full economic rent while he was living there: see the Finance Act 1986 s 102, Sch 20 para 6(1)(a) as amended (42–44 Halsbury's Statutes (4th Edn) TAXATION) which provides that occupation of land by the donor is not regarded as a reservation of benefit where the land is rented for full consideration in money or money's worth. As to reservation of benefit generally see Paragraph 290 [749] et seq ante. For an investment clause authorising the purchase of a residence for a beneficiary see Form 142 [1568] post. See also Form 139 note 1 [1563] ante. Under the Trustee Act 2000 Pt III (ss 8–10) (48 Halsbury's Statutes (4th Edn) TRUSTS AND SETTLEMENTS) there is no power to purchase land outside the UK.

       When this clause is inserted in a document the defined terms in { } must be altered to suit those used in the document.

2   The words in square brackets may be omitted if the settlement is intended to include an interest in possession since the trustees would then have the power to divert income away from the person entitled to it and this could result in the settlement being taxed as one with no interest in possession for inheritance tax purposes. This will depend on whether a power to apply income in this way is an administrative or dispositive power: see Introduction to Section H [1586] post and see *Pearson v IRC* [1981] AC 753, [1980] 2 All ER 479, HL and see Paragraph 287 [730] ante.

3   See note 2 above.

[1565]

141

Property of any kind at discretion of trustees with advice[1]

0.1   The purchase of or at interest upon the security of such investments and property of whatsoever nature and wheresoever situated as the {Trustees} shall in their absolute discretion think fit

0.2   PROVIDED that the {Trustee} in making any investment shall have regard to the need for diversification of investments so far as is appropriate to the circumstances of the trust created by this settlement and to the suitability to the trust of investments of the description of the investment proposed and that the investment proposed is an investment of that description

0.3   AND PROVIDED also that before exercising any power of investment authorised by this settlement the {Trustees} shall have obtained and considered proper advice on the question whether the investment is satisfactory having regard to the need for diversification and to the suitability

0.4   For the purposes of this clause proper advice means the advice given in writing or subsequently confirmed in writing of a person who is reasonably believed by the {Trustees} to be qualified by his ability in and practical experience of financial matters and such advice may be given by a person notwithstanding that he gives it in the course of his employment as an officer or servant and notwithstanding that he is a trustee of this settlement giving advice required pursuant to these provisions by his co-trustee or co-trustees

[1566]

1   The provisos to this clause are adaptations of the Trustee Act 2000 ss 4 and 5 (48 Halsbury's Statutes (4th Edn) TRUSTS AND SETTLEMENTS) which relate to the duty of trustees in choosing investments. The power to invest or to purchase property 'of whatsoever nature and wheresoever situated' is wider than the power given by the Trustee Act 2000 ss 3 (general investment power) and 8 (power to acquire land). As to the duty to obtain advice before investing see Paragraph 243 [594] ante.

       When this clause is inserted in a document the defined terms in { } must be altered to suit those used in the document.

[1567]

142

Purchase of a residence for a beneficiary and improvements on it[1]

Trust capital may be invested in:

0.1   the purchase of a residence for [*(beneficiary)* or any one or more of the {Beneficiaries}]

0.2   the purchase of vacant land for the purpose of building a residence for [*(beneficiary)* or any one or more of the {Beneficiaries}] and

0.3   erecting repairing improving decorating making alterations to and demolishing and rebuilding any house or other building on any land subject to the trusts of this settlement and in particular this includes works in the nature of improvements the cost of which is not authorised to be defrayed out of capital under the Settled Land Act 1925[2]

[1568]

PROVIDED that:

0.4   any residence or vacant land so purchased may be either freehold or leasehold for a term of which more than 60 years shall be unexpired at the time of purchase and shall be held on trust of land

0.5   before purchasing such residence or land the trustees shall obtain a report as to its value from a professionally qualified surveyor or valuer and

0.6   any such residence or land shall be in the United Kingdom [or in *(add any other countries allowed)*]

[1569]

1   Trustees are given wide powers to purchase land in the UK including power to purchase land for use as a residence for a beneficiary: see the Trustee Act 2000 s 8 (48 Halsbury's Statutes (4th Edn) TRUSTS AND SETTLEMENTS) and the Trusts of Land and Appointment of Trustees Act 1996 s 6(3) as amended by the Trustee Act 2000 s 40(1), Sch 2 paras 45(1) (37 Halsbury's Statutes (4th Edn) REAL PROPERTY) and see further Form 139 note 1 [1563] ante. If the Trustees are to be entitled to purchase land in Scotland this should be expressly provided for. For a clause requiring trustees to permit beneficiaries to occupy land held on trust see Form 210 [1727] post; but see also as to the inheritance tax consequences Paragraph 287.3 [734] ante.

        When this clause is inserted in a document the defined terms in { } must be altered to suit those used in the document.

2   As to improvements under the Settled Land Act 1925 (48 Halsbury's Statutes (4th Edn) TRUSTS AND SETTLEMENTS) see vol 40(2) (2001 Reissue) TRUSTS AND SETTLEMENTS Part 9 [4101].

[1570]

143

Purchase of chattels for residence of a beneficiary[1]

Chattels for the decoration furnishing and equipment of the residence of any of the {Beneficiaries} [which has been purchased pursuant to clause *(number)*]

1   There is no equivalent statutory power in the Trustee Act 2000 (48 Halsbury's Statutes (4th Edn) TRUSTS AND SETTLEMENTS). When this clause is inserted in a document the defined terms in { } must be altered to suit those used in the document.

[1571]

144

Purchase of chattels for investment with provision for income based on value[1]

0.1   With the advice of a professionally qualified valuer furniture pictures and objects d'art [at a price not exceeding £... for any one object or set of objects [and not exceeding in the aggregate £...]]

[0.2   PROVIDED that there shall be paid to any of the {Beneficiaries} entitled for the time being to the income of this settlement out of the capital of this settlement a sum equal to …% per year [above the base lending rate of *(name of bank)*] on the purchase price for the first [5] years after the purchase and subsequently on the value of the object as ascertained below any such sum to be treated as if it were income from the investments under this settlement

0.3   Every [5] years after such a purchase a valuation shall be obtained from a qualified valuer for the purpose of calculating such sum]

---

1   Although the payment in sub-clause 0.2 above is out of the capital of the trust fund, it is thought that it would be taxed as income in the beneficiary's hands. When this clause is inserted in a document the defined terms in { } must be altered to suit those used in the document.

[1572]

145

Prohibited investments by reference to schedule[1]

The {Trustees} shall not invest in any of the investments set out in the schedule ('the Prohibited Investments')

---

1   When this clause is inserted in a document the defined terms in { } must be altered to suit those used in the document.

[1573]

146

Retention of investments by reference to schedule

The {Trustees} shall retain and not sell any investments set out in the schedule without the consent of the [{Settlor}][1]

---

1   Clauses such as this are sometimes employed where the settlement comprises part of the settlor's shareholding in his family company and he wishes to ensure that no shares in that company can be sold without his consent. When this clause is inserted in a document the defined terms in { } must be altered to suit those used in the document.

[1574]

147

Ethical investment (trustees' discretion)[1]

To select only investments which the {Trustees} in their absolute discretion consider to be ethically acceptable without being liable for any loss which might thereby result to the {Trust Fund}

1   As to ethical investment see Paragraph 245 [598] ante. The settlor may wish, in a non-binding letter of wishes, to indicate the main considerations that should guide the trustees in exercising the above power. Consider also Forms 148 [1576], 149 [1577] post. When this clause is inserted in a document the defined terms in { } must be altered to suit those used in the document.

[1575]

148

Power to invest only in ethical investments[1]

0.1   Money for the time being subject to the trusts of this settlement and requiring investment shall be invested or laid out in the purchase or otherwise in the acquisition of shares stock debentures loan stock or other securities of companies which or the subsidiaries of which are engaged in one or some or other of the following activities: *(insert details)*

0.2   The general power of investment contained in the Trustee Act 2000 Section 3 shall not apply to this settlement

1   As to ethical investment see Paragraph 245 [598] ante. A clause on these lines will result in a somewhat narrow power of investment. It would be more usual to have a wide power of investment or adopt the general power of investment under the Trustee Act 2000 s 3 (48 Halsbury's Statutes (4th Edn) TRUSTS AND SETTLEMENTS) but exclude certain categories of investment considered by the Settlor to be unethical: see Form 149 [1577] post.

[1576]

149

Prohibition on certain (non-ethical) investments[1]

Notwithstanding the provisions of *(the preceding sub-clause)* the {Trustees} shall not (whether in exercise of the power of investment conferred by *(that sub-clause)* or of the general power of investment contained in the Trustee Act 2000 Section 3) invest in the shares stock debentures loan stock or other securities of any company which is or any of the subsidiaries of which are engaged in any of the following activities: *(insert details)*

1   As to ethical investment see Paragraph 245 [598] ante. This is a precedent for a sub-clause, following another which conferred a wide power of investment, excluding from its ambit the general power of investment under the Trustee Act 2000 s 3 (48 Halsbury's Statutes (4th Edn) TRUSTS AND SETTLEMENTS) and certain investments which the settlor considers 'unethical'. The general power of investment may be excluded: see the Trustee Act 2000 s 6(1). When this clause is inserted in a document the defined terms in { } must be altered to suit those used in the document.

[1577]–[1585]

H: CLAUSES CONCERNING DISPOSITIVE POWERS OF TRUSTEES

1: INTRODUCTION

The distinction between administrative and dispositive powers

The term a 'dispositive power' as opposed to an 'administrative power' was first expounded in the capital transfer tax case of *Pearson v IRC*[1]. It was there defined as a power to dispose of the net income[2] and the mere existence of such a power was considered fatal to the existence of an interest in possession. The borderline with administrative powers is not easy to draw[3]. In this section of Forms, the term is used more widely to embrace any discretionary power affecting a beneficiary's enjoyment of either income or capital. Hence, powers of maintenance and advancement are included, as are powers to lend money and to pay and apply the trust fund. In the context of the power to lend (as also of a power to permit a beneficiary to occupy trust property), it is assumed that such powers will be exercised in accordance with the beneficial trusts. Thus, whilst a house may be purchased under the Trustee Act 2000 Section 8 for occupation by a life tenant, it would be inappropriate for the power to be exercised in favour of the remainderman. In the case of discretionary trusts, when trustees have wide power to apply income and capital for the class of beneficiaries, it is thought that a house may be purchased for occupation by any member of that class on the basis that it amounts to an exercise of the trustees' discretion in his favour. Similar comments may be made of the power conferred on trustees by Form 162 [1624] post.

[1586]

1   *Pearson v IRC* [1981] AC 753, [1980] 2 All ER 479, HL. For a discussion of this case see Paragraph 286.3 [727] ante.
2   See Paragraph 287.2 [731] ante.
3   See, for example, *Miller v IRC* [1987] STC 108, Court of Sess. See also the views of the Court of Appeal on the nature of the Trustee Act 1925 s 32 (48 Halsbury's Statutes (4th Edn) TRUSTS AND SETTLEMENTS) powers of advancement in *Inglewood v IRC* [1983] 1 WLR 366 at 373, CA. See also the distinction drawn in the Trustee Act 2000 Pt IV (ss 11–27) (48 Halsbury's Statutes (4th Edn) TRUSTS AND SETTLEMENTS) between 'delegable' and 'non-delegable' functions which was adopted after the Law Commission felt that the distinction between dispositive or distribution powers (ie powers which should not be delegable) and administrative powers (which should be delegable) did not satisfactorily deal with all cases: *Trustees' Powers and Duties* (Law Com No 260) para 4.8. In particular, powers to appoint and replace trustees, although not dispositive in nature, were considered to be inappropriate powers to delegate.

[1587]

2: FORMS

150

Power for trustees to accumulate income for 21 years[1]

In addition and without prejudice to any other power of accumulation conferred upon them[2] the {Trustees} may during the period of 21 years from the date of this settlement accumulate such of the income of the {Trust Fund} as shall not have been paid or applied under the provisions of clause *(number)* or any part or parts of it by way of compound interest by investing the same and the resulting income of it in any of the investments authorised under this settlement and shall hold such accumulations and the resulting income as an accretion to and augmentation of the capital of the {Trust Fund} and as one fund with it for all purposes [PROVIDED that the {Trustees} may apply the accumulations of any preceding year and the resulting income of it as if such accumulations and the resulting income were income arising in the then current year]

[1588]

1   As to the permitted periods of accumulation see Paragraph 83 [194] ante. Note in the case of accumulation and maintenance trusts the restrictions on accumulation imposed by the Inheritance Tax Act 1984 s 71 (42–44 Halsbury's Statutes (4th Edn) TAXATION): see Paragraph 127 [316] ante and vol 40(2) (2001 Reissue) TRUSTS AND SETTLEMENTS Part 11 [6301]. When this clause is inserted in a document the defined terms in { } must be altered to suit those used in the document.

2   These words preserve the statutory power of accumulation during the minority of a beneficiary. It is not considered that they are necessary since the power to accumulate during a minority would apply (if the appropriate conditions were satisfied) in any event.

[1589]

151

Power of maintenance enlarged to include minors outside the statutory power[1]

0.1   The {Trustees} may apply all or a part of the income of the {Trust Fund} as in their discretion they think fit for or towards the maintenance education or benefit of any minor or minors who may be absolutely or presumptively or contingently entitled to the {Trust Fund} or any share in it and whether or not so entitled to the intermediate income or who may be or become members of a class so entitled and may either themselves so apply the same or may delegate such application to others and such minors if more than one may be maintained or educated either together as a class or individually

0.2   During such minority the {Trustees} shall invest any surplus income in authorised investments to be held as augmentations of the capital producing such income

[1590]

1   In view of the powers of maintenance given by the Trustee Act 1925 s 31 as amended by the Family Law Reform Act 1969 s 1(3), Sch 1 Pt I and the Trustee Act 2000 s 40(1), Sch 2 para 25 (48 Halsbury's Statutes (4th Edn) TRUSTS AND SETTLEMENTS) (see Paragraph 235 [568] ante) this specific power is unlikely to be required except:

    (a)   where there is a trust of a contingent interest which does not carry the intermediate income;

    (b)   in the rather unusual case of settlements of foreign property where the Act might not apply;

(c)   where some other variation from the statutory power is required; or

(d)   where the property might not be considered to be 'held by the trustees on trust' for the beneficiary within the meaning of the Trustee Act 1925 s 31 as it has not been appropriated in the exercise of a discretion.

For a modification of the statutory power see Form 152 [1592] post. When this clause is inserted in a document the defined terms in { } must be altered to suit those used in the document.

[1591]

152

Variation of statutory powers of maintenance[1]

The provisions of the Trustee Act 1925 Section 31 as amended by the Family Law Reform Act 1969 and the Trustee Act 2000 shall apply to this settlement and (subject to and in default of appointment to the contrary) to any appointment made under this settlement as if:

0.1   the words 'as the Trustees shall in their absolute discretion think fit' were substituted for the words 'as may, in all the circumstances, be reasonable' in Section 31(1)(i)

0.2   the proviso to Section 31(1) had been omitted

0.3   throughout Section 31 the age of *(state age)*[2] was substituted for 18 and infancy was to mean the period before the attainment of *(state age above)* and

0.4   the {Trustees} were empowered at any time during the infancy of any of the {Beneficiaries} on whose account income may have been accumulated under Section 31 to apply such accumulations or any part of them as if they were income arising in the then current year and as if they were applicable for the benefit of any others or other of the {Beneficiaries} and not only for the benefit of the {Beneficiary} on whose account they were made[3]

[1592]

1   As to the statutory power of maintenance under the Trustee Act 1925 s 31 as amended by the Family Law Reform Act 1969 s 1(3), Sch 1 Pt I and the Trustee Act 2000 s 40(1), Sch 2 para 25 (48 Halsbury's Statutes (4th Edn) TRUSTS AND SETTLEMENTS) see Paragraph 235 [568] ante. When this clause is inserted in a document the defined terms in { } must be altered to suit those used in the document.

2   Inclusion of this sub-clause will defer entitlement to income to the stated age which in many cases may be the age at which the beneficiary is to obtain a vested interest in capital: for the income tax consequences of vested and contingent interests in income see Paragraph 349 [970] et seq ante; see further vol 40(2) (2001 Reissue) TRUSTS AND SETTLEMENTS Part 11 [6301]. If the stated age exceeds 25 years, it will prevent the beneficiary from receiving a vested interest in income before reaching 25 years with the result that the settlement cannot qualify as an accumulation and maintenance settlement for inheritance tax purposes. For the capital gains tax consequences of deferring entitlement to income to an age coinciding with the ending of an accumulation and maintenance settlement see vol 40(2) (2001 Reissue) TRUSTS AND SETTLEMENTS Part 11 [6301].

3   If the power given by this modification is exercised in favour of children of the settlor who are unmarried and have not attained the age of 18 years, this will result in the funds so applied being treated as the income of the settlor for income tax purposes: see the Income and Corporation Taxes Act 1988 s 660B(2) as inserted by the Finance Act 1995 s 74, Sch 17 para 1 (42–44 Halsbury's Statutes (4th Edn) TAXATION) and Paragraph 356 [1002] et seq ante. For the tax treatment of accumulations applied under this power, see Paragraph 127 [316] ante and vol 40(2) (2001 Reissue) TRUSTS AND SETTLEMENTS Part 11 [6301].

[1593]

153

Power of advancement[1]

The {Trustees} may advance to any of the {Beneficiaries} any sum [not exceeding one-half] out of the share to which he or she is absolutely presumptively or contingently entitled for his or her advancement or benefit as the {Trustees} in their discretion think fit[2]

1   Advancement is provided for in the Trustee Act 1925 s 32 as amended by the Trusts of Land and Appointment of Trustees Act 1996 s 25(1), Sch 3 para 3(8) (48 Halsbury's Statutes (4th Edn) TRUSTS AND SETTLEMENTS): see Paragraph 238 [573] ante. This clause will not be required where the section applies, unless it is desired to enlarge the power by omitting the words in square brackets (this is commonly done in modern settlements). The section does not apply to capital money arising under the Settled Land Act 1925: Trustee Act 1925 s 32(2) as substituted by the Trusts of Land and Appointment of Trustees Act 1996 s 25(1), Sch 3 para 3(8). For the exercise of a power of advancement see Form 290 [2029] post.

　　　When this clause is inserted in a document the defined terms in { } must be altered to suit those used in the document.

2   As to the making of further advances after an initial advance of up to one-half the fund in circumstances where the trust property has increased in value see *Re Marquess of Abergavenny's Estate Act Trusts, Marquess of Abergavenny v Ram* [1981] 2 All ER 643, [1981] 1 WLR 843. Consider whether a proviso should be added requiring the consent of a beneficiary with a prior income entitlement (as is found in the Trustee Act 1925 s 32).

[1594]

154

Power to advance capital to husband and wife—for use in marriage settlement where one fund and where husband and wife have interests in income only[1]

At any time or times during the lives of the {Husband} and the {Wife} or the life of the survivor of them the {Trustees} being 2 in number or a trust corporation may if they think fit transfer pay or apply the whole [or any part or parts not exceeding altogether more than *(specify fraction)*] of the capital of the {Trust Fund} to or for the benefit of the {Husband} and the {Wife} or either of them or the survivor of them to hold the same on trust for the {Husband} and the {Wife} or either of them or such survivor absolutely freed from the trusts and provisions of this settlement[2] PROVIDED always that during the joint lives of the {Husband} and the {Wife} this power shall not be exercised in favour of one of them without the prior consent in writing of the other

[1595]

1   Advancement is provided for in the Trustee Act 1925 s 32 as amended by the Trusts of Land and Appointment of Trustees Act 1996 s 25(1), Sch 3 para 3(8) (48 Halsbury's Statutes (4th Edn) TRUSTS AND SETTLEMENTS): see Paragraph 238 [573] ante. See further Form 153 note 1 [1594] ante. Note that the statutory power only permits advancements to beneficiaries with an entitlement to capital. Express provision is therefore needed (along the lines of this Form and Forms 155 [1597], 156 [1599] post) if advancements are to be made to beneficiaries interested only in income. For the inheritance tax consequences of the exercise of this power, see Paragraph 300.5 [777] ante; for capital gains tax consequences see Paragraph 342 [919] et seq ante.

　　　When this clause is inserted in a document the defined terms in { } must be altered to suit those used in the document.

2   For the capital gains tax implications, see *Swires v Renton* [1991] STC 490.

[1596]

155

Power to advance capital to husband and wife where each spouse's fund is held on separate trusts and when the husband and wife have interests in income only

At any time or times during the lifetime of the [{Wife} *or* {Husband}] the {Trustees} being 2 in number or a trust corporation may if they think fit transfer pay or apply [the whole *or* any part or parts not exceeding altogether more than *(specify fraction)*][1] of the capital of the [{Wife's Fund} *or* {Husband's Fund}] to or for the benefit of the [{Wife} *or* {Husband}] to hold the same on trust for the [{Wife} *or* {Husband}] absolutely freed from the trusts of this settlement[2] PROVIDED always that during the joint lives of the {Husband} and the {Wife} this power shall not be exercised without the prior consent in writing of the [{Husband} *or* {Wife}]

[1597]

1   Advancement is provided for in the Trustee Act 1925 s 32 as amended by the Trusts of Land and Appointment of Trustees Act 1996 s 25(1), Sch 3 para 3(8) (48 Halsbury's Statutes (4th Edn) TRUSTS AND SETTLEMENTS): see Paragraph 238 [586] ante. See further Form 153 note 1 [1594] ante. When this clause is inserted in a document the defined terms in { } must be altered to suit those used in the document.
2   For the capital gains tax implications, see *Swires v Renton* [1991] STC 490.

[1598]

156

Power to advance capital or make loans to the life tenant[1]

The {Trustees} may if they consider such to be to the advantage of the {Life Tenant} at any time or times pay to or apply for the benefit of the {Life Tenant} the whole or any part of the capital of the {Trust Fund} (including any accumulations of income forming part of it) freed from the trusts of this settlement or may lend the same or any part of it to the {Life Tenant} on such terms as to interest and repayment and with or without security as the {Trustees} shall think fit or agree [PROVIDED that the above powers shall not be exercised during the life of the {Settlor} without the consent of the {Settlor} in writing]

[1599]

1   This clause may be of advantage if it is considered likely that the trustees will acquire assets as part of the trust property which produce no or very little income so as to leave the life tenant with insufficient income. As to the inheritance tax consequences of interest free loans to beneficiaries see Paragraph 287.4 [736] ante.
    A power to lend may be usefully used in a settlement in which it is desired to make up the income of a life tenant to a certain amount out of capital. Outright capital payments so made in some circumstances can be treated as income of the recipient for income tax purposes: see Paragraph 353 [982] ante, although if there is no obligation laid on the trustees and the sums are clearly identified as capital, it is not considered that this will be the case.
    When this clause is inserted in a document the defined terms in { } must be altered to suit those used in the document.

[1600]–[1610]

157
Powers in the wider and narrower form[1]

(a) Introduction

The classification of trustee powers following *Bond v Pickford*

In *Bond v Pickford* [1983] STC 517, CA, Slade LJ moved away from the old distinction between powers of appointment and powers of advancement to a classification of powers in the wider form (which enable assets to be removed from the original settlement) and powers in the narrower form (under which the assets remain comprised in the original settlement). The relevant clauses form the basis of this precedent.

For capital gains tax purposes, if property passes into a new settlement there is a deemed disposal under the Taxation of Chargeable Gains Act 1992 Section 71 as amended by the Finance Act 1999 s 75(1) and consequent charge to tax (unless hold-over relief is available). Accordingly, it is important for settlements to contain powers enabling the existing trusts to be modified (eg by exercise of a special power of appointment) as well as powers enabling property to be resettled. In some circumstances a resettlement will be intended, in others the intention will be for property to remain comprised in the original settlement. Even if a new settlement is created, the original settlor is the settlor of that trust for tax purposes.

The intention of trustees when exercising such powers is a factor that will be considered in determining whether the exercise of a power in the wider form has created a new settlement[2]. Trustees should therefore include as a recital a statement of their intentions in exercising the relevant power. For other illustrations of powers in the narrower and wider forms see vol 40(2) (2001 Reissue) TRUSTS AND SETTLEMENTS Part 11 [6501].

[1611]

---

1   Ie under the Taxation of Chargeable Gains Act 1992 s 77 as substituted by the Finance Act 1995 Sch 17 para 27 and amended by the Finance Act 1998 s 121(3), Sch 21 para 6(1) (42–44 Halsbury's Statutes (4th Edn) TAXATION).

2   See *Swires v Renton* [1991] STC 490 in which the court accepted that the intention of the trustees was not to create a new settlement in exercising a power in the wider form. The power in this case was 'to pay or apply any part or parts of ...the Trust Fund... freed and released from the trusts affecting the same' to or for the benefit of any member of the class of beneficiaries. A power in the narrower form cannot, of course, be exercised so as to create a new settlement.

[1612]

(b) Forms

157(1) Power to 'pay or apply' capital—power in the wider form[1]

Until the {Vesting Day} the {Trustees} may in their absolute discretion from time to time pay or apply the whole or any part or parts of the capital of the {Trust Fund} to or for the benefit of all or such one or more of the {Beneficiaries} for the time being living in such shares if more than one and in such manner as the {Trustees} shall in their absolute discretion think fit

---

1   When this clause is inserted in a document the defined terms in { } must be altered to suit those used in the document.

[1613]

157(2) Powers in the narrower form and in the wider form[1]

Without prejudice to the generality of the foregoing the {Trustees} may apply capital for the benefit of one or more of the {Beneficiaries} for the time being and whether an infant or not by:

0.1   allocating or appropriating to such {Beneficiary} such sum or sums out of or investments forming part of the capital of the {Trust Fund} as the {Trustees} think fit absolutely or contingently upon the attainment by him or her of a specified age or the happening of a specified event before the {Vesting Day} and so that the provisions of the Trustee Act 1925 Section 31 and the powers of the {Trustees} to invest and vary investments so allocated shall apply to any money or investments so allocated[2]

0.2   settling the same on such trusts for the benefit of any such {Beneficiary} and any spouse of him or her and his or her widower as the {Trustees} may think fit and so that any such settlement may confer on the {Trustees} thereof or on the person for whose benefit the same is made or on any other person such powers of appointment and otherwise in relation to the fund thereby settled and the income thereof as the {Trustees} may determine PROVIDED that any such powers of appointment shall specifically exclude the {Settlor} or any wife of the {Settlor} and all interests created by any such settlement shall become vested interests before the {Vesting Day}[3]

0.3   purchasing an annuity for the life of any one of the {Beneficiaries} or for any less period

[1614]

1   When this clause is inserted in a document the defined terms in { } must be altered to suit those used in the document.

2   This clause contains powers in the narrower form under which the assets remain comprised in the original settlement.

3   This clause contains powers in the wider form enabling assets to be removed from the original settlement.

[1615]

158

Power to lend generally[1]

The {Trustees} may from time to time and at any time lend any money subject to the trusts of this settlement to any persons or corporations whatsoever and wheresoever situated or resident (other than the {Settlor} or any spouse of the {Settlor}) and upon such terms and conditions as to repayment interest premiums or otherwise and whether upon security or upon personal credit only and subject to such other provisions as the {Trustees} may in their absolute and unfettered discretion think fit [PROVIDED always that no money for the time being subject to the trusts of this settlement shall be lent under the above power during the life of the {Settlor} without the prior consent of the {Settlor} in writing]

[1616]

1   As to when this power (and the similar power to permit a beneficiary to occupy or enjoy trust property) may be exercised, see Introduction to this section [1586] ante.

     This is the widest power of its kind that can be conferred upon the trustees. Specific authority is necessary to enable the trustees to make unsecured loans: see further 48 Halsbury's Laws (4th Edn 2001 Reissue) para 898. For alternative powers permitting loans to beneficiaries see Form 4 schedule paragraph 23 [1100] ante and Form 169 [1642] post.

     When this clause is inserted in a document the defined terms in { } must be altered to suit those used in the document.

[1617]

159

Loans to life tenant charged upon life interest under the settlement on security of life policy

From time to time at the request in writing of *(life tenant)* to [raise by sale or mortgage of the {Trust Property} and] lend to the *(life tenant)* any sum or sums not exceeding in the whole £... on the security of a policy or policies of insurance on the life of the *(life tenant)* in such sum not being less than the amount so lent and in such office as the {Trustees} may determine and with such covenant by the *(life tenant)* to pay the premiums on such policy or policies but with power for the {Trustees} if occasion should arise to pay such premiums out of the capital or income[1] of the residue of the {Trust Property} or upon such other security to be provided by the *(life tenant)* as the {Trustees} may in their discretion deem adequate at such rate of interest and upon such terms and for such period as the {Trustees} may think proper and the {Trustees} may continue such loans for so long during the life of *(life tenant)* as they think fit and shall not be liable for any loss which may arise of any money so lent

[1618]

1   It is understood that the Inland Revenue accepts that if this power is exercised so that premises are paid out of income, then even though that expense may be capital in nature it does not infringe the requirements for an interest in possession for inheritance tax purposes (on the basis that the power is administrative rather than dispositive). See Introduction to this section [1586] ante. When this clause is inserted in a document the defined terms in { } must be altered to suit those used in the document.

[1619]

160

Power to lend capital to beneficiaries generally[1]

The {Trustees} may from time to time lend any money for the time being forming part of the capital of the {Trust Fund} to any one or more of the {Beneficiaries} at such rate or rates of interest [if any] and with and subject to such terms as to repayment security or otherwise as may be agreed between the {Trustees} and such of the {Beneficiaries} to whom such money is to be lent and in default of any such agreement any such money lent to any of the {Beneficiaries} shall on the death of that {Beneficiary} be repayable with simple interest at the rate of ...% per year

[1620]

1   This clause may be of advantage if it is considered likely that the trustees will acquire assets as part of the trust property which produce no or very little income so as to leave the life tenant with insufficient income. As to the inheritance tax consequences of interest-free loans to beneficiaries see Paragraph 287.4 [736] ante.
    A power to lend may be usefully used in a settlement in which it is proposed to make up the income of a life tenant to a certain amount out of capital. Outright capital payments so made in such circumstances could be treated as income of the recipient for income tax purposes: see Paragraph 353 [982] ante.
    When this clause is inserted in a document the defined terms in { } must be altered to suit those used in the document.

[1621]

161

Occupation and use of trust property[1]

0.1   Where any person is for the time being [or if he had attained the Relevant Age would be][2] beneficially interested in possession in any land or chattel comprised in the {Trust Fund} the {Trustees} may permit him to occupy reside in or use that land or chattel (whether for domestic purposes or for the purposes of any trade profession or business carried on by him whether alone or in partnership with others) for any period and upon any terms they think fit

0.2   Without limitation to the generality of sub-clause [0.1] in the exercise of the power conferred by that clause the {Trustees} may impose any conditions as to the payment of rates community charges taxes and other expenses and outgoings and as to insurance repair decoration cultivation or use that they think fit

[1622]

---

1   As with the power to make loans, this power will normally only be exercisable in favour of a beneficiary with an interest in possession in the settled property or in favour of a member of a discretionary class which could benefit from the income of the Trust Fund. When this clause is inserted in a document the defined terms in { } must be altered to suit those used in the document.

2   The words in square brackets will be relevant when beneficiaries of an accumulation and maintenance trust become entitled to an interest in possession on attaining a specified age (in this Form 'Relevant Age').

[1623]

162

Power to effect a policy for the education of beneficiaries[1]

The {Trustees} may from time to time and at any time if they shall think fit effect any policy of insurance under which it is provided that any sum or sums of money may in any contingency be payable to or applicable for the maintenance education or benefit of any of the {Beneficiaries} for the time being entitled to benefit from any trust or power contained in this settlement or apply income of the {Trust Fund} for the maintenance education or benefit of such of the {Beneficiaries} and may apply any such income subject to any such trust or power in paying or contributing towards the payment of the premiums or costs of any such policy of insurance

---

1   In appropriate circumstances trustees may be given powers to invest in a long-term care bond for the benefit of one or more beneficiaries. When this clause is inserted in a document the defined terms in { } must be altered to suit those used in the document.

[1624]

163

Power to pay income or capital to the parent or guardian of a minor[1]

The {Trustees} may pay or transfer to the parents or either of them or to the guardian or guardians of any minor any sum of money being income of the {Trust Fund} intended to be applied for the maintenance education or benefit of that minor or any sum of money or other property forming part of the capital of the {Trust Fund} which it is intended should be applied for the advancement or benefit of that minor upon receiving from any such parents parent guardian or guardians an undertaking in writing to apply any such sums of money or other property in the manner intended and the receipt of any such parents parent guardian or guardians shall be a complete discharge to the {Trustees} provided that no exercise of any of the powers conferred by or created by this clause shall operate in any way to confer any benefit on the {Settlor} or spouse of the {Settlor}

[1625]

1   If the minor is entitled to benefit under the statutory power of maintenance conferred by the Trustee Act 1925 s 31 as amended by the Family Law Reform Act 1969 s 1(3), Sch 1 Pt I and the Trustee Act 2000 s 40(1), Sch 2 para 25 (48 Halsbury's Statutes (4th Edn) TRUSTS AND SETTLEMENTS) (see Paragraph 235 [568] ante), this provision will affect the exercise of that statutory power, in that section 31 does not call for an undertaking from the parents of the minor that the money will be used for the purpose for which it is paid to them. It is considered that this clause is likely to be of greater use in those settlements to which the statutory powers of maintenance and advancement do not apply. A minor cannot, in general, give a valid receipt to trustees.

   When this clause is inserted in a document the defined terms in { } must be altered to suit those used in the document.

[1626]

164

Power to accelerate or defer entitlement to income[1]

This clause shall apply when a {Beneficiary} has a contingent interest in the capital of the trust property:

0.1   the {Trustees} may by deed or deeds declare at any time while the {Beneficiary}'s interest remains contingent that the {Beneficiary} shall from that time have a vested interest in the future income of the whole or some specified part of the property in which he or she has the interest and clause [0.2] or clause [0.3] as the case may be shall then apply

0.2   if the declaration is made at a time when the {Beneficiary} is under the age of 18 years then until he or she reaches that age:
   0.2.1   the {Trustees} shall have the power to apply the whole or any part of that income for his or her maintenance education or benefit as they in their absolute discretion think fit
   0.2.2   the {Trustees} shall retain the rest of that income on trust for such {Beneficiary} absolutely and
   and when the {Beneficiary} reaches 18 years the {Trustees} shall pay that income to that {Beneficiary}

0.3   if the declaration is made at a time when the {Beneficiary} has already reached the age of 18 years then the {Trustees} shall pay that income to that {Beneficiary}

0.4   The Trustee Act 1925 Section 31 shall not apply to that income.

[1627]

1   If the powers provided by this clause are exercised by the trustees, the effect may be to accelerate the beneficiary's entitlement to income so as to give a vested interest in income at a time prior to which it would normally be obtained; ie at age 18 years, or to defer entitlement given that the Trustee Act 1925 s 31 as amended by the Family Law Reform Act 1969 s 1(3), Sch 1 Pt I (48 Halsbury's Statutes (4th Edn) TRUSTS AND SETTLEMENTS) has been excluded. The exercise of this power results in income tax being payable at the basic rate see further Paragraph 347 [956] et seq ante. Giving a beneficiary a vested interest in income creates an interest in possession for inheritance tax purposes: see further

Paragraph 285 [722] et seq ante. If income is not to be paid to a beneficiary over the age of 18, then it is envisaged that it will be accumulated and an appropriate accumulation period should be selected.

When this clause is inserted in a document the defined terms in { } must be altered to suit those used in the document.

[1628]

165

Power to appropriate and fix values of interests of persons absolutely entitled[1]

0.1   The {Trustees} may at any time or times at their discretion appropriate any part of the {Trust Fund} in its then actual state of investment in or towards satisfaction of the whole or any part of any share in the same to which any person or persons beneficially interested under this settlement has or have become absolutely entitled

0.2   In making such appropriation the {Trustees} may themselves estimate the value of the component parts of the {Trust Fund} or may employ such persons to make such valuations as in the circumstances the {Trustees} may select or deem proper[2]

0.3   Any appropriation so made shall be final and binding on all persons beneficially interested under the trusts of this settlement

[1629]

1   Trustees of land have power to partition land under the Trusts of Land and Appointment of Trustees Act 1996 s 7 (37 Halsbury's Statutes (4th Edn) REAL PROPERTY): see Paragraph 223 [536] ante and see vol 40(2) (2001 Reissue) TRUSTS AND SETTLEMENTS Part 8 [3001]. The power of appropriation given in the Administration of Estates Act 1925 s 41 as amended (17 Halsbury's Statutes (4th Edn) EXECUTORS AND ADMINISTRATORS) does not apply to trustees. When this clause is inserted in a document the defined terms in { } must be altered to suit those used in the document.

2   This is wider than the power to value given by the Trustee Act 1925 s 22(3) as amended by the Trustee Act 2000 s 40(1), Sch 2 para 22(b) (48 Halsbury's Statutes (4th Edn) TRUSTS AND SETTLEMENTS) which only extends to valuation by 'duly qualified agents'. As to the power to value trust property see Paragraph 262 [647] ante.

[1630]

166

General power to appropriate[1]

The {Trustees} may appropriate any part of the {Trust Fund} in the actual condition or state of investment of the same at the time of appropriation in or towards the satisfaction of the share or interest of any person or persons in the {Trust Fund} as to the {Trustees} may seem just and reasonable according to the respective rights of the persons interested in the {Trust Fund}

1   The power of appropriation given in the Administration of Estates Act 1925 s 41 as amended (17 Halsbury's Statutes (4th Edn) EXECUTORS AND ADMINISTRATORS) does not extend to trustees. When this clause is inserted in a document the defined terms in { } must be altered to suit those used in the document.

[1631]

167

Power to transfer assets between separate funds[1]

The {Trustees} may at any time or times in their absolute discretion transfer any asset assets or capital money forming part of a fund under the settlement held upon trusts for the time being distinct from any other fund thereunder to that other fund in consideration of the transfer of any asset assets or capital money of equal open market value from that other fund to the first mentioned fund

1   Often accumulation and maintenance trusts result in separate funds being established for the individual beneficiaries. Assets appropriated to one fund may not be exchanged for assets in that other fund in the absence of an express power. When this power is included trustees should also be given a power to have assets valued 'for any purpose and in such manner as the trustees shall in their discretion think fit'. Given that there will normally be a single composite settlement in such cases it is not thought that the exercise of this power will give rise to a capital gains tax charge. When this clause is inserted in a document the defined terms in { } must be altered to suit those used in the document.

[1632]–[1640]

I: CLAUSES CONCERNING ADMINISTRATIVE POWERS OF TRUSTEES

168

Power to borrow[1]

The {Trustees} may raise any money required at any time for any one or more of the purposes of this settlement (including the making of any desired investment)[2] [upon personal security or] by mortgage charge sale or surrender of the {Trust Fund} or any part or parts of it in such manner and upon such terms or conditions whatever as they shall think proper in the circumstances and no purchaser or lender paying or advancing money on a sale mortgage or charge purporting to be made by the {Trustees} under or for any of the purposes of this settlement shall be concerned to see that the money is wanted or that no more than is wanted is raised for any of the stated purposes or otherwise as to the propriety of the transaction or application of any such money [PROVIDED that no money may be borrowed from the {Settlor} or any spouse of the {Settlor}]

1   When this clause is inserted in a document the defined terms in { } must be altered to suit those used in the document.
2   There is no general power to borrow for investment purposes: see *Re Suenson-Taylor's Settlement, Moores v Moores* [1974] 3 All ER 397, [1974] 1 WLR 1280.

[1641]

169

Power to effect all kinds of dealings in land[1]

The {Trustees} may sell lease demise let mortgage charge license and generally manage and deal with any land which or the proceeds of sale of which may at any time form part of the {Trust Fund} as if the {Trustees} were the beneficial owners of it absolutely entitled

1   Trustees are given wide powers by the Trustee Act 2000 s 8(3) (48 Halsbury's Statutes (4th Edn)
        TRUSTS AND SETTLEMENTS) under which they have all the powers of an absolute owner in relation
        to the land that they have acquired. A similar power is given to trustees of land by the Trusts of Land
        and Appointment of Trustees Act 1996 s 6(1). Most draftsmen, therefore, consider this sort of express
        provision unnecessary. When this clause is inserted in a document the defined terms in { } must be
        altered to suit those used in the document.

[1642]

170
Power to form a sinking fund[1]

The {Trustees} may establish and maintain capital reserves management funds and any
form of sinking fund in order to pay or contribute towards all fees costs and other
expenses arising in relation to the {Property} and so that the {Trustees} may make
provision for such fund out of income or capital at such time or times as they think fit
and the {Trustees} may invest and deal in and with such fund (not immediately required
for the aforesaid purposes) in such manner as they shall from time to time determine

[1643]

1   It is unusual to see a clause of this type. It raises a number of issues, notably that if income is to be
        retained for this purpose it may amount to an accumulation. In so far as it is applied for repairs (ie
        income expenses) on the property this is not thought to be the case and trustees are thought to have
        power to reserve out of one year's rents for repairs to be accrued in future years: see generally, Underhill
        and Hayton *Law of Trusts and Trustees* (5th Edn, 1995) p 534 et seq. Given that the power is classified
        as administrative, rather than dispositive, in nature it is also considered that it will not give rise to
        inheritance tax problems relating to the existence of an interest in possession. Of course 'sinking fund'
        trusts are from time to time created and these are a species of purposes trust: as to which see vol 40(2)
        (2001 Reissue) TRUSTS AND SETTLEMENTS Part 13 [7501].
              When this clause is inserted in a document the defined terms in { } must be altered to suit those
        used in the document.

[1644]

171
Power to improve land[1]

The {Trustees} may in their uncontrolled discretion and from time to time apply any
money for the time being forming part of the capital [or income][2] of the {Trust Fund}
in improving or developing in any manner whatsoever any land which or the proceeds
of sale of which may for the time being be subject to the trusts of this settlement or in
building rebuilding erecting enlarging decorating or improving any buildings or other
structure upon such land

[1645]

1   Note that the powers of trustees of land given by the Trusts of Land and Appointment of Trustees Act
        1996 s 6(1) (37 Halsbury's Statutes (4th Edn) REAL PROPERTY) are limited to the land itself and would
        not include the power to use any part of the trust capital eg to improve the land. As to the Trusts of
        Land and Appointment of Trustees Act 1996 s 6 as amended see Paragraph 221 [532] ante and vol 40(2)
        (2001 Reissue) TRUSTS AND SETTLEMENTS Part 8 [3001]. By contrast, the powers given under the
        Trustee Act 2000 are not so restricted. When this clause is inserted in a document the defined terms in
        { } must be altered to suit those used in the document.
2   The words in square brackets may be omitted if the settlement is intended to include an interest in
        possession since the trustees would then have the power to divert income away from the person entitled
        to it and this could result in the settlement being taxed as one with no interest in possession for
        inheritance tax purposes. This will depend on whether a power to apply income in this way is an
        administrative or dispositive power: see Introduction to Section H [1586] ante; and see *Pearson v IRC*
        [1981] AC 753, [1980] 2 All ER 479, HL and see Paragraph 287.2 [731] ante.

[1646]

172
Express power of leasing[1]

Until the land now settled on trust for sale ('the Land') shall be sold the {Trustees} may at any time or times [with the consent in writing of *(life tenant)* and after [his] death at the discretion of the {Trustees}] demise the Land or any part or parts of it for any term of years absolutely or lesser period or otherwise and either at a rack rent or taking a premium and either subject or not subject to stipulations as to repairing or building and may grant any such lease subject to such covenants and conditions at such progressive or other rents and otherwise in such manner in all respects as the {Trustees} may think fit as if they were beneficially entitled to the Land and may [with the same consent and at the same discretion] enter into any contract or contracts for the granting of any such lease and may also rescind abandon or vary the terms of every or any such contract which may have been entered into for any such lease upon such terms and conditions as the {Trustees} may think fit and any money or other consideration to be received as a premium for the granting of any such lease shall be held upon such trusts as are declared or referred to in this settlement concerning the money to arise from the sale of the property now granted

[1647]

1   For the general powers of trustees of land see the Trusts of Land and Appointment of Trustees Act 1996 s 6 as amended by the Trustee Act 2000 s 40(1), Sch 2 para 45(1)–(3), Sch 4 Pt II (37 Halsbury's Statutes (4th Edn) REAL PROPERTY) and Paragraph 221 [532] ante. For the continued use of trusts for sale see Paragraph 108 [267] ante. The powers conferred by the Trusts of Land and Appointment of Trustees Act 1996 s 6 as amended are limited to land in the UK. For the powers given to all trustees, see the Trustee Act 2000 Pt III (ss 8–10) (48 Halsbury's Statutes (4th Edn) TRUSTS AND SETTLEMENTS).
     When this clause is inserted in a document the defined terms in { } must be altered to suit those used in the document.

[1648]

173
Power to determine whether expenditure to fall on capital or income[1]

The {Trustees} may in their absolute discretion from time to time and at any time pay or appropriate any part of the capital or income of the {Trust Fund} in meeting defraying or otherwise providing for any costs expenses or other liabilities incurred by the {Trustees} in the administration of the property for the time being forming part of the {Trust Fund} and may charge the same with the payment of any sums of money payable in respect of any such liabilities

[1649]

1   As to the allocation of expenses to capital and income see generally Paragraph 144 [351] et seq ante. It is not considered that the Trustee Act 2000 s 31 has effected any change in the law. This clause (and Form 174 [1651] post) should be avoided where it is intended that the settlement should contain an interest in possession for inheritance tax purposes because of the risk that the clause confers dispositive powers on trustees: see Form 171 note 2 [1645] ante. For the income tax position see *Carver v Duncan* [1985] AC 1082, [1985] 2 All ER 645, HL and Paragraph 348.1 [961] ante.
     When this clause is inserted in a document the defined terms in { } must be altered to suit those used in the document.

[1650]

174

Power to determine whether receipts are capital or income[1]

The {Trustees} may if they in their absolute discretion think fit from time to time and at any time decide whether any property received by them as such trustees shall be treated as income or as capital for the purposes of any one or more of the trusts powers and other provisions contained in or conferred by this settlement

[1651]

1   This clause is sometimes found in old trusts and, more often, in overseas trusts. Its use in United Kingdom trusts raises difficult problems: for example, to what extent can trustees be allowed to decide whether receipts are trust capital or trust income? That trustees can decide whether trust expenses will be paid out of trust income or capital, irrespective of the true nature of those expenses, is accepted (see Form 173 [1649] ante) and so, albeit indirectly, trustees do have the ability to determine the quantum of income and capital. To go further and give trustees the power to characterise receipts may, however, be to go too far although it should be stressed that this is not a matter which has been finally decided by the courts.

In *Miller v IRC* [1987] STC 108, a Scottish case, the deceased was entitled under a marriage settlement which she made on alimentary liferent (non assignable life interest) for herself; thereafter the trust fund was held on further alimentary trusts for her husband and children. There then followed a declaration empowering the trustees to:

'striking the free income or produce of any year … to appropriate such portion of revenue as they may think proper for meeting (1) depreciation of the capital value of any of the assets with regard to which they may think it prudent to provide for depreciation, and (2) for any other reason or purpose which the trustees may in their sole discretion deem to be advisable or necessary; and the trustees shall have power to decide what sums received by them fall to be treated as revenue and what as capital, and what payments made by them fall to be charged to revenue and what to capital.'

[1652]

The liferentrix died in 1982 and the trustees claimed that no tax was then payable on the basis that the effect of the above declaration was to prevent her having an interest in possession in the trust fund. The Scottish Court of Session held unanimously that the trustees' power to apply income in the manner set out above was administrative, not dispositive, and that therefore the liferentrix did have an interest in possession. Lord Kingcraig, giving the leading judgment, referred to Viscount Dilhorne's dicta in *Pearson v IRC* [1981] AC 753, [1980] 2 All ER 479, HL to the effect that a dispositive power has the effect of enabling income to be diverted so that it benefits others (see Paragraph 287 [730] ante). The powers here were intended merely to preserve the trust capital for the benefit of the beneficiaries as a whole. In contrast to *Pearson v IRC*, the initial gift was the deceased's liferent, the powers being a burden on that gift. Their purpose was to maintain the land and buildings comprised in the trust fund for the benefit of all the beneficiaries, including the liferentrix, not to divert income away from her for the benefit of others. The clause in this case was more restrictive than the precedent under consideration, being confined as the statement indicates to diverting income to make good depreciation in the trust capital.

Recent problems involving corporate demergers effected by a distribution of shares and enhanced scrip dividends, have pointed to the benefits that could result from incorporating such a clause in the trust deed: in the demerger situation, for instance, *Sinclair v Lee* [1993] Ch 497, [1993] 3 All ER 926 went only part of the way to solving the problem of whether the demerger shares were an income or capital receipt since the judgment was limited to the so-called 'indirect' demerger. Whether shares received under a 'direct' demerger are trust income or capital remains unclear: in common sense, the shares should be capital and trustees armed with a clause along the lines of this Form would doubtless so decide (for the attitude of the Inland Revenue, see Inland Revenue Statement of Practice SP4/94 (17 May 1994)). One option for the trust draftsman to consider is to limit the clause to catch particular problem areas: for instance the case where because of a shareholding, trustees receive further shares from the relevant company. See further the Trust Law Committee, Consultation Paper, 'Capital and Income of Trusts' (June 1999).

When this clause is inserted in a document the defined terms in { } must be altered to suit those used in the document.

[1653]

175

Power to determine whether receipts are capital or income and whether expenditure to fall on capital or income—long form[1]

To treat as income or as capital or to apportion between income and capital any dividends stock dividends bonus shares rights interests rents issues and profits derived from any property at any time comprised in the {Trust Fund} and generally to determine as the {Trustees} shall deem just and reasonable according to the respective rights and interests of the persons interested what part of the receipts of the trust is income and what is capital and whether or not such property is wasting or unproductive or was purchased at a premium or discount and notwithstanding the time when such dividend stock dividends bonus shares rights interest rents issues or profits were earned accrued declared or paid to make such reserves out of income or capital as the {Trustees} deem proper for expenses taxes and other liabilities of the trust to pay from income or from capital or to apportion between income and capital any expenses of making or changing investments and of selling exchanging or leasing including brokers' commissions and charges and generally to determine what part of the expenses of the trust shall be charged to capital and what part to income and to determine as between separate funds and separate parts or shares the allocation of income gains profits and losses and distributions

1   For a short form power to determine whether expenditure falls on capital or income see Form 173 [1649] ante. For a short form power to determine whether receipts are capital or income see Form 174 [1651] ante. When this clause is inserted in a document the defined terms in { } must be altered to suit those used in the document.

[1654]

176

Power of exchange including property abroad[1]

0.1   The {Trustees} may dispose of transfer and convey in exchange for other land immovable property tenements rentcharges easements or like incumbrances whatever over or affecting land or immovable property wherever situated whether in the United Kingdom or abroad and held for an estate in fee simple in possession (if situated in England and Wales) or absolutely all or any part of the land conveyed to them to be held on the trusts of this settlement to any person or persons for such an equivalent or recompense in land immovable property tenements rentcharges or easements or incumbrances whatever over or affecting land or immovable property as to the {Trustees} shall seem reasonable and on any such exchange may give or receive any money for equality of exchange

0.2   The {Trustees} shall [with all convenient speed after effecting any such exchange] pay and apply any money to be received for equality of exchange in or on such of the trusts now declared of the net money to be produced by the sale of such property [conveyed to the {Trustees} on trust for sale] as shall then be subsisting and capable of taking effect

[1655]

1   As to stamp duty on exchanges of property see Information Binder: Stamp Duties [1] Table of Duties (Exchange or Excambion). A tenant for life has a statutory power of exchange: Settled Land Act 1925 s 38(iii) (48 Halsbury's Statutes (4th Edn) TRUSTS AND SETTLEMENTS). However, that power excludes the giving of settled land in England or Wales in exchange for land outside England or Wales:

see the Settled Land Act 1925 s 40(3). Trustees of land are given wider powers by the Trusts of Land and Appointment of Trustees Act 1996 s 6 as amended by the Trustee Act 2000 s 40(1), Sch 2 para 45(1)–(3), Sch 4 Pt II (37 Halsbury's Statutes (4th Edn) REAL PROPERTY) in relation to land situated in the UK: see Paragraph 221 [532] ante and vol 40(2) (2001 Reissue) TRUSTS AND SETTLEMENTS Part 8 [3001]. This clause is more extensive than the statutory power, and may be useful if the settlement comprises or may comprise land abroad.

    When this clause is inserted in a document the defined terms in { } must be altered to suit those used in the document.

[1656]

177

Power to take a reduced deposit on sale of land and appoint a stakeholder[1]

On the occasion of any sale transfer demise exchange grant or other transaction affecting any trust property the {Trustees} shall have the following powers:

0.1   to agree to the payment of a deposit representing less than 10% of the total consideration (or equality money on exchange) payable under any contract [provided that any such deposit shall not be less than 2.5% of the sum so payable]

0.2   to permit any deposit of whatever amount to be held by a stakeholder under the terms of any contract to which they are a party

and the {Trustees} shall not be liable for any loss arising from or in consequence of the exercise of such powers[2]

[1657]

1   Trustees may be open to criticism if they take a deposit of less than 10% under a contract for the sale of trust property in circumstances where such deposit is customary. Should the purchaser default, the deposit received may not cover any loss on resale in a falling property market, remedies against the purchaser having been exhausted. Standard conveyancing contracts which usually incorporate some form of Standard Conditions, typically the Standard Conditions of Sale (3rd Edn), for which see vol 35 (1997 Reissue) SALE OF LAND Form 7 [1416], or the Standard Commercial Property Conditions (1st Edn), for which see vol 38(1) (2000 Reissue) SALE OF LAND Form 2 [1071], which provide for a 10% deposit to be held by the seller's solicitor as stakeholder. Arguably, the trustees would be committing a breach of trust by allowing trust property (ie the deposit as part of the sale proceeds) to be held by a third party who is not their agent for the purpose of receiving the deposit. This clause overcomes these difficulties by allowing the taking of a reduced deposit and the appointment of a stakeholder, although it is envisaged that the first power would only be exercised to accommodate a purchaser who was short of immediate funds.

     When this clause is inserted in a document the defined terms in { } must be altered to suit those used in the document.

2   If not included in the trust deed, the clause could be adapted to provide for an authorisation and indemnity in appropriate circumstances.

[1658]

178

Additional powers to manage farms and woodlands[1]

If the {Trustees} shall purchase any farm agricultural land or woodlands they shall in addition to the powers conferred on them by the Trusts of Land and Appointment of Trustees Act 1996 Section 6 and by the Trustee Act 2000 Section 8[2] have power to manage stock and cultivate such farm agricultural land or woodlands [including power subject to obtaining any necessary planning or other permission to use the land so purchased for commercial or sporting purposes such as and including fishing clay pigeon pheasant grouse or other game shooting and recreational activities such as and including off-road driving paintballing adventure training and camping] and to employ and expend such part of the capital [or income]³ of the {Trust Fund} as they shall think fit for that purpose or for the purpose of compensating outgoing tenants (whether such compensation be paid for improvements or in consideration of the surrender of a lease or otherwise) with power also to hire engage dismiss and pay managers bailiffs agents labourers and workmen and to buy and sell live and dead farm stock and to employ the same in the management and cultivation of such farm agricultural land or woodlands and generally to act in all matters relating to such farm agricultural land or woodlands as if they were the absolute owners of them and the {Trustees} shall be free from all responsibility and be fully indemnified out of the {Trust Fund} in respect of any loss arising in the exercise of this power

[1659]

1   This clause is included for use primarily where it is contemplated that agricultural land may be acquired. Trustees are naturally reluctant to engage in any business in the absence of the clearest express power and indemnity. When this clause is inserted in a document the defined terms in { } must be altered to suit those used in the document.

2   As to the Trusts of Land and Appointment of Trustees Act 1996 s 6 as amended by the Trustee Act 2000 s 40(1), Sch 2 para 45(1)–(3), Sch 4 Pt II (37 Halsbury's Statutes (4th Edn) REAL PROPERTY) see Paragraph 221 [532] ante and vol 40(2) (2001 Reissue) TRUSTS AND SETTLEMENTS Part 8 [3001]. As to the Trustee Act 2000 s 8 (48 Halsbury's Statutes (4th Edn) TRUSTS AND SETTLEMENTS) see Paragraph 244 [596] ante.

3   The words in square brackets may be omitted if the settlement is intended to include an interest in possession since the trustees would then have the power to divert income away from the person entitled to it, and this could result in the settlement being taxed as one with no interest in possession for inheritance tax purposes. This will depend on whether a power to apply income in this way is an administrative or dispositive power: see Introduction to Section H [1586] ante, see *Pearson v IRC* [1981] AC 753, [1980] 2 All ER 479, HL and see Paragraph 287.2 [731] ante.

[1660]

179

Powers of management of property and carrying on any business—short form¹

The {Trustees} shall in respect of any property of whatsoever nature which shall for the time being be subject to the trusts of this settlement have all the powers of disposition leasing management repair building development equipment furnishing insurance improvement and all other powers of any beneficial owner absolutely entitled including in particular and without prejudice to the generality of this clause full power to carry on equip and finance any business or promote any corporation for that purpose in any part of the world and may in that behalf or for that purpose expend any part or parts of the capital [or income]² of the {Trust Fund}

[1661]

1   If trustees need to carry on a business they should be given express powers in the trust instrument. This clause does not allow the trustees to carry on business with one or more of themselves as partners in their own right: if this power is desired Form 180 [1633] post should be adapted. For a wider general power see Form 186 [1665] post. When this clause is inserted in a document the defined terms in { } must be altered to suit those used in the document.

2   See Form 178 note 3 [1660] ante.

[1662]

180

Power to carry on existing business[1]

The {Trustees} may for such time as they in their absolute discretion consider it to be for the benefit of those persons beneficially interested under this settlement carry on or assist in carrying on by themselves or in partnership with any other person [including one or more of themselves][2] the business described in Part I of the schedule ('the Business') the assets of which are described in Part II of the schedule as forming part of the {Trust Fund} and for that purpose may retain such assets in their actual state without being liable for loss and may employ in the same such additional capital whether or not forming part of the {Trust Fund} as they shall think fit and may employ or concur in employing any managers of the Business [including one or more of themselves] and may act generally in all matters relating to the Business as if they were beneficially entitled to it and may delegate all or any of the powers contained in this settlement to any persons or person whom they may think fit

[1663]

1   This clause may be necessary when assets comprising a business are settled. The clause provides for the trustees to carry on a specified business only. If a general power to carry on businesses is required then either Form 179 [1661] ante or Form 181 [1665] post should be used. When this clause is inserted in a document the defined terms in { } must be altered to suit those used in the document.
2   These words should be included if the assets consist of a share in a partnership in which the trustees are or are likely to be interested as partners.

[1664]

181

Power to start and carry on business—additional power to form company for purpose of carrying on business[1]

0.1   The {Trustees} may from time to time carry on or assist in carrying on whether by themselves or singly or in partnership with any other persons or corporation (whether or not such persons or corporation shall be beneficially or otherwise interested under the trusts of this settlement) any business which they shall in their absolute discretion consider to be for the benefit of the persons for the time being beneficially interested under this settlement and for that purpose may employ in any such business any part or parts of the capital of the {Trust Fund} [not exceeding in total more than one-half of its value] as they shall from time to time see fit to advance for the purposes of such business and for this purpose may engage or concur in engaging on such terms as they shall think fit any managers (whether corporate or not) and other employees of the business and may delegate any of the powers vested in them by this sub-clause to any person or persons or corporations and may otherwise act in relation to such business as if they were beneficially entitled to it

[1665]

0.2   The {Trustees} may at any time promote or join in promoting any company wherever situated or resident for the purpose of carrying on or taking over any such business as is mentioned in clause [0.1] or concur in any scheme or arrangement for the reconstruction of any such company or for its amalgamation with any other company or for the transfer of any such business to another company in such manner as they shall think fit or may sell or transfer any such business or the property (including the goodwill) of any such business or any part of it to any such company in consideration for the issue to them of shares stock debentures or debenture stock or of the payment of cash or otherwise whether the same be issued transferred or payable immediately or by instalments and any such shares stock debentures debenture stock cash or other property whatsoever received by the {Trustees} in consideration for any such transfer shall be held by them as forming part of the capital of the {Trust Fund} PROVIDED that any expense incurred by the {Trustees} in the promotion of any such company or in entering into any such scheme or arrangement as is contemplated above shall be payable out of the capital of the {Trust Fund}

[1666]

0.3   The {Trustees} or any of them may act as officers of any such company as is referred to in clause [0.2] without being accountable for any remuneration or other benefits received by them or him as such and notwithstanding that the appointment of them or him was procured directly or indirectly by the exercise or as the result of the non-exercise of voting and other rights attaching to any shares stock debentures or debenture stock for the time being forming part of the {Trust Fund}[2]

0.4   All contracts or arrangements made or entered into by the {Trustees} or any of them in pursuance of the exercise of any of the powers contained in this clause shall be valid and effectual notwithstanding that the {Trustees} or any of them shall be promoters or a promoter of any such company or partners or a partner in any such business or otherwise interested in the same otherwise than as the {Trustees} or one of them under this settlement

[1667]

1   This clause is intended for use in settlements conferring the widest powers on trustees. Trustees have, in general, no power to carry on a business. For a power to carry on any business (short-form) see Form 179 [1661] ante and for a power to carry on a specified business only see Form 180 [1663] ante. When this clause is inserted in a document the defined terms in { } must be altered to suit those used in the document.

2   For the equitable position in the absence of this provision, see Paragraph 153 [372] ante.

[1668]

182

Power to form limited liability partnerships[1]

Any partnership formed by the {Trustees} to carry on any business pursuant to [the proceeding sub-clause] may be a limited liability partnership under the Limited Liability Partnership Act 2000 and the Trustees may agree with the other partners therein (who may include any beneficiary or beneficiaries under the trusts of this settlement) such terms and conditions of the partnership as they shall think fit

1   The Limited Liability Partnership Act 2000 (32 Halsbury's Statutes (4th Edn) PARTNERSHIP) may be of use to trustees mindful of their personal liability for business debts which would apply if it was carried on as a 'sole trade' or through the medium of a simple partnership. As to limited liability partnerships generally see vol 30 (1996 Reissue) PARTNERSHIP Paragraph 246 [354] et seq. When this clause is inserted in a document the defined terms in { } must be altered to suit those used in the document.

[1669]

183

Power to hold directorships and retain remuneration[1]

Any {Trustee} may act as an officer or employee of any company in which the {Trust Fund} or any part of it may be invested or as an officer or employee of any subsidiary of any such company and may retain for himself any remuneration or other benefits which he may receive by virtue of his position as such officer or employee notwithstanding that any votes or other rights attached to any such investment may have been instrumental either by themselves or in combination with other votes or rights whether or not of a similar nature or by reason of the non-exercise of any such votes or rights in procuring or maintaining for himself his position as such officer or employee

1   For the position in the absence of a provision such as this see Paragraph 153 [372] ante. When this clause is inserted in a document the defined terms in { } must be altered to suit those used in the document.

[1670]

184

Power to retain and invest in property not producing income[1]

None of the {Beneficiaries} shall be entitled to compel the sale or other realisation of any property or investments not producing income [or to insist on the investment of any part of the {Trust Fund} in property or investments which produce income]

1   For a discussion on trustees' powers of investment see Paragraph 241 [591] et seq ante. Older cases considered that an 'investment' had to produce income; in the Trustee Act 2000 the word 'investment' is not defined but in recent years judges have commented favourably on trustees being judged according to 'modern portfolio theory'. When this clause is inserted in a document the defined terms in { } must be altered to suit those used in the document.

[1671]

185

Powers to be exercised within perpetuity period[1]

No discretion or power conferred on the {Trustees} or on any other person by this settlement or by any appointment made under it shall be exercised or become exercisable in any circumstances whatsoever [after the end of the {Trust Period}[2] or outside the {Perpetuity Period}[3]]

[1672]

1   When this clause is inserted in a document the defined terms in { } must be altered to suit those used in the document.
2   This clause assumes that the trust period has already been defined in the definition section of the deed; eg 'the Trust Period' means the period starting on the date of this deed and ending 80 years afterwards which period shall be the perpetuity period applicable to the trusts under this deed. Of course, the term 'the Trust Period' need not be the same as the perpetuity period. As to perpetuities see further Paragraph 77 [183] ante.
3   Normally the administrative powers of trustees can be exercised outside the perpetuity period applicable to the settlement: see the Perpetuities and Accumulations Act 1964 s 8(1) (33 Halsbury's Statutes (4th Edn) PERPETUITIES).

[1673]

186

Power to restrict the exercise of a power by releasing part of fund or income, or by restricting purposes or means of exercise[1]

PROVIDED that the {Trustees} from time to time and at any time may by deed or deeds restrict the exercise of the preceding power by releasing the whole or any part or parts of the [income of the] {Trust Fund} from the exercise of the preceding power [or by restricting or extinguishing either wholly or in part any one or more of the purposes for or means by which such power can be exercised as to the whole or any part or parts of the {Trust Fund}] but so that no such release restriction or extinguishment shall operate so as to invalidate any prior exercise of the above power

1   This clause, still often found in offshore trusts, should be avoided. For public policy reasons an attempt to oust the jurisdiction of the court is void: see *re Wynn* [1952] Ch 271, [1952] 1 All ER 341. This Form will be appropriate where it is desired to put an end to an accumulation. When this clause is inserted in a document the defined terms in { } must be altered to suit those used in the document.

[1674]

187

Powers of trustees to be uncontrolled and unfettered[1]

The discretions and powers conferred on the {Trustees} by this settlement shall be absolute and uncontrolled discretions and powers and any such powers or discretions appertaining to the management or administration of any property for the time being forming part of the {Trust Fund} shall be exercisable by the {Trustees} as if they were beneficially entitled to it and none of the {Trustees} shall be held liable for any loss or damage to the {Trust Fund} or any part of it arising as a result of the exercise or failure to exercise or of the concurring or failing to concur in any such power or discretions

1   This clause, still often found in offshore trusts, should be avoided. For public policy reasons an attempt to oust the jurisdiction of the court is void: see *re Wynn* [1952] Ch 271, [1952] 1 All ER 341. Further, limits will be imposed by the courts based on the 'irreducible trust core' despite the apparent width of the protection afforded to trustees: see, for instance, *Armitage v Nurse* [1998] Ch 241, [1997] 2 All ER 705, CA and Paragraph 94 [227] ante.
        When this clause is inserted in a document the defined terms in { } must be altered to suit those used in the document.

[1675]

188

Power to effect transactions and exercise powers though personally interested[1]

Notwithstanding any rule of law or equity to the contrary the {Trustees} may validly effect any of the following transactions PROVIDED that every trustee personally interested in the transaction shall have acted in good faith and that at least one of the {Trustees} shall have no interest in the transaction save in his capacity as one of the trustees of the settlement:

0.1   the sale or other disposal of any property or any estate right or interest in or over any property to the {Trustees} as part of the {Trust Fund}

0.2   the purchase of any property forming part of the {Trust Fund} or any estate right or interest in or over such property

0.3   the loan of money to the {Trustees} as part of the {Trust Fund} on the security of the {Trust Fund} or otherwise and on such terms as to interest and repayment as may be agreed between the {Trustees}

0.4   the borrowing of money forming part of the {Trust Fund} on such terms as to interest and repayment as may be agreed between the {Trustees}

[1676]

0.5   the leasing or agreeing to lease or the hire of any property to the {Trustees} so as to form part of the {Trust Fund} on such terms and conditions as to rent and otherwise as may be agreed between the {Trustees}

0.6   the taking on lease or the hire of any property forming part of the {Trust Fund} on such terms and conditions as to rent or otherwise as may be agreed between the {Trustees}

0.7   the acceptance of payment of money by instalments with or without security

0.8   the expenditure of capital money in the repair improvement development decoration or rebuilding of any land or other immovable property whatsoever or wheresoever situated held by the {Trustees} as part of the {Trust Fund}

0.9   the provision of security for any account due from the {Beneficiaries} otherwise than to the {Settlor} or any spouse of the {Settlor}

0.10   any other transaction concerning the property for the time being forming part of the {Trust Fund} or the management of it notwithstanding that the {Trustees} have a personal interest in it

[1677]

1   This Form confers a wide exemption on the trustees from the rule that a trustee must not profit from his trust: see Paragraph 208 [495] ante. Its width can be reduced by excluding one or more of the transactions mentioned. For a power to enter into transactions with other trusts of which the trustees may also be trustees see Form 4 schedule para 24 [1101] ante. When this clause is inserted in a document the defined terms in { } must be altered to suit those used in the document.

  Different problems may arise if a trustee is also a beneficiary when the question is whether he can exercise a dispositive discretion in his own favour.

[1678]

189

Administrative powers relating to a settled share of an undivided estate[1]

0.1   Except in cases in which in the exercise of the powers in that behalf contained below the {Trustees} shall think fit to defer or modify the execution of this trust the {Trustees} shall so soon as may be required and if need be compel the payment or transfer to them of the property constituting the share now assigned ('the Assigned Share')

0.2   The {Trustees} shall at such time or times as they may consider most expedient realise such (if any) part of the Assigned Share as shall consist of investments other than such as are authorised by this settlement and shall either retain or at any time or times [with the consent of the {Spouses} or the survivor of them and after the death of that survivor] at their discretion realise all or any part of the Assigned Share in the form of investments now or by law authorised and shall invest in manner now or by law authorised the proceeds of any such realisation and also any part of the Assigned Share which shall be paid to them in money

0.3   The {Trustees} may at any time if they think fit accept in satisfaction of part of the Assigned Share any equitable undivided part of any land buildings and property or any undivided part of any mortgage debts and securities for the same although the entireties of the same mortgage debts and securities shall remain vested in the trustees for the time being of the will of *(testator)* ('the Will Trustees' which shall include all future trustees of the same will) or in other persons approved for the purposes by the {Trustees} [PROVIDED that the Will Trustees or such other persons shall have delivered to the {Trustees} a declaration of trust approved by the {Trustees} of such debts and securities a part of which shall be accepted as stated above as part of the Assigned Share]

[1679]

[0.4   The {Trustees} may at any time at their discretion concur with the Will Trustees and any other persons interested in the property subject to the trusts of the residuary estate of *(testator)* ('the Residuary Estate') in any partition of all or of any part of the Residuary Estate and may accept from the Will Trustees in substitution for the Assigned Share or for any part of it any severed part of the Residuary Estate which the {Trustees} shall judge to be equivalent to (as the case may require) the whole or the part of the Assigned Share in substitution for which the {Trustees} shall accept that severed part and every such partition so concurred in by the {Trustees} shall be binding on all persons who by virtue of this settlement are or may become interested in the Assigned Share with respect to the interests now acquired by them][2]

0.5   The {Trustees} may at such discretion as stated above allow such time as they shall in any case think it proper or expedient to allow the Will Trustees for the payment or transfer of the Assigned Share or of any property constituting or substituted for the same or any part of it

0.6   The {Trustees} shall not be bound (though they shall be at full liberty) to investigate the accounts of the Will Trustees and the course of the administration of their trust or any part of it and they shall not be bound [(save on the request in writing of some person beneficially interested under this settlement)] (although they shall be at liberty) to make or insist on or by any proceedings in any court of law or equity to seek to enforce any claim or claims which the {Trustees} might enforce against the Will Trustees or any other person or persons with respect to or on account of any inaccuracy in such accounts or any act or acts or omission or omissions in the course of such administration

[1680]

1   This Form is intended to provide for the case where the property settled is a share in other property (in this Form the property is comprised in a will trust) in which the settlor has an interest held jointly with others. When this clause is inserted in a document the defined terms in { } must be altered to suit those used in the document.

2   Power to agree the amount or value of their share, and to concur with the owners of other individual shares, is given by the Trustee Act 1925 ss 22(1), 24 as amended by the Trustee Act 2000 s 40(1), Sch 2 para 22(a) and the Trusts of Land and Appointment of Trustees Act 1996 s 25(1), Sch 3 para 3(6) (48 Halsbury's Statutes (4th Edn) TRUSTS AND SETTLEMENTS): see Paragraph 265 [653] ante. It will in most cases be sufficient to rely on these provisions unless it is desired to extend them or make special provision for some particular matter; eg partition, in the case of land, may be effected under the Trusts of Land and Appointment of Trustees Act 1996 s 7 (37 Halsbury's Statutes (4th Edn) REAL PROPERTY).

[1681]

190

Power to accept an interest under another trust[1]

The {Trustees} may accept any interest under any estate or trust which may with their consent be assigned to them and will in addition have the following incidental powers:

0.1   the {Trustees} may agree and settle without further investigation the accounts of the trustees of any estate or trust in which any interest assigned to them subsists and for that purpose may execute and give releases and discharges whether or not those trustees are strictly entitled to them;

0.2   the {Trustees} will not be liable for any failure to proceed against or to direct any investigation of the accounts of any person who has or may have committed a breach of the trust in which any interest assigned to the {Trustees} subsists; and

0.3   the {Trustees} may join with any other person or persons beneficially interested in the estate or trust concerned in securing such variation of the trusts affecting the estate or trust as the {Trustees} consider desirable including the partition of the funds subject to those trusts between different beneficiaries

In exercising the powers under this clause the {Trustees} may rely entirely upon the advice of any person reasonably believed by them to be qualified to give that advice and may agree to any proposal which that person may advise is or may be for the benefit of this settlement

[1682]

---

1   It is a common inheritance tax saving arrangement for a remainder interest to be settled: for instance on accumulation and maintenance trusts for the settlor's children. The interest is (generally) excluded property for inheritance tax (see the Inheritance Tax Act 1984 s 48 as amended by the Finance Act 1996 Sch 28 para 8 (42–44 Halsbury's Statutes (4th Edn) TAXATION)) and its transfer will not normally attract a capital gains tax charge (see the Taxation of Chargeable Gains Act 1992 s 76(1) as amended by the Finance Act 1998 s 128(1)(a) (42–44 Halsbury's Statutes (4th Edn) TAXATION)); but note the growing list of exceptions: see Paragraph 315 [811] ante.

     When this clause is inserted in a document the defined terms in { } must be altered to suit those used in the document.

[1683]

191

Power of trustees to insure the lives of the settlor and any of the beneficiaries[1]

The {Trustees} shall have power at any time to effect any policy of insurance of whatever nature upon the life of the {Settlor} and the lives of any of the {Beneficiaries} and to pay or apply any part of the capital or income (including accumulations of income)[2] of the {Trust Fund} in or towards the payment of any premium for effecting or maintaining any such policy or to borrow from any person or corporation (including any one or more of themselves) the whole or any part of the money required for the payment of any such premium whether or not the loan is secured upon the whole or any part of the {Trust Fund} and upon such terms as to interest repayment and otherwise as the {Trustees} shall see fit to agree to the intent that the {Trustees} shall hold any such policy and the proceeds of it and all money arising from it as an accretion to the capital of the {Trust Fund}

[1684]

1   This power may be considered useful when it is desired to insure against the possible liability of the
        trustees to inheritance tax arising on the death of the settlor within seven years of effecting the
        settlement or against a similar liability on the death of any of the beneficiaries. The scope of this clause
        is not restricted to policies designed to provide for inheritance tax which might arise on the death of
        the settlor or any of the beneficiaries.
              When this clause is inserted in a document the defined terms in { } must be altered to suit those
        used in the document.
2   It is considered that a power to apply income in this way is administrative in nature: see Introduction
        to Section H [1586] ante, *Pearson v IRC* [1981] AC 753, [1980] 2 All ER 479, HL and Paragraph 287.2
        [731] ante. For the income tax position when premiums are paid out of income see *Carver v Duncan*
        [1985] AC 1082, [1985] 2 All ER 645, HL and see Paragraph 348.1 [961] ante.

[1685]

192

Power to dispense with consents[1]

Where under the provisions of this settlement any consent is required to be given in
writing or otherwise to the exercise of any trust or power now declared or conferred the
{Trustees} shall apply personally or by letter addressed to the last address known to them
of the person or persons whose consent is required for consent to any transaction
proposed by the {Trustees} and if any such person shall within [21] days or such time as
the {Trustees} may require [either] fail to consent [or shall refuse to consent][2] to such
transaction the {Trustees} may dispense with the consent of the person so failing to
consent [or refusing to consent] and may perform the trust or exercise the power as if
the consent of such person had not been required

1   When this clause is inserted in a document the defined terms in { } must be altered to suit those used
        in the document.
2   It would be unusual to include the words in square brackets which have the effect of reducing the
        obligations of the trustees to notification of the relevant person. In the case of an offshore trust, the
        consent of a Protector is commonly required before trustees distribute the trust fund.

[1686]

193

Residuary power to do all other acts in the administration of the trust considered for the benefit of the trust fund[1]

The {Trustees} may enter into and execute any agreements business arrangements
dealing dispositions dedications whatsoever and do all other acts and things whatever
which the {Trustees} may in their absolute discretion think expedient in the interests of
any person or persons for the time being beneficially interested in the trusts of
this settlement

1   When this clause is inserted in a document the defined terms in { } must be altered to suit those used
        in the document.

[1687]

194

Power of trustees to confer additional powers on themselves or nominees[1]

If in the course of the management or administration of the assets for the time being subject to the trusts of this settlement the {Trustees} shall consider that any transaction is expedient but the same cannot be effected by reason of the presence or absence of any power for that or any other purpose vested in the {Trustees} by this settlement or by law and the transaction is such as that defined in the Settled Land Act 1925 Section 64[2] or mentioned in the Trustee Act 1925 Section 57[3] the {Trustees} may by any deed revoke vary or confer upon themselves or on their nominees either generally or in any particular instance the necessary power for that purpose without the necessity of obtaining an order of the court

[1688]

1   This Form might be included for convenience but note that although it appears to give the trustees freedom to include almost any administrative provision, it is probable that it would be construed as restricted to the inclusion only of those powers which the court would consider for the benefit of the beneficiaries. It probably would not allow export of the trust. For an alternative clause, see Form 4 clause 8.3 [1089] ante.
         When this clause is inserted in a document the defined terms in { } must be altered to suit those used in the document.
2   As to settlements of land under the Settled Land Act 1925 (48 Halsbury's Statutes (4th Edn) TRUSTS AND SETTLEMENTS), see generally vol 40(2) (2001 Reissue) TRUSTS AND SETTLEMENTS Part 9 [4101].
3   As to this section generally see Paragraph 234 [567] ante.

[1689]

195

Clause providing for collective delegation by trustees of their administrative powers including delegation to beneficiaries[1]

0.1   Power to delegate all or any of the powers of the {Trustees} contained in the [schedule] and any administrative powers conferred by law (and all or any of the duties and discretions of the {Trustees} relating to the exercise of such powers) to any person or persons (not being the {Settlor} or any spouse of the {Settlor}) subject to such conditions (if any) and upon such terms (including the remuneration of any such delegate) as the {Trustees} shall think fit (without being liable for the acts or defaults of any such delegate) and to revoke or modify any such delegation or conditions or terms

0.2   The persons in whose favour the {Trustees} may delegate all or any of such powers include any one or more of the {Trustees} and any one of more of the beneficiaries under the trusts of this settlement (but other than and excluding the Settlor or any spouse of the {Settlor})

0.3   A delegation by the {Trustees} under the foregoing power to two or more persons may authorise such delegates to exercise the powers duties and discretions delegated either jointly or jointly and severally

0.4   The Trustee Act 2000 Section 11 shall not apply to this deed[2]

[1690]

1   The power to delegate under the Trustee Act 2000 s 11 (48 Halsbury's Statutes (4th Edn) TRUSTS
       AND SETTLEMENTS) cannot be exercised in favour of a beneficiary. This precedent permits trustees
       to delegate administrative powers to any person (other than the settlor or his spouse) including a
       beneficiary. It also permits joint and several delegation; cf the Trustee Act 2000 s 12(2). As to powers
       providing for delegation by trustees, whether collectively or individually, see Form 316 [2194] et
       seq post.
             When this clause is inserted in a document the defined terms in { } must be altered to suit those
       used in the document.
2   The power to delegate contained in the Trustee Act 2000 s 11 may be excluded: see the Trustee Act
       2000 s 26(b). The duty to keep the arrangements with an agent under review and to intervene
       contained in the Trustee Act 2000 s 22 may also, if desired, be excluded in connection with this express
       power: see the Trustee Act 2000 s 21(3).

                                                                                                   [1691]

196

Power to vest trust fund in nominees[1]

0.1   The {Trustees} may from time to time cause any property forming part of the
         {Trust Fund} to be registered in the name or names of any other persons or
         corporations whatsoever and wheresoever resident or situated on behalf of the
         {Trustees} and may pay any expenses in connection with the same out of the
         capital or income of the {Trust Fund} as may be proper and the {Trustees} shall
         not be liable for any loss to the {Trust Fund} which may be occasioned by the
         exercise of this power

0.2   The {Trustees} may in the exercise of the above power cause any shares in any
         company to be registered in the name of any one of their number for the
         purpose of qualifying such {Trustee} as a director of such company

                                                                                                   [1692]

1   This Form is wider than the power conferred by the Trustee Act 2000 s 16 (48 Halsbury's Statutes
       (4th Edn) TRUSTS AND SETTLEMENTS). The introduction of CREST has made the use of nominees
       desirable, if not essential, for trustees. As to CREST see generally vol 11 COMPANIES Paragraph 265
       [2414].
             When this clause is inserted in a document the defined terms in { } must be altered to suit those
       used in the document.

                                                                                                   [1693]

197

Power to remove forum of trust from the United Kingdom[1]

0.1   The {Trustees} may (without infringing the rule against perpetuities or the
         rules relating to excessive accumulation) pay or transfer all or any part of the
         {Trust Fund} to or into the names or control of the trustees of any other
         settlement existing at the date of such payment or transfer under which any of
         the [{Beneficiaries} *or (specify class of beneficiaries)*] is beneficially interested and
         the receipt of the trustees of such other settlement shall afford a good and
         sufficient discharge to the {Trustees} without themselves being responsible for
         seeing to the application of the assets so paid or transferred and the power now
         conferred may be exercised notwithstanding that the trustees or some of the

trustees of such other settlement are resident outside the United Kingdom and that the proper law of such other settlement is some law other than English law and that the general or any part of the administration of the trusts of such other settlement is carried on outside the United Kingdom PROVIDED that no exercise of any of the powers conferred by the provisions of this clause shall operate either directly or indirectly to confer any benefit on the {Settlor} or the spouse of the {Settlor}[2]

[1694]

0.2   The {Trustees} may transfer the general or any part of the administration of the trusts of this settlement or of any trust created or constituted under this settlement outside the United Kingdom and for any such purpose may exercise the power of appointment conferred by clause (number) by appointing that the {Trust Fund} or any part of it shall be held on trusts the general or any part of the administration of which is carried on outside the United Kingdom or the proper law of which is not English law and the trustees or some of the trustees of which are resident outside the United Kingdom and whether or not such trusts are the same or substantially the same as the trusts of this settlement and for that purpose may free and discharge the {Trust Fund} or any part of it so appointed from the trusts of this settlement and execute and do or concur in the execution and doing of all such documents and things as may be necessary for any such purpose

[1695]

1   This clause may be considered suitable where the incidence of taxation is likely to bear heavily on the settled funds. As to the exporting of a United Kingdom trust see vol 40(2) (2001 Reissue) TRUSTS AND SETTLEMENTS Part 15 [8701]. The capital gains tax advantages that at one time were afforded to offshore trusts have largely been removed.

Due to the uncertainties over whether trustees have an inherent power to export a trust should it ever become desirable to do so, wide powers of this type may be considered necessary having regard to the difficulty which may be encountered in obtaining the approval of the court to such a scheme under the Variation of Trusts Act 1958 (48 Halsbury's Statutes (4th Edn) TRUSTS AND SETTLEMENTS): see *Re Weston's Settlements, Weston v Weston* [1969] 1 Ch 223, [1968] 3 All ER 338, CA. The United Kingdom means Great Britain and Northern Ireland and does not include the Channel Islands or the Isle of Man. For a declaration as to proper law together with a power to change the proper law applicable to the trust see Form 249 [1809] post. For a Jersey trust see vol 40(2) (2001 Reissue) TRUSTS AND SETTLEMENTS Part 15 [8701].

When this clause is inserted in a document the defined terms in { } must be altered to suit those used in the document.

2   Cf *IRC v Botnar* [1999] STC 711, CA.

[1696]

198

Power to act by majority[1]

If the {Trustees} or any of them shall at any time disagree or differ from the others or other of the {Trustees} as to the exercise of any of the powers and discretions now or by law or by any instrument executed under this settlement conferred on the {Trustees} or as to the manner of the exercise of any such power or discretion then such power or discretion and all other powers and acts incidental to it shall become exercisable by a majority of the {Trustees} not being less than [2] in number wishing to exercise such power or discretion PROVIDED that the majority so exercising any such power or discretion shall keep records in writing of the exercise of it and shall without undue delay inform the minority of the {Trustees} not joining in such exercise of the manner in which the majority have exercised the power or discretion [and so that no purchaser mortgagee lessee or other person dealing with the {Trustees} not being less than 2 in number shall be concerned or entitled to inquire whether or not a majority of the {Trustees} have agreed to act for the purposes of the transaction concerned]

1   Notwithstanding such a clause, all the trustees who are estate owners of trust land (or registered proprietors in the case of registered land) must join in to effect a disposition of it (in the absence of intervention by the court to enforce the majority decision). When this clause is inserted in a document the defined terms in { } must be altered to suit those used in the document.

[1697]

199

Powers in relation to company affairs—intervention not compellable and compromise of share and other rights[1]

0.1   The {Trustees} shall not be bound or required to interfere in the management or conduct of the affairs or business of any company or corporation in which the {Trust Fund} or any part of it may for the time being be invested (whether or not they have the control of such company or corporation) but so long as they shall have no notice of any act of dishonesty or misappropriation or misapplication of money or other property on the part of the directors or other persons having such management or conduct they may leave the same (including the payment or non-payment of dividends) wholly to such directors or other persons and no {Beneficiary} shall be entitled as such beneficiary in any way whatsoever to compel control or forbid the exercise or the exercise in any particular manner of any voting or other rights which may at any time be vested in the {Trustees} with regard to such company or corporation

0.2   The {Trustees} may at any time or times enter into any compromise or arrangement with respect to any release or forbear to exercise all or any of their rights as debenture holders debenture stockholders creditors stockholders or shareholders of any company and whether in connection with a scheme of reconstruction or amalgamation or otherwise and may accept in or towards satisfaction of all or any such rights such consideration in such form or forms (and whether or not comprising and including money) as they shall in their discretion think fit

[1698]

1   Formerly the Trustee Act 1925 s 10(3) as amended by the Trustee Investments Act 1961 s 9(1) (48 Halsbury's Statutes (4th Edn) TRUSTS AND SETTLEMENTS) gave trustees various powers in relation to the reconstruction or amalgamation of companies in which trustees hold shares. The Trustee Act 1925 s 10(3) was repealed, and not replaced, by the Trustee Act 2000 and, hence, the only statutory powers possessed by trustees are comprised within the general power of investment given by the Trustee Act 2000 s 3 (48 Halsbury's Statutes (4th Edn) TRUSTS AND SETTLEMENTS). Sub-clause 0.2 above deals with the resulting lacuna.

When this clause is inserted in a document the defined terms in { } must be altered to suit those used in the document.

[1699]

200

Powers in relation to company affairs—rearrangements etc and voting[1]

0.1   In relation to any securities of a company for the time being forming part of the
        {Trust Fund} to concur in any scheme or arrangement for the reconstruction
        of the company or for the sale of all or any part of the property and undertaking
        of the company to another company or for the acquisition of the securities of
        the company or of control thereof by another company or for the amalgamation
        of the company with another company or for the release modification or
        variation of any rights privileges or liabilities of any denomination or
        description of the reconstructed or purchasing or new company in lieu of or in
        exchange for all or any of the original securities and with power to retain any
        securities so accepted as above for any period for which the original securities
        could have been retained

0.2   To exercise or concur in exercising the voting and other rights attaching to any
        securities for the time being forming part of the {Trust Fund} so as to become
        a director or other officer or employee of any company and to be entitled to
        vote for and to be paid and to retain for the {Trustees'} use and benefit
        reasonable remuneration for the {Trustees'} services

1   See Form 199 note 1 [1699] ante. When this clause is inserted in a document the defined terms in { }
        must be altered to suit those used in the document.

[1700]

201

Limitation on extent of trustees' powers so as not to prevent the existence of an interest in possession[1]

It is provided that none of the additional powers contained in clause *(number)* shall be
capable of being exercised in such a way as would or might prevent an interest in
possession of any of the {Beneficiaries} from subsisting or continuing to subsist in the
whole or any part of the {Trust Fund} in any case where such an interest otherwise
would subsist or continue to subsist

1   For the meaning of an 'interest in possession' see Paragraph 286 [723] ante. When this clause is inserted
        in a document the defined terms in { } must be altered to suit those used in the document.

[1701]

202

Limitation on extent of trustees' powers so as not to breach provisions of the Inheritance Tax Act 1984 Section 71[1]

It is provided that none of the powers conferred on the {Trustees} by the terms of this
settlement or the general law shall be capable of being exercised in such a way as would
prevent Section 71 of the Inheritance Tax Act 1984 (or any modification or re-
enactment of it) from applying in respect of the whole or any part of the {Trust Fund}
in any case where that section (or modification or re-enactment) would otherwise so
apply

[1702]

1   As to the inheritance tax consequences of an accumulation and maintenance settlement as defined by the Inheritance Tax Act 1984 s 71 (42–44 Halsbury's Statutes (4th Edn) TAXATION) see vol 40(2) (2001 Reissue) TRUSTS AND SETTLEMENTS Part 11 [6301]. This Form can be included in a settlement where it might otherwise be argued that certain powers possessed by the trustees could be exercised in such a way as to infringe the conditions required to bring a settlement within the section (eg the statutory power of advancement).

When this clause is inserted in a document the defined terms in { } must be altered to suit those used in the document.

[1703]

203

Limitation on extent of trustees' powers so as not to be able to confer any benefit on settlor or settlor's spouse[1]

Notwithstanding anything in the terms of this settlement expressed or implied no power or discretion conferred on the {Trustees} or on any other persons shall be exercisable and no money or other assets subject to its trusts shall in any circumstances be paid transferred or applied in any manner or in any circumstances to or for the benefit of the {Settlor} or any spouse for the time being of the {Settlor}

[1704]

1   The reason for including this type of clause will be apparent from that part of the commentary dealing with taxation, particularly that concerning the inheritance tax rule on reservation of benefit and the income tax and capital gains tax rules taxing the settlor who has reserved a benefit in the trust: see Paragraph 290 [749] et seq ante. It is desirable both as a reminder to the trustees and so that an argument that the settlor might in fact derive some benefit under the settlement can be forestalled. For the construction of such clauses see *IRC v Botnar* [1999] STC 711, CA; *Fuller v Evans* [2000] 1 All ER 636, [2000] 2 FLR 13 and *Netherton v Netherton* [2000] 1 WTLR 1171.

When this clause is inserted in a document the defined terms in { } must be altered to suit those used in the document.

[1705]

204

Power to exclude beneficiaries[1]

The {Trustees} (being at least 2 in number or a trust corporation) may at any time or times during the {Trust Period} by any deed during the {Trust Period} revocably or irrevocably declare that any one or more of the {Beneficiaries} shall cease to be a beneficiary or beneficiaries and upon the execution of any such deed this settlement shall be construed and take effect accordingly

1   For an alternative clause enabling trustees to include persons as beneficiaries and to exclude persons from being beneficiaries see Form 4 clause 6 [1087] ante. When this clause is inserted in a document the defined terms in { } must be altered to suit those used in the document.

[1706]

205

Power to institute proceedings and compromise claims[1]

To institute prosecute and defend any suits or actions or other proceedings affecting the {Trustees} as trustees of this settlement or the {Trust Fund} and to compromise any matter of difference or to submit any such matter to arbitration and to compromise compound or abandon any debts owing to the {Trustees} as such trustees or any other claims and to adjust any dispute in relation to debts or claims against them as such trustees upon evidence that the {Trustees} shall deem sufficient and to make partition upon such terms (including if thought fit the payment or receipt of equality money) as the {Trustees} shall deem desirable with co-owners or joint owners besides the trust having any interest in any properties in which the {Trustees} as trustees of this settlement are interested and to make such partition either by sale or by set-off or by agreement or otherwise [and so that the {Trustees} shall not be responsible for any loss occasioned by any act or thing so done by them in good faith]

[1707]

1   When trustees are in any doubt as to how they should act it is recommended that they seek directions of the court; provided that they act in accordance with those directions they will be absolutely protected. See generally Underhill and Hayton *Law of Trusts and Trustees* (15th Edn, 1995) ch 19 and note the terms of CPR Sch 1 RSC Order 85 r 2. On the position of costs see *Re Beddoe, Downes v Cottam* [1893] 1 Ch 547, CA; and on acting unreasonably see *Re Spurling's Will Trusts, Philpot v Philpot* [1966] 1 All ER 745, [1966] 1 WLR 920.

For the statutory power to compound liabilities see the Trustee Act 1925 s 15 (48 Halsbury's Statutes (4th Edn) TRUSTS AND SETTLEMENTS) and note that the statutory duty of care in the Trustee Act 2000 (48 Halsbury's Statutes (4th Edn) TRUSTS AND SETTLEMENTS) applies to trustees exercising the statutory or any equivalent express power. The duty can be excluded. In this Form the words in square brackets restore the position to what it had been before 1 February 2001 (the commencement date of the Trustee Act 2000).

When this clause is inserted in a document the defined terms in { } must be altered to suit those used in the document.

[1708]

206

Power to pay incidental costs[1]

The {Trustees} may pay out of the {Trust Fund} the costs of and incidental to the preparation and completion of this settlement (including any stamp duty payable on it)

1   Clauses of this type are commonly included in settlements as they were in the days of estate duty. Nevertheless, the inheritance tax reservation of benefit position cannot be regarded as clear cut: does the power operate to reduce the value of the property originally settled or is it the case that given that the costs will be paid (or not) swiftly, the reservation (if so it be) ceases soon after the settlement is established? Of course, if the power is not exercised but it remains open to the trustees to make the payment, the latter argument does not hold good. If the trustees have a duty to pay costs, the argument that there is a reduction in the value of the gift and hence no reservation is strengthened. As to the reservation of benefit rules, see Paragraph 290 [749] et seq ante.

When this clause is inserted in a document the defined terms in { } must be altered to suit those used in the document.

[1709]–[1720]

J: DIRECTIONS AS TO LAND AND OTHER PROPERTY HELD OR PURCHASED

207

Directions as to tenure of land purchased as part of the trust fund if in England or Wales[1]

Any land purchased under the powers of investment contained above shall (if in England or Wales) be of freehold tenure or of leasehold tenure held for a term of which at least [60] years shall be unexpired whether subject to leases or tenancies or not such land to be assured to the {Trustees} upon the trusts and with and subject to the powers and provisions (including the power contained in this settlement of investing in the purchase of land) as those with and subject to which the money so invested would then have been held had no such investment of it been made

1   This provision is designed to control the exercise of the trustees' powers when land is purchased in pursuance of a specific power contained in the settlement. The trustees may otherwise be directed to rely on the powers given by the Trusts of Land and Appointment of Trustees Act 1996 (37 Halsbury's Statutes (4th Edn) REAL PROPERTY). As to these powers see Paragraph 221 [532] et seq ante and for further commentary on the provisions of the Trusts of Land and Appointment of Trustees Act 1996 see vol 40(2) (2001 Reissue) TRUSTS AND SETTLEMENTS Part 8 [3001]. As to the power to purchase land as a residence for beneficiaries: see Form 139 note 1 [1563] ante.

[1721]

208

Directions as to nominees holding land and other property purchased as part of the trust fund if not in the United Kingdom[1]

Any land or other property (whether movable or immovable) purchased under the powers of investment conferred above on the {Trustees} (other than property situated in the United Kingdom) may be assured either to the {Trustees} or into the name of a nominee or nominees or in any other manner giving the {Trustees} control over such land or other property that the {Trustees} may consider appropriate and so that any land or immovable property so purchased shall be held by the {Trustees} or such nominee or nominees with power to sell the same

[1722]

1   When originally enacted the Trusts of Land and Appointment of Trustees Act 1996 (37 Halsbury's Statutes (4th Edn) REAL PROPERTY) only applied to land situated in England or Wales: see Paragraph 221 [532] et seq ante and see generally vol 40(2) (2001 Reissue) TRUSTS AND SETTLEMENTS Part 8 [3001]. The Trustee Act 2000 s 8 (48 Halsbury's Statutes (4th Edn) TRUSTS AND SETTLEMENTS) has widened the application to land situated in the UK. It remains appropriate in the case of other land to expressly empower the use of nominees and to give a power of sale. For the general power of trustees to sell trust property see Underhill and Hayton *Law of Trusts and Trustees* (15th Edn, 1995) p 676 et seq. When this clause is inserted in a document the defined terms in { } must be altered to suit those used in the document.

[1723]

209

Directions as to land—large estates[1]

The {Trustees} shall hold any land or other immovable property and any building or other structures whatever upon such land or other immovable property and any chattels real and all rights of whatever nature appurtenant to any such land or other immovable property whether situated in the United Kingdom or elsewhere which may for the time being be subject to the trusts of this settlement with and subject to the following directions powers and discretions:

0.1   any property within the above description shall if situated in the United Kingdom be either freehold or leasehold as defined in the Trustee Act 2000 s 8(2) for a term of years of which not less than [60] years is unexpired at the time of acquisition by the {Trustees} and shall be conveyed transferred or assigned to the {Trustees} and if situated elsewhere than in the United Kingdom shall be of any tenure equivalent to freehold tenure and shall be conveyed transferred or assigned to the {Trustees} with power to sell the same[2]

0.2   the {Trustees} shall stand possessed of any such property so acquired and as part of the {Trust Fund} and with and subject to any of the other trusts powers and provisions by this settlement expressly or by law impliedly imposed or conferred upon or otherwise applicable to the {Trustees} or the trusts of this settlement

0.3   with reference to any property so acquired the {Trustees} may raise and pay out of the capital or income of the {Trust Fund} any money required to be paid on the exercise of the powers or discretions by this settlement or by statute conferred and in the uncontrolled opinion of the {Trustees} properly payable out of capital or income as the case may be and in so far as such property shall be situated outside the United Kingdom the powers conferred by law on the {Trustees} shall apply as if such property were situated in the United Kingdom

[1724]

0.4   the {Trustees} shall have all the powers conferred on them by the Trusts of Land and Appointment of Trustees Act 1996 Section 6 as amended and extended by the Trustee Act 2000 s 40(1), Sch 2 para 45(1) SUBJECT to the restrictions imposed by this clause

0.5   the {Trustees} may build rebuild erect demolish[3] repair equip extend improve decorate redecorate protect and insure any house building or other structure on any land or other immovable property and install maintain erect and insure any plant or machinery on any land and may erect lay out or maintain fences roadways wires pipes ditches paths watercourses reservoirs yards pleasure gardens and may carry out any other works whatsoever incidental to any land wheresoever subject to the trusts of this settlement and with the same purpose may open or work any mines or quarries on such land and may take and carry away minerals or stone from any such land and may plant cultivate maintain and cut timber growing on such land without being impeachable for waste and may farm any such land and do all operations incidental to the same and may otherwise carry on business on or develop any such land in any way they think fit

0.6   the {Trustees} may in performing or exercising any of the above obligations and powers employ or engage any person or corporation whatsoever or wheresoever as an agent servant or independent contractor to do any of the acts or to exercise any of the discretions or carry out any of the obligations by this settlement conferred or imposed on the {Trustees} on such terms and conditions as to remuneration or payment or otherwise on such conditions as the {Trustees} think fit and so that the {Trustees} shall not be liable or responsible for any loss arising to the {Trust Fund} through the acts or defaults of any such person or corporation in carrying out any of the above objects

[1725]

1   These powers in connection with the management of any land purchased by the trustees are intended for use in the case of only the largest estates where it is contemplated that there will be substantial holdings of land. In other cases short directions would probably suffice: see, for example, Forms 207 [1721], 208 [1722] ante.

When this clause is inserted in a document the defined terms in { } must be altered to suit those used in the document.

2   Under the Trusts of Land and Appointment of Trustees Act 1996 (37 Halsbury's Statutes (4th Edn) REAL PROPERTY) trustees of land are given wide powers to purchase land whether freehold or leasehold: see the Trusts of Land and Appointment of Trustees Act 1996 s 6(3) as amended by the Trustee Act 2000 s 40(1), Sch 2 para 45(1). Express provisions are therefore needed if this power is to be restricted: eg in the case of leasehold interests requiring a certain unexpired term. The Act only applies to land in the United Kingdom: Trusts of Land and Appointment of Trustees Act 1996 s 6(3) as amended by the Trustee Act 2000 s 40(1), Sch 2 para 45(1) (the amendment to section 6(3) effectively replaces 'England and Wales' with 'the United Kingdom': see the Trustee Act 2000 s 8). In relation to land acquired elsewhere trustees should be given an express power of sale. For the general power of trustees to sell trust property see Underhill and Hayton *Law of Trusts and Trustees* (15th Edn, 1995) p 676 et seq. As to the Trusts of Land and Appointment of Trustees Act 1996 see Paragraph 221 [532] et seq ante and for a section by section discussion of the provisions of the Act see vol 40(2) (2001 Reissue) TRUSTS AND SETTLEMENTS Part 8 [3001].

3   It will be necessary for the Trustees to obtain planning permission and/or listed building consent etc as applicable before demolition, alteration, building etc is undertaken. Demolition should not be undertaken lightly but in some cases, where the principal dwelling is in a ruinous condition, is of little or no architectural merit and would be uneconomic to repair or rebuild, demolition may be the only commercially acceptable course open to the trustees.

[1726]

210

Trustees to permit beneficiaries to occupy land held on trust for sale[1]

0.1   Until the {Property} shall be sold the {Trustees} shall permit [the {Spouses} or the survivor of them *or* any persons or person contingently or otherwise interested in the {Trust Fund} or any part of it[2] *or* the {Life Tenant}] to occupy rent free or upon such terms as the {Trustees} shall determine all or any part of the {Property} or to receive the rents and profits of it [such persons or person [or in the case of minors the {Trustees}] *or* the {Life Tenant}] keeping the {Property} in repair and insured against loss by fire *(specify any other risks)* and the {Trustees} shall receive the rents and profits (if any) of such of the {Property} as [the {Spouses} or the survivor of them *or* such persons or person[3] *or* the {Life Tenant}] shall not occupy or of which [such persons or person *or* the {Life Tenant}] shall not receive the rents and profits

[0.2   After the death of the [survivor of the {Spouses} *or* {Life Tenant}] if and when any issue [of the {Marriage}] who shall be living at the death of [that survivor *or* the {Life Tenant}] shall be under the age of 18 years and unmarried the {Trustees} shall if they think fit so to do permit any [issue of the {Marriage} *or* children of the {Life Tenant}] to live in and occupy any house or houses and land forming part or all of the {Property} on such terms as above and shall let at rent the residue of the {Property}]

[1727]

1   For the right of an interest in possession beneficiary to occupy land held on a trust of land see the Trusts of Land and Appointment of Trustees Act 1996 ss 12, 13 (37 Halsbury's Statutes (4th Edn) REAL PROPERTY) and Paragraph 228 [545] ante. It is thought that these provisions will apply when the land is held on a trust of land simpliciter or on an express trust for sale: see Paragraph 108 [267] ante. To some extent the statute renders express provisions of this type redundant; but note that the Act only applies to land situated in the United Kingdom (see Form 209 note 2 [1726] ante) and this Form may require the trustees to allow occupation by a beneficiary other than one enjoying an interest in possession in the land. As to when the Trusts of Land and Appointment of Trustees Act 1996 ss 12, 13 can be excluded see Paragraph 228 [545] ante and for further commentary on these provisions see vol 40(2) (2001 Reissue) TRUSTS AND SETTLEMENTS Part 8 [3001]. See also the Trustee Act 2000 s 8 in relation to the acquisition of land for the occupation of a beneficiary. This power is not dispositive in nature and, hence, only beneficiaries entitled to income or who could be appointed income (eg under the terms of a discretionary trust) should benefit from the exercise of the power.

        When this clause is inserted in a document the defined terms in { } must be altered to suit those used in the document.

2   If this optional wording is inserted sub-clause 0.2 above may be omitted.

3   See note 2 above.

[1728]

211

Power to allow beneficiaries the use and enjoyment of chattels[1]

The benefit of the use or enjoyment of any chattels for the time being subject to the trusts of this settlement may at the discretion of the {Trustees} and upon such terms and conditions in all respects as they may think fit be granted to any one or more of the {Beneficiaries} and the {Trustees} may at any time in their discretion apply any money subject to the trusts of this settlement in the purchase or otherwise in the acquisition of any chattels for the purpose of enabling the same to be used or enjoyed accordingly

1   Commonly such beneficiaries would be required to insure the chattels and in appropriate cases provide adequate security arrangements. As with the power to allow occupation of land this power is not dispositive in nature. The Trustee Act 2000 (48 Halsbury's Statutes (4th Edn) TRUSTS AND SETTLEMENTS) does not give trustees a power to acquire assets other than land for occupation by a beneficiary. When this clause is inserted in a document the defined terms in { } must be altered to suit those used in the document.

[1729]

212

Insurance of trust property—trustees liable to insure[1]

The {Trustees} shall insure and keep insured at the expense of [income *or* capital] to their full value the buildings [(if any)] and chattels for the time being subject to this settlement against loss from or damage by fire storm [flood] theft *(specify any other risks)* and may insure against loss or damage from such other causes as they in their absolute discretion may think fit and at the expense of income or capital or partly of either in such proportions as they may think fit [PROVIDED that all insurance shall be with an office of repute]

1   As to the trustees' power to insure under the Trustee Act 1925 s 19(1) as substituted by the Trustee Act 2000 s 34(1) (48 Halsbury's Statutes (4th Edn) TRUSTS AND SETTLEMENTS) see Paragraph 69 [165] and Paragraph 259 [641] ante. As to the power of trustees under the Trusts of Land and Appointment of Trustees Act 1996 s 6 as amended by the Trustee Act 2000 s 40(1), Sch 2 para 45(1)–(3), Sch 4 Pt II (37 Halsbury's Statutes (4th Edn) REAL PROPERTY) to insure see Paragraph 69 [165] and Paragraph 259 [641] ante. For the inheritance tax consequences of a power enabling trustees to pay premiums out of income or capital see *Carver v Duncan* [1985] AC 1082, [1985] 2 All ER 645, HL.

        When this clause is inserted in a document the defined terms in { } must be altered to suit those used in the document.

[1730]

213

Insurance of trust property—discretion as to insurance and protection of chattels[1]

The {Trustees} shall not be liable for any loss depreciation or damage (howsoever caused) which may happen at any time to any chattels for the time being subject to the trusts of this settlement but may in their discretion (but without being under any liability or obligation to do so) from time to time take at the expense of the income or capital of the {Trust Fund} any steps which they may think proper for the insurance repair protection renewal or custody of such chattels or any of them or otherwise in relation to the same

1   As to the trustees' power to insure under the Trustee Act 1925 s 19(1) as substituted by the Trustee Act 2000 s 34(1) (48 Halsbury's Statutes (4th Edn) TRUSTS AND SETTLEMENTS) see Paragraph 69 [165] and Paragraph 259 [641] ante. As to the power of trustees under the Trusts of Land and Appointment of Trustees Act 1996 s 6 as amended by the Trustee Act 2000 s 40(1), Sch 2 para 45(1)–(3), Sch 4 Pt II (37 Halsbury's Statutes (4th Edn) REAL PROPERTY) to insure see Paragraph 69 [165] and Paragraph 259 [641] ante. For the inheritance tax consequences of a power enabling trustees to pay premiums out of income or capital see *Carver v Duncan* [1985] AC 1082, [1985] 2 All ER 645, HL.
       When this clause is inserted in a document the defined terms in { } must be altered to suit those used in the document.

[1731]

214

Exclusion of apportionment of income accruing on property settled

The provisions of the Apportionment Act 1870 shall not apply to the trusts of this settlement and accordingly all dividends and other income received by the {Trustees} shall be treated as income accruing at the date of receipt whether or not such dividends or income shall have been earned and accrued wholly or partially in respect of a period prior to the date of receipt[1]

1   By the Apportionment Act 1870 (23 Halsbury's Statutes (4th Edn) LANDLORD AND TENANT), dividends and other periodical payments are to be considered as accruing from day to day and are apportionable in respect of time accordingly, unless there is a stipulation to the contrary: see Paragraph 156 [381] ante. When this clause is inserted in a document the defined terms in { } must be altered to suit those used in the document.

[1732]

215

Powers relating to remainder interests comprised in the settlement[1]

0.1   The {Trustees} may at any time and from time to time [(but during the life of *(name)* not without [his] consent in writing)] sell call in or convert into money or other property the whole or any part of the above remainder interest expectant on the death of *(life tenant)* and may invest the net proceeds of any such sale calling in and conversion in the investments authorised by this settlement

0.2   The {Trustees} may at any time and from time to time [(but during the life of *(name)* not without [his] consent in writing)] borrow any money required for any of the purposes of this settlement upon the security of the whole or any part of the above remainder interest expectant on the death of *(life tenant)* and upon such terms as to interest repayment and otherwise as the {Trustees} shall see fit to agree

0.3   The {Trustees} shall so soon as may be after the death of *(life tenant)* require and compel payment and transfer or payment or transfer to them as the case may require of such money or investments as the {Trustees} shall in their absolute discretion judge to be equivalent to the value of the undivided share to which they have become entitled[2]

[1733]

1   These provisions are designed for use (if desired) in cases where one of the assets comprised in the settlement is a reversionary interest. See also Form 37 [1288] ante for the trustees' powers to accept a remainder interest as settled property. They may be used independently or together, as the circumstances may dictate. When this clause is inserted in a document the defined terms in { } must be altered to suit those used in the document.

2   This final provision assumes a situation in which the remainder interest consists of an undivided share. Its main effect is to convert the powers which the trustees would have in any case under the Trustee Act 1925 s 22 as amended by the Trustee Act 2000 s 40(1), Sch 2 para 22 (48 Halsbury's Statutes (4th Edn) TRUSTS AND SETTLEMENTS) (see Paragraph 265 [653] ante) into obligations. Note that the statutory duty of care (provided for in the Trustee Act 2000 s 1 and Sch 1 (48 Halsbury's Statutes (4th Edn) TRUSTS AND SETTLEMENTS)) will apply unless excluded.

[1734]–[1740]

K: INDEMNITY, EXONERATION, CHARGING AND AUDIT

(For general commentary on the issues that arise in relation to exculpation clauses and for a discussion of the case of Armitage v Nurse [1998] Ch 241, [1997] 2 All ER 705, CA, see Paragraph 192 [471] et seq ante. For forms of releases and indemnities see vol 40(2) (2001 Reissue) TRUSTS AND SETTLEMENTS *Part 20 [9821]. For a form of trustee protection clause see Form 4 clause 13 [1090] ante and see Form 4 note 24 [1105] ante for comments thereon. For a more restricted exoneration clause see the Standard Provisions of the Society of Trust and Estate Practitioners at Form 3 provision 12 [1071] ante. See further 'Trustee Exemption Clauses', a Consultation Paper of the Trust Law Committee (November 1998). The matter has now been referred to the Law Commission for consideration. Before inserting indemnity, exoneration and charging clauses, it is essential that the settlor is made fully aware of how these operate and agrees to their inclusion: see generally Part 2 Introduction to Section B [1061] ante.)*

[1741]

216

Power for trustee personally interested to refrain from acting

Any individual {Trustee} who or whose spouse or issue may benefit from or be otherwise interested in the result of the exercise of any power or discretion conferred in this settlement upon the {Trustees} may abstain from acting in the execution of the same and allow his co-trustees **[(being at least 2 in number or a trust corporation)]** to act in the execution of the same and concur merely as a formal party[1]

1   Although it is thought that a trustee can confer benefits on himself as beneficiary provided that he is not the sole trustee, some practitioners fear that such conduct could be challenged and therefore use a clause along these lines. For an alternative clause, see Form 4 clause 12 [1090] ante. When this clause is inserted in a document the defined terms in { } must be altered to suit those used in the document.

[1742]

217

Power to pay income to agent or banker[1]

Upon the request in writing of the *(beneficiary)* the {Trustees} may so long as they shall think fit pay any income of the *(beneficiary)* to any banker or other agent selected by [him *or* her] and [until such request be revoked and the revocation communicated to the {Trustees}] the receipt of such banker or agent shall be sufficient discharge to the {Trustees} for such income

1   When this clause is inserted in a document the defined terms in { } must be altered to suit those used
       in the document.

[1743]

218

No requirement for trustees to give bond or security[1]

None of the {Trustees} shall be required to give a bond or security for the due and faithful administration of the {Trust Fund} or for the discharge of the trusts by this settlement created

1   When this clause is inserted in a document the defined terms in { } must be altered to suit those used
       in the document.

[1744]

219

Exclusion of the duty of care under the Trustee Act 2000 Section 1[1]

The duty of care contained in the Trustee Act 2000 Section 1 shall not apply to the {Trustees} in the exercise of any of the powers conferred on them by this settlement nor to any duties relating to the exercise of such powers nor to the exercise by the {Trustees} of any powers contained in or duties imposed by the Trustee Act 2000 the Trustee Act 1925 the Trusts of Land and Appointment of Trustees Act 1996 or any other statute where that duty of care is expressed to be applicable[2]

[1745]

1   The duty of care can be excluded in the trust instrument: see the Trustee Act 2000 Sch 1 para 7
       (48 Halsbury's Statutes (4th Edn) TRUSTS AND SETTLEMENTS). As an alternative to excluding the
       duty, draftsmen (obviously after agreeing the matter with the settlor) may prefer to deal with the matter
       in an exoneration clause: see further Form 221 [1749] post. Of course this will mean that there may
       still be a breach of duty (albeit not actionable because of the exculpation clause) and if such breach was
       serious and repeated, a court might remove the trustees.
             When this clause is inserted in a document the defined terms in { } must be altered to suit those
       used in the document.
2   Consider, as an alternative, replacing the statutory duty with a lesser obligation, 'to act in good faith':
       see the now-repealed Trustee Act 1925 s 23(1) (48 Halsbury's Statutes (4th Edn) TRUSTS AND
       SETTLEMENTS).

[1746]

220

Exoneration of trustees—short form[1]

No {Trustee} shall be liable for any loss or damage which may happen to the {Trust Fund} or any part thereof or the income thereof at any time or from any cause whatsoever unless such loss or damage shall be caused by his own actual fraud

[1747]

1   When this clause is inserted in a document the defined terms in { } must be altered to suit those used in the document.

This clause was considered by the Court of Appeal in *Armitage v Nurse* [1998] Ch 241 at 252, [1997] 2 All ER 705 at 713. A trustee exoneration clause will be effective to protect trustees against the consequences of mistake or negligence. A clause will not, however, be valid if it seeks to cover any dishonest intention eg if it purported to afford protection to trustees who had been fraudulent or recklessly indifferent to their fiduciary duties. Such a clause would offend 'the irreducible trust core' which was explained as follows by Millett LJ in *Armitage v Nurse* :

'there is an irreducible core of obligations owed by the trustees to the beneficiaries and enforceable by them which is fundamental to the concept of a trust. If the beneficiaries have no rights enforceable against the trustees there are no trusts. But I do not accept the further submission that these core obligations include the duties of skill and care, prudence and diligence. The duty of the trustees to perform the trusts honestly and in good faith for the benefit of the beneficiaries is the minimum necessary to give substance to the trusts, but in my opinion it is sufficient.'

As a result this clause will be effective to protect trustees against a negligent breach of the statutory duty of care: it will also protect trustees who commit a 'judicious' breach of trust. However, it is not sufficient for the trustee to believe that he is acting in the interests of the beneficiaries by committing a breach of trust if that belief was so unreasonable that no reasonable solicitor-trustee could have held it: see the preliminary decision of the Court of Appeal in *Walker v Stones* [2000] 4 All ER 412, [2001] 2 WLR 623. Note that at the time of writing the case of *Walker v Stones* is on appeal before the House of Lords, whose judgment is expected shortly.

The clause can be relied upon by the person who drafted it provided (and this is a general requirement for the validity of such clauses) that it had been agreed by the settlor or testator. Normally this will be presumed from his execution of the trust or will: see *Bogg v Raper* [1998] CLY 4592, (1998) Times, 22 April, CA.

[1748]

221

Exoneration of trustees—long form[1]

No {Trustee} being an individual [who gives his services gratuitously] shall be liable for any loss to the capital or income of the {Trust Fund} caused by any improper investment or purchase made by him in good faith or for the negligence or fraud of any agent employed by him or by any other {Trustee} although the employment of such agent may not have been strictly necessary or resulting from any other cause whatever other than wilful and individual fraud or wrongdoing on the part of the {Trustee} who is sought to be made liable

[1749]

1   Note that this clause is an expanded version of Form 220 [1747] ante. The words in square brackets limit the protection to lay trustees and to professionals acting without charge. Compare the restrictive provisions in the Standard Provisions of the Society of Trust and Estate Practitioners at Form 3 clause 12 [1071] ante. When this clause is inserted in a document the defined terms in { } must be altered to suit those used in the document.

[1750]

222

Clause negativing vicarious liability[1]

A {Trustee} shall be liable and accountable only for money and property actually received by [him] and (subject to the provisions of clause *(specify)* of this deed) only for [his] own acts receipts omissions and defaults and not for those of any other {Trustee}

[1751]

1   Despite the repeal of the Trustee Act 1925 s 30(2) by the Trustee Act 2000 s 40(1), (3), Sch 2 para 24, Sch 4 Pt II (48 Halsbury's Statutes (4th Edn) TRUSTS AND SETTLEMENTS) it is not considered that a trustee is vicariously liable for the acts of his co-trustee: see Paragraph 185 [456] ante. To put the matter beyond doubt, a cautious draftsman might include this clause, even in cases where the trustees were not otherwise protected by an exoneration clause. When this clause is inserted in a document the defined terms in { } must be altered to suit those used in the document.

[1752]

223

Exoneration from duty to investigate accounts[1]

The {Trustees} shall be responsible only for so much of the {Trust Fund} as shall be actually paid and transferred to them respectively and nothing contained in this settlement shall cast any obligation upon the {Trustees} or any of them to investigate the accounts of the trustees of the will of *(testator)* or to recover or (save at the request in writing of some person beneficially interested under this settlement [and if so requested on a sufficient indemnity as to costs]) sue for the money stocks funds securities and property forming part of the {Trust Fund} or any part or parts of it respectively as shall not have been paid or transferred to them by the trustees of the above will and no neglect or omission in that respect shall be chargeable as a breach of trust

[1753]

1   This Form and Form 220 [1747] and Form 224 [1755] provide, in effect, for a modification of the statutory exemptions conferred by the Trustee Act 1925 s 61 and the Trustee Act 2000 s 23 (48 Halsbury's Statutes (4th Edn) TRUSTS AND SETTLEMENTS): see further Form 220 note 1 [1748] ante. When this clause is inserted in a document the defined terms in { } must be altered to suit those used in the document.

[1754]

224

Indemnity to trustees by joint settlors[1]

The {Settlors} jointly and severally covenant with the {Trustees} and with each of them that the {Settlors} and each of them will at all times in future keep indemnified the {Trustees} and each of them and their respective personal representatives and estates from and against all actions proceedings claims and demands which may be brought claimed or recovered by or on behalf of the {Settlors} or any of them for or in consequence of:

0.1   either any performance of any trust or trusts or the exercise of any power or powers by this settlement reposed in or conferred on the {Trustees}

0.2   any act or default (being one not made or committed dishonestly) in the performance of such trusts or of any of them or in the exercise of such powers or any of them or

0.3   any act (not being a dishonest one) purporting and believed by the person doing it to be done in performance or exercise of any of such trusts or powers although the same shall not have been required or authorised by the same respectively

and in addition to the indemnity and reimbursement clause implied in this settlement by the Trustee Act 1925 Sections 26, 27 and 28 and the Trustee Act 2000 Sections 23 and 31 inclusive the {Trustees} may from time to time reimburse themselves or pay or discharge out of the {Trust Property} all expenses incurred by them in or about the performance of any acts purporting and supposed to be done by them in performance of such trusts or any of them or in exercise of such powers or of any of them although the same acts shall not have been required by any of the trusts or authorised by any of the powers

[1755]

1   This Form and Forms 220 [1747] and 222 [1751] ante provide, in effect, for a modification of the statutory exemptions conferred by the Trustee Act 1925 s 61 and the Trustee Act 2000 s 23 (48 Halsbury's Statutes (4th Edn) TRUSTS AND SETTLEMENTS): see further Form 220 note 1 [1748] ante.

When this clause is inserted in a document the defined terms in { } must be altered to suit those used in the document.

[1756]

225

Indemnity to trustees out of the trust fund[1]

A {Trustee} shall be entitled to exoneration and indemnity out of the {Trust Fund} for any liability loss or expense incurred under this settlement and for any judgment recovered against and paid by such {Trustee} other than liability loss expense or judgment arising out of his own wilful and individual fraud wrongdoing or neglect

1   Compare the Trustee Act 2000 s 31 (48 Halsbury's Statutes (4th Edn) TRUSTS AND SETTLEMENTS). When this clause is inserted in a document the defined terms in { } must be altered to suit those used in the document.

[1757]

226

Power to charge the trust fund[1]

The {Trustees} may charge the property and assets comprised in the {Trust Fund} or any part of it to secure obligations incurred by them for valuable consideration

1   This clause enables specific assets to be charged: see further Law Reform Committee 23rd Report (Cmnd 8733) where a clause conferring the power to create a floating charge over the trust fund is suggested. See also the Report published by the Trust Law Committee in June 1999 Rights of Creditors against Trustees and Trust Funds.

When this clause is inserted in a document the defined terms in { } must be altered to suit those used in the document.

[1758]

227

Payment of annuities to trustees[1]

Every {Trustee} [not being the {Settlor} or any spouse of the {Settlor}] [other than a solicitor or professional trustee or member of a firm who or whose firm is employed or entitled to be paid for his services or those of such firm] shall be entitled while he shall continue to be a {Trustee} to receive yearly the sum of £... by equal half-yearly payments for his services and responsibility relating to the trusts of this settlement

[1759]

1   This clause is designed to remunerate the 'non-professional' trustee (eg a family trustee) by means of an annual annuity. For the usual taxation reasons the settlor and his spouse should be excluded. A professional trustee is now able to charge in the absence of an express charging clause so long as his co-trustees have agreed in writing that he should be entitled to do so: Trustee Act 2000 s 29(2) (48 Halsbury's Statutes (4th Edn) TRUSTS AND SETTLEMENTS). A trust corporation is entitled to charge whether it is the sole trustee or not and regardless of whether, in the latter case, the agreement of the co-trustee is obtained or not: Trustee Act 2000 s 29(1). Where an express provision is included the statutory provisions are excluded. It remains desirable to provide expressly for the remuneration of trustees: see Form 233 [1769] post.

     When this clause is inserted in a document the defined terms in { } must be altered to suit those used in the document.

[1760]

228

Power to retain commissions and brokerages[1]

Any of the {Trustees} who shall be an individual shall be entitled to retain any share of brokerage or any commission (or share of commission) paid to him or his firm by any broker agent or insurance office in connection with any acquisition of or dealing with any investments or property or the effecting of or payment of any premiums on any policy of insurance subject or intended to become subject to the trusts of this settlement

1   This clause ousts the 'self-dealing' rule, see Paragraph 209 [497] ante. When this clause is inserted in a document the defined terms in { } must be altered to suit those used in the document.

[1761]

229

Power to retain director's fees etc[1]

No {Trustee} shall be accountable for any remuneration or other benefit received by him or any other of the {Trustees} from any company in which shares stock debentures or other securities are for the time being held whether directly or indirectly by the {Trustees}

1   This clause ousts the 'self-dealing' rule, see Paragraph 209 [497] ante. When this clause is inserted in a document the defined terms in { } must be altered to suit those used in the document.

[1762]

230

Audit[1]

The {Trustees} may cause the accounts of the trust to be audited annually by such professional accountant as they may appoint for the purpose and may in their discretion determine out of what part or parts of the {Trust Fund} or the income of it the costs of such audit shall be defrayed and may make any apportionments of such costs as they think desirable

1   This clause extends the statutory power of audit under the Trustee Act 1925 s 22(4) (48 Halsbury's Statutes (4th Edn) TRUSTS AND SETTLEMENTS). See further Paragraph 206 [491] and Paragraph 266 [655] ante. When this clause is inserted in a document the defined terms in { } must be altered to suit those used in the document.

[1763]

231

Audit and accounts[1]

0.1   The {Trustees} [shall *or* may in their discretion] cause the accounts of the {Trust Estate} and the {Trust Fund} ('the Accounts') to be audited annually by a qualified accountant from time to time appointed by the {Trustees} ('the Accountant') and shall furnish to the Accountant such vouchers consents and information as he may require

0.2   A copy or summary of the Accounts shall be signed by the Accountant and a copy of the document so signed ('the Summary') shall be delivered or sent by post to every person for the time being entitled to the income of the {Trust Estate} or the {Trust Fund} or whose consent is by this settlement required to the exercise of the trusts or powers conferred by the settlement on the {Trustees} or by law implied or if any such person be a minor to his or her guardian or guardians

0.3   Every person entitled to receive a copy of the Summary shall furnish the {Trustees} from time to time with an address within the United Kingdom to which the same may be addressed and if such person fails so to do it shall be sufficient if the same is sent by post to the last address of such person known to the {Trustees} and the accidental omission to address or send by post any such copy of the Summary to any person entitled to the same or the delivery or sending the same to the wrong address shall not prejudice the conclusive nature of the Accounts and Summary for the purpose provided in clause [0.4] below

0.4   The Accounts or Summary when signed as stated in clause [0.2] above shall be conclusive evidence of the matters stated in them and that all consents or requests by this settlement or by law required to any transaction appearing in them or reasonably to be inferred from them have been properly given or made

0.5   Within [6 months] after the delivery or posting of the copies of the Summary any person interested may require the rectification of the Accounts or Summary and if the {Trustees} and the Accountant fail to agree to such requisition may take proceedings for that purpose or to set aside any transaction appearing in them or reasonably to be inferred from them

[1764]

1   As to the right of beneficiaries to inspect accounts and other trust documents see 48 Halsbury's Laws
     (4th Edn 2000 Reissue) para 855 et seq and Paragraph 207 [493] ante. This Form is probably only of
     use in very large settlements. When this clause is inserted in a document the defined terms in { } must
     be altered to suit those used in the document.

[1765]

232
Disclosure of documents—confidentiality[1]

Without prejudice to any right under the general law of the {Trustees} to refuse
disclosure of any document it is declared that the {Trustees} shall not be bound to
disclose to any person any of the following documents that is to say:

0.1   any document disclosing any deliberations of the {Trustees} (or any of them)
        as to the manner in which the {Trustees} should exercise any power or any
        discretion conferred upon the {Trustees} by this settlement or disclosing the
        reason for any particular exercise of any such power or any such discretion or
        the material upon which such reasons shall or might have been based

[1766]

0.2   any other document relating to the exercise or proposed exercise of any power
        or any discretion conferred on the {Trustees} by this settlement

1   For the rules on the obligation of trustees with regard to the provision of information to beneficiaries
     see *Re Londonderry's Settlement, Peat v Walsh* [1965] Ch 918, [1964] 3 All ER 855, CA; *Lemos v Coutts
     & Co* [1992–3] CILR 490; Re Rabaiotti Settlement (2000) WTLR 953, Royal Ct (Jer) and Paragraph
     207 [493] ante. When this clause is inserted in a document the defined terms in { } must be altered to
     suit those used in the document.

[1767]

233
Remuneration of Trustees[1]

0.1   Any of the {Trustees} who shall be an individual engaged in any profession or
        business [which consists of or includes the administration of trusts or the
        management of assets of a type comprised in the {Trust Fund} or the advising
        of trustees either generally or in respect of any particular aspects of their
        functions or obligations] either alone or in partnership shall be entitled to
        charge and be paid and to retain all professional or other charges for any business
        done or time spent or services rendered by him or his firm in connection with
        the trusts powers and provisions of this settlement and shall also be entitled to
        retain any share of brokerage or commission paid to him or his firm by any
        broker agent or insurance office in connection with any acquisition of or
        dealing with any investments or property or the effecting or payment of any
        premium on any policy of insurance subject or intended to become subject to
        the trusts of this settlement[2]

0.2   None of the {Trustees} holding any directorship or other office or employment
        or retainer in relation to any company all or any of whose shares stock or
        securities shall at any time be subject to any trusts of this settlement shall be
        accountable for any remuneration received in connection with such
        directorship office employment or retainer[3]

0.3   Notwithstanding anything contained in this clause neither the {Settlor} nor any spouse of the {Settlor} who may for the time being be one of the {Trustees} shall be entitled to charge or be paid or retain all or any share of any professional or other charges by reason of this clause or be relieved thereby from any liability to account as a trustee for any money or assets[4]

[1768]

1   When this clause is inserted in a document the defined terms in { } must be altered to suit those used in the document.

2   Clause 0.1 above is concerned with the question of which trustees should be remunerated: should only professionals whose business involves acting as and advising trustees be entitled to remuneration? The Trustee Act 2000 s 28(5) (48 Halsbury's Statutes (4th Edn) TRUSTS AND SETTLEMENTS) limits statutory remuneration to trustees acting 'in a professional capacity': see Paragraph 213 [513] ante. Include the words in square brackets if the statutory restriction is required: if, on the other hand, it is desired to enable trustees who exercise any profession or vocation to charge, then delete these words. There may be some uncertainty as to what is included in the term 'profession or business': is it limited to a self employed person? If so, it excludes employees, including (say) the senior investment manager of a merchant bank who may be the ideal trustee for a particular trust. It is arguable (although rather weakly) that such a person carries on a business (see Kessler *Drafting Trusts and Will Trusts* (5th Edn, 2000) para 18.56). Given these doubts it may be safer to employ a wider clause along the lines of the following:

> 'Any trustee, whether he is engaged in a profession or business or merely acts in a personal capacity shall be entitled to charge and be paid all normal professional or other reasonable charges for business done services rendered or time spent by such trustee personally or by such trustee's firm or company in the administration of these trusts including acts which a trustee not engaged in any profession or business could have done personally'

The wider formulation of this clause prohibits a lay trustee from receiving remuneration but would, allow (say) a self-employed plumber or carpenter to be paid! It may be thought that although this clause is widely used in practice, it is unsatisfactory in trusts where trustees other than solicitors and accountants are involved.

3   Clause 0.2 above is required to exclude the self-dealing rule illustrated in cases such as *Re Dover Coalfield Extension Ltd* [1908] 1 Ch 65, CA: see further *Snell's Equity* (30th Edn) para 11-76. As to the self-dealing rule see Paragraph 209 [497] ante.

4   Clause 0.3 above is designed to ensure the neither the settlor nor his spouse can benefit in any way from the trust and is primarily dictated by tax considerations: see Paragraph 62 [145] and Paragraph 289 [749] et seq ante.

[1769]–[1780]

L: APPOINTMENT AND REMOVAL OF TRUSTEES

(As to the appointment and retirement of trustees under the Trusts of Land and Appointment of Trustees Act 1996 Part II and as to the change of trustees generally, see vol 40(2) (2001 Reissue) TRUSTS AND SETTLEMENTS Part 10 [5201].

234

Power to appoint new trustees

The power of appointing new or additional {Trustees} shall vest in the {Settlor} during [his *or* her] life and afterwards in *(name)*[1] but so that neither the {Settlor} nor any spouse of the {Settlor} [nor any of the {Beneficiaries}][2] shall be appointed as one of the {Trustees}

1   Particularly in discretionary trusts it may be desirable (as a way of controlling the trustees) to provide for the principal beneficiary to have the power to appoint new trustees; for example, the power could be given successively to the settlor's son, grandson etc. The draftsman should consider whether to

include a power to remove trustees: for such a power see Form 242 [1792] post. Consider also the impact of the Trusts of Land and Appointment of Trustees Act 1996 Pt II (ss 19–21) (37 Halsbury's Statutes (4th Edn) TRUSTS AND SETTLEMENTS).

    When this clause is inserted in a document the defined terms in { } must be altered to suit those used in the document.

2   The words in square brackets should be inserted where under the provisions of the settlement a sole trustee acting alone could appoint the trust fund to himself.

[1781]

235

Power of each party to appoint a new trustee[1]

(first party) shall have the power during [his] life to appoint new {Trustees} or a new {Trustee} in place of *(first trustee)* and [his] successors in the office of trustee and *(second party)* during [her] life shall have the power of appointing new {Trustees} or a new {Trustee} in place of *(second trustee)* and [his] successors in the office of trustee

1   Provisions of this type may be inserted into divorce settlements. When this clause is inserted in a document the defined terms in { } must be altered to suit those used in the document.

[1782]

236

Power to appoint new trustees including non-resident trustees

0.1   The power of appointing new {Trustees} shall vest in the {Settlor} during [his] life and shall include power to appoint as {Trustees} (in addition to the power contained above to appoint as {Trustee} a trust corporation [or any other company][1]) any person or persons (or company) whether resident (or incorporated) in the United Kingdom or not PROVIDED that neither the {Settlor} nor any spouse of the {Settlor} shall be appointed a trustee of this settlement nor of any trusts created or dispositions made under the settlement

0.2   Such appointment may be made notwithstanding that as a result of it (or of any retirement occurring in connection with it) all or a majority of the {Trustees} are persons resident (or incorporated) outside the United Kingdom and the provisions of the Trustee Act 1925 Section 36 (as amended)[2] in their application to this settlement shall be varied so that it shall not be a ground for the replacement of a {Trustee} that [he] has resided out of the United Kingdom for more than 12 months

[1783]

1   See Form 239 note 1 [1789] post. When this clause is inserted in a document the defined terms in { } must be altered to suit those used in the document.

2   Ie Trustee Act 1925 s 36 as amended by the Mental Health Act s 149(1), Sch 7 Pt I, by the Trusts of Land and Appointment of Trustees Act 1996 s 25(1), Sch 3 para 3(11), Sch 4 and by the Trustee Delegation Act 1999 s 8 (48 Halsbury's Statutes (4th Edn) TRUSTS AND SETTLEMENTS).

[1784]

237

Power to appoint trust corporation as trustee

0.1 A trust corporation falling within the meaning given to those words by the Law of Property Act 1925[1] may be appointed to be the sole {Trustee} or one of the {Trustees}

0.2 Every trust corporation so appointed shall be entitled to charge remuneration according to its scale [but shall in no case be entitled to remuneration at a rate higher than the Public Trustee if appointed would be entitled to charge]

0.3 A trust corporation if a bank shall be entitled to transact every form of banking business with the {Trustees} and the {Beneficiaries} and although such business shall concern the {Trust Fund} and although the trust corporation is a {Trustee} (whether or not a sole {Trustee}) it shall not be liable to account for any of the profits so made[2]

0.4 Where a trust corporation is a {Trustee} together with other {Trustees} the trust corporation shall have the custody of all documents and securities relating to the trust

[1785]

1   As to the meaning of 'trust corporation' see the Law of Property Act 1925 s 205(1)(xxviii) as extended by the Law of Property (Amendment) Act 1926 s 3 (37 Halsbury's Statutes (4th Edn) REAL PROPERTY). When this clause is inserted in a document the defined terms in { } must be altered to suit those used in the document.

2   In the absence of such an exemption from accounting, a trustee would have to account for profits on the general principle that a trustee is not allowed to profit from the trust. For a case in which a trust corporation was liable for breach of fiduciary duty in the circumstances contemplated by this Form see *Re Paulings Settlement Trusts, Younghusband v Coutts & Co* [1964] Ch 303, [1963] 3 All ER 1, CA.

[1786]

238

Power to appoint trust corporation or company (including foreign company) as trustee

Any trust corporation or company[1] whether or not incorporated or resident in the United Kingdom which is empowered to act as a trustee may be appointed to be a trustee of this settlement or of any trust or other disposition constituted by virtue of the exercise of any power contained in this settlement or by law implied and upon such appointment shall have the powers rights and benefits as to remuneration and otherwise as may be agreed in writing prior to any such appointment between such trust corporation or company and the person or persons entitled under this settlement or under any disposition made under this settlement to appoint such trustees or in default of such agreement in accordance with the published terms and conditions of such trust corporation or the usual terms and conditions as to the acceptance and carrying out of trusts at the date of the appointment of such trust corporation or company and if such trust corporation or company has power to act as a bank it shall be entitled to act as banker to make advances to the trust under the power contained above without being liable to account for any profits so made and in all respects as if it were not a trustee of this settlement

1   See Form 239 note 1 [1789] post.

[1787]

239

Power to appoint corporation as trustee and to remove[1]

0.1   If at any time or times it shall be considered necessary or expedient to do so the persons or person having the power to appoint new {Trustees} under this settlement may appoint either as the sole {Trustee} or jointly with any existing {Trustees} or {Trustee} and either as a general trustee or custodian trustee any incorporated body (whether or not a trust corporation) which such persons or person shall consider to be a suitable trustee and may agree the amount of the remuneration payable to such body and whether such remuneration shall be payable out of capital or income or both

0.2   PROVIDED always that if any such body shall be appointed to be a {Trustee} [and afterwards the {Spouses} or the survivor of them or the guardian of any minor interested in possession in the {Trust Fund} or any part of it shall be dissatisfied with the conduct of the body so appointed] the person or persons having the power to appoint new {Trustees} may by deed remove that body from the trusteeship and appoint such other person or corporation as a trustee of such of the trusts as shall be subsisting in the place of such body and jointly with any other then existing {Trustee} or solely as the case may require

[1788]

1   Power to appoint as trustee a company which is not a trust corporation is uncommon. The power of such a company to give, as sole trustee, a valid discharge by a written receipt for money, securities and other personal property and effects should be considered and note that the settlement cannot deprive it of such power: see the Trustee Act 1925 s 14(1), (3) as amended by the Trustee Act 2000 s 40(1), Sch 2 para 19 (48 Halsbury's Statutes (4th Edn) TRUSTS AND SETTLEMENTS). That power does not apply to proceeds of sale or other capital money arising under a trust of land or capital money arising under the Settled Land Act 1925 (48 Halsbury's Statutes (4th Edn) TRUSTS AND SETTLEMENTS): Trustee Act 1925 s 14(2) as amended by the Trusts of Land and Appointment of Trustees Act 1996 s 25(1), Sch 3 para 3(3). Corporate trustees are commonly found in company pension schemes: often a subsidiary company of the company which promoted the scheme and which is the main employer. For an express power to remove trustees see Form 242 [1792] post.

    When this clause is inserted in a document the defined terms in { } must be altered to suit those used in the document.

[1789]

240

Provision for automatic retirement of a trustee[1]

0.1   The power of appointing a new trustee or trustees in place of any of the {Trustees} shall be exercisable by the {Principal Beneficiary} during [his] lifetime and subject thereto the power of appointing new or additional trustees of this {Settlement} shall be exercisable by the {Settlor} during [his] lifetime and subject thereto by such person or persons as the {Settlor} shall by any deed or deeds revocable or irrevocable nominate for this purpose

0.2   At each [five-year] anniversary of the creation of the {Settlement} and without prejudice to any other occasion on which a person may cease to be a trustee one of the {Trustees} shall retire from the trusteeship and the person having power to appoint a trustee to act in [his] place may on or before the anniversary appoint some other person not already one of the {Trustees} to act in [his] place (failing which the trustee shall continue as if reappointed)

0.3   As between any two of the {Trustees} the one to retire first under clause [0.2] shall be the one whose appointment (or most recent appointment including an occasion on which [he] continued as if reappointed) occurred first and subject thereto the elder shall retire first

1   When this clause is inserted in a document the defined terms in { } must be altered to suit those used in the document.

[1790]

241

Number of trustees[1]

The number of {Trustees} shall (so far as is practicable) be not less than 2 individuals at any one time and if at any time the number of {Trustees} shall fall below 2 immediate steps shall be taken (so far as is practicable) to appoint a new or additional {Trustee} or {Trustees} so as to constitute at least 2 persons as {Trustees} PROVIDED that any trust corporation appointed under the power contained in this settlement may be appointed and act as sole {Trustee} and it shall not be necessary to appoint any other person or corporation to act with such trust corporation as {Trustee}

1   When this clause is inserted in a document the defined terms in { } must be altered to suit those used in the document.

[1791]

242

Power to remove trustees[1]

(name) may at any time by deed remove any {Trustee} from his office of trustee of the trusts created by this settlement and may by deed appoint any other person to be a {Trustee} either jointly with any then continuing {Trustee} or solely if after such removal there shall not be any continuing {Trustee} but in every such case as last mentioned more than one {Trustee} must be appointed and then the trust property shall by vesting declaration conveyance transfer or other assurance as may be necessary or expedient be vested jointly in the persons who shall then become the {Trustees}[2]

[1792]

1   In principle there should be nothing unusual about a power to remove trustees. The Trustee Act 1925 s 36(2) (48 Halsbury's Statutes (4th Edn) TRUSTS AND SETTLEMENTS) makes express provision for the consequences of the exercise of such a power. Clauses of this type are, however, rarely encountered in practice: probably because of concern at possible conflicts of interest or the possibility of improper use of the power. Such a power is probably fiduciary and cannot properly be used to 'pack' the body of trustees to ensure that there is a majority who will follow the appointor's directions: *IRC v Schroder* [1983] STC 480 at 500. The tax implications where such a power is vested in the settlor may also need to be considered.

          The power may be expressed to be exercisable either by the settlor or a named person (eg a 'protector') or by the rest of the trustees (not being less than 2) apart from the person being removed. It may be useful where, for example, a senile trustee cannot be shown to be 'unfit' or 'incapable' or 'refusing' to act. It is also possible to have provisions for automatic retirement of trustees on attaining a specified age.

          When this clause is inserted in a document the defined terms in { } must be altered to suit those used in the document.

2   In relation to real property subject to a strict settlement, the property is, and remains, vested in the current tenant for life. There is no requirement to vest the property in the trustees; there is simply a need, in the case of registered land, for the restriction on the register to be amended so as to refer to the new trustees in place of the old trustees. The restriction is that contained in the Land Registration Rules 1925, SR & O 1925/1093 r 58(1), Sch 2 Form 9 (as amended by SI 1996/2975 and SI 1999/2097).

[1793]–[1800]

M: MISCELLANEOUS PROVISIONS

243

Covenant by trustees to pay inheritance tax on creation of a trust[1]

The {Trustees} covenant with the {Settlor} that they will pay all or any inheritance tax which may be payable by reason of the transfer to the {Trustees} of the securities mentioned in the first schedule

1   Inheritance tax may be immediately payable (eg in the case of a discretionary trust) or only payable if the settlor dies within seven years (in the case of a failed potentially exempt transfer). It is not thought that this provision gives rise to problems under the reservation of benefit provisions: see further Paragraph 290 [749] et seq ante. When this clause is inserted in a document the defined terms in { } must be altered to suit those used in the document.

[1801]

244

Covenant by trustees to reimburse settlor in respect of capital gains tax payable by settlor on settlement gains[1]

The {Trustees} jointly covenant with the {Settlor} that they or the survivor of them or other the trustees or trustee for the time being of the settlement will on demand being made by the {Settlor} or [his] personal representatives pay to [him] or them all capital gains tax assessed on and paid by the {Settlor} or [his] personal representatives in respect of any chargeable gains made by the trustee or trustees for the time being of the settlement by reason of the provisions of the Taxation of Chargeable Gains Act 1992 Section 77[2] or any statutory re-enactment or modification of it for the time being in force

[1802]

1   When this clause is inserted in a document the defined terms in { } must be altered to suit those used in the document.

2   Taxation of Chargeable Gains Act 1992 s 77 as substituted by the Finance Act 1995 s 74, Sch 17 para 27 and amended by the Finance Act 1998 s 121(3), Sch 21 para 6(1) (42–44 Halsbury's Statutes (4th Edn) TAXATION). When this section operates gains realised by the trustees are not charged on those trustees, but instead are treated as accruing to the settlor who is then given a right of recovery against the trustees under the Taxation of Chargeable Gains Act 1992 s 78 as amended by the Finance Act 1995 s 74, Sch 17 para 28. For the position of the settlor charge under the Taxation of Chargeable Gains Act 1992 s 86 as amended by the Finance Act 1998 s 121(3), Sch 21 para 6(2) in relation to offshore trusts, see vol 40(2) (2001 Reissue) TRUSTS AND SETTLEMENTS Part 15 [8701].

[1803]

245

Covenant by parent of spouse to pay sum on death[1]

0.1   In consideration of the {Marriage} the {Father} covenants with the {Trustees} that his personal representatives will within 6 months from his death pay to the {Trustees} the sum of £... with interest at the rate of ... % per year from his death unless he shall have previously paid that sum to the {Trustees} which he shall be at liberty to do

0.2   The {Trustees} shall hold the sum of £... when paid to them and the investments representing the same on the trusts declared by this settlement and then subsisting concerning the [{Trust Fund} *or* {Husband's Fund} *or* {Wife's Fund}] and shall apply the interest (if any) on it until payment as if it were income of the same fund

---

1   When this clause is inserted in a document the defined terms in { } must be altered to suit those used in the document.

[1804]

246

Covenant by parent to settle equal share of his estate[1]

0.1   The {Father} covenants with the {Trustees} that if the [{Wife} *or* {Husband}] or any issue of the {Marriage} shall survive him his personal representatives will so soon as may be after his death pay or assure to the {Trustees} money or investments at least equal in value to such share or proportion of his net residuary estate as if the same were divided in equal shares between the children of the {Father} [by his wife] who shall be living at his death or be then dead leaving issue then living and of an amount as would be equivalent to one such share

0.2   PROVIDED that in ascertaining such share or proportion the {Trustees} shall bring into hotchpot any property given or transferred to the {Trustees} by the {Father} either directly or through the [{Wife} *or* {Husband]} and also that any legacy or property bequeathed by the will of the {Father} or any codicil to it to the {Trustees} or the {Wife} or {Husband} or both of them or their children or issue shall unless the contrary be directed by such will or codicil be brought into hotchpot and reckoned as partly or wholly in satisfaction of such share

0.3   *(continue with declaration of trust)*[2]

[1805]

---

1   A covenant to this effect is often desired but a covenant to pay a lump sum (see Form 245 [1804] ante) is to be preferred. When this clause is inserted in a document the defined terms in { } must be altered to suit those used in the document.

2   For a declaration of trust which may be adapted as appropriate see Form 245 clause 0.2 [1804] ante.

[1806]

247

Covenant by parents not to exercise power of appointment in their marriage settlement so as to reduce share settled on their child[1]

[After the {Marriage} has taken place] *(parents of wife)* will not nor will either of them exercise any of the powers of appointment given to them and the survivor of them by their marriage settlement dated *(date)* (of which *(trustee)* and *(trustee)* are the present trustees) so as by any means to reduce the share of the {Wife} in the trust funds and property now or in future subject to the trusts of such settlement to a lesser amount than the share to which the {Wife} would be entitled in default of any exercise of such powers of appointment or any of them and if the property subject to such trusts had wholly devolved under the trusts for issue in default of appointment contained in the same settlement

1   When this clause is inserted in a document the defined terms in { } must be altered to suit those used in the document.

[1807]

248

Power of wife to release protected life interest on appointment of capital to child[1]

If at any time or times the {Wife} shall concur with the {Husband} in exercising the power of appointment of the {Trust Fund} or of any part of it to take effect after the death of the survivor of the {Spouses} for the benefit of any issue of the {Marriage} and the {Husband} and {Wife} shall desire to accompany that appointment with an assignment or release to or for the benefit of such issue of the life interests of the {Spouses} in the {Trust Fund} or in such part of it and if the {Trustees} shall be of opinion that in the then existing circumstances of the {Spouses} and the children or more remote issue it is expedient for such desire to be carried into effect then notwithstanding that her life interest in the {Trust Fund} is held upon protective trusts for her benefit the {Wife} may with the consent in writing of the {Trustees} so release or assign her life interest and any such release or assignment by her shall be as effectual as it would have been if she had been absolutely entitled to her life interest

[1808]

1   The purpose of this clause is to allow the wife to release her interest without bringing into operation the statutory protective trusts set out in the Trustee Act 1925 s 33(1) (48 Halsbury's Statutes (4th Edn) TRUSTS AND SETTLEMENTS). In general, the consent of the protected life tenant to the exercise of an express or statutory power of advancement will not operate to work a forfeiture of the life interest when the statutory protective trusts apply. The clause is, however, of use in settlements in which it is intended to rely on express provisions in the settlement as creating the protective trusts rather than the statutory provisions of the Trustee Act 1925 s 33(1). As to protective trusts see Paragraph 123 [305] ante and for a detailed consideration see vol 40(2) (2001 Reissue) TRUSTS AND SETTLEMENTS Part 12 [6901].
    When this clause is inserted in a document the defined terms in { } must be altered to suit those used in the document.

[1809]

249
Declaration as to proper law together with power to change the proper law applicable to the trust[1]

0.1   It is declared that (subject as is provided below) this settlement shall be construed and take effect according to the law of England and Wales whose law shall be the proper law of the settlement and that the rights of all persons beneficially entitled under this settlement and the construction of each and every provision of this settlement shall (subject as is provided below) be governed exclusively by such law

0.2   Notwithstanding the provisions of sub-clause [0.1] above but subject to sub-clause [0.4] below the {Trustees} (being at least 2 in number or a trust corporation) may at any time and from time to time during the subsistence of the trusts of this settlement but before the {Ultimate Date} by deed declare that this settlement shall from the date of such deed take effect in accordance with the law of some other place in any part of the world and that the proper law of the settlement shall from such time be the law of that place and this settlement shall from such time be construed and take effect according to and be governed exclusively by such law (but subject to the power conferred by this sub-clause [0.2] and until any further declaration is made under this settlement)

0.3   So often as any such declaration as stated above shall be made the {Trustees} (being at least 2 in number or a trust corporation) may at any time or times afterwards but before the {Ultimate Date} by deed make such consequential alterations in the trusts powers and provisions of this settlement as the {Trustees} in their absolute discretion shall consider necessary or desirable to secure that so far as may be possible such trusts powers and provisions shall be as valid and effective under the law of the place named in such declaration as they are under the law of England and Wales

[1810]

0.4   Notwithstanding anything contained in this clause:
    0.4.1   the {Trustees} shall not at any time have the power to take any action under this clause which:
        0.4.1.1   might directly or indirectly result in this settlement becoming revocable or unenforceable or
        0.4.1.2   might in any way make any alteration in the beneficial trusts and powers of this settlement (or in the persons beneficially entitled under this settlement) which could not then have been made by the {Trustees} in exercise of the powers conferred on them by this settlement insofar (if at all) as such powers are then still subsisting and exercisable with immediate effect
    0.4.2   the {Trustees} (being at least 2 in number or a trust corporation) may at any time or times before the {Ultimate Date} by deed or deeds extinguish (or restrict the future exercise of) the powers respectively conferred by sub-clauses [0.2] and [0.3]

[1811]

1   This clause both declares the proper law and gives the trustees power to change the proper law applicable to the trust. For a power to remove the forum of trust from the United Kingdom see Form 197 [1694] ante. When this clause is inserted in a document the defined terms in { } must be altered to suit those used in the document.

[1812]

250

Exclusion of settlor from benefit—variation to exclude settlor's spouse[1]

Notwithstanding anything above declared or implied no power or discretion by this settlement or by law conferred on the {Trustees} or any of them or on any other persons whatsoever shall be exercisable and no provision contained in this settlement shall operate in any manner so as to cause any property for the time being subject to the trusts of this settlement or any part of the income of it to be paid or applied in any manner or in any circumstances whatsoever to or for the benefit of the {Settlor} [or any spouse for the time being of the {Settlor}][2]

[1813]

1　　Although the powers and discretions of trustees and appointors may normally only be exercised so as to benefit the objects of the trust, it may be desirable to insert a proviso such as that contained in this clause in order both to remind the trustees not to exercise their powers so as to confer a benefit on the settlor and also to resolve any doubts as to whether or not the settlor can in fact benefit. For the adverse tax consequences that may result from the settlor's obtaining any benefit or any part of the trust property see Paragraph 290 [749] et seq (inheritance tax) and Paragraph 359 [1011] ante (income tax). These problems do not arise in relation to the settlor's widow or widower.

　　When this clause is inserted in a document the defined terms in { } must be altered to suit those used in the document.

2　　A divorced spouse is not included and nor is the settlor's widow or widower: *Lord Vestey's Executors v IRC* [1949] 1 All ER 1108, HL. The spouse should not be named, since otherwise he or she will be prohibited from benefit after the settlor's death or after divorce, and any future spouse of the settlor would not be excluded under this clause. In cases where there are joint settlors each settlor, together with spouses, should be excluded. Any person who provides property for the benefit of the settlor becomes (to that extent) a settlor and under the tax legislation so too does a person providing funds indirectly. In practice, it is rare for a settlor exclusion clause to be drafted so as to catch such persons: for a consideration of whether this is desirable see Kessler *Drafting Trusts and Will Trusts: A Modern Approach* (5th Edn, 2000) para 9.53. See also *IRC v Botnar* [1999] STC 711; *Fuller v Evans* [2000] 1 All ER 636, [2000] 2 FLR 13 and *Netherton v Netherton* (2000) 1 WTLR 1171. See also Form 4 clause 14 [1091] ante and Form 4 note 5 [1103] ante.

[1814]

251

Exclusion of community of property[1]

It is hereby declared that any part of the {Trust Fund} to which any {Beneficiary} may become entitled or which is applied for the benefit of such {Beneficiary} shall not become subject to any provisions for the community of property to which in the absence of this declaration it would become subject but shall be and remain the sole separate and exclusive property of such {Beneficiary} and should such {Beneficiary} be married or marry in community of property then any benefit accruing to such {Beneficiary} shall be expressly excluded from the community and in the case of the {Beneficiary} being female such benefit shall also be free from the interference control or marital power of any husband of such {Beneficiary} PROVIDED always that for the purpose of this sub-clause the word 'benefit' shall where the context so admits include movable and immovable property and the provisions of this sub-clause shall apply moreover not only to the benefits accruing to any {Beneficiary} but also to any and all benefits at any time afterwards directly or indirectly acquired by means of the proceeds of such

1　　Community of property is a concept widely applied in civil law jurisdictions. When this clause is inserted in a document the defined terms in { } must be altered to suit those used in the document.

[1815]–[1840]

PART 6: DOCUMENTS SUBSIDIARY TO, MODIFYING AND EXTINGUISHING TRUSTS

Forms and Precedents

A: LETTERS OF WISHES

252

Letter of wishes for use with fully discretionary or flexible life interest trusts—detailed guidance[1]

To: The trustees of a settlement dated *(date)* and made between *(parties)* ('the Settlement').

This letter contains my wishes in respect of the administration of the Settlement. It is not intended to create any legally binding trust direction or obligation.

[1841]

It is my wish that the property which is the subject of the Settlement should be held on the following trusts:

1.1   If my wife, *(wife)*, survives me, everything to her absolutely.

1.2   If my wife predeceases me but one or both of my children, *(child)* and *(child)*, survive:

        1.2.1   70% of the assets to such of *(child)* and *(child)* as survive and if they both survive in equal shares. I request that they have an entitlement to income for life and that you have a discretion to advance capital to them;

        1.2.2   before dividing up the remaining 30% of the assets, I request that you consider what provision, if any, should be made for my father, *(father)*, who lives at *(address)* and what additional provision is needed for my mother-in-law, *(mother-in-law)*, who lives at *(address)*. Subject to these considerations:

            1.2.2.1   15% to my sister, *(sister)*, who lives at *(address)*, with an entitlement to income for life and you have discretion to advance capital to her, and after her death her share should go to her children in equal shares absolutely once they attain the age of 25 years;

            1.2.2.2   5% to my mother-in-law, *(mother-in-law)*, absolutely;

            1.2.2.3   5% to my wife *(wife)*'s nieces, *(niece)* and *(niece)*, who live at *(address)*, in equal shares once they attain the age of 25 years absolutely; and

            1.2.2.4   5% to *(name)* absolutely.

[1842]

1.3   If my wife and my children, *(child)* and *(child)*, predecease me, I request that you consider the matters as in paragraph 1.2.2 above, subject to these considerations:

    1.3.1   75% of the assets to my sister, *(sister)*, with an entitlement to income for life and you have power to advance capital to her, and after her death her share should go to her children in equal shares absolutely once they attain the age of 25 years;

    1.3.2   15% to my mother-in-law, *(name)*, absolutely;

    1.3.3   5% to my wife *(wife)*'s nieces, *(name)* and *(name)*, in equal shares once they attain the age of 25 years absolutely; and

    1.3.4   5% to *(name)* absolutely.

In considering whether and how to exercise your discretions, I request that you consult with *(executor)*, one of the executors of my will.

Dated: *(date)*

(signature of the settlor)

[1843]

1   This letter gives detailed guidance to trustees whilst Form 253 [1845] post is more general. It should be stressed that the settlor's wishes are not binding on the trustees; any attempt to make them binding might result in the letter being treated as incorporated in the trust document. To avoid any possibility of this, it may be sensible for the letter to be signed a few days after the trust has been established. Letters of wishes may, of course, be updated by the settlor from time to time. Both Forms deal with the exercise of dispositive powers by trustees of either fully discretionary or flexible life interest trusts. For alternative ways of retaining some control over the trustees after death, and ensuring that due weight is given to the letter of wishes, the draftsman should consider giving the main beneficiary the power to appoint (and possibly dismiss) trustees: for a power to remove trustees see Form 242 [1792] ante. There is some authority that such a letter is confidential so that a beneficiary is not entitled to see it unless he shows a prima facie case that:

    (a)   the trust terms should include the letter as being incorporated into the trust; or

    (b)   the trustees have exercised their discretions capriciously.

In those two cases the beneficiary is entitled to discovery of the letter: see *Hartigan Nominees Pty Ltd v Rydge* (1992) 29 NSWLR 405, CA but contrast *Re Rabaiotti Settlement* (2000) WTLR 953, Royal Ct (Jer). When discussing the contents of the letter with the settlor, it is therefore important to consider whether the letter should be made available to the beneficiaries. If so, this should be explicitly stated in the letter.

[1844]

253

Letter of wishes for use with fully discretionary or flexible life interest trusts— general guidance[1]

To: My executors and trustees.

This letter sets out in general terms my wishes with regard to the various settlements which I have created and the provisions of my will. It should be borne in mind that they may be overtaken by future events and I wish you to use your own judgement to decide how matters should be dealt with in the future.

[1845]

My intention is to make proper provision for my former wife during her life and to provide for my present wife and my two children.

I would ask you to bear in mind that whilst my wife and the children are living in *(property)* I would not wish you to take any steps to sell the house. If circumstances changed: for instance, if the children left home or if my wife decided to remarry then you would need to consider carefully what should be done. My main concern would be that my dependants are properly provided for. Subject to these general remarks my wishes are as follows:

1   So far as the settlement of *(date)* is concerned, the main purpose of this trust is to pay benefits to my former wife during her life. She should be maintained out of income and (where necessary) capital. After her death I would envisage this fund being used primarily for the benefit of my children.

                                                                                                      [1846]

2   So far as the declaration of trust dated *(date)* is concerned, my main objective is to make proper provision for my wife. Accordingly, I would regard her as the prime beneficiary and would expect her to receive maintenance in the form of income and, if appropriate, capital. In the event of her remarrying you would need to consider carefully whether she should still receive income or if she was then fully provided for whether the income (and capital) should be paid out to the children.

3   Turning to my will there is first a trust of the inheritance tax nil-rate band and you will see that the beneficiaries are my wife and the children. My general remarks apply here and I would expect the income to be paid for the benefit of my wife. The residue clause of the will gives a life interest to my wife which can be terminated at your discretion. Again I would expect you to leave this life interest in being until circumstances changed.

I would like you to consider any suggestions jointly put to you by my wife and the children and if you consider them wise, to act on them.

Dated: *(date)*

(signature of the settlor)

1   See Form 252 note 1 [1844] ante.

                                                                                                      [1847]

254

Letter of wishes to trustees of a discretionary trust of life policy requesting the proceeds to be used in the payment of inheritance tax on death[1]

To: The trustees of a settlement dated *(date)* and made between *(parties)*.

The purpose of this letter is to indicate to you how I would wish you to exercise certain discretions vested in you as trustees of the settlement known as my '1993 Discretionary Settlement'. That settlement had transferred to it a life policy to a value of £500,000.

                                                                                                      [1848]

The life policy is a convertible term policy for a term of 15 years. The purpose of the policy is to protect against the inheritance tax which will be payable on my interest in my late father's will trust and to discharge any tax that may be payable on lifetime gifts as a result of my death. Should there be an excess of funds for any reason (for instance, because inheritance tax rates have fallen or the value of my interest in the settlement is less than anticipated) then I would wish you to hold any surplus funds for the benefit of my issue, failing whom any surplus funds should be distributed in accordance with the terms of my will as if they formed part of my residuary estate.

Dated: *(date)*

(signature of the settlor)

1   It is normal inheritance tax planning to take out insurance to cover tax liabilities arising on death. Protection against a tax charge on lifetime gifts can be obtained by the use of term assurance: in this Form the main purpose is to cover tax payable in respect of an interest in possession in settled property. The trust containing the life policy should contain a wide class of beneficiary and give the trustees power to add to the class. For the tax consequences of creating and operating a flexible trust of a life policy see Form 6 note 1 [1135] ante.

[1849]

B: TRUSTEE RESOLUTIONS ETC

255

Resolution exercising power of advancement[1]

We *(trustee)* of *(address)* and *(trustee)* of *(address)* being the present trustees of the settlement ('the Settlement') dated *(date)* and made between *(parties)* in exercise of the power of advancement contained in the Trustee Act 1925 Section 32 as extended by clause *(number)* of the Settlement resolve immediately to advance and transfer the investments described in the schedule (being part of that property now subject to the trusts of the Settlement to which *(beneficiary)* is absolutely entitled contingent on [him] attaining 21 years of age) to *(beneficiary)* absolutely freed and discharged from the trusts powers and provisions in the Settlement declared and contained

[1850]

Dated: *(date)*

SCHEDULE

The Investments

(describe investments)

(signatures of the trustees)

1   As to the power of advancement see Paragraph 238 [573] et seq ante and for a request for advancement see Form 265 [1879] post. The statutory power of advancement and most express powers to 'pay or apply' may be exercised by trustee resolution, although a deed is often used in practice: see further

Introduction to Section E [1951] post. In this Form there is no prior interest where consent is required: see Form 266 [1881] post for a typical consent. For capital gains tax purposes there will be a deemed disposal under the Taxation of Chargeable Gains Act 1992 s 71 as amended by the Finance Act 1999 s 75(1) (42–44 Halsbury's Statutes (4th Edn) TAXATION) given that the settlement is brought to an end as a result of the trustee resolution. For inheritance tax purposes if the person advanced already has an interest in possession there is no charge: Inheritance Tax Act 1984 s 53(2) (42–44 Halsbury's Statutes (4th Edn) TAXATION). If the trust is one of accumulation and maintenance there will be no inheritance tax charge because of Inheritance Tax Act 1984 s 71(4). As to accumulation and maintenance trusts generally see Paragraph 127 [316] ante and vol 40(2) (2001 Reissue) TRUSTS AND SETTLEMENTS Part 11 [6301].

[1851]

256

Resolution exercising power of advancement by way of transfer to a new settlement[1]

We *(trustee)* of *(address)* and *(trustee)* of *(address)* being the present trustees of the settlement ('the Settlement') dated *(date)* and made between *(parties)* in exercise of the power of advancement contained in the Trustee Act 1925 Section 32 as extended by clause *(number)* of the Settlement resolve immediately to advance and transfer the investments described in the schedule (being part of that property now subject to the trusts of the Settlement) by way of resettlement for the benefit of *(beneficiary)* to *(trustee)* of *(address)* and *(trustee)* of *(address)* as trustees of a settlement dated *(date)* absolutely freed and discharged from the trusts powers and provisions in the Settlement to the intent that the same shall be held by them upon the trusts and with and subject to the powers and provisions declared and contained in that settlement as an addition and as one fund for all purposes

[1852]

Dated: *(date)*

SCHEDULE

The Investments

(describe investments)

(signatures of the trustees)

1   This Form makes it clear that property is being transferred to a new settlement; in other cases the position may be less certain. The trustees will make a deemed disposal of the investments advanced for capital gains tax purposes: see the Taxation of Chargeable Gains Act 1992 s 71 as amended by the Finance Act 1999 s 75(1) (42–44 Halsbury's Statutes (4th Edn) TAXATION). The trustees must ensure that the power is being exercised intra vires: eg that the perpetuity rule is not being infringed. For a deed of advancement effecting a resettlement see Form 290 [2020] post.

[1853]

257

Exercise of power of advancement by trustee resolution—a 'settled advance'[1]

WHEREAS:

(1)   We *(trustee)* of *(address)* and *(trustee)* of *(address)* being the present trustees of the settlement ('the Settlement') details of which are set out in the schedule

(2)   In the events which have happened we own *(insert details)* ('the Property')

(3)   The power to advance capital contained in the Trustee Act 1925 Section 32 has been expressly incorporated into the Settlement by clause [2] and we have decided [with the consent of *(life tenant)*[2]] to exercise this power for the benefit of *(beneficiary)* as set out below

[1854]

WE HEREBY RESOLVE in exercise of the power of advancement conferred on us by clause [2] of the Settlement and of *(insert details)* all other relevant powers to apply the Property for the benefit of *(beneficiary)* by declaring that from the date of this resolution we will hold the Property by way of amendment[3] of the existing trusts of the Settlement upon the following trusts:

1   The income (if any) of the Property shall be paid to *(beneficiary)* during his lifetime

2   The Trustees may at any time during *(beneficiary)*'s life pay or apply the whole or any part of the Property in which his interest in possession is for the time being subsisting to him or for his advancement or otherwise for his benefit in such manner as the Trustees shall in their discretion think fit. In exercising the powers conferred by this clause the Trustees shall be entitled to have regard solely to the interests of *(beneficiary)* and to disregard all other interests or potential interests in the Property

3   Subject as above the capital and income of the Property shall be held upon trust for *(remainder beneficiary)* absolutely[4]

4   The trusts powers and provisions contained in this Settlement shall continue to be applicable to the Property so far as consistent with the provisions of this resolution[5]

[5   *(Life tenant)* hereby consents as required by the Trustee Act 1925 Section 32(1) to the exercise of the power of advancement contained in this resolution]

Dated *(date)*

SCHEDULE

The Settlement

(insert details of the settlement)

(signatures of the trustees)
[1855]

---

1   For the power of advancement, see Paragraph 238 [573] ante. The power may be exercised by resolution but sometimes a deed is preferred: see Form 153 [1594] post. For 'settled advances' see *Pilkington v IRC* [1964] AC 612, [1962] 3 All ER 622, HL and *Re Hampden Settlement Trusts* [1977] TR 177. The power is in the 'wider form' and, hence, may be used to create a new settlement for capital gains tax purposes: see Paragraph 342 [919] ante. However, it may be exercised in the 'narrower form' so that a new settlement (and consequent risk of a capital gains tax charge) is not created: see *Swires v Renton* [1991] STC 490.

2   Consent is required of 'any prior life or other interest': Trustee Act 1925 s 32(1)(c) (48 Halsbury's
         Statutes (4th Edn) TRUSTS AND SETTLEMENTS).
3   The intention is not to create a new settlement: see clause 4 above and note 1 above.
4   If desired a life interest trust in favour of the beneficiary's spouse may be included: this will avoid an
         inheritance tax charge on the beneficiary's death.
5   No new settlement is intended: see note 1 above.

[1856]

258

Resolution exercising the power of appropriation[1]

We *(trustee)* of *(address)* and *(trustee)* of *(address)* being the present trustees of the settlement
('the Settlement') dated *(date)* and made between *(parties)* in relation to the presumptive
share of *(beneficiary)* in the Trust Fund (as defined in the Settlement) under the trusts
declared in clause *(number)* of the Settlement now resolve that in exercise of the power
of appropriation conferred on us by clause *(number)* of the Settlement we now
appropriate the investments described in the schedule as part of the presumptive share of
(beneficiary) to be held on the trusts and with and subject to the powers and provisions
declared and contained in the Settlement

Dated: *(date)*

SCHEDULE

The Investments

(describe investments)

(signatures of the trustees)
[1857]

1   The Administration of Estates Act 1925 s 41 as amended (17 Halsbury's Statutes (4th Edn)
         EXECUTORS AND ADMINISTRATORS) confers a power of appropriation on personal representatives
         but not on trustees: see further Paragraph 74 [170] ante. For express powers of appropriation conferred
         on trustees see Form 4 schedule paragraph 11 [1096] and Forms 165 [1629], 166 [1631] ante.

[1858]

259

Resolution to transfer assets to a beneficiary pursuant to an express power in the trust deed[1]

We *(trustee)* of *(address)* and *(trustee)* of *(address)* being the present trustees of the settlement
('the Settlement') dated *(date)* and made between *(parties)* resolve as follows:

1   To transfer and pay immediately the investments and sum of cash described in
         the schedule (which investments and sum of cash are comprised in *(beneficiary)*'s
         Fund as defined in clause *(number)* of the Settlement) to *(beneficiary)* for his
         absolute use and benefit freed and discharged from the trusts powers and
         provisions contained in the Settlement

[1859]

2   Until the date of such transfer and payment to hold such investments and sum of cash for *(beneficiary)* absolutely subject to any lien vested in us as such trustees in respect of any costs or taxes payable in respect of such investments and sum of cash

Dated: *(date)*

SCHEDULE

Investments and Cash Sum

(describe investments and cash sum)

(signatures of the trustees)

1   For the taxation consequences see Form 255 note 1 [1851] ante.

[1860]–[1870]

C: CONSENTS AND AUTHORITIES ETC GIVEN TO TRUSTEES

260

Consent to postponement of sale of freehold land subject to trusts of will (or request to sell such freehold land) by persons interested under a will[1]

To *(names and addresses of trustees)* the trustees of the will of *(testator)*.

We *(names and addresses of beneficiaries)* [a majority according to value of] the persons of full age beneficially interested in possession [in the rents and profits until sale][2] of a freehold estate situated at *(address)* and known as the *(name)* Estate ('the Estate') under the will of *(testator)* deceased [consent to the postponement of the sale of the Estate for a period of *(number)* months from the date below *or* request you so soon as conveniently may be to take steps for effecting a sale of the Estate and premises][3].

Dated *(date)*

(signatures of beneficiaries)
[1871]

1   Power to postpone a sale of land held on trust for sale is implied in all cases by the Trusts of Land and Appointment of Trustees Act 1996 s 4(1) (37 Halsbury's Statutes (4th Edn) REAL PROPERTY): see Paragraph 108 [267] ante and, for detailed commentary on this provision, see vol 40(2) (2001 Reissue) TRUSTS AND SETTLEMENTS Part 8 [3001]. Given the general power to postpone sale, an express consent to postponement will only be required under special circumstances for the protection of the trustees.
2   These words are appropriate when the land is held on a trust for sale.
3   Trustees of land have a duty to consult the beneficiaries entitled to an interest in possession in the land in exercising any function relating to the land and to give effect to their wishes so far as consistent with the general interest of the trust: see the Trusts of Land and Appointment of Trustees Act 1996 s 11. For a discussion of this provision see Paragraph 225 [540] ante and see vol 40(2) (2001 Reissue) TRUSTS AND SETTLEMENTS Part 8 [3001].

[1872]

261

Authority and direction to trustees of settlement to make change in investments of the settled funds[1]

To *(names and addresses of trustees)* trustees of the settlement described below.

We *(tenant for life)* of *(address)* and *(remainderman)* of *(address)* authorise and direct you to sell £... *(name of stock)* held by you as trustees of a settlement dated *(date)* and made between *(parties)* and to invest the proceeds of sale in the purchase of £... *(name of stock)* to be held by you upon the trusts of such settlement.

Dated *(date)*

(signatures of tenant for life and remainderman)

---

1   As to powers of investment generally see Paragraph 241 [591] et seq ante.

[1873]

262

Authority and direction to trustees of settlement to call in mortgage and reinvest money received[1]

To *(names and addresses of trustees)* trustees of the settlement described below.

[I *(tenant for life)* of *(address)* or We *(names and addresses)* [a majority of] the persons interested] authorise and direct you as trustees of a settlement dated *(date)* and made between *(parties)* to call in the sum of £... advanced by you as such trustees to *(mortgagor)* of *(address)* upon mortgage of certain freehold property situated at *(address)* and to invest such sum when received (after payment out of it of all incidental expenses) [upon such investments authorised by the trusts of the settlement as you shall deem fit *or* in the purchase of a sum of *(name of stock)* as that money shall suffice to purchase].

Dated *(date)*

(signature of tenant for life or beneficiaries)
[1874]

---

1   This Form and Form 264 [1877] post may be used where the settlement or will makes the consent of the tenant for life necessary to an investment of the trust funds. If the investment directed is a breach of trust, the Forms will afford evidence on which the court can impound the beneficiary's interest under the Trustee Act 1925 s 62 as amended by the Married Women (Restraint upon Anticipation) Act 1949 s 1(4), Sch 2 (48 Halsbury's Statutes (4th Edn) TRUSTS AND SETTLEMENTS). Where trustees are required to invest in such investments as the tenant for life directs, he may if acting bona fide, direct a purchase from himself: *Re Hart's Will Trusts, Hart v Hart* [1943] 2 All ER 557.

[1875]

263

Request by wife to trustees of settlement to enforce husband's covenant

To *(names and addresses of trustees)* the trustees of the settlement described below.

I *(wife)* wife of *(covenantor)* of *(address)* request and direct you to call in and compel payment of the sum of £... now due and owing under the provisions of a settlement dated *(date)* and made between *(parties)* under which the sum of £... yearly was made payable to you in trust for me during the joint lives of myself and my husband and by which you were directed not to call in and compel payment of the same unless requested so to do in writing under my hand.

Dated *(date)*

(signature of wife)
[1876]

264

Authority and direction to trustees of will to sell stock and invest proceeds of sale upon mortgage[1]

To *(names and addresses of trustees)* the trustees of the will of *(testator)*.

I *(tenant for life)* of *(address)* authorise and direct you to sell so much of £... *(name of stock)* standing in your names as trustees of the will of *(testator)* deceased as will realise the sum of £... and to advance such sum when realised (after payment out of it of all incidental expenses) to *(intended mortgagor)* of *(address)* upon mortgage of certain freehold property situated at *(address)* such mortgage to bear interest at the rate of ...% per year.

Dated *(date)*

(signature of tenant for life)
[1877]

1   This Form and Form 262 [1874] ante may be used where the settlement or will makes the consent of the tenant for life necessary to an investment of the trust funds. If the investment directed is a breach of trust, the Forms will afford evidence on which the court can impound the beneficiary's interest under the Trustee Act 1925 s 62 as amended by the Married Women (Restraint upon Anticipation) Act 1949 s 1(4), Sch 2 (48 Halsbury's Statutes (4th Edn) TRUSTS AND SETTLEMENTS). Where trustees are required to invest in such investments as the tenant for life directs, he may if acting bona fide, direct a purchase from himself: *Re Hart's Will Trusts, Hart v Hart* [1943] 2 All ER 557.

[1878]

265

Request for an advancement[1]

To: The trustees of the *(name)* settlement ('the Settlement').

I *(beneficiary)* of *(address)* being entitled contingently upon my attaining the age of 21 years or marrying to a one equal third share in the property subject to the trusts declared in the Settlement request you in exercise of the power of advancement contained in the

Trustee Act 1925 Section 32 (as amended by the Trusts of Land and Appointment of Trustees Act 1996) to advance such of the property comprised in my contingent share as is described in the schedule to me absolutely freed and discharged from the trusts powers and provisions of the Settlement.

Dated: *(date)*

SCHEDULE

The Property

(describe property)

(signature of the beneficiary)
[1879]

1   On the power of advancement see Paragraph 238 [573] et seq ante. For the exercise of that power see Forms 289 [2011], 290 [2020] post. It may be for the benefit of a wealthy adult beneficiary for the trustees to make payments to a charity selected by that beneficiary in discharge of his moral obligations: see *Re Clore's Settlement Trusts, Sainer v Clore* [1966] 2 All ER 272, [1966] 1 WLR 955. From a taxation point of view the availability of income tax relief by way of gift aid should not be overlooked: there may be attractions in a cash gift being made directly by the relevant beneficiary. As to gift aid see vol 17(2) (2000 Reissue) GIFTS Paragraph 53 [746] et seq. For the taxation (and, especially, the capital gains tax) consequences of property being advanced to a beneficiary absolutely see Form 255 note 1 [1851] ante.

[1880]

266

Consent by a beneficiary entitled to a prior interest to the exercise of the power of advancement[1]

I *(beneficiary)* of *(address)* being entitled to a prior interest in the settlement *(insert details)* consent to the advancement of *(describe property)* to *(beneficiary)* of *(address)*.

Dated: *(date)*

(signature of the beneficiary)

1   As to the requirement for consent on an advancement by trustees under the Trustee Act 1925 s 32 as amended by the Trusts of Land and Appointment of Trustees Act 1996 s 25(1), Sch 3 para 3(8) (48 Halsbury's Statutes (4th Edn) TRUSTS AND SETTLEMENTS) see Paragraph 240 [577] ante.
   If there is a possibility of this Form being used where the beneficiary is one of two or more who have become absolutely entitled together, then the practitioner should consider whether it may be a qualifying conveyance for the purposes of the Land Registration Act 1925 s 123 as inserted by the Land Registration Act 1997 s 1 (37 Halsbury's Statutes (4th Edn) REAL PROPERTY). This is because it could be argued that, in such a situation, the beneficiary is receiving the specific property in exchange for foregoing his entitlement to a share in the whole of the assets held by the trustees. This may count as 'valuable or other consideration' for the purposes of the Land Registration Act 1925 s 123(6)(a)(i).

[1881]–[1890]

D: CONVEYANCES AND DECLARATIONS ETC IN FAVOUR OF BENEFICIARIES ABSOLUTELY ENTITLED

267

Conveyance by trustees holding upon trust for sale under a will to beneficiary absolutely entitled and wishing to take the property as land[1]

THIS CONVEYANCE is made the ...... day of ....

BETWEEN:

(1)   *(trustees)* of *(addresses)* ('the Trustees') and

(2)   *(beneficiary)* of *(address)* ('the Grantee')

WHEREAS

(1)   By his will dated *(date)* ('the Will') *(testator)* late of *(address)* ('the Testator') appointed the Trustees to be the executors and trustees of the Will and after giving various specific and pecuniary legacies gave all the residue of his real and personal estate to the Trustees upon trust that they should sell the same and out of the proceeds pay his funeral and testamentary expenses debts and legacies and invest the residue in the manner described in the Will and should hold the residue and the investments in trust to pay the income from it to *(life tenant)* ('the Life Tenant') during her life and from and after her death to hold the residue and the investments in trust for the Grantee absolutely and the Testator gave the Trustees power in their absolute discretion to postpone the sale of any part of his real estate

[1891]

(2)   The Testator died on *(date)* and the Trustees proved the Will on *(date)* in the [Principal Registry of the Family Division of the High Court *or (name)* District Probate Registry]

(3)   The Testator was at his death seised of certain property for an estate in fee simple in possession free from incumbrances and by an assent dated *(date)* the Trustees assented to such property vesting in themselves upon trust to sell the same and to hold the proceeds of sale upon the trusts declared concerning the same in the Will

(4)   The Life Tenant died on *(date)*

(5)   [No part *or* Part] of the vested property has been sold and the property now subject to the trusts of the assent[2] is described in the schedule ('the Property')

(6)   The Grantee does not wish the Property to be sold and converted under the above trust for sale but wishes it to be taken and enjoyed by him as land and has requested the Trustees to convey the Property to him in the manner described below[3]

[1892]

NOW THIS DEED WITNESSES as follows:

1   Conveyance

The Trustees [with limited title guarantee] convey to the Grantee the Property TO HOLD to the Grantee in fee simple for his own benefit absolutely discharged from the above trust for sale

[2   Declaration of discharge

The Trustees pursuant to the Trusts of Land and Appointment of Trustees Act 1996 Section 16(4) declare that they are discharged from the trust created by the Will in relation to the Property][4]

3   Stamp duty certificate

It is hereby certified that this instrument falls within category 'F' in the schedule to the Stamp Duty (Exempt Instruments) Regulations 1987[5]

IN WITNESS etc

SCHEDULE

The Property

(describe the Property)

(signatures of the parties)[6]

(signatures of witnesses)

[1893]

1   As to stamp duty see Information Binder: Stamp Duties [1] Table of Duties (Conveyance or transfer). It should be noted that an express trust for sale has been incorporated into the will which, apart from the inclusion of a power to postpone sale, remains unaffected by the Trusts of Land and Appointment of Trustees Act 1996 (37 Halsbury's Statutes (4th Edn) REAL PROPERTY). Note also that trustees of land are given power in the Trusts of Land and Appointment of Trustees Act 1996 s 6(2) to convey land to a beneficiary absolutely entitled even if not called upon to do so: see Paragraph 222 [534] ante and, for commentary on this provision, see vol 40(2) (2001 Reissue) TRUSTS AND SETTLEMENTS Part 8 [3001].
    On the death of the life tenant he is treated as making a transfer of value of the settled property and inheritance tax may be payable by the trustees, who should ensure that this has been discharged before they convey the land to the grantee: for a salutary case, see *Howarth's Executors v IRC* [1997] STC (SCD) 162. There is a tax-free uplift of property values for capital gains tax purposes.
    This conveyance, as no receipt has to be given for any purchase or capital money, can be made by a single trustee.

2   Assent is used here because the assent recited in recital (3) [1892] above created an independent trust for sale. If the assent is simply upon the trusts of the will, then 'Will' should be substituted in recital (5) [1892] above for 'assent'.

3   The recitals contained in this deed will after 20 years be sufficient evidence in favour of a purchaser of the facts recited, except in so far as they may be proved to be inaccurate: see the Law of Property Act 1925 s 45(6) (37 Halsbury's Statutes (4th Edn) REAL PROPERTY). The period can be shortened by a special condition of sale, and the recitals made conclusive evidence.

4   The Trusts of Land and Appointment of Trustees Act 1996 s 16(4)(a) appears to contemplate a separate deed of discharge being executed by the trustees, although the general view is that the discharge can be contained in the conveyance and that it is not necessary to have a separate deed of discharge. If desired this clause can be omitted and a separate deed of discharge executed. As to the Trusts of Land and Appointment of Trustees Act 1996 s 16 see Paragraph 229 [547] ante and, for detailed commentary on that provision, see further vol 40(2) (2001 Reissue) TRUSTS AND SETTLEMENTS Part 8 [3001].

5   Ie the Stamp Duty (Exempt Instruments) Regulations 1987, SI 1987/516. As to the inclusion of such a certificate see Information Binder: Stamp Duties [1] Table of Duties (Exempt Instruments Regulations).

6   As to the statutory requirements for the valid execution of a deed see vol 12 (1994 Reissue) DEEDS, AGREEMENTS AND DECLARATIONS.

[1894]

268

Transfer of the whole of registered freehold land by trustees to beneficiaries absolutely entitled[1]

Use Land Registry Form TR1, for which see vol 37 (2001 Reissue) SALE OF LAND *Form 1 [51], and insert the wording shown below in the panels specified*

Panel 1 Stamp duty
I/We hereby certify that this instrument falls within category 'F' in the Schedule to the Stamp Duty (Exempt Instruments) Regulations 1987[2]

Panel 5 Transferor
(names of trustees)

Panel 6 Transferee
(name(s) of beneficiary or beneficiaries)

Panel 9 Consideration
The transfer is not for money or anything which has a monetary value

Panel 10 Title guarantee
limited title guarantee

Panel 11 Declaration of trust
(complete as appropriate)[3]

Panel 12 Additional provisions
12.1   This transfer is made in consideration of the Transferee[s] being [together] absolutely entitled[4] to the property in the events that have happened

[12.2   The parties apply to the Registrar for the restriction registered as entry number *(number)* in the proprietorship register to be cancelled][5]

[1895]

---

1   As to stamp duty see the Information Binder: Stamp Duties [1]: Table of Duties: Conveyance or transfer. As to Land Registry fees see the Information Binder: Property [1]: Property fees: Land Registration fees. This Form gives effect to a transfer of registered land held by trustees to one or more beneficiaries who have become absolutely entitled to the land either as beneficial joint tenants, tenants in common or on trusts declared in a separate deed. As to trusts of land generally see vol 35 (1997 Reissue) SALE OF LAND Paragraph 970 [1266] et seq. Form TR1 is the Land Registry form of transfer of the whole of freehold or leasehold land prescribed by the Land Registration Rules 1925, SR & O 1925/1093 r 98 as substituted by SI 1999/128, Sch 1 Form TR1 as inserted by SI 1997/3037. Reference should be made to vol 37 (2001 Reissue) SALE OF LAND Form 9 [132] for an illustration of the method of inserting clauses in Land Registry Form TR1, a selection of common form clauses including definition, incumbrance and indemnity clauses, detailed notes on matters common to many forms of transfer and for cross references to the commentary in vol 35 (1997 Reissue) SALE OF LAND and for the location of alternative transfer clauses. As to completion of panels other than those dealt with in this Form see vol 37 (2001 Reissue) SALE OF LAND Form 1 [51]. For the forms of execution of transfers prescribed by SR & O 1925/1093 Sch 3 as inserted by SI 1997/3037 see vol 37 (2001 Reissue) SALE OF LAND Form 8 [123]. As to the statutory requirements for the valid execution of a deed see vol 12 (1994 Reissue) DEEDS, AGREEMENTS AND DECLARATIONS. As to the method of reproduction of Land Registry forms see vol 37 (2001 Reissue) SALE OF LAND Form 9 note 1(5) [137].

2   Ie the Stamp Duty (Exempt Instruments) Regulations 1987, SI 1987/516. This certificate is applicable
       provided that the dealing with the equitable interest preceding the transfer was not for money or
       money's worth: see vol 35 (1997 Reissue) SALE OF LAND Paragraph 578 [764].

[1896]

3   Where there is more than one beneficiary, the Registrar requires sufficient information to enable him
       to consider whether or not to retain the restriction referred to in the Land Registration Act 1925 s 58(3)
       (37 Halsbury's Statutes (4th Edn) REAL PROPERTY) and SR & O 1925/1093 r 213 as substituted by
       SI 1996/2975, Sch 2 Form 62 (as substituted by SI 1989/801 and amended by SI 1996/2975 and
       SI 1997/3037). The beneficiaries should make an express declaration of trust for the sake of certainty
       and to avoid any future difficulties with regard to the determination of beneficial interests. As to the
       effect of an express declaration see *Goodman v Gallant* [1986] Fam 106, [1986] 1 All ER 311, CA; *Turton
       v Turton* [1988] Ch 542, [1987] 2 All ER 641, CA. Where the transfer refers to a separate deed declaring
       the trusts upon which the land is to be held, there is no need to lodge a copy because neither the
       Registrar nor any other person dealing with a registered estate or charge is affected with notice of any
       trust and, so far as possible, such trusts are to be excluded from the register: see the Land Registration
       Act 1925 s 74.
4   Where there is a sole beneficiary, or there are joint beneficiaries who hold as beneficial joint tenants,
       it is appropriate for any restriction entered on the register in the form of SR & O 1925/1093 Sch 2
       Form 62 (as substituted by SI 1989/801 and amended by SI 1996/2975 and SI 1997/3037) to be
       removed. However, the Registrar needs to be satisfied that the parties are entitled to apply for the
       restriction to be removed: see the Land Registration Act 1925 s 58(3) and SR & O 1925/1093 r 213
       as substituted by SI 1996/2975 and amended by SI 1997/3037. The Registrar therefore must be
       satisfied as to the equitable title and he may, in some cases, require confirmation by statutory declaration
       that the beneficial interests have not been dealt with other than in accordance with the documents
       produced.
             Where a deed has been executed by the trustees under the Trusts of Land and Appointment of
       Trustees Act 1996 s 16(4) (37 Halsbury's Statutes (4th Edn) REAL PROPERTY) declaring that they are
       discharged from the trusts in relation to that land, the Registrar is entitled to assume that the land is not
       subject to the trust unless he has actual notice that the trustees were mistaken in their belief that the
       land was conveyed to the beneficiaries absolutely entitled to the land under the trust and of full age and
       capacity: see the Land Registration Act 1925 s 94(5) as inserted by the Trusts of Land and Appointment
       of Trustees Act 1996 Sch 3 para 5(8)(c). The trustees are not required to execute a deed because the
       Trusts of Land and Appointment of Trustees Act 1996 s 16 does not apply to registered land: Trusts of
       Land and Appointment of Trustees Act 1996 s 16(5).
5   For the modifications needed if the property is subject to a charge see vol 37 (2001 Reissue) SALE OF
       LAND Form 183 [1353].

[1897]

269

Conveyance by trustees (one not being an original trustee) holding upon trust for sale under a will to a surviving joint tenant desiring to take the property as land—indemnity by beneficiary[1]

THIS CONVEYANCE is made the ...... day of ....

BETWEEN:

(1)   *(first trustee)* of *(address)* and *(second trustee)* of *(address)* ('the Trustees') and

(2)   *(surviving joint tenant)* of *(address)* ('the Grantee')

[1898]

WHEREAS

(1)   By his will dated *(date)* ('the Will') *(testator)* late of *(address)* ('the Testator')
        appointed *(first trustee)* and *(deceased trustee)* ('the Original Trustees') to be the
        executors and trustees of the Will and after giving various specific and pecuniary
        legacies gave all the residue of his real and personal estate to the Original

Trustees upon trust that they should sell the same and out of the proceeds pay his funeral and testamentary expenses debts and legacies and invest the residue in the manner described in the Will and should hold the residue and the investments in trust for *(deceased joint tenant)* and the Grantee as joint tenants absolutely and the Testator gave his trustees power in their absolute discretion to postpone the sale of any part of his real estate

[1899]

(2)   The Testator died on *(date)* and the Original Trustees proved the Will on *(date)* in the [Principal Registry of the Family Division of the High Court *or (name)* District Probate Registry]

(3)   The Testator was at his death seised of certain property for an estate in fee simple in possession free from incumbrances and by an assent dated *(date)* the Original Trustees assented to such property vesting in themselves upon trust to sell the same and to hold the proceeds of sale upon the trusts declared concerning the same in the Will

(4)   *(deceased trustee)* died on *(date)*

(5)   By a deed of appointment dated *(date)* *(first trustee)* appointed *(second trustee)* to be a trustee of the assent

(6)   *(deceased joint tenant)* died on *(date)*

(7)   By a conveyance dated *(date)* the Trustees conveyed *(describe property)* being part of the vested property to *(purchaser)*

(8)   The Grantee being absolutely entitled to the proceeds of sale of the remaining vested property described in the schedule ('the Property') and wishing that the Property should not be sold and converted under the trust for sale but should be taken and enjoyed by him as land has requested the Trustees to convey the Property to him in the manner appearing below[2]

[1900]

NOW THIS DEED WITNESSES as follows:

1   Conveyance

The Trustees [with limited title guarantee] at the request and by the direction of the Grantee convey to the Grantee the Property TO HOLD to the Grantee in fee simple for his own benefit absolutely discharged from the trust for sale

2   Indemnity

The Grantee covenants with the Trustees that he will keep the Trustees and each of them indemnified against all claims proceedings costs and expenses in respect of the Property and in respect of the execution of this deed

[3   Declaration of discharge

The Trustees pursuant to the Trusts of Land and Appointment of Trustees Act 1996 Section 16(4) declare that they are discharged from the trust created by the Will in relation to the Property][3]

4   Stamp duty certificate

It is hereby certified that this instrument falls within category 'F' in the Schedule to the Stamp Duty (Exempt Instruments) Regulations 1987[4]

IN WITNESS etc

SCHEDULE

The Property

(describe the Property)

(signatures of the parties)[5]
(signatures of witnesses)
[1901]

1   As to stamp duty see Information Binder: Stamp Duties [1] Table of Duties (Conveyance or transfer). For the existence of a trust for sale in such circumstances see Form 267 note 1 [1894] ante.
2   The recitals contained in this deed will after 20 years be sufficient evidence in favour of a purchaser of the facts recited, except in so far as they may be proved to be inaccurate: see the Law of Property Act 1925 s 45(6) (37 Halsbury's Statutes (4th Edn) REAL PROPERTY). The period can be shortened by a special condition of sale, and the recitals made conclusive evidence.
3   The Trusts of Land and Appointment of Trustees Act 1996 s 16(4)(a) (37 Halsbury's Statutes (4th Edn) REAL PROPERTY) appears to contemplate a separate deed of discharge being executed by the trustees, although the general view is that the discharge can be contained in the conveyance and that it is not necessary to have a separate deed of discharge. If desired this clause can be omitted and a separate deed of discharge executed. As to the Trusts of Land and Appointment of Trustees Act 1996 s 16 see Paragraph 229 [547] ante and, for detailed commentary on that provision, see vol 40(2) (2001 Reissue) TRUSTS AND SETTLEMENTS Part 8 [3001].
4   Ie the Stamp Duty (Exempt Instruments) Regulations 1987, SI 1987/516. As to the inclusion of such a certificate see Information Binder: Stamp Duties [1] Table of Duties (Exempt Instruments Regulations).
5   As to the statutory requirements for the valid execution of a deed see vol 12 (1994 Reissue) DEEDS, AGREEMENTS AND DECLARATIONS.

[1902]

270

Declaration by sole trustee holding upon trust for sale under a will who is now the sole beneficiary and wishes to take the property as land—unregistered land[1]

THIS DECLARATION is made the ...... day of .... by *(declarant)* of *(address)* ('the Declarant')

WHEREAS

(1)   By his will dated *(date)* ('the Will') *(testator)* late of *(address)* ('the Testator') appointed *(deceased trustee)* and the Declarant (together called 'the Trustees') as executors and trustees of the Will and after giving various specific and pecuniary legacies gave all the residue of his real and personal estate to the Trustees upon trust that they should sell the same and out of the proceeds pay his personal and testamentary expenses debts and legacies and invest the residue and hold the investments in trust to pay the income to *(life tenant)* during his life and from and after his death to hold the residue and the investments in trust for the Declarant absolutely and he gave the Trustees power in their absolute discretion to postpone the sale of any part of his real estate

[1903]

(2)   The Testator died on *(date)* and the Trustees proved the Will on *(date)* in the [Principal Registry of the Family Division of the High Court *or (name)* District Probate Registry]

(3)   The Testator was at his death seised of certain property for an estate in fee simple in possession free from incumbrances and by an assent dated *(date)* the Trustees assented to such property vesting in themselves upon the trusts declared concerning the same in the Will

(4)   *(life tenant)* died on *(date)*

(5)   *(deceased trustee)* died on *(date)*

(6)   [No part *or* Part] of the vested property has been sold and the property now subject to the trusts of the Will is described in the schedule ('the Property')

(7)   The Declarant wishes to enjoy the Property as land and makes the following declaration[2]

[1904]

THE DECLARANT DECLARES that the Property is vested in the Declarant in fee simple for his own absolute use and benefit free from incumbrances and discharged from the trust for sale

IN WITNESS etc

SCHEDULE

The Property

(describe the Property)

(signature of the declarant)[3]
(signatures of witnesses)
[1905]

1   For the existence of a trust for sale in such circumstances see Form 267 note 1 [1894] ante.
2   The recitals contained in this deed will after 20 years be sufficient evidence in favour of a purchaser of the facts recited, except in so far as they may be proved to be inaccurate: see the Law of Property Act 1925 s 45(6) (37 Halsbury's Statutes (4th Edn) REAL PROPERTY). The period can be shortened by a special condition of sale, and the recitals made conclusive evidence.
3   As to the statutory requirements for the valid execution of a deed see vol 12 (1994 Reissue) DEEDS, AGREEMENTS AND DECLARATIONS.

[1906]

271

Application by sole trustee holding registered land upon trust for sale under a will who is now the sole beneficiary and wishes to take the property as land— to withdraw a restriction[1]

HM LAND REGISTRY

LAND REGISTRATION ACTS 1925 to 1986

[Administrative area]   *(insert details)*
Title number   *(title number)*
Property   *(describe property)*
Date   *(date)*

I *(registered proprietor or trustee)* of *(address)* hereby apply to the Registrar to withdraw the restriction[s][2] registered on the *(date)* against the title above referred to

(signature of registered proprietor)
[1907]

---

1   For the existence of a trust for sale in such circumstances see Form 267 note 1 [1894] ante. The trustee will already be registered as proprietor of the land, but it is anticipated that a restriction will also have been entered pursuant to Land Registration Rules 1925, SR & O 1925/1093 rr 213, 236, (both substituted by SI 1996/2975) Sch 2 Form 62 (as substituted by SI 1989/801 and amended by SI 1996/2975 and SI 1997/3037). In order to obtain unrestricted ownership, this application must be made and the Registrar will require evidence of the equitable title: see SR & O 1925/1093 rr 16(b) (as substituted by SI 1996/2975), 214. Accordingly, the application will normally be required to be accompanied by a statutory declaration by the applicant setting out the events entitling him to the property: alternatively, the evidence may take the form of a certificate by the applicant's solicitor explaining what has occurred. Additional evidence may also be required such as a copy of the will, etc: see, further, vol 25(1) (1999 Reissue) LAND REGISTRATION Form 78 note 1 [3647].
    This Form is based on the prescribed form of application in SR & O 1925/1093 r 236B (as substituted by SI 1999/128 and further substituted by SI 2001/619), Sch 2 Form 77 (as substituted by SI 1996/2975 and amended by SI 1999/128). An application to withdraw or modify a restriction is required to be in this Form: SR & O 1925/1093 r 236B.

2   A plural alternative is provided as in some cases the restriction contained in SR & O 1925/1093 rr 59A, 106A (as inserted by SI 1996/2975), 236 (as substituted by SI 1996/2975), Sch 2 Form 11A (as inserted by SI 1996/2975) may also be on the register: ie where the powers of trustees of a trust of land are limited by virtue of the Trusts of Land and Appointment of Trustees Act 1996 s 8 (37 Halsbury's Statutes (4th Edn) REAL PROPERTY). The Registrar will require satisfactory evidence that the restriction no longer applies.

[1908]

272

Declaration by survivor of two tenants in common, who is devisee of the share of the deceased tenant in common, that he holds the entirety beneficially free from any trust for sale or the statutory trusts—variation where survivor is sole statutory beneficiary on intestacy[1]

THIS DECLARATION is made the ...... day of .... by *(declarant)* of *(address)* ('the Declarant')

WHEREAS

(1)   By a conveyance dated *(date)* ('the Conveyance') and made between (1) *(grantor)* and (2) *(deceased tenant in common)* ('the Deceased') and the Declarant the property described in the schedule ('the Property') was conveyed to the Deceased and the Declarant in fee simple [upon trust to sell the same and to stand possessed of the net proceeds of sale and of the net rents and profits until sale in trust for themselves as beneficial tenants in common *or* as beneficial tenants in common][2]

[1909]

(2)   [The Deceased died on *(date)* having made his will dated *(date)* ('the Will') by which he appointed *(executor)* and *(executor)* ('the Executors') to be the executors and gave all his share and interest in the Property to the Declarant and the Will was on *(date)* proved by the Executors in the [Principal Registry of the Family Division of the High Court *or* *(name)* District Probate Registry]

or

The Deceased died on *(date)* intestate and a widower leaving one child only him surviving namely the Declarant and leaving no other person entitled on his intestacy and letters of administration to his estate were on *(date)* granted to the Declarant out of the [Principal Registry of the Family Division of the High Court *or* *(name)* District Probate Registry]]

[(3)   The Executors [by an assent in writing dated *(date)*][3] assented to the gift contained in the Will of the Deceased of all his share and interest in the Property to the Declarant]

(4)   The Declarant wishes to enjoy the Property as land and to make the following declaration[4]

[1910]

THE DECLARANT DECLARES that the Property is now vested in the Declarant in fee simple for his own absolute use and benefit discharged from [any trust for sale arising under the Conveyance *or* any trust arising by virtue of the provisions of the Law of Property Act 1925 as amended by the Trusts of Land and Appointment of Trustees Act 1996][5] or otherwise

IN WITNESS etc

SCHEDULE

The Property

(describe the Property)

(signature of the Declarant)[6]
(signatures of witnesses)
[1911]

1   This Form is a declaration made by the survivor of two original beneficial tenants in common that he is now entitled to the land in question absolutely. With the conversion of implied trusts for sale to trusts of land (as from 1 January 1997) by the Trusts of Land and Appointment of Trustees Act 1996 (37 Halsbury's Statutes (4th Edn) REAL PROPERTY) the optional wording in recital (1) [1909] above and the declaration caters for the following possibilities:

     (a)   Where the original conveyance imposed an express trust for sale. In this (somewhat unusual) case, the trust for sale continues and the declarant must state that the land is held free from those trusts (ie incorporate the first alternative in square brackets).

     (b)   Where the original conveyance did not impose an express trust for sale, but was executed before 1 January 1997 an implied trust for sale automatically arose. The imposition of a trust for sale in these circumstances, was abolished by the Trusts of Land and Appointment of Trustees Act 1996 s 5 and therefore the second alternative should be used. The declaration will in this case declare that the property is held freed from the statutory trusts (which are now a trust of land) and will not mention any trust of land. Of course if the conveyance had been on or after 1 January 1997, a trust for sale would not have been imposed.

     The Form is suitable for use in the case of unregistered land. For a Form applicable to registered land where the registered proprietor has become solely and beneficially entitled see Form 271 [1907] ante.

2   The recital should follow the wording of the original conveyance, which may or may not have contained an express trust for sale. See note 1 above.

3   The assent need not be in writing as it does not relate to a legal estate in land and consequently the Administration of Estates Act 1925 s 36(4) (17 Halsbury's Statutes (4th Edn) EXECUTORS) does not apply.

4   The recitals contained in this deed will after 20 years be sufficient evidence in favour of a purchaser of the facts recited, except in so far as they may be proved to be inaccurate: see the Law of Property Act 1925 s 45(6) (37 Halsbury's Statutes (4th Edn) REAL PROPERTY). The period can be shortened by a special condition of sale, and the recitals made conclusive evidence.

5   See note 1 above.

6   As to the statutory requirements for the valid execution of a deed see vol 12 (1994 Reissue) DEEDS, AGREEMENTS AND DECLARATIONS.

[1912]

273

Assignment of the whole of an unregistered leasehold interest by trustees to a beneficiary absolutely entitled[1]

THIS ASSIGNMENT is made on the ...... day of ....

BETWEEN:

(1)   *(trustees)* of *(addresses)* ('the Trustees') and

(2)   *(the beneficiary)* of *(address)* ('the Beneficiary')

NOW THIS DEED WITNESSES as follows:

[1913]

1   Definitions and interpretation

In this assignment:

1.1   'the Covenants' mean the covenants conditions and other obligations on the part of the tenant contained or referred to in the Lease

1.2   'the Lease' means the lease of the Property particulars of which are set out in schedule 1

1.3   'the Property' means the land [and buildings] more particularly described in the Lease and briefly described in schedule 2

1.4   'the Term' means the term granted by the Lease

[1.5   words importing one gender shall be construed as importing any other gender]

[1.6   words importing the singular shall be construed as importing the plural and vice versa]

[1.7   words importing persons shall be construed as importing a corporate body and/ or a partnership and vice versa]

[1.8   the clause headings do not form part of this assignment and shall not be taken into account in the construction or interpretation of it]

[1.9   any reference to a clause paragraph or schedule is to one in this assignment so numbered]

[1914]

2   Recitals

2.1   By the Lease the Property was demised [to the Trustees] for the Term at the [initial] rent mentioned in schedule 1

2.2   The Property is now vested in the Trustees for the unexpired residue of the term [at the current rent mentioned in schedule 1] subject to the Covenants but otherwise free from incumbrances

2.3   The Beneficiary is now absolutely entitled to the proceeds of the sale of the Property and has requested that it should not be sold and converted under the trust for sale but should be assigned to him

[2.4   The consent of *(landlord)* has been obtained as required by the Lease]

3   Assignment

The Trustees assign the Property to the Beneficiary to hold to the Beneficiary for the unexpired residue of the Term subject to [the exceptions and reservations in the Lease and] performance of the Covenants

4   Title guarantee

4.1   This assignment is made with limited title guarantee

4.2   It is agreed that the covenants implied by the Law of Property (Miscellaneous Provisions) Act 1994 Section 4 shall be limited so as not to extend to any breach of the Covenants relating to the repair and decoration of the Property

[4.3   The parties apply to the Registrar to enter on the register in an appropriate manner a note that such implied covenants have been modified in the manner set out above]

[1915]

[5   Indemnity

(where the lease being assigned does not create a new tenancy within the meaning of the Landlord and Tenant (Covenants) Act 1995 Section 1(3))

With the object and intention of affording to the Trustees a full and sufficient indemnity but not further or otherwise the Beneficiary covenants with the Trustees that he and his successors in title will:

5.1   during the Term pay the rents reserved in the Lease and perform all the Covenants

5.2   keep the Trustees indemnified against all actions claims demands losses costs damages or liabilities whatsoever by reason of any future breach of the Covenants]

6   Declaration of discharge

The Trustees pursuant to the Trusts of Land and Appointment of Trustees Act 1996 Section 16(4) declare that they are discharged from the trust created by the Will in relation to the Property][2]

7   Stamp duty certificate

It is hereby certified that this instrument falls within category 'F' in the schedule to the Stamp Duty (Exempt Instruments) Regulations 1987[3]

IN WITNESS etc

SCHEDULE 1

The Lease

(insert details)

SCHEDULE 2

The Property

(describe the property)

(signatures of the parties)[4]

(signatures of witnesses)

[1916]

1   As to stamp duty see the Information Binder: Stamp Duties [1]: Table of Duties: Conveyance or transfer. Reference should be made to vol 37 (2001 Reissue) SALE OF LAND Form 63 [513] for detailed notes on matters common to many forms of assignment, for cross references to the relevant part of the commentary in vol 35 (1997 Reissue) SALE OF LAND and for the location of alternative forms of clauses. As to the liability of sellers after assignment generally, see vol 35 (1997 Reissue) SALE OF LAND Paragraph 890 [1181] et seq. As to Land Registry fees see the Information Binder: Property [1]: Property fees: Land Registration fees. An assignment of a lease having more than 21 years to run, which is not for valuable consideration, nor by way of gift, and does not give effect to a court order, is not subject to compulsory registration. However, it is susceptible to voluntary registration. Accordingly, a transfer made under the Land Registration Rules 1925, SR & O 1925/1093 r 72 may be used where the unregistered lease has more than 21 years to run and the transferee is clear that a voluntary application will be made following the assignment. In the case where the lease has more than 21 years to run, and the beneficiary is one of two or more who have become absolutely entitled together, then the practitioner should consider whether it may be a qualifying conveyance for the purposes of the Land Registration Act 1925 s 123 as inserted by the Land Registration Act 1997 s 1 (37 Halsbury's Statutes (4th Edn) REAL PROPERTY). This is because it could be argued that, in such a situation, the beneficiary is receiving the specific property in exchange for foregoing his entitlement to a share in the whole of the assets held by the trustees. This may count as 'valuable or other consideration' for the purposes of the Land Registration Act 1925 s 123(6)(a)(i).

2   The Trusts of Land and Appointment of Trustees Act 1996 s 16(4)(a) (37 Halsbury's Statutes (4th Edn) REAL PROPERTY) appears to contemplate a separate deed of discharge being executed by the trustees, although the general view is that the discharge can be contained in the assignment and that it is not

necessary to have a separate deed of discharge. If desired this clause can be omitted and a separate deed of discharge executed. As to the Trusts of Land and Appointment of Trustees Act 1996 s 16 see Paragraph 229 [547] ante and, for detailed commentary on this provision, see vol 40(2) (2001 Reissue) TRUSTS AND SETTLEMENTS Part 8 [3001].

3   Ie the Stamp Duty (Exempt Instruments) Regulations 1987, SI 1987/516. As to the inclusion of such a certificate see Information Binder: Stamp Duties [1] Table of Duties (Exempt Instruments Regulations).

4   As to the statutory requirements for the valid execution of a deed see vol 12 (1994 Reissue) DEEDS, AGREEMENTS AND DECLARATIONS.

[1917]

274

Transfer of the whole of registered leasehold land by trustees to beneficiaries absolutely entitled[1]

Use Land Registry Form TR1, for which see vol 37 (2001 Reissue) SALE OF LAND Form 1 [51], and insert the wording shown below in the panels specified

Panel 1 Stamp duty

I/We hereby certify that this instrument falls within 'F' in the Schedule to the Stamp Duty (Exempt Instruments) Regulations 1987[2]

Panel 5 Transferor

(names of trustees)

Panel 6 Transferee

(name(s) of beneficiary or beneficiaries)

Panel 9 Consideration

The transfer is not for money or anything which has a monetary value

Panel 10 Title guarantee

limited title guarantee

It is agreed that the covenants implied by the Law of Property (Miscellaneous Provisions) Act 1994 section 4 shall be limited so as not to extend to any breach of the covenants relating to the repair and decoration of the property[3]

Panel 11 Declaration of trust

(complete as appropriate)[4]

Panel 12 Additional provisions

12.1   In this transfer:

12.1.1   'the Covenants' means the covenants conditions and other obligations on the part of the tenant contained or referred to in the Lease

12.1.2   'the Lease' means the lease of the property particulars of which are set out in the register

12.1.3   'the Term' means the term granted by the Lease

[12.2   Indemnity covenant[5]
        (where the lease being transferred does not create a new tenancy within the
        meaning of the Landlord and Tenant (Covenants) Act 1995 s 1(3))
        With the object and intention of affording to the Transferor a full and sufficient
        indemnity but not further or otherwise the [Transferee covenants *or* Transferees
        [jointly and severally] covenant] with the Transferor that [he *or* they] and [his
        or their] successors in title will:
        12.2.1   during the Term pay the rents reserved in the Lease and perform all
                  the Covenants
        12.2.2   keep the Transferor indemnified against all actions, claims, demands,
                  losses, costs, damages and liabilities whatsoever by reason of any
                  [future] breach of the Covenants]

[12.3   The parties apply to the Registrar to enter on the register in an appropriate
         manner a note that the implied covenants for title are modified in the manner
         set out in panel 10][6]

12.4   This transfer is made in consideration of the Transferee[s] being [together]
         absolutely entitled[7] to the property in the events that have happened

[12.5   The parties apply to the Registrar for the restriction registered as entry number
         (number) in the proprietorship register to be cancelled][8]

                                                                            [1918]

1   As to stamp duty see the Information Binder: Stamp Duties [1]: Table of Duties: Conveyance or
     transfer. As to Land Registry fees see the Information Binder: Property [1]: Property fees: Land
     Registration fees. This Form gives effect to a transfer of registered land held by trustees to one or more
     beneficiaries who have become absolutely entitled to the land either as beneficial joint tenants, tenants
     in common or on trusts declared in a separate deed. As to trusts of land generally see vol 35
     (1997 Reissue) SALE OF LAND Paragraph 970 [1266] et seq. Form TR1 is the Land Registry form of
     transfer of the whole of freehold or leasehold land prescribed by SR & O 1925/1093 r 98 as substituted
     by SI 1999/128, Sch 1 Form TR1 as inserted by SI 1997/3037. Reference should be made to vol 37
     (2001 Reissue) SALE OF LAND Form 9 [132] for an illustration of the method of inserting clauses in
     Land Registry Form TR1, a selection of common form clauses including definition, incumbrance and
     indemnity clauses, detailed notes on matters common to many forms of transfer and for cross references
     to the commentary in vol 35 (1997 Reissue) SALE OF LAND and for the location of alternative transfer
     clauses. As to completion of panels other than those dealt with in this Form see vol 37 (2001 Reissue)
     SALE OF LAND Form 1 [51]. For the forms of execution of transfers prescribed by SR & O 1925/1093
     Sch 3 as inserted by SI 1997/3037 see vol 37 (2001 Reissue) SALE OF LAND Form 8 [123]. As to the
     statutory requirements for the valid execution of a deed see vol 12 (1994 Reissue) DEEDS,
     AGREEMENTS AND DECLARATIONS.
         As to the method of reproduction of Land Registry forms see vol 37 (2001 Reissue) SALE OF
     LAND Form 9 note 1(5) [137].
2   Ie the Stamp Duty (Exempt Instruments) Regulations 1987, SI 1987/516. This certificate is applicable
     provided that the dealing with the equitable interest preceding the transfer was not for money or
     money's worth: see vol 35 (1997 Reissue) SALE OF LAND Paragraph 578 [764].

                                                                            [1919]

3   As to limitation of liability under the implied covenants for title see vol 37 (2001 Reissue) SALE OF
     LAND Form 61 note 8 [510].
4   Where there is more than one beneficiary, the Registrar requires sufficient information to enable him
     to consider whether or not to retain the restriction referred to in the Land Registration Act 1925 s 58(3)
     (37 Halsbury's Statutes (4th Edn) REAL PROPERTY) and SR & O 1925/1093 r 213 as substituted by
     SI 1996/2975, Sch 2 Form 62 (as substituted by SI 1989/801 and amended by SI 1996/2975 and
     SI 1997/3037). The beneficiaries should make an express declaration of trust for the sake of certainty
     and to avoid any future difficulties with regard to the determination of beneficial interests. As to the
     effect of an express declaration see *Goodman v Gallant* [1986] Fam 106, [1986] 1 All ER 311, CA; *Turton
     v Turton* [1988] Ch 542, [1987] 2 All ER 641, CA. Where the transfer refers to a separate deed declaring
     the trusts upon which the land is to be held, there is no need to lodge a copy because neither the
     Registrar nor any other person dealing with a registered estate or charge is affected with notice of any
     trust and, so far as possible, such trusts are to be excluded from the register: see the Land Registration
     Act 1925 s 74.

5   As to the different ways in which an indemnity covenant may be given see vol 37 (2001 Reissue) SALE OF LAND Form 61 note 17 [512].

6   As to reference in the register to modification of the implied covenants for title see vol 37 (2001 Reissue) SALE OF LAND Form 61 note 20 [512].

7   Where there is a sole beneficiary, or there are joint beneficiaries who hold as beneficial joint tenants, it is appropriate for any restriction entered on the register in the form of SR & O 1925/1093 Sch 2 Form 62 (as substituted by SI 1989/801 and amended by SI 1996/2975 and SI 1997/3037) to be removed. However, the Registrar needs to be satisfied that the parties are entitled to apply for the restriction to be removed: see the Land Registration Act 1925 s 58(3) and SR & O 1925/1093 r 213 as substituted by SI 1996/2975 and amended by SI 1997/3037. The Registrar therefore must be satisfied as to the equitable title and he may, in some cases, require confirmation by statutory declaration that the beneficial interests have not been dealt with other than in accordance with the documents produced.

   Where a deed has been executed by the trustees under the Trusts of Land and Appointment of Trustees Act 1996 s 16(4) (37 Halsbury's Statutes (4th Edn) REAL PROPERTY) declaring that they are discharged from the trusts in relation to that land, the Registrar is entitled to assume that the land is not subject to the trust unless he has actual notice that the trustees were mistaken in their belief that the land was conveyed to the beneficiaries absolutely entitled to the land under the trust and of full age and capacity: see the Land Registration Act 1925 s 94(5) as inserted by the Trusts of Land and Appointment of Trustees Act 1996 Sch 3 para 5(8)(c). The trustees are not required to execute a deed because the Trusts of Land and Appointment of Trustees Act 1996 s 16 does not apply to registered land: Trusts of Land and Appointment of Trustees Act 1996 s 16(5).

8   For the modifications needed if the property is subject to a charge see vol 37 (2001 Reissue) SALE OF LAND Form 183 [1353].

[1920]

275

Conveyance of mortgaged freehold land by sole surviving trustee for sale to a beneficiary who has become absolutely entitled following deaths of co-beneficiaries[1]

THIS CONVEYANCE is made the ...... day of ....

BETWEEN:

(1) *(surviving trustee for sale)* of *(address)* ('the Trustee') and

(2) *(beneficiary)* of *(address)* ('the Grantee')

WHEREAS

(1) By his will dated *(date)* ('the Will') *(testator)* late of *(address)* ('the Testator') appointed the Trustee and *(deceased trustee)* ('the Deceased Trustee') to be the executors and trustees of the Will and gave to them all his real and personal property upon trust for sale and conversion and directed them out of the proceeds of sale to pay his debts and funeral expenses (all of which have been duly paid) and to hold the residue of such proceeds upon trust for all his children who should attain the age of 21 years

[1921]

(2) The Testator died on *(date)* and the Will was on *(date)* proved in the [Principal Registry of the Family Division of the High Court *or (name)* District Probate Registry] by the Trustee and the Deceased Trustee

(3) The Testator was at the date of his death seised of the property described in the schedule ('the Property') for an estate in fee simple in possession subject only to a mortgage ('the Mortgage') dated *(date)* and made between *(parties)* by which the Property was charged to *(mortgagee)* by way of a legal mortgage to secure the payment of the sum of £... and interest on it as mentioned in the Mortgage

(4)   By an assent in writing dated *(date)* the Trustee and the Deceased Trustee assented to the vesting in themselves of the Property for an estate in fee simple subject to the Mortgage upon trust to sell the same and to hold the proceeds upon the trusts declared concerning the same by the Will

(5)   The Testator had 3 children and no more who attained the age of 21 years namely the Grantee and *(first deceased child)* ('the First Deceased Child') and *(second deceased child)* ('the Second Deceased Child')

(6)   The First Deceased Child died on *(date)* having by her will dated *(date)* which was proved on *(date)* in the [Principal Registry of the Family Division of the High Court *or (name)* District Probate Registry] by *(executor)* (the sole executor named in the will) given her share and interest in the proceeds of sale of the Property to the Grantee absolutely

[1922]

(7)   On *(date) (executor of the First Deceased Child)* assented to the vesting in the Grantee of all the interest of the First Deceased Child in the proceeds of sale of the Property[2]

(8)   The Second Deceased Child died on *(date)* intestate leaving the Grantee his sole statutory beneficiary under the Administration of Estates Act 1925 and letters of administration to his estate were on *(date)* granted out of the [Principal Registry of the Family Division of the High Court *or (name)* District Probate Registry] to the Grantee

(9)   The Deceased Trustee died on *(date)*

(10)   The Grantee being absolutely entitled to the proceeds of sale of the Property has requested the Trustee to convey it to him subject to the Mortgage which the Trustee has agreed to do upon the Grantee giving him such indemnity as is contained in this deed

[1923]

NOW THIS DEED WITNESSES as follows:

1   Conveyance

The Trustee [with limited title guarantee] conveys to the Grantee the Property TO HOLD to the Grantee in fee simple for his own benefit subject to the Mortgage and the principal and interest secured by it but discharged from the trust for sale

2   Indemnity

The Grantee covenants with the Trustee that the Grantee or the persons deriving title under him will pay all money now due or to become due under the Mortgage and will at all times keep the Trustee and his estate and effects and the estate and effects of the Testator indemnified from and against all actions proceedings costs claims and demands in respect or on account of the same and in respect of the execution of this deed

[3   Declaration of discharge

The Trustee pursuant to the Trusts of Land and Appointment of Trustees Act 1996 Section 16(4) declares that he is discharged from the trust created by the Will in relation to the Property][3]

4   Stamp duty certificate

It is certified that this instrument falls within category 'E' in the Schedule to the Stamp Duty (Exempt Instruments) Regulations 1987[4]

[1924]

IN WITNESS etc

SCHEDULE

The Property
(describe the Property)

(signatures of the parties)[5]
(signatures of witnesses)
[1925]

1   As to stamp duty see Information Binder: Stamp Duties [1] Table of Duties (Conveyance or transfer) and see note 4 below. It is assumed that an express trust for sale has been incorporated into the will which, apart from the inclusion of a power to postpone sale, remains unaffected by the Trusts of Land and Appointment of Trustees Act 1996 (37 Halsbury's Statutes (4th Edn) REAL PROPERTY).
       Where property is conveyed subject to a mortgage, it will be prudent first to check the terms of the mortgage to see whether the mortgagee's consent is required to the conveyance and, if so, to seek such consent before the conveyance is effected. Otherwise the mortgagee may be entitled to realise its security following breach of the terms of the mortgage. It would be advisable, if possible, for the trustee to persuade the mortgagee to join in the deed to release him and for a new covenant to be taken by the mortgagee directly from the beneficiary: see Form 276 clauses 12.4 and 12.5 [1927] post.
2   This assent, as it does not relate to land, need not be in writing.
3   The Trusts of Land and Appointment of Trustees Act 1996 s 16(4)(a) appears to contemplate a separate deed of discharge being executed by the trustee, although the general view is that the discharge can be contained in the conveyance and that it is not necessary to have a separate deed of discharge. If desired this clause can be omitted and a separate deed of discharge executed. As to the Trusts of Land and Appointment of Trustees Act 1996 s 16 see Paragraph 229 [547] ante and, for detailed commentary on this provision, see vol 40(2) (2001 Reissue) TRUSTS AND SETTLEMENTS Part 8 [3001].
4   Ie the Stamp Duty (Exempt Instruments) Regulations 1987, SI 1987/516 reg 2(2), Schedule category E as amended by SI 1999/2539. As to the inclusion of such a certificate see Information Binder: Stamp Duties [1] Table of Duties (Exempt Instruments) Regulations.
5   As to the statutory requirements for the valid execution of a deed see vol 12 (1994 Reissue) DEEDS, AGREEMENTS AND DECLARATIONS.

[1926]

276

Transfer of the whole of registered freehold land subject to a registered or noted charge by trustees to beneficiaries absolutely entitled[1]

Use Land Registry Form TR1, for which see vol 37 (2001 Reissue) SALE OF LAND Form 1 [51], and insert the wording shown below in the panels specified

Panel 1 Stamp duty

I/We hereby certify that this instrument falls within category 'F' in the Schedule to the Stamp Duty (Exempt Instruments) Regulations 1987[2]

Panel 5 Transferor

(names of trustees)

Panel 6 Transferee

(name(s) of beneficiary or beneficiaries)

Panel 9 Consideration

The transfer is not for money or anything which has a monetary value

Panel 10 Title guarantee

limited title guarantee

Panel 11 Declaration of trust

(complete as appropriate)[3]

Panel 12 Additional provisions

12.1   This transfer is made in consideration of the Transferee[s] being [together] absolutely entitled to the property in the events that have happened

12.2   In this transfer
   [12.2.1   'The Chargee' means *(proprietor of charge)* [company registration number] of *(address) or* whose registered office is at *(address)*
   12.2.2   'The Charge' means the charge [in favour of the Chargee *or* of which the Chargee is the proprietor][4] dated *(date)* [which is noted in the register *or* registered on *(date)*][5] and under which £… is owing in respect of the principal [and interest *or* but all interest has been paid to the date of this transfer[6]]]

12.3   The Property is transferred subject to the Charge

12.4   The Transferee covenants with the Transferor [and the Chargee][7] from the date of this transfer to pay the principal interest and all other monies due under the Charge and to comply with the Transferor's obligations in the Charge in accordance with its terms and to indemnify the Transferor against all claims and demands arising out of any failure to do so[8]

12.5   The Transferor warrants to the Transferee that the total amount outstanding under the Charge at the date of this transfer is as stated in clause 12.2.2 and is made up as there stated[9]

[12.6   The parties apply to the Registrar for the restriction registered as entry number (number) in the proprietorship register to be cancelled][10]

[1927]

---

1   As to stamp duty see the Information Binder: Stamp Duties [1]: Table of Duties: Conveyance or transfer. As to Land Registry fees see the Information Binder: Property [1]: Property fees: Land Registration fees. This Form transfers the equity of redemption, the property remaining subject to a registered charge. As to transfers of charged land generally see vol 35 (1997 Reissue) SALE OF LAND Paragraph 582 [770] et seq. It is not strictly necessary for the chargee's charge certificate to be lodged when the land is transferred subject to the charge, but it is desirable for this to be arranged, if the certificate is not already on deposit, so that it may be brought up to date.

   This Form leaves the transferor (as the original borrower) still liable to the lender under the covenants in the mortgage. If the transferor is to be released a form based on vol 37 (2001 Reissue) SALE OF LAND Form 116 [989] should be used. The transferee should check the terms of the mortgage to ensure that there is no restriction preventing the transferor from disposing of the equity of redemption. If there is a restriction, as is commonly the case, the transferor can still validly transfer the property to the transferee, but the transfer is a breach of the conditions of the mortgage that gives the lender the right to call in the outstanding mortgage money. The lender may, if he wishes, simply consent to the transfer, in which case this Form may be used, or he may join in the transfer to take new covenants from the transferee, in which case a form based on vol 37 (2001 Reissue) SALE OF LAND Form 116 [989] should be used. If the lender does not consent to the transfer, it may be possible to avoid or minimise the effect of the restriction by transferring the equitable interest in the property. The rules of a particular lender, eg a building society, may require certain conditions to be fulfilled by a borrower, eg ownership of shares in the society. If so these conditions must be fulfilled by the transferee.

Form TR1 is the Land Registry form of transfer of the whole of freehold or leasehold land prescribed by the Land Registration Rules 1925, SR & O 1925/1093 r 98 as substituted by SI 1999/128, Sch 1 Form TR1 as inserted by SI 1997/3037. Reference should be made to vol 37 (2001 Reissue) SALE OF LAND Form 9 [132] for an illustration of the method of inserting clauses in Land Registry Form TR1, a selection of common form clauses including definition, incumbrance and indemnity clauses, detailed notes on matters common to many forms of transfer and for cross references to the commentary in vol 35 (1997 Reissue) SALE OF LAND and for the location of alternative transfer clauses. As to completion of panels other than those dealt with in this Form see vol 37 (2001 Reissue) SALE OF LAND Form 1 [51]. For the forms of execution of transfers prescribed by SR & O 1925/1093 Sch 3 as inserted by SI 1997/3037 see vol 37 (2001 Reissue) SALE OF LAND Form 8 [123]. As to the statutory requirements for the valid execution of a deed see vol 12 (1994 Reissue) DEEDS, AGREEMENTS AND DECLARATIONS. As to the method of reproduction of Land Registry forms see vol 37 (2001 Reissue) SALE OF LAND Form 9 note 1(5) [137].

2 Ie the Stamp Duty (Exempt Instruments) Regulations 1987, SI 1987/516. This certificate is applicable provided that the dealing with the equitable interest preceding the transfer was not for money or money's worth: see vol 35 (1997 Reissue) SALE OF LAND Paragraph 578 [764].

[1928]

3 Where there is more than one beneficiary, the Registrar requires sufficient information to enable him to consider whether or not to retain the restriction referred to in the Land Registration Act 1925 s 58(3) (37 Halsbury's Statutes (4th Edn) REAL PROPERTY) and SR & O 1925/1093 r 213 as substituted by SI 1996/2975, Sch 2 Form 62 (as substituted by SI 1989/801 and amended by SI 1996/2975 and SI 1997/3037). The beneficiaries should make an express declaration of trust for the sake of certainty and to avoid any future difficulties with regard to the determination of beneficial interests. As to the effect of an express declaration see *Goodman v Gallant* [1986] Fam 106, [1986] 1 All ER 311, CA; *Turton v Turton* [1988] Ch 542, [1987] 2 All ER 641, CA. Where the transfer refers to a separate deed declaring the trusts upon which the land is to be held, there is no need to lodge a copy because neither the Registrar nor any other person dealing with a registered estate or charge is affected with notice of any trust and, so far as possible, such trusts are to be excluded from the register: see the Land Registration Act 1925 s 74.

4 Where the charge is noted use the first alternative form of wording in the square brackets. Where the charge is registered use the second form of wording.

5 See note 4 above.

6 The amount owing under the charge is important for the transferee. The breakdown may also be important to the transferee. If the chargee is not a party to this transfer the statement will not be binding on him and the transferee should obtain written confirmation from the lender as to the amount outstanding. The chargee will be a party if he takes a direct covenant as in clause 12.4 [1927] above.

7 Because the charge was created by the transferor and the transferee is not party to it, the chargee usually requires the transferee to covenant directly with the chargee to observe the mortgage conditions; otherwise the chargee's only recourse will be against the property itself or the transferor as the original party to the charge who, in practice, may subsequently prove untraceable.

8 The transferor normally requires a covenant from the transferee to observe the mortgage conditions and for indemnity, because he continues to remain liable under the terms of the charge unless actually released by the chargee, although in the case of a sale of the whole of the mortgaged property the transferee is under an implied obligation to indemnify the transferor provided the property is expressly sold subject to the mortgage: *Waring v Ward* (1802) 7 Ves 332 at 337, *Bridgman v Daw* (1891) 40 WR 253; see also *Re Law Courts Chambers Co Ltd* (1889) 61 LT 669. An express covenant excludes the implied obligation: *Mills v United Counties Bank Ltd* [1912] 1 Ch 231, CA. The benefit of the covenant is not assignable: *Rendall v Morphew* (1914) 84 LJ Ch 517. Although the transferee may make himself liable directly to the lender by a fresh covenant, such liability will not be implied merely from the payment of the mortgage interest: *Re Errington, ex p Mason* [1894] 1 QB 11. For an example of such a covenant see vol 37 (2001 Reissue) SALE OF LAND Form 117 [991].

9 A statement of the amount outstanding under the charge may amount to a covenant or warranty that the figures are correct, but a cautious transferee may wish to obtain a specific warranty to that effect on which he could sue if the figures prove to be understated. He should also obtain confirmation from the lender of the accuracy of the figures, and if he does so the lender himself may be estopped from claiming that the mortgage debt is greater than the figure he has stated and be left with any remedy he may have against the transferor/borrower.

10 Where there is a sole beneficiary, or there are joint beneficiaries who hold as beneficial joint tenants, it is appropriate for any restriction entered on the register in the form of SR & O 1925/1093 Sch 2 (as substituted by SI 1989/801 and amended by SI 1996/2975 and SI 1997/3037) to be removed. However, the Registrar needs to be satisfied that the parties are entitled to apply for the restriction to be removed: see the Land Registration Act 1925 s 58(3) and SR & O 1925/1093 r 213 as substituted by SI 1996/2975 and amended by SI 1997/3037. The Registrar, therefore, must be satisfied as to the equitable title and he may, in some cases, require confirmation by statutory declaration that the beneficial interests have not been dealt with, other than in accordance with the documents produced.

Where a deed has been executed by the trustees under the Trusts of Land and Appointment of Trustees Act 1996 s 16(4) (37 Halsbury's Statutes (4th Edn) REAL PROPERTY) declaring that they are discharged from the trusts in relation to that land, the Registrar is entitled to assume that the land is not subject to the trust unless he has actual notice that the trustees were mistaken in their belief that the land was conveyed to the beneficiaries absolutely entitled to the land under the trust and of full age and capacity: see the Land Registration Act 1925 s 94(5) as inserted by the Trusts of Land and Appointment of Trustees Act 1996 Sch 3 para 5(8)(c). The trustees are not required to execute a deed because the Trusts of Land and Appointment of Trustees Act 1996 s 16 does not apply to registered land: Trusts of Land and Appointment of Trustees Act 1996 s 16(5).

[1929]

277

Transfer of mortgage of unregistered land by surviving trustee of a settlement to two beneficiaries absolutely entitled[1]

THIS TRANSFER OF MORTGAGE is made the ...... day of ………

BETWEEN:

(1)   *(surviving trustee)* of *(address)* ('the Transferor') and

(2)   *(beneficiaries)* of *(addresses)* ('the Transferees')

WHEREAS

(1)   This deed is supplemental to a mortgage ('the Mortgage') dated *(date)* and made between (1) *(mortgagor)* ('the Mortgagor') and (2) *(deceased trustee)* ('the Deceased Trustee') and the Transferor by which the property described in the schedule was charged by the Mortgagor to the Deceased Trustee and the Transferor by way of legal mortgage to secure the payment to the Deceased Trustee and the Transferor of £... ('the Principal Sum') with interest on it at the rate of ...% per year in the manner set out in the Mortgage

[1930]

(2)   The Deceased Trustee died on *(date)*

(3)   The Principal Sum remains owing on the security of the Mortgage **[**but all interest on it to the date of this deed has been paid *or* together with interest on it from *(date)***]**

(4)   The Transferees are entitled in equity to the Principal Sum and the interest on it and have requested the Transferor to make this transfer in the manner described below

NOW THIS DEED WITNESSES that in consideration of the above the Transferor **[**with limited title guarantee**]** transfers to the Transferees the benefit of the Mortgage

IN WITNESS etc

SCHEDULE

The Property

(describe the mortgaged property)

(signatures of the parties)[2]
(signatures of witnesses)
[1931]

1   This Form may be used where settled funds are invested on mortgage and two or more persons have become absolutely entitled to the funds. The trusts are invariably kept off the title. After execution of this transfer, the transferees should execute a declaration of trust that the respective transferees are entitled in equal shares or specified amounts of the sum secured by the transfer. Notice of the transfer should be given to the mortgagor.

2   As to the statutory requirements for the valid execution of a deed see vol 12 (1994 Reissue) DEEDS, AGREEMENTS AND DECLARATIONS.

[1932]

278

Transfer of a registered charge by surviving trustees of a settlement to two beneficiaries absolutely entitled[1]

Use Land Registry Form TR3, for which see vol 25(1) (1999 Reissue) LAND REGISTRATION *Form 43 [3351], and insert the wording shown below in the panels specified*

Panel 5 Transferor

(names of trustees)

Panel 6 Transferee

(name(s) of beneficiary or beneficiaries)

Panel 9 Consideration

The transfer is not for money or anything which has a monetary value

Panel 10 Title guarantee

limited title guarantee

Panel 11 Additional provisions

The transfer is made in consideration of the Transferee(s) being absolutely entitled [in equal *or* (as the case may be)] in equity to all monies due under the charge whether principal or interest.

1   Form TR3 is the Land Registry form of transfer of charge prescribed by the Land Registration Rules 1925, SR & O 1925/1093 r 153 (as substituted by SI 1999/128), Sch 1 Form TR3 (as inserted by SI 1997/3037).

[1933]

279

Disposition between beneficiaries to put an end to trust for sale[1]

THIS DEED is made the ...... day of ....

BETWEEN:

(1)   *(executors and trustees of will of testator)* of *(addresses)* ('the Will Trustees')

(2)   *(son of testator)* of *(address)* ('the Son')

(3)   *(daughter of testator)* of *(address)* ('the Daughter') and

(4)   *(trustees of daughter's marriage settlement)* of *(addresses)* ('the Daughter's Trustees')

WHEREAS

(1)   By his will dated *(date)* ('the Will') *(testator)* ('the Testator') late of *(address)* after making certain specific and pecuniary bequests gave the residue of his real and personal estate to the Will Trustees upon trust for sale and to stand possessed of the net proceeds of sale upon trust for the Son and the Daughter as tenants in common in equal shares and the Testator appointed the Will Trustees to be executors of the Will

[1934]

(2)   The Testator died on *(date)* and the Will was on *(date)* proved in the [Principal Registry of the Family Division of the High Court *or (name)* District Probate Registry] by the Will Trustees

(3)   The Testator's net residuary estate after payment of his debts funeral and testamentary expenses and the duties payable on his death consists of the freehold property described in the first schedule ('the Property') the mortgage debt and investments described in the second schedule ('the Mortgage Debt and Investments') and £... cash ('the Cash')

(4)   The parties to this deed desire to put an end to the trust for sale affecting the Property and to divide the testator's net residuary estate equally as described below

(5)   By a settlement ('the Daughter's Settlement') dated *(date)* and made between *(parties)* on the marriage shortly afterwards solemnised of the Daughter with *(name of husband)* the Daughter covenanted and agreed that her after-acquired property should be vested in the Daughter's Trustees as mentioned in the Daughter's Settlement

(6)   It is intended that the Mortgage Debts and Investments shall immediately be transferred to or into the names of the Daughter's Trustees and that the Cash be paid on the execution of this deed as to £... to the Son and as to £... to the Daughter's Trustees and it has been agreed that the Property shall be conveyed to the Son in the manner described below

[1935]

NOW THIS DEED WITNESSES as follows:

1   Intention to execute assent and transfer

In consideration of the above and at the request of the Son and the Daughter and the Daughter's Trustees the Will Trustees covenant that they will by an assent under hand intended to bear even date with but to be executed immediately after this deed assent to the vesting in the Son of all the Property in fee simple discharged from the trust for sale[2] and further covenant that they will at the same time transfer the Mortgage Debt and Investments to the Daughter's Trustees to be held on the trusts of the Daughter's Settlement as one fund with the same

2   Declaration of trust of mortgage debt and investment

The Daughter's Trustees shall hold the Mortgage Debt and Investments when transferred to them upon the trusts and with and subject to the powers and provisions respectively affecting them under or by virtue of the Daughter's Settlement

[1936]

3   Release

In consideration of the payment of the sum of £... to the Son and of the sum of £... to the Daughter's Trustees (the receipt and payment of which the Son and Daughter and the Daughter's Trustees acknowledge) and of the assent in respect of the Property and the transfers of the Mortgage Debt and Investments so intended to be made and subject to the due execution of the said assent and transfers the Son the Daughter and to the extent of their interest in the same the Daughter's Trustees release the Will Trustees from all actions proceedings claims and demands in respect of the Testator's residuary estate or the income from it and every part of such estate or income

IN WITNESS etc

FIRST SCHEDULE

The Property

(describe the Property)

SECOND SCHEDULE

Mortgage Debt and Investments

(describe the Mortgage Debt and Investments)

(signatures of the parties)[3]
(signatures of witnesses)
[1937]

1   It is assumed that an express trust for sale has been incorporated into the will which, apart from the inclusion of a power to postpone sale, remains unaffected by the Trusts of Land and Appointment of Trustees Act 1996 (37 Halsbury's Statutes (4th Edn) REAL PROPERTY). It is assumed that this Form is in effect a partition agreement which is not intended to vary the value of the beneficial interests and that the son and the daughter's trustees are taking property of equal value. It may be possible to achieve the same result more simply by the personal representatives exercising a power of appropriation.

        For the position when land is conveyed to a beneficiary absolutely entitled see the Trusts of Land and Appointment of Trustees Act 1996 s 16(4) (37 Halsbury's Statutes (4th Edn) REAL PROPERTY). As to the Trusts of Land and Appointment of Trustees Act 1996 s 16 see Paragraph 229 [547] ante and, for detailed commentary on this provision, see vol 40(2) (2001 Reissue) TRUSTS AND SETTLEMENTS Part 8 [3001].

        No charge will arise to inheritance tax because the two beneficiaries are each entitled to a one-half share of the estate and the assets that each are taking are equivalent to a one-half interest. For capital gains tax purposes the matter is covered by the Taxation of Chargeable Gains Act 1992 s 62(4) (42–44 Halsbury's Statutes (4th Edn) TAXATION).

2   Whilst it would be possible for the will trustees by this deed to convey the freehold property to the son, it is better to keep the trusts off the title and to assure the property to him by means of a separate assent.

3   As to the statutory requirements for the valid execution of a deed see vol 12 (1994 Reissue) DEEDS, AGREEMENTS AND DECLARATIONS.

[1938]–[1950]

E: DEEDS EXERCISING DISPOSITIVE POWERS— ADVANCEMENT, PAY OR APPLY, APPOINTMENT

1: INTRODUCTION

Scope of this section

This section provides forms to be used when trustees are exercising dispositive powers, that is powers to distribute trust property for the objects of the trust[1]. It should be noted that certain forms found in other sections involve the exercise of a dispositive power: for instance resolutions exercising powers of advancement[2]. In exercising such powers 'trustees must act in good faith, responsibly and reasonably. They must inform themselves, before making a decision, of matters which are relevant to the decision'[3]. This requires the trustee to make 'such a survey of the range of objects or possible beneficiaries ... as will enable him to carry out his fiduciary duties'. He must find out 'the permissible area of selection and then consider responsibly, in individual cases, whether a contemplated beneficiary was within the power and whether, in relation to other possible claimants, a particular grant was appropriate[4].' The trustees must obey the trust instrument and cannot make an appointment that is not authorised by it.

The decision of a trustee may be challenged:

1   if it can be shown that he did not act in good faith having properly informed himself[5].

2   if it is shown that the trustee did not 'consider' the appointment but acted on the direction of another eg the settlor[6].

3   if, under the so-called '*Hastings-Bass* principle', it can be shown that the trustees would not (or perhaps, might not) have exercised the power in the way that they did had they considered all the facts (eg, had they realised that the result would create a perpetuity or lead to a tax charge)[7].

To what extent can such powers be exercised to create discretionary trusts and to transfer property to trustees of a separate trust? The question in all cases turns on a construction of the wording of the relevant power and it is common for a settlor expressly to permit the creation of discretionary or protective trusts and the transfer of property to trustees of a separate trust[8]. In the absence of express wording a restrictive view may be taken of the power based in part on adherence to the maxim *delegatus non potest delegare*.

Finally it may be noted that a power to pay or apply capital for the benefit of a beneficiary may permit incidental benefits to be conferred on persons who are not beneficiaries provided that the payment can be shown to be for the benefit of the beneficiary[9].

[1951]

---

1   See *Trustees' Powers and Duties* (Law Com No 260) para 4.7 where the distinction is drawn between dispositive powers and powers to administer the trust: see further Paragraph 287.2 [731] ante and Part 5 Introduction to Section H [1586] ante.
2   See Form 255 [1850] et seq post.
3   Per Robert Walker J in *Scott v National Trust* [1998] 2 All ER 705 at 717.
4   *McPhail v Doulton* [1971] AC 424 at 449, 457 quoted by Megarry VC in *re Hay's Settlement Trusts* [1981] 3 All ER 786, [1982] 1 WLR 202. In making the decision the trustee is not subject to the rules of natural justice, ie he is not obliged to hear the person affected by his decision: see Robert Walker J in

Scott v National Trust (as above): 'but [the trustees] are not a court or an administrative tribunal. They are not under any general duty to give a hearing to both sides' and see R v Charity Commrs, ex p Baldwin (7 July 2000, unreported).

5   Klug v Klug [1918] 2 Ch 67 and on the giving of reasons by trustees see re Beloved Wilkes' Charity (1851) 20 LJ Ch 588, 3 Mac & G 440; Dundee General Hospitals Board of Management v Walker [1952] 1 All ER 896 and Robert Walker J in Scott v National Trust.

6   In Turner v Turner [1984] Ch 100, [1983] 2 All ER 745 the appointments were held void.

7   Re Hastings-Bass [1975] Ch 25, [1974] 2 All ER 193; Mettoy Pension Trustees v Evans [1991] 2 All ER 513, [1990] 1 WLR 1587; Stennard v Fisons Pensions Trust [1992] 1 RLR 27; Green v Cobham (19 January 2000, unreported).

8   See Form 5 clause 3.2.2 [1112] ante, Form 98 [1474] ante and Form 288 [1991] post.

9   See the 'settled advance' cases of Pilkington v IRC [1964] AC 612, HL; Re Hampden Settlement Trusts [1977] TR 177 and Re Clore's Settlement Trusts [1966] 2 All ER 272, [1966] 1 WLR 955.

[1952]

2: FORMS

280

Deed of appointment terminating discretionary trust—appointments in favour of adult beneficiary absolutely and in favour of minor beneficiary contingently on his attainment of specified age[1]

THIS DEED OF APPOINTMENT is made the ...... day of .... by *(trustees)* of *(addresses)* ('the Trustees')

WHEREAS

(1)   This deed is supplemental to [the will of *(testator)* late of *(address)* dated *(date)* ('the Will') *or* a settlement dated *(date)* and made between *(parties)* ('the Settlement')]

(2)   The Trustees are the present trustees of the [Will *or* Settlement]

(3)   The property now subject to the trusts of the [Will *or* Settlement] consists of the investments [and cash] set out in the schedule

(4)   The Trustees intend by this deed to exercise the power of appointment given to them by clause *(number)* of the [Will *or* Settlement]

[1953]

NOW THIS DEED WITNESSES as follows:

1   Exercise of power

1.1   The Trustees in exercise of their power of appointment conferred by clause *(number)* of the [Will *or* Settlement] and of all other powers them enabling [irrevocably *or* subject to clause 1.4 below][2] appoint the property set out in the schedule as and from the date of this deed to be held upon the following trusts:

      1.1.1   as to the property set out in Part I of the schedule upon trust as to both capital and income for *(adult beneficiary)* absolutely

      1.1.2   as to the property set out in Part II of the schedule upon trust as to both capital and income for *(minor beneficiary)* but contingently upon his attaining the age of [18 *or* 21] years

      1.1.3   *(set out trusts (if any) in favour of other beneficiaries)*

1.2   PROVIDED that if any person named in clause 1.1.2 [and clause 1.1.3][3] above shall die before attaining a vested interest but leaving a child or children living at his death then such child or children shall take absolutely and if more than one in equal shares so much of the trust property and the income of it as that person would have taken had he attained a vested interest[4]

[1954]

1.3   [PROVIDED also that if at any time the trusts declared by clause 1.1.2 [and clause 1.1.3] above read in conjunction with clause 1.2 above shall fail then from the date of failure the property which was the subject of those trusts and the income from it shall be held upon trust *(set out alternative trusts)*

or

PROVIDED also that if at any time the trusts declared by clause 1.1.2 [and clause 1.1.3] above in conjunction with clause 1.2 above in respect of a share of the trust property shall fail then from the date of such failure that share (and any part of the trust property which may already have accrued to it under this provision) shall accrue to the other share or shares (and equally if more than one) the trusts of which shall not at that date have failed and be held upon the trusts from time to time affecting such other share or shares][5]

[1.4   PROVIDED also that the Trustees or other the trustees or trustee for the time being of the [Will *or* Settlement] shall have power at any time or times by deed or deeds wholly or partially to revoke or otherwise vary those trusts declared by this deed which create contingent interests and by the same deed to declare such other trusts (concerning the same) as may be authorised by clause *(number)* of the [Will *or* Settlement]][6]

[1955]

2   Powers of maintenance and advancement

The trusts contained in clause 1.1.2 [and clause 1.1.3] above shall carry the intermediate income and the statutory powers of maintenance accumulation and advancement contained in the Trustee Act 1925 Sections 31 and 32 (as amended by the Family Law Reform Act 1969 by the Trusts of Land and Appointment of Trustees Act 1996 and by the Trustee Act 2000) shall apply to them with the following variations:

2.1   in the case of the said Section 31 the substitution in subsection (1)(i) of the words 'the trustees in their absolute discretion think fit' for the words 'may in all the circumstances be reasonable' and the omission of the proviso to subsection (1) and

2.2   in the case of the said Section 32 the omission of the words 'one-half of ' from proviso (a) to subsection (1)

3   Administrative provisions

The administrative provisions of the [Will *or* Settlement] which are contained in clauses *(specify clauses)* shall apply to the trusts declared by this deed in the same way as they applied to the trusts of the [Will *or* Settlement] itself so far as the same are not inconsistent with the trusts and provisions above declared and contained [save only for the following modifications: *(specify)*][7]

[1956]

[4   Exclusion of apportionment

All income of the property set out in Part I and Part II of the schedule received by or on behalf of the Trustees or other trustees or trustee for the time being of the [Will *or* Settlement] from and after the date of this deed shall be treated as if it had arisen wholly after such date and the Apportionment Act 1870 shall not be applicable to it][8]

IN WITNESS etc

SCHEDULE

Part I

(describe property to be held on trust for beneficiary specified in clause 1.1.1 [1954] above)

Part II

(describe property to be held on trust for beneficiary specified in clause 1.1.2 [1954] above)
(continue with further parts as appropriate)[9]

(signatures of the trustees)[10]
(signatures of witnesses)
[1957]

1   Trustees holding property on discretionary trusts may wish to terminate the discretionary trusts by appointing the trust property amongst all or some of the beneficiaries. They can do this only if the document creating the trusts enables them to do so; if the beneficiaries are all *sui juris* and in agreement; or they proceed under the Variation of Trusts Act 1958 (48 Halsbury's Statutes (4th Edn) TRUSTS AND SETTLEMENTS). This Form is for use when the trustees are acting under powers in the trust instrument and assumes that the trustees wish to terminate the discretionary trust once and for all, and that they have power to do so.

       This Form presupposes that the trust property is still in the form of investments and that these are being appointed *in specie* amongst beneficiaries some of whom are not yet of age. So far as adult beneficiaries are concerned, the effect of the Form is that they become absolutely entitled to the shares appointed to them, and these shares can then be transferred to them by the trustees in exchange for formal receipts. The tax position is as follows:

(a)   *Inheritance tax:* the property ceases to be held on non-interest in possession trusts as a result of the appointment and hence an 'exit charge' may arise: see Paragraph 319 [830] et seq ante. Trustees should ensure that they retain sufficient money to pay this tax.

(b)   *Capital gains tax:* the apportionment in favour of beneficiaries who are absolutely entitled triggers a deemed disposal under the Taxation of Chargeable Gains Act 1992 s 71 (42–44 Halsbury's Statutes (4th Edn) TAXATION): see Paragraph 341.3 [911] ante. In such cases any charge may be postponed by the making of a hold-over election: see the Taxation of Chargeable Gains Act 1992 s 260 (as amended by the Finance Act 1995 ss 67, 72, Sch 13 paras 1, 4) and for the prescribed form of election see Form 299 [2086] post. The appointments in favour of beneficiaries on attaining [18 *or* 21] years result in the property continuing to be settled and do not result in a disposal for capital gains tax purposes.

       The trusts on which the trustees may appoint the property are governed, as to beneficiaries, by the provisions of the original discretionary will or settlement. The trusts on which the trustees may appoint are also governed by the rule against perpetuities; the perpetuity period will normally be declared in the original will or settlement and any appointment must keep within it.

[1958]

2   Where some of the interests appointed are contingent (eg the interest appointed by clause 1.1.2 [1954] above), the appointors can reserve power to revoke the relevant trusts. In such a case, the first option in square brackets should be omitted and clause 1.4 [1955] above included in the Form. The reservation of a power of revocation would mean that the relevant trusts did not qualify (for inheritance tax purposes) as accumulation and maintenance and hence the property would continue to be held on non-interest in possession trusts.

3   The clause numbers of those clauses appointing contingent interests should be set out.

4   The interests of the children mentioned in clause 1.2 [1954] above are not made contingent on their attaining a specified age and so are vested from the outset. This is partly to make the trusts declared in their favour less likely to infringe the perpetuity rule, and partly to safeguard their families if they should die young leaving a wife or children.

5   Clause 1.3 [1955] above is a longstop provision. The trustees could name here an adult beneficiary who
       (or whose estate) they would wish to benefit in these circumstances. Alternatively, they could provide
       that property of which the trusts failed (eg because a minor died before attaining a vested interest and
       without leaving children) should accrue to property the trusts of which had not failed, in which case
       the second of the two alternative forms of clause 1.3 should be used.
6   See note 2 above.
7   By this clause the trustees give themselves administrative powers (eg of investment, charging, insurance,
       etc). Their power to do this, and its extent, depend on the wording of the power of appointment
       contained in the original will or settlement. It is assumed in the present case that the trustees have
       power, and wish to give themselves the same powers as they had under the original will or settlement.
       They may also be able to give themselves other powers, for instance, a wide power of advancement
       which in the nature of things would not have been included in the original will or settlement: if the
       trustees wish to do this, they should so provide.
8   This clause should be included if it is wished to exclude the operation of the Apportionment Act 1870
       (23 Halsbury's Statutes (4th Edn) LANDLORD AND TENANT) to accruing income. If further parts are
       added to the schedule the clause should be amended as appropriate.
9   The schedule will set out all the trust property and will be divided into as many parts as there are
       beneficiaries in whose favour an appointment is made.
10   As to the statutory requirements for valid execution of a deed see vol 12 (1994 Reissue) DEEDS,
       AGREEMENTS AND DECLARATIONS.

[1959]

281

Deed of appointment of share in trust fund[1]

THIS DEED OF APPOINTMENT is made the …… day of ……… by *(original trustees)*
of *(addresses)* ('the Original Trustees')[2]

WHEREAS

(1)   This deed is supplemental to a settlement ('the Settlement') dated *(date)* and
        made between (1) *(settlor)* ('the Settlor') and (2) the Original Trustees

[1960]

(2)   In this deed the expressions[3] 'the Trustees' 'the Trust Fund' 'the Beneficiaries'
        and 'the Vesting Day' have the same meaning as in the Settlement

(3)   It was provided by the Settlement that the Trustees might apply capital for the
        benefit of any one or more of the Beneficiaries for the time being living by
        appointing allocating or appropriating to such Beneficiary such sum or sums out
        of or investments forming part of the capital of the Trust Fund as the Trustees
        should think fit either absolutely or contingently upon the attainment by him
        or her of a specified age or the happening of a specified event before the Vesting
        Day and so that the provisions of the Trustee Act 1925 Section 31 (as amended
        by the Family Law Reform Act 1969 and the Trustee Act 2000)[4] and the
        powers of the Trustees to invest and vary investments should apply to any
        money or investments so allocated or appropriated

(4)   The Original Trustees are the trustees for the time being of the Settlement

(5)   The assets described in the first schedule are now comprised in the Trust Fund

(6)   All the persons named in the second schedule are Beneficiaries

(7)   The Trustees have decided to exercise their above recited power in the manner
        described below

[1961]

NOW THIS DEED WITNESSES as follows:

[1   Appointment of assets

The Trustees in exercise of the above recited and all other (if any) of the powers enabling them irrevocably appoint allocate and appropriate to the persons named in Part I of the second schedule the assets specified opposite their respective names for their respective use and benefit absolutely][5]

2   Appointment on attaining specified age

The Trustees in exercise of the above recited and all other (if any) of the powers enabling them irrevocably appoint allocate and appropriate the assets specified in [Part II of] the second schedule to such of the persons named in [Part II of] the second schedule as shall attain the age of 25 years and if more than one in equal shares absolutely[6]

3   Intermediate income

It is declared and confirmed that the trusts of the appointment allocation and appropriation directed by clause [2] above shall carry the intermediate income and that the provisions of the Trustee Act 1925 Section 31 (as amended by the Family Law Reform Act 1969 and the Trustee Act 2000) shall apply to them accordingly[7]

[1962]

4   Continuation of Settlement terms

Subject to all the trusts powers and provisions of this deed applicable to the assets specified in [Part II of] the second schedule and if and so far as (for any reason whatsoever) not wholly disposed of by the same such assets and the income of them shall continue to be held upon and with and subject to the trusts powers and provisions declared and contained in the Settlement[8]

5   Administrative provisions

The administrative and other powers and provisions contained in clauses *(number)* to *(number)* (inclusive) of the Settlement shall so far as not inconsistent with the trusts powers and provisions in this deed declared and contained concerning the assets specified in [Part II of] the second schedule continue to apply to such assets during the subsistence of such trusts and provisions

[6   Exclusion of apportionment

All income of the assets specified in the second schedule received by or on behalf of the Trustees from and after the date of this deed shall be treated as if it had arisen wholly after such date and the Apportionment Act 1870 shall not be applicable to it]

[1963]

IN WITNESS etc

FIRST SCHEDULE
(details of assets comprised in the Trust Fund)

SECOND SCHEDULE

[Part I

(names of beneficiaries receiving assets absolutely and details of the assets)][9]

[Part II]

(names of beneficiaries receiving an interest in the resettled assets and details of the assets)

IN WITNESS etc

(signatures of the parties)[10]
(signatures of witnesses)
[1964]

1   This Form is a suggested deed of appointment of the trust fund of a discretionary settlement partly to certain beneficiaries absolutely and partly to other (minor) beneficiaries on accumulation and maintenance trusts. See further the notes to Form 280 [1953] ante and on the question of what constitutes a resettlement for capital gains tax purposes see Inland Revenue Statement of Practice SP 7/84 (11 October 1984) and Paragraph 342 [919] ante. As to accumulation and maintenance trusts see Paragraph 127 [316] ante and see vol 40(2) (2001 Reissue) TRUSTS AND SETTLEMENTS Part 11 [6301]. In this Form the property remains held on the original trusts for capital gains tax purposes: ie the appointment does not trigger any disposal under the Taxation of Chargeable Gains Act 1992 s 71 (42–44 Halsbury's Statutes (4th Edn) TAXATION)

2   It is necessary to consider on the terms of the settlement itself whether the consent of anyone has to be obtained; for example the consent of the settlor.

3   Clearly the appropriate definitions and terminology used in the settlement must be carefully followed.

4   Ie the Trustee Act 1925 s 31 as amended by the Family Law Reform Act 1969 s 1(3), Sch 1 Pt I and by the Trustee Act 2000 s 40(1), Sch 2 para 25 (48 Halsbury's Statutes (4th Edn) TRUSTS AND SETTLEMENTS).

5   This part of the appointment is to beneficiaries absolutely. If no beneficiaries are to take an absolute interest this clause should be omitted.

6   This part of the appointment creates an accumulation and maintenance trust under the provisions of the Inheritance Tax Act 1984 s 71 (42–44 Halsbury's Statutes (4th Edn) TAXATION).

7   See note 4 above.

8   This clause will assist in showing that the property remains comprised in the original settlement for capital gains tax purposes: see Inland Revenue Statement of Practice SP 7/84 (11 October 1984) and Paragraph 342 [919] ante.

9   If no beneficiaries are to take an absolute interest this part of the schedule should be omitted.

10   As to the statutory requirements for valid execution of a deed see vol 12 (1994 Reissue) DEEDS, AGREEMENTS AND DECLARATIONS.

[1965]

282

Clause appointing trust fund absolutely[1]

The {Trustees} appoint and direct that they shall from and after the date of this deed stand possessed of the {Trust Fund} in trust for *(beneficiary)* absolutely

1   This Form assumes an appointment of the entire trust fund in favour of a beneficiary absolutely. For capital gains tax purposes there will be a deemed disposal under the Taxation of Chargeable Gains Act 1992 s 71(1) (42–44 Halsbury's Statutes (4th Edn) TAXATION): see further Paragraph 341.3 [911] ante. When this clause is inserted in a document the defined terms in { } must be altered to suit those used in the document.

[1966]–[1975]

283

Clause appointing trust fund absolutely contingent on attaining an age[1]

The {Trustees} appoint and direct that they shall from and after the date of this deed stand possessed of the {Trust Fund} in trust for *(beneficiary)* absolutely contingent on his attaining the age of **[18]** years

---

1   This Form assumes an appointment of the entire trust fund in favour of a beneficiary contingently. For capital gains tax purposes a deemed disposal will occur when the beneficiary satisfies the contingency: see *Tomlinson v Glyn's Executor and Trustee Co* [1970] Ch 112, [1970] 1 All ER 381, CA and see Paragraph 341.3 [911] ante. When this clause is inserted in a document the defined terms in { } must be altered to suit those used in the document.

[1976]

284

Appointment terminating discretionary trust in favour of 25 year accumulation and maintenance settlement[1]

THIS DEED OF APPOINTMENT is made the ...... day of .... by *(trustees)* of *(addresses)* ('the Present Trustees')

[1977]

WHEREAS

(1)   This deed is supplemental to a settlement ('the Settlement') dated *(date)* and made between (1) *(settlor)* ('the Settlor') and (2) *(original trustees)*

(2)   The Present Trustees are the present trustees of the Settlement

(3)   By clause *(number)* of the Settlement the trustees for the time being of the Settlement were directed to stand possessed of the Trust Fund (as defined in the Settlement) and all the income of it upon trust for all or any of the Beneficiaries (as defined in the Settlement) at such time or times and if more than one in such shares and with such discretionary or other trusts and such powers of appointment advancement maintenance and other discretionary powers (of whatever nature and whether relating to capital or income) to be vested in any person or persons whether or not the trustees or trustee for the time being of the Settlement and with such gifts over and generally in such manner for the benefit of the Beneficiaries or any one or more of them as such trustees (being at least 2 in number or a trust corporation) should by deed revocable or irrevocable from time to time or at any time during the Trust Period (as defined in the Settlement) appoint

[1978]

(4)   The expression 'the Beneficiaries' as used in the Settlement was defined in clause *(number)* of the Settlement as including (inter alia) all the Settlor's children or remoter issue living at the date of the Settlement or afterwards to be born during the Trust Period and all the wives and husbands widows and widowers of such children or remoter issue of the Settlor

(5)   The class of the Beneficiaries therefore includes the 3 children of the Settlor's son *(son)* namely *(first grandson)* (who was born on *(date)* *(second grandson)* (who was born on *(date)*) and *(third grandson)* (who was born on *(date)*) and all further

children or remoter issue of the Settlor's son born during the Trust Period and
the wives and husbands and widows and widowers of such children or remoter
issue of the Settlor's son

(6)   The power of appointment referred to in recital (3) above and contained in
        clause *(number)* of the Settlement has not yet been exercised

(7)   The Present Trustees wish to make such appointment as is contained below

[1979]

NOW THIS DEED WITNESSES as follows:

1   Definitions

In this deed the following expressions have where the context permits the following
meanings:

1.1   'the Trustees' means the Present Trustees or the survivor of them or other the
        trustees or trustee for the time being of the Settlement

1.2   'the Trust Fund' 'the Accumulation Period' and 'the Trust Period' have the
        same meanings as are given to those expressions respectively in clause *(number)*
        of the Settlement[2]

1.3   'the Primary Class' means the three children of the Settlor's son *(son)* namely
        (first grandchild) (second grandchild) and *(third grandchild)* and all further children
        born to the Settlor's son during the Trust Period (by any marriage)

1.4   'the Wider Class' means:
        1.4.1   the members of the Primary Class
        1.4.2   the wives and husbands and widows and widowers (whether or not
                  remarried) of the members of the Primary Class and
        1.4.3   the children and remoter issue of the members of the Primary Class
                  born during the Trust Period

1.5   'interest in possession' has the same meaning as in the inheritance tax legislation

1.6   'the substituted age' means the age that will be attained (if he or she so long
        lives) by a beneficiary presumptively entitled to the income of the Trust Fund
        or a share of it under the trusts appointed and declared below on his or her
        birthday last preceding the termination of the Accumulation Period if (but only
        if) that age is greater than 18 years and less than 25 years

[1980]

2   Exercise of power

In exercise of the power of appointment conferred on them by clause *(number)* of the
Settlement and of any and every other power enabling them the Present Trustees now
irrevocably appoint and direct that from and after the date of this deed the Trustees shall
stand possessed of the Trust Fund and the income of it upon and with and subject to the
trusts powers and provisions declared and contained below in respect of the same

3   Principal trusts[3]

3.1   The Trust Fund and the income of it shall be held (subject as provided below)
        on such trusts in favour or for the benefit of all or any one or more of the
        members of the Wider Class and with and subject to such powers and provisions
        for their maintenance education advancement and benefit and such powers and

provisions for accumulation of income during the Accumulation Period or any other permissible period (including if thought fit discretionary trusts and powers to be exercised or executed by any person or persons and notwithstanding any delegation of discretion and including powers and provisions of an administrative nature) and in such manner generally as the Trustees by any deeds or deed revocable or irrevocable executed during the Trust Period appoint

[1981]

3.2　Notwithstanding anything contained above:

3.2.1　no appointment in exercise of the power contained in clause 3.1 above shall be made and no such appointment shall be revoked in such a way as to affect any income previously received or receivable by the Trustees (unless it has been validly accumulated) and nor shall any such appointment or revocation affect any capital previously transferred paid or applied to or for the benefit of any person under any applicable power

3.2.2　no such appointment shall be made or revoked so as to terminate or override a subsisting interest in possession in the whole or any part of the Trust Fund unless such interest has subsisted as an interest in possession therein for a period of at least 3 calendar months[4]

3.2.3　if and so long as the conditions specified in the following clause 3.3 below are for the time being satisfied in respect of the Trust Fund or any part of it (below called 'the Restricted Property') no such appointment shall be made or revoked except in such a way that those conditions shall also be satisfied in respect of the Restricted Property after such appointment or revocation[5]

[1982]

3.3　The conditions mentioned in clause 3.2.3 above are that:

3.3.1　one or more individuals (below called 'Minor Beneficiaries') under the age of 25 years at the time of the revocation or appointment in question will (if and so far as they do not become so entitled immediately on the revocation or appointment) become beneficially entitled to (or to an interest in possession in) the Restricted Property on or before attaining a specified age not exceeding 25 years and

3.3.2　no interest in possession subsists in the Restricted Property (unless and except so far as created immediately by the appointment or revocation) and its income is in the meantime to be accumulated so far as not applied for the maintenance education or benefit of one or more of the Minor Beneficiaries

and for this purpose 'individuals' includes unborn persons but the condition in clause 3.3.1 above shall not be satisfied unless after the appointment or revocation in question there is at least one Minor Beneficiary then living

3.4　The Trustees (being at least 2 in number or a trust corporation) may at any time or times during the Trust Period by deed extinguish (or restrict the future exercise of) the power contained in clause 3.1 above

[1983]

4　Trust for Primary Class

Subject to and in default of and until any exercise of the power of appointment contained above the Trust Fund and the income of it shall be held in trust for such members of the Primary Class (born before the first member of the class to do so attains a vested interest hereunder) as shall attain the age of 25 years during the Trust Period or shall be living and under that age on the expiry of the Trust Period and if more than one in equal shares absolutely

5   Powers of maintenance and advancement

The trust declared in clause 4 above shall (subject to the above powers and provisions of this deed) carry the intermediate income and Sections 31 and 32 of the Trustee Act 1925 (as amended by the Family Law Reform Act 1969 by the Trusts of Land and Appointment of Trustees Act 1996 and by the Trustee Act 2000) shall apply to it with the following variations:

5.1   in the case of the said Section 31 the substitution in subsection (1)(i) of the words 'the trustees in their absolute discretion think fit' for 'may in all the circumstances be reasonable' and the omission of the proviso to subsection (1)

5.2   in its application to the share of a beneficiary during the Accumulation Period the said Section 31 shall be deemed to be further modified by the substitution of references in the case of a beneficiary who has a substituted age to attaining the age of 18 years or to infancy of references to attaining the substituted age or as the case may be to the period during which that beneficiary is under the substituted age

5.3   in the case of the said Section 32 the omission of the words 'one-half of ' from proviso (a) to subsection (1)

5.4   the power conferred by the said Section 32 shall not at a time when there is no subsisting interest in possession in the whole or some part of the Trust Fund be exercised so as to apply any capital of the fund for the benefit of a beneficiary in a way which would or might prevent that beneficiary becoming entitled to it (or to an interest in possession in it) on or before attaining the age of 25 years or in such a way that the income of the property might in the meantime be applied otherwise than by being accumulated so far as not used for the maintenance education or benefit of that beneficiary

[1984]

6   Accumulation

Subject to all the trusts powers and provision declared and contained above and so far as not disposed of by the same the income of the Trust Fund shall be accumulated during the Accumulation Period and so that such accumulations shall be added as an accretion to the capital of the Trust Fund as one fund with it for all purposes

7   Continuation of Settlement terms

Subject to all the trusts powers and provisions of this deed affecting the same and if and so far as (for any reason whatsoever) not wholly disposed of by the same the Trust Fund and the income of it shall continue to be held upon and with and subject to the trusts powers and provisions declared and contained in the Settlement

8   Exclusion of apportionment

8.1   All income of the Trust Fund received by or on behalf of the Trustees from and after the date of this deed shall be treated as if it had arisen wholly after such date and the Apportionment Act 1870 shall not be applicable to it

8.2   Furthermore wherever under the trusts appointed and declared above concerning the Trust Fund there is a change in the person or persons beneficially or prospectively beneficially entitled to the income of the Trust Fund or any part of it (whether due to the birth or death of any person or for any other reason whatever) the provisions of the Apportionment Act 1870 shall also not apply

[1985]

9   Administrative provisions

During the subsistence of the trusts powers and provisions appointed declared and contained in this deed the administrative and other powers and provisions contained in clauses *(number)* to *(number)* (inclusive) of the Settlement shall (so far as they are not inconsistent with the trusts powers and provisions in this deed appointed and declared and contained) continue to apply to the Trust Fund and the income of it

IN WITNESS etc

(signatures of the trustees)[6]
(signatures of witnesses)
[1986]

1   For a typical clause in a discretionary trust conferring wide powers of appointment on the trustees, see Form 4 clause 2 [1084] ante. By irrevocably exercising such powers the trustees are in this appointment limiting the beneficiaries to persons falling within the definition of an accumulation and maintenance trust for inheritance tax purposes: see the Inheritance Tax Act 1984 s 71 (42–44 Halsbury's Statutes (4th Edn) TAXATION), Paragraph 127 [316] ante and see vol 40(2) (2001 Reissue) TRUSTS AND SETTLEMENTS Part 11 [6301]. The exercise of this power is not a disposal for capital gains tax purposes. For inheritance tax purposes the termination of the discretionary trust may result in an 'exit charge': see Paragraph 319 [830] et seq ante. For income tax purposes the Income and Corporation Taxes Act 1988 s 686 as amended (42–44 Halsbury's Statutes (4th Edn) TAXATION) provides for liability at the 'rate applicable to trusts' to apply throughout: see Paragraph 348 [959] ante.

2   The perpetuity and accumulation periods are taken from the settlement.

3   Because the beneficiaries are members of the 'wider class' which includes issue of the settlor's children, the requirement of the Inheritance Tax Act 1984 s 71(2)(b)(i) is not satisfied; accordingly, this trust will attract accumulation and maintenance status for only 25 years from the date of the appointment: Inheritance Tax Act 1984 s 71(2)(a).

4   The power to revoke an interest in possession can only be exercised after that interest has subsisted for three months to remove any suggestion that it has no 'reality': see *Hatton v IRC* [1992] STC 140; and compare *Fitzwilliam v IRC* [1993] STC 502, HL.

5   In exercising this power of appointment by clause 2 [1981] above the trustees intend to convert the discretionary trust into a qualifying accumulation and maintenance trust. To satisfy the requirements for the accumulation and maintenance trust, there must be no overriding powers vested in the trustees which could be exercised so as to prevent the accumulation and maintenance conditions from being satisfied. Therefore the power of appointment in clause 3 [1981] above is hedged about with restrictions. Clauses 3.3.1 [1983] and 3.3.2 [1983] above contain the basic requirements to be satisfied if a trust is to qualify as an accumulation and maintenance settlement under the Inheritance Tax Act 1984 s 71(1); these requirements are imported into the exercise of the clause 3 power in cases where prior to the relevant exercise or revocation of the power the relevant part of the fund qualified as an accumulation and maintenance trust. It is not, for example, possible to postpone the entitlement of any beneficiary beyond the age of 25 years by exercising the clause 3 power of appointment. Similarly, the revocation of any appointment is likewise restricted where under the terms of the appointment accumulation and maintenance trusts are in being. By contrast, if under the appointment in question the beneficiary has already become entitled to an interest in possession in that part of the fund (so that it is no longer held on accumulation and maintenance trusts) then the restrictions in clause 3.2.3 [1982] above are inapplicable.

6   As to the statutory requirements for valid execution of a deed see vol 12 (1994 Reissue) DEEDS, AGREEMENTS AND DECLARATIONS.

[1987]

285

Clause revoking prior revocable appointment[1]

In pursuance of the power given to them by the {Appointment} and all other powers (if any) enabling them the {Trustees} wholly revoke the appointment contained in the {Appointment}

1   When this clause is inserted in a document the defined terms in { } must be altered to suit those used in the document.

[1988]

286

Clause revoking prior appointment and making new appointment—power of revocation reserved[1]

0.1   In pursuance of the power given to them by the {Appointment} and all other powers (if any) enabling them the {Trustees} wholly revoke the appointment contained in the {Appointment}

0.2   The {Trustees} appoint and direct that they shall from and after the date of this deed stand possessed of the {Trust Fund} in trust for *(beneficiary)* absolutely contingent on his attaining the age of **[18]** years

0.3   Notwithstanding anything contained above the {Trustees} may at any time or times during the {Trust Period} by any document or documents revoke or vary either wholly or partly the appointment in favour of *(beneficiary)* contained in clause 0.2 above

1   When this clause is inserted in a document the defined terms in { } must be altered to suit those used in the document.

[1989]

287

Clause partially revoking prior appointment and making irrevocable new appointment[1]

0.1   The {Trustees} partially revoke the appointment contained in clause *(number)* of the {Appointment} to the extent only necessary to permit the appointment in clause **[0.2]** below

0.2   In exercise of the power of appointment conferred upon the {Trustees} by clause *(number)* of the {Settlement} and of all other powers (if any) enabling them the {Trustees} irrevocably appoint and direct that the sum of £... shall immediately be raised and paid to *(beneficiary)* out of the {Trust Fund} and shall as from the date of this deed be held upon trust for *(beneficiary)* absolutely

1   When this clause is inserted in a document the defined terms in { } must be altered to suit those used in the document.

[1990]

288

Transfer of property on to the trusts of a new settlement pursuant to an express power[1]

THIS DEED is made the ...... day of ....

BETWEEN:

(1)   *(trustees of existing settlement)* of *(addresses)* ('the Present Trustees') and

(2)   *(trustees of new settlement)* of *(addresses)* ('the New Trustees')

WHEREAS

(1)   This deed is supplemental to:

      (1.1)   a settlement ('the Present Settlement') dated *(date)* and made between (1) *(settlor)* ('the Settlor') and (2) the Present Trustees and

      (1.2)   a settlement ('the New Settlement') dated *(date)* and made between (1) *(the settlor)* and (2) the New Trustees

[1991]

(2)   In this deed the following expressions have where the context permits the following meanings respectively that is to say:

      (2.1)   the expression 'the Trust Fund' 'the Trust Period' and 'the Beneficiaries' shall have the meanings given to them respectively by the Present Settlement

      (2.2)   'the New Settlement Trust Fund' means the trust fund defined in clause *(number)* of the New Settlement

(3)   By clause *(number)* of the Present Settlement the trustees for the time being of such settlement have power (notwithstanding the trusts and provisions declared and contained in clauses *(numbers)* (inclusive) to the Present Settlement) at any time or times during the Trust Period if in their absolute discretion they shall so think fit to pay or transfer any income or capital of the Trust Fund to the trustees of any other trust wherever established or existing under which any one or more of the Beneficiaries is or are interested if the trustees for the time being of the Present Settlement shall in their absolute discretion consider such payment or transfer to be for the benefit of such one or more of the Beneficiaries as is or are interested under such other trust

[1992]

(4)   The above recited power is subject to the proviso contained in clause *(number)* of the Present Settlement that no payment or transfer of income or capital shall be made to the trustees of another trust under such power if the Settlor or any spouse for the time being of the Settlor is interested under such other trust

(5)   The New Settlement is a settlement in favour and for the benefit of a number of persons who are all members of the class of the Beneficiaries under the Present Settlement

(6)   At the date of this deed the Trust Period has not yet expired

(7)   The Trust Fund now includes the investments specified in the schedule ('the Investments')

(8)   Nothing in the New Settlement infringes any rule against perpetuities applicable to the Present Settlement and neither the Settlor nor any spouse for the time being of the Settlor is interested under the trusts of the New Settlement[2]

(9)   The Present Trustees consider that it would be for the benefit of those members of the class of the Beneficiaries under the Present Settlement who are interested under the trusts of the New Settlement for the Investments (but not any other part of the Trust Fund) to be transferred to the New Trustees as the trustees of the New Settlement to be held by them as part of the New Settlement Trust Fund and have determined to exercise the power in that behalf contained in clause *(number)* of the Present Settlement accordingly in the manner appearing below

(10)   The New Trustees have joined in this deed to accept the Investments (subject as is mentioned below) as an addition to the New Settlement Trust Fund upon and with and subject to the trusts powers and provisions of the New Settlement

[1993]

NOW THIS DEED WITNESSES as follows:

1   Transfer of Investments

The Present Trustees as the trustees of the Present Settlement in exercise of the power contained in clause *(number)* of such settlement and of any and every other power them enabling irrevocably resolve determine and direct that the whole of the Investments (but not any other part of the Trust Fund) shall immediately be transferred to the New Trustees as the trustees of the New Settlement to the intent that upon such transfer being made (which has taken place contemporaneously with the execution of this deed) the Investments shall from that time cease to be held upon and with and subject to the trusts powers and provisions of the Present Settlement and shall (with the future income of the sale) for all purposes become subject to the trusts powers and provisions contained in the New Settlement and form part of the New Settlement Trust Fund

2   Acceptance

In exercise of the power in that behalf contained in clause *(number)* of the New Settlement and of any and every other power them enabling the New Trustees accept the Investments as an addition to the New Settlement Trust Fund as one fund with it for all purposes

[1994]

3   Indemnity

It is declared that the transfer of the Investments is subject to the payment out of them of all taxes and duties of a capital nature due or becoming due (whether in the United Kingdom or in any other country) in respect of such assets on their transfer into the names of the New Trustees and the New Trustees (in exercise of the power in that behalf contained in clause *(number)* of the New Settlement) jointly and severally covenant with the Present Trustees to keep the Present Trustees and all other the trustees or trustee for the time being of the Present Settlement indemnified against all such taxes and duties

IN WITNESS etc

SCHEDULE

The Investments

(describe investments)

(signatures of the parties)[3]
(signatures of witnesses)

[1995]

1   This transfer is made pursuant to an express power: for an example of such a power see Form 98 [1474] ante. For capital gains tax purposes there will be a deemed disposal within the Taxation of Chargeable Gains Act 1992 s 71(1) (42–44 Halsbury's Statutes (4th Edn) TAXATION); only in limited circumstances is hold-over relief available. As to capital gains tax in relation to resettlements see Paragraph 342 [919] ante.
2   For an example of an advancement onto new trusts which infringed the perpetuity rule see *Pilkington v IRC* [1964] AC 612, [1962] 3 All ER 622, HL.
3   As to the statutory requirements for valid execution of a deed see vol 12 (1994 Reissue) DEEDS, AGREEMENTS AND DECLARATIONS.

[1996]–[2010]

289

Exercise of express power to transfer or apply property for the benefit of the principal beneficiary under a protective trust[1]

THIS DEED is made the …… day of ……… by *(trustees)* of *(addresses)* ('the Present Trustees')

WHEREAS

(1)   This deed is supplemental to a deed of settlement ('the Settlement') dated *(date)* and made between (1) *(settlor)* and (2) the Present Trustees

[2011]

(2)   It was provided in clause *(number)* of the Settlement that notwithstanding the protective trusts for the benefit of the Principal Beneficiary (as defined in the Settlement) contained in such settlement the trustees for the time being of it might at any time or times during the lifetime of the Principal Beneficiary (inter alia) pay transfer or apply in any manner to or for the benefit of the Principal Beneficiary the whole or any part of the Trust Fund (as defined in clause *(number)* of the Settlement) [discharged from all the trusts powers and provisions of the Settlement][2]

(3)   The sum of cash and the mortgage debts described in the schedule ('the Specified Assets') are amongst the assets comprised in the Trust Fund at the date of this deed

(4)   The Present Trustees consider that the Principal Beneficiary would be benefited if the Specified Assets were applied for his benefit by being appropriated and held by the Present Trustees and their successors on the trusts declared below [to the intent that the Specified Assets remain part of the settlement for capital gains tax purposes][3]

[2012]

NOW THIS DEED WITNESSES as follows:

1   Definitions and interpretation

In this deed the following expressions have where the context permits the following meanings:

1.1   'the Trustees' means the Present Trustees or other the trustees or trustee for the time being of this deed

1.2   'the Advanced Fund' means the Specified Assets all property at any time added to them by way of further settlement accumulation of income capital appreciation or otherwise and all property from time to time representing the same

2   Exercise of express power

2.1   The Present Trustees as the trustees of the Settlement in exercise of the power conferred on them by clause *(number)* of the Settlement and of any and every other power them enabling irrevocably resolve determine and direct that the Advanced Fund shall be and is now applied for the benefit of the Principal Beneficiary by appropriating the same to be held by the Trustees as and from the date of this deed upon the trusts and with and subject to the powers and provisions declared and contained below

2.2   The Advanced Fund is so applied together with (without any apportionment) all accrued or accruing income of such fund received by the Trustees on or after the date of this deed (and so that the provisions of the Apportionment Act 1870 shall not apply)

[2013]

3   Trusts of the Advanced Fund

The Trustees shall pay the income of the Advanced Fund to the Principal Beneficiary during his life and subject to this (and to the power conferred by clause 4 below and any interest appointed under such clause) shall hold the Advanced Fund upon trust (both as to capital and income) for all or such one or more exclusively of the others or other of the children or remoter issue of the Principal Beneficiary at such ages or times and if more than one in such shares and with such provisions for their respective maintenance education and advancement and benefit generally (at the discretion of the Trustees or any other person or persons) as the Principal Beneficiary shall by deed or deeds revocable or irrevocable or by will or codicil appoint and in default of and subject to any and every such appointment upon trust for all or any the children or child of the Principal Beneficiary who attain the age of 21 years or marry and if more than one in equal shares PROVIDED that no child of the Principal Beneficiary who or whose issue shall take any part of the Advanced Fund under an appointment by virtue of the power last above conferred shall in default of appointment to the contrary be entitled to any share of the unappointed part of the Advanced Fund without bringing the share or shares appointed to him or her or to his or her issue into hotchpot and accounting for the same accordingly

4   Interest of a surviving spouse

The Principal Beneficiary shall have power to appoint by will or codicil to or for the benefit of any spouse of the Principal Beneficiary who may survive the Principal Beneficiary an interest for the life of such spouse or any less period in the whole or any part of the income of the Advanced Fund and any such appointment may (due regarding being had to the law concerning remoteness) be made upon protective trusts or otherwise for the benefit of such spouse and subject to any conditions which the Principal Beneficiary may think proper

[2014]

5   Default trusts

Subject to the trusts powers and provisions above and to the powers vested in the Trustees by this deed or by law the Advanced Fund and the income of such fund (if and so far as not wholly disposed of as mentioned above) shall be held in trust for the Principal Beneficiary's brother *(brother)* if he shall be living at the death of the Principal Beneficiary absolutely and if such brother shall not then be living then in trust for all or any the children or child of *(brother)* living at the death of the Principal Beneficiary who attain the age of 21 years or marry and if more than one in equal shares absolutely [and subject thereto on the trusts of the settlement insofar as the same are then subsisting and capable of taking effect][4]

6   Power to advance capital

6.1   Notwithstanding all or any of the trusts contained in this deed the Trustees (being at least 2 in number or a trust corporation) shall be at liberty if in their absolute discretion they think fit at any time or times during the life of the Principal Beneficiary to transfer pay or apply in any manner to or for the benefit of the Principal Beneficiary the whole or any part or parts of the capital of the Advanced Fund discharged from all the trusts powers and provisions of this deed

6.2   The Trustees (being at least 2 in number or a trust corporation) may at any time or times with the consent in writing of the Principal Beneficiary by deed or deeds extinguish (or restrict the exercise of) the above power or powers

6.3   In deciding whether or not to exercise the power contained in clause 6.1 above the Trustees shall have regard primarily to the interests of the Principal Beneficiary and need not be deterred from exercising such power by reason only of the fact that the interests of the person entitled following the death of the Principal Beneficiary under the trusts above declared will be diminished or defeated

[2015]

7   Powers of maintenance and advancement

The Trustee Act 1925 Sections 31 and 32 (as amended by the Family Law Reform Act 1969 by the Trusts of Land and Appointment of Trustees Act 1996 and by the Trustee Act 2000) (relating to maintenance accumulation and advancement) shall apply to the trusts declared in default of appointment in clause 3 above (subject to all subsisting prior interests) and shall so apply subject to the following modifications:

7.1   in the case of the said Section 31 the substitution in subsection (1)(i) of the words 'the trustees in their absolute discretion think fit' for the words 'may in all the circumstances be reasonable' and the omission of the proviso to subsection (1)

7.2   in the case of the said Section 32 the omission of the words 'one-half of' from proviso (a) to subsection (1)

[7.3   if capital is applied in exercise of the power conferred by Section 32 for the benefit of any person who has not attained the age of 25 years in such a way that the capital so applied is to remain in trust the trusts shall be such that:
　　7.3.1   that person will become entitled to (or to an interest in possession in) the capital so applied on or before attaining that age
　　7.3.2   the income is in the meantime to be accumulated so far as not applied for his maintenance education or benefit]

[2016]

8   Apportionment

Where under the trusts for the time being affecting the Advanced Fund there is a change in the person or persons beneficially or prospectively beneficially entitled to the income of the Advanced Fund or any part of it (whether due to the death or birth of any person or for any other reason whatsoever) no apportionment shall be made of income accrued or accruing or of outgoings expended which relate to a period partly before and partly after such death birth or other event causing such change and any such item of income or of expenditure shall be treated as having accrued or having become a proper liability wholly after such death birth or other event as the case may be

## 9	Administrative powers

The administrative and other powers and provisions contained in clauses *(numbers)* of the Settlement respectively shall continue to apply to the Advanced Fund so far as the same are consistent with the beneficial trusts declared above but with the substitution for references to 'the Settlor' and 'the Trust Fund' of references to 'the Principal Beneficiary' and 'the Advanced Fund' wherever the former references occur in such clauses and sub-clauses of the Settlement respectively

[2017]

## 10	Power to pay taxes etc

The Trustees shall (in addition to all other powers vested in the Trustees by this deed or by law) have power to settle and pay out of the Advanced Fund all legal and other costs of and incidental to the preparation and execution of this deed

## 11	Clause headings

The headings to the clauses of this deed are for the purposes of information only and are not part of and shall not be used in the construction of this deed or any part of it

IN WITNESS etc

SCHEDULE

The Specified Assets

(describe cash and mortgage debts)

(signatures of the trustees)[5]
(signatures of witnesses)
[2018]

1	On the exercise of the power of advancement to resettle property see *Pilkington v IRC* [1964] AC 612, [1962] 3 All ER 622, HL. As to capital gains tax in relation to the exercise of powers of advancement, appointment etc see further Paragraph 342 [919] ante. For protective trusts see vol 40(2) (2001 Reissue) TRUSTS AND SETTLEMENTS Part 12 [6901]. In this case the express power given in the settlement is being exercised to remove property from the protective trusts, which gives the principal beneficiary a full life interest with power to appoint a similar interest to a surviving spouse, and with power to appoint capital and income amongst his children.
2	A power to transfer or apply property may be exercised to create a new settlement or within the framework of the existing trusts. A recital that the assets remain comprised in the settlement and the express inclusion of default trusts whereby the assets remain held on the trusts of the settlement, point to the property remaining comprised in that settlement. By contrast, a recital that the property is discharged from those trusts points to the creation of a new settlement. The draftsman should therefore delete or incorporate the wording in square brackets as appropriate.
3	See note 2 above.
4	See note 2 above.
5	As to the statutory requirements for valid execution of a deed see vol 12 (1994 Reissue) DEEDS, AGREEMENTS AND DECLARATIONS.

[2019]

290

Exercise of power of advancement under the Trustee Act 1925 Section 32 to effect a resettlement[1]

THIS DEED is made the ...... day of .... by *(trustees)* of *(addresses)* ('the Present Trustees')

WHEREAS

(1)   This deed is supplemental to a deed of settlement ('the Settlement') dated *(date)* and made between (1) *(settlor)* and (2) *(trustees)*

[2020]

(2)   By the terms of the Settlement the trustees for the time being of the Settlement were directed to hold the Trust Fund (as defined in the Settlement) upon trust to divide the same into four equal parts and inter alia to hold one such equal part (defined in the Settlement as and in this deed called the 'Second Daughters Fund') upon the trusts and with and subject to the powers and conditions declared and contained concerning the Second Daughter's Fund[2]

(3)   The Present Trustees are the trustees for the time being of the Settlement as regards the trusts relating to the Second Daughter's Fund

(4)   The Second Daughter's Fund is held by the Present Trustees in accordance with the terms of the Settlement upon trust for *(beneficiary)* if [he] shall attain the age of 21 years or marry

(5)   The investments specified in the schedule ('the Investments') are among the assets for the time being comprised in the Second Daughter's Fund

(6)   The Present Trustees consider that it would be to the material benefit of *(beneficiary)* that the Investments should be set aside and held by the Present Trustees and their successors on the trusts declared below which *(beneficiary)* has requested them to do

(7)   The Present Trustees have accordingly determined to exercise the power of advancement contained in the Trustee Act 1925 Section 32 (as amended by the Trusts of Land and Appointment of Trustees Act 1996) for the benefit of *(beneficiary)* in the manner appearing below (being satisfied that the Investments do not exceed in value one half of the Second Daughter's Fund[3])

[2021]

NOW THIS DEED WITNESSES as follows:

1   Definitions and interpretation

In this deed the following expressions have where the context permits the following meanings:

1.1   'the Trustees' means the Present Trustees or other the trustees or trustee for the time being of this deed

1.2   'the Advanced Fund' means the Investments all property at any time added to them by way of further settlement accumulation of income capital appreciation or otherwise and all property from time to time representing the same

1.3   'the Vesting Date' means *(date)*

2 Exercise of power of advancement

The Present Trustees as the trustees of the Settlement in exercise of the power contained in the Trustee Act 1925 Section 32 and of any and every other power them enabling for the benefit of *(beneficiary)* irrevocably direct and declare that the Advanced Fund shall from the date of this deed be held by the Trustees as a separate fund upon the trusts and with and subject to the powers and provisions declared and contained below and so that all accrued or accruing income of such fund received by the Trustees on or after the date of this deed shall be dealt with as if it had accrued after such date (and so that the provisions of the Apportionment Act 1870 shall not apply)

[2022]

3 Trusts of the Advanced Fund

The Trustees shall stand possessed of the Advanced Fund upon the following trusts that is to say:

3.1 upon trust as to capital and income including intermediate income for *(beneficiary)* if **[he]** shall be living at the Vesting Date absolutely and subject to this for such of *(beneficiary)*'s children as shall attain the age of 21 years before the Vesting Date or be living at the Vesting Date and if more than one in equal shares absolutely

3.2 subject to clause 3.1 upon trust for *(default beneficiary)* absolutely

4 Powers of maintenance and advancement

The trusts contained in clause 3 above shall carry the intermediate income and the statutory powers of maintenance accumulation and advancement contained in the Trustee Act 1925 Sections 31 and 32 (as amended by the Family Law Reform Act 1969 by the Trusts of Land and Appointment of Trustees Act 1996 and by the Trustee Act 2000) shall apply to this settlement but with the following modifications:

4.1 in the case of the said Section 31 the substitution in subsection (1)(i) of the words 'the trustees in their absolute discretion think fit' for the words 'may in all circumstances be reasonable' and the omission of the proviso to subsection (1) and

4.2 in the case of the said Section 32 the omission of the words 'one-half of' from proviso (a) to subsection (1) and the insertion of a further proviso to the effect that in any case where the said statutory power of advancement contained in the said Section is exercised so as to apply capital money for the advancement or benefit of a person who immediately prior to such exercise does not have an interest in possession in the capital money in question then such capital money must be vested either absolutely or for an interest in possession in the person in question immediately upon such application being made or (if such person is then under the age of 25 years) before he or she shall have attained the age of 25 years and in such manner that conditions (a) and (b) of the Inheritance Tax Act 1984 Section 71(1) shall be satisfied

[2023]

5 Apportionment

Where under the trusts for the time being affecting the Advanced Fund there is a change in the person or persons beneficially or prospectively beneficially entitled to the income of the Advanced Fund or any part of it (whether due to the death or birth of any person or for any other reason whatsoever) no apportionment shall be made of income accrued or accruing or of outgoings expended which relate to a period partly before and partly after such death birth or other event causing such change and any such item of income or of expenditure shall be treated as having accrued or having become a proper liability wholly after such death birth or other event as the case may be

6   Investment powers

(continue with required investment powers)[4]

7   Appropriation

The Trustees shall have power from time to time to set such a value upon any investments or other property forming part of the Advanced Fund as the Trustees shall think fit and to appropriate if they shall think fit any such investments or property at such value in or towards the satisfaction of any share or interest under the trusts affecting the same

[2024]

8   Trustee indemnity

8.1   In the professed execution of the trusts and powers of this deed or of any assurance of immovable property upon trust such that the property or the net proceeds of sale[5] are to be held on the trusts of this deed none of the Trustees (being an individual) shall be liable for any loss arising by reason of any improper investment made in good faith or the retention of any improper investment or any failure to see to the insurance of or preservation of any chattels or the making or revising of any inventory of them or for the negligence or fraud of any agent employed by him or by any other of the Trustees (although the employment of such agent was not strictly necessary or expedient) or by reason of any other matter or thing whatever except wilful and individual fraud or wrongdoing on the part of that one of the Trustees who is sought to be made liable

8.2   The Trustees shall not be bound or required to interfere in the management or conduct of the affairs or business of any company in respect of which the Trustees shall hold or control the whole or a majority or any part of the shares carrying the control of the company or other the voting rights of the company and so long as there shall be no notice of any act of dishonesty or misappropriation of money on the part of the directors having the management of such company the Trustees shall be at liberty to leave the conduct of its business (including the payment or non-payment of dividends) wholly to such directors

[2025]

9   Trustee's charges and remuneration

9.1   Any of the Trustees who shall be an individual engaged in any profession or business either alone or in partnership shall be entitled to charge and be paid and to retain all professional or other proper charges for any business done or time spent or services rendered by him or his firm in connection with the trusts powers and provisions of this deed or of any assurance of immovable property upon trust such that the property or the net proceeds of sale[6] are to be held on the trusts of this deed and shall also be entitled to retain any share of brokerage or commission paid to him or his firm by any broker agent or insurance office in connection with any acquisition of or dealing with any investments or property or the effecting or payment of any premium on any policy of insurance subject or intended to become subject to the trusts of this deed or any such assurance

9.2   None of the Trustees holding any directorship or other office or employment or retainer in relation to any company all or any of whose shares stock or securities shall at any time be subject to any trusts of this deed shall be accountable for any remuneration received in connection with such directorship office employment or retainer

[2026]

10   Trust corporation

10.1   A corporation (whether or not a trust corporation) may at any time be appointed to be one of the Trustees on such reasonable terms as to remuneration and charging and otherwise however as shall be agreed at the time when the appointment is made between the person or persons making the appointment on the one hand and the corporation on the other

10.2   The provisions of the Trustee Act 1925 Section 37 in their application to this deed shall be varied so that for each reference to 'a trust corporation' there shall be substituted a reference to 'a corporation (whether or not a trust corporation)'

11   Clause headings

The headings to the clauses of this deed are for the purposes of information only and are not part of and shall not be used in the construction of this deed or any part of it

IN WITNESS etc

SCHEDULE

The Investments

(describe investments)

(signatures of the trustees)[7]
(signatures of witnesses)
[2027]

1   On the exercise of the power of advancement to make a 'settled advance' see *Pilkington v IRC* [1964] AC 612, [1962] 3 All ER 622, HL. As to capital gains tax in relation to resettlements see further Paragraph 342 [919] ante.

2   The relevant beneficiary is contingently absolutely entitled to the Second Daughter's Fund: there is no prior interest whose consent is required.

3   See the Trustee Act 1925 s 32(1)(a) (48 Halsbury's Statutes (4th Edn) TRUSTS AND SETTLEMENTS); the one-half restriction is often expressly removed in trust deeds.

4   For investment clauses for use in trusts and settlements see Form 124 [1543] et seq ante. For an example of an express power of investment see Form 4 schedule paragraph 1 [1092] ante.

5   These words provide for the possibility of land being acquired by the trustees and held either on a trust for sale or a simple trust of land. In order to keep the beneficial trusts off the title there is a separate trust of the conveyance or transfer.

6   See note 5 above.

7   As to the statutory requirements for valid execution of a deed see vol 12 (1994 Reissue) DEEDS, AGREEMENTS AND DECLARATIONS.

[2028]

291

Clause stating that the power has been exercised revocably[1]

The {Appointer} declares that it shall be lawful for [him] at any time or times in the future by deed or deeds executed during the {Trust Period} wholly or partly to revoke or vary the appointment contained in clause *(specify)* above

1   When this clause is inserted in a document the defined terms in { } must be altered to suit those used in the document.

[2029]–[2070]

F: NOTICES

292

Notice by one joint tenant to other or others severing joint tenancy in equity under the Law of Property Act 1925 Section 36(2)[1]

To *(joint tenants)* of *(addresses)*.

I, the undersigned *(joint tenant)* of *(address)*, give you notice of my desire to sever as from this day the joint tenancy in equity of and in the property described in the schedule ('the Property') now held by you and me as joint tenants both at law and in equity so that the Property shall from the date of this notice belong [to you and me as tenants in common in equal shares *or (specify)*].

Dated *(date)*

SCHEDULE
(describe the Property)

(signature of joint tenant giving the notice)

. . . .

Received a notice of which the above is a duplicate

Dated *(date)*[2]

(signature of joint tenant receiving the notice)
[2071]

1   For the power conferred by the Law of Property Act 1925 s 36(2) as amended by the Law of Property (Amendment) Act 1926 s 7, Schedule and by the Trusts of Land and Appointment of Trustees Act 1996 s 5(1), Sch 2 para 4 (37 Halsbury's Statutes (4th Edn) REAL PROPERTY) to sever a joint tenancy in land by notice, and as to the advisability of indorsing a memorandum of severance on the assurance by which the property was vested in the joint tenants, see Form 25 notes 1 [1221] and 3 [1222] ante. In view of the Law of Property (Joint Tenants) Act 1964 s 1(1) proviso (a) (37 Halsbury's Statutes (4th Edn) REAL PROPERTY), it is thought that the date of severance should appear on the notice. It is also desirable that the size of the shares should be specified: cf *Radziej (otherwise Sierkowska) v Radziej* [1967] 1 All ER 944, [1967] 1 WLR 659; affd [1968] 3 All ER 624, [1968] 1 WLR 1928, CA.
      In the case of registered land, application must be made to enter a restriction on the register pursuant to the Land Registration Rules 1925, SR & O 1925/1093 rr 213, 236 (both substituted by SI 1996/2975), Sch 2 Form 62 (as substituted by SI 1989/801 and amended by SI 1996/2975 and SI 1997/3037).

       The regulations respecting the service, etc, of notices which are contained in the Law of Property Act 1925 s 196 apply to the giving of notice under the Law of Property Act 1925 s 36(2): see *Re 88 Berkeley Road, London NW9, Rickwood v Turnsek* [1971] Ch 648, [1971] 1 All ER 254 where, by virtue of the Law of Property Act 1925 s 196(4), a notice contained in a properly addressed prepaid letter sent by recorded delivery was held to have been sufficiently served although not received by the addressee.

2   This receipt should be added to a duplicate of the notice and, after signature, the duplicate should be retained by the joint tenant giving notice.

[2072]

293

Notice by joint tenants of full age, in whom legal estate is vested, to minor joint tenant in equity severing equitable joint tenancy[1]

To *(minor joint tenant)* of *(address)* a minor.

We, the undersigned *(joint tenants)* of *(addresses)*, give you notice that each of us wishes to sever as from this day the joint tenancy in equity of and in the property described in the schedule ('the Property') which is now vested in us as trustees upon trust for ourselves and you as joint tenants so that the Property shall from the date of this notice belong to [each of us and to you in equal shares as tenants in common *or (specify)*].

Dated *(date)*

SCHEDULE
(describe the Property)

(signatures of joint tenants giving the notice)

. . . .

Received a notice of which the above is a duplicate

Dated *(date)*

(signature of guardian of the minor joint tenant)
[Father of the above named *(minor joint tenant)* or
(describe other capacity in which he is such guardian)]

[2073]

1   The Law of Property Act 1925 s 36(2) as amended by the Law of Property (Amendment) Act 1926 s 7, Schedule and by the Trusts of Land and Appointment of Trustees Act 1996 s 5(1), Sch 2 para 4 (37 Halsbury's Statutes (4th Edn) REAL PROPERTY) makes no exception for a case where a joint tenant is a minor and it is, therefore, apprehended that severance by notice is possible where one joint tenant is a minor. The notice should be addressed to the minor and handed to his guardian. This will ensure as far as possible that in due course it will come to the knowledge of the minor when he attains full age.

     In view of the Law of Property (Joint Tenants) Act 1964 s 1(1) proviso (a) (37 Halsbury's Statutes (4th Edn) REAL PROPERTY), it is thought that the date of severance should appear on the notice. It is also desirable that the size of the shares should be specified: cf *Radziej (otherwise Sierkowska) v Radziej* [1967] 1 All ER 944, [1967] 1 WLR 659; affd [1968] 3 All ER 624, [1968] 1 WLR 1928, CA. As to the regulations respecting the service of notices, see Form 292 note 1 [2072] ante.

[2074]

294

Notice to trustees holding upon the statutory trusts applicable to property held in undivided shares of assignment of beneficial interest of tenant in common[1]

To *(trustees)* of *(addresses)*.

I, the undersigned *(assignee)* of *(address)*, give you notice that by an assignment dated *(date)* and made between (1) *(assignor)* ('the Assignor') and (2) myself the *(specify)* share of the Assignor in *(describe property)* the entirety of which you hold as trustees upon the statutory trusts was assigned to me absolutely.

Dated *(date)*

(signature of assignee)

. . . .

We acknowledge to have received a notice of which the above is a duplicate

Dated *(date)*

(signatures of trustees)
[2075]

---

1   Land to which persons are beneficially entitled in possession as tenants in common is, unless it is held upon express trust for sale, held upon a statutory trust of land: see the Law of Property Act 1925 s 34 as amended by the Trusts of Land and Appointment of Trustees Act 1996 ss 5, 25(2), Sch 2 para 3, Sch 4 (37 Halsbury's Statutes (4th Edn) REAL PROPERTY). As to the persons to whom notice should be given, the custody and production of notices and indorsement in lieu of notice, see the Law of Property Act 1925 s 137 as amended by the Trusts of Land and Appointment of Trustees Act 1996 s 25(1), Sch 3 para 4(15). As to the regulations respecting the service of notices, see Form 292 note 1 [2072] ante.

[2076]

295

Notice to trustees by purchaser or assignee of reversionary interest

To: *(trustees)* of *(addresses)* the trustees of a settlement dated *(date)* and made between (1) *(settlor)* and (2) *(original trustees)*.

I, the undersigned *(assignee)* of *(address)*, give you notice that by a deed dated *(date)* and made between (1) *(assignor)* ('the Assignor') and (2) myself the Assignor assigned to me [by way of gift *or* for the consideration stated in such assignment] absolutely all that the [one half *or* *(as the case may be)*] share to which the Assignor was entitled in reversion expectant upon the death of *(life tenant)* in the funds subject to the trusts of the above settlement.

Dated: *(date)*

(signatures of the trustees)

. . . .

I acknowledge receipt of notice of which the above is a duplicate.

Dated: *(date)*

(signatures of the trustees)
[2077]

296
Notice to trustees of appointment under special or general power[1]

To: *(trustees)* of *(addresses)* the trustees of a settlement dated *(date)* and made between (1) *(settlor)* and (2) *(original trustees)*.

I, the undersigned *(appointor)* of *(address)*, give you notice that by a deed dated *(date)* and made by me a copy of which is annexed to this notice, I exercised irrevocably the power of appointment conferred on me by clause *(number)* of the above settlement.

Dated: *(date)*

(signature of appointor)

. . . .

I acknowledge receipt of notice of which the above is a duplicate.

Dated: *(date)*

(signature of recipient)

1   For a detailed discussion of powers of appointment see vol 31 (1999 Reissue) POWERS OF APPOINTMENT Paragraph 1 [3001] et seq. As to the regulations respecting the service of notices, see Form 292 note 1 [2072] ante.

[2078]

297
Request that a life assurance policy be issued to the applicant as trustee[1]

WHEREAS *(applicant)* of *(address)* ('the Settlor') has made application to *(name and address of life office)* ('the Company') to effect the policy of assurance ('the Policy') to be issued by the Company namely:

Date of application	Nature of assurance	Life or lives assured

[2079]

The Settlor requests and authorises the Company to issue the Policy to the Settlor as trustee upon the trusts expressed below:

1   The trustee or trustees for the time being ('the Trustee') shall hold the Policy and the full benefit of it and all money which may become payable under it and all assets which may from time to time represent the Policy ('the Trust Fund') and all income of it upon trust for such of the settlor's children as shall attain 21 years and if more than one in equal shares

2   The power of appointing new or additional trustees is vested in the Settlor while living

3   The Settlor shall not have any right by lien or otherwise to reimbursement of any sum paid or provided as premium on the Policy [and the Trust Fund shall at all times be held to the exclusion of the Settlor and of any benefit to the Settlor by contract or otherwise]

[2080]

4   The Trustee shall have the following powers in addition to all relevant powers conferred by law:

    4.1   to exercise any power election or option available under the terms and conditions of the Policy or otherwise as if the Trustee was the absolute beneficial owner of the Policy

    4.2   to invest the Trust Fund in income producing or non-income producing assets including policies of assurance as if the Trustee was the absolute beneficial owner of it and to make loans with or without interest to beneficiaries or to persons accountable for payment of tax on property in which such beneficiaries may have a beneficial interest PROVIDED that this power shall not be exercised except in conformity with the beneficial trusts powers and provisions for the time being governing the Trust Fund (or the part of it from which such loan is to be made) and the income of it[2]

[2081]

5   Unless otherwise directed by the trusts expressed above the Trustee may:

    5.1   apply for the maintenance education or benefit of any beneficiary who has not attained the age of 18 years all or part of the income of the share of the Trust Fund to which that beneficiary is absolutely contingently or defeasibly entitled as the Trustee may think fit and subject to this the Trustee shall accumulate such income or the remainder at compound interest by investing the same and the resulting income in any of the investments now authorised and adding such accumulation to the capital of such share

    5.2   advance freed and discharged from the above trusts the whole or such part as the Trustee may think fit of the capital of any beneficiary's presumptive or defeasible share in the Trust Fund for the benefit of that beneficiary in such manner in all respects as the Trustee in his discretion shall think fit and

    5.3   accept as a good and sufficient discharge a receipt given by the parent or guardian of a minor beneficiary to whom or for whose benefit any payment of income or capital is made

[2082]

6   Any Trustee (other than the Settlor or a spouse of the Settlor) being a person engaged in any profession business or trade shall be entitled to be paid all usual professional business or trade charges for business transacted time expended and work done by him or by any employee or partner of his in connection with the above trusts [including acts which a trustee not being in any profession business or trade could have done personally][3] and a trust corporation may be appointed as trustee upon terms and conditions as published or as agreed with the Settlor or Trustee as at the date of appointment

Dated: *(date)*

(signature of settlor)

---

1   As to stamp duty see Information Binder: Stamp Duties [1] Table of Duties (Declaration of trust).
2   For the investment powers of trustees generally pursuant to the Trustee Act 2000 (48 Halsbury's Statutes (4th Edn) TRUSTS AND SETTLEMENTS) see Paragraph 241 [591] ante.
3   The words in square brackets are no longer necessary as a result of the Trustee Act 2000 s 28(2).

[2083]

298

Notice of assignment of insurance policy on the creation of a life insurance trust[1]

To *(insurance company)*

We *(solicitors)* of *(address)* as solicitors for *(assignor)* now give you notice that by a deed of assignment and declaration of trust dated *(date)* and made between (1) *(assignor)* ('the Assignor') and (2) *(trustees)* ('the Trustees') the Assignor assigned to the Trustees the benefit of the policy of insurance described in the schedule below and all money assured by or to become payable under or by virtue of it and all benefits and advantages of it to be held by the Trustees upon the trusts and with and subject to the powers and provisions contained in the assignment

Dated *(date)*

SCHEDULE

Issuing Society	Policy Number	Sum Assured	Annual Premium

(signature of solicitors)

1   For a life insurance settlement see Form 6 [1120] ante.

[2084]

299

Capital gains tax hold–over relief on the creation of a trust or on the termination of a trust[1]

HELP SHEET *IR295*

For the Capital Gains Pages

Claim for hold-over relief - Sections 165 and 260 TCGA 1992

Transferor		Transferee	
Name		Name	
Address		Address	
Inland Revenue office		Inland Revenue office	
Tax reference		Tax reference	

Except in case of a gift in settlement, the claim must be made by both transferor and transferee. If the transferor or transferee has no Inland Revenue office or reference please explain why.

We/I hereby claim relief under Section 165 / Section 260 TCGA 1992 in respect of the transfer of the asset specified below. The particulars given in this claim are correctly stated to the best of my/our information and belief.

Description of asset and date of disposal

√ one box

The gain held over is £ ___   A calculation is attached   ☐

We apply for deferment of valuations and have completed the second page of the claim form.   ☐

We qualify for relief because

√ one box

- the asset is used for the business of ___   ☐
  Please insert name of person

- the asset consists of unlisted shares or securities of a trading company or holding company of a trading group   ☐

- the asset is agricultural land   ☐

- the asset consists of listed shares or securities of the transferor's personal company or, where trustees are the transferors, a company in which they had 25% of the voting rights   ☐

- the disposal was a chargeable transfer, but not a Potentially Exempt Transfer, for Inheritance Tax purposes   ☐

- the disposal was exempt from Inheritance Tax under IHTA Section ___   ☐
  Please insert Section number

Signed ___   Signed ___

Date ___ / ___ / ___   Date ___ / ___ / ___

[2085]

HELP SHEET IR295

For the Capital Gains Pages

Request for valuations to be deferred

The disposal meets the conditions of Inland Revenue Statement of Practice SP8/92. We jointly request that SP8/92 be applied, so that formal agreement of values can be deferred. We accept the terms upon which SP8/92 applies. We are satisfied that the value of the asset at the date of transfer is such that there would be a chargeable gain but for the claim.

Transferor

Signed

Date   /   /

Transferee

Signed

Date   /   /

The details required are as follows; where estimated figures are used please use the codes at the bottom of the form.

If there is insufficient space or you find it more convenient, please give the details on a separate sheet. You can give the information in the form of a calculation if you prefer.

1 Date of acquisition and cost   /   /

2 Date and cost of additional allowable expenditure   /   /   £

3 Value at 31 March 1982 if relevant   £

4 Value of asset at date of transfer   £

5 Details of any relevant bonus issues or reorganisations if asset consists of shares or securities

6 If the disposal is a part disposal, details of and value of part retained

Notes

- The disposal of part of a shareholding may be a part disposal. If there is an entry in box 6, the figures at boxes 1 to 3 are those for the whole asset, not just the part disposed of.

- Where the figures given are values and not actual costs, please write whichever of the following letters is appropriate in the box, after the figures:

  A: Value agreed by Inland Revenue

  V: Valuation by professional valuer but not agreed by Inland Revenue

  E: Our estimate of the value.

- Acceptance of the claim does not bind the Inland Revenue to accepting the values shown. The claimants are not bound by the values shown.

1   This Form is taken from Inland Revenue Help Sheet IR295: *Relief for Gifts and Similar Transactions*. A hold-over election is available on the creation of a settlement provided that either the property settled comprises business assets, or the creation of the trust is a chargeable transfer for inheritance tax purposes (eg if trust is in discretionary form): see the Taxation of Chargeable Gains Act 1992 ss 165, 260 as amended (42-44 Halsbury's Statutes (4th Edn) TAXATION). The election is made by the settlor alone as transferor. It should be noted that the Taxation of Chargeable Gains Act 1992 s 260 provides for other limited cases of hold-over.

A hold-over election is also available on the termination (in whole or in part) of a trust comprising business assets, or of a discretionary trust, and when a beneficiary becomes absolutely entitled to property comprised in an accumulation and maintenance trust: see the Taxation of Chargeable Gains Act 1992 ss 165, 260 as amended. The election is made by the trustees as transferors and the Inland Revenue consider that the beneficiaries must also join in the election as transferees (this despite the deemed disposal that occurs under the Taxation of Chargeable Gains Act 1992 s 71). In most cases, accumulation and maintenance trusts are replaced by interest in possession trusts so that (unless the property settled comprises business assets) capital gains tax hold-over relief is not available if that beneficiary subsequently becomes absolutely entitled to the property. There may, therefore, be cases where it is possible and desirable to convert the interest in possession trust back into accumulation and maintenance form in order to take advantage of hold-over relief: see vol 40(2) (2001 Reissue) TRUSTS AND SETTLEMENTS Part 11 [6301].

An election in similar form is required when property is resettled: both old and new trustees (often the same persons) should elect. On the ending of an interest in possession trust any chargeable gain that arises may only be held over if (or to the extent that) the property settled comprises business assets (for the occasions when property is resettled, see Paragraph 342 [919] ante).

No specific time period is laid down for the making of hold-over elections: accordingly, the provisions of the Taxes Management Act 1970 s 43(1) as amended by the Finance Act 1994 Sch 19 para 14 (42-44 Halsbury's Statutes (4th Edn) TAXATION) apply and prescribe a five-year period running from 31 January following the tax year in which the disposal occurred. For the option to defer the calculation of held-over gain see Inland Revenue Statement of Practice SP8/92. The making of a hold-over election results in a loss of the transferor's accrued taper relief on the asset(s) transferred.

[2087]–[2100]

G: DISENTAILING ASSURANCES

300

Deed of disentail by tenant in tail in possession[1]

THIS DISENTAILING DEED is made the …… day of ………

BETWEEN:

(1)   *(tenant in tail)* of *(address)* ('the Grantor') and

(2)   *(trustees)* of *(addresses)* ('the Trustees')

WHEREAS

(1)   This deed is supplemental to the settlement and other documents and events specified in the schedule ('the Settlement')

(2)   Under the subsisting limitations or trusts of the Settlement the Grantor is tenant in tail [male] in possession of the Settled Property as defined in the Settlement[2]

(3)   The Grantor wishes to bar absolutely the entail in the Settled Property

[2101]

NOW THIS DEED WITNESSES as follows:

Conveyance

The Grantor conveys assigns and disposes of to the Trustees all the Settled Property to which the Grantor is entitled for such entailed interest in possession TO HOLD the same to the Trustees in fee simple or absolutely according to the nature of the property discharged from all entailed interests of the Grantor in it under the terms of the Settlement and from all estates rights interests and powers to take effect after the determination or in defeasance of such entailed interests but subject to any relevant existing charges and so discharged in trust for the Grantor in fee simple and absolutely according to the nature of the property[3]

IN WITNESS etc

SCHEDULE

The Settlement

(insert details of the Settlement)

(signatures of the parties)[4]
(signatures of witnesses)
[2102]

1   As to stamp duty see the Information Binder: Stamp Duties [1]: Table of Duties: Conveyance or transfer. This Form can only be used in respect of an entailed interest created by an instrument coming into force before 1 January 1997. Any purported grant of an entailed interest by an instrument coming into operation after that date operates instead to create an absolute interest: Trusts of Land and Appointment of Trustees Act 1996 s 2, Sch 1 para 5 (37 Halsbury's Statutes (4th Edn) REAL PROPERTY). As to the barring of entail interests generally see Paragraph 277 [691] et seq ante.
        On a disentailment by a tenant in tail in possession the tenant in tail becomes absolutely entitled as against the trustees of the property and there is a deemed disposal and immediate reacquisition at market value for capital gains tax purposes: see the Taxation of Chargeable Gains Act 1992 s 71(1) (42–44 Halsbury's Statutes (4th Edn) TAXATION) and see Paragraph 345.1 [911] ante. For inheritance tax purposes, a disentail by a tenant in possession is not chargeable: Inheritance Tax Act 1984 ss 51(1), 53(2) (42–44 Halsbury's Statutes (4th Edn) TAXATION).
2   There is no advantage in specifying the settled property in detail since the deed of disentail is not a document forming part of the legal title as it only deals with equitable interest.
3   The effect of this deed is to convey the Grantor's entailed (ie equitable) interest to the Trustees. The Trustees will then convey the resulting equitable fee simple or absolute interest (depending on the nature of the property) usually to the Grantor. The Trustees are usually the trustees of the settlement for the purposes of the Settled Land Act 1925 (48 Halsbury's Statutes (4th Edn) TRUSTS AND SETTLEMENTS). If the property is land and it is vested in the Grantor as tenant for life, he should not execute a deed in his own favour but appoint trustees. The reconveyance to the Grantor will be by assent if the settlement was made by will, or by conveyance if inter vivos. The Grantor will then hold on fee simple or absolutely (depending on the nature of the property) free from any trustee interest. If the property is registered land, the legal estate will usually be vested in the Grantor as tenant for life under the Settled Land Act 1925. A Form 9 restriction, under the Land Registration Rules 1925, SR & O 1925/1093 r 58, Sch 2 as amended by SI 1996/2975 and SI 1999/2097, will have been registered. On the conveyance of the equitable fee simple to the Grantor, the Trustees will apply for the restriction to be cancelled, leaving the Grantor as absolute owner.
        A vesting instrument is only required where, not withstanding the disentailing assurance, some trust interest continues (such as a subsisting joint use or a power of charging) and, on cessation of the settlement, a deed of discharge under the Settled Land Act 1925 s 17 will be required.
        It is common for a resettlement to take place upon trusts appointed by the Grantor, the Trustees then holding pursuant to these trusts.
4   As to the statutory requirements for valid execution of a deed see vol 12 (1994 Reissue) DEEDS, AGREEMENTS AND DECLARATIONS.

301

Deed of disentail by tenant in tail in remainder with consent of protector[1]

THIS DISENTAILING DEED is made the ...... day of ....

BETWEEN:

(1)   *(tenant for life)* of *(address)* ('the Protector')

(2)   *(tenant in tail)* of *(address)* ('the Grantor') and

(3)   *(trustees)* of *(addresses)* ('the Trustees')

WHEREAS

(1)   This deed is supplemental to the settlement and other documents and events specified in the schedule ('the Settlement')

(2)   Under the subsisting limitations or trusts of the Settlement the Protector is tenant for life of the Settled Property as defined in the Settlement[2] and protector of the Settlement and the Grantor is tenant in tail [male] in remainder under it expectant upon the determination of the life interest of the Protector

(3)   The Grantor wishes to bar absolutely the entail in the Settled Property

[2104]

NOW THIS DEED WITNESSES as follows:

Conveyance

The Grantor with the consent of the Protector (testified by his execution of this deed) conveys assigns and disposes of to the Trustees all the Settled Property to which the Grantor is entitled for such entailed interest in remainder TO HOLD the same to the Trustees subject to the interest of the Protector in fee simple or absolutely according to the nature of the property discharged from all entailed interests of the Grantor in it under the terms of the Settlement and from all estates rights interests and powers to take effect after the determination or in defeasance of such entailed interests and so discharged in trust for the Grantor in fee simple and absolutely according to the nature of the property[3]

IN WITNESS etc

SCHEDULE

The Settlement

(insert details of the Settlement)

(signatures of the parties)[4]
(signatures of witnesses)
[2105]

---

1   As to stamp duty see the Information Binder: Stamp Duties [1]: Table of Duties: Conveyance or transfer. This Form can only be used in respect of an entailed interest created by an instrument coming into force before 1 January 1997. Any purported grant of an entailed interest by an instrument coming into operation after that date operates instead to create an absolute interest: Trusts of Land and Appointment of Trustees Act 1996 s 2, Sch 1 para 5 (37 Halsbury's Statutes (4th Edn) REAL PROPERTY). As to the barring of entail interests generally see Paragraph 277 [691] et seq ante.

      This Form is more commonly seen than a disentailing assurance by a tenant in tail in possession. It normally precedes a resettlement on trusts jointly appointed by the Protector (tenant in tail in possession) and the Grantor.

In this Form, on a disentailment by a tenant in tail in remainder with the consent of the protector, the tenant in tail does not become absolutely entitled as against the trustees of the property so that there is no disposal for capital gains tax purposes. For inheritance tax purposes, the nature of the Grantor's interest in the property (it is excluded property) does not change. The tax position will, of course, change if there is a resettlement: see Form 304 [2113] post.

2   There is no advantage in specifying the settled property in detail since the deed of disentail is not a document forming part of the legal title as it only deals with equitable interest.

3   See Form 300 note 3 [2103] ante.

4   As to the statutory requirements for valid execution of a deed see vol 12 (1994 Reissue) DEEDS, AGREEMENTS AND DECLARATIONS.

[2106]

302

Deed of disentail by trustee in bankruptcy in tail in possession[1]

THIS DISENTAILING DEED is made the ...... day of ....

BETWEEN:

(1)   *(trustee in bankruptcy)* of *(address)* ('the Trustee in Bankruptcy')

(2)   *(tenant in tail)* of *(address)* ('the Bankrupt') and

(3)   *(trustees)* of *(addresses)* ('the Trustees')

WHEREAS

(1)   This deed is supplemental to the settlement and other documents and events specified in the schedule ('the Settlement')

(2)   Under the subsisting limitations or trusts of the Settlement the Bankrupt was at the date of the Bankruptcy Order mentioned below the tenant in tail [male] in possession of the Settled Property as defined in the Settlement[2]

(3)   On *(date)* a Bankruptcy Order was made against the Bankrupt and on *(date)* the Trustee in Bankruptcy was appointed to be the trustee of the estate of the Bankrupt

(4)   By Schedule 5 Part II paragraph 13 of the Insolvency Act 1986 the Trustee in Bankruptcy is given the power to deal with any property comprised in the Bankrupt's estate to which the Bankrupt is beneficially entitled as tenant in tail in the same manner as the Bankrupt might have dealt with it

[2107]

NOW THIS DEED WITNESSES as follows:

Conveyance

For the purpose of barring the entail the Trustee in Bankruptcy in pursuance and exercise of the powers vested in him by statute as set out above and all other powers enabling him conveys assigns and disposes of to the Trustees all the Settled Property to which at the date of the adjudication mentioned above the Bankrupt was entitled for such entailed interest in possession TO HOLD the same to the Trustees in fee simple or absolutely according to the nature of the property discharged from all entailed interests of the

Bankrupt in it under the terms of the Settlement and from all estates rights interests and powers to take effect after the determination or in defeasance of such entailed interests and so discharged in trust for the Trustee in Bankruptcy as trustee of the estate of the Grantor in fee simple and absolutely according to the nature of the property[3]

IN WITNESS etc

SCHEDULE

The Settlement

(insert details of the Settlement)

(signatures of the parties)[4]
(signatures of witnesses)
[2108]

1   This Form can only be used in respect of an entailed interest created by an instrument coming into force before 1 January 1997. Any purported grant of an entailed interest by an instrument coming into operation after that date operates instead to create an absolute interest: Trusts of Land and Appointment of Trustees Act 1996 s 2, Sch 1 para 5 (37 Halsbury's Statutes (4th Edn) REAL PROPERTY). As to the barring of entail interests generally see Paragraph 277 [691] et seq ante. As to the power of the trustee in bankruptcy to deal with the entailed interests of a bankrupt see the Insolvency Act 1986 s 314(1)(b), Sch 5 para 13 (4 Halsbury's Statutes (4th Edn) BANKRUPTCY AND INSOLVENCY).
2   There is no advantage in specifying the settled property in detail since the deed of disentail is not a document forming part of the legal title as it only deals with equitable interest.
3   See Form 300 note 3 [2103] ante.
4   As to the statutory requirements for valid execution of a deed see vol 12 (1994 Reissue) DEEDS, AGREEMENTS AND DECLARATIONS.

[2109]

303

Deed of disentail under the Mental Health Act 1983 Section 96(1)[1]

THIS DISENTAILING DEED is made the ...... day of ....

BETWEEN:

(1)   *(patient)[2]* ('the Grantor') acting by *(receiver)* of *(address)* ('the Receiver') pursuant to the order recited below and

(2)   *(trustees)* of *(addresses)* ('the Trustees')

WHEREAS

(1)   This deed is supplemental to the settlement and other documents and events specified in the schedule ('the Settlement')

(2)   Under the subsisting limitations or trusts of the Settlement the Grantor is tenant in tail [male] in possession of the Settled Property as defined in the Settlement[3]

(3)   By an Order of the Master of the Court of Protection made on *(date)* in the matter of the Grantor the Receiver was directed to execute such disentailing deed to give effect to the terms of the draft disentailing deed mentioned in the Order as should be settled and approved by the Court of Protection

[2110]

NOW THIS DEED made in pursuance of the order mentioned above WITNESSES as follows:

Conveyance

The Grantor acting by the Receiver conveys assigns and disposes of to the Trustees all the Settled Property to which the Grantor is entitled for such entailed interest in possession TO HOLD the same to the Trustees in fee simple or absolutely according to the nature of the property discharged from all entailed interests of the Grantor in it under the terms of the Settlement and from all estates rights interests and powers to take effect after the determination or in defeasance of such entailed interests and so discharged in trust for the Grantor in fee simple and absolutely according to the nature of the property

IN WITNESS etc

SCHEDULE

The Settlement

(insert details of the Settlement)

(signatures of the parties)[4]
(signatures of witnesses)
[2111]

1   As to stamp duty see the Information Binder: Stamp Duties [1]: Table of Duties: Conveyance or transfer. This Form can only be used in respect of an entailed interest created by an instrument coming into force before 1 January 1997. Any purported grant of an entailed interest by an instrument coming into operation after that date operates instead to create an absolute interest: Trusts of Land and Appointment of Trustees Act 1996 s 2, Sch 1 para 5 (37 Halsbury's Statutes (4th Edn) REAL PROPERTY). As to the barring of entail interests generally see Paragraph 277 [691] et seq ante.
        The Court of Protection has very wide powers to authorise and direct the disentailment of the entailed property of a patient and its resettlement: see the Mental Health Act 1983 s 96(1)(d), (k), (2) (28 Halsbury's Statutes (4th Edn) MENTAL HEALTH). The practice of the court is to direct a settlement of the disentailed property rather than sanctioning a disentail so that the property vests in the patient absolutely: for that reason there will normally be a contemporaneous trust deed giving effect to the directions of the Court of Protection.
2   No address should be given.
3   There is no advantage in specifying the settled property in detail since the deed of disentail is not a document forming part of the legal title as it only deals with equitable interest
4   The deed will be executed on behalf of the patient by the receiver; for a suitable attestation clause see vol 12 (1994 Reissue) DEEDS, AGREEMENTS AND DECLARATIONS. As to the statutory requirements for valid execution of a deed see vol 12 (1994 Reissue) DEEDS, AGREEMENTS AND DECLARATIONS.
[2112]

304

Deed of disentail and partition, property being partitioned between tenant for life and tenant in tail on an actuarial basis[1]

THIS DISENTAILING DEED is made the ...... day of ....

BETWEEN:

(1)   *(tenant for life)* of *(address)* ('the Protector')

(2)   *(tenant in tail)* of *(address)* ('the Grantor') and

(3)   *(trustees)* of *(addresses)* ('the Trustees')

WHEREAS

(1)   This deed is supplemental to the settlement and other documents and events specified in Part I of the schedule ('the Settlement')

[2113]

(2)   Under the subsisting limitations or trusts of the Settlement the Protector is tenant for life of the Settled Property as defined in the Settlement[2] and protector of the Settlement and the Grantor is tenant in tail [male] in remainder under it expectant upon the determination of the life interest of the Protector

(3)   The Protector and the Grantor have agreed that the Settled Property shall be disentailed in the manner below

(4)   The Protector and the Grantor being together absolutely entitled to the Settled Property free from all charges and incumbrances have further agreed to partition the Settled Property on the basis of the actuarial values of their respective interests

(5)   The Protector and the Grantor have been advised by a duly qualified actuary[3] that at the date of this deed the property and investments specified in Part II of the schedule represent the actuarial value of the Grantor's reversionary interest in the Settled Property and the property and investments in Part III of the schedule represent the actuarial value of the Protector's life interest in the Settled Property

[2114]

NOW THIS DEED WITNESSES as follows:

1   Conveyance

The Grantor with the consent of the Protector (testified by his execution of this deed) conveys assigns and disposes of to the Trustees all the Settled Property to which the Grantor is entitled for such entailed interest in remainder TO HOLD the same to the Trustees subject to the interest of the Protector in fee simple or absolutely according to the nature of the property discharged from all entailed interests of the Grantor in it under the terms of the Settlement and from all estates rights interests and powers to take effect after the determination or in defeasance of such entailed interests and so discharged in trust for the Grantor in fee simple and absolutely according to the nature of the property

2   Assignment of life interest

The Protector conveys assigns and releases to the Grantor the life interest of the Protector in the property and investments specified in Part II of the schedule to hold the same to the Grantor absolutely to the intent that the Grantor may immediately become absolutely entitled in possession to the property and investments specified in Part II of the schedule and that the same may now be transferred by the Trustees to the Grantor[4]

[2115]

3   Assignment of reversion

The Grantor conveys assigns and transfers to the Protector his interest expectant on the death of the Protector in the property and investments specified in Part III of the schedule TO HOLD the same unto the Protector to the intent that the life interest of the Protector may be enlarged into an absolute interest and that the same property and investments may now be transferred by the Trustees to the Protector[5]

4   Inheritance tax

It is agreed and declared that any inheritance tax liability resulting from this partition in respect of the Grantor's share shall be borne by that share and any capital gains tax resulting from this partition shall be borne by the Protector and the Grantor in the same proportions as they become absolutely entitled to the Settled Property but that nothing in this deed shall prejudice or impair any right or lien to which the Trustees are entitled in respect of any claim for costs charges or expenses or so as to protect themselves against any tax liabilities[6]

IN WITNESS etc

SCHEDULE

Part I

(insert details of the Settlement)

Part II

(insert details of the property and investments to be transferred to the Grantor)

Part III

(insert details of the property and investments to be transferred to the Protector)

(signatures of the parties)[7]
(signatures of witnesses)
[2116]

1   As to stamp duty see the Information Binder: Stamp Duties: [1]: Table of Duties: Conveyance or transfer. This Form can only be used in respect of an entailed interest created by an instrument coming into force before 1 January 1997. Any purported grant of an entailed interest by an instrument coming into operation after that date operates instead to create an absolute interest: Trusts of Land and Appointment of Trustees Act 1996 s 2, Sch 1 para 5 (37 Halsbury's Statutes (4th Edn) REAL PROPERTY). As to the barring of entail interests generally see Paragraph 277 [691] et seq ante. For the inheritance tax consequences of a partitioning of a settled fund see Paragraph 300.4 [776] ante. For capital gains tax purposes, both the tenant for life and tenant in tail become absolutely entitled to the settled property resulting in a deemed disposal by the trustees with subsequent charge: see Paragraph 341.3 [911] ante.

2   There is no advantage in specifying the settled property in detail since the deed of disentail is not a document forming part of the legal title as it only deals with the equitable interest. The specific property subject to partition must be set out in detail in the schedule.

3   The partition should be made on an actuarial basis which should take account of any inheritance tax saving resulting from a partition during lifetime rather than allowing the life tenant's interest in possession to terminate on death.

4   Since this deed is not part of the legal title, any land must be vested in the recipient in the usual way on the determination of a settlement. The conveyance or transfer referred to in the deed is of the Grantor or Protector's equitable entitlement only. The legal title still needs to be transferred or conveyed.

5   See note 4 above.

6   This clause ensures that in the event of the life tenant not surviving seven years, any inheritance tax will be borne by the grantor's share. This will avoid any grossing up. It also provides for any capital gains tax to be borne by the parties in proportion to the value of the settled property taken by each. The fact that some assets may have a higher potential liability than others is something which would be taken into account when agreeing the basis of the division. Notwithstanding what the life tenant and grantor have agreed, the trustees retain any rights they may require to protect themselves, particularly against tax liabilities. This is important since they will be liable for any inheritance tax due on the grantor's share if the life tenant dies within seven years, as well as being liable, if the donee beneficiary defaults or emigrates, for the tax on any chargeable gain which was the subject of a hold-over election. Provision may also be made for the costs and expenses incurred in connection with the preparation of this deed and with the apportionment of income: see further Form 314 clauses 6 [2166] and 7 [2167] post.

7   As to the statutory requirements for valid execution of a deed see vol 12 (1994 Reissue) DEEDS, AGREEMENTS AND DECLARATIONS.

[2117]–[2130]

H: MISCELLANEOUS DOCUMENTS MODIFYING AND ENDING EXISTING TRUSTS

1: MODIFICATIONS TO AN EXISTING TRUST

(The Forms contained in this section are not intended to be exhaustive since an existing trust may be modified in a variety of ways not considered in this section, for instance: by the exercise of powers of appointment and advancement (for such dispositive powers, see Section E [1951] ante); by the exercise of (and by the acquisition of further) administrative powers and by extraneous events such as the death or bankruptcy of a beneficiary.)

305

Deed adding property to an existing trust[1]

THIS DEED is made the ...... day of ....

BETWEEN:

(1)   *(donor)* of *(address)* ('the Donor') and

(2)   *(trustees)* of *(addresses)* ('the Trustees')

WHEREAS

(1)   The Trustees are the present trustees of a settlement ('the Settlement') dated *(date)* and made between (1) *(settlor)* ('the Settlor') and (2) the Trustees being a settlement made by the Settlor for the benefit of his children and other issue

(2)   The Donor wishes to make an addition of property to the Trustees to be held upon the trusts of the Settlement such property comprising the sum of £... cash

[2131]

NOW THIS DEED WITNESSES as follows:

1   Declaration

The Trustees stand possessed of the sum of £... transferred to them by the Donor as an addition to the property subject to the trusts of the Settlement and as part of the Trust Fund described in and defined by clause *(number)* of the Settlement and upon the trusts and with and subject to the power and provisions contained in the Settlement

2   Stamp duty certificate

It is hereby certified that this instrument falls within category 'L' in the Schedule to the Stamp Duty (Exempt Instruments) Regulations 1987[2]

IN WITNESS etc

(signatures of the parties)[3]
(signatures of witnesses)
[2132]

1   As to stamp duty see Information Binder: Stamp Duties [1] Table of Duties (Voluntary dispositions). It is common for property to be added to an existing trust without any formality (eg, to a pilot trust). Commonly, all that is considered necessary is for the property to be validly transferred into the names of the trustees.

2   Ie the Stamp Duty (Exempt Instruments) Regulations 1987, SI 1987/516. As to the inclusion of such a certificate see Information Binder: Stamp Duties [1] Table of Duties (Exempt Instruments Regulations).

3   As to the statutory requirements for valid execution of a deed see vol 12 (1994 Reissue) DEEDS, AGREEMENTS AND DECLARATIONS.

[2133]

306

Deed adding further beneficiary[1]

THIS DEED is made the ...... day of .... by *(trustees)* of *(addresses)* ('the Trustees')

WHEREAS

(1)   This deed is supplemental to a deed of settlement ('the Settlement') dated *(date)* and made between *(parties)*

[2134]

(2)   The Trustees are the present trustees of the Settlement

(3)   By clause *(number)* of the Settlement the Trustees have power by deed or deeds to add one or more persons to the Beneficiaries (as defined in the Settlement)

(4)   The Trustees now wish to add the persons specified in the schedule ('the Additional Beneficiaries') to the Beneficiaries

NOW THIS DEED WITNESSES as follows:

1   Declaration

In exercise of the power given to them by clause *(number)* of the Settlement the Trustees declare that the Additional Beneficiaries shall be added to the Beneficiaries for all the purposes of the Settlement

[2135]

2   Date of addition

The addition shall take effect from the date of this deed

IN WITNESS etc

SCHEDULE

Additional Beneficiaries

(specify Additional Beneficiaries)

(signatures of the parties)[2]
(signatures of witnesses)

1   For a power to add or remove beneficiaries see Form 4 clause 6 [1087] ante.

2   As to the statutory requirements for valid execution of a deed see vol 12 (1994 Reissue) DEEDS, AGREEMENTS AND DECLARATIONS.

[2136]

307

Deed excluding beneficiary[1]

THIS DEED is made the ...... day of .... by *(trustees)* of *(addresses)* ('the Trustees')

WHEREAS

(1)   This deed is supplemental to a deed of settlement ('the Settlement') dated *(date)* and made between *(parties)*

[2137]

(2)   The Trustees are the present trustees of the Settlement

(3)   By clause *(number)* of the Settlement the Trustees have power to declare by deed that one or more of the Beneficiaries (as defined in the Settlement) shall be revocably or irrevocably excluded in whole or in part from benefit in the Settlement

(4)   The Trustees now wish revocably to exclude the persons specified in the schedule ('the Excluded Persons') from benefit under the Settlement

NOW THIS DEED WITNESSES as follows:

1   Declaration

In exercise of the power given to them by clause *(number)* of the Settlement the Trustees revocably declare that the Excluded Persons shall be excluded from any benefit from the Settlement

[2138]

2   Date of exclusion

The exclusion shall take effect from the date of this deed

IN WITNESS etc

SCHEDULE

Excluded Persons

(specify Excluded Persons)

(signatures of the parties)[2]
(signatures of witnesses)

1   For a power to add or remove beneficiaries see Form 4 clause 6 [1087] ante.
2   As to the statutory requirements for valid execution of a deed see vol 12 (1994 Reissue) DEEDS, AGREEMENTS AND DECLARATIONS.

[2139]

308

Clause releasing power of the trustees[1]

The {Trustees} now release the power conferred upon them by clause *(number)* of the {Settlement} so that the power shall not from the date of this deed be capable of exercise by the {Trustees} in relation to the {Trust Fund}

1   It may be possible for the release to be revocable so that the effect of this clause may be undone in the
           future. If this is both possible and intended the words 'provided that the Trustees may revoke this deed
           by further deed executed at any time during the Trust Period' should be added. This cannot be done
           unless there is a clause expressly permitting such revocation in the settlement. For release of powers
           generally, see Thomas *Powers* (1998) at 15-02 et seq.
                When this clause is inserted in a document the defined terms in { } must be altered to suit those
           used in the document.

[2140]

309

Release of power of appointment by beneficiary[1]

The {Life Tenant} releases the power conferred on [him] by clause *(number)* of the
{Settlement} to the intent that the power shall not from the date of this deed be
exercisable by the {Life Tenant} in relation to the {Specified Fund} (but for the
avoidance of doubt such power shall continue to be exercisable in relation to the balance
of the {Trust Fund})

1   When this clause is inserted in a document the defined terms in { } must be altered to suit those used
           in the document.

[2141]

310

Assignment of reversionary interest on trust[1]

THIS ASSIGNMENT is made the ...... day of ....

BETWEEN:

(1)   *(settlor)* of *(address)* ('the Settlor') and

(2)   *(names)* of *(addresses)* ('the Original Trustees')

WHEREAS

(1)   This deed is supplemental to:
           (1.1)   a settlement dated *(date)* ('the Settlement') made between (1) the
                     Settlor and (2) the Original Trustees
           (1.2)   the will dated *(date)* ('the Will') of *(testator)* late of *(address)* ('the
                     Testator') who died on *(date)* which was proved in the [Principal
                     Registry of the Family Division of the High Court *or (name)* District
                     Probate Registry] on *(date)* by *(executors)*

(2)   The Original Trustees are still the trustees of the Settlement and the testator's
           widow *(name of widow)* is still alive

(3)   By clause *(number)* of the Will the trustees of the Will are directed to stand
           possessed of the Testator's net residuary estate (being the property in the Will
           called 'my Residuary Estate')
           (3.1)   upon trust to pay the income to the Testator's widow *(name)* during
                     her lifetime and
           (3.2)   upon trust from and after her death to hold the same for the Settlor
                     absolutely

(4)   The Settlor now wishes to assign his reversionary interest under clause *(number)* of the Will to the Original Trustees as an addition to the trust fund subject to the Settlement and to be held by them (or other the trustees or trustee for the time being of the Settlement) upon and with and subject to the trusts powers and provisions declared and contained in the Settlement

[2142]

NOW THIS DEED WITNESSES as follows:

1   Definitions

In this deed the following expressions have where the context permits the following meanings namely:

1.1   'the Testator's Residuary Estate' means the Testator's net residuary estate (being the property in the Will called 'my Residuary Estate')

1.2   'the Assigned Reversionary Interest' means all that the reversionary interest of the Settlor in the Testator's Residuary Estate under clause *(number)* of the Will

1.3   'the Settlement Trust Fund' means the trust fund subject to the Settlement (being the 'Trust Fund' described in and defined by clause *(number)* of the Settlement)

2   Assignment

The Settlor assigns to the Original Trustees the Assigned Reversionary Interest TO HOLD to the Original Trustees absolutely

3   Trusts

The Original Trustees (or other the trustees or trustee for the time being of the Settlement) shall stand possessed of the Assigned Reversionary Interest and the property from time to time representing the same as an addition to the property subject to the trusts of the Settlement and as part of the Settlement Trust Fund and (together with the future income of it) upon the trusts and with and subject to the powers and provisions declared and contained in the Settlement

4   Stamp duty certificate

It is hereby certified that this instrument falls within category 'L' in the Schedule to the Stamp Duty (Exempt Instruments) Regulations 1987[2]

IN WITNESS etc

(signatures of the parties)[3]
(signatures of witnesses)
[2143]

---

1   As to stamp duty see Information Binder: Stamp Duties [1] Table of Duties (Voluntary disposition). For the capital gains tax position on an assignment of a reversionary interest see Taxation of Chargeable Gains Act 1992 s 76 (43 Halsbury's Statutes (4th Edn) TAXATION) and for inheritance tax purposes see Inheritance Tax Act 1984 s 48 (42 Halsbury's Statutes (4th Edn) TAXATION).

2   Ie the Stamp Duty (Exempt Instruments) Regulations 1987, SI 1987/516. As to the inclusion of such a certificate see Information Binder: Stamp Duties [1] Table of Duties (Exempt Instruments Regulations).

3   As to the statutory requirements for the valid execution of a deed see vol 12 (1994 Reissue) DEEDS, AGREEMENTS AND DECLARATIONS.

[2144]

311
Surrender of life interest[1]

0.1   The {Life Tenant} assigns surrenders and releases to the {Trustees} [his] life interest in the {Specified Fund} to the intent that the provisions contained in clause *(number)* of the {Settlement} (or such of them as shall for the time being be capable of taking effect) shall be accelerated and take effect on the release of such interest as if the {Life Tenant} were actually dead

0.2   All income of the {Specified Fund} received by or on behalf of the {Trustees} from and after the date of this deed shall be treated as if it had arisen wholly after such date and the Apportionment Act 1870 shall not be applicable to it

---

1   When this clause is inserted in a document the defined terms in { } must be altered to suit those used in the document.

[2145]

312

Agreement with beneficiary for occupation of a trust property pursuant to the Trusts of Land and Appointment of Trustees Act 1996 Section 13[1]

THIS AGREEMENT is made the ...... day of ....

BETWEEN:

(1)   *(trustees)* of *(addresses)* ('the Trustees') and

(2)   *(beneficiary)* of *(address)* ('the Beneficiary)

WHEREAS

(1)   The Trustees are the present trustees of (a) a conveyance dated *(date)* and made between *(parties)* and (b) settlement of even date with and made between the same parties in the same order as the conveyance

(2)   The freehold property known as *(specify)* ('the Property') is vested in the Trustees and is held on trusts whereunder the Beneficiary is entitled to an interest in possession therein

(3)   The Trustees have determined in accordance with the provisions of the Trusts of Land and Appointment of Trustees Act 1996 Section 13 and it has been agreed with the Beneficiary that the Beneficiary will pursuant to the right conferred on him by Section 12 of that Act occupy the Property on the terms and conditions hereinafter contained including the payment by the Beneficiary to AB (who is also entitled to an interest in possession under the trusts affecting the Property) of such annual sums as are hereinafter provided

[2146]

NOW IT IS HEREBY AGREED as follows:

1   Pursuant to the Trusts of Land and Appointment of Trustees Act 1996 Sections 12 and 13 the Beneficiary shall be entitled to occupy the Property until this Agreement is determined in accordance with the provisions hereinafter contained

2   The Beneficiary hereby undertakes to pay to the said AB the annual sum of £... by equal half yearly instalments payable in arrears throughout the currency of this Agreement so long as the said AB shall be entitled to an interest in possession under the trusts affecting the Property the first such instalment to be paid on *(date)* and subsequent instalments to be paid on the ... day of ... and the ... day of ... in each year and the last payment to be made on the termination of this Agreement or on such earlier date as the said AB shall cease to be entitled to an interest in possession under the trusts affecting the Property (whether due to the death of the said AB or for any other reason) and to be a proportionate payment

3   The Beneficiary agrees with the Trustees:

    3.1   to pay all council tax water rates and all other taxes impositions and outgoings which are now or may at any time during the currency of this Agreement be assessed levied charged or imposed on the Property or on the owner or occupier in respect thereof

    3.2   not to use the Property except as a residence for the Beneficiary and his family

    3.3   to keep the interior of the dwellinghouse on the Property and all fixtures and fittings therein (other than electrical wiring or pipes and apparatus for the supply of hot and cold water) in proper repair and good decorative condition throughout the currency of this Agreement

    3.4   to pay direct to the various supply authorities for all gas water and electricity consumed on the Property and the rent of the meters to regulate such supplies and to pay for the rental of any telephone or telephones installed at the Property and the costs of all calls

    3.5   to maintain the garden at the Property in a neat and tidy condition

    3.6   to insure and keep insured the dwellinghouse on the Property against loss from fire and all other perils usually covered by a householders' comprehensive policy in the names of the Trustees in an insurance office nominated by the Trustees and to produce a receipt for any premium paid to the Trustees or their agent on demand

[2147]

    3.7   to permit the Trustees and their surveyors and agents at all reasonable times during the currency of this Agreement with or without workmen and others and with or without appliances to enter on the Property to view the state of repair and condition of the same and to repair the same

    3.8   not to make or allow to be made during the currency of this Agreement any new building on the Property or make or allow to be made any alteration or addition to the dwellinghouse on the Property

    3.9   not to do or permit anything to be done on the Property which may be or become a nuisance or annoyance or cause damage or inconvenience to the owners or occupiers of any adjoining or neighbouring property and

    3.10   forthwith on receipt of any notice or order or any proposal for the same from a planning or other authority to give full particulars to the Trustees or their agents and if required to do so to produce the same to the Trustees or their agents

4   Nothing contained in this agreement shall create the relationship of landlord and tenant between the Trustees and the Beneficiary

5   This Agreement shall automatically determine on the death of the Beneficiary or on the termination for any other reason of the Beneficiary's interest in possession in the Property:

    5.1   if at any time during the continuance of this Agreement the Trustees wish to sell the Property they shall be entitled to give the Beneficiary three months' notice to cease occupation of the Property and the Beneficiary shall cease occupation at the end of such period[2]

    5.2   if at any time during the continuance of this Agreement the Beneficiary shall be in breach of any of the terms and conditions of this Agreement the trustees shall be entitled to give the Beneficiary three months' notice to cease occupation of the Property and the Beneficiary shall cease occupation at the end of such period and the right to terminate the Beneficiary's occupation in respect of any breach of any terms or conditions shall not be waived solely by reason of any earlier waiver by the Trustees of any previous or continuing breach of that or any other condition

6   The Beneficiary may at any time give to the Trustees one month's notice of his intention to vacate the Property and on the expiry of such period of one month this Agreement shall determine

7   The expression 'the Trustees' herein shall include the trustees or the trustee for the time being of the said conveyance and the said settlement

8   The expression 'interest in possession' herein shall have the same meaning as that expression has for the purposes of the Trusts of Land and Appointment of Trustees Act 1996

(signatures of the trustees)

(signature of the beneficiary)

[2148]

---

1   This Form gives a beneficiary occupation of a dwelling house on terms that he is subject to interior repairs and the payment of all outgoings, and also subject to his making annual payments to another beneficiary entitled to an interest in possession. It is thought that the arrangement would be construed as a licence and not a tenancy in view of the fact that it is in favour of a beneficiary within a trust, and gives effect to the right of occupation of a beneficiary and the attendant powers of the trustees under the Trusts of Land and Appointment of Trustees Act 1996 ss 12, 13 (37 Halsbury's Statutes (4th Edn) REAL PROPERTY).

    For the inheritance tax implications of permitting a beneficiary to reside in the property see Paragraph 287.3 [734] ante. As to the right of beneficiaries to occupy trust land, see Paragraph 228 [545] ante.

2   The trustees can give notice to terminate the agreement if they wish to sell the property but the beneficiary would still be in occupation if he did not leave willingly and would come within the terms of the Trusts of Land and Appointment of Trustees Act 1996 s 13(7). In such circumstances the trustees would have to go to court to secure his removal.

[2149]–[2160]

2: ENDING THE TRUST

313

Revocation of voluntary settlement in exercise of a power contained in it by indorsement on the settlement deed

I *(settlor)* the within-named settlor in exercise of the power of revocation reserved to me in that behalf by clause *(number)* of the within-written settlement and of all other relevant powers [with the consent of the within-named trustees as testified by their execution of this indorsement] now wholly revoke all the trusts powers and provisions declared and contained in the within-written settlement and declare that the within-named trustees shall as and from the date of this indorsement stand possessed of the Trust Fund (as defined in the within-written settlement) and the income of it in trust for myself absolutely.

IN WITNESS etc

(signature of the settlor)[1]
(signatures of witnesses)
[2161]

1   As to the statutory requirements for valid execution of a deed see vol 12 (1994 Reissue) DEEDS,
       AGREEMENTS AND DECLARATIONS. The trustees should also execute if their consent is required to
       the revocation. Unless the contrary is stated in the trust deed voluntary settlements are irrevocable. For
       a recent illustration of a settlement under which a settlor could recover the property, see *Melville v IRC*
       [2000] STC 628.

[2162]

314

Deed of partition of trust fund between life tenant and remainderman[1]

THIS DEED OF PARTITION is made the ...... day of ....

BETWEEN:

(1)   *(life tenant)* of *(address)* ('the Life Tenant')

(2)   *(remainderman)* of *(address)* ('the Remainderman') and

(3)   *(trustees)* of *(addresses)* ('the Trustees')

[2163]

WHEREAS

(1)   This deed is supplemental to a deed of settlement ('the Settlement') dated *(date)* and made between *(parties)*

(2)   Under the trusts and provisions declared and contained in the Settlement [and in the events that have happened] the Trust Fund (as defined in the Settlement) is held by the Trustees (who are the present trustees of the Settlement) upon trust to pay the income of it to the Life Tenant during his life and subject to such life interest upon trust as to both capital and income for the Remainderman absolutely

(3)   At the date of this deed the Trust Fund consists of the investments and the sum of capital cash described in the schedule

(4)   The Life Tenant and the Remainderman have agreed to partition the Trust Fund between themselves and have agreed to divide the Trust Fund and to make mutual exchanges of their interests in such fund without the payment of any equality money in the manner appearing below

[2164]

NOW THIS DEED WITNESSES as follows:

1   Definition

In this deed the expression 'the Trust Fund' shall where the context permits have the meaning given to that expression in clause *(number)* of the Settlement

2   Assignment by the Life Tenant

The Life Tenant assigns and surrenders to the Remainderman ALL THAT the interest of the Life Tenant in the income arising during his lifetime in …% of the Trust Fund TO HOLD to the Remainderman to the intent that such interest of the Life Tenant in the income of the Trust Fund shall merge in the reversion expectant upon his death and the Remainderman shall be entitled to such proportion of the Trust Fund absolutely

3   Assignment by the Remainderman

The Remainderman assigns and transfers to the Life Tenant ALL THAT his interest expectant upon the death of the Life Tenant in …% of the Trust Fund TO HOLD to the Life Tenant to the intent that such interest of the Life Tenant shall be enlarged and that he shall be entitled to such proportion of the Trust Fund absolutely

[2165]

4   Capital gains tax

It is agreed between the Life Tenant and the Remainderman that the capital gains tax payable in respect of the assets comprised in the Trust Fund by virtue or in consequence of the partition effected by this deed and in respect of any actual disposals made by the Trustees prior to the date of this deed and where such tax has not yet been paid shall be borne and paid as to …% by the Life Tenant and as to …% by the Remainderman

5   Lien

It is agreed between the Life Tenant and the Remainderman and the Trustees that the Trustees shall have a lien over the investments and sum of cash specified in the schedule for the amount of the capital gains tax assessable on the Trustees by virtue or in consequence of the partition by this deed effected and in respect of any actual disposals made by the Trustees prior to the date of this deed and where such tax has not yet been paid (but without prejudice to any liens vested in the Trustees by statute in respect of any United Kingdom taxes)

6   Costs and expenses

It is agreed between the Life Tenant and the Remainderman that all costs and expenses in connection with and incidental to the negotiation preparation and completion of this deed (including any stamp duty payable on it) and the implementation of its provisions shall be borne and paid as to …% by the Life Tenant and as to …% by the Remainderman

[2166]

7   Apportionment

All income of the Trust Fund and any assets comprised in such fund received by or on behalf of the Trustees from and after the date of this deed shall be treated as if it had arisen wholly after such date and the Apportionment Act 1870 shall not apply

IN WITNESS etc

SCHEDULE

Investments and Cash

(specify investments and capital cash)

(signatures of the parties)[2]
(signatures of witnesses
[2167]

1   As to stamp duty see Information Binder: Stamp Duties [1] Table of Duties (Exchange or Excambion) and (Partition or Division). The partition will result in the property ceasing to be settled for capital gains tax purposes and so there will be a deemed disposal under the Taxation of Chargeable Gains Act 1992 s 71 (42–44 Halsbury's Statutes (4th Edn) TAXATION). For inheritance tax purposes that portion of the capital which under the terms of the partition passes to the remainderman will involve a potentially exempt transfer by the life tenant. See also Form 304 [2113] ante which is a deed of disentail and partition.

2   As to the statutory requirements for valid execution of a deed see vol 12 (1994 Reissue) DEEDS, AGREEMENTS AND DECLARATIONS.

[2168]

315

Deed of release and surrender by cohabitant of any potential right to claim a beneficial interest[1]

THIS DEED OF RELEASE AND SURRENDER is made the ...... day of ....

BETWEEN:

(1)   *(owner of property)* of *(address)* ('AB') and

(2)   *(cohabitant)* of *(address)* ('BC')

NOW THIS DEED WITNESSES as follows:

1   Recitals

1.1   AB is the [estate owner *or* registered proprietor] of the freehold property known as *(describe property)* [and registered at HM Land Registry under title number *(title number)*] ('the Property')

1.2   BC [has lived at the Property since *or* will live at the Property from] *(date)*
[2169]

2   Residence

AB will [continue to provide *or* provide] accommodation to BC

3   Beneficial interest

BC renounces releases and surrenders to AB all if any rights [she] may have at any time to claim any beneficial interest in the Property or any income derived from the Property regardless of any contributions including but not limited to:

3.1   contribution or payment of any mortgage on the Property and

3.2   contributions to [her] living expenses or any outgoings on the Property

3.3   any repairs or improvements to the Property

4   Alienation

Nothing in this deed removes the right of AB at any time during [his] life or by will to transfer all or any part of [his] legal estate and/or beneficial interest in the Property to BC

5   Acknowledgement

BC acknowledges that [she] understands the nature and effect of this deed and further acknowledges that:

5.1   [she] has received independent legal advice as to its provisions and nature and effect and

5.2   [she] is entering into this deed freely and voluntarily

IN WITNESS etc

(signatures of the parties)[2]
(signatures of witnesses)
[2170]

---

1   Where property is vested in one party only, a cohabitant may establish ownership of a beneficial share. In order to do so, the claimant must show that the parties had a common intention that both should have a beneficial interest in the property acquired, and that the claimant has acted to his or her detriment on the basis of that common intention: see *Grant v Edwards* [1986] Ch 638, [1986] 2 All ER 426, CA and *Lloyds Bank plc v Rosset* [1991] 1 AC 107, [1990] 1 All ER 1111, HL.

This Form expresses the agreement between the parties that the beneficial interest is owned exclusively by one party. The Form will also effectively prevent the inference of any common intention that the beneficial ownership should be shared. For a deed of variation specifying an increased beneficial interest where one co-owner has made a substantial improvement to the property see vol 16(2) (1996 Reissue) FAMILY Form 17 [1107].

If the deed is executed after the parties have occupied the property for a period of time so that BC may already have acquired an interest in the property then: (a) the property will at the relevant time be held on a trust of land; and (b) the effect of the surrender may be to give rise to a potentially exempt transfer for inheritance tax purposes.

2   As to the statutory requirements for valid execution of a deed see vol 12 (1994 Reissue) DEEDS, AGREEMENTS AND DECLARATIONS.

[2171]–[2190]

PART 7: TRUSTEE DELEGATION

Forms and Precedents

A: INTRODUCTION

Powers providing for delegation by trustees—as a body or individually

This section is divisible into two parts:

1   **Collective delegation**: by which the trustees as a body delegate functions to an agent. The Trustee Act 2000 Part IV[1] provides for the widespread delegation of administrative powers and discretions by trustees. Form 318 [2198] and Form 319 [2200] below provide for the common situation where trustees wish to delegate the management of the trust investments. Practitioners may consider that the restrictions on delegation imposed under the Trustee Act 2000 Section 12[2], are unsatisfactory. Form 316 [2194] below is an express power to delegate (both collectively and individually) which excludes the provisions of the Trustee Act 1925.

2   **Individual delegation**: the law relating to the delegation of trustee functions by powers of attorney has been amended by the Trustee Delegation Act 1999[3]. The main features to note are:

    2.1   The legislation is concerned with individual rather than collective delegation.

    2.2   In general, trustee functions can be delegated for periods of up to 12 months (see Form 320 [2205] below which is the form of delegation set out in the legislation).

[2191]

    2.3   Delegation can be to a sole co-trustee but the 'two-trustee rule' is preserved (indeed strengthened) by the Trustee Delegation Act 1999 Section 7[4].

    2.4   Delegation can be by enduring power of attorney but, in line with the general rule, the power is only effective for a period of up to 12 months (see Form 323 [2221] below)[5].

    2.5   The Trustee Delegation Act 1999 Section 1 introduces a new power which can be used where land is held on trust and the delegating trustee has a beneficial interest in that land. This provision is intended to deal with co-ownership of land but, because of the way in which it is drafted, it also applies when a trustee is a beneficiary of (say) the family's landed estate. The power of delegation under the Trustee Delegation Act 1999 Section 1 can be exercised by an ordinary (ie non-trustee) power of attorney, by an enduring power of attorney (so that delegation will continue even after the donor trustee becomes mentally incapable) or by a trustee power (limited to a period of 12 months under the Trustee Act 1925 Section 25[6]). Forms 324 [2230]–326 [2234] post are concerned with Section 1 delegation[7].

[2192]

1   Ie the Trustee Act 2000 Part IV (ss 11–27) (48 Halsbury's Statutes (4th Edn) TRUSTS AND SETTLEMENTS). As to the power of collective delegation conferred on trustees by the Trustee Act 2000 see Paragraph 246 [611] et seq ante.
2   As to the restrictions set out in the Trustee Act 2000 s 12 see Paragraph 247 [613] ante.
3   The principal Acts amended by the Trustee Delegation Act 1999 (48 Halsbury's Statutes (4th Edn) TRUSTS AND SETTLEMENTS) are the Trustee Act 1925 , the Powers of Attorney Act 1971 and the Enduring Powers of Attorney Act 1985.
4   As to the application of the 'two-trustee rule' see Paragraph 258 [634] ante.
5   As to the power to delegate for a period not exceeding 12 months see Paragraph 256 [630] ante.
6   The Trustee Act 1925 s 25 as substituted by the Trustee Delegation Act 1999 s 5(1), (2) (48 Halsbury's Statutes (4th Edn) TRUSTS AND SETTLEMENTS).
7   As to delegation under the Trustee Delegation Act 1999 s 1 see Paragraph 257 [632] ante.

[2193]

B: POWERS PROVIDING FOR COLLECTIVE DELEGATION

316

Power for trustees to delegate both collectively and individually—exclusion of the Trustee Act 1925 Section 25[1]

Power for the {Trustees} collectively or for any of them individually (with the consent of the others or other of them) to delegate to any person or persons (not being the {Settlor} or any spouse of the {Settlor} but including in the case of delegation by an individual {Trustee} any other {Trustee} and including also any beneficiary or beneficiaries under the trusts of this deed) at any time and for any period and in any manner and on any terms and conditions all or any of the trusts powers and discretions herein declared or conferred by this deed or by law and the Trustee Act 1925 Section 25 (as substituted by the Trustee Delegation Act 1999) shall not apply to this deed.

[2194]

1   This express power ousts the statutory restrictions on trustee delegation in Trustee Delegation Act 1999 ss 1, 5 which recast the Trustee Act 1925 s 25 (48 Halsbury's Statutes (4th Edn) TRUSTS AND SETTLEMENTS). The delegation does not need to be by deed. It can be made 'in any manner', hence permitting the use of both enduring powers of attorney and general powers under the Powers of Attorney Act 1971 s 10 as amended by the Trustee Delegation Act 1999 s 3 (1 Halsbury's Statutes (4th Edn) AGENCY). It removes the restrictions of the Trustee Act 1925 s 25 (48 Halsbury's Statutes (4th Edn) TRUSTS AND SETTLEMENTS): eg, as to a maximum duration of 12 months. Notice however that the 'two-trustee rule' under the Trustee Delegation Act 1999 s 7 is mandatory and may create problems if a sole co-trustee has been appointed as attorney. For collective delegation see Form 317 [2196] post.
      When this clause is inserted in a document the defined terms in { } must be altered to suit those used in the document.

[2195]

317
Collective power to delegate[1]

0.1   Power to delegate all or any of the powers of the {Trustees} contained in the schedule and any administrative powers conferred by law (and all or any of the duties and discretions of the {Trustees} relating to the exercise of such powers) to any person or persons (not being the {Settlor} or any spouse of the {Settlor}) subject to such conditions (if any) and upon such terms (including the remuneration of any such delegate) as the {Trustees} shall think fit (without being liable for the acts or defaults of any such delegate) and to revoke or modify any such delegation or conditions or terms

0.2   The persons in whose favour the {Trustees} may delegate all or any of such powers include any one or more of the {Trustees} and any one of more of the {Beneficiaries} under the trusts of this settlement (but other than and excluding the {Settlor} or any spouse of the {Settlor})

0.3   A delegation by the {Trustees} under the foregoing power to two or more persons may authorise such delegates to exercise the powers duties and discretions delegated either jointly or jointly and severally

0.4   The Trustee Act 2000 Section 11 shall not apply to this deed[2]

[2196]

1   The power to delegate under the Trustee Act 2000 s 11 (48 Halsbury's Statutes (4th Edn) TRUSTS AND SETTLEMENTS) cannot be exercised in favour of a beneficiary. This Form permits trustees to delegate administrative powers to any person (other than the settlor or his spouse) *including* a beneficiary. It also permits joint and several delegation: cf the Trustee Act 2000 s 12(2).
       When this clause is inserted in a document the defined terms in { } must be altered to suit those used in the document.

2   The power to delegate contained in the Trustee Act 2000 s 11 may be excluded: see the Trustee Act 2000 s 26(b). The duty to keep the arrangements with an agent under review and to intervene contained in the Trustee Act 2000 s 22 may also, if desired, be excluded in connection with this express power: see the Trustee Act 2000 s 21(3).

[2197]

318
Delegation of investment decisions by letter[1]

To: *(company's name)*

We *(trustees)* being the present trustees of a settlement dated *(date)* and made between *(parties)* in exercise of the power contained in [clause *(number)* of the settlement *or* the Trustee Act 2000 Section 11] hereby delegate to you [the power of investment and the power to sell convert and transpose investments contained in clauses *(number)* and *(number)* of the settlement respectively] [the general power of investment contained in the Trustee Act 2000 Section 3] in respect of the investments and moneys from time to time comprised in the Trust Fund (as defined in the settlement) such powers to be exercised upon the terms and conditions set out in a letter of even date herewith and addressed by us to you a copy of which is annexed hereto.

You are empowered to exercise any of the powers and discretions relating to investment or ancillary to it conferred on us as the trustees of the settlement by the settlement or by law including the power contained in [clause *(number)* of the settlement *or* the Trustee Act 2000 Section 16] to place investments in the names of nominees and to give instructions to such nominees.

The delegation made hereby shall be revocable at any time by written notice given by us (or the survivor of us) to you or by you to us (or the survivor of us) but so that any person dealing with you in good faith shall be entitled to assume that no notice has been given by either of us to the other revoking this delegation.

Dated: *(date)²*

(signatures of the trustees)

[2198]

1   This Form is intended for use in conjunction with a letter on the lines of that contained in Form 319 [2200] post, containing the terms of the delegation and the policy statement.

2   The delegation of the investment power is not by power of attorney as this is not a requirement of the power contained in the Trustee Act 2000 s 11 (48 Halsbury's Statutes (4th Edn) TRUSTS AND SETTLEMENTS), nor usually of express powers to collectively delegate administrative powers. However, if any number of productions of the instrument of delegation are required, there is a practical advantage in using a power of attorney as copies, duly certified, can be used to prove its contents under the Powers of Attorney Act 1971 s 3 as amended by the Courts and Legal Services Act 1990 s 125(2), Sch 17 para 4 (1 Halsbury's Statutes (4th Edn) AGENCY). Any number of registrations or productions can then be dealt with at the same time and no harm ensues if a copy is lost or an institution fails to return one.

[2199]

319

Collective delegation of investment decisions—letter to a fund manager incorporating the 'policy statement'[1]

(date)

Dear Sirs

This letter is written in connection with the appointment by us today of you as our delegates in the exercise of our powers of investment under the settlement ('the Settlement') dated *(date)* and made between *(parties)* of which we are the present trustees.

The terms of the client agreement which is annexed to this letter will apply to your appointment except insofar as they are inconsistent with the terms set out in this letter.

We confirm that your appointment authorises you to make purchases and sales of investments on our behalf without previous reference to us in connection with the funds of this Settlement. The appointment is revocable at any time by written notice given by the trustees of the Settlement for the time being to you.

There are stated in the third schedule our powers of investment as trustees of the Settlement. We confirm that, within the scope of those powers, and subject to the duties placed on trustees in selecting investments by the general law and to what is stated in the next paragraph, you are authorised to purchase stocks and shares throughout the world and units in all unit trusts and offshore funds, including unit trusts under your own management[2].

[2200]

You will find listed in the first schedule:

1   any investments which are not to be sold without our specific authority; and

2   any investments in which we do not wish you to invest.

We will give you notice of any change in either of these categories of investment.

Subject to the duty imposed upon trustees by the general law to have regard to the interests of all beneficiaries, both present and future, and whether in capital or income, we have indicated in the second schedule the balance between income and capital growth which we consider appropriate to the circumstances of the Settlement. We will give you notice of any shift in emphasis that we may from time to time consider desirable. Valuations of the investments in the Settlement should be sent to us at least once a year.

Any cash forming part of the portfolio which is not immediately required for the purpose of any transactions may, at your discretion, be placed on deposit in any currency at normal commercial rates of interest, but small balances of less than £... may temporarily be held on current account.

[2201]

We will pay your service charges (plus VAT where appropriate) in accordance with your current scale of stated charges as amended from time to time by prior written notice, which may be deducted from any cash balances held by you.

Please sign and return to us the attached copy of this letter to indicate your acceptance of its terms.

Yours faithfully

(signatures of the trustees)

FIRST SCHEDULE

1   We do not wish the following holdings to be sold without our prior consent: [No investments in this category at present *or (specify)*].

2   We do not wish any holdings to be bought in the following countries, companies or sectors: [No investments in this category at present *or (specify)*].

[2202]

SECOND SCHEDULE

We wish your investment policy for this account to be based on an even balance between income and capital growth.

THIRD SCHEDULE

Powers set out in the *(name)* settlement:

'Trust money may be invested or laid out in the purchase or otherwise in the acquisition of or at interest upon the security of any shares stocks funds securities policies of insurance or other investments or property (movable or immovable) of whatsoever nature and wheresoever situated and whether or not productive of income and whether involving liability or not or upon such personal credit with or without security in all respects as the Trustees shall in their discretion think fit to the intent that the Trustees shall have the same full and unrestricted powers of investing transposing investments and dealing with trust money and buying or selling property in all respects as if they were absolutely entitled beneficially[3]'.

ANNEXURE
(client agreement)

[2203]

1 The Trustee Act 2000 Pt IV (ss 11–27) (48 Halsbury's Statutes (4th Edn) TRUSTS AND SETTLEMENTS) gives trustees statutory powers to delegate to agents. In connection with the delegation of fund management on a discretionary basis, note in particular:

    (a)   the definition of 'delegable function' in the Trustee Act 2000 s 11(2), which permits the delegation of administrative discretions;

    (b)   the restriction on who may act as an agent under the statutory power contained in the Trustee Act 2000 s 12(2), (3) which makes it desirable for an express power to delegate to be given in trust deeds and to be used when an appointment is made (see Form 316 [2194] ante);

    (c)   the terms of agency set out in the Trustee Act 2000 s 14 (and see note 2 below);

    (d)   the special power in the Trustee Act 2000 s 15 regulating asset management and especially the requirement that the agreement should be in writing and that the trustees should formulate guidance in the form of a 'policy statement';

    (e)   the wide definition of asset management functions in the Trustee Act 2000 s 15(5).

2 See the Trustee Act 2000 s 14(3)(c): it is thought that allowing a fund manager to invest in funds under his own management is 'reasonably necessary' within the Trustee Act 2000 s 14(2).

3 This express power mirrors the general power of investment given by the Trustee Act 2000 s 3. Amongst other matters that may be included in a 'policy statement', consider:

    (a)   tax factors: for instance, if the trust has unused capital losses which are being carried forward the trustees should ensure that these are used (they will be wasted if still unused when the trust ends); also, cash may be needed to pay tax: eg, the charge on a discretionary trust on the occasion of a tenth anniversary;

    (b)   the income requirements of a beneficiary (eg life tenant) may dictate the nature of the investments; likewise if the life tenant's needs are modest, a policy of capital growth may be pursued;

    (c)   investing in a collective investment fund may be attractive especially for the relatively modest trust fund; the acquisition of such an investment may also be attractive in preserving capital gains tax taper relief (viz the sale of the investments comprised in the fund does not effect the running of taper relief on the units held by the trustees).

[2204]

C: POWERS PROVIDING FOR INDIVIDUAL DELEGATION

320

Statutory power of delegation under the Trustee Act 1925 Section 25 as amended[1]

THIS GENERAL TRUSTEE POWER OF ATTORNEY is made on *(date)* by *(name of donor)* of *(address of donor)* as trustee of *(details of trust)*

I appoint *(name of one donee)* of *(address)* to be my attorney *(insert either date on which delegation commences or period for which it continues, or both)* in accordance with Section 25(5) of the Trustee Act 1925

IN WITNESS etc

(signatures of the parties)[2]
(signatures of witnesses)
[2205]

1   This is the form for individual trustee delegation under the Trustee Act 1925 s 25(6) as substituted by
     the Trustee Delegation Act 1999 s 5(1), (2) (48 Halsbury's Statutes (4th Edn) TRUSTS AND
     SETTLEMENTS). There is no stamp duty chargeable on powers of attorney. Note in particular:
     (a)   this Form envisages a single donor and a single attorney;
     (b)   a trustee may delegate for a period of 12 months commencing from a future date. A delegation
            without a specified time limit or for a period exceeding 12 months is valid for 12 months from
            the date of execution of the instrument that creates the power or from such later date as the
            instrument may specify: see the Trustee Act 1925 s 25(2) as substituted (see above).
2   As to the statutory requirements for valid execution of a deed see vol 12 (1994 Reissue) DEEDS,
     AGREEMENTS AND DECLARATIONS. As to the execution of a power of attorney specifically, see vol
     31 (1999 Reissue) POWERS OF ATTORNEY Paragraph 7 [4009].

[2206]

321

Delegation of individual trusteeship by way of power of attorney[1]

THIS POWER OF ATTORNEY is made on the ...... day of .... by *(trustee)* of
(address) ('the Donor')

[2207]

WHEREAS

(1)   The Donor and *(remaining trustees)* are the present trustees of a settlement ('the
       Settlement') dated *(date)* and made between *(parties)*

(2)   The Donor wishes to appoint *(attorney)* of *(address)* ('the Attorney') to be his
       attorney in the manner appearing below

NOW in exercise of the power conferred by the Trustee Act 1925 Section 25 as
amended by the Trustee Delegation Act 1999 Section 5 and of all other powers

THIS DEED WITNESSES as follows:

1   Delegation
The Donor delegates to the Attorney for the period of one year from *(date)* the execution
of the trusts powers and discretions of the Settlement including all trusts and powers
implied or conferred by statute in relation to it

[2208]

2   Appointment
In order to give effect to this delegation the Donor appoints the Attorney to be attorney
for the Donor and on behalf of the Donor and in the name of the Donor or the name
of the Attorney to execute any deeds or instruments and do all other things which in the
opinion of the Attorney shall be required to be executed and done in or about the
execution of such trusts powers and discretions or any of them including the statutory
and other powers mentioned in the Trustee Act 1925 Section 25(6) as amended

[3   Ratification
The Donor agrees to ratify and confirm whatever the Attorney shall in good faith do in
connection with the above][2]

IN WITNESS etc

(signature of the Donor)[3]
(signatures of witnesses)
[2209]

1   As to the power to delegate for a period not exceeding 12 months see Paragraph 256 [630] ante. As to the form of notice to a co-trustee of delegation of trusteeship by way of power of attorney, see Form 322 [2211] post. There is no stamp duty chargeable on powers of attorney.

2   Clause 3 above is not included in the statutory form set out in the Powers of Attorney Act 1971 s 10, Sch 1 and ratification will rarely be appropriate. In respect of acts of the donee pursuant to the power it will not be necessary; in so far as the power is exceeded the donor is not bound by his donee's acts. Accordingly, only if the power is defective for a reason not apparent on its face, is it thought that ratification may be appropriate.

3   As to the statutory requirements for valid execution of a deed see vol 12 (1994 Reissue) DEEDS, AGREEMENTS AND DECLARATIONS. As to the execution of a power of attorney specifically, see vol 31 (1999 Reissue) POWERS OF ATTORNEY Paragraph 7 [4009].

[2210]

322

Notice to co-trustee of delegation of trusteeship by way of power of attorney[1]

(name) Settlement

To: *(co-trustee)*

Take notice that I did on *(date)* by a power of attorney coming into operation on *(date)* delegate to *(attorney)* of *(address)* for a period of one year from *(date)* the execution and exercise in my name of the trusts powers and discretions vested in me as trustee of the settlement because *(state reason for giving power)*.

Dated: *(date)*

(signature of the trustee)

1   As to the requirement to give notice under the Trustee Act 1925 s 25(4) as substituted by the Trustee Delegation Act 1999 s 5(1), (2) (48 Halsbury's Statutes (4th Edn) TRUSTS AND SETTLEMENTS), see Paragraph 256 [630] ante.

[2211]–[2220]

323

Enduring power as a trust power under the Trustee Act 1925 Section 25 (as amended)[1]

Part A: About using this form

1. **You may choose one attorney or more than one.** If you choose one attorney then you must delete everything between the square brackets on the first page of the form. If you choose more than one, you must decide whether they are able to act:
   - Jointly (that is, they must all act together and cannot act separately) or
   - Jointly and severally (that is, they can all act together but they can also act separately if they wish).

   On the first page of the form, show what you have decided by crossing out one of the alternatives.

2. **If you give your attorney(s) general power** in relation to all your property and affairs, it means that they will be able to deal with your money or property and may be able to sell your house.

3. **If you don't want your attorney(s) to have such wide powers,** you can include any restrictions you like. For example, you can include a restriction that your attorney(s) must not act on your behalf until they have reason to believe that you are becoming mentally incapable; or a restriction as to what your attorney(s) may do. Any restrictions you choose must be written or typed where indicated on the second page of the form.

4. **If you are a trustee** (and please remember that co-ownership of a home involves trusteeship), you should seek legal advice if you want your attorney(s) to act as a trustee on your behalf.

5. **Unless you put in a restriction preventing it** your attorney(s) will be able to use any of your money or proprety to make any provision which you yourself might be expected to make for their own needs or the needs of other people. Your attorney(s) will also be able to use your money to make gifts, but only for reasonable amounts in relation to the value of your money and property.

6. **Your attorney(s) can recover the out-of-pocket expenses** of acting as your attorney(s). If your attorney(s) are professional people, for example solicitors or accountants, they may be able to charge for their professional services as well. You may wish to provide expressly for remuneration of your attorney(s) (although if they are trustees they may not be allowed to accept it).

7. **If your attorney(s) have reason to believe** that you have become or are becoming mentally incapable of managing your affairs, your attorney(s) will have to apply to the Court of Protection for registration of this power.

8. **Before applying to the Court of Protection for registration** of this power, your attorney(s) must give written notice that that is what they are going to do, to you and your nearest relatives as defined in the Enduring Powers of Attorney Act 1985. You or your relatives will be able to object if you or they disagree with registration.

9. **This is a simplified explanation** of what the Enduring Powers of Attorney Act 1985 and the Rules and Regulations say. If you need more guidance, you or your advisers will need to look at the Act itself and the Rules and Regulations. The Rules are the Court of Protection (Enduring Powers of Attorney) Rules 1986 (Statutory Instrument 1986 No. 127). The Regulations are the Enduring Powers of Attorney (Prescribed Form) Regulations 1990 (Statutory Instrument 1990 No. 1376).

10. **Note to Attorney(s)**
    After the power has been registered you should notify the Court of Protection if the donor dies or recovers.

11. **Note to Donor**
    Some of these explanatory notes may not apply to the form you are using if it has already been adapted to suit your particular requirements.

YOU CAN CANCEL THIS POWER AT ANY TIME BEFORE IT HAS TO BE REGISTERED

Part B: To be compelted by the 'donor' (the person appointing the attorney(s))

Don't sign this form unless you understand what it means

Please read the notes
in the margin which
follow and which are
part of the form
itself.

Donor's name and
address.

Donor's date of birth.

See note 1 on the
front of this form. If
you are appointing
only one attorney,
you should cross out
everything between
the square brackets.
If appointing more
than two attorneys,
please give additional
name(s) on an
attached sheet.

Cross out the one
which does not apply
(see note 1 on the
front of this form).

Cross out the one
which does not apply
(see note 2 on the
front of this form).
Add any additional
powers.

If you don't want the
attorney(s) to have
general power, you
must give details here
of what authority you
are giving to the
attorney(s).

Cross out the one
which does not
apply.

[   ]

of

born on

appoint

of

• [and

    of

• jointly
• jointly and severally]

to be my attorney for the purpose of the Enduring Powers of Attorney Act 1985
• with general authority to act on my behalf
• with authority to do the following on my behalf

in relation to
• all my property and affairs
• the following property and affairs

the trust fund vested in me and X as trustees of a settlement dated the [ ] day of
[ ] [ ] and made between A of the one part and B and C of the other part and the
execution and exercise of all or any of the trust powers and discretions vested in me
and X jointly as the trustees of that settlement.

Part B: Continued

Please read the notes in the margin which follow and which are part of the form itself.

If there are restrictions or conditions, insert them here; if not cross out these words if you wish (see note 3 on the front of this form).

If this form is being signed at your direction:
-the person signing must not be an attorney or any witness (to Parts B or C)
-you must add a statement that this form has been signed at your direction
-a second witness is necessary (please see below).

Your signature (or mark).

Date.

Someone must witness your signature.

Signature of witness

Your attorney(s) cannot be your witness. It is not advisable for your husband or wife to be your witness.

Signature of second witness.

A second witness is only necessary if this form is not being signed by you personally but at your direction (for example, if a physical disability prevents you from signing).

- subject to the following restrictions and conditions:

The delegation under this power (made pursuant to section 25 of the Trustees Act 1925) is to commence on the [   ] day of [   ] [   ] and to continue only for nine months.

I intend that this power shall continue even if I become mentally incapable

I have read or have had read to me the notes in Part A which are part of, and explain this form

Signed by me as a deed..
and delivered

on

in the presence of

Full name of witness

Address of witness

in the presence of

Full name of witness

Address of witness

Part C: To be completed by the attorney(s)

Note: 1. This form may be adapted to provide for execution by a corporation.

2. If there is more than one attorney additional sheets in the form as shown below must be added to this Part C.

Please read the notes in the margin which follow and which are part of the form itself.	I understand that I have a duty to apply for the Court for registration of this form under the Enduring Powers of Attorney Act 1985 when the donor is becoming or has become mentally incapable.
Don't sign this form before the donor has signed Part B or if, in your opinion, the donor was already mentally incapable at the time of signing Part B.	I also understand my limited power to use the donor's property to benefit persons other than the donor.
If this form is being signed at your direction: -the person signing must not be an attorney or any witness (to Parts B or C) -you must add a statement that this form has been signed at your direction -a second witness is necessary (please see below).	I am not a minor.
Signature (or mark) of attorney.	Signed by me as a deed... and delivered
Date.	on
Signature of witness.	in the presence of
The attorney must sign the form and his signature must be witnessed. The donor may not be the witness and one attorney may not witness the signature of the other.	Full name of witness Address of witness
Signature of second witness.	in the presence of
A second witness is only necessary if this form is not being signed by you personally but at your direction (for example, if a physical disability prevents you from signing).	Full name of witness Address of witness

1   This Form based on the form prescribed by the Enduring Powers of Attorney (Prescribed Form) Regulations 1990, SI 1990/1376 reg 2(1), Schedule made under the Enduring Powers of Attorney Act 1985 (1 Halsbury's Statutes (4th Edn) AGENCY). For the prescribed form see vol 31 (1999 Reissue) POWERS OF ATTORNEY Form 137 [4601]. This Form has been modified for use as an enduring power under the Trustee Act 1925 s 25 as substituted by the Trustee Delegation Act 1999 s 5(1), (2) (48 Halsbury's Statutes (4th Edn) TRUSTS AND SETTLEMENTS). Omissions or deletions of one of the various pairs of prescribed alternatives on the statutory form is permitted, and so too is the exclusion of any corresponding marginal notes: SI 1990/1376 reg 2(2)(a)(ii), (b)(iii). Whilst explanatory information cannot be omitted additional information can be incorporated. Where a permitted deletion of a prescribed alternative is carried out, it is not a requirement that the deletion be initialled. As to the formalities when creating an enduring power of attorney see vol 31 (1999 Reissue) POWERS OF ATTORNEY Paragraph 32 [4454]. This Form must be executed by the donee as well as the donor.

Note that this Form:

(a)   delegates the trustee functions of the donor from a date that is set out in the instrument (as an alternative it could have specified from the date when the power was registered);

(b)   is limited to a period of nine months (the maximum permitted period under the Trustee Act 1925 s 25 is 12 months);

(c)   delegates all the trustee's functions.

[2229]

324

Power of attorney pursuant to the Trustee Delegation Act 1999 Section 1[1]

THIS POWER OF ATTORNEY is made the ...... day of .... by *(donor)* of *(address)* ('the Donor')

WHEREAS

(1)   The property known as *(describe property)* ('the Property') is registered in the names of the Donor and AB as proprietors at HM Land Registry with title absolute under Title No *(title number)*[2]

(2)   The Property is vested in the Donor and AB as trustees upon trust for themselves as tenants in common in equal shares[3]

(3)   The Donor wishes to appoint *(name)* of *(address)* ('the Attorney') to be [his] attorney for the purposes hereafter mentioned

(4)   The provisions of the Trustee Delegation Act 1999 Section 1 apply to this power

(5)   In this power the expression 'the other trustee' means where the context permits the said AB or other the trustees or trustee in whom the Property shall for the time be vested with the Donor as trustees.

[2230]

NOW THIS DEED WITNESSES as follows:

1   The Donor HEREBY APPOINTS the Attorney to be [his] attorney to sell together with the other trustee the Property and for that purpose to employ agents and agree the terms and conditions of sale and together with the other trustee to receive the purchase money from the purchaser or purchasers and to deal with all matters ancillary to such sale and the Donor hereby delegates to the Attorney all trusts powers and discretions relating to such sale and matters

ancillary to such sale vested in the Donor and the other trustee jointly and appoints the Attorney in [his] name and on his behalf to execute and do all deeds documents and acts required to be executed or done in the execution and exercise of such trusts powers and discretions[4]

[2   The Donor agrees to ratify and confirm whatever the Attorney shall in good faith do in the premises][5]

IN WITNESS etc

(signature of the Donor)[6]
[2231]

1   This Form is a general power satisfying the requirements of the Powers of Attorney Act 1971 s 10 as amended by the Trustee Delegation Act 1999 s 3 (1 Halsbury's Statutes (4th Edn) AGENCY). It is not a trustee power under the Trustee Act 1925 s 25 as substituted by the Trustee Delegation Act 1999 s 5(1), (2) (48 Halsbury's Statutes (4th Edn) TRUSTS AND SETTLEMENTS) and, accordingly, may last for longer than 12 months. There is no stamp duty chargeable on powers of attorney.
2   Crucially the power falls within the Trustee Delegation Act 1999 s 1 (48 Halsbury's Statutes (4th Edn) TRUSTS AND SETTLEMENTS): see in particular recital (2) above which indicates that the Donor has a beneficial interest in possession in land of which he is a trustee.
3   Had the donor so wished he could have appointed the named trustee as his attorney. In such a case AB could not, acting alone, give a good receipt for capital monies arising on a sale of the land and, because the conditions of the Trustee Delegation Act 1999 s 8 are not met, the donor and AB would together have had to act in that regard.
4   The power is limited to the sale of a particular property and matters ancillary thereto. It could, of course, have been granted in terms wide enough to allow the attorney to exercise all the donor's trustee functions.
5   Clause 2 above is not included in the statutory form set out in the Powers of Attorney Act 1971 s 10, Sch 1 and ratification will rarely be appropriate. In respect of acts of the donee pursuant to the power it will not be necessary; in so far as the power is exceeded the donor is not bound by his donee's acts. Accordingly, only if the power is defective for a reason not apparent on its face, is it thought that ratification may be appropriate.
6   Powers of attorney, other than enduring powers under the Enduring Powers of Attorney Act 1985 (1 Halsbury's Statutes (4th Edn) AGENCY), are normally executed by the donor alone. As to the statutory requirements for valid execution of a deed see vol 12 (1994 Reissue) DEEDS, AGREEMENTS AND DECLARATIONS.

[2232]

325

Statement pursuant to the Trustee Delegation Act 1999 Section 2(2)[1]

To: *(purchaser)*

The transfer dated the *(date)* made between AB and CD of the one part and you of the other part, by which the freehold property known as *(describe of property)* was transferred to you by AB and CD in consideration of the sum of £... was executed on behalf of AB by me as his attorney under a general power of attorney made by AB on the *(date)* appointing me to be his attorney in accordance with the Powers of Attorney Act 1971 Section 10. I now state and confirm that at the date of this transfer AB was, subject to the contract for the sale of this property made between him and CD and you, beneficially entitled to this freehold property as joint tenant with CD.

Dated: *(date)*

(signature of attorney)

1   This Form deals with the common situation where a land registry sale by joint tenants has been completed by a transfer executed on behalf of one of the owners by an attorney. It will not normally be satisfactory to incorporate the statement into the transfer since that would involve making the attorney a party to the document in his own right.

[2233]

326

Clause excluding the operation of the Trustee Delegation Act 1999 Section 1[1]

The provisions of sub-section (1) of Section 1 of the Trustee Delegation Act 1999 shall not apply to any trustee or trustees for the time being of this settlement

1   In the case of a settlement (as opposed to a statutory trust arising in cases of co-ownership) the operation of the Trustee Delegation Act 1999 s 1 (48 Halsbury's Statutes (4th Edn) TRUSTS AND SETTLEMENTS) may give rise to anomalies, and delegation under section 1 lacks the safeguards provided for in Trustee Act 1925 s 25 as substituted by the Trustee Delegation Act 1999 s 5(1), (2) (48 Halsbury's Statutes (4th Edn) TRUSTS AND SETTLEMENTS). Hence it will be desirable to include a provision in the settlement deed along the lines of this Form, especially when the trust fund includes, or may include, land.

[2234]–[2999]

INDEX

References are to the numbers in square brackets which appear
on the right hand side of the text